ROCK ART SCIENCE

THE SCIENTIFIC STUDY OF PALAEOART

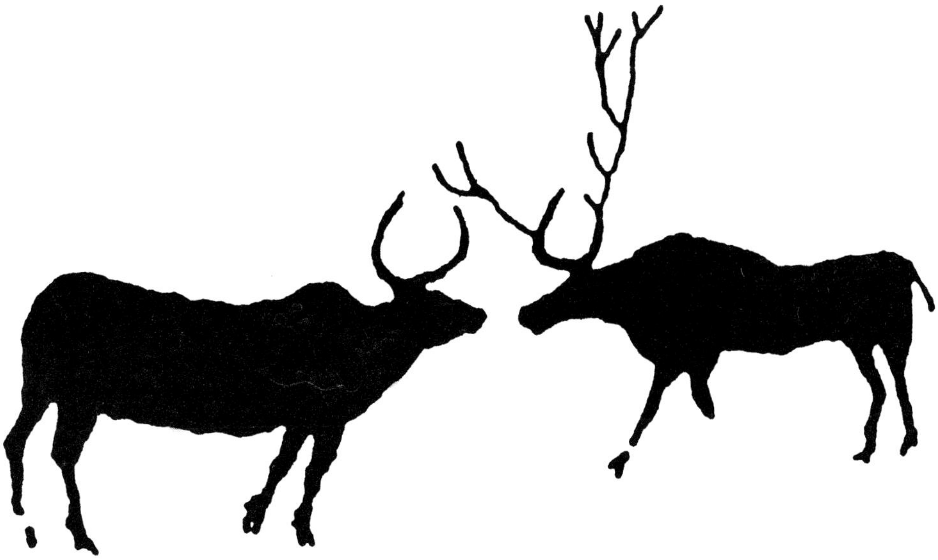

ROCK ART SCIENCE

THE SCIENTIFIC STUDY OF PALAEOART

ROBERT G. BEDNARIK

ARYAN BOOKS INTERNATIONAL
New Delhi

ROCK ART SCIENCE

The Scientific Study of Palaeoart

ISBN-81-7305-318-9 (HB)
81-7305-319-7 (PB)

This volume was first published by Brepols Publishers NV, Belgium, in 2001. This is a revised version.

Published in **2007** by:
ARYAN BOOKS INTERNATIONAL
Pooja Apartments, 4B, Ansari Road, Darya Ganj, New Delhi-110 002 (India)
Tel.: 23287589, 23255799; Fax: 91-11-23270385; E-mail: aryanbooks@vsnl.com

Computer Typeset and Printed in India at
ABI Prints & Publishing Co., New Delhi

PREFACE

An earlier version of this volume was published by Brepols in 2001, being the first academic textbook on the topic of the scientific study of palaeoart. Although the subject of early art forms had been studied, in one form or another, for centuries, and quite intensively for the entire 20th century, all of this work had been undertaken without the existence of a formal discipline, without a universal methodology, terminology and any relevant international standards. Until the final decade of the 20th century, numerous individuals and groups worldwide, all of whom had worked in relative academic isolation, had investigated the pre-Historic rock arts and portable arts of the world. This has fostered countless modern re-interpretations of ancient symbolic systems and a great variety of idiosyncratic models, jargons and disagreements. Since its formation in 1988, the International Federation of Rock Art Organisations, under my leadership, has sought to create a discipline rendering palaeoart studies more rigorous, transforming the general endeavour into a scientific pursuit. It has done this by setting international research standards, determining an ethical code, establishing a uniform terminology — but most of all, by initiating the creation of a comprehensive scientific methodology that simply did not exist before. This volume summarises the results of these efforts so far. The present edition takes into consideration the crucial developments between 1995 and 2005, up to the time of its publication.

Rock art specialists have praised the first edition of this work as a watershed publication opening up a whole new discipline. It has been criticised by some archaeologists as being overly critical of their discipline. In this edition I have made an attempt to limit criticism to what is absolutely necessary to convey the gravity of issues. Many of the world's leading rock art researchers are also archaeologists, and I am thrilled and grateful to see them working in this field. But it is unavoidable, in debating the issues honestly, to clarify that rock art science has an agenda that differs significantly from the politics of archaeology, and that most archaeologists do lack the knowledge and experience to deal with palaeoart expeditiously. This is hoped to lead to academic introspection, not antagonism, and to a better dialogue between archaeologists and rock art scientists. I ask archaeologists to consider this book as an attempt to communicate with them constructively.

I thank Vikas Arya for taking on the task of bringing this volume to a greater readership, by producing an updated edition of what since 2001 already has become the foundation of the discipline of palaeoart studies. The world's largest rock art concentrations occur outside of Europe, and this renders it most important that this volume be made available especially in those regions that are richest in rock art. India, for instance, has one of the world's largest and scientifically most important concentrations of rock art. With this edition go my hopes that this book can contribute to the development of sound research traditions in this fascinating field, in India and around the world.

Robert G. Bednarik
Melbourne, July 2006

CONTENTS

1. ROCK ART SCIENCE : AN INTRODUCTION

APROPOS OF ROCK ART

Rigorous demands of taxonomy require that a phenomenon be defined to the exclusion of any similar phenomena, and in an objective fashion that would be acceptable to any intelligent organism in this universe. This excludes sapiens-centric definitional devices of many kinds, such as those involving intentionality, communication, intellect, simplistic concepts of what art is, and so forth. There are many forms of rock markings that may, in rare cases, resemble rock art so closely that archaeologists have mistaken them for rock art, when in fact they are the result of non-anthropic processes (e.g. geomorphological markings; see Ch. 3). There are rock markings made by non-human species that may closely resemble rock art to our sensory perceptions, and they may even be the result of some 'intentional' activity. An example would be the scratch marks made by cave bears, produced to communicate certain information to other members of that species (Bednarik 1988). They are not regarded as rock art, hence semiotic properties are not a distinguishing characteristic of rock art, or indeed of any 'art'.

In defining rock art we might begin by considering some fundamental issues: if rock markings were produced by intelligent interstellar organisms, would we regard their handiwork as rock art? Irrespective of our preferred answer, we need to consider that such alien organisms might well produce rock markings that are not readily detectable by humans (for instance, arrangements of anisotropically discrete properties, or any other 'intentional' arrangements of magnetic, chemical, crystallographic or petrographic properties that may readily be perceptible to an alien, but not to a human being). Would we include them under the heading of 'rock art'? Probably not. It follows that the definition of rock art is deliberately self-referential to one particular species — ours.

A scientific definition of rock art, then, is that it consists of markings occurring on rock surfaces that were 'intentionally' produced by members of the genus *Homo* (i.e. anthropic markings), that are detectable by 'normal' human sensory faculties, and that are concept-mediated externalisations of a 'conscious' awareness of some form of perceived reality.

This may sound somewhat esoteric, perhaps a little over-rigorous. But I wanted to start this book by emphasising that it represents a deliberate attempt to address its subject matter in a scientific rather than 'empirical', archaeological or humanistic fashion. This book is free of rhetoric about the 'aesthetics' of rock art, for aesthetics can only be relevant to science if it is meaningful to the interstellar organism who lacks a sense of vision, touch and hearing — not to mention anthropocentric perception. There will be no confident guesses in this volume of what has been depicted in rock art, because what they tell us about the perception of the observer is not relevant to the study of rock art, only to the study of the neural system of that observer. The fact that certain paint residues on a rock face resemble the shape of an elephant to me is of scientific consequence only to the study of how my perception decodes visual information. If I claimed that my perception is identical to that of the maker of the figure I would be well advised to present some persuasive evidence why that proposition should be accepted. No such claims are testable by refutation, hence they are of little use to proper science. No prospects of falsifiability and repeatability of experiments, the cornerstones of science, are readily apparent in them. It should therefore be of more than a little concern to us that a great deal of what has been presented in the name of 'rock art research' over the past couple of centuries has consisted to a great extent of people's self-conscious responses to rock art: what it reminded them of, and how similar it seemed to something else they had seen. This is the creation of a modern rock art mythology, largely the kind of scholarship so far presented in this field. It is the explicit purpose of this book to show that scientific approaches are possible in the study of rock art.

A workable definition of rock art is an essential prerequisite in such an endeavour. But because of the fossilised state of disciplinary definitions and the all-pervading anthropocentrism in 'scholarly pursuits', the acquisition of a rigorous definition involves some seemingly pedantic points of epistemology that need to be made. While it is true that a great deal of rock art would be detectable by the human tactile sense, it is fair to say that this is merely incidental; rock art appears to be squarely aimed at the visual sense of our species. In establishing what constitutes rock art it is therefore particularly relevant to consider what properties of rock art render it perceptible to the human sensory faculties. The distinguishing property of rock art, and palaeoart generally, is this: its crucial characteristics must all be determined by the visual sense of humans. There is no other surviving entity in the entire experience of early humans about which the same could be said: all other phenomena in the physical world can be presumed to possess crucial characteristics that are not detectable by humans. Hence palaeoart constitutes the only surviving phenomena of the world of early humans whose common crucial denominators of phenomenon categories (those variables that determine the category into which a phenomenon would belong, irrespective of human experience) must be detectable by human vision. Indeed, art is the major aspect in human experience about which humans can think objectively (Bednarik 1994a). It has no other role but to communicate to members of our species, or be contemplated by them, which can be said about very few other tangible aspects of reality. This definition of art turns on its head the traditional belief that art is subjective, science as practiced today is objective. In a truly objective system, the roles are reversed: much of what postures as science is entirely anthropocentric and subjective (most scientific efforts in the world today are a 'prostituted' form of science, being in the service of the destruction of humans, in the service of the preservation of humans, or in the service of human expansion, e.g. through space exploration), while art is the only sensory experience of humans about which mere humans can consistently utter objective statements.

First, a little epistemology

Human beings are 'intelligent organisms' on a minor planet in one of the countless galaxies of the universe, who have developed what they themselves rather pompously define as 'conscious' constructs of reality. These are essentially an 'unintended by-product' of their cognitive evolution. The 'true' status of our consciousness, or the nature of the relationship between our constructs of reality and 'objective reality' (assuming that such a state does exist), are profoundly unknown to us; they have remained inaccessible so far, after millennia of human philosophy. The issue of our inability to comprehend real reality — our anthropocentrism — is readily illustrated by a similar conceptual limitation: our assumption that all other human groups experience reality in the same way as we do individually. This fallacy is readily evident, there is no single common reality even among extant human groups, there are in fact many human constructs of reality in use currently. Some of them have little regard for the concept of linear time, others have far more complex ideas of space than the conglomerate of ontologies we usually define as the 'Western world view'. Moreover, it is very reasonable to assume that the cosmovision of any extinct human groups also differed significantly from that of the investigating archaeologist. All human groups probably believe and believed in the validity of their own construct of reality, including modern archaeologists who are strongly conditioned by cultural and academic biases, causing them to believe that they are somehow 'objective'. Yet no human being is even remotely objective, all our constructs of reality merely reflect contingent prejudices whose origins are very complex indeed.

We thus arrive at a very interesting point. The origins of human constructs of reality could be studied by objective organisms through the examination of physical remains of the processes that formed them, particularly early expressions of symbolism. The major corpus of such evidence is collectively called palaeoart, and it occurs mostly in the form of rock art. It follows that, if we were capable of studying rock art *objectively*, we might discover how humans developed their ontologies. This, I propose, might well be the most important pursuit in a science serving our species, because it would illuminate how the conceptual constructs humans have perceived as realities came into being, and how they might relate to a Kantian objective reality 'out there'. It is therefore most unfortunate that the principal store of information we would have in this quest has so far only been considered as a source of creative mythologies about pre-literate peoples. It is my contention here that we as researchers need to perform significantly better if we are to ever glimpse some of the real potential of our discipline.

To do so I propose that we could discontinue the time-honoured practice of inventing mythologies about rock art. Our 'research' so far has produced precious little except a cacophony of hypotheses about 'what it all means'. Rock art research seems to boast the highest ratio, in any scholarly quest, of interpretations or models to the quantity of secure data actually available. The number of idiosyncratic theories, taxonomies, even terminologies is immense, bearing in mind that only a few thousand scholars have contributed to this diversity, and there could well be as many different methodologies as there are practitioners. In this discipline there might be seen to be an inverse proportion of the number of hypotheses produced to the quantity of scientific information actually available. One only needs to consider one small example to see this: the Upper Palaeolithic art of a small part of Europe, especially south-western

Europe. This ill-defined corpus (it includes many fakes and unauthenticated claims) has attracted almost countless explanations, all of which have one thing in common: they cannot be applicable to the entire body of such art as there are always numerous exceptions. There have been shamanistic interpretations, hunting and sexual hypotheses, special water and sound-inspired hypotheses, topographical hypotheses, as well as structuralist, deconstructionist, Marxist, feminist, adaptationist, diffusionist, behaviourist and art-for-art's-sake hypotheses of various kinds. Interpretations of individual anthropomorphous motifs included in this art corpus, for instance, range from 'shamans' to 'Neanderthals' and to fertility symbols and caricatures — an endless procession of unfounded, often downright puerile guesses. The public which funds this hobby is being hoodwinked into accepting this pursuit as having some scientific credibility. Indeed, we seem to have as many meanings and interpretations for this Palaeolithic art as there have been researchers examining it, and yet we have not even devised comprehensive scientific means of determining what is and what is not Palaeolithic art (as attested by the recent Côa controversy; cf. Gonçalves 1998). This provides a fair indication of the desperate state of affairs this discipline is in, academically speaking. Moreover, the multitude of hypotheses we face is not just contradictory, all are unfalsifiable and therefore vigorously defended by their promoters. Many practitioners who have contributed to this sorry catalogue of humbug are deeply entrenched and highly sensitive to criticism. When we add to all of these complications and the personal feuds they have spawned the lack of terminological uniformity, which often leads to misunderstandings and further discord, it becomes obvious that uniform standards of terminology and methodology are as essential as is agreement as to what is and what is not science, and what constitutes rock art science.

This book is intended to offer such uniform standards, and it advocates a sharp division between scientific rock art research and other forms of rock art studies. Bearing in mind that humans lack access to objective reality, proper science offers a framework of knowledge claims that need to be testable by refutation. This means essentially that a proposition has to be presented in such a way that the conditions under which it may be refuted are either evident, or they can be formulated. A proposition that cannot be refuted outside the brain of the proposer is not scientific. This would include my impression that the paint residues on the rock form a picture of an elephant, as it would include the proposition that *Homo erectus* created rock art. Neither claim is refutable, whereas the proposition that *Homo erectus* created no rock art is refutable. Another benefit of this strategy, apart from being scientific, is that it favours refutation over confirmation, an intellectually corrupting system which so much dominates archaeology.

It is not the a priori intention of this book to cast out traditional or non-scientific approaches to rock art, or even to disparage them. These practices of inventing mythologies have in many ways benefited the discipline, rendering rock art interesting and valuable, drawing public attention to it, and they have thus assisted in its appreciation and preservation. There is no reason why poets, artists and dreamers should not deal with rock art on their own terms, enjoy it, and help others to do so. In this sense, fanciful and dramatic interpretations, such as in terms of complex shamanistic beliefs, may greatly contribute to an appreciation of rock art, and should not be discouraged or ridiculed. Societies preceding ours had to deal with rock art made before their time, and they did so by inventing their own interpretations, by attaching meanings to specific features of an art they had no direct understanding of. It is entirely legitimate for modern-day societies to re-interpret rock art from their own perspectives, and science certainly has no right to discourage such practices. It may comment on them, it may analyse them, but the only right science may ethically claim in this context is the demand that such pursuits not be labelled 'scientific'. They are not, and to claim so is to misrepresent and discredit science.

Which raises the question, what are scientific claims about rock art, and how do we generate refutable propositions from the data it may yield. In this book it will be attempted to provide some of the answers. Rock art research is a very young discipline, still in its embryonic stage. This is reflected in the volume in hand, which is in no way intended to provide a comprehensive summary of all the scientific approaches possible to rock art. All I can provide here is a review of scientific work conducted so far, and perhaps add some ideas of how such a quest might proceed in the years to come. I am well aware of the limitations of this young discipline and the difficulties it faces, but in creating a working basis we have to start from some common frame of reference. This is what I wish to present here.

About terminology

Scientific work depends heavily on a precise terminology and its correct use. Here we strike the first problem in rock art research: there is no widely agreed terminology. As noted, this discipline has probably spawned the greatest diversity of idiosyncratic terminologies relative to the number of practitioners. In Australia, the two major attempts to create rock art terminologies are those of McCarthy (1967, 1968) and Maynard (1977). Globally, some degree of standardisation has been introduced since the advent of *Rock Art Research* (in 1984) and the International Federation of Rock Art Organisations (IFRAO, in 1988), but agreement on terms remains elusive. This is confusing to the newcomer, it continues to fuel systematic disagreements between researchers, and it is often directly related to issues concerning technology. To see this it is useful to examine the debate between McCarthy (1989) and Maynard (1989).

Maynard, whose proposed system is more consistent and analytically relevant than McCarthy's (essentially for the reasons she states; Maynard 1977), considers the need for a typology paramount: without it, quantitative analysis is impossible. She compares this need with the prerequisite typology for stone tool studies, apparently considering that the lithic taxonomies created by archaeologists are valid outside of archaeological constructs. Recognising how typologies are not usually designed by sound principles, but 'grow, like mushrooms, in the dark' (Maynard 1977: 388), she offers a comprehensive classification system based on her own understanding of Australian rock art. In analysing inconsistencies in McCarthy's nomenclature, Maynard observes for instance the ambiguity in using the term 'engraving' both as a major term (in the sense of 'petroglyph') and for a specific technique (incising, scratching or cutting action). In her own system, based on the variables of technique, form, motif, size and character, she lists three headings for reductive-technique rock art forms (petroglyphs) according to whether the figures were made by friction, percussion or rotation. Under 'percussion' she offers the sub-headings 'direct percussion' (pounding) and 'indirect percussion' (pecking). In other words: percussion petroglyphs were made either by using a hammer in one hand ('pounded'), or a hammer in one hand and a chisel (or bit, punch or gad) in the other ('pecked'). The term pecking (or peck marks, pecked designs etc.) has been widely adopted and is one of the most frequently used technological terms one now reads in rock art descriptions.

If indirect percussion was used in producing petroglyphs, with a stone 'chisel' and a stone hammer, this should have resulted in vast numbers of discarded stone implements with distinctive bipolar damage (similar to the 'fabricator' or *outil écaillé*). Almost no such tools have been reported from petroglyph sites. The idea of indirect percussion is an unsupported, academic pronouncement ('academic' in the sense of 'impractical') and its advocates have not demonstrated the technique by replication (Bednarik 1991: 117). It might require between 25 000 and 100 000 impact nicks per square metre of pecked petroglyph area (many figures are larger than that), and on completion the artist's fingers would probably require amputation. I have seen sites with over 1000 m^2 of 'pecked' area. If we assume that each chisel can make 100 nicks before it is too worn and that each such slug weighs just 25 g, we should have at least 25 tons of such slugs at these sites. None have been reported.

Preoccupation with the question of direct *versus* indirect percussion seems to result from an over-emphasis of difference between motifs with precisely directed, deep percussion marks, and those with more diffuse, shallow and apparently less well directed marks, and the conclusion that the two must be attributable to two different production methods. In reality, other variables are more likely to account for technological differences. These variations might include the type of rock, depth and state of weathering zone, presence of case hardening, direction of impact, presence of moisture, and various attributes of the percussion tool used. The tendency of explaining different impact marks as the result of different techniques is consistent with other archaeological interpretations: that the specialist is capable of distinguishing taxonomic entities among the physical evidence considered to be of archaeological relevance (Bednarik 1994a). A less superficial treatment of rock art technology is offered in Chapter 4.

Maynard's endeavour to establish a technology-based classification system led her to point out that very few Australian petroglyphs are 'engravings' (i.e. have been produced by a method similar to that of traditional metal engraving), and yet the term 'engraving' continues to be used widely by Australian and British archaeologists in describing all rock art made by the removal of mineral mass. Again, this misuse of technology-derived terminology is attributable to a misunderstanding of technology: an 'engraving', as Maynard points out, is a marking made with a burin or graver. In palaeoart studies it typically refers to a subtractive process producing markings on portable objects (stone, bone, ivory, ostrich eggshell, amber etc.) and to similar markings on rock. These were, as Maynard argues, made by friction (or, to be more specific, by incision, scratching or abrasion), and certainly not by percussion of any type. The use of 'engraving' to describe a percussion petroglyph therefore seems to indicate lack of technological understanding.

Insistence upon the use of rigorous terminology is not mere pedantry; terminological confusion reflecting poor understanding of technology is likely to result in unrigorous, poorly founded models and, more serious still, in neglect of crucial archaeological evidence (as will be shown in this book, cf. Ch. 4).

Globally, rock art motifs can be divided into two principal classes on the basis of their method of manufacture: those made by a reductive process (petroglyphs), and those made by an additive process (pictograms, which include paintings, drawings, stencils, beeswax figures etc.). This distinction is mirrored in the two main classes of geoglyphs (positive and negative geoglyphs), and it is not only practical and sensible, but widespread in rock art. It affects site preservation and management practices; and, perhaps most importantly, it is reflected in the way we conduct *rock art science*. For instance, the methods used in determining the possible ages of rock art differ greatly according to whether the art was made by an additive or a reductive process. Similarly, methods of preservation differ between pictograms and petroglyphs. Therefore this basic division will be observed here, but it needs to be mentioned that some rock art traditions combined both treatments, or that some petroglyphs have been, or may have been, coloured. This does not contradict the said division, it merely reminds us that taxonomic models are usually not absolute, but are merely useful reference frames in scientific work.

A lack of understanding of the technology of petroglyphs leads to a misuse of terminology. The names used for additive rock art forms are more appropriate than those often applied to petroglyphs, precisely because they are technology-derived terms: stencils, paintings (applied wet), drawings (applied dry), beeswax figures etc. Reductive rock art (petroglyphs) is often defined by subjective technological labels: engraving (often misused), carving (technologically inappropriate), pecking (possibly always misused), pounding, etching (a possibly inappropriate description from South America), boring or drilling (doubtful that it was used).

Petroglyphs come in two basic morphological forms: as sgraffiti (defined by colour contrast) or as relief petroglyphs (defined by relief depth). Both of these types can be made either by percussion or abrasion. The sgraffito method has been widely used on ceramics in the past and is still used with cement render on building facades. The majority of the world's petroglyphs were sgraffiti. Sgraffito petroglyphs have a very limited life span (Bednarik 1994b, 1995); in most cases they remain visible only for as long as it takes the rock surface to repatinate fully. This applies particularly to rock art sgraffiti made by merely bruising a varnish cover. In archaeology, the technological definition of sgraffito has remained almost unknown in relation to rock art (Bednarik 1979: Note 1), and false chronologies were based on this taphonomic misapprehension of how technique may determine longevity (Bednarik 1994b: Fig 1). Indeed, inadequate understanding of taphonomy is a major factor in misinterpreting rock art quantitatively as well as qualitatively. It is also closely related to misapprehensions about technology (see Ch. 8).

The effects of the lack of a uniform terminology in rock art research are evident throughout the relevant literature. This issue is quite easily resolved by a wide agreement on a 'benchmark' terminology and its consistent implementation. An endeavour to create such a standard through consensus was announced in September 1997, at which time a very preliminary list of words was published that might possibly merit inclusion in such a dictionary of rock art research (Bednarik 1997). Through a process of consultation a draft was developed and published in August 1999, the *Proposed glossary of rock art research* (Bednarik 1999). This was offered for international commentary, and corrections and additions were expressly invited. More researchers responded and assisted in the shaping of a final version, which was eventually published in November 2000, thus being the result of over three years of consultation (Bednarik 2000). This concise dictionary was then adopted by the International Federation of Rock Art Organisations (IFRAO) as the *IRAG*, the International Rock Art Glossary. It now forms the international standard terminology in this field of research and has been translated into various major languages (Bednarik et al. 2003). The *IRAG*, which represents the internationally agreed official terminology of the IFRAO publications, appears as Chapter 12 of this book, and this book represents a systematic application of it.

REFERENCES

BEDNARIK, R. G. 1979. The potential of rock patination analysis in Australian archaeology — part 1. *The Artefact* 4: 14–38.

BEDNARIK, R. G. 1988. Comment on D. Mania and U. Mania, 'Deliberate engravings on bone artefacts of Homo erectus'. *Rock Art Research* 5: 96–100.

BEDNARIK, R. G. 1991. Standardisation in rock art terminology. In C. Pearson and B. K. Swartz (eds), *Rock art and posterity: conserving, managing and recording rock art*, pp. 116–118. Occasional AURA Publication 4, Australian Rock Art Research Association, Melbourne.

BEDNARIK, R. G. 1994a. On the scientific study of palaeoart. *Semiotica* 100(2/4): 141–68.

BEDNARIK, R. G. 1994b. A taphonomy of palaeoart. *Antiquity* 68: 68–74.

BEDNARIK, R. G. 1995. Metamorphology: in lieu of uniformitarianism. *Oxford Journal of Archaeology* 14(2): 117–22.

BEDNARIK, R. G. 1997. Proposed dictionary of rock art research. *AURA Newsletter* 14(2): 15–16.

BEDNARIK, R. G. 1999. Proposed glossary of rock art research. *AURA Newsletter* 16(1): 3–10.

BEDNARIK, R. G. 2000. Rock art glossary. *Rock Art Research* 17: 147–55.

BEDNARIK, R. G., M. CONSENS, A. MUZZOLINI, D. SEGLIE and J. SHER 2001. *Rock Art Glossary: a multilingual dictionary*. IFRAO-Brepols Series 2, Turnhout.

GONÇALVES, E. M. 1998. Science, controversy and participation. The case of the Foz Côa rock art engravings. *Journal of Iberian Archaeology* 0: 7–31.

McCARTHY, F. D. 1967. *Australian Aboriginal rock art* (3rd edn). Australian Museum, Sydney.

McCARTHY, F. D. 1968. Recording art on rock surfaces. In D. J. Mulvaney (ed.), *Australian archaeology: a guide to field techniques*, pp. 125–155. Australian Institute of Aboriginal Studies, Canberra.

McCARTHY, F. D. 1989. Rock art sequences: a matter of clarification. *Rock Art Research* 5: 16–42.

MAYNARD, L. 1977. Classification and terminology in Australian rock art. In P. J. Ucko (ed.), *Form in indigenous art*, pp. 387–402. Gerald Duckworth and Co. Ltd., London.

MAYNARD, L. 1989. Comment on F. D. McCarthy, 'Rock art sequences: a matter of clarification'. *Rock Art Research* 5: 30.

2. The study of rock art in a historical perspective

In the beginning

The contemplation of rock art is probably almost as old as its production. We may reasonably assume that the Palaeolithic visitors who defaced and vandalised previously produced rock paintings in Cosquer Cave, France, perhaps around 19 000 years ago (Clottes et al. 1992), did not do this entirely without reason. We may never know what their motivation was, but whatever moved them to this action, it indicates a keen awareness of the earlier created rock art. It also implies the formulation of some kinds of concepts about what it signified to these Solutrean observers. Modern researchers also tend to formulate mental constructs derived from the contemplation of visual perception of surviving traces of this palaeoart, an activity they choose to define as 'study'. In that sense there are no fundamentally different cognitive activities involved: the Solutrean rock art vandal and the modern rock art researcher are both members of an intelligent species whose attention is drawn to specific visual characteristics of rock markings signifying the semiotic involvement of other intellects, be they those of members of the same species, another intelligent species, or perceived deities of some form (e.g. creation ancestors). The contemplation preceding the reaction of both these beholders of the rock art is an essential prerequisite for any of their reactions.

The modern researcher might feel that his contemplation is at a more sophisticated level or intellectually more comprehensive, which may well be true in principle. But the same would be said by a being of vastly greater intellect than that averaged by modern humans, in assessing the merits of our 'study' of rock art, hence this is certainly very much a relativism. It is perhaps true that there has been a change towards increased intellectual sophistication in human reactions to rock art over time, but we have no clear evidence that such change was in the form of some gradual evolution towards betterment. We may argue that surely each generation of rock art students would have had the benefit of standing on the shoulders of those before them. But this can be a deceptive argument, because of the inertness of rock art to cultural analysis: if the paradigms, methods or working hypotheses of those before us were faulty then it would be pointless to expect veracity even from their most sophisticated outcomes. They may simply be sophistries, and one should not invoke some Darwinist model of a discipline based on ultimately unfalsifiable propositions: ever-increasing sophistication does not necessarily lead to betterment; it may lead to an amplification of falsities. We have excellent examples of such developments in archaeology, and in epistemologies generally.

Thus it may be judicious not to judge the responses of previous beholders of rock art, or assume that our own responses are always necessarily 'superior'. Ever since rock art was first made, over a hundred thousand years ago (Bednarik 2001), it has been available for human contemplation, and has no doubt been subjected to ethnoscientific consideration at times. The earliest known evidence we have of considered responses in the form of written records comes from China, where about 2250 years ago the philosopher Han Fei (280–233 B.C.) reported observing rock art. Almost 700 years later, the Northern Wei Dynasty geographer Li Daoyuan (A.D. 386–434) described in some detail numerous sites of rock pictures from many parts of the country (Chen 1988). He also mentions hearing about rock art further west, in today's regions of India and Pakistan. A few centuries later, the rock paintings at Xianzitan, Huaan, Fujian Province, were recorded, together with a legend about them, by Zhang Yue of the Tang Dynasty (in *Xuan Shi Zhi*, eighth century A.D.) (Bednarik and Li 1991). All of these early reports precede those of other continents significantly. Interestingly, the first 'direct datings' (see Ch. 7) of Chinese rock art, referring to prominent painting sites, have yielded antiquities in the order of 2000–3000 years. At the huge site of Huashan, Guangxi Zhuang Province, some paintings appear to be between 2115 and 2370 years old, and at Cangyuan, Yunnan Province, radiocarbon dates ranging from 2960 to 3100 years were secured from the paintings, compared to dates between 2735 and 2895 from the site's occupation deposits (Bednarik and Li 1991). More recently Tang and Gao (2004) have shown by microerosion analysis that a great deal of rock art in western China is two to four millennia old. Hence the earliest written records of Chinese rock art are from the time when much of it was being made.

The earliest published reproductions of rock art, however, are from South America. Ambrósio Fernandes Brandão, who reported that in 1598 a Captain De Carvalho found twenty-four 'inscriptions' in a cave on the Rio Araçuagipe while raiding the Petiguas Indians, published schematised drawings of diverse motifs in 1618 (Brandão 1930). This was preceded by several briefly mentioned observations of rock art in Mexico during the sixteenth century, including those by Fray Juan de Torquemada, Comendador Christobal de Salazar in 1579, Fray Diego de Azevedo in 1592, and in the following century, in 1615, by Padre Rodrigo de Cabredo. Numerous further reports of rock art followed, from many parts of Latin America (e.g. Ramos Gavilán 1621; Ruiz de Montoya 1639). The first full recording of a New World petroglyph panel comes from Peru, where Antonio de Calancha copied a panel measuring several metres at Calango near Lima and published it (Calancha 1638). In Colombia, the Padre Simón reported deeply cut petroglyphs south-west of Bogotá, found about 1620 (Simón 1882–92, II: 283). De Zemora reported further petroglyphs in Colombia in 1635 (Cabrera Ortiz 1946: 237), while Padre Alonso Ramos Gavilan provided the first published report of Bolivian rock art in 1621, mentioning four sites. In Venezuela, petroglyphs were first reported from the Orinoco in 1671 (Rivero 1883), followed by Schabel's (1965: 304) report in 1704 of petroglyphs near what is now Ciudad Bolívar. The first report of rock art from the Lesser Antilles is from Breton and dates from 1635 (Bouge 1947). All of these reports were by Christian missionaries, who in many cases attributed the rock art to St Thomas.

In Guyana, rock art was discovered by a German surgeon, Nikolas Horstman in 1740 (Schomburgk 1841: 147), but Dubelaar (1986) regards this material as European; and in the same year by Pieter Tollenaer in the upper Rupununi region. The Jesuit missionary Gilli (1780–84) described rock art from the Orinoco in Venezuela which the Tamanaco Indians told him was made by the creator god Amalivaca. The Franciscan Padre Ramón Bueno recorded further petroglyphs near the Orinoco at the end of the century but his manuscript was lost in a flood (Von Humboldt and Bonpland 1814–25, II: 624).

One of the most interesting aspects of this period in Latin America is the policy of Christian missionaries to destroy or deface indigenous rock art. When I analysed a rock painting site in Bolivia, Peña Escrita, in 1987, I proposed that the defacement of the art and the superimposed petroglyphs of crosses represent evidence of religious iconoclasm or attempts to exorcise or neutralise the potency the site represented for the local autochthons (Bednarik 1988, 1992). I suggested that the defacement was systematic, proceeded from the left to the right of the site, and could have been performed in front of an audience of indigenes. Within a few years Querejazu Lewis (1994) located historical evidence that an Idols Eradication Policy was declared in the Resolutions of the Provincial Council in the City of Kings (now Lima, Peru) in 1567. De Calancha, the first to record a full petroglyph panel, himself a missionary, reported in 1638 that the Calango petroglyphs had been ground down by the Spanish, and a cross placed at the head of the rock to counter the continuing worshipping of the site by the indigenes.

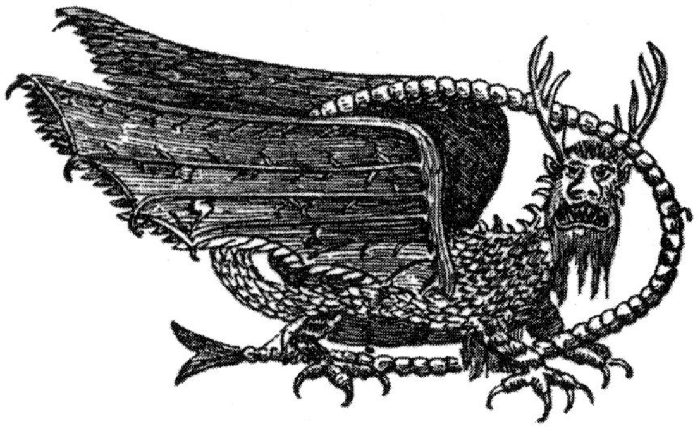

Figure 1. Interpretation by William Dennis in 1825 of a subsequently destroyed petroglyph at the mouth of the Piasa Creek, Illinois, first recorded by Jacques Marquette in 1673.

The earliest known report of rock art north of Mexico is more recent than in the south, dating from 1673, but also comes from a Catholic missionary. The elaborate petroglyph of a dragon-like figure Jacques Marquette recorded on the Piasa Creek near Alton, Illinois, was not destroyed by iconoclasm, however, but by quarrying activities in 1856. We have several fanciful recordings of it, such as a pen-and-ink sketch from 1825 (Figure 1). The petroglyphs at Dighton Rock, Massachusetts, were first recorded by Danforth in 1680, and several times again in the following century. La Roche-á-l'Oiseau, a rock painting site in Quebec, seems to be the first rock art site reported in Canada. It was mentioned in 1686 that tobacco was thrown at the panel, which brings to mind Querejazu's (1994) report of offerings of chewed coca leaves having been made at a Bolivian rock art site still in recent times.

In Europe, rock art recording had its debut in Scandinavia, with a comparatively detailed drawing of petroglyphs at Backa in Brastad near Tanum, Bohuslän. It was lodged by Peder Alfssön in the archives of Copenhagen in 1627, and eventually published by Suhm (1784). The same panel has been recorded many times since, and Nordbladh (1981) illustrates how the various recordings were affected by specific preoccupations of the times in question. While Alfssön included nonexisting bird depictions in his freehand drawing, Hilfeling added runes to his scale drawing (Tham 1794: Pl. VII), and several subsequent recorders improved precision, even including the rendering of the background rock texture.

In central Europe, the Vallée des Merveilles seems to have attracted the first attention resulting in a published mention, by Abbé Pietro Gioffredo,

c. 1650. The megalithic rock art of western Europe received its first mention in a letter by Edward Lhwyd, who visited Newgrange in Ireland in 1699 (Bahn 1998). In Spain and Portugal, rock art attracted less interest than that of the colonies, with the first mentions in Portugal by Padre António Carvalho da Costa in 1706 and Debrie's etching (Contador de Argote 1734) which Bahn (1998) describes as the earliest published picture of European rock art. To the east, in Russia and Siberia, rock art also attracted interest during the 17th century. For instance Prince Nikolai Milesku Spafarii mentioned petroglyphs on the Yenisei in 1675, and Nicolaas Witsen (1692) described rock paintings. Daniil-Gotlieb Messerschmidt and Philip Johann Tabbert von Strahlenberg, who commenced archaeological excavations in Siberia, both recorded petroglyphs in the Yenisei region during the 1720s (von Strahlenberg 1730), ushering in scientific investigation in Siberia earlier than elsewhere.

In Africa, rock art was occasionally mentioned in the 18th century, beginning with 1721. Most of these brief references reported the European sighting of Bushman paintings in the continent's far south, and there appears to be no European mention of the vast corpus of northern African rock art until the early 19th century. It is important to appreciate that all of the 'discoveries' listed are fundamentally Eurocentric in the sense that most rock art had always been 'known' since it was made. For instance there is no consideration in the European literature of, say, Arab reports of north African rock art, which most probably do exist from the same period. Similarly, in Australia it is Governor Arthur Phillip who is generally credited with the first 'discovery' of rock art, which is almost certainly false, in the sense that he was probably not the first European to see such art. But in the tradition of British society, which also ignores the achievements of, for instance, convicts, a 'discovery' only counts when made by a gentleman and an officer. Many Europeans and Asians (Macassans) were in Australia before the First Fleet in 1788 and it would be very odd indeed if none of them had seen Aboriginal rock art. Some Western Australian petroglyphs were probably made by Macassans, and one European even engraved the date 1771 at a Pilbara petroglyph site, while a Dutchman seems to be the author of a 1714 inscription in a limestone cave on the Western Australian coast.

Rock art appreciation is often characterised by explaining the significance of the art in terms of the metaphysical constructs of the time. It is easy for us to see that this applied in previous centuries; we may be more reluctant to accept that the same rule still applies today. It is then a sobering thought to consider how researchers of future centuries will judge our own inadequate efforts in this field. There are several very early recorded attempts to attribute Latin American petroglyphs to St Thomas, a Catholic saint said to have travelled in those regions. Elsewhere, rock art was interpreted as the work of witches, barbarians, of the Devil, of Druids, of the world creators, of Vikings and other early peoples. This tradition of explaining rock art survives in specific forms to the present time, for instance by attributing it to space travellers, aliens or shamans.

Scholarly interest in rock art

Roughly with the beginning of the 19th century there appears a first concern with rock art as a source of data for scholarly contemplation, manifested by deliberate endeavours to record not only what one thinks one sees on a panel, but also relative relationships, particularly of size and juxtaposition of motifs. This was probably only in part a result of an appreciation that such relationships also need to be considered in interpretation. There was perhaps also a developing desire to resist the impulse to interpret, because the academic climes of the time valued more objective approaches in other fields. It is interesting that two centuries later we are still struggling with the same kinds of problems in the study of rock art, the struggle between the 'interpreters' and the 'rock art scientists'.

The initial development of the discipline is neatly illustrated by the various recordings of the above-mentioned Backa panel in Sweden. C. G. Brunius made a drawing of it between 1814 and 1816 that was accomplished with a grid and is just about correctly proportioned (Brunius 1868). Brunius' work, which survives in Stockholm's Topographical Archives, was particularly painstaking and he recognised the importance of lighting, including artificial lighting. A. E. Holmberg's (1848: Pls 33,34) lithographs of the same panel also approach best modern recording standards. The wood engraving of L. Baltzer, who experimented for decades with documentation methods, traced the Backa panel with linen and then reduced the recording painstakingly, showing even details of the rock fabric surrounding the motifs (Montelius 1874–79: 163; Baltzer 1881–90). Baltzer chose lithographic printing as the preferred means of publishing his meticulous recordings, printing them himself. Some of his work is so precise that subsequent weathering of the petroglyphs he recorded can be observed.

Similar developments are apparent elsewhere. For instance, the petroglyphs at Lake Onega in Russia, 'discovered' by Constantin Grewingk in 1848, were first recorded by him (Grewingk 1855) and Peter Schwed (Shved 1850). They produced good freehand drawings of the standard usual at that time, which were republished several times, and it was not until the early 20th century that the first true scale drawings were made (Hallström 1914). In much of Europe little progress was made in the study of rock art, however. For instance the pre-Historic age of Alpine petroglyphs was only recognised in 1877, by Emile Rivière at Mount Bego. Most rock art regions began to attract interest in the 1860s and 1870s. In 1879 it was still possible to flatly reject the possibility of Pleistocene rock art, as the discoverer of Altamira, Don Marcelino Santiago Tomás Sanz de Sautuola (1831-1888) learnt to his detriment. The rejection he suffered led to his premature death. It took in fact to 1895 to establish a case for Palaeolithic rock art in France, with the discovery of art in La Mouthe, a cave whose entrance was blocked by occupation deposits of that period, and Daleau's (1896) excavation of petroglyphs in Pair-non-Pair.

In most parts of the world this period in the historical development of rock art studies is dominated by observant travellers, naturalists, explorers and geographers. This is particularly evident in Africa, where Belzoni (1820) considered the antiquity of petroglyphs on the upper Nile, Jean-Jacques Ampère noted those in Nubia in 1848, and David Livingstone mentioned Angolan rock art in 1857. Much more detailed was the work of Heinrich Barth in Libya, who located numerous rock art sites in the Fezzan and at Telizzharen between 1849 and 1855, initiating Saharan rock art research (Barth 1857–58). Like Belzoni, Barth realised that the petroglyphs belonged to different cultural periods. Henri Duveyrier (1876) recorded Tassili petroglyphs and observed the need to interpret some rock art as indicating significantly better environmental conditions in the Sahara's past. In the continent's south, too, rock art began to attract the attention of travellers, such as Sir James Alexander who reported Bushman paintings in 1837, or the geologist George Stow who began recording rock art in 1867. Joseph Orpen's ethnographic work prompted that of Wilhelm Bleek and his relative, Lucy Lloyd, who together produced practically all the ethnographic knowledge we have today about the Bushmen and their rock art.

In South America, travels by scientific investigators such as Von Humboldt, who was the first to mention rock art in Ecuador, led to brief reports about rock art which are now marked by more scholarly preoccupations than previously. Others were Rivero and Von Tschudi (1851) in Peru, and later Erland Nordenskiöld (1910) in Peru and Bolivia, and d'Orbigny (1826–33) in Bolivia, while in Argentina rock art was reported by Francisco P. Moreno in 1877 (Moreno 1901). A detailed history of the discovery of rock art in South America during the 19th century is provided by Theodor Koch-Grünberg (1907). Sir Robert H. Schomburgk (1851) first reported cave art in the Dominican Republic. In North America, early reports are from the eastern states and progressively from further west (1804 in West Virginia, 1816 in Missouri, 1846 in New Mexico, 1850 in California, 1852 in Utah), culminating in the sustained work of Garrick Mallery through the 1880s (Mallery 1893). This work ushered in systematic rock art studies in the United States.

Australia, too, experienced this phase of scholarly interest in rock art by explorers, beginning with Matthew Flinders' (1814), and including George Grey (1841) and Ludwig Leichhardt in the 1840s. Systematic work, however, had to wait until well into the 20th century. In India, another British colony with major rock art bodies, much the same pertains. The first detailed study of Indian rock art began in the 1860s, with Archibald Carllyle's explorations in the northern Vindhya Ranges, in the Mirzapur district of Uttar Pradesh (Carllyle 1885), followed by the research there of Cockburn in the late 1800s (Cockburn 1883, 1888, 1894). Actually, the earliest reference we seem to have of Indian rock art relates to petroglyphs at Almora and dates from 1856 (Chakravarty and Bednarik 1997).

ARCHAEOLOGICAL STUDY OF ROCK ART

Carllyle was first assistant to the Archaeological Survey of India, and it is during the last decades of the 19th century that the then comparatively young discipline of archaeology began to take a sustained interest in rock art of some parts of the world. This applies in northern Africa and various parts of Eurasia, whereas it occurred somewhat delayed in Australia and South America, during the early decades of the 20th century. In North America, some researchers lament the 'lack of interest' among archaeologists still today (Chippindale 1993; Clottes 1994), whereas in China rock art studies became annexed by art history rather than archaeology. In most Muslim countries the study of rock art has found little or no official encouragement until very recent times. Thus the processes of the development of rock art research in the 20th century present a complex global mosaic, determined by historical currents, by the direction of previous work, political and religious preoccupations and, perhaps most importantly, the impact of influential scholars. In western Europe, for instance, there developed a distinct preoccupation with Pleistocene rock art right from the beginning of the century, whereas in all other continents this bias is either muted or absent. In Australia, which probably possesses most surviving Pleistocene rock art, archaeologists developed no preoccupation at all with this aspect.

Apart from these quite significant regional differences in the development of the discipline, the

20th century is characterised by an increasing influence of archaeology in most of the world. Archaeology as a discipline depends greatly upon the invention of styles, be they of stone tools, ceramic pots or arrow heads. Rock art is a particularly fertile field for the invention of styles. Once published, these constructs took on a life of their own, and they were used to prop up a series of hypotheses, often guided by diffusionist concepts or farflung cultural connections. Such stylistic constructs were most particularly valued in the creation of chronological sequences. Those of the Upper Palaeolithic cave art are especially important because they influenced model-building elsewhere. They were developed throughout the 20th century, and while those of individual leading proponents differed in various details, they all agreed on the evolutionary notion that there must have been an increase in the complexity of art with time. Palaeoart, according to these sequences, began either with the Perigordian or the Aurignacian, as simple 'signs' and primitive iconic motifs, developing through subsequent periods as progressively more complex traditions. It culminated in the polychrome paintings and pictures of extraordinary artistic sophistication in the Magdalenian 20 000 or 25 000 years later, followed by a period of 'decline'.

In its essential features this model persisted for nearly the entire 20th century, honed and refined by generations of researchers who accepted it as gospel. This is not to say that there was no debate, on the contrary, there was extensive and sometimes heated debate. But it always concerned minor details, which only served to reinforce the paradigm's underlying structure. Researchers invented and rejected artistic sub-phases and styles, and developed great expertise in recognising the diagnostic features of the styles they themselves had created. Two developments in 1995 led to the sudden collapse of the underlying structure of this intricate stylistic chronology (Bednarik 1995). It remains difficult to assess the effects of these changes, because generations of researchers have modelled their thinking on the now discredited chronology, and there is strong opposition to reform within the discipline. If remedial processes were left to archaeology it would take generations to escape the ingrained half-truths it has created about rock art.

While this was a local European issue, it determined the direction of the discipline elsewhere. European Upper Palaeolithic rock art research has for a century served the rest of the world as an implicit model of how to conduct research. For instance, Asian and in some cases even North American researchers have searched for 'stylistically Upper Palaeolithic' rock art in their quest to locate Pleistocene traditions, failing entirely to find similar traditions. Yet there is almost no evidence that the Final Pleistocene graphic arts of most of Eurasia, east of a line through Germany and Italy, resembled those of Franco-Cantabria, so this search inspired by an inappropriate and now discredited model was entirely in vain. Consequently what we know today about the Pleistocene arts of the rest of Eurasia is minute, disjointed and profoundly incomplete (Bednarik 1994). The European procedure of archaeologically inventing styles, giving them labels and attaching them to archaeologically perceived traditions was also widely adopted. Yet archaeology is incapable of defining emic cultures reliably, it merely classifies material residues of human populations and then makes the untestable assumption that these taxonomic constructs define distinctive peoples or cultural traditions. This used to be taken so far that the perceived movement of technological traits or behaviour patterns was equated with the migration of actual peoples, in the absence of any other evidence.

Rock art, with its numerous potential variables, offers almost unlimited scope for the invention of stylistic markers. Archaeology has made ample use of this. This is not to say that such deductions necessarily need to be false, rock art traditions certainly do possess stylistic parameters. The valid issue is that these are not self-evident, and they may not be detectable in the way the alien researchers often imagine. The claims of archaeologists that they have the ability of correctly identifying valid stylistic markers in rock art need to be discounted, not because they are *always* false, but because they are *often* false; one has no way of knowing when they are. Major rock art sites usually consist of cumulative records of successive traditions, and without identifying these traditions individually archaeology can only create false concepts of traditions. Indeed, this practice is comparable to excavating the tools of many traditions, and then lumping them all together and defining them as a single cultural assemblage. This is the most anti-archaeological way one could treat the layers of an excavation, yet in rock art this is precisely how archaeologists treat the evidence. For instance, many such cumulative site inventories in Australia are described as 'Panaramitee style', even though they clearly consist of many chronologically discrete components. Or to give a better known example: the rich rock art of Lascaux Cave in France probably consists of a cumulative record spanning Palaeolithic and post-Palaeolithic traditions of at least 10 000 years (Bahn 1994), yet for over half a century it has been held up as a paragon of one single tradition. If archaeology defines its traditions of rock art in this haphazard manner and then bases all kinds of secondary hypotheses on such fallacious data (e.g. that another corpus of rock art must be the same age as that of Lascaux, because it comprises stylistically similar elements), then these traditions are probably misleading constructs and can only lead to further errors.

Archaeologists are likely to reject my harsh description of what they have contributed to rock art research, but it is necessary to consider how their long domination of the discipline has retarded it. Many of the methods of scientific examination of rock art have been available in other disciplines for much if not all of the 20th century. For instance many of the methods of forensic science are highly appropriate for the analysis of rock art, much more so than any archaeological method. Their introduction and that of many others, particularly dating methods, has consistently been discouraged by archaeologists, in favour of orthodox archaeological approaches which inevitably centred on style and meaning. As a consequence rock art studies became an impoverished and backward field of research. The paradox is that, without some idea of its age, rock art is of no use whatsoever to archaeology. Yet the introduction of scientific methods to the field, including for age estimation, was actively resisted by archaeologists who objected to their discipline 'being taken over by the scientists', as one archaeologist observed in 1995.

THE ADVENT OF ROCK ART SCIENCE

As in any historical development in research, there were precursors and many isolated endeavours of introducing scientific methods of enquiry into this field for many decades. Indeed, some were envisaged as early as 185 years ago (Belzoni 1820). If the discipline had not been taken over by archaeology a century ago, it would almost certainly have reached its scientific phase much earlier. Since the middle of the 20th century, archaeology has experienced a continuous crisis of confidence, brought about by a variety of circumstances. First the introduction of carbon isotope dating coincided with the discovery of the Piltdown hoax. This was followed by the quick succession of often contradictory theoretical paradigms in the following decades, and the rising opposition to archaeological practices from various quarters, such as ethnic groups. The discipline became increasingly defensive and in this climate the endeavours of researchers to adopt a scientific, i.e. non-archaeological, epistemology were not welcomed. Archaeology does make extensive use of the hard sciences, in an opportunistic way rather than by adopting a scientific universal theory (such as taphonomic logic).

This state of affairs pertained in the 1970s and into the early 1980s. The change brought about in the 1980s is attributable not to any particular developments in scientific technology, but to a combination of structural changes in the discipline. Most of all, rock art research organisations had begun to appear in several parts of the world. The first, the Canadian Rock Art Research Associates (CRARA), was founded in 1969 by Selwyn Dewdney. Although it became defunct in the early 1980s without having effected any significant changes, it did lead to the formation by Klaus Wellmann of the considerably more robust American Rock Art Research Association (ARARA) in 1975. The real breakthrough came with the Australian Rock Art Research Association (AURA), founded by me in 1983. Within a few years it advanced to the most effective force in the discipline, establishing its premier journal, *Rock Art Research*, and in 1988 staging the first world congress of rock art research. This brought together, for the first time, the world's foremost specialists in the field. Until then, individual rock art researchers as well as rock art organisations around the world operated largely without being aware of the work conducted in other parts of the world — sometimes even in their own country or region of activity. As a result the discipline had experienced a great diversity of research approaches and terminologies, reflected in a multitude of idiosyncratic constructs, sequences, chronologies, names and definitions. Communication was limited, and where it did occur it often led to misunderstandings, and clarifications sometimes led to academic feuds.

At the First AURA Congress, held in Darwin in 1988, the International Federation of Rock Art Organisations (IFRAO) was formed, initially by nine members. By the advent of the 21st century it had some forty member organisations representing many thousands of researchers in all parts of the world. These developments had profound implications for the discipline, particularly in standardisation of terminology and methodology, in the establishment of universal deontological standards and, perhaps most importantly, in a far-reaching reappraisal of conservation and site management practices and conditions. Centuries of neglect and abuse of rock art, including by researchers, became the subject of debate, and rock art specialists found themselves involved in pitched battles with state archaeological agencies in a few countries. The fact that these dramatic changes in the way the discipline operated occurred under the auspices of a fully democratic international federation led by very dedicated and resourceful scholars who, effectively, co-ordinated its strategies caught an antiquated establishment off-guard in some cases. As the new century commences, these changes are far from complete, but it has already become adequately clear that the progress made in the discipline in the last fifteen years of the 20th century exceeds in magnitude that of the previous 200 years.

Within these last few years rock art research has adopted a plethora of new methods, all contributed by scientific disciplines. They include a wide range of physical and chemical analyses of rock art and rock art-related materials, such as the identification of inclusions in paint residues and in mineral accretions, ranging from fibres to pollen and graphite crystals. Much of this work is directed at questions of antiquity, but numerous other issues also attract attention now. For instance, the technology of paints used in rock art, as well as of their application, are being analysed. The nano-stratigraphy of paints and mineral accretions has shown how sequences of rock art can be studied scientifically rather than by archaeological intuition. Numerous approaches are being developed in the ever-crucial question of the age of rock art. Field microscopy of rock art has been developed for several purposes, including dating, petrography and technological analyses. The discrimination between anthropic and nonanthropic rock markings, which has been a significant difficulty for archaeologists, has been developed into a fine art. Much the same has been done for portable art objects, as well as the detection of fakes. Replication studies have been attempted, although they remain still in their infancy. The related subject of production processes of petroglyphs has received some close attention. The psychology of iconicity and its decipherment have been considered, and the distinction between mental and artistic representations. Similarly, an interest has been developed in the relationships between ontogenic and phylogenic development of logic and symbolism, and in the more general utilisation of universals in palaeoart studies. Of particular importance is the development of taphonomic logic, which is crucial in developing a science of rock art. Rigorously framed statistical approaches are being developed. In all of these many new approaches to rock art, developed in the last fifteen years, the epistemology applied to the formulation of theories and the interpretation of palaeoart has become central. In this, rock art science differs fundamentally from the epistemology of traditional archaeological approaches. The principal difference, after all, is that in science all propositions need to be refutable, whereas orthodox archaeology relies traditionally on the lack of refutability in its claims of knowledge.

None of this is intended to suggest that archaeology has no further role to play in the study of palaeoart. On the contrary, many archaeologists have already adapted their work to the new scenario, and now work in collaborative projects with scientists. Most certainly the archaeologist has a role to play in the future development of the discipline, but the difference will be that he or she will be one member in a team of several researchers, and will no longer be able to dictate the terms of research priorities or the direction of the discipline. Archaeologists, like their colleagues from art history, anthropology, ethnography, geography, semiotics, geomorphology, geochemistry, nuclear physics, conservation science and so forth will contribute their diverse talents to this complex discipline if they have the flexibility to collaborate in such ways. But the agenda will no longer be that of the past: that the main role of rock art is to explain archaeology. Not only is it quite doubtful that rock art will ever have any great explanatory role in archaeology, its ultimate research potential is not closely connected with archaeology. Rather, rock art science serves the endeavour of understanding the cognitive and intellectual world of past and present societies, and ultimately perhaps in determining how our species acquired its very concepts of reality. In comparison to the significance of such a profound philosophical issue, the contribution of rock art in the interpretation of archaeology is entirely trivial.

REFERENCES

BAHN, P. G. 1994. Lascaux: composition or accumulation? *Zephyrvs* 47: 3–13.

BAHN, P. G. 1998. *The Cambridge illustrated history of prehistoric art.* Cambridge University Press, Cambridge.

BARTH, H. 1857-58. *Reisen und Entdeckungen in nord- und Zentral-Afrika in den Jahren 1849 bis 1855*, 5 volumes. J. Perthes, Gotha. (French translation, 4 volumes, 1860–63, F. Didot – A. Lacroix-Verbroeckhoven et Cie, Paris-Bruxelles-Leipzig.)

BALTZER, L. 1881–90. *Glyphes des rochers du Bohuslän (Suède).* Goteborg.

BEDNARIK, R. G. 1988. El arte rupestre Boliviano visto desde el exterior. *SIARB Boletín* 2: 22–28.

BEDNARIK, R. G. 1992. Acerca de la motivación del re-uso del arte rupestre: un ejemplo del Período Colonial de Bolivia. In R. Querejazu Lewis (ed.), *El arte rupestre colonial y republicano de Bolivia y paises vecinos*, pp. 28–35. Contribuciones al Estudio del Arte Rupestre Sudamericano 3. SIARB, La Paz.

BEDNARIK, R. G. 1994. A taphonomy of palaeoart. *Antiquity* 68: 68–74.

BEDNARIK, R. G. 1995. Refutation of stylistic constructs in Palaeolithic rock art. *Comptes Rendus de L'Académie de Sciences Paris* 321(série IIa, No. 9): 817–21.

BEDNARIK, R. G. and LI FUSHUN 1991. Rock art dating in China: past and future. *The Artefact* 14: 25–33.

BEDNARIK, R. G. 2001. The oldest known rock art in the world. *Anthropologie* 39(2): 81–89.

BELZONI, G. 1820. *Narrative of the operations and recent discoveries within the pyramids, temples, tombs and excavations in Egypt and Nubia*, Vol. 1. London.

BOUGE, L. J. 1947. Objets lithiques et pétroglyphes des Antilles, à l'origine, à l'arrivée de C. Colomb, après la conquête. *Compte-Rendu du Congrès International des Américanistes* 28: 587–98.

BRANDÃO, A. F. 1930 (1618). *Diálogos das Grandezas do Brasil* (ed. J. Capistrano de Abreu). Rio de Janeiro.

BRUNIUS, C. G. 1868. *Försök till förklaring öfver häll-ristningar.* Lund.

CABRERA ORTIZ, W. 1946. Pictógrafos y petroglifos. *Boletín de Arqueología* (Bogotá) 2(3): 231–53.

CALANCHA, A. DE LA 1638. *Coronica moralizada del orden de San Augustín en el Perú.* Barcelona.

CARLLYLE, A. 1885. *Report of tours in Gorakhpur and Ghazipur.* Archaeological Survey Report 22, Calcutta.

CHAKRAVARTY, K. K. and R. G. BEDNARIK 1997. *Indian rock art and its global context.* Motilal Banarsidass Publishers Private Limited, Delhi, and Indira Gandhi Rashtriya Manav Sangrahalaya, Bhopal.

CHIPPINDALE, C. 1993. Australia: towards secure knowledge of prehistoric pictures. *Cambridge Archaeol ogical Journal* 3: 141–53.

CHEN ZHAOFU 1988. *Découverte de l'art prehistorique en Chine.* Albin Michel, Paris.

CLOTTES, J. 1994. Rock art in the USA: an outsider's view. *International Newsletter on Rock Art* 9: 23–4.

CLOTTES, J., J. COURTIN and H. VALLADAS 1992. A well-dated Palaeolithic cave: the Cosquer Cave at Marseille. *Rock Art Research* 9: 122–29.

COCKBURN, J. 1883. A short account of the petrographs in the caves and rock shelters of the Kaimur Range in Mirzapore District. *Proceedings of the Asiatic Society of Bengal* 52: 125–26.

COCKBURN, J. 1888. On Palaeolithic implements from the Ken Ravines in south Mirzapur. *Journal of the Anthropological Institute* 62: 57–65.

COCKBURN, J. 1894. On flint implements from the Kon Ravines of south Mirzapore. *Journal of the Asiatic Society of Bengal* 63: 21–37.

CONTADOR DE ARGOTE, J. 1734. *Memórias para a história eclesiástica de Arcebispado de Braga.*

DALEAU, F. 1896. Les gravures sur roche de la caverne de Pair-non-Pair. *Actes de la Société Archeologique de Bordeaux* 21: 235.

D'ORBIGNY, A. 1826-33. *Voyage dans l'Amérique Méridionale.* Paris.

DUBELAAR, C. N. 1986. *South American and Caribbean petroglyphs.* Foris Publications, Dordrecht.

DUVEYRIER, H. 1876. Sculptures antiques de la province marocaine de Soûs découvertes par le rabbin Mardochée. *Bulletin de la Société de géographie de Paris* 12: 129–44.

FLINDERS, M. 1814. *A voyage to Terra Australis*, 2 volumes. Nicol, London.

GILLI, F. S. 1780–84. *Saggio di storia Americana, o sia, storia naturale, civile e sacra de'regni e delle provincia spagnuole di Terra-Ferma nell'America Meridionale.* Rome.

GREWINGK, C. 1855. Über die in Granit geritzten Bildergruppen am Ostufer des Onega-Sees. *Bulletin de la Classe des Sciences historiques, philologiques et politiques de l'Académie Impériale des Sciences de Saint-Pétersbourg* 12: 97–103.

GREY, G. 1841. *Journals of two expeditions of discovery.* Boone, London.

HALLSTRÖM, G. 1914. Issledovaniye kamennogo veka u Belogo morya i Onezhskogo ozera v 1910 godu. In *Trudy XV arkheologicheskogo syezda v Novgorode 1911*, 1: 100.

HOLMBERG, A. E. 1848. *Skandinaviens hällristningar.* P. G. Berg, Stockholm.

HUMBOLDT, A. VON and A. BONPLAND 1814–25. *Voyage aux régions equinoxiales du nuveau continent; rélation historique.* Paris.

KOCH-GRÜNBERG, T. 1907. *Südamerikanische Felszeichnungen.* Berlin.

MALLERY, G. 1893. *Picture-writing of the American Indians.* Tenth Annual Report of the Bureau of American Ethnology, 1888–89, Washington.

MONTELIUS, O. 1874-79. Bohusländska hällristningar. *Bidrag till kännedom om Göteborgs och Bohusläns fornminnen och historia*, pp. 146–165, 423–424. Stockholm.

MORENO, F. P. 1901. Notes on the anthropogeography of Argentina. *Journal of the Royal Geographical Society of London* 18: 574–89.

NORDBLADH, J. 1981. Knowledge and information in Swedish petroglyph documentation. In C.-A. Moberg (ed.), *Similar finds? Similar interpretations*, pp. G1–G79. Department of Archaeology, University of Göteborg, Göteborg.

NORDENSKIÖLD, E. 1910. *Archäologische Untersuchungen im Grenzgebiet von Peru und Bolivien.* Stockholm.

QUEREJAZU LEWIS, R. 1994. Contemporary indigenous use of traditional rock art sites at Yaraque, Bolivia. *Rock Art Research* 11: 3–9.

RAMOS GAVILÁN, A. 1621. *Historia del celebre y milagroso santuario de la insigne imagen de Nuestra Señora de Copacabana y sus milagros e invención de la crux de Carabuco.* Lima.

RIVERO, J. 1883. *Historia de las misiones de los llanos de Casanere y los ríos Orinoco y Meta, escrita el año de 1736.* Bogotá.

RIVERO, M. E. and J. D. DE TSCHUDI 1851. *Antigüeda-des Peruanas.* Vienna.

RUIZ DE MONTOYA, A. 1639. *Conquista esperitual hecha por los religiosos de la Compañia de Jesús, en las provincias del Paraguay, Paraná, Uruguay y Tapé.* Madrid.

SCHABEL, M. A. 1965. *Relación de su viaje (1704).* Anuario del Instituto de Antropología e Historia de la Fakultad de Humanidades y Educación de la Universidad Central de Venezuela, Vol. 2, Caracas.

SCHOMBURGK, R. H. 1841. *Robert Hermann Schomburgks Reisen in Guiana und am Orinoko, während der Jahre 1835–1839. Nach seinen Berichten und Mittheilungen an die Geographische Gesellschaft in London.* O. A. Schomburgk, Leipzig.

SCHOMBURGK, R. H. 1851. Ethnological researches in Santo Domingo. *Meetings of the British Association for the Advancement of Science* 21: 90–92.

SHVED, P. 1850. Krestovyi i Peli mysy. *Geograficheskiye izvestiya, izdavayemye Imperatorskim Russkim geograficheskim obshcestvom* 1: 68–71.

SIMÓN, P. 1882–92. *Noticias historiales de las conquistas de tierra firme en las Indias occidentales (1623–1627).* Bogotá.

STRAHLENBERG, P. J. T. VON 1730. *Das Nord- und Östliche Theil von Europa und Asien.*

SUHM, P. F. 1784. *Samlinger til den danske historie.* B 2. H.3.

TANG HUISHENG and GAO ZHIWEI 2004. Dating analysis of rock art in the Qinghai-Tibetan Plateau. *Rock Art Research* 21: 161–72.

THAM, P. 1794. *Göthiska monumenter.* Stockholm.

WITSEN, N. 1692. *Nord und Ost Tartaray.*

3. THE DISCRIMINATION OF NATURAL AND ARTIFICIAL ROCK MARKINGS

INTRODUCTION

The discrimination between natural rock markings and those made intentionally by humans is obviously fundamental to a scientific study of rock art. Indeed, unless we can have full confidence in this ability of recognising whether or not a particular rock marking represents what we define as rock art, there can be no effective analysis of this phenomenon. After all, there would be no merit in speculating about the style, significance or archaeological age of a rock marking, or how to preserve it, when it is in fact a purely natural phenomenon.

There are numerous instances on record of archaeologists having identified natural rock markings as rock art. Some practitioners have even 'dated' or otherwise 'analysed' such misidentified markings. Similarly, rock art has occasionally been described as natural by archaeologists, although much less frequently. This general problem of recognising whether a phenomenon is man-made (artificial) or natural is not limited to rock surfaces, it is also widespread among portable objects of various types, especially portable palaeoart (beads, pendants, plaques, carvings, figurines). As demonstrated by almost innumerable instances, an archaeological training provides no protection against such fallacies, and the discrimination of the two classes of markings or objects is a specialist task. It falls into the realm of palaeoart science, and in the case of rock art is best investigated from the perspective of the geomorphologist or geochemist.

While markings on rock surfaces are extremely numerous, rock art (intentional non-utilitarian anthropic rock markings) accounts for considerably less than one millionth of them. Among the truly astronomical number of natural markings, a small proportion resembles rock art and can conceivably be misidentified as such.

Much the same problem exists with stone implements: their secure identification is not possible in archaeology. Around the world numerous instances exist of whole assemblages of flaked stone fragments whose unresolved status bears witness to this truism. Practitioners cannot agree on the criteria for discriminating between artefacts or 'nature-facts' (also called 'geofacts'; natural products that resemble artificially flaked stone). Some celebrated recent examples are finds from Pedra Furada (Brazil), Calico Hills (California), Riwat (Pakistan) and Diring-Ur'akh (Siberia). The frequent misidentification of fractured stone illustrates how the pronouncements of archaeologists are unfalsifiable, or can be tested only with great difficulty. A naturally fractured piece of flint may appear to resemble an artefact in every conceivable respect, and yet it was formed entirely by natural processes (impact, pressure, *Salzsprengung*, regelation, temperature changes and so forth). Under certain conditions, tens of thousands of such naturally formed stone flakes may occur at a site. Their number may then be cited in support of an anthropic explanation for such a concentration. A good example is provided by the Calico Hills site in California, where well over 100 000 naturefacts have been excavated, the 'best' specimens of which seem to resemble Lower Palaeolithic artefacts very closely. Nevertheless, there is in my view not a single humanly made tool among them (except in the uppermost 10 cm of the deposit). Such sites have been found in all continents, illustrating how tool definitions used in Pleistocene archaeology may simply be predicated on stylistic claims about formal attributes.

It is important here to appreciate the subjectivity of the stone tool classes invented by archaeology, because precisely the same kinds of limitations apply to archaeological taxonomies imposed on rock art (see Ch. 1). Even the motif classes the archaeologist applies to an art corpus are entirely arbitrary, created as the subjective perception of the modern, usually 'Western' observer dictates. These classes are defined in such a way that sometimes they can easily include rock markings that are not made by humans at all. Archaeologists are academically and cognitively predisposed to look for patterning in evidence. When they believe to discern patterns, they tend to see this as an indication of human involvement (signifying 'intentionality'). In archaeological work such perceived patterning may relate to any one of numerous phenomena: the arrangement of 'post holes' or stone slabs in an excavation, the occurrence of sites in a given landscape, the consistent way an assemblage of animal bones is fractured, and so forth. Archaeological training requires the development of such an ability to detect patterning, and combined with the idea that stylistic templates apply in all cultural remains, this ability is crucial to archaeological studies.

It does, however, bring some drawbacks to the discipline as well. Patterning can of course indicate the involvement of an intelligent organism, but it also occurs as the result of numerous natural phenomena. Taphonomy, for instance, creates patterning in the evidence, as do countless other 'natural' processes, including weathering, animal behaviour, vulcanism and so forth. When naturally patterned evidence resembles cultural patterning, archaeologists may show a predisposition towards favouring the latter explanation. Archaeologically untutored observers with a good understanding of natural processes, such as foresters, naturalists, indigenes leading relatively traditional lives and peasants in remote regions are not so predisposed. They often experience no difficulties in recognising the natural or cultural status of a rock marking. This applies even in cases when they are confronted for the very first time with the need to consciously discriminate between the two types of markings or objects. It could then be said that the difficulties some specialists have in distinguishing between artefacts and naturefacts are, paradoxically, attributable to their academic training, their mental conditioning.

In order to avoid misidentifications of this nature we need to understand the cognitive processes involved in them. Naïve empiricism, which remains well entrenched in the disciplines, derives its confidence from the belief that it can create order in disorder, that it can detect the laws ruling natural systems. Although quantum mechanics has shown that these systems and laws seem to be a great deal more complex than previously thought, archaeology follows the traditional mode of positivism, treating the discipline as if it were subject to some system resembling the periodic table of elements, or the species biology chooses to acknowledge. 'Taxonomisation', as the process of creating nomenclatures based on inadequate understanding of the system(s) in question has been called (Bednarik 1994a), creates classes of data and entities, and having done so, the discipline pretends that they are real. In the case of archaeology it is then claimed that some of these 'egofacts' (Consens 2000) are, e.g., side scrapers, whereas others are end scrapers, *because practitioners say so.* The implicit logic is that we can readily 'recognise' the taxa, hence they exist and the pigeonhole created is justified. Taxonomisation is both necessary for, and detrimental to, science. The way to minimise the detrimental aspects and maximise the beneficial ones is to always remember that the taxonomies of science are temporary or tentative, and usually not real. They are, like the model of reality humans have themselves created, merely a crutch on which to support our frail disciplines. In reality, a taxonomy can only be constructed convincingly of entities whose common crucial denominator(s) of the phenomenon category in question we can identify. This is usually not possible because as mere humans we have, as noted in the first chapter, no access to reality.

Discriminating cultural and natural rock markings involves a thorough knowledge of the ranges of both phenomena, and of the processes of alteration affecting both types. The following sub-chapters explore the various types of rock markings that are not rock art, and then place rock art into a taxonomy that has some semblance of objectivity. In practical terms it is usually possible to discount most of the natural interpretations of rock markings quite readily, and if none of the categories described here fit, and the marking under investigation does resemble a non-utilitarian anthropic rock marking, then — and only then — are we justified in accepting the marking in question as rock art. This discussion divides rock markings initially into geological and biological classes, totalling twelve types (Table 1). Rock art itself is one of the six types of the biological class. It is to be emphasised that this taxonomy is not absolute, there are often intermediate forms of markings, or marks that may fall into two or more of the categories below. Hence this is merely a practical framework to assist in identification, not some periodic table of elements.

G. Geological rock markings

GP. Petrographic markings
- GP1. Inclusions in igneous rocks
- GP2. Naturally enhanced inherent markings

GW. Weathering markings
- GW1. Solution marks
- GW2. Exfoliation marks

GK. Kinetic markings
- GK1. Taphonomic marks
- GK2. Clastic movement marks

B. Biological rock markings

BP. Plant markings
- BP1. Kinetic plant marks
- BP2. Chemical plant marks

BA. Animal markings
- BA1. Animal scratches
- BA2. Animal polish

BH. Humanly-made markings
- BH1. Unintentional or utilitarian anthropic marks
- BH2. Non-utilitarian marks (rock art)

Table 1. A tentative taxonomy of markings on rock surfaces which are readily perceptible by humans, and which have been, or could conceivably be, identified as petroglyphs.

GP. PETROGRAPHIC MARKINGS

Petrographic markings on rock surfaces are attributable to intrinsic structures or inclusions found in rocks, and are divided into two basic types: those which derive their crucial characteristics of visibility from inherent factors of specific areas of rock surface (Type GP1), and those in which this visibility has been enhanced or accentuated by secondary processes, notably selective solution or corrosion (Type GP2). The overriding common characteristic of these markings, and one which they share with no other type of rock marking, is that the structures they are associated with always extend beneath the surface of the rock, over distances ranging from under a millimetre to many centimetres, even metres. In other words, these markings are attributable to forms present in the rock structure which happen to have been truncated at the present surface, and were rendered visible by some characteristic or process. Quite obviously, they can easily be distinguished from petroglyphs by sectioning of the rock, to examine whether their formation extends beneath the surface. However, this is neither always readily possible, nor is it desirable to destroy the rock in the process of determining the nature of a marking. Hence it is requisite to possess some understanding of such phenomena. In most cases a careful examination can resolve the matter conclusively and, in any event, only specific rock types seem susceptible to such markings.

GP1. Inclusions in igneous rocks

The phenomena considered under this heading have not been significantly affected by weathering processes. The marking on the rock surface is attributable to a distinctive variation in the rock's texture. Such xenoliths formed in igneous rocks when, during solidification of the magma, selective crystallisation occurred locally. Patterns of crystallisation in these rocks are largely determined by cooling rates, which will favour some of the component minerals over others. A variety of visually and often structurally distinctive formations may be the result, and where they become exposed on a rock surface, they may resemble artificial rock markings. An example used here for illustration is on basalt near Maryborough, Australia (Figure 2).

Such xenolithic phenomena have been commonly identified as petroglyphs. One aspect that might invite errors if this kind could be that these features tend to occur in localised groups, and this clustered distribution might emphasise their apparent artificiality and the concept of 'site'. An example are the 'whale and fish petroglyphs' at the Canadian littoral site Point no Point (Hill and Hill 1974: 63), which occur on a single panel and which are certainly petrographic marks that have not been enhanced by humans. It should be noted, however, that weathering may commonly apply to these phenomena, so a clear demarcation between GP1 and GP2 markings is not realistically possible.

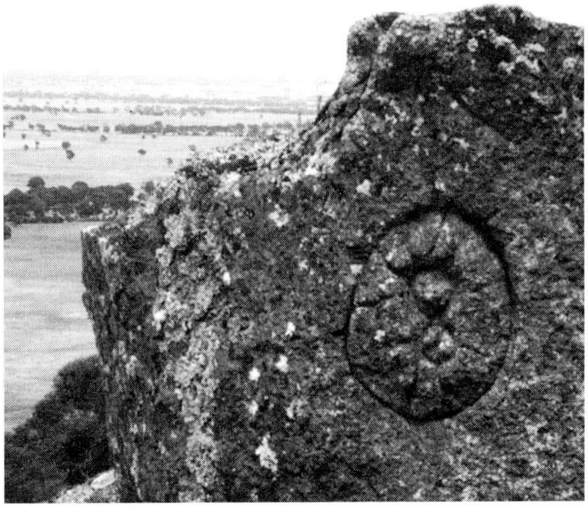

Figure 2. Natural petrographic marking on basalt near Maryborough, Victoria, Australia.

Markings attributable to xenolithic inclusions in igneous rocks, attributable to rock fragments that differ from their former lava matrix petrologically, may resemble petroglyphs very closely, particularly when they are of suitable dimensions or form distinctive 'motifs'. They can be identified by close petrographic examination, especially microscopic assessment of crystallisation states, and also by surveying the nearby rock surfaces to establish the full range of markings present. As with many other types of natural rock marks, there is often a spectrum of morphology, ranging from those that resemble petroglyphs very closely to markings that certainly do not, by any stretch of the imagination. Once such a range has been identified, it is often easy to see that the 'most convincing' markings must be seen in their full context of surface phenomena existing at the locality in question (Figure 3).

Surface markings that are attributable to inclusions in the rock fabric are not restricted to igneous rocks; they can be found in most other types of rock. Among them are bedding strata and other formations in sandstone, fossil casts in a variety of rocks, patches of exotic minerals, products of replacement processes, and many more. However, their nature is usually fairly obvious and serious students of rock art have not experienced any difficulties with them. They are therefore not considered here.

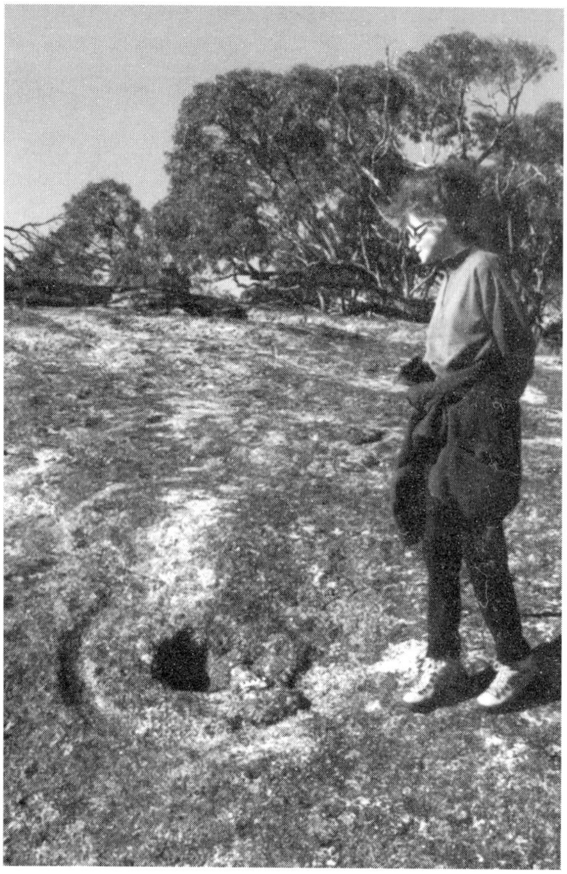

Figure 3. Large natural petrographic marking on granite at the peak of Mt Korong, near Wedderburn, Victoria, Australia.

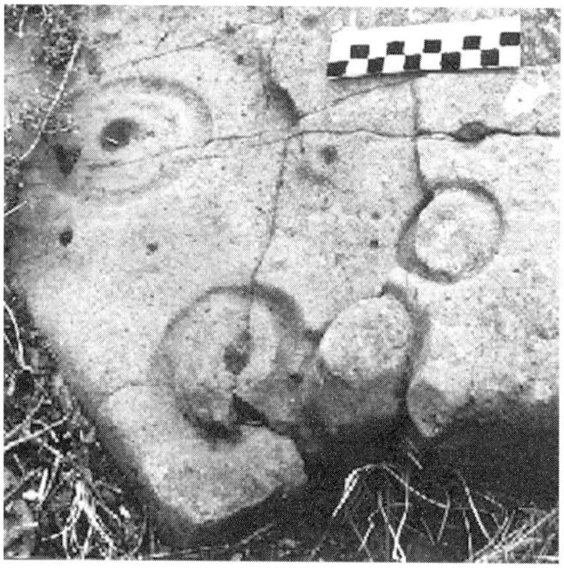

Figure 4. Natural petrographic markings on basalt at the peak of Mt Loch, Victoria, Australia.

GP2. Naturally enhanced inherent markings

Numerous distinctive rock markings occur at the summit of Mt Loch in the Australian Alps of Victoria, an extrusive basalt cone (Figure 4). Most are circles of up to 10 cm in diameter; there are also concentric circles, circles with central pit, and joined circles or ellipses. Circles are often well-shaped, and in many cases the groove widths, depths and sections closely resemble those of archaic Australian petroglyph traditions. Archaeologists have therefore considered the possibility of human manufacture.

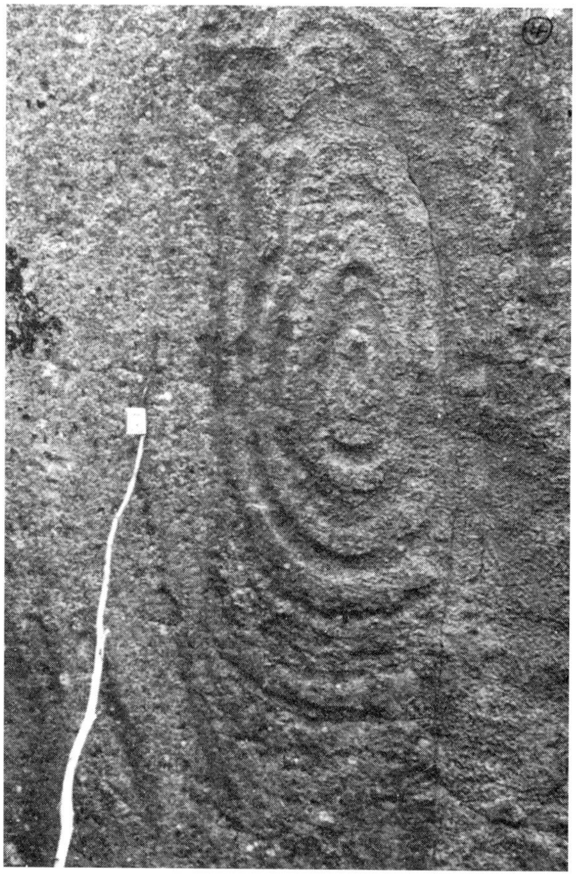

Figure 5. Large petrographic marking on vertical dolerite surface, about 2 m high, central Tasmania.

The basalt facies in a small area contains xenolithic inclusions from its igneous phase, which are rounded, often elongate and cigar shaped, but which are petrographically similar to their matrix. Where they are sectioned on the rock surface they form circles. At the contact joints between each inclusion and the matrix occur iron-rich minerals, which promote local acceleration of erosional processes. The result is a distinctive groove following the outline of the truncated inclusion. The joint itself may not be visible on the corroded base of the groove, and the markings they form resemble very ancient petroglyphs, particularly where more recent fractures cross through them. Besides the dominant circular markings, there are also some more complex 'designs'. However, none of them is the work of humans, nor is there any evidence that the grooves might have been emphasised by human intervention. These are purely natural phenomena, and they are attributable to a combination of diagenetic factors and recent weathering. A similar explanation probably pertains to a prominent and large set of concentric circular markings on a dolerite boulder, discovered in central Tasmania in 1995 (Bednarik 1999). They, too, were described as petroglyphs, and even assigned an approximate age without evidence (Figure 5).

Phenomena of this specific type are comparatively rare and may be restricted to igneous rock, in which such inclusions could form during crystallisation. This is not to suggest that there are no inclusions of other types (for instance, fossil casts or vesicle formations), but it seems that the surface markings they might conceivably cause cannot be mistaken for petroglyphs by a reasonably experienced observer, even if there has been an emphasising process at work.

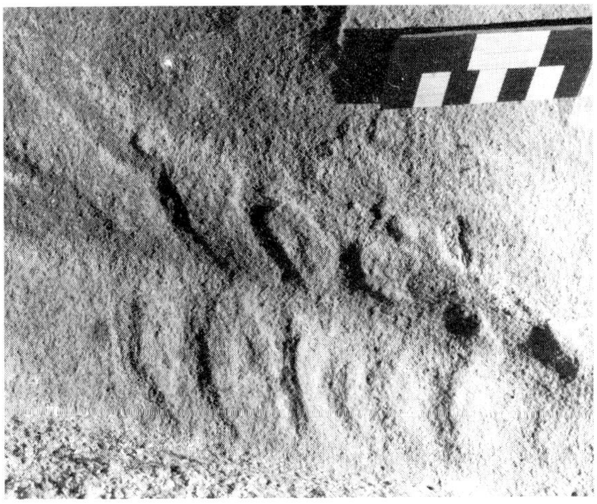

Figure 6. Part of a concentric arrangement of natural markings on sandstone, attributable to weathering of inherent sandstone strata. Gariwerd (Grampians), Victoria, Australia.

Other types of 'naturally enhanced inherent markings' are not restricted to igneous rocks; they have been observed on many types of rock, including sedimentary facies, even limestones. They are still attributable to some inclusion, formation or other feature inherent in the rock fabric. These features include the laminations often found in sedimentary rocks, especially sandstones, thin lamellae of intruded minerals, bedding planes or minute joints, and other textural disconformities. Where they are truncated by the rock surface, their structures may be subjected to differential solution or corrosion, which emphasise visibility of the phenomena. The markings so formed may then be an interplay of the geometries of the geological disconformity, and the relief or topography of the rock surface where the two intersect. For example, a sequence of parallel rock laminations intersected by a concave surface will result in concentric arcs or semicircles, as in Figure 6. The set of concentric arcs resembles the archaic petroglyph 'style' of Australia very closely, including the groove section and pitted appearance typical of pounded motifs. The markings are attributable to laminae of the sandstone, exposed by weathering processes (granular mass-exfoliation) that formed the curved wall of the recess in which the markings occur.

The next example was found in the same region, just south of Horsham. At this location occur several panels densely covered by cup-marks of typical cupule appearance, a type of petroglyph frequently found in northern Australia and in many other world regions (Bednarik 1993a, 2000). There are several hundred such cup-shaped marks on hard siliceous sandstone at the Horsham site, all between 5 and 10 cm in diameter, and a few centimetres deep.

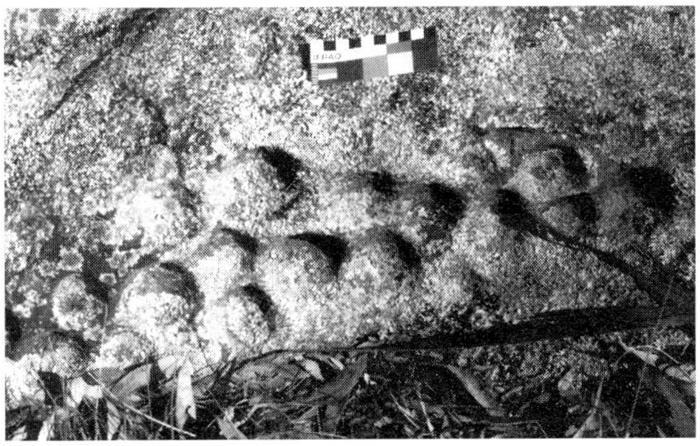

Figure 7. Cupule-like natural markings on lichen-covered sandstone, near Horsham, Victoria, Australia.

Superficially they are indistinguishable from anthropic cupule panels, and yet they are entirely natural products (Figure 7). They are the result of a complex lithological process at the time the rock formed, in which a layer of highly water-sorted (evenly sized) spherical cobbles laying on quartz sand was covered by a thin, ferruginous lamina. The sand bed was metamorphosed to a slightly quartzitic sandstone. Erosive processes then removed the pebble conglomerate, presumably because it was less weathering resistant than the silica cement of the sandstone. The iron deposit was mostly removed, and the remaining negative impressions of the pebbles were exposed to weathering action. Once weathered, the dense groups of hemispherical depressions became almost indistinguishable from cupules, and the temptation of seeing them as cupules is considerable.

Tectonic fracture lines in limestone caves are often emphasised at the rock surface by solution and other processes resulting in grooves. Sometimes these marks resemble rock art, but in the vast majority of cases their geomorphological nature is quite apparent. Nevertheless, there have been cases of misidentification, including one of the most spectacular cases in the literature. Rogers (1981) reported discovering 'the first examples in Britain of Palaeolithic parietal cave art'. He had found what he thought were engraved pictures of two animals outside a cave in the Wye Valley. The grooves were described as possibly being 'inlaid with malachite', a technique never before reported in Pleistocene art. There were several other aspects of the article, which should have suggested that the report was either a hoax or a misidentification, but none of this prevented it from being published in a supposedly prestigious journal — and in fact *after* it had been examined by several specialists and unanimously rejected by them. The figures were found to be entirely natural markings (one fracture line, possible frost damage, some 'current bedding micro-structures' and recent exfoliation), and the 'inlay' in some of the grooves forming them was algae (Sieveking 1982). Indeed, the 'cave' is only a shallow rockshelter and a Pleistocene petroglyph would have been most unlikely to have survived in such an exposed location.

GW. WEATHERING MARKINGS

The rock markings listed under this heading exhibit no readily apparent evidence that they are attributable to some inherent structural disconformities, inclusions or flaws in the rock. Rather, they appear to be the result of weathering processes that are active only at the interface of lithosphere and atmosphere, although it is possible that in some cases there may be a structurally given predisposition. However, these markings never extend beneath the surface layer, so one might define them as 'two-dimensional' to contrast them with the 'three-dimensional' nature of class GP markings. Also, weathering markings are largely restricted to the types of rock that are not usually susceptible to the GP markings; they are especially prominent on sedimentary rocks. Two types in this class are again distinguished: the marks caused by solution, which are particularly common on carbonate rocks; and the marks predominantly caused by granular exfoliation, which is typically active on sandstone facies. The secure identification of both types is contingent upon good field experience in observing geomorphological phenomena, particularly karst features and sandstone weathering patterns. It is certainly inappropriate that the discrimination of such markings (and subsequent heritage management decisions) be left to archaeologists.

GW1. Solution marks

Solution is a basic form of chemical weathering, in which solids are dissolved in water or aqueous solution. Susceptibility to solution of any mineral can vary significantly, being a function of such factors as temperature, pressure, pH, turbulence and the presence of catalysts. Solution contributes to many weathering processes, for instance to granular exfoliation or biologically caused weathering, but for some types of rock, notably carbonates, it is the principal weathering agent.

The limestones or dolomites of karsts are susceptible to solution processes, which result in rock markings that may resemble petroglyphs and have in a number of instances been misinterpreted as such. Essentially, these rocks are readily soluble in aqueous carbon dioxide, which is formed by atmospheric water and respiratory carbon dioxide. Solution of limestone is active primarily at or near the surface, and not subterraneously as is often thought. Solution within caves is mostly phreatic, because vadose water (which has percolated through the closed system of the rock strata above) is generally bicarbonate enriched (or super-saturated due to the higher pressure in the rock's closed system) and therefore has no solvent potential upon entering a cave (in fact it often has to precipitate surplus solute then, which leads to the formation of speleothems). This means that solution markings inside limestone caves are exceedingly rare, and seem to occur only in two forms: where atmospheric run-off has access, usually near the entrance, or in the form of root channels (see below, under plant marks).

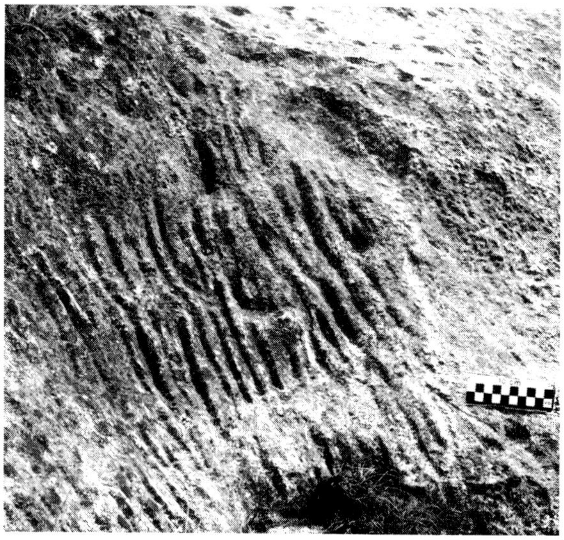

Figure 8. *Rillenkarren* on Tertiary limestone just outside Picaninnie Cave, Mt Gambier, South Australia.

Outside caves, solution markings can be common, especially where water runs over a rock slope after draining from a higher-lying soil deposit. This may result in *Rillenkarren*: sets of linear, subparallel grooves of surprisingly regular spacing, always orientated in the direction of natural water flow (Figure 8). Their regular arrangements may be most suggestive of artificial rock markings, particularly in such countries where similar arrangements are known to occur in rock art. *Karren* tend to deepen with age, and eventually can be as deep as one metre.

Karren are not as common in Australian karsts as they are in those of other regions (central Europe, Brazil, Caribbean), although they do occur in some Australian areas, such as near Fitzroy Crossing, Kimberley. They do co-occur with similar-looking rock art in Orchestra Shell Cave near Perth (Bednarik 1987a). Although closely resembling the finger flutings in that cave, their identification presents no difficulty for the experienced observer. Another karst weathering phenomenon, *kamenitsa*, occurs on the Nullarbor plain. In some parts of the world, these depressions have been mistaken by archaeologists for grinding grooves, mortars or petroglyphs, notably at some sites in western U.S.A. These features are attributable to the natural propensity of the slightest depression to retain moisture and acidic matter (e.g. decomposing leaf litter) longer than the adjacent areas, which leads to accelerated solution, and the deepening in turn accelerates the process.

Some rock markings in this category are less readily explainable, such as petroglyph-like grooves on a basaltic escarpment near Castlemaine, Victoria. They are 15–40 mm wide, of rounded section, and usually peter out without distinct ends. No recognisable arrangements are formed, but neither is there a natural solution process that seems to account for the markings. The rock is dissected by some layers of vesicle-rich material, which is somewhat more resistant to weathering, and where these are crossed by the grooves, the veins project distinctly into the grooves. This discounts the possibility that the grooves were made by people, because impact would have worn the veins as much as the adjacent matrix. However, it does not explain the markings themselves. A solution process is probably responsible for these grooves.

Other types of solution marks have led to spectacular misidentifications by archaeologists and epigraphers, the latter notably in North America. One of the better-known controversies concerns the purported Phoenician messages on the 'written stones' of Quebec, which are among the literally hundreds 'deciphered' by epigraphers. Having been interpreted in 1974 as Phoenician by an archaeologist from Laval University in Canada who had identified several such 'writings' along the American Atlantic coast, they were then identified as Libyan and deciphered by another archaeologist, famous for his deciphering of inscriptions (most of which, conversely, were no inscriptions at all). Dubois (1985), who investigated these two panels as well as several other, similar finds in the area, reports that the markings occur in strata with numerous solution grooves that are narrow and distinctively V-shaped in section. Many of the lines contain constrictions that render a production even with metal tools entirely impossible. Similar markings were found in granite and gneiss as well as in a sandstone. In the former rocks they were attributable to selective weathering of aligned plagioclases, in the latter to the corrosive spray of seawater. Dubois' conclusion is relevant to all potentially doubtful rock markings: 'While the issue may have been archaeology, the object of attention was rock and, as such, subject to geomorphological processes'. It is interesting that natural processes that result in such 'inscriptions' occur of course in all continents, but the phenomenon of their identification as writing seems endemic to North America. Most of them seem to be natural markings and plough marks.

GW2. Exfoliation marks

Exfoliation of rock occurs through several processes, which vary according to rock type and environmental conditions. Their scale of magnitude ranges from microscopic flaking of particles due to salt formation, to the large-scale mass-exfoliation of, say, unloading of granite masses. In contrast to solution, a continuous or periodic process, exfoliation of each particle is an instantaneous event, even though many such events may be required to cumulatively result in the production of a rock marking. The processes responsible are always physical, although chemical processes or changes may have precipitated the stresses leading to exfoliation. In other forms, the exfoliation is caused by physical factors alone, among them insolation, *Kernsprung*, lightning strike, *Salzsprengung* (wedging by salt crystallisation), stress fracture attributable to ancient material stresses or recent thermal stresses, hydration, and simple gravitational force. When a rock mass is detached, the fracture surface may bear stress marks of various types, including concentric arcs, radial patterns or subparallel furrows. Incredibly, such markings have been considered to be humanly made, on occasion, by rock art scholars, which confirms the power of the human propensity for seeking order in chaos, and how it affects those who search for rock art.

Exfoliation scars can also resemble non-art anthropic markings, such as grinding grooves. Dickson (1980: 160) determined experimentally that granite is one of the worst media in which to grind stone axes/hatchets. He considered it likely that the few instances of apparent grinding grooves on granite are attributable to alternative agencies. Wade (1941), who described such granite grooves, expressed similar reservations. Granite is less susceptible than sandstone to weathering phenomena that resemble anthropic marks, but several processes do result in markings likely to be misinterpreted. *Tafoni* and scalloping occur usually just above ground level (Ollier 1965), and they are related to the breaching of case hardening. The exfoliation process operates inwards and upwards on a boulder, eventually forming alcoves and scallops, but it never extends below ground level. The sculptures resulting from this have sometimes been considered to be artificial. *Tafoni* are shallow, rounded weathering hollows in granite-like rocks and sandstones. They are rarely, if indeed at all, associated with evidence of aeolian sand blasting, and are attributable principally to chemical decay resulting from prolonged moisture presence and the effects of cyclical wetting and drying.

Sandstone is more likely than granite to bear surface markings that are prone to interpretation as petroglyphs. For instance, Sims (1977), who examined the authenticity of twenty petroglyph sites reported in Tasmania, and who rejected seven out of the nineteen he could locate, reported most of the misidentifications from sandstone sites. Sandstone is obviously most susceptible to granular mass-exfoliation, the shedding of mass, grain by grain. Where such processes are influenced by even minor diagenetic characteristics, such as stratigraphic laminations, they are bound to result in various types of surface grooves and pits, which may resemble artificial marks closely. There is a clear overlap between them and the type GP2 marks. The tendency of true petroglyphs on sandstone to weather comparatively rapidly only facilitates misidentification, because weathered petroglyphs may resemble exfoliation scars. Moreover, sandstone is perhaps the rock type that is most susceptible to case hardening, and this leads to many forms of erosion products, which resemble artificial marks. Case hardening may be visually obvious, through the deposition of a surface lamina of distinctive colour or consistency. Other forms of it are not readily visible, but are a form of induration of the surface-near layer, usually up to several centimetres deep. In both instances, the case hardening protects the much more erosion-prone inner material, until weathering or other causes puncture the cutaneous zone locally and lead to the breakdown of the core. This then results in *tafoni* and similar alveolar formations. Moisture retention is the crucial factor in all of these processes: the surface aspects most susceptible to them are those most likely to retain atmospheric or capillary moisture longer. This is why the upper part of a sandstone formation, which dries most quickly after rain because of its greater exposure to sun and wind, is the most indurated, and thus the most exfoliation resistant. Once again, an erosion process is accelerated by the geometry of its own products: depressions become progressively more cavernous, and as they do they retain moisture longer again; the formation process is self-accelerating.

Although not well understood, granular exfoliation is probably a combination of several factors. The cement of all sandstones is more soluble and less resistant than the sand grains. A complex regime of salt removal, temperature change of salt solution, chemical conversion of mineral components and subsequent change in bulk (including subflorescence) and other factors weaken coherence in the rock's fabric. Hydration of clay components, kaolin or gypsum is often a major influence. Small flakes or individual grains are detached, and no doubt aeolian action or surface wash can contribute to their removal. Interestingly, sandstone that is subjected to fairly continuous high moisture levels is just as erosion resistant as sandstone that remains dry, and there seems to be very little, if any, exfoliation below ground level. Sandstone exfoliation, irrespective of whether it occurs at the granular level or as spalls of up to a several centimetres in thickness, seems to operate primarily in conditions where salts are neither being flushed nor stable, which are those areas where moisture remains longest but still evaporates regularly. This is perhaps the simplest general rule, even if it may in fact be an over-simplification.

The thousands of pit markings on tesselated sandstone pavements in the Sydney region are the subject of an ongoing controversy. The tessellation itself does not concern us here, because it is generally agreed that it is a natural phenomenon (Branagan and Cairns 1993), even though it remains unexplained. This often extensive lattice of deeply eroded grooves divides some twenty-five known pavements into mosaics of sometimes geometric accuracy. The inherent tessellation characteristics extend perhaps 20 cm below the surface, and they have given rise to selective weathering which formed the grooves. The largest of these pavements, the Elvina Track site, measures about 6500 square metres (Figure 9).

Most of its thousands of polygonous panels bear a number of pits of 20–50 mm diameter. Many specialists, including eminent geologists and rock art scholars of extensive field experience (Cairns and Branagan 1992: 29), accept the pits as humanly-made cupules. However, most Australian rock art specialists believe that they are natural markings (Bednarik 1990). The aspect that most prompts observers to favour an anthropic origin is the pattern of distribution of the pits within the polygon panels: none of the pits occur near the grooves bordering each polygon, and they seem often evenly, 'intentionally' spaced. This is perhaps a classic example of selective natural processes resulting in physical aspects of a regularity that lead to the idea that intentionality must be involved: the human propensity, even scientific predisposition, of perceiving patterns imposes order and then interprets this very order as being intentional, because natural processes are perceived as random. Natural processes can thus 'mimic' intentionality.

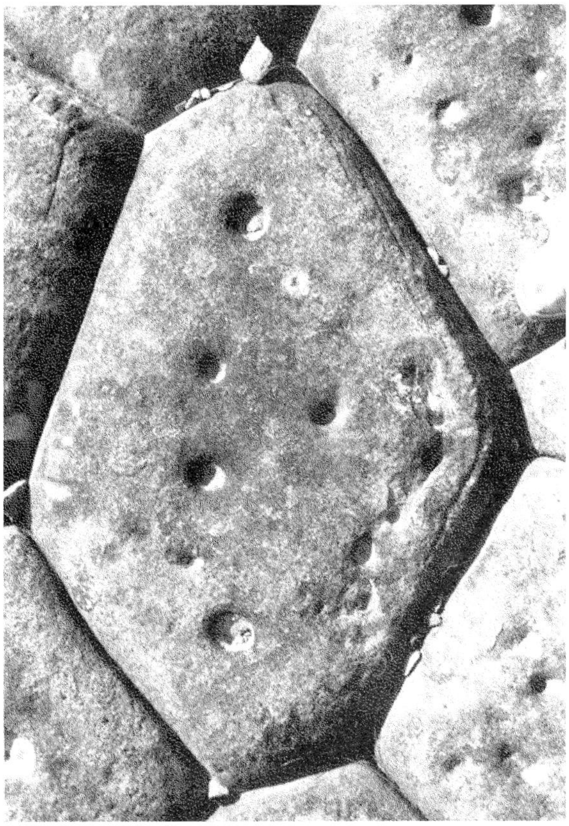

Figure 9. Section of polygonous tesselation on sandstone, with cupule-like but natural depressions. Elvina Track site, near Sydney, Australia.

Each polygon at the Sydney tesselated pavements has similar run-off characteristics: near the borders, the profile curves gently towards the surrounding groove, into which rainwater drains readily. Drainage is slower in the more central parts of the polygon, and water will remain in even the slightest depressions there. Uneven exfoliation is the result, leading to drainage towards the deepening depression. This process favours regular spacings as watersheds are established in the micro-topography of each polygon. Once under way, it leads inevitably to foci of erosional activity, and ever-accelerating rates of erosion in just one location, the pit forming in the middle of each local drainage zone. The result is a natural pattern of regularity, which the uncritical observer is likely to interpret as intentional.

GK. KINETIC MARKINGS

These may not be as easily identifiable as one might be tempted to think; they have presented great difficulties for archaeologists as well as rock art scholars. In the majority of cases, their attribution tends to be easy, once they have been carefully considered in their environmental context. But there have also been cases where an unusual context responsible for them no longer exists, and if such markings are sufficiently complex they can be most baffling even for the specialist. Kinetic markings are always attributable to the movement of an active component (the marking element) relative to the passive component (the rock being marked). The former is often harder than the latter, but not necessarily so, especially where a great deal of kinetic force is involved. Kinetic rock markings could be sub-divided according to various definitions, but most of the possible taxonomic criteria are difficult to establish. They are divided here fairly arbitrarily into 'general taphonomic marks' on portable clasts, and 'clastic movement marks' that are usually found on stationary rock surfaces that have been affected by clasts moving over or past them.

GK1. Taphonomic marks

The term taphonomy, derived from palaeontology, is a fairly recent introduction to archaeology. It refers to the modifications experienced by materials since the time they became part of what is considered to form the 'archaeological record' (Bednarik 1994b). The term has also a secondary, epistemic sense (see Ch. 8). In the present context, taphonomic markings are those that are not attributable to intentional human agency, but were acquired through movement of rock clasts within or relative to a sediment matrix, by such processes as cryoturbation, solifluction, trampling, or even by human agency. For instance, if a human stepped or sat on a rock slab, its underside might be marked by harder sand grains caught between it and the bedrock. Such markings would then not be intentional, and even though they would be anthropic, for the present purpose they would be biospheric taphonomic marks. Even if a rock slab had been used as support in some manufacturing process — such as the cutting of skins or meat, thereby sustaining cut marks — this would still apply from a geologist's point of view; but in the present context it would be more appropriate to consider such marks under BH1 below.

Australian examples of archaeological misidentification of taphonomic markings are the 'engraved plaques' from Trench 9 of Devil's Lair Cave, in the south-western corner of the continent (Dortch 1976). They consist of 'extremely friable' aeolian calcarenite and bear a network of random striations on one of the flat faces of each plaque. The rock is so soft that many striations were added when a specimen was cleaned with a fine nylon brush. Dortch discounts natural causes of the numerous incised markings without discussion, but in 1996 he made the collection of six 'engraved plaques' as well as other controversial finds from Devil's Lair available for specialist study (Bednarik 1998). The presumed limestone plaques were found to bear a variety of taphonomic marks as well as two types of animal scratch marks (see Ch. 10).

Similar markings can be found on clastic material at many sites the world over. For instance, dozens of specimens from just one site in Brazil (Toca do Sítio do Meio, southern Piauí) with what archaeologists had identified as tens of thousands of anthropic markings were found to bear taphonomic markings (Bednarik 1989). In this sandstone shelter, a layer of very fine-grained sedimentary rock exfoliates from the roof as angular blocks of 25–40 cm length. Microscopic examination showed that the marks are of greatly varying ages, widths and depths, ranging from barely perceptible examples to 4 mm wide grooves. There are clear sets of two or more subparallel marks, some of which may be interrupted only to continue as different arrangements, perhaps by changing direction. Another hallmark of these typical taphonomic marks is the point of commencement, with a distinct, impact-like impression. The angular edges of the clasts are also very worn and rounded. There are essentially three potential explanations to account for such marks: they could be attributable either to trampling by humans or other animals; to movement of the slab relative to a rock surface, with loose quartz grains caught between the two surfaces; or to general detrital movement. Quite probably, a combination of these factors applies to the densely marked material.

In periglacial regions, detrital movement is often attributable to cryoturbation, the movement of sediments by freezing and thawing cycles, or to solifluction, the collapse of sloping sediments when saturated by moisture upon thawing. Cryoturbation can be most effective in producing markings on rock, which have been reported even on obsidian tools (in Hungary). Clearly these marks are very common at archaeological sites, but they have hardly any archaeological significance.

The great variety of forms in which taphonomic marks occur is illustrated by the following example. Cave divers had discovered a panel of incised markings in a limestone cave near Mt Gambier, South Australia, under 7 m of water, in a downward sloping passage. If they were human markings, as the divers thought, they would probably be of Pleistocene age, because the passage would have been flooded during the Holocene. The preserved finger markings found below seawater in Cosquer Cave, France, which are of the Pleistocene (Clottes et al. 1992), show that such markings can survive below water. However, my detailed examination of the submerged Australian markings revealed no evidence of human involvement; they seemed to be taphonomic marks. Their occurrence on the wall of a recess in the passage seemed puzzling, but the water-filled caves in the region frequently contain ancient tree trunks with their roots and branches that had fallen into sinkhole entrances. Perhaps such an ancient log had become lodged in this position and, buffeted by water flow, produced the incisions with its limbs. It is not a proven explanation by any means, but perhaps the most realistic one under the circumstances.

GK2. Clastic movement marks

These are among the most common rock markings in the world: glacial striae alone would probably account for millions of times as many marks as rock art motifs do. The great majority of these marks can be readily identified, if only because of their enormous numbers, but there are still exceptions. Clastic movement is a common phenomenon at many types of archaeological sites, and it can be attributed to a variety of causes. Fluviatile sedimentary movement, animal burrowing, and simple gravity are among them, but also tectonic adjustments. This applies especially in limestone caves, where several processes can effect large-scale detrital movement. Many cave systems form above a sub-floor phreatic reservoir, and where the clastic breakdown from roof falls causes the floor to settle progressively, blocks move not only relative to each other, but also down along the walls of the cave. Often this results in deeply incised wall markings (for a photograph of a good example, see Maynard and Edwards 1971: Pl. 32). Similar movement of talus clasts is caused by seismic events, and even by eustatic fluctuations. The aquifer level in coastal karst regions falls with the sea level, which means that huge masses of boulders that were submerged in water become exposed as the water drains from these systems. The boulder structures may have been tectonically stable as long as they remained submerged, but they are not once they are above water, during stadials. Finally, tectonic subsidence can be caused by certain mining methods (Sefton 1995), and this could conceivably result in similar kinetically caused rock markings.

The deep incisions occasioned by gravitational movement of clasts or other detrital matter, be it in limestone caves or other types of sites, are fairly easy to identify where they are relatively fresh. However, if they are very corroded, patinated and considered in isolation it is quite possible to mistake them for anthropic marks, especially where several occur together and they seem to form 'arrangements'. Another type of rock marking occasioned by clastics movement is easy to recognise. Glacial striae were made by rocky detritus dragged or pushed by glaciers over stationary rock surfaces, which had often been planed smooth in the process. Such glacial pavements are most common in the Northern Hemisphere, and they often form the support surfaces of petroglyphs (Figure 10), for instance in Val Camonica (Italy), Britain, Scandinavia, Karelia and Canada. The direction of the striae is generally uniform, they are inevitably aligned with the flow of the most recent glacier. Their sizes range in width from barely perceptible incisions, under a millimetre wide, to massive gouges of about one metre width and many tens of metres length. Irrespective of their size, they bear a number of distinctive morphological features. These permit the clear determination of the direction in which the marking point was moved over the rock, through the configuration of transverse tear marks, the serrated patterns at the longitudinal edges of the margins, and the form of the point of commencement, including comet-like marks. Some of these features are similar to those observed in other types of kinetic markings, both natural and anthropic, and even on materials other than rock (e.g. on ostrich eggshell). The transverse tear marks, for instance, have been observed at the microscopic level in pre-Historic engravings on portable stone objects (d'Errico 1988). They have also been reported at the macroscopic level, in the finger flutings found on formerly soft speleothem deposits in caves (Bednarik 1986a, 1992a). These stress marks can be found even in the largest glacial striae. They are arcuate and always curved in the direction the boulder was dragged over the pavement (i.e. the convex side points in the direction of movement). Where a boulder scraped over an elevated aspect of the panel topography, the impact mark is obviously on the oncoming side. The comet-like arrangements sometimes seen at the point of commencement may indicate where the boulder first struck, and then either bounced or turned slightly, affecting the morphology of the resulting mark.

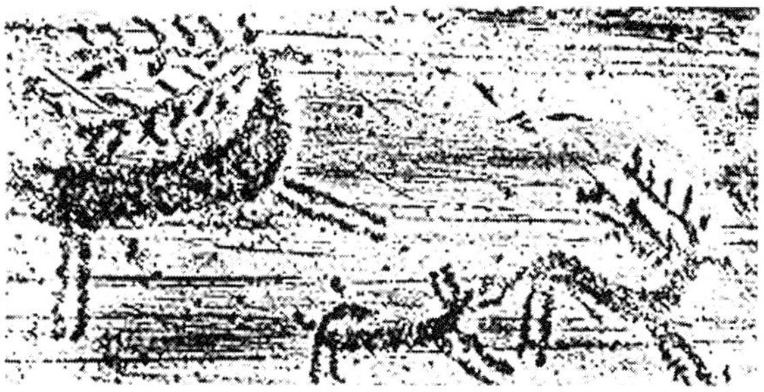

Figure 10. Petroglyphs surrounded by subparallel glacial striations, Val Camonica, Italy.

Usually it is not just the distinctiveness of striae that enable their secure identification, but also their abundance, typical location and direction. Other kinetic movement marks may be extremely rare and thus much harder to identify. While examining the Siberian rock art site Tal'ma II (near the upper Lena river), I noted sets of parallel grooves high up on the vertical cliff face, about 6 m from the ground, on very smooth rock. Unable to reach them, I inspected them through binoculars to determine what caused them. However, I remained unable to form an opinion: intuition told me the marks were natural, but they were clearly attributable to mechanical force or impact, and there seemed no natural agency that could have caused such repetitive marks. Subsequently I located similar marks at two more Siberian sites, again high on steep cliffs overlooking a river, managing in one case to reach and examine them. They certainly looked like man-made impact grooves, but microscopic inspection revealed no evidence of actual impact. Rather, there was dense crushing of grains evident, as if the marks had been pressed into the rock with considerable force. I then hypothesised that perhaps there had been a rock tower leaning loosely against the cliff, and if a hard clast had become lodged between it and the cliff, it might have slowly wandered downwards with each minute movement, only to be pressed against the cliff by the weight of the tower, in each successive position.

It seemed a desperate explanation at the time but it turned out to be valid. Soon afterwards I found a clast that had become stuck in such a position between a sheer cliff and a detached rampart, and had already produced several pressure marks. Each time there was movement in the tower, be it seismic, tectonic, or caused by temperature change, moisture, freezing or thawing, the clast dropped a few centimetres. This observation shows poignantly how even the most unlikely explanation may turn out to be correct, and how judicious and wary the researcher really needs to be in pursuing natural explanations for unusual phenomena.

BP. PLANT MARKINGS

The second major division are biological rock markings. Again, they are divided into three classes: those made by plants (BP), non-human animals (BA), and humans (BH). In each class, two types are again distinguished.

The division of plant markings into kinetic and chemical types is as obvious as it is opportune. Such rock marks can readily be identified by the specialist, but they have been a source of difficulty for many writers and commentators, and there is no shortage of misidentifications of both types listed here.

BP1. Kinetic plant marks

Although it is a distinguishing characteristic of all species of the vegetable kingdom that they lack the power of locomotion, that does not prevent them from producing kinetic rock markings. These are only possible where vegetation occurs immediately adjacent to rock, and the necessary energy is provided mostly by the wind. If a tree, shrub or even a large tuft of grass stands next to a rock surface, it may rub against the rock. A pliable limb, stalk or tuft may perform a semi-circular movement for months and years, and this can result in distinctive arcuate marks even on hard rock, such as granite (Twidale et al. 1983: Fig. 8). Much softer rocks may incur markings of some depth, and these may consist of multiple arcs. Obviously once the plant has died, the cause of the rock mark may not be apparent. It is then quite possible to misinterpret it as artificial, particularly after modification by weathering.

Dickson (1980) describes another type of kinetic plant mark, which he observed on sandstone. It is

> shallow with no definite shape and is a natural phenomenon. It is produced by a low tree branch moving with the wind so as to rub against the sandstone. On examining one of these grooves still being formed the branch was found to be worn half-way through and a month later it had broken away.

He reports that this type of broad and shallow groove can resemble axe grinding grooves, but he cites no examples of known misidentifications (nearly all of the 1967 axe grinding sites reported in eastern Australia are on sandstone; Hiscock and and Mitchell 1993: 34).

Another type of sandstone marking sometimes produced by plants has been misidentified in this manner on occasion. It occurs usually on the past or present margins of rock exposures. A tree growing in such a location is likely to hug the rock for support with its roots. Every time it sways in the wind, there is a minute movement in its main roots just below the ground. Together with soil and fine sand acting as an abrasive, this is sufficient to produce quite deep grooves on the rock, which in turn improve the tree's hold on its support. Over the tree's lifetime, such grooves can become up to 10 cm deep. After the tree disappears and the soil erodes, the grooves remain, consisting of sometimes under-cut but usually quite short, meandering and randomly orientated, rounded furrows. At the Amphitheatre petroglyph site near Laura, Cape York Peninsula, northern Australia, the pavement edge on which they occur is now more than two metres above the surrounding sediment floor, and in such cases it may be difficult to perceive how these markings could have been made by the roots of a tree. However, in Ku-ring-gai chase National Park near Sydney, there are many such grooves, and it was there that a park ranger informed me that he had observed the phenomenon where a tree had been uprooted by the wind.

BP2. Chemical plant marks

The second type of marks produced by vegetation is entirely different. Numerous plant species have symbiotic associations between the mycelium of fungi and their roots (conifers, for instance). In endotrophic mycorrhiza, the fungi penetrate deep into the internal cells of the root, while in ectotrophic mycorrhiza they only enter the epidermis. Mycorrhizal associations are complex and remain inadequately understood. In many species of plants they extend to bacteria within the root systems whose presence remains largely unexplained. Presumably they relate to the plant's metabolism, assisting it in dissolving salts (the function of roots, besides providing support, is to supply the plant with water and nutrients, *i.e.* salts). The respiratory carbon dioxide of these micro-organisms reacts with moisture in the soil to form carbonic acid, which dissolves calcium carbonate locally. The mycorrhizal relationship thus supports the nutrient exchange system and at the same time provides certain plant species with the means of attacking limestone bedrock and utilising it for mechanical support. For instance, in south-western Australian caves, the roots of some eucalypts have penetrated more than 20 m of solid limestone in this fashion (Bednarik 1991a). It is relevant to consider that the CO_2 content of air is in the order of 0.03%, while the CO_2 content of a soil atmosphere (the gaseous component of a soil) can be 300 times as high (Ollier 1969: 40). This carbon dioxide is largely the result of the respiration of soil microbiota (for a detailed discussion of the relevant chemical processes see Hendy 1971).

The resulting markings have been studied in detail on portable objects of the Pleistocene, notably on objects of ivory (Russia), bone (China) and ostrich eggshell (India) (Bednarik 1993b, 1993c). These materials consist collectively of organically derived, mineralised calcareous materials dominated by carbonates (or surviving largely as carbonates once fossilised), and they are susceptible to chemical markings by roots in the same way as limestone is. However, the root markings on them are generally smaller, usually 1–2 mm wide. Those observed in limestone caves may be as wide as 10 mm (larger ones can probably be found), but they are as well rounded in section and of the same morphology (Figure 11).

Hundreds of markings on sandstone near Remarkable Cave, Tasmania, which had earlier been considered to be rock carvings (Reid 1962), have also been identified as root marks (Both 1963), although it is not clear whether these are chemical or kinetic grooves. At another Tasmanian site, this time on granite, presumed petroglyphs (Sharland 1957) appear to be the result of both plant abrasion (type BP1) and 'acid leaching' (type BP2) (cf. Ellis 1958). Nevertheless, chemical plant markings on rock are most commonly found on carbonate rocks, notably limestone, and on carbonate-cemented sandstone. The roots of at least some plant species are most effective in invading fine cracks and then enlarging their bulk with the help of solution, sometimes prising apart rock masses. Where the resulting fracture surfaces become exposed, as on a wall of a cave, the root channels survive as well-rounded grooves that may resemble finger grooves on soft rock, or petroglyphs on harder surfaces. However, the experienced observer can readily discriminate between these markings in probably all cases.

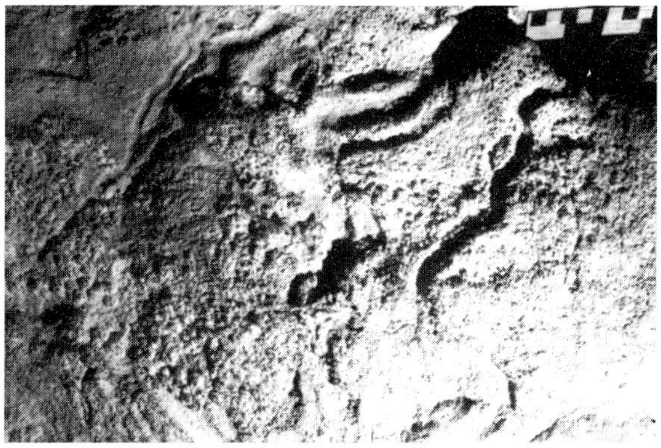

Figure 11. Solution grooves caused by roots, Wombat Cave, Naracoorte, South Australia.

BA. ANIMAL MARKINGS

The same does not apply to animal markings on rock surfaces. In particular, animal scratches in caves, which have presented such difficulties to archaeologists in the past (Bednarik 1991a), are not in all cases reliably identifiable — not even by the most experienced observers (cf. Sharpe 2004). Nevertheless, this applies only in exceptional circumstances, and the overwhelming majority of such cave markings can be convincingly attributed. This is a specialist task, however, involving considerable relevant experience. Most importantly, cave markings are subjected to several very common alteration processes, the products of which vary greatly, and an observer needs to be fully conversant with these. For instance, the processes of speleothem growth, maturation and deterioration need to be well understood. In the following section the markings of non-human animals are considered, those of human animals are discussed last.

BA1. Animal scratches

No more than a most rudimentary account of animal scratch markings is provided here, more detailed analyses are available (Bednarik 1981, 1991a, 1993d, 1998). It should be stated from the outset that animal markings are not restricted to rock; they occur on many surfaces regularly and in patterns of great consistency. For instance, numerous animal species, ranging from insects to birds and mammals, mark tree trunks. Some examples are the red-necked sap sucker (*Sphyrapicus varius*), a North American bird that constructs ladder-like, geometric arrangements of deeply sculptured squares; or the yellow bellied glider (*Petaurus australis reginae*) of eastern Australia, which carves trident or V-shaped dendroglyphs (Bednarik 1994c) into its feeding trees (they resemble petroglyphs in the same region closely); or a variety of large mammalian carnivores (Felidae, Ursidae) which mark tree trunks with their claws to communicate with other members of their species. Elephants 'draw' with their trunks in the dust and can learn to use a paintbrush (Diamond 1991). The abilities of non-human primates have been well documented by dozens of authors. Here we are only considering animal marks on rock, even though it is useful to perceive rock markings by animals within the greater context of general animal markings and their ethology.

Animal scratch marks are among the most common rock markings in the world, and while they are usually most conspicuous in limestone caves (Bednarik 1991a), they occur also at open air sites. Their common occurrence in caves is a purely taphonomic phenomenon; surfaces are far more often marked outside of caves, but they are then exposed to weathering processes and such markings rarely survive for any great length of time. Within deep caves, even faint scratch marks can survive for periods of tens of millennia. The same principle, obviously, applies to rock art: few open Pleistocene rock art sites have been identified so far, most have not survived, while many of those in caves probably have. The long survival of animal scratches in caves means that markings of greatly differing ages often occur together, particularly in 'natural animal traps' (caves with vertical entrances) in regions with clawed animals of poor climbing abilities. On the other hand, many claw marks are by species with superb climbing abilities that entered caves habitually. The most numerous animal markings in caves, however, are those of airborne individuals, especially bats. Chiroptera produce rock markings on soft surfaces with their wings as well as with their digital claws, and these are usually of distinctive spatial distribution within a cave's topography. Birds mark such surfaces with their primaries, claws and possibly their mandibles; ungulates do so with horns and antlers on occasion. In Kenya, elephants consuming mineral deposits in caves mark the walls with their tusks. Clawed animals which have marked cave walls include reptiles, but the claw markings of mammalian species are the most common, ranging from those of the tiniest rodents or Chiroptera to those of extinct megafaunal species.

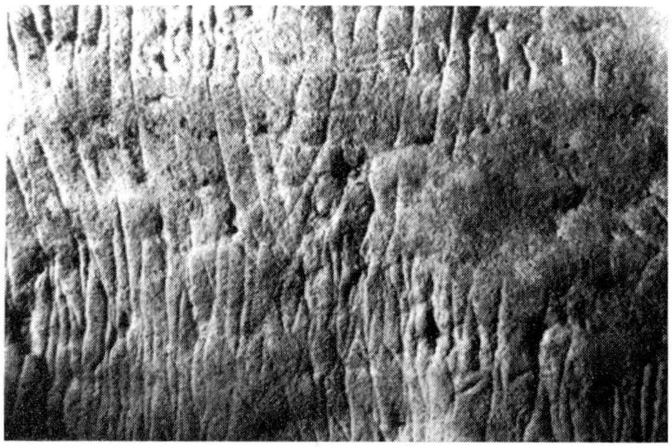

Figure 12. Cave bear claw marks, Grotte des Endrevies, Dordogne, France.

The most common among the latter are the claw marks of the European cave bear (*Ursus spelaeus*), a powerful animal that once ranged from Spain to the Urals (Bednarik 1993d). Having studied its markings in some fifty caves, I distinguish seven types according to the apparent reasons why they were made. In some European caves, ursine claw markings cover the walls for kilometres (Figure 12), and in Chauvet Cave they match those found with tracks on the clay floor of the cave. Megafaunal cave markings are also common in southern Australia, particularly in the Mt Gambier karst region. Some have tentatively been attributed to species on the basis of claw spacing and size, inferred mobility of forelegs, body size, climbing ability, and occurrence of skeletal remains within the cave in question. In many cases, sinkholes and other caves with vertical entrances contain vast deposits of osteal remains, of individuals that fell into the caves and were unable to escape. Hundreds of such sites have been examined in several continents (Bednarik 1992b), and the behaviour of confined animals has been studied from various traces they left (Bednarik 1991a). Australian megafauna species also entered caves voluntarily, and there is some evidence that individuals may have perished in the search for subterranean water (Figure 13). Megafaunal scratch marks in Australia postdate parietal art in some cases, just as they do in Europe, thus indicating the Pleistocene age of the underlying rock art. There is no known site of 'cave art' in Australia that does not also contain animal scratches, and the latter are usually far more numerous. Discriminating the two types of marks is the crucial precondition for any informed assessment of the rock art component.

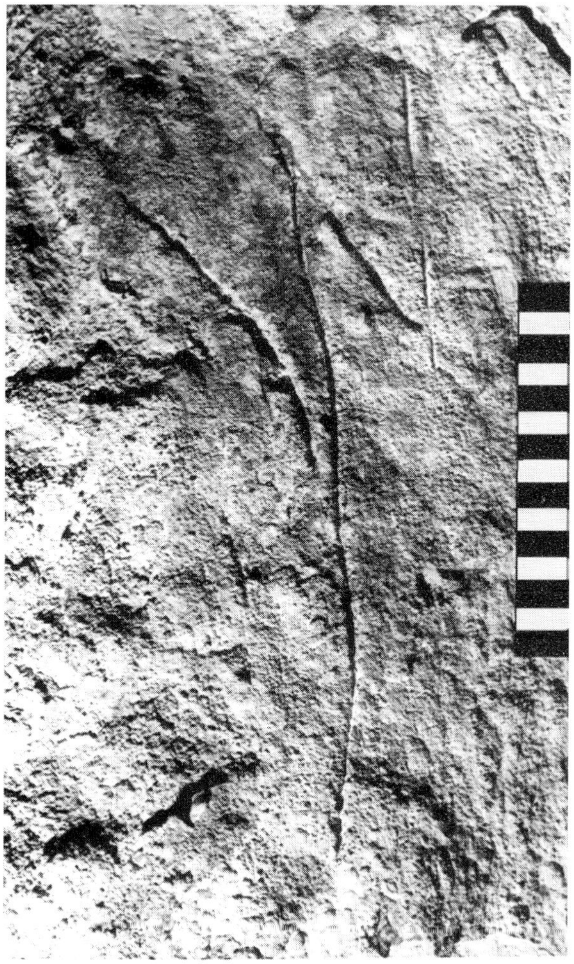

Figure 13. Ceiling markings in Robertson Cave, South Australia, attributed to *Thylacoleo carnifex*.

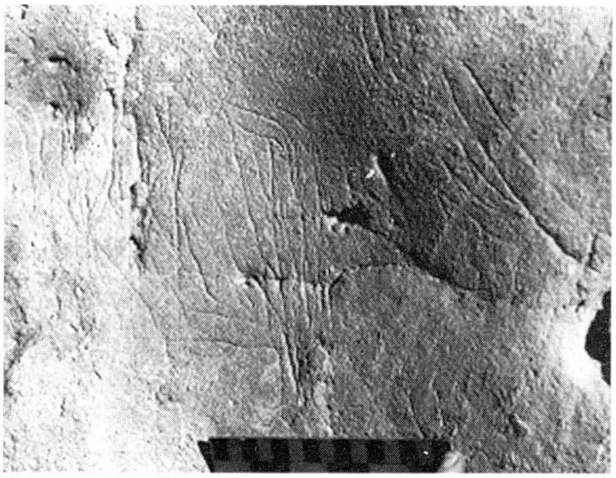

Figure 14. Typical animal climbing marks, several metres above the floor of Robertson Cave, South Australia.

In Australia, four quite distinctive mammalian scratch marks are defined, apart from bat markings: 'climbing marks' (primarily by possums; Figure 14), 'gouged symmetrical marks' (certain extant species lacking any climbing ability; Figure 15), 'megafaunal marks' and 'exploratory marks' (Bednarik 1991a). These distinctive forms do not comprise the entire spectrum of marks present, they are merely frequent, prominent and typical modes of occurrence in one particular geographic region. Obviously the types of animal marks differ in various parts of the world, according to regional animal species, ethology, geomorphological factors and preservation conditions. Our knowledge differs according to the research conducted, which is inadequate in a few regions, and practically absent in the rest of the world. In the same way that rock art in caves may have suffered considerable modification through time, animal scratches may have been greatly modified over the millennia, and their visual appearance altered by one or more of several speleo-morphological processes.

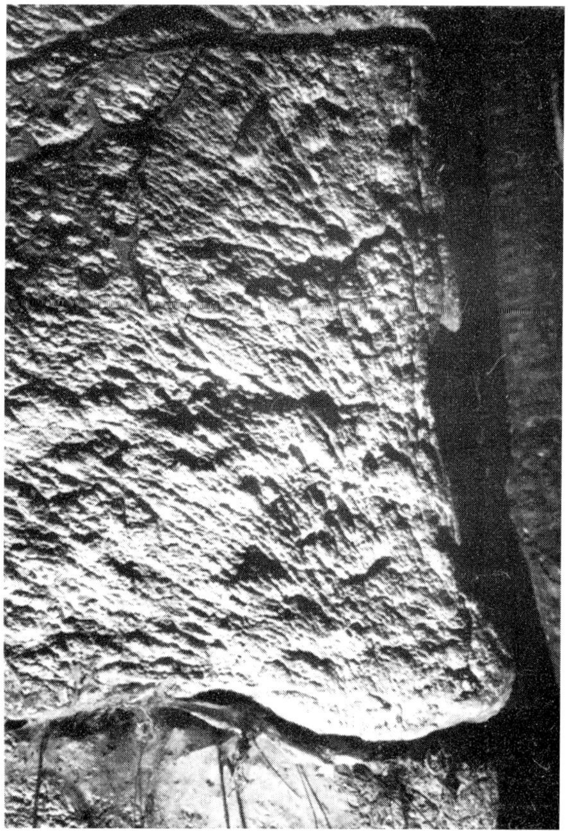

Figure 15. Typical gouged symmetrical animal marks, Gran Gran South Cave, South Australia.

In view of this entirely inadequate state of our knowledge it is inappropriate that the status of cave markings be commented upon by non-specialists.

The subject is far too complex to allow such commentary to be related to management decisions or research findings. Many examples of misidentifications of cave markings by 'trained' researchers are known, and some have been cited in the past. Just one of them is rehearsed here: the 'human hand' prominently engraved on the upper left hand corner of the rock art panel in the famous Palaeolithic site of Bara Bahau, France (Bednarik 1986b: Fig. 6), has been described as the oldest work of art in the world by various writers, and has been admired by vast numbers of tourists and scholars over four decades. It is almost certainly the handiwork of a cave bear (Bednarik 1981, 1991a: 31, 1993d).

BA2. Animal polish

Claw scratches are not the only type of wall markings cave bears produced. The second type is very different, but has also been inadequately studied. The *Bärenschliffe* are panels of polished rock surface, on cave walls as well as on the sides of large floor boulders. They are particularly common in central Europe, and where there has been no subsequent change of floor level they are typically found between 0.4 and 1.4 m above the floor. These polished panels can occur up to a few kilometres into a cave system. They were produced by generations upon generations of cave bears using the same paths in the dark. As their bodies rubbed against the walls, the sand and silt embedded in their shaggy fur acted as an abrasive, gradually smoothing the rock surface (Bednarik 1993d). The reason for the bears' forays deep into caves was to reach hibernation dens, which were typically located in warm air syphons where the air trapped may have been of a considerably higher ambient temperature than that outside the caves, during the harsh winters of stadial peaks. On well-preserved cave bear polishes, numerous striations can be found, caused by quartz grains lodged in the animals' fur. Some of the first purported Pleistocene rock art reported in central Europe (Hahn 1991) consists of several dozen fragments of such panels with random grooves (Bednarik 2002), which had later exfoliated and become stratified in the cave floor. (There is, in fact, no known rock art of the Pleistocene in central Europe; Bednarik 2002.)

Numerous other species have produced rock surface polish, particularly in caves and rockshelters. They range from those climbing habitually in and out of caves (e.g. possums in Australia; Bednarik 1991a), to species using such sites as lairs (e.g. cave hyena in Europe, Tasmanian devil in Australia etc.), and to those sheltering in cave entrances and rockshelters. Rock art conservators are particularly concerned with the habits of some ungulates, such as feral pigs and water buffaloes, of rubbing their bodies on rock to rid themselves of parasites. Rock paintings can be rapidly destroyed in this fashion. Not only does this habit result in surface polish, there may also be a deposition of accretionary salts, including perhaps oxalates (Watchman 1990: 48). Breck Parkman has recently identified a series of extensive rock polishes in the Unites States, which appear to be attributable to mammoths and other megafauna. He has also demonstrated that extant elephants, too, create polished surfaces on rock outcrops. Quite possibly, these phenomena are more common than we have appreciated in the past. However, of all the rock markings considered in this chapter, animal polish is the least likely to be mistaken as anthropic, it is listed merely for completeness.

BH. Humanly-made markings

While these are the only types of rock markings that are of interest to the archaeologist, the rock art scientist cannot afford to ignore all the others discussed above. Even though the humanists among hominin ethologists are primarily concerned with 'intentionality' of rock markings, the class of anthropogenic rock markings is best divided into the following two types: those that are the result of some human activity in which there was no conscious desire to leave 'meaningful' marks on the rock; and those in which there was such an intention. This division is adopted here, distinguishing between utilitarian and non-utilitarian humanly-made marks, rather than just between intentional and unintentional marks. The reason for this is that there are many intentional but still utilitarian marks.

BH1. Unintentional and utilitarian anthropic marks

This definition is quite self-explanatory, but it includes a great variety of markings, some of which may even have archaeological significance. Among them are the marks remaining from mining or quarrying activities, such as the long grooves in Gran Gran Cave, Australia, made by long wooden stakes driven into the limestone to expose a chert seam (Bednarik 1992c). They could easily be mistaken for petroglyphs. Modern mining tools of various types produce a variety of rock markings, as does construction machinery and other heavy equipment: rock drills, core drills, steel tracks of track-mounted vehicles, or gouge marks where a vehicle brushed past a rock face, drag marks on rock pavements, or grooves cut by steel cables being pulled over rock. In short, there is a considerable variety possible and, particularly if such marks have become weathered, they may easily resemble petroglyphs.

Surprisingly, these marks made by modern machinery have posed significant difficulties for numerous practitioners, and many such marks have been misidentified as pre-Historic rock art by professional prehistorians. It is impossible to devise a set of rules to help avoid such pitfalls, because there will always be 'unusual' specimens that will baffle the researcher, and there will always be rock markings of this type that do resemble petroglyph motifs very closely. The following two groups of such marks have been misidentified most often.

Several instances of *dragmarks* come to mind, including one seen during a post-congress field trip after the Second AURA Congress, in 1992. A classic example occurred in 1990, when a petroglyph site in Russia was examined by over twenty scholars. A one-metre-long groove was located on the slope of a granite hill overlooking a lake, on the top of which was a lighthouse. The petroglyphs were all on the lakeshore, and this solitary mark lay half way up the hill. Most of the specialists were prepared to accept its authenticity, but it was clear that it could not possibly be a petroglyph, despite its weathered appearance. The groove had been incised in one single abrasive motion, uphill rather than downhill. It was aligned with the lighthouse above, so I proposed that some heavy piece of equipment might have been dragged up the hill, perhaps with the help of a tugboat. It could have been a cannon, for instance. Later it was confirmed that artillery was positioned on the hill, which has no road access, during World War 2.

Dragmarks can be very deep, but they are often non-symmetrical in section, very even longitudinally, and they lack the pitted surface of percussion petroglyphs. The edges may be so steep that the mark can only have been made with metal and with great kinetic force. On a vertical surface they may be parallel to the surface of movement, or they are aligned with the most likely direction of movement. For instance where they are attributable to heavy vehicular construction machinery, they are parallel to the road. Abrasion marks are rare on hard rock (granite, quartzite, diorite etc.); they are far more common on dolomite, soft sandstone, limestone etc., so where they do occur on plutonic rock they are more likely to be interpreted as petroglyphs. In North America, plough marks have occasionally posed problems for archaeologists. With a long duration of mechanised agriculture in that continent, such marks may be quite weathered and thus appear more ancient than they actually are.

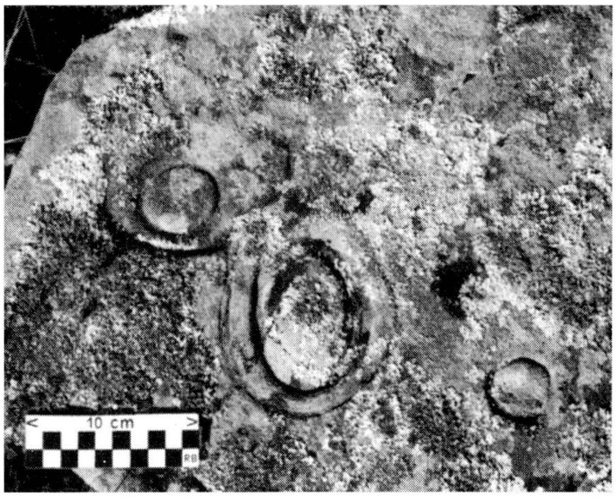

Figure 16. Semi-circular marks on sandstone, made with metal machine tools. Sutherland Creek site, Victoria, Australia.

Circular rock marks may resemble petroglyphs, and again several examples come to mind. However, their archaeological misidentification as petroglyphs is quite unnecessary. Rotating machine tools, such as core drills, can produce perfectly circular marks, which will be distorted if the tool slipped laterally whilst it was applied to the rock surface. Such marks have been found on both horizontal and vertical rock surfaces, and in one case, from Germany, were of about one metre diameter. The circular rock marks found on a loose sandstone slab at Sutherland Creek, near Geelong, Victoria (Bolger 1979), were authenticated by archaeologists and compared to circular petroglyphs in Tasmania and the 'Cleland Hills Type' of Northern Territory. Yet the markings had been cut with rotating metal tools of two distinctive (imperial) sizes. It would be impossible to reproduce them with stone tools, with their vertical walls in each groove and the narrow groove widths of only a few millimetres (Figure 16).

A very different type of circular mark, also from the Geelong district, consists of countless narrow, concentric circular marks of varying diameters, forming a deep depression on a boulder of basalt. When consulted I judged it to be the result of a rotating metal object, suggesting that it might have served to test an early type of rock drill, or that the block might have been used to hold the axle of some machine in place. Some months later I was informed that the type of machine that produced such marks had been located: a 19th century rock drill.

This great variety of modern utilitarian rock markings needs to be considered before judging any markings on rock surfaces. From the archaeologist's point of view, they may not be very interesting, but other rock markings produced by pre-Historic societies were both utilitarian and intentional. The first examples springing to mind in Australia are perhaps axe/hatchet-grinding grooves. They are a widespread phenomenon, occurring at thousands of sites (as mentioned above, nearly 2000 sites have been registered in the three eastern mainland states alone), almost always on sandstone. A better example of this type of rock marking are the 'grinding sites drainage grooves'. Caryll Sefton (pers. comm. 1989) reported observing patterns of long grooves on sandstone pavements in the general Sydney region, which she had seen at about twenty sites. They seem to be effective in draining water during rain, and they can occur at petroglyph sites. These long grooves are hammered into the sandstone with stone tools in precisely the same fashion as petroglyphs, they are certainly anthropogenic, and they can form networks of many metres. Their usual archaeological interpretation is that they are un-completed petroglyphs. After examination I mooted the hypothesis that some of these lines are drainage systems to manage the hydrology of axe reduction workshop sites — keeping them dry, crystalline and hard (Bednarik 1990: 3).

While this remains a hypothesis, it does offer a logical explanation: the effective life span of a grinding area depends on how long the case hardened surface remains hard, and nothing weakens the coherence of the stone's grains as much as prolonged presence of water. On a near-horizontal pavement, moisture is retained far longer than on a sloping site. If there is a natural hollow in the rock that retains water for weeks, it provides an ideal reservoir of the moisture that would have been used in the axe/hatchet reduction grinding. However, the second site requirement was the presence of hardened grinding surfaces; without them the site had no value for the production of ground stone tools.

Archaeological rock markings which are intentional but utilitarian (and consequently are not rock art) occur in many forms in various parts of the world, depending on ecological and geological factors. They are not reviewed here as they have rarely presented problems to archaeologists.

BH2. Non-utilitarian anthropic marks (rock art)

In defining the subject of non-utilitarian anthropic rock markings as art we would do well to consider what art actually is, and to do so outside the concepts of Westerners. Indeed, this question can be properly answered only by taking it outside the conceptual framework of hominins altogether, and by responding in a fashion that would satisfy an extra-terrestrial being of superior intelligence.

No-one has managed to provide a definition of art that is both philosophically correct and acceptable to the majority of practitioners. For instance art has been defined as the medium conveying the artist's awareness of perceived reality to human sensory perception. It therefore serves to externalise human concepts of reality (Bednarik 1991b). In a more esoteric, but philosophically more satisfying definition, art is the phenomenon in human experience of which there can be no crucial common denominators of phenomenon categories that are inaccessible to humans. Art thus consists of the collective phenomena about which academically unencumbered humans could be able to think about objectively (Bednarik 1990/91). This definition has the benefits of being mindful of epistemological demands, and of being valid outside an anthropocentric frame of reference.

However, it would not distinguish, in the case of the graphic arts, between 'graffiti', fine arts, 'utilitarian' art, children's drawings, or the cupules of archaic *Homo sapiens*. Non-utilitarian rock markings are therefore likely to comprise many forms of 'symbolic' expression, ranging from graffiti to 'establishment art' (e.g. shamanistic art, emblemic art, art embodying cultural, social or political messages). Hence a great variety of forms must be expected, and there is no golden rule to separate rock art from other rock markings, based on simply recognising the former. It is true that most rock art is fairly easily recognised, although care is always required even in apparently clear-cut cases. Here we are mostly concerned with that small proportion of rock markings that provide no clear indication of what they are, or which are not what they seem to be. Unfortunately, doubtful cases are not necessarily solvable by summoning up previous cognitive experience or academic training, and secure discrimination can involve considerable 'analytical creativity' on the part of the analyst. Moreover, it must be emphasised that several instances of rock markings have been encountered, particularly in caves that have resisted all attempts to define their origins. They are, however, extremely rare.

NATURAL AND ARTIFICIAL COLOUR MARKINGS ON ROCK

Instances of the misidentification of pictograms and natural colourations are also quite rare in comparison to the surprising frequency of misidentifications of petroglyphs. This subject is therefore not given much space here, but it should be mentioned that there have been many cases, nevertheless, perhaps beginning with 1912 (when Breuil and Sollas thought they had found cave paintings in a Welsh cave, Bacon's Hole; it turned out that the red stripes had been made by a workman in 1894; Daniel 1992: 27–28).

Rock paintings and other pictograms lacking clear definition as recognisable motifs are perceived by their colour contrast, and to a lesser degree by the fact that only a limited range of colours is normally used. Paint colours such as green, blue, bluish and grey are exceedingly rare in world rock art, red being by far the most common colour (Bednarik 1992d). Misidentification as a pictogram is only possible where there are natural discolourations on a rock surface that appear to form a motif. These may either be due to pigment that has been applied by a non-human agency, they may be natural petrographic colours (e.g. related to weathering), or they may consist of an accretionary deposit of coloured matter.

No coloured rock markings by a non-human mammal are known, but a number of insect species do produce such motifs. Most particularly, a variety of wasps (e.g. in South America and Australia) constructs mud structures on sheltered rock surfaces. Where they use a mud that is rich in pigments such as red clay or iron oxides, the pigment may penetrate a sandstone support surface. Once the mud nest has weathered away, a distinctive pigment stain may remain. Such mud-daubing wasp nests tend to be divided into a number of small chambers of remarkably regular patterning, which will produce distinctive 'motifs'. In some cases, these may resemble actual rock art motifs. For instance, a wasp of north-eastern Brazil constructs nests of oval form, divided into large chambers with parallel walls (Bednarik 1989). The red stains they leave on the rock consist of ovals with distinctive internal barring, which is a motif commonly found in various rock arts, including that of the region in question. Other species produce different patterns (e.g. in northern as well as southern Australia).

Inherent colouration of rock or coloured patches caused by weathering should not present difficulties of identification. Nevertheless, accretionary deposits can be tricky, as indicated by the following few instances of such misidentification. At the well-known petroglyph site of Rochester Creek in Utah, a roughly triangular patch of red colour was found below the surface upon excavation of some sediment, and this patch was identified as a rock painting by some dozens of scholars in the early 1980s. An archaeologist then secured a charcoal sample from nearby and, assuming it to be stratigraphically related to the 'painting', obtained a radiocarbon date from it which he tried to relate to the red patch. Microscopic examination of the site found that no pigment deposition was evident (Bednarik 1987b). The entire panel was covered by a dark-brown varnish that had become locally discoloured within a small area of roughly triangular shape. Right above it was a scar where a flake had become detached by thermal fracture (Figure 17). It appears therefore that a fire had once been lit at the foot of the vertical panel, altering the rock varnish locally. Most likely this had involved the dehydration of goethite to haematite, which would account for

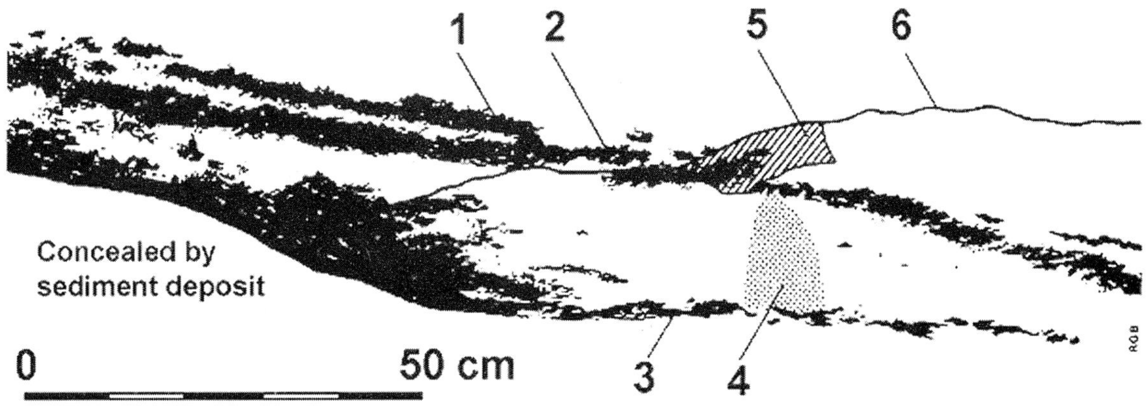

Figure 17. Lower part of vertical petroglyph panel of Rochester Creek site, Emery, Utah, USA. The present sediment level is indicated by the uppermost of the three carbonate accretions shown in black. The scale drawing shows the spatial relationships of (1) the uppermost carbonate band, which postdates some petroglyphs; (2) the middle carbonate band, which occurs below all petroglyphs and postdates feature 5; (3) the lower carbonate horizon; (4) the red patch misidentified as a pictogram, apparently contemporary with features 3 and 5; (5) scar of thin thermal spall; and (6) a natural fracture predating all five preceding features.

the colour change from brown towards a reddish hue — a process frequently manifested in the field.

At Laurie Creek, in the Northern Territory of Australia, an AMS radiocarbon date was derived from what was defined as blood residues in a weathered dark-red paint residue. At the time the 20 000-year date was reported it was the oldest direct date in the world from a pictogram. Nelson (1993), the group's radiocarbon scientist, was sceptical enough to resample the deposit, and found that it consisted neither of pigment, nor did it contain human blood as reported; in fact the material dated was not even proteinaceous. The deposit was simply a natural weathering product of iron oxides, and Nelson found that organic material was often present on the site's rock surfaces (concerning the presence of organics in weathering zones, see direct dating discussion in Ch. 7). The date obtained has therefore no archaeological significance whatsoever.

A French researcher reported the discovery of paintings in a cave on Mount Bego in the western Alps, which in 1996 led to a heated public debate with other researchers working in the area. One professor of archaeology who had worked in the region for thirty years argued that there were no paintings in the cave, only lichens and algae, but that there were some petroglyphs which his opponent had failed to detect. The conservator under whose jurisdiction the site lies recognised the existence of the pictograms, but argued that the art is recent. Surface deposits were then analysed by two laboratories and the presence of ochres was demonstrated. But when the first researcher returned to the site she reported that her paintings had disappeared, had been scraped off to discredit her. In the process of this vandalism, petroglyphs had emerged beneath the paintings. Two independent researchers were then called in to resolve the matter, who found no trace of paint, petroglyphs or vandalism.

SUMMARY

It is again clear from these examples, which all refer to errors by highly regarded professional archaeologists of many years' experience, that archaeological identifications of rock marks as rock art should not necessarily be relied upon. This is a specialist task that comes under the aegis of rock art science. Some archaeologists are very experienced in the study of rock art, but this is due to their specific research orientation. Some are also experienced in geochemistry, but that does not mean that all archaeologists are experts in geochemistry. Precisely the same applies to rock art science, which is just as distant from orthodox archaeology as is geochemistry, and which also involves a great deal of specialised knowledge of which none is conveyed by a traditional archaeological training.

There is, however, a more exasperating dimension to the traditional domination of rock art science by archaeology. The scientific study of rock art lags significantly behind current progress in comparable disciplines. It is fair to say that the state of a discipline that is incapable of defining reliably the object of its study is not adequately equipped to deal with it, and it is apparent that this state is attributable to the preoccupations of archaeologists working with rock art — with stylistic and iconographic but unfalsifiable claims about the art, and with preserving reputations and influence. Scientific study of rock art has been marginalised for the best part of two centuries by these circumstances, and for this reason rock art science lags around fifty years behind other disciplines. This is readily obvious when we consider that stock-in-trade methods of forensic science, which are most suitable for rock art studies (e.g. matching microscopic striations or identifying blood traces), have not been introduced in this field, even though they have routinely been in use elsewhere for many decades. Instead we have been fed a diet of opinions about what rock art means, why it was made, and which invented style it belongs to — none of them testable, none scientific.

REFERENCES

BEDNARIK, R. G. 1977. A survey of prehistoric sites in the Tom Price region, north Western Australia. *Archaeology and Physical Anthropology in Oceania* 7: 51–76.

BEDNARIK, R. G. 1981. On natural rock markings. Unpubl. MS, 71 p., held in the Archive of the Australian Rock Art Research Association, Melbourne.

BEDNARIK, R. G. 1986a. Parietal finger markings in Europe and Australia. *Rock Art Research* 3: 30–61, 159–70.

BEDNARIK, R. G. 1986b. Cave use by Australian Pleistocene man. *Proceedings, University of Bristol Spelaeological Society* 17: 227–45.

BEDNARIK R. G. 1987a. The cave art of Western Australia. *The Artefact* 12: 1–16.

BEDNARIK, R. G. 1987b. No pictographs at end of Rochester Creek rainbow. *La Pintura* 14(2+3): 14–17.

BEDNARIK, R. G. 1989. On the Pleistocene settlement of South America. *Antiquity* 63: 101–11.

BEDNARIK, R. G. 1990. Annual AURA Meeting 1989. *AURA Newsletter* 7(1): 2–3.

BEDNARIK, R. G. 1990/91. Epistemology in palaeoart studies. *Origini* 15: 57–78.

BEDNARIK, R. G. 1991a. On natural cave markings. *Helictite* 29(2): 27–41.

BEDNARIK, R. G. 1991b. Standardisation in rock art terminology. In C. Pearson and B. K. Swartz (eds), *Rock art and posterity: conserving, managing and recording rock art,* pp. 116–118. Occasional AURA Publication 4, Australian Rock Art Research Association, Melbourne.

BEDNARIK, R. G. 1992a. Base pour des etudes de pointe des debuts de l'art. *L'Anthropologie* 96(2-3): 369–74.

BEDNARIK, R. G. 1992b. Adventures in the exploration of Samson's Shaft in Brazil. *Purakala* 2: 81–84.

BEDNARIK, R. G. 1992c. Early subterranean chert mining. *The Artefact* 15: 11–24.

BEDNARIK, R. G. 1992d. Mehr über die rote Farbe in Vorgeschichte. *Almogaren* 23: 179–89.

BEDNARIK, R. G. 1993a. About cupules. *Rock Art Research* 10(2): 138–39.

BEDNARIK, R. G. 1993b. About Palaeolithic ostrich eggshell in India. *Indo-Pacific Prehistory Association Bulletin* 13: 34–43.

BEDNARIK, R. G. 1993c. Palaeolithic art in India. *Man and Environment* 18(2): 33–40.

BEDNARIK, R. G. 1993d. Wall markings of the cave bear. *Studies in Speleology* 9: 51–70.

BEDNARIK, R. G. 1994a. On the scientific study of palaeoart. *Semiotica* 100(2/4): 141–68.

BEDNARIK, R. G. 1994b. Archaeology: empiricist determinism or cultural synthesis? *South African Archaeological Bulletin* 49(160): 96–99.

BEDNARIK, R. G. 1994c. No sex, please, we're gliders! *AURA Newsletter* 11(1).

BEDNARIK, R. G. 1998. Microscopic analysis of 'engraved plaques' and other objects from Devil's Lair. *Journal of the Royal Society of Western Australia* 81: 23–33.

BEDNARIK, R. G. 1999. Just a natural phenomenon? *The Age* 30 November: 14.

BEDNARIK, R. G. 2000. Age estimates for the petroglyph sequence of Inca Huasi, Mizque, Bolivia. *Andean Past* 6: 277–87.

BEDNARIK, R. G. 2002. Paläolithische Felskunst in Deutschland? *Archäologische Informationen* 25(1-2): 107–17.

BOLGER, P. 1979. Aboriginal engravings from Sutherland Creek, Maude, Victoria. *Victorian Naturalist* 96: 69–71.

BOTH, R. A. 1963. Rock markings on Tasman Peninsula. Unpubl. report, Tasmanian Museum, Hobart.

BRANAGAN, D. F. and H. C. CAIRNS 1993. Tesselated pavements in the Sydney region, New South Wales. *Journal and Proceedings, Royal Society of New South Wales* 126: 63–72.

CAIRNS, H. C. and D. F. BRANAGAN 1992. Artificial patterns on rock surfaces in the Sydney region, New South Wales: evidence for Aboriginal time charts and sky maps? In J. McDonald and I. P. Haskovec (eds), *State of the art: regional rock art studies in Australia and Mela-nesia,* pp. 25–31. Occasional AURA Publication 6, Australian Rock Art Research Association, Melbourne.

CLOTTES, J., I. COURTIN and H. VALLADAS 1992. A well-dated Palaeolithic cave: the Cosquer Cave at Marseille. *Rock Art Research* 9: 122–29.

CONSENS, M. 2000. Between artefacts and egofacts: the power of assigning names (abstract). In R. G. Bednarik (ed.), *Third AURA Congress, program and congress handbook,* p. 10. Occasional AURA Publication 11, Australian Rock Art Research Association, Inc., Melbourne.

DANIEL, G. E. 1992. *Writing for antiquity.* Thames & Hudson, London.

D'ERRICO, F. 1988. Lecture technologique de l'art mobilier gravé. Nouvelles méthodes et premiers résultats sur les galets gravés de Rochedane. *L'Anthropologie* 92: 101–22.

DIAMOND, J. 1991. *The rise and fall of the third chimpanzee.* Radius, London.

DICKSON, F. P. 1980. Of grinding grooves. *Archaeology and Physical Anthropology in Oceania* 15: 157–61.

DORTCH, C. E. 1976. Two engraved stone plaques of Late Pleistocene age from Devil's Lair, Western Australia. *Archaeology and Physical Anthropology in Oceania* 11: 32–44.

DUBOIS, J.-M. M. 1985. The 'written stones' of Quebec: history and mithology [sic]. *Bollettino del Centro Camuno di Studi Preistorici* 22: 63–66.

ELLIS, W. F. 1958. Examination of rock markings. *Walkabout* 24(2): 40.

HAHN, J. 1991. Höhlenkunst aus dem Hohlen Fels bei Schelklingen, Alb-Donau-Kreis. *Archäologische Ausgrabungen in Baden-Württemberg* 19: 19–21.

HENDY, C. H. 1971. The isotopic geochemistry of speleothems. *Geochimica et Cosmochimica Acta* 35: 801–24.

HILL, B. and R. HILL 1974. *Indian petroglyphs of the Pacific Northwest.* Hancock House, Saanichton, B.C.

HISCOCK, P. and S. MITCHELL 1993. *Stone artefact quarries and reduction sites in Australia: towards a type profile.* Technical Publications Series 4, Australian Heritage Commission, Canberra.

MAYNARD, L. and R. EDWARDS 1971. Wall markings. In R. V. S. Wright (ed.), *Archaeology of the Gallus Site, Koonalda Cave,* pp. 61-80. Australian Institute of Aboriginal Studies, Canberra.

NELSON, D. E. 1993. Second thoughts on a rock-art date. *Antiquity* 67: 893–95.

OLLIER, C. D. 1965. Some features of granite weathering in Australia. *Zeitschrift für Geomorphologie* 9: 285–304.

OLLIER, C. D. 1969. *Weathering.* Longman, London.

REID, O. W. 1962. Further discoveries of Aboriginal rock carvings in Tasmania. *Papers and Proceedings, Royal Society of Tasmania* 96: 87–89.

ROGERS, T. 1981. Palaeolithic cave art in the Wye Valley. *Current Anthropology* 22: 601–602.

SEFTON, C. 1995. Sandstone overhangs and subsidence: monitoring rock art for effects of mining activities. In A. Thorn and J. Brunet (eds), *Preservation of rock art*, pp. 55–59. Occasional AURA Publication 9, Australian Rock Art Research Association, Melbourne.

SHARLAND, M. S. R. 1957. Symbols of an extinct race. *Walkabout* 23(10): 38–42.

SHARPE, K. 2004. Line markings: human or animal origin? *Rock Art Research* 21: 57–84.

SIEVEKING, G. de G. 1982. Palaeolithic art and natural rock formations. *Current Anthropology* 23: 567–69.

SIMS, P. C. 1977. Variations in Tasmanian petroglyphs. In P. J. Ucko (ed.), *Form in indigenous art*, pp. 429–38. Prehistory and Material Culture Series 13, Australian Institute of Aboriginal Studies, Canberra.

TWIDALE, C. R., E. M. CAMPBELL and J. A. BOURNE 1983. Granite forms, karst and lunettes. In M. J. Tyler, C. R. Twidale, J. K. Ling and J. W. Holmes (eds), *Natural history of the South East*, pp. 25–37. Royal Society of South Australia Inc., Adelaide.

WADE, A. 1941. Note on a grooved and polished granite surface near Eulo, western Queensland. *Proceedings of the Royal Society of Queensland* 53: 101–104.

WATCHMAN, A. 1990. A summary of occurrences of oxalate-rich crusts in Australia. *Rock Art Research* 7: 44–50.

4. THE TECHNOLOGY OF ROCK ART

TECHNOLOGY OF PETROGLYPHS

Most archaeologists commenting on the technology of petroglyphs seem unfamiliar with any replicative studies or ethnographic observations of petroglyph making, and some have created a purely theoretical system of taxonomy which is essentially impractical and derived from confirmation-based deductions (science is falsification based). As noted in Chapter 1, petroglyphs (reductive forms of rock art) are usually described by subjective technological labels. For instance, the term 'engraving' is used as a collective name for all petroglyphs, instead of being reserved for true engravings. An often seen term is 'rock carving', which seems to refer to the meaning of 'to carve initials into a tree'. This is inappropriate as a corresponding technological process would only be effective on very soft rock, and there is no evidence that it was frequently used, if at all. In South America, it has been claimed that petroglyphs were produced by etching the rock with corrosive plant juices. There is no evidence of this and it, too, should be regarded it as archaeolore until credible ethnographic or geochemical evidence is presented in support. The method of drilling or boring, i.e. using a stone tool in a rotational movement, has also been suggested to have been used. No microscopic, ethnographic or other indication suggests that petroglyphs might have been made by such a technique. Then there is the term 'pecking', which Maynard (1977) decreed refers to indirect percussion, and which involves the use of two tools: a chisel-like stone tool and a hammer stone. As mentioned in Chapter 1, this method was either never used, or so rarely that its results are most uncommon. Yet the term appears so often in the literature that it seems to be regarded as synonymous with percussion petroglyph. Maynard's term for direct percussion, pounding, which accounts either for most or all percussion petroglyphs, is by contrast notoriously rare in the literature.

One could argue that it does not matter if archaeologists invent a mythology about rock art; it does no harm. But this is not strictly true. They are often placed in positions of executive control over rock art sites; they often excavate at rock art sites. Most archaeologists are unable to recognise the tools used in the production of petroglyphs, so they will not find or recognise such implements in sediments below or near petroglyphs. Such finds will go unreported even though they are of profound importance to the archaeology of the site in question. For example, petroglyph tools in stratified sediments might be able to be dated. Since they were associated directly with some of the petroglyphs present they may provide reliable age estimations for the rock art.

Numerous archaeological excavations have been conducted at petroglyph sites, but there are no reports of stratified petroglyph-producing tools from nearly all of them. Since such tools have often been observed as surface finds by a few specialists (see below) it is to be expected that they should also occur below ground. The explanation is probably to be found in the inability of most archaeologists to recognise such tools. Any such tools from stratified contexts would provide crucial archaeological evidence at a petroglyph site, probably the most important evidence available from such a site. Therefore these excavations can be defined as needless destruction of crucial archaeological evidence (cf. Swartz 1997: 73, in reference to a recent instance).

Another issue concerns the inability of most archaeologists to distinguish between rock markings made by stone points, metal or other materials (e.g. animal claws). The difficulties in discriminating between, say, animal scratches and similar human marks have already been illuminated in Chapter 3, but they are compounded by those of identifying tool materials in cases of clearly anthropic markings. For instance, there are cases such as those from Portugal in which archaeologists claimed that rock marks made with metal tools date from the Palaeolithic period, are of a Solutrean style and 20 000 years old. This is again an issue of technology, and one that cannot be resolved by archaeological reasoning about style; it must be examined scientifically, by methods of replication and falsification.

In this chapter some of the most pressing aspects of petroglyph technology are briefly reviewed. Much more detailed research of the issues broached here is required, especially in the acquisition of more comprehensive data than are currently available. It is appropriate to begin with some ethnographic reports.

ETHNOGRAPHIC OBSERVATIONS

The most extensive ethnographic information we possess about rock art is that of Australia, where painting on rock continues to the present day. Aboriginal painting traditions have not only survived, they thrive today on media such as bark and canvas. Knowledge about the cultural context and the techniques used in rock painting continues to be collected (e.g. Mulvaney 1996). Numerous Aboriginal communities across the country perceive recent rock art traditions as ongoing — as externalisations of living culture (Ward 1992).

Petroglyphs, on the other hand, are usually ascribed to 'the ancients' (as are some paintings), or are considered to be of non-human origins. They may have been made by ancestral heroes, or they are attributed to the time 'when the rocks were still soft' (Flood 1995a; Mowaljarlai and Vinnicombe 1995). Although there is certainly a distinct paucity of ethnographic data concerning the production of petroglyphs, detailed accounts nevertheless do exist in Australia. For instance, Mountford (1955, 1976) has witnessed and photographed the making of petroglyphs on several occasions. In 1937 he observed the production of sgraffito petroglyphs (figures produced by the removal of a layer of material of colour different to that of the material exposed) at The Granites, Northern Territory, and reported that the artist used a 'small rounded pebble held in the hand' (Mountford 1976: 76). His photographs (Pls 19, 20) show the left-handed use at a pavement site of a fist-sized, flattish cobble of about ten centimetres. A further illustration (Pl. 21) shows a man using a thin cobble of probably much less than 200 grams mass to produce a petroglyph by striking a vertical wall at eye level.

Mountford subsequently observed many recent petroglyphs along the Mann and Musgrave Ranges, and photographed Tjanjundina creating a narrative scene commemorating an emu hunt that had just taken place (Mountford 1976: Pl. 22). Here, the stone hammer held by Tjanjundina is so small it is concealed by his hand.

Much earlier reports are available from the Pilbara, Western Australia. Stokes (1846: 169), in describing the Depuch Island petroglyphs, recognised that images were made by pounding away the dark-brown rock varnish (sgraffito technique), but appears not to have witnessed the making of any petroglyphs. Withnell (1901: 29), also writing about the coastal Pilbara, mentions how the outline of a motif was first sketched with chalk or ochre, and then a 'sharp hard stone' was used to create impact grooves of about four millimetres depth. His description was confirmed by Clement (1903: 9), reporting from the same region. Clement also thought that chalk or charcoal was used to outline the figures, but that they were then hammered with 'a stone axe'. The latter practice seems very unlikely, for two reasons: stone axes are absent or very rare in the Pilbara (cf. Bednarik 1973, 1977: 68), and their sharp edges would not be used for such damaging tasks. So perhaps McCarthy (1961: 143) is right in assuming that Clement and Withnell merely surmised, but never actually saw petroglyphs made. Clement's illustration of a petroglyph-making implement (1903: Pl. 3) is not of an axe, but of a thin cobble, similar to that which Mountford (1976: 81, footnote 9) described from The Granites. On the other hand, Bates (n.d.) reported that petroglyphs were still made at Port Hedland when she was there, and Tindale has mentioned that a petroglyph was made there during his visit (Wright 1968: 71). Further evidence (Crawford 1964: 44) implies that outlines on Depuch Island were at least sometimes drawn with a sharp object before the petroglyphs were hammered in, which would tend to support Withnell's and Clement's accounts.

Evidence of the use of a pointed tool to initially outline the form of petroglyphs subsequently made by percussion is not limited to Australia. There are many examples among the Côa valley petroglyphs in Portugal which were first outlined with a stone point, then struck with a stone hammer (Bednarik 1995a). I have observed similar treatment elsewhere, including in Asia (e.g. Siberia) and South America (e.g Peru).

There are further factors suggesting that petroglyph production in the Pilbara continued into the last century. When I visited a petroglyph and occupation site near Tom Price (Site 2: Bednarik 1977) in the company of four Indjibandi men in early 1968, one of the men, who was in his seventies then, spontaneously produced a new petroglyph. He made a complex linear, to me non-iconic, motif within ten or twelve minutes. I was curious about several aspects of this event, including whether he had seen this done before. He stated, through a translator, that he had seen the old people do it when he was very young, and that he had done it himself as a child. On the occasion I observed then he used only a single tool, an untrimmed quartz cobble with a pointed end, about seven centimetres long, to strike the rock panel directly.

IMPLEMENTS FOR THE PRODUCTION OF PETROGLYPHS

Not having attempted any replication work prior to 1968, I had falsely assumed that to create the impact necessary to achieve the indentations on hard rock (such as diorite, as in the Tom Price example), a tool mass well in excess of a kilogram would be required. I was surprised to see such a small tool (of about 150 to 200 g) used so effectively, and subsequently began to look for suitable tools at petroglyph sites, in Australia as well as in the other continents.

Others have done much the same. In Anati's work, for instance, there are various references to the tools he observed at petroglyph sites (Anati 1976a: 41, 1976b: 28), which he sometimes even found on the carved surfaces themselves (e.g. Anati 1981: 14–15, showing examples from Negev Desert). This prodigious author's principal work is in the Val Camonica of northern Italy, where he has collected many petroglyph-making stone implements (Anati 1994: Fig. 40). A series of such tools can be seen at the Centro Camuno di Studi Preistorici in Capo di Ponte. They show that those found in Europe were practically identical to those I had observed elsewhere since 1968 (Figure 18). At nearby Valtellina, similar tools were found in crevices of the large monolith of Rupe Magna, near Grosio (Arcà 1995: Fig. 112). Edwards (1964: 650) mentioned the stone tools at the Australian petroglyph site Pitcairn Station, Wilman (1968) those at South African sites. Percussion stone tools supposedly used in petroglyph manufacture have also been reported from several American sites, specifically in the Southwest (Kearns et al. 1975: 325; Ives 1986; Wallace and Holmlund 1986: 26; Moore 1992).

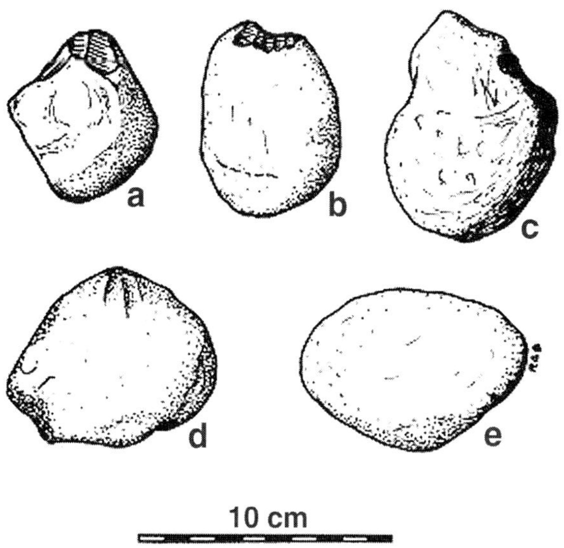

Figure 18. Quartzite mur-e excavated at Luine, a petroglyph site in Val Camonica, northern Italy.

The problem Australian archaeologists have experienced in speculating about the manufacture of petroglyphs (of which their frequent use of the term 'engraving' in the place of 'petroglyph' is symptomatic) has its several parallels in other parts of the world. The perhaps best example is provided by their Russian colleagues, in relation to the heavily researched Karelian petroglyph sites. Ravdonikas (1936a, 1936b, 1937, 1938) favoured the indirect percussion hypothesis, as did other Russian archaeologists (e.g. Linewski 1978: 194) (Figure 19). However, Savvateyev's (1970, 1973, 1976, 1977) detailed research failed to produce such percussion tools from the region's numerous excavations. He mentions dozens of excavations close to petroglyph sites, which have not produced a single tool used for indirect percussion. He did, however, find many 'impact stones', as he calls them: fist-sized quartz cobbles that fit well into the hand, with the working point distinguished by impact-scarring. He reports finding dozens near the mouth of the River Vyg, where Karelia's largest petroglyph site complex is located. Of particular relevance are the petroglyph making implements he excavated immediately below the Besovy Sledky rock ledge, which bears a very dense concentration of 470 figures covering just a few square metres (Bahn et al. 1995).

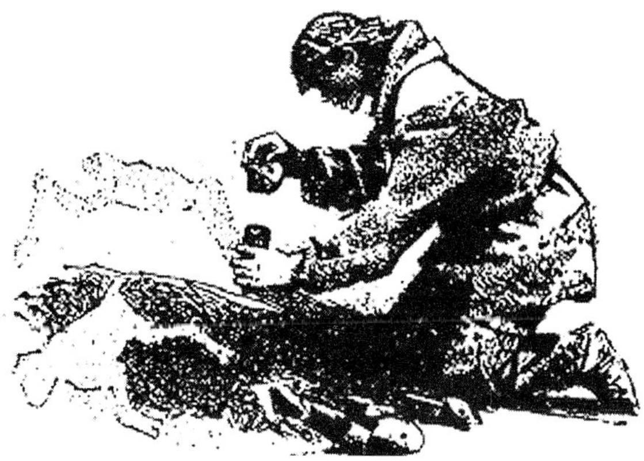

Figure 19. Artistic reconstruction depicting how percussion petroglyphs are falsely assumed to have been made (after A. M. Linewski).

Recently I have replaced the cumbersome term '*petroglyph-making implement*' with an Aboriginal word from the Booandik language, *mur-e* (Smith 1880: 129). In its scientific usage, mur-e (singular and plural) refers generically to a tool that has been used in fashioning a petroglyph, and as an adopted word it is not italicised (Bednarik 1998).

Percussion mur-e

Since becoming aware in 1968 of what to look for, I have observed mur-e, especially those used in percussion, at many sites, and used facsimiles of them in replicative experiments well away from the art. In the Pilbara region of north-western Australia, where I recorded hundreds of petroglyph sites during the

1960s, I had ample opportunity to search the barren rock pavements and rock piles with their often large numbers of motifs, usually being the first non indigenous person to examine these sites. Mur-e were easy to find in such conditions of very minimal sediment formation and vegetation cover (Figure 20). In the early 1970s I extended my search to various other regions of Australia, increasingly using scientific methods to study mur-e. For instance, in 1971 I examined several at Sturts Meadows, and removed the specimen shown in Figure 21 for detailed analysis. The dark discolouration clearly visible on its impact fractured point is dark-brown mineral matter. It consisted mainly (in descending order) of SiO_2, Al_2O_3, Fe_2O_3, MnO and TiO_2, and the trace elements Ba, Sr, Cu, Ni, Pb, V, Co and Cr. The composition of the pavement varnish nearby, sampled at the same time, provided a result so similar that there should be no doubt that this white quartz cobble was used to make petroglyphs at the site.

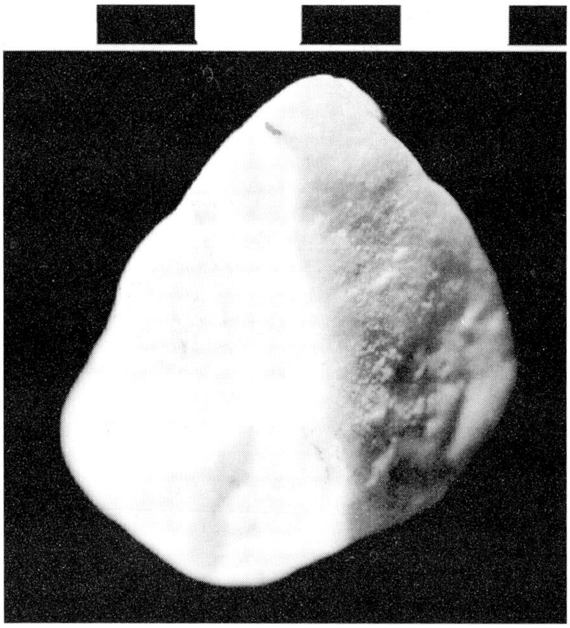

Figure 21. White quartz mur-e from Stuart's Meadows, near Broken Hill, Australia. A residue of rock varnish is visible on the point, and an impact fracture extends towards the viewer.

During the subsequent thirty years I have examined percussion mur-e in all continents except Antarctica. While there are no strict consistencies among them in material type or preparation, several striking characteristics should be noted:

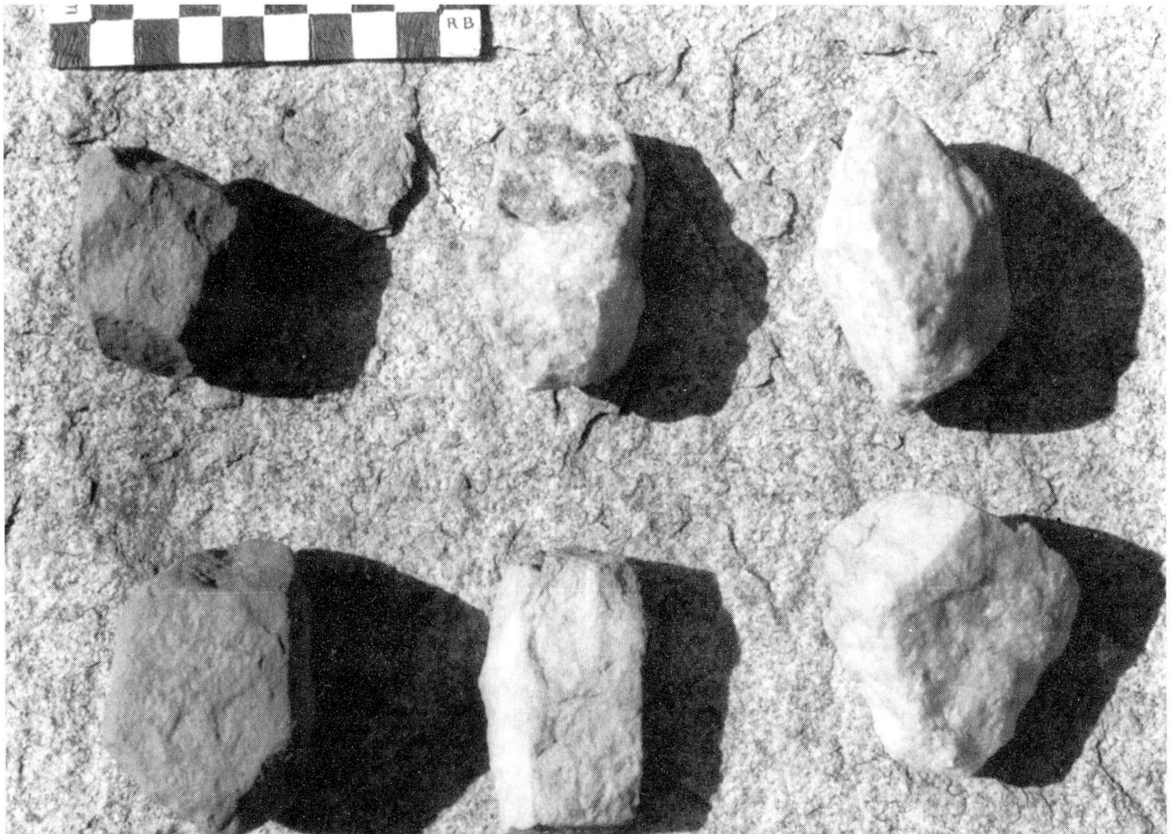

Figure 20. Six mur-e collected in 1968 at a dense petroglyph concentration on Burrup peninsula, north-western Australia, but left at the site.

Size: percussion mur-e are rarely large. As I have not taken scales to the field, and have rarely removed the finds from the sites, I cannot offer detailed statistics. However, percussion mur-e are usually under 150 g, and very rarely over 250 g. Weights of 100 to 130 grams are very common. Depending on the shape and relative density, this would correspond to a maximum dimension of 6 to 8 cm.

Shape: the axis of maximum dimension usually coincides with the direction of application. There is considerable variation in shape, but overall there is a global preference for pieces with a thick end to be held in the hand, and a vaguely pointed end with which to strike the rock surface and which bears the wear marks. There are, however, also flat and elongate shapes represented, and for patina-bruising even quite round pebbles or cobbles have been used. Finally, there are also specimens that were used at more than one point (sometimes accounting for more than 25% of the mur-e present at a site).

Materials: in regions with an abundant variety of alluvial cobbles or clastic rocks, there is a distinctive preference for dense quartzites and crystalline quartz of various types. However, in regions of soft rock facies such as schists, carbonates or poorly consolidated sandstones, alternative materials have been used for mur-e.

Preparation: contrary to a common assumption, few mur-e seem to have been prepared by prior flaking, in Australia and elsewhere. Flaking around the working point is probably use-wear rather than intentional trimming. If small flakes are removed around the point as a result of impact, they actually tend to lead to a more acute point rather than a blunting. However, at least 80% of percussion mur-e bear no macroscopic flaking at all, be it use-wear or intentional preparation.

Wear: this is by far the most important and consistent aspect of percussion mur-e. Its characteristics are a direct function of the tool material properties, the rock panel's physical properties, and aspects of application of the tool to the rock panel. If the first two are well understood (see replication work, below), we can reasonably speculate about the third factor. The typical, most common wear-pattern to be observed is that generally acquired by quartzite mur-e when used on sandstone, variations of which are also found when applied to other rock types. There is an elongate, discrete area of bruising, convex (often of 4 to 5 mm latitudinal radius) and of a highly distinctive morphology. The microscopic relief of this facet is greatest at the margins, amounting to just a few microns of depth in the central part. Individual grains are rarely cracked, but their surface has a distinctly 'frosted' appearance when fresh. This wear-pattern cannot be identified with the unaided eye.

Wear-patterns on quartz are quite different. Microscopic conchoidal flake scars are found around minute depressions or faults within the wear facet. They measure usually from 50 to 150 μm. On a highly metamorphosed coarse quartzite, microscopic flaking and deeply developed macroscopic impact fractures can be observed adjacent to the principal impact area. Naturally there are also significant differences according to the type of rock and its weathering zone that caused the mur-e wear. Recognition and interpretation of these features is a specialist task. It should be possible, on the basis of experimentation, to estimate the duration of time a mur-e was used (i.e. approximately how many nicks it produced, or what length of engraved line).

Abrasion mur-e

A great variety of other materials may have been used to produce petroglyphs, especially where the rock is comparatively soft. The softest rock ever used in the making of petroglyphs is a carbonate speleothem called moonmilk (*Mondmilch*, *Montmilch*, *Bergmilch* etc.), a substance of pure calcite that may have the appearance, consistency and crystal structure (in the macroscopic sense) of freshly fallen snow. In dry situations it resembles fibres microscopically, but it often turns into a dough-like mass containing a great quantity of moisture. It can be marked by the slightest finger touch, and it has been marked in this way to produce petroglyphs called finger flutings (digital flutings, *sillons digitaux paralleles* etc.) during the past thirty or more millennia (Bednarik 1986), in at least France, Spain, Australia and New Guinea (Figure 22).

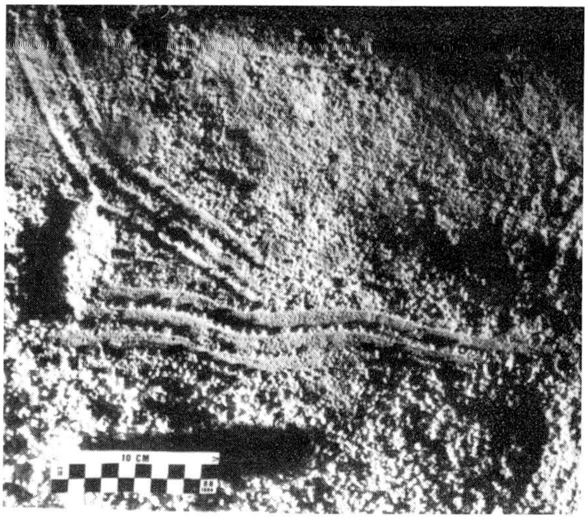

Figure 22. Detail of finger fluting on now fossilised *Montmilch*, Karlie-ngoinpool Cave, near Mt Gambier, South Australia.

This is one of the most widespread forms of early cave art in the world, having survived in at least seventy limestone caves despite its fragility. It survived either because of the extremely stable speleoclimates of deep caves (free of diurnal and seasonal air temperature fluctuations, stable relative air humidity), or because the formerly soft deposit has hardened. Under particularly favourable conditions these markings can become rock-hard and survive practically uncorroded, preserving every finest detail, such as tiny tear-marks indicating the direction of application. There are often other features providing similar information, such as the arrangements of the fingers at one or both ends of an individual set of fingers, or small ridges alongside finger grooves and the 'shavings' curling up from them.

Other types of cave petroglyphs offer even more scope for technological analysis. Engravings made with implements (rather than fingers) occur in numerous limestone caves in south-western Europe and southern Australia. Their detailed study (Bednarik 1984, 1986, 1987, 1992a, 1994a, 1997) uses aspects of the methods pioneered by Marshack (1972, 1975, 1986, 1989), and experimentally developed by d'Errico (1987, 1991, 1992, 1994) for portable art objects of antiquity. Foremost in the application of these methods to cave engravings is the use of field optical microscopy, still used only by myself. As in the study of portable engravings (i.e. markings made with burins or similar tools), such as those of the Upper Palaeolithic of western Europe, microscope-assisted 'internal analysis' can clarify many aspects of the production of cave engravings. These include the direction of abrasion, the point of commencement, and priority of markings in a superimposition sequence. Markings made with the same instrument can sometimes be identified, although the claims of both Marshack and d'Errico, that they can also identify tool changes in what are said to be notational sets, are rejected (cf. Bednarik 1991a). Two very different markings can be made by the same stone tool point, by simply turning it slightly. Therefore sameness in two marks may demonstrate that they were made with the same point, but difference does not prove the use of different tools. Consequently it is impossible to identify notations securely by microscopic study.

Cave engravings have sometimes survived in superb detail, especially where a formerly soft wall deposit hardened soon after it was marked. This hardening is partly attributable to desiccation, but primarily to the filling of voids in the carbonate precipitates' delicate crystal structure with more calcite deposition — resulting in what might loosely be described as a 'fossilised' surface. At some of the Australian sites, the types of stone tool material used in abrading mur-e were determined through replication studies from the striation patterns. In particular, at Mandurah Cave in Western Australia, experiments on a medium similar to the cave deposit showed that neither the end of a green branch, a dry branch, polished wood (boomerang) or chert produced markings whose microscopic striation patterns matched those on the cave walls, whereas the local calcarenite clasts produced striation spacings and patterns closely resembling the rock art (Bednarik 1987). In Nung-kol Cave, South Australia, the rock art was engraved into harder surfaces. Similar matching succeeded in showing that most rock markings there had apparently been made with local limestone clasts, but some had been cut with flaked chert (Figure 23).

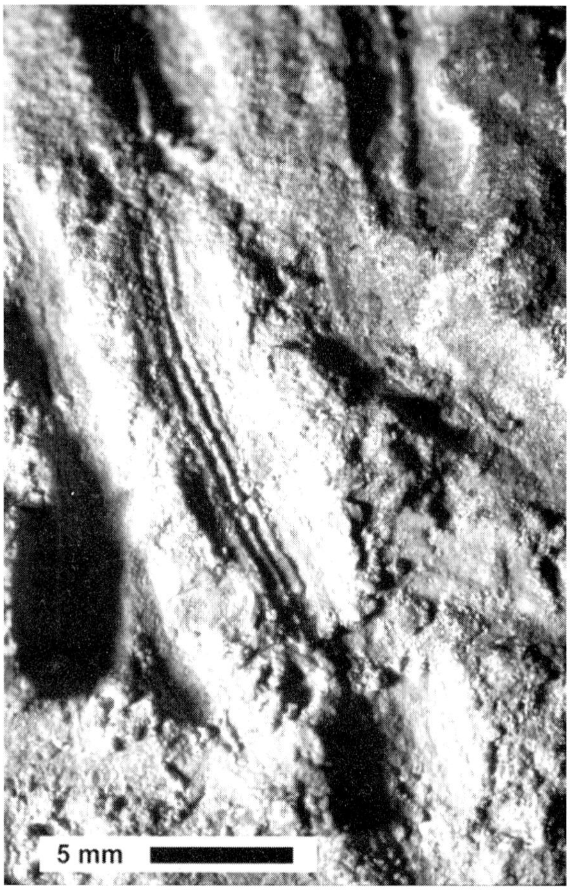

Figure 23. Detail of stone tool marks on formerly soft cave wall in Nung-kol Cave, near Mt Gambier, South Australia, showing details of tool applications and striations. Three different tool points can be discerned on the basis of striations and point cross-section.

The limestone is of different texture (grain structure) at the two caves, but in both regions the marks match those made experimentally with local material. It seems that the people who incised these markings into cave walls often used the resource most readily available — the clasts from the cave floor they were standing on.

This raises an important issue in the study of petroglyph technology: to what extent is it possible to determine whether engraved marks were made with stone or metal points. 'Engraved marks' are abraded markings, often made with a single continuous stroke. It needs to be emphasised that combinations of abraded and hammered marks often occur in rock art, in which either of these two techniques is superimposed on the other. The percussion marks are always distinguished by impact pits with coarse surfaces and diffuse shapes. Their morphology has not been studied in any detail so far, but it is obviously a function not only of rock type and tool point, but also of weathering state, mode and force of application, moisture and so forth. Nevertheless, technological details may be recoverable. They certainly are in abrasion petroglyphs, particularly where weathering has remained minimal.

The discrimination of engraving marks that were made with stone or metal tools can be of particular importance, because metal marks can only be of limited antiquity. After years of replicative work in the laboratory (mostly on slate and schist) I find it is possible to recognise marks of metal tools with a reliability of 98-99% in blind tests, but definite identification of stone tool marks remains elusive. In other words, specific traits are endemic to metal tools, but others are shared with stone tools. Nevertheless, while this applies under the stringent experimental conditions, it is of less concern in the field. This is because the problem relates primarily to the use of broken steel and bronze points, which are jagged and can resemble stone tool points. Since it is not very likely that such tools were frequently used in rock art production, the field conditions are perhaps some-what less rigorous. The types of metal tools most likely used to score rock surfaces are perhaps knives, nails, millstone roughing rods, chisels, swords, daggers, bayonets, pins and horseshoe nails.

Stone tool marks usually bear irregular longitudinal striations, and if the tool point was slightly rotated during an application, as was often the case, this would be reflected in the striae and in the groove cross section. Stone tool points are usually of irregular shape, often featuring multiple micro-points, and this characteristic can also occur on broken metal objects. Other features commonly seen in stone tool marks are '*stries parasites*' and 'duplication marks' (Bednarik 1995a: 96), but the most reliable indication that stone was used are 'fracture steps'. There are two main types of the first group, lateral parasitic striae and end parasitic striae (d'Errico 1994: 27-30), as well as others, and in their study it is important to consider convexities in the engraved surface. In a duplication mark ('*sillon rectilignes*') a lateral parasitic striation essentially takes over from the first micro-point whose mark peters out. This is because the position of the tool relative to the surface being engraved upon changed gradually: the tool might be turned, its angle of application might have changed, or the surface contour itself has changed. Cases of more than two duplicate marks occur (Bednarik 1995a: 96). Unfortunately these features are also possible with broken metal points. 'Fracture steps', however, occur where a point snaps partly (spalling) or completely, and they are typical of stone tool marks. Other features to study are crossings of two grooves, junctions, changes of direction, and points of commencement.

Tool grooves that lack any striations and, seen in section, feature steep walls, even undercut walls, or where an abrasive tool application involved considerably force were made with metal tools. They can be quite reliably identified by an experienced observer. Eastham (1999: 98) needed to examine a bovid figure on Penascosa panel 3 only briefly and without magnification to recognise that it had been cut with a carbon steel tool, yet numerous archaeologists had pronounced the same figure to be of the Upper Palaeolithic — which has yielded no steel tools so far. At another of the Côa sites in Portugal, panel 2 at Ribeira dos Piscos, I had scanned several hundred engraved lines on a small panel microscopically for many hours, without finding a single mark that bore any of the characteristics of stone tool marks. An anthropomorphous caricature among these marks bore the unmistakable hallmarks of a metal tool, and yet it was attributed to the Palaeolithic period. The figure had been engraved in one single movement, with numerous changes of direction, yet the groove width remained uniform around each curve, with distinct U-shape. In view of the rock's hardness it would have had to be engraved with a steel tool rather than one of bronze.

REPLICATIVE EXPERIMENTS

The great significance of replicative experimentation in the study of petroglyph technology has been emphasised repeatedly in papers on fundamental rock art science (Bednarik 1991b [see chapter' Replicative experiments'], 1992a, 1998). Replication studies of percussion petroglyphs have been conducted on numerous occasions in several continents. Crawford (1964: 44), in considering the technique used in making the petroglyphs on Depuch Island, Western Australia, remarked on how easy he found it to make petroglyphs 'in a minute or two' with 'a few taps on the stone'. McCarthy has conducted various experiments; for instance, he used 'the sharp corner of a piece of ironstone or ferruginous sandstone' to create direct percussion petroglyphs on Sydney sandstone (McCarthy 1967: 19). McCarthy's (1962: 44) experiments at Port Hedland using whelk shells to bore rather than to pound the oolite pavement led to Maynard's (1977) inclusion of the category 'drilled petroglyphs' in her schema. Wright (1968:34), conducting his own replication experiments, found that he could produce only very small pits in the limestone by rotating the point of a sharp stick. He suggests that sharp hard rocks were used, which is consistent with my own observations at the Port Hedland sites in 1967, later confirmed by microscopy.

Among the examples of replicative petroglyphs later examined with the microscope, some Russian experiments are particularly impressive. Many were made under controlled conditions, some were recorded on film. Savvateyev (1977) used mur-e collected from nearby excavations at Belomorsk, on the White Sea, to produce a filled-in image of a whale, similar to pre-Historic figures, in 30 minutes by direct percussion. The most difficult part, he reports, was to pound a precise edge; he attributes this to his lack of experience. His replication studies, like those of other Russian researchers working in Karelia (such as, more recently, Arsen Faradjev), were conducted on massive, frequently un-patinated granite pavements.

Sierts (1968), a sculptor, undertook petroglyph replication experiments with several materials on dolerite, diabase and sandstone after he had visited three art sites. He produced a few petroglyphs, timing himself and keeping records. His samples are quite elaborate, yet he reports that they took substantially less time to make than his colleagues estimated. Sierts took only one hour to create three petroglyphs which others estimated to have taken him forty to fifty hours. He rejects the indirect percussion method (pecking) as 'absolutely unsuitable', providing a photograph of the kind of tool flakes indirect percussion yields. His work was repeated by Weeks (2001), with similar results: the intermediary tools used in indirect percussion were shattered by the compressive force, and such lithics seem absent at sites. Previous American work has been reported from Arizona (Bruder 1983; Pilles 1976) and Montana (Loendorf 1984).

In my own replicative experiments, conducted from 1968 to the present on many lithologies, I found that the physical effort involved in producing percussion petroglyphs varied enormously according to the rock type, its weathering state or patination (Bednarik 1979), and to a lesser degree on the type of mur-e and technique employed. It is entirely impossible to generalise from isolated experiences, and all variables need to be fully recorded and quantified in such experimentation. For instance, rock types on which percussion petroglyphs were most frequently made are the facies of sandstones found in the sections of the Gondwana plate. Having conducted experiments on these Gondwana sandstones in southern Africa, India, Australia and South America, I have asked scholars how long they think it would take to create (a) a hammered and abraded groove of ten cm length and one cm depth, and (b) a cupule of 12 mm depth, on well-weathered sandstone (Figure 24). The true answers are (a) one minute and (b) two minutes respectively, but all estimates I was given were very significantly higher (ranging from 15 minutes to 6 hours). This is a fair indication of the effects of an acute lack of experimental work in petroglyph technology, and of inadequately published results of experiments.

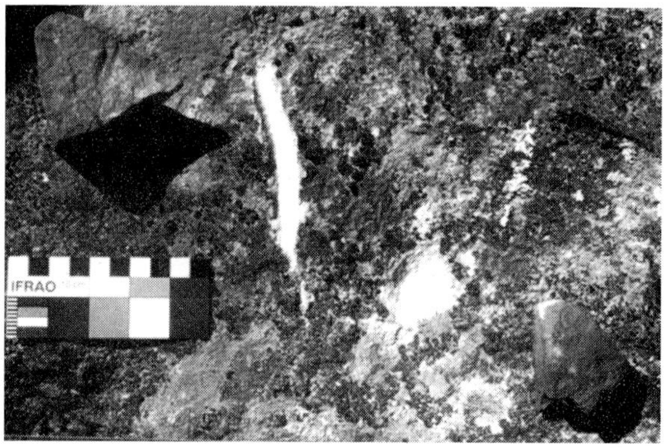

Figure 24. Standard petroglyph replicas, consisting of a 10-cm-long hammered and abraded groove of 10 mm depth and a cupule of 12 mm depth. The mur-e used for each marking is shown next to it.

While it would be inappropriate to conduct intervention experiments at actual rock art sites, there are good reasons to replicate open site petroglyphs at nearby rock surfaces, and to record all details of their production. I have found such replicas, including those I made decades ago, most useful in studying weathering and patination processes. Such studies, in turn, may be relevant to dating research and conservation work. What is therefore required are not only comprehensive records, but a central repository of these records so that future taphonomic studies of petroglyphs can be based on sound information rather than conjecture. Such records, to be adequate for future reference, perhaps centuries from now, need to include the following minimum details:

a. Precise location, including GPS co-ordinates, so that the actual marking(s) can be found again. The location must be referenced to permanent features, not vegetation, sediment or unstable rock features.
b. Condition and aspects of the rock surface at the time: depth of weathering rind; details of patination; exposure to rain, insolation and wind. Is the rock dry or wet? Which direction is the replica petroglyph facing?
c. Petrology of support rock substrate; rainwater acidity at the site; annual precipitation details.
d. Type and material of mur-e used; their weight; microscopic description of tool wear.
e. Description of manufacturing technique used; time taken.
f. Recording of true colours by photography with a colour scale calibrated for digitised colour re-constitution (IFRAO Standard Scale — Bednarik and Seshadri 1995).

This type of work can produce invaluable new information, not just concerning petroglyph dating and conservation, but also concerning chemical and physical erosion rates, chemical changes in rock subsurfaces, lichenometry, the formation of rock varnish or other accretionary mineral deposits, and so forth. All of this can help other disciplines besides rock art research. The *ad hoc* approach to the need of replicative experimentation that seems evident from the literature needs to be replaced with a systematic program of research. Such a program could be guided or even administered by the International Federation of Rock Art Organisations (IFRAO).

THE DATING OF MUR-E

The most recent development in the study of mur-e is their use in the dating of petroglyph-making activity. The practice of dating the mur-e rather than the petroglyphs was first applied in Bolivia in 1997. The difficulties in dating petroglyphs by a 'direct' method (see Ch. 7) are well appreciated. Essentially, those very few methods that might provide reliable results are notoriously imprecise and their application is limited to specific rock types and site morphologies. Other methods do exist but they are without exception fraught with difficulties (Bednarik 1979, 1996; Dorn 1996). One possibility that has not been explored so far is to determine when any mur-e found at petroglyph sites were used. It cannot usually be known on which motif they were used, but if the number of motifs present is small and they seem to be of similar ages, this might suffice to arrive at an estimate of the age of those motifs. Where several mur-e are available from a single site they may be used to estimate the times when different marking traditions were in use. This has been successfully done at several sites.

As in the case of petroglyphs there are two fundamentally different ways of estimating mur-e ages. One is by archaeological methods, using deductive reasoning. Generally this would involve indirect dating of some kind, probably radiocarbon determination of charcoal found in apparent association with the mur-e. Results acquired by these means may well be valid, but it must be cautioned that, as in the case of petroglyphs dated by indirect, archaeological means, there is no simple way to refute the proposition: we have to accept inductive pronouncements on trust (e.g. that the validity of the chronological association of charcoal and mur-e has not been negated by taphonomic factors).

The second method of determining the time a mur-e was used (or last used) is to estimate the age of the wear marks on it. The only technique used so far is that of microerosion analysis applied to microscopic fracture edges of percussion mur-e (Bednarik 1998). This can only be applied to mur-e (or their fragments) found on the surface, preferably on an open rock pavement, and with the certainty that they have not been covered by any sediment since their use. Moreover, it is limited to the kind of rocks suitable for microerosion analysis, particularly the quartz or quartzite fortunately often used for mur-e. A further limitation, one which affects precision rather than reliability, is the absence of calibration curves (which continues to hamper the application of microerosion dating generally).

A series of petroglyph sites on the foot of Cerro Tunari, near Cochabamba, Bolivia, consists of monolithic outcrops, several hundred metres apart, that dot the glacial valley floor. The outcrops measure several metres across and are a few metres high, and are usually steep sided. The petroglyphs have been made on their upper platform surfaces. Tiny slivers of white quartz were found in the cracks of the decorated platform at Kalatrancani 3. At nearby Kalatrancani 1, a mur-e of white quartz was found a few metres from the outcrop. Microscopic examination indicated that the mur-e had been used to pound a hard surface, and quartz fragments at site 3 were collected for detailed analysis. Since they were found on top of the steep-sided rock, several metres above the surrounding plain, it seems highly likely that they have remained from the petroglyph making activity.

Preliminary examination of seven quartz chips from Kalatrancani 3, all under 11 mm long, suggests that they derive from a crystalline quartz morphologically similar to the mur-e from Kalatrancani 1. They were detached about 500 to

600 years ago, which suggests that the petroglyphs among which they were recovered — or at least some or one of them — were made shortly before the arrival of the Spanish in South America. The mur-e from the second site was used slightly earlier.

The small sandstone cave of Toro Muerto, in the Mizque valley, central Bolivia, contains a dense concentration of petroglyphs. The barren rock shelf in front of the cave is strewn with hundreds of stone tools, from amongst which the five best mur-e were collected, based on clarity of bruising marks and their susceptibility to microerosion dating. Microerosion data secured from them indicate that the three most recently used date from about the same time, one is almost twice as old, while the fifth has clearly been used on two different occasions, separated by about 3500 years (Bednarik 1998). This study shows that, under favourable conditions, it is possible to estimate the ages of a series of petroglyphs without excavating any sediments or even examining the motifs.

In the case of estimating the age of percussion mur-e, the microscopy takes place in the laboratory. Most other microscopic work with petroglyphs, however, necessitates a good knowledge of field microscopy. This is one of the most important factors in a scientific study of rock art, being indispensable in many areas, such as conservation, dating, internal analysis, technological study, nano-stratigraphy, sample removal, petrology and geomorphology. Microscopy is essential in rock art science, which is perhaps most glaringly obvious in the area of technological analysis. Some aspects of field microscopy are considered in Chapter 9.

TECHNOLOGY OF PICTOGRAMS

Ethnographic observations

Numerous observations have been made concerning the mining or collection of pigment materials, especially ochre, and the preparation of paints and their application, most commonly perhaps in southern Africa and Australia. Ochres were used in southern Africa (and elsewhere) much earlier than the first settlement of Australia, and were extensively mined there in the Middle Stone Age. Massive ochre mines occur in both regions (e.g. Ngwenya, Wilgie Mia). Ethnographic observations about the mining of ochre are available from the 19th century, and in Australia even from the 20th century. Bleek and Lloyd (1911: 379) report how /Xam miners feared sorcerers dwelling in small holes in the mines. In 1834 George Augustus Robinson described the mining operations at the Tasmanian site Mount Rowland (Plomley 1966), one of thirteen ochre mines recorded just in Tasmania. The hard work, with wooden wedges and hammerstones, was conducted exclusively by women, who drove narrow tunnels into the rock. Robinson describes how one of the women became stuck in such a tunnel and had to be pulled out by her legs. The 20-m-deep and up to 30-m-wide mine of Wilgie Mia, Western Australia, where about 40 000 tonnes of ochre were extracted with the help of scaffolds, heavy stone mauls and fire-hardened wooden wedges, has served countless generations. Here, as elsewhere on the Australian mainland, the mining was done by men. The rock was broken up, ground and worked with water into balls for transport and trading. This massive mining operation continued as recently as 1939 (Flood 1995b: 273). The ochre deposit was formed when the Spirit Being Mondong speared a great kangaroo. The red ochre represents its blood, the yellow its liver, and the green minerals its gall (McCarthy 1967: 35). The kangaroo died at another hill nearby, Little Wilgie, which appears to have been mined before Wilgie Mia, perhaps in the Pleistocene. As in southern Africa, the indigenes regarded the Wilgie Mia mine with trepidation. They had to leave it walking backwards, erasing their tracks so Mondong could not follow them. Other major ochre mines were at Bookartoo and Yarrakinna in South Australia, Ulpunyaii, Karrku and Lawa in central Australia, and Gunnodjbedjahjam in Arnhem Land. Yarrakinna's bounty represented the blood of a sacred emu killed by a pack of dingoes. Extraction of the mineral was accompanied by rituals to appease the emu's spirit. There is considerable evidence of ochre mining by 'pre-Upper Palaeolithic societies' available in other parts of the world (Bednarik 1992b; Sagona 1994). One of the largest known Pleistocene mines occurs in Lion Cavern, Swaziland, where it has been dated to over 43 000 BP (Beaumont 1973). It includes thousands of mining tools of the Middle Stone Age.

There is also ethnographic information available about the preparation and application of rock art paints. It was surveyed in southern Africa by Rudner (1982), generally from a limited number of 19th century sources. In Australia, rock painting traditions continue, on a very small scale, to the present time, including the repainting of existing art (Ward 1992). For instance, the western Arnhem Land artist Najombolmi produced rock art until recently, and Haskovec and Sullivan (1989) were able to identify 604 motifs at 46 sites as his work. Kimberley artists David Mowaljarlai and George Djommeri repainted the Mirila shelter in 1985. Also in the 1980s, a Japanese television production featured the execution of a rock painting in Djalama territory, Northern Territory. Later that decade, the repainting of several sites in the Gibb River region of the Kimberley took place. It became the centre of a controversy that has been extensively debated in the following years, beginning with the First AURA Congress in 1988 and leading to the publication by AURA of a volume dedicated to this issue (Ward 1992). At that major academic event, traditional artist Dick Nangulei Murrumurru demonstrated his outstanding rock painting skills to hundreds of international rock art scholars (Chaloupka 1992) (Figure 25). In central Australia, Jawoyn artists Peter Manabaru and Jack Chadum allowed their production of rock paintings to be filmed in May 1992 (Smith 1993). Further ethnographic examples are provided by Gould (1969: 147), Taçon (1992), Chaloupka (1993) and Flood (1997: 18-24). Mulvaney (1996) collected valuable ethnographic information about rock art among the Mirriuwung and Gadjerong, located between the Kimberley and Katherine. Even in the 1990s, rock paintings were still produced, for instance by Stewart Davies, a Ngaanyatjarra man from Warburton, who painted in a rockshelter at a site complex known as Kalkakutjarra (Bednarik 2000: 22). These are just some recent examples permitting ethnographic analysis of rock painting production in Australia, many more are available from earlier times.

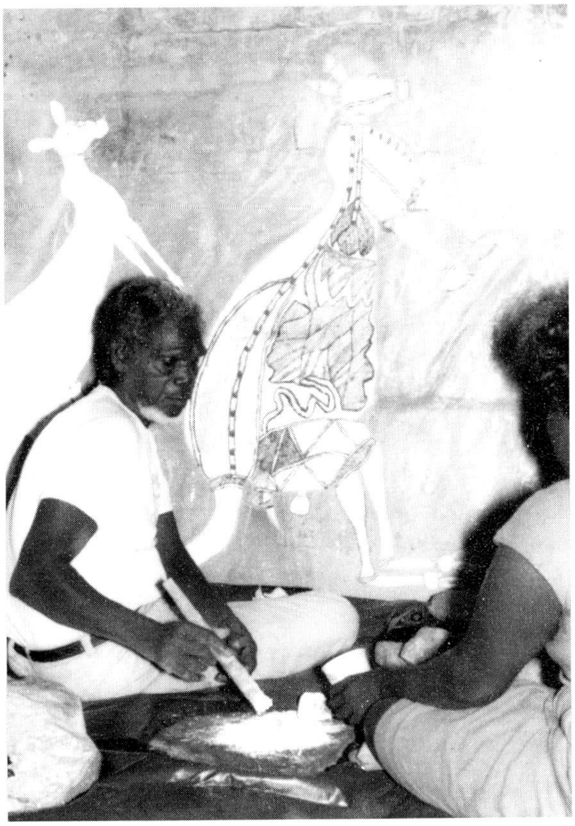

Figure 25. Aboriginal artist Dick Nangulei Murrumurru demonstrating rock art painting skills and techniques on a rock wall replica made from fibreglass. First AURA Congress, Darwin, 1 September 1988.

While such recent and comprehensive information is not available elsewhere, it would be wrong to assume that these traditions have necessarily ceased to be active in the rest of the world. Soon after I predicted that some Bolivian rock art traditions would be found to be extant (Bednarik 1988), Querejazu Lewis (1994) provided the first tentative evidence of this kind. Similar indications exist elsewhere, especially in India (e.g. in Bihar), even though clear evidence about a continuation of rock art production remains elusive so far.

Be that as it may, there is a good deal of ethnographic information available about the technology of pictograms, albeit most of it does come from Australia. There, good-quality red ochre was a highly valued and widely traded commodity. Substitutes were also used, including yellow or brown limonite that had been roasted to a red colour. White was frequently obtained from kaolin, huntite, enstatite, carbonates, gypsum or selenite, even from finely ground minerals such as quartz, microcline, muscovite and jarosite. Black pigments are most commonly of charcoal or manganese oxide. Yellow and various hues of brown were obtained from iron minerals, clay, from the dust inside termite nests, siderite, and locally from a fungus. Glauconite (Elkin 1948) and, after European contact, a textile bleach called Reckitt's Blue (Spencer 1928: 851) provided the rare bluish colours.

Hard pigments were pounded, ground or abraded into a powder, and ground patches of rock are a ubiquitous feature at thousands of rock art sites. Various liquids provided the solvent, suspender or binder required in paint production, including water, urine, blood, semen, honey, eggwhite, or the fat of various animals. A particularly effective binder or fixative is orchid juice (*Dendrobium* sp.) (Mountford 1956: 11; Levitt 1981: 146). Numerous other binders were used, mostly derived from plants, including resinous substances or tree sap, which were added to the paint in pulverised form (Brandl 1973: 105). There is an extensive literature on binders used in painting on bark or artefacts (for a review, see Cole and Watchman 1992) and it can be assumed that most of the materials observed were also used for the production of rock paintings.

Similarly, there is a copious literature on the Australian use of paintbrushes and the application of paint to rock surfaces. In Arnhem Land, brushes were recently made from stringy-bark, other tree bark, pandanus leaves, kapok bush, palm leaf fibres or twigs whose ends were chewed (Mountford 1956; Edwards and Guerin 1969; Brandl 1973). Cole and Watchman (1992) report the use of bark and stems of the native kapok bush and small bundles of wallaby grass. However, paints were also frequently applied with fingers or whole hands, in Australia as well as elsewhere. The prepared paint was sometimes contained in the mouth of the artist from which the brush was replenished (Brandl 1973: 105), or in a suitable container, such as a seashell or piece of bark.

A very distinctive form of pictogram is the stencil, in which an object is placed against the rock surface and the artist then sprays the paint directly from his mouth along the object's margins. The hand stencil is one of the most widely distributed rock art motifs in the world, occurring in all continents and as far back in time as the Upper Palaeolithic. In Australia, however, stencil production has been developed into a major art tradition, especially in central Queensland. It includes besides hand silhouettes also those of numerous objects of material culture, such as wooden artefacts, weapons, as well as animal feet, human feet and even entire human bodies. Needless to say, this provides an excellent source of information about the overall form and type of tool kits used at the time the art was made. The stencil technique was not limited to the production of object silhouettes, however. Linear pictograph motifs, too, were often produced without brushes, by spraying the paint directly from the mouth through a narrow gap formed by the hands, which were quickly moved over the rock. This is a more effective form of paint application than the use of brushes, especially on rough and porous support surfaces, because sprayed paint tends to have better penetration and adherence. In the far north of Australia there is yet another form of paint application, in which paint-soaked missiles of vegetation, usually perhaps grass, were thrown against the rock panel, often high up and well out of reach, to leave behind paint imprints (Chaloupka 1984; Welch 1990).

Paintings and stencils are not the only forms of pictograms. Rock drawings were made with hand-held pieces of pigment, applied dry to the rock surface in the fashion of a crayon. This was a widespread technique but its results seem to be more fugitive than those of wet-applied pigments. Therefore taphonomic biases would favour an under-representation of drawings in the existing record. Drawings can often be distinguished from paintings, especially microscopically. The crayons used in rock drawings are sometimes found at sites, even in sediment layers. They may bear wear facets, and where these are well preserved on haematite, striations can usually be recognised on them. Such pigment crayons have been found from the Lower Palaeolithic onwards (of Europe, Asia and Africa), even though no pigmented rock art is known from either the Lower or the Middle Palaeolithic period. They provide an indication that the practice of colouring rock surfaces dates back significantly earlier than the first known pictograms (Bednarik 1990).

Finally, an unusual form of rock art, limited to certain parts of the Top End of the Northern Territory and the Kimberley in Australia, are beeswax figures (Welch 1995). They were made by the application of thin strips or dots of beeswax on rockshelter walls, which were pressed onto the rock while still soft and pliable. This is therefore an additive method of creating rock art, and its results thus fall under pictograms. The wax ages soon but it has been preserved for up to about 4000 years (Nelson 2000; Nelson et al. 1993).

Analyses of paint residues

Globally, ethnographic information about the technology of rock paintings is, however, very limited. There are then two alternative approaches to the issue: analytical and replicative studies. In replication work, the experimenter attempts to reproduce rock art as closely as possible, using identical materials as determined by material analysis of the art, and attempting to copy the presumed application method as deduced from a variety of visual clues. Therefore replicative experiments are entirely dependent upon the prior acquisition of various types of analytical data about the original art. Such information concerns the composition of paint residues and physical traces relating to painting technique.

Relevant inorganic analytical methods of rock paints began to be introduced in the 1970s, starting with x-ray diffraction (XRD) (Koski et al. 1973; Taylor et al. 1975; Clarke 1976; Ballet et al. 1979), but were used only intermittently until the 1990s. XRD provides information about the atomic and molecular structure of crystalline substances, i.e. most minerals. Geochemical analyses of pigments were also obtained by electron microscopes fitted with energy dispersive x-ray analysers (SEM-EDXA, or SEM-EDS), also beginning with Koski et al. (1973). Applied frequently in the 1990s, the method was often used in tandem with XRD (e.g. Clarke and North 1991; Cole and Watchman 1992; Scott and Hyder 1993; Chaffee et al. 1994; David et al. 1995; Hyman et al. 1996; Mawk et al. 1996; Meneses L. 1996; Watchman and Hatte 1996; Barker et al. 1997; Watchman et al. 1997; Mawk and Rowe 1998; Ward et al. 1999). A third analytical method used is Fourier transform infrared spectroscopy (FTIR). Its application to pictograms was pioneered by Brunet et al. (1987) and Moffatt et al. (1989), and it has also found wide acceptance during the 1990s, especially in Australia (Clarke and North 1991; Watchman 1993; Morwood et al. 1994; MacLeod et al. 1995; Watchman and Hatte 1996; Barker et al. 1997). Less commonly used is an alternative method of elemental analysis, proton-induced x-ray emission (PIXE), first applied to rock art pigments by Clottes et al. (1990) and Peisach et al. (1991), then by David et al. (1993).

Rock art paint residues comprise not only mineral matter, many pigments were of organic origin, including charcoal, cochineal, fungal matter and berry juices. Also, numerous types of inclusions can occur in such samples, either added intentionally (organic solvents, binders or extenders) or as incidental additions (particularly brush fibres and bark remains, but airborne matter and a host of other substances as well). Therefore several techniques targeting organics have also been applied to paint samples. Chromatography was probably introduced by Denninger (1971), in his unsuccessful attempt to estimate the age of albuminous binders in South Africa. He used paper chromatography, in which prepared filter paper is dipped into a solvent containing the sample, whereas in gas-liquid chromatography, separation of the components occurs as a gaseous mixture is passed through a coiled tube and past a detector. Only limited use has been made of this method in pictogram analysis (Scott et al. 1996), as well as of a combination of gas chromatography and mass spectrometry (Pepe et al. 1991; Petit and Valot 1992). Scott et al. (1996) also used crossover immunoelectrophoresis in their study of a Chumash paint cake, intended to detect blood plasma. However, the identification of blood traces in both rock art and on stone artefacts remains fraught with uncertainties, after the doubts arising from Loy's work at two Australian sites (see Ch. 7 for details; Loy et al. 1990; cf. Nelson 1993; Loy 1994; Tuross and Barnes 1996; Gillespie 1997).

All of these methods simply attempt to determine the components of paint residues or their organic inclusions. Other analytical methods have attracted less attention but can provide vital information about the processes of paint preparation and application. Three innovative studies stand out particularly. Lorblanchet et al. (1990) described detailed experiments of how red pigments in Cougnac, France, appear to have been made from local siderolithic clays rather than imported ochre. These authors suggest that the initially yellow clays were mixed with water, decanted to remove sand, after which the fine fractions were dried and roasted for several hours until they became red. Clottes et al. (1990) pioneered the analysis of paint residues to determine differences and similarities in paint recipes. Taking fifty-nine minute samples from pictograms in Niaux, also in France, they detected four distinctive paint recipes among them, based on the presence or combination of mineral additions which they proposed were extenders. This is possible in the case of talcum powder, present in one group, while barite, feldspar and biotite could have been added to the paint unintentionally, during grinding of the pigment minerals. Perhaps the most informative analytical work with rock art paints is Cole and Watchman's (1992), targeting vegetable materials present in paint samples from northern Queensland, Australia. They located plant fibres in twenty-five samples from several sites near Laura and tried to identify them, often from minute particles of cellular structures. It appears that about one half of the samples are from plant matter introduced as binders, the other half could be from brushes or other implements. Most of the latter were thought to be from kapok bush (*Cochlospermum fraseri*), which would confirm ethnographic information from the same locality that the bark and stems of kapok were used in paint application.

The possibility of applying 'internal analysis' (see Ch. 8) to pictograms, of the type used on portable objects and rock engravings, has apparently attracted no interest so far. This is probably related to the general lack of enthusiasm for field microscopy, which would be the principal method of such studies. Some information of this type, however, can be gained by inspection with a magnifying glass. In particular, paint tends to build up on the side of surface grains or protrusions facing the direction from which it was applied, while the lee-side of such minute topographic features may bear little or no paint. This area of study clearly needs to be developed.

Another research topic relating to the technology of pictograms is the sourcing of pigments. This is sometimes mentioned as an aside in reports, but has not attracted a great deal of focused research. Lorblanchet et al. (1990) have shown the utility of such work in yielding useful data. Bruno David (pers. comm.) is assembling a sample collection from ochre sources near rock art regions which may eventually present the opportunity to establish links between quarries and rock art motifs on a broader scale. This is, however, not as readily possible as it may seem. There is considerable local variation in the chemical and petrographic composition of most mineral matter quarried for use as pigment, especially ochres, and 'fingerprinting' of known mines may not be an easy process.

Finally, some brief commentary about nano stratigraphy (see Ch. 9) is germane here. Where pictograms were subjected to repainting over time, this leads to sometimes very complex stratigraphies, revealing a long history of site use. Some painting episodes may be separated by thin strata of accretionary mineral deposits, be they silicas, oxalates, carbonates or whatever. Substantial sequences of superimposed painting events have been found at sites across northern Australia, even at locations where no paintings were visible on the rock surface. Recent nano-stratigraphic work has convincingly shown the great analytical value of such studies (Watchman 2000; Campbell 2000), but current technology still demands physical sampling of these sequences. Future techniques may permit us to detect concealed motifs without such interference, by using radiation that can differentiate between specific paint compositions to home in on individual layers. I have expressed this hope before, only to be told that I was daydreaming. But who could have predicted the effects of the technical sophistication developed in recent decades, often as a by-product of space exploration. In 1984 I predicted that the rapid commercial development of computer software would, purely as a by-product, deliver incredibly powerful image management systems then only possible on huge mainframe computers. Others were sceptical then, but fifteen years later, such systems and the PCs to run them had become so readily available that students used them. Most rock art can easily survive a few more centuries if left undisturbed; the kinds of technologies then available are unimaginable to us.

CONCLUSION

The close nexus between the technology of petroglyph studies and terminological constructs is obvious. The names used for additive rock art forms (pictograms) are more appropriate than those often applied to petroglyphs, precisely because they are technology-derived terms: stencils, paintings (applied wet), drawings (applied dry), bees-wax figures etc. Reductive rock art (petroglyphs) is often defined by subjective technological labels that bear no relation to the method of their production: engraving, carving, pecking, etching, boring or drilling. Petroglyphs come in two basic forms: as sgraffiti (defined by colour contrast) or as relief petroglyphs (defined by relief depth). Both of these types can be made either by percussion or abrasion. The majority of the world's petroglyphs were sgraffiti. Sgraffito petroglyphs have a limited life span (Bednarik 1994b, 1995b); in most cases they remain visible only for as long as it takes the rock surface to repatinate fully. This applies particularly to rock art sgraffiti made by merely bruising a varnish cover. In archaeology, the technological definition of sgraffito has remained almost unknown (Bednarik 1979: Note 1), and false rock art chronologies were based on this taphonomic misapprehension of how technique may determine longevity (Bednarik 1994b: Fig 1). Taphonomic logic predicts that sgraffiti are massively under-represented, and that the impact of this distortion increases sharply with age. However, inadequate understanding of taphonomy is a major factor in misinterpreting rock art quantitatively as well as qualitatively, and it is closely related to misapprehension about technology as it relates to petroglyphs.

On the whole it is fair to say that the technology of rock art, particularly of petroglyphs, has been largely disregarded by archaeology. This has led to significant misinformation in terminology, and to failing to appreciate the significant interplay between technology, taphonomy, recording and interpretation. The technological aspects of rock art are of just as much importance as is its dating, for instance, but they have been treated in a cavalier fashion so far, and most of the limited information about this subject contained in the literature is either inadequate or false. There are telling similarities in the way the methodology of Semenov (1964), which should have been such a boon for archaeology, was ignored or misunderstood for many years. It is one of the major tasks of rock art science to develop this field in the years ahead.

REFERENCES

ANATI, E. 1976a. *Evolution and style in Camunian rock art.* Archivi 6, Capo di Ponte.

ANATI, E. 1976b. *Metodi di rilevamento e di analisi dell'arte rupestre.* Studi Camuni 7, Edizione del Centro Camuni di Studi Preistorici, Capo di Ponte.

ANATI, E. 1981. *Felskunst im Negev und auf Sinai.* Gustav Lübbe Verlag, Bergisch Gladbach.

ANATI, E. 1994. *Valcamonica rock art: a new history for Europe.* Studi Camuni 13, Edizione del Centro Camuni di Studi Preistori-ci, Capo di Ponte.

ARCÀ, A. 1995. Rilevamento e documentazione. In A. Arcà et al. (eds), *Rupe Magna: la roccia incisa più grande delle Alpi*, pp. 111–117. Consorzio per il Parco delle Incisioni Rupestri di Gro-sio, Sondria.

BAHN, P. G., R. G. BEDNARIK and J. STEINBRING 1995. The Peterborough Petroglyph Site: reflections on massive intervention in rock art. *Rock Art Research* 12: 29–41.

BALLET, O., A. BOCQUET, R. BOUCHEZ, J. M. D. COEY and A. CORNU 1979. Étude technique des poudres colorées de Lascaux. In *Lascaux Inconnu*, pp. 171–174. XXIe Supplément, *Gallia Préhistoire*.

BARKER, B., K. SALE and A. WATCHMAN 1997. Authentication of rock art in the Whitsunday Islands, Queensland, Australia. *Rock Art Research* 14: 113–23.

BATES, D. n.d. Volume 9 of collected papers (unpubl.) held in the National Library of Australia, Canberra.

BEAUMONT, P. B. 1973. The ancient pigment mines of southern Africa. *Southern African Journal of Science* 69: 140–52.

BEDNARIK, R. G. 1973. Wohnhöhlen bei Tom Price (Nordwest-Australien). *Die Höhle* 24: 140–45.

BEDNARIK, R. G. 1977. The lithic objects from Tom Price. Unpubl. catalogue, 33 pp., AURA Archive, Melbourne.

BEDNARIK, R. G. 1979. The potential of rock patination analysis in Australian archaeology — part 1. *The Artefact* 4: 14–38.

BEDNARIK, R. G. 1984. Die Bedeutung der paläolithischen Fingerlinientradition. *Anthropologie* 23: 73–79.

BEDNARIK, R. G. 1986. Parietal finger markings in Europe and Australia. *Rock Art Research* 3: 30–61, 159–70.

BEDNARIK, R. G. 1987. The cave art of Western Australia. *The Artefact* 12: 1–16.

BEDNARIK, R. G. 1988. El arte rupestre Boliviano visto desde el exterior. *SIARB Boletín* 2: 22–28.

BEDNARIK, R. G. 1990. An Acheulian haematite pebble with striations. *Rock Art Research 7: 75.*

BEDNARIK, R. G. 1991a. Comment on F. d'Errico, 'Microscopic and statistical criteria for the identification of prehistoric systems of notation'. *Rock Art Research* 8: 89–91.

BEDNARIK, R. G. 1991b. A basis for advanced studies in palaeoart. *Rock Art Quarterly* 2(3–4): 80-3.

BEDNARIK, R. G. 1992a. Base pour des études de pointe des débuts de l'art. *L'Anthropologie* 96(2-3): 369–74.

BEDNARIK, R. G. 1992b. Early subterranean chert mining. *The Artefact* 15: 11–24.

BEDNARIK, R. G. 1994a. On the scientific study of palaeoart. *Semiotica* 100(2/4): 141–68.

BEDNARIK, R. G. 1994b. A taphonomy of palaeoart. *Antiquity* 68(258): 68–74.

BEDNARIK, R. G. 1995a. The age of the Côa valley petroglyphs in Portugal. *Rock Art Research* 12: 86–103.

BEDNARIK, R. G. 1995b. About sgraffiti. *Pictogram* 8(1): 29–30.

BEDNARIK, R. G. 1996. Only time will tell: a review of the methodology of direct rock art dating. *Archaeometry* 38(1): 1–13.

BEDNARIK, R. G. 1997. An engraved slate fragment from Walyunga, Western Australia. *Records of the Western Australian Museum* 18: 317–21.

BEDNARIK, R. G. 1998. The technology of petroglyphs. *Rock Art Research* 15: 23–35.

BEDNARIK, R. G. (ed.) 2000. *Program and congress handbook: Third AURA Congress.* Occasional AURA Publication 11, Australian Rock Art Research Association, Melbourne.

BEDNARIK, R. G., G. KUMAR, A. WATCHMAN and R. G. ROBERTS 2005. Preliminary results of the EIP Project: the status at the end of 2004. *Rock Art Research* 22.

BEDNARIK, R. G. and K. SESHADRI 1995. Digital colour re-constitution in rock art photography. *Rock Art Research* 12: 42–51.

BLEEK, W. H. I. and L. LLOYD 1911. *Specimens of Bushman folklore.* George Allen, London.

BRANDL, E. J. 1973. *Australian Aboriginal paintings in western and central Arnhem Land.* Australian Aboriginal Studies 52, Australian Institute of Aboriginal Studies, Canberra.

BRUDER, S. J. 1983. *Archaeological investigation at the Hedgpeth Hills petroglyph site.* Research Report 28, Museum of Northern Arizona, Flagstaff.

BRUNET, J., S. DEMAILLY and P. VIDAL 1987. Étude de prelevements des peintures rupestres du Plateau du Tadjilahine (Tassili n'Ajjer) — Algerie. *ICOM Committee for Conservation, Proceedings of the 8th Triennial Meeting*, Vol. 3, Sydney, 6-11 September, pp. 1141–47. The Getty Conservation Institute, Los Angeles.

CAMPBELL, J. B. 2000. The Chillagoe and Laura laser-AMS dating project. In G. K. Ward and C. Tuniz (eds), *Advances in dating Australian rock-markings*, pp. 80–83. Occasional AURA Publication 10, Australian Rock Art Research Association, Melbourne.

CHAFFEE, S. D., M. HYMAN, M. W. ROWE, N. COULAM, A. SCHROEDL and K. HOGUE 1994. Radiocarbon dates on the All American Man. *American Antiquity* 59: 769–81.

CHALOUPKA, G. 1984. *From palaeoart to casual paintings.* Monograph 1, Northern Territory Museum of Arts and Sciences, Darwin.

CHALOUPKA, G. 1992. Retouch events. In G. K. Ward (ed.), *Retouch: maintenance and conservation of Aboriginal rock imagery*, pp. 12–16. Occasional AURA Publication 5, Australian Rock Art Research Association, Melbourne.

CHALOUPKA, G. 1993. *Journey in time.* Reed, Sydney.

CLARKE, J. 1976. Two Aboriginal rock art pigments from Western Australia, their properties, use and durability. *Studies in Conservation* 21: 134–42.

CLARKE, J. and N. NORTH 1991. Pigment composition of post-estuarine rock art in Kakadu National Park. In C. Pearson and B. K. Swartz (eds), *Rock art and posterity: conserving, managing and recording rock art*, pp. 80–87. Occasional AURA Publication 4, Australian Rock Art Research Association, Melbourne.

CLEMENT, E. 1903. Ethnographic notes on the Western Australian Aborigines. *Internationales Archiv für Ethnography* 16: 1–29.

CLOTTES, J., M. MENU and P. WALTER 1990. New light on the Niaux paintings. *Rock Art Research* 7: 21–26.

COLE, N. and A. WATCHMAN 1992. Painting with plants: investigating fibres in Aboriginal rock paintings at Laura, north Queensland. *Rock Art Research* 9: 27–36.

CRAWFORD, I. M. 1964. The engravings of Depuch Island. In W. D. L. Ride and A. Neumann (eds), *Depuch Island*, pp. 23–63. Western Australian Museum Special Publication 2, Perth.

DAVID, B., E. CLAYTON and A. WATCHMAN 1993. Initial results of PIXE analysis on northern Australian ochres. *Australian Archaeology* 36: 50–57.

DAVID, B., A. WATCHMAN, R. GOODALL and E. CLAYTON 1995. The Maytown ochre source. *Memoirs of the Queensland Museum* 38: 441–45.

DENNINGER, E. 1971. The use of paper chromatography to determine the age of albuminous binders and its application to rock paintings. Rock paintings in southern Africa, supplement to the *South African Journal of Science*, Special Issue, 2: 80–84.

D'ERRICO, F. 1987. Nouveaux indices et nouvelles techniques microscopiques pour la lecture de l'art gravé mobilier. *Comptes Rendus de l'Académie des Sciences de Paris* 304: 761–64.

D'ERRICO, F. 1991. Microscopic and statistical criteria for the identification of prehistoric systems of notation. *Rock Art Research* 9: 83–93.

D'ERRICO, F. 1992. The study of engraved notches and their statistical analysis. *Rock Art Research* 9: 131–32.

D'ERRICO, F. 1994. *L'art gravé azilien*. 31e supplément, Gallia Préhistoire, CNRS Éditions, Paris.

DORN, R. I. 1996. A change of perception. *La Pintura* 23(2): 10–11.

EASTHAM, M. 1999. The analysis of scan sequences embedded in Palaeolithic parietal images. *Rock Art Research* 16: 89–108.

EDWARDS, R. 1964. Rock engravings and stone implements of the Pitcairn Station, northeastern South Australia. *Records of the South Australian Museum* 14: 645–62.

EDWARDS, R. and B. GUERIN 1969. *Aboriginal bark paintings*. Rigby, Adelaide.

ELKIN, A. P. 1948. Grey's northern Kimberley cave-paintings re-found. *Oceania* 19(1): 1–15.

FLOOD, J. 1995a. Copying the Dreamtime: anthropic marks in early Aboriginal Australia. Paper presented to Symposium A1, International Rock Art Congress, Turin.

FLOOD, J. 1995b. *Archaeology of the Dreamtime* (revised edition). Angus and Robertson, Sydney.

FLOOD, J. 1997. *Rock art of the Dreamtime. Images of ancient Australia*. Angus and Robertson, Sydney.

GILLESPIE, R. 1997. On human blood, rock art and calcium oxalate: further studies on organic carbon content and radiocarbon age of materials relating to Australian rock art. *Antiquity* 71: 430–37.

GOULD, R. A. 1969. *Yiwara: foragers of the Australian desert*. William Collins, London and Sydney.

IVES, G. A. 1986. Rock art of the Dolores River valley. In A. E. Kane, W. D. Lipe, T. A. Kohler and C. K. Robinson (eds), *Dolores Archaeological Program: research design and initial survey results*, pp. 235–252. U.S. Department of the Interior, Bureau of Reclamation, Denver.

HASKOVEC, I. and H. SULLIVAN 1989. Reflections and rejections of an Aboriginal artist. In H. Morphy (ed.), *Animals into art*, pp. 57–74. Unwin, London.

HYMAN, M., S. A. TURPIN and M. E. ZOLENSKY 1996. Pigment analyses from Panther Cave, Texas. *Rock Art Research* 13: 93–103.

KEARNS, T. M., M. R. POLK and L. S. TEAGUE 1975. Archaeological resources, Orme Reservoir, Phase II, Verde Arm. In V. Canouts (ed.), *An archaeological survey of Orme Reservoir*, pp. 275–373. Cultural Resource Management Section, Arizona State Museum, Tucson.

KOSKI, R. A., E. H. McKIE and D. H. THOMAS 1973. Pigment composition of prehistoric pictographs of Gatecliff Shelter, central Nevada. *American Museum Novitates* 2521: 1–9.

LEVITT, D. 1981. *Plants and people: Aboriginal uses of plants on Groote Eylandt*. Australian Institute of Aboriginal Studies, Canberra.

LINEWSKI, A. M. 1978. *Kivikirjan sivuja*. Suomentanut O. Kukkonen, Karjala, Petroskoi.

LOENDORF, L. L. 1984. *Documentation of rock art: Petroglyph Canyon, Montana (24 Cb 601)*. Department of Anthropology and Archaeology Contribution 207, University of North Dakota, Grand Forks.

LORBLANCHET, M., M. LABEAU, J. L. VERNET, P. FITTE, H. VALLADAS, H. CACHIER and M. ARNOLD 1990. Palaeolithic pigments in the Quercy, France. *Rock Art Research* 7: 4–20.

LOY, T. H. 1994. Direct dating of rock art at Laurie Creek (NT), Australia: a reply to Nelson. *Antiquity* 68: 147–48.

LOY, T. H., R. JONES, D. E. NELSON, B. MEEHAN, J. VOGEL, J. SOUTHON and R. COSGROVE 1990. Accelerator radiocarbon dating of human blood proteins in pigments from Late Pleistocene art sites in Australia. *Antiquity* 64: 110–16.

McCARTHY, F. D. 1961. The rock engravings of Depuch Island, north-west Australia. *Records of the Australian Museum* 28: 121–48.

McCARTHY, F. D. 1962. *The rock engravings at Port Hedland, north-western Australia*. Papers of the Kroeber Anthropological Society 26, University of California.

McCARTHY, F. D. 1967. *Australian Aboriginal rock art* (3rd edn). Australian Museum, Sydney.

MACLEOD, I. D., P. HAYDOCK and E. CHARTON 1995. Avian guano and its effects on the preservation of rock paintings. In A. Torn and J. Brunet (eds), *Preservation of rock art*, pp. 60–64. Occasional AURA Publication 9, Australian Rock Art Research Association, Melbourne.

MARSHACK, A. 1972. *The roots of civilization*. McGraw-Hill, New York and Toronto, and Weidenfeld, London.

MARSHACK, A. 1975. Exploring the mind of Ice Age man. *National Geographic* 147(1): 64–89.

MARSHACK, A. 1986. Theoretical concepts that lead to new analytic methods, modes of enquiry and classes of data. *Rock Art Research* 3: 95–111.

MARSHACK, A. 1989. Methodology in the analysis and

interpretation of Upper Palaeolithic image: theory versus contextual analysis. *Rock Art Research* 6: 17–38.

MAWK, E. J., M. F. NOBBS and M. W. ROWE 1996. Analysis of white pigments from the Olary region, South Australia. *Rock Art Research* 13: 31–37.

MAWK, E. J. and M. W. ROWE 1998. Effect of water on Lower Pecos River rock paintings in Texas. *Rock Art Research* 15: 12–16.

MAYNARD, L. 1977. Classification and terminology of Australian rock art. In P. J. Ucko (ed.), *Form in indigenous art: schematisation in the art of Aboriginal Australia and prehistoric Europe*, pp. 385–402. Australian Institute of Aboriginal Studies, Canberra.

MENESES LAGÉ, M. C. S. 1996. Análise química de pigmentos de arte rupestre do sudeste do Piauí. *Revista de Geologia* 9: 83–96.

MOFFATT, E. A., P. J. SIROIS, S. YOUNG and I. N. M. WAINWRIGHT 1989. Analysis of wall painting fragments from Dunhuang. *Canadian Conservation Institute Newsletter* February: 9–10.

MOORE, R. A. 1992. The lithic assemblage from a Pueblo petroglyph site. In M. S. Duran and D. T. Kirkpatrick (eds), *Artifacts, shrines, and Pueblos: papers in honor of Gordon Page*, pp. 167–182. Archaeological Society of New Mexico 20, Albuquerque.

MORWOOD, M. J., G. L. WALSH and A. WATCHMAN 1994. The dating potential of rock art in the Kimberley, N.W. Australia. *Rock Art Research* 11: 79–87.

MOUNTFORD, C. P. 1955. An unrecorded method of Aboriginal rock marking. *Records of the South Australian Museum* 11(4): 345–51.

MOUNTFORD, C. P. 1956. Art, myth and symbolism of Arnhem Land. *Records of the American-Australian Expedition to Arnhem Land, 1948*, Vol. 1

MOUNTFORD, C. P. 1976. *Nomads of the Australian desert*. Rigby, Adelaide.

MOWALJARLAI, D. and P. VINNICOMBE 1995. Perspectives of the origin of rock images in the western Kimberley. In G. K. Ward and L. A. Ward (eds), *Management of rock imagery*, pp. 42–52. Occasional AURA Publication 9, Australian Rock Art Research Association, Melbourne.

MULVANEY, K. 1996. What to do on a rainy day: reminiscences of Mirriuwung and Gadjerong artists. *Rock Art Research* 13: 3–20.

NELSON, D. E. 1993. Second thoughts on a rock-art date. *Antiquity* 67: 893–95.

NELSON, D. E. (ed.) 2000. *The beeswax art of northern Australia*. Compact disk, Simon Fraser University, Burnaby, Canada.

NELSON, D. E., C. CHIPPINDALE, G. CHALOUPKA, P. TAÇON and J. R. SOUTHON 1993. AMS dating of beeswax rock art in northern Australia. *The Artefact* 16: 52.

PEISACH, M., C. A. PINEDA and L. JACOBSON 1991. Nuclear analytical study of rock paintings. *Journal of Radioanalytical and Nuclear Chemistry* 151: 221–27.

PEPE, C., J. CLOTTES, M. MENU and P. WALTER 1991. Le liant des peintures paléolithiques ariégoise. *Comptes Rendus de l'Académie des Sciences Paris* 312: 929–34.

PETIT, J. and H. VALOT 1992. A propos de peinture préhistorique. *La Recherche* 23: 744.

PILLES, P. J. 1976. Appendix I: Consultant's report on the petroglyphs of the ash disposal area. In D. R. Keller and D. M. Goddard (eds), *Final report for the Cholla power plant expansion: ash disposal area impact mitigation studies*, pp. 1–10. Museum of Northern Arizona, Flagstaff.

PLOMLEY, N. J. B 1966. *Friendly mission. The Tasmanian journals and papers of George Augustus Robinson 1829–1834*. Hobart.

QUEREJAZU LEWIS, R. 1994. Contemporary indigenous use of traditional rock art sites at Yaraque, Bolivia. *Rock Art Research* 11: 3–9.

RAVDONIKAS, V. I. 1936a. *Naskal'nye izobrazenija Onezskogo ozera i Belogo morya*. Izdatel'stvo Akademii Nauk SSSR, Moscow-Leningrad.

RAVDONIKAS, V. I. 1936b. K izuceniju naskal'nych izobrazenij Onezskogo ozera i Belogo morja. *Sovetskaya Arkheologiya* 1: 9–50.

RAVDONIKAS, V. I. 1937. Sledy totemiceskich pred-stavleny v obrazach naskal'nych izobrazenij Onezskogo ozera i Belogo morya. *Sovetskaya Arkheologiya* 3: 3–32.

RAVDONIKAS, V. I. 1938. *Naskal'nye izobrazenija Onezskogo ozera i Belogo morya*, Part 2. Izdatel'stvo Akademii Nauk SSSR, Moscow-Leningrad.

RUDNER, I. 1982. Khoisan pigments and paints and their relationship to rock paintings. *Annals of the South African Museum* 87: 1–281.

SAGONA, A. (ed.) 1994. *Bruising the red earth: ochre mining and ritual in Aboriginal Tasmania*. Melbourne University Press, Melbourne.

SAVVATEYEV, J. 1970. *Zalavruga. Arkhelolgicheslie pamyatniki nizov'ya reki Vyg. Chast' pervaya. Petrogliphy*. Nauka, Leningradskoe otdelenie, Leningrad.

SAVVATEYEV, J. A. 1973. Petroglify Karelii. *Voprosy Istorii* 6: 132–46.

SAVVATEYEV, J. A. 1976. *Petroglify Karelii*. Nauka SSSR, Petrozavodsk.

SAVVATEYEV, J. A. 1977. *Zalavruga, cast' II. Stojanki*. Nauka, Leningradskoe otdelenie, Leningrad.

SCOTT, D. A. and W. D. HYDER 1993. A study of some Californian Indian rock art pigments. *Studies in Conservation* 38: 155–73.

SCOTT, D. A., M. NEWMAN, M. SCHILLING, M. DERRICK and H. P. KHANJIAN 1996. Blood as binding medium in a Chumash Indian pigment cake. *Archaeometry* 38: 103–12.

SEMENOV, S. A. 1964. *Prehistoric technology* (transl. By M. W. Thompson). Cory, Adams and Mackay, London.

SIERTS, W. 1968. How were rock engravings made? *South African Journal of Science* 64: 281–85.

SMITH, Christine 1880. *The Booandik tribe of South Australian Aborigines: a sketch of their habits, customs, legends, and language.* E. Spiller, Adelaide.

SMITH, Claire 1993. *Yungayi care for country.* Film video, Australian Rock Art Research Association, Melbourne.

SPENCER, W. B. 1928. *Wanderings in wild Australia.* Macmillan, London.

STOKES, J. L. 1846. *Discoveries in Australia ... during the voyage of H.M.S. Beagle in the years 1837–43.* T. and W. Boone, London.

SWARTZ, B. K. 1997. An evaluation of rock art conservation practices at Foz Côa, northern Portugal. *Rock Art Research* 14: 73–75.

TAÇON, P. S. C. 1992. 'If you miss all this story, well bad luck': rock art and the validity of ethnographic interpretation in western Arnhem Land, Australia. In M. J. Morwood and D. R. Hobbs (eds), *Rock art and ethnography,* pp. 11–18. Occasional AURA Publication 5, Australian Rock Art Research Association, Melbourne.

TAYLOR, J. M., R. M. MYERS and I. N. M. WAINWRIGHT 1975. An investigation of the natural deterioration of rock paintings in Canada. *Conservation in archaeology and the applied arts,* pp. 87–91. The International Institute for Conservation of Historic and Artistic Works, London.

TUROSS, N. and I. BARNES 1996. Protein identification of blood residues on experimental stone tools. *Journal of Archaeological Science* 23: 289–96.

WALLACE, H. D. and J. P. HOLMLUND 1986. *Petroglyphs of the Picacho Mountains, south-central Arizona.* Anthropological Papers 6, Institute for American Research, Arizona.

WARD, G. K. (ed.) 1992. *Retouch: maintenance and conservation of Aboriginal rock imagery.* Occasional AURA Publication 5, Australian Rock Art Research Association, Melbourne.

WARD, I. C. PATTERSON and A. WATCHMAN 1999. The environment and condition of multi-layered Aboriginal paintings at Kennedy-A in the wet tropics, north Queensland. *Rock Art Research* 16: 25–35.

WATCHMAN, A. 1993. Evidence of a 25 000-year-old pictograph in northern Australia. *Geoarchaeology* 8: 465–73.

WATCHMAN, A. 2000. Micro-excavation and laser extraction methods for dating carbon in silica skins and oxalate crusts. In G. K. Ward and C. Tuniz (eds), *Advances in dating Australian rock-markings,* pp. 35–39. Occasional AURA Publication 10, Australian Rock Art Research Association, Melbourne.

WATCHMAN, A. and E. HATTE 1996. A nano approach to the study of rock art. *Rock Art Research* 13: 85–92.

WATCHMAN, A., G. L. WALSH, M. J. MORWOOD and C. TUNIZ 1997. AMS radiocarbon age estimates for early rock paintings in the Kimberley, N.W. Australia: preliminary results. *Rock Art Research* 14: 18–26.

WEEKS, R. 2001. Indirect percussion: fact or fiction? *American Indian Rock Art* 27: 117–21.

WELCH, D. 1990. The bichrome art period in the Kimberley, Australia. *Rock Art Research* 7: 110–24.

WELCH, D. 1995. Beeswax rock art in the Kimberley. *Rock Art Research* 12: 23–28.

WHITNELL, J. G. 1901. *Customs and traditions of Aboriginal natives of north western Australia.* Privately published, Roeburne.

WILMAN, M. 1968. *The rock-engravings of Griqualand West and Bechuanaland, South Africa* (2nd edn). A. A. Balkema, Cape Town.

WRIGHT, B. J. 1968. *Rock art of the Pilbara region, north-west Australia.* Occasional Papers in Aboriginal Studies 11, Australian Institute of Aboriginal Studies, Canberra.

5. The recording of rock art

Introduction

The purpose of rock art recording is to create a visual register of those aspects of the art that are deemed 'important', and a data base for rock art conservation and management. The principal difficulty in addressing the subject of rock art recording is that whatever I may advocate here, much is likely to be outdated within a very few years. There should be no doubt that the extraordinary developments we have witnessed in recent years in electronic data handling will have a massive influence on all aspects of this topic. Indeed, it seems almost self-evident that much of the future of rock art recording lies in digital image processing, a field developing so rapidly that last year's software is already superseded this year. Spurned on by incredible economic benefits, this field of technology forges ahead on the back of corporate enthusiasm.

Nevertheless, the recording of rock art is a multifaceted subject whose diversity is the result of historical development, differences in regional practices, and individual preferences. Nearly all of this development predates the ready availability of computer equipment, and much of it does not become superseded by new technology, nor does the use of digitised data manipulation and storage render other techniques obsolete. On the contrary, it should prompt us to guard against becoming too reliant on one set of methods and thus neglect other, valuable and promising approaches. This has happened in the past and continues to be the case. For instance, we would do well to remember that one of the most valuable rock art recording practices, rock surface cartography, has been most inadequately utilised in the past, is likely to be further marginalised by 'glamorous' computer applications, and essentially does not benefit from the new methodology. As in the case of rock art preservation issues (Ch. 6), it would be most unwise to place 'all of our eggs into one basket'. Too much is at stake.

Another important factor is that not all rock art recorders in the world have the same degree of access to equipment and facilities. This is in part a matter of institutional support, and in part dependent on the particular world region one works in. Having worked extensively in countries where the monthly salary of an academic is in the order of the cost of a slide film, I am acutely aware under what difficult conditions many colleagues work. Similarly, many rock art researchers who have no institutional support at all, funding their own work, need access to low-cost methods. Fortunately the quality of rock art recordings is not related much to one's resources, but primarily to one's competence and dedication. Therefore it is not a valid excuse for inadequate work to point to poor support: the principal ingredients for good recording work are time, skill and determination. Nevertheless, relevant knowledge is required, especially to decide one's strategy. This chapter is intended to provide a basic understanding of the options, in the form of a 'cook book approach', listing useful approaches.

Traditional methods of recording rock art

Early rock art recordings (see Ch. 2) are generally freehand drawings of varying quality, and this basic method still does remain in use. The recorder draws what he or she perceives on the rock surface, and the result is often highly subjective. There are numerous cases described in the literature of numbers of motifs on a panel remaining unrecorded, or of motifs recorded quite inaccurately, sometimes having apparently false meanings attributed to them. One of the troublesome characteristics of rock art motifs is that iconographically they can be quite ambiguous. They were usually made by artists whose conditioned perception differed significantly from that of today's recorder, and in the case of horizontally orientated motifs there is no objective indication of which way the figure is meant to be viewed. Another common problem with this simple recording method is that many variables of a motif, such as line thickness or groove depth, which may be important to the motif's interpretation, find no consideration, and that minor features, attributable to technique rather than intention (e.g. individual poorly directed nicks on the rock, or careless strokes in the painting), tend to be given significant interpretations ('hunchback', 'broken limb' etc.), or features that are intentional are interpreted in the artistic conventions that conditioned the recorder's perception. In freehand reproductions, the features the recorder considers crucial in interpreting the motif are inevitably emphasised, and those the artist might have considered crucial may well be neglected or omitted. Therefore such recordings are unreliable, they are invariably *interpretations* of what is on the rock, not *recordings* of it.

Another difficulty to contend with in freehand drawings is that dimensions are distorted, be they those of motifs and their parts, or the spaces between motifs. This has been readily overcome by one of three means: the use of a string grid and graph paper, the use of transparent sheets placed over the art onto which the art is recorded in full size, or copying from photographic records, usually from slides projected onto paper. Each of these methods has its strengths and drawbacks, and it is not my intention to advocate here one or the other. A variety of factors determine the favoured choice in fieldwork, and in the hands of the conscientious rock art recorder every method yields worthwhile results. However, the wide use of these three basic methods has led to a variety of supplementary practices, some of which require special mention here. For instance, in some parts of southern Europe, the use of transparent sheets has been widely adopted for the recording of petroglyphs, but it was found that details of figures were often hard to detect. The use of pigments was introduced to achieve a sharper contrast between pecked surfaces and incidental and natural depressions (e.g. weathering scars). Pigments were applied directly on the petroglyph panels, usually in the form of white paint, sometimes followed by the application of a black substance. This is particularly effective on the glacially polished rocks of the southern Alps, where the black soot preparation readily delineates the smooth panel surface, and the finest details of abrasion and percussion petroglyphs stand out in stark contrast, offering ideal recording conditions.

However, the procedure also results in badly disfigured panels, and while the recorders availing themselves of this method emphasised that the paints they use are 'degradable' and 'organic', paint residues remain present for many decades. The method has been adopted in other parts of the world, and thousands of square metres of petroglyphs have been contaminated in this way. Both the white gouache (usually casein-based, flour and similar preparations) and the black soot introduce significant organic contamination into the geochemical fabric of the micro-subsurface (weathering zone, accretions and phenomena collectively defined as patina), which is one of the most important analytical aspects of any rock art panel. Such contamination, for instance, prejudices several scientific dating methods, such as carbon isotope analysis. Obviously the pavements so treated are unsuitable now for various forms of scientific work. Besides, some of this treatment may still conjure up future conservation problems, as there are claims that the surfaces so treated are now 'more resistant to weathering'. This is ominous, because if there is indeed any change in the subsurface chemistry or fabric of the rock it is almost inevitable that this will lead to cutaneous exfoliation in the long term.

This is only one of several examples of selfish and short-sighted recording methods that were developed over the past century, in which the priorities and convenience of rock art recorders were given precedence over the physical integrity of the rock art and the priorities of rock art scientists. Rock art recorders or connoisseurs have availed themselves of a number of liquids which, when applied to rock art (especially paintings) enhance colour contrast considerably and so facilitate the production of better photographic records. Dousing the rock with a transparent liquid cancels the optical effect of the diffuse, weathered surface or porous precipitate by filling the pores temporarily. The liquid most commonly used for such enhancement is water, either plain or distilled. The idea that it is acceptable to spray distilled water on paintings seems to have originated in India, and it is attributable to a misunderstanding. In 1981, at a conference in Bhopal, Professor Emmanuel Anati explained the use of poultices to remove salt deposits from rock paintings. Apparently assuming that distilled water was being used for this because it would have no effect on the rock, scholars thought that there was no objection to using it regularly for photographic enhancement. Indian rock paintings occur mostly on sandstone which contains a variety of water soluble salts, and it makes little difference whether the water regularly applied to it is distilled or not. Salts are mobilised and as their solvent evaporates, they precipitate on the surface, covering the paintings with an opaque, whitish crust that only encourages more vigorous water application.

The method is certainly not limited to India, it has, for instance, caused much damage to Saharan paintings. Nor is water the only liquid used for this purpose, to my knowledge three other liquids have been applied to enhance rock paintings: motor oil (in South Africa), clear lacquer and apparently kerosene. The last-mentioned is of particular interest here. Professor Marvin Rowe's team secured an AMS radiocarbon date from an American rock painting that seemed excessively high: 32 900 ± 900 years BP! It was obtained from pigment attached to a sandstone block that had fallen from the panel of the type site of the 'Barrier Canyon style' in Utah, which is thought to be of the late Holocene. Upon closer scrutiny the sandstone block was found to have been contaminated by a hydrocarbon derivative, probably kerosene. The implication is that this liquid had been applied in the past by someone who wanted to enhance photographic contrast (Chaffee et al. 1993: 71).

Another enhancement substance very commonly used in rock art recording is chalk (Bock 1981; Leen 1981; Bednarik 1987a, 1990a; Francis et al. 1993; Loendorf 2001). Its use to highlight petroglyphs, and even rock paintings, has been documented in literally thousands of published photographs. This method prejudices nearly all currently used methods of direct dating (see Ch. 7). Chalk consists largely of calcium carbonate. Its calcium distorts the cation-ratio of rock varnish where it is present, and its carbon is essentially radiocarbon dead: although it is derived from mineralised organic remains, these are usually millions of years old. However, if it has been dissolved and reprecipitated, its radiocarbon content becomes the expression of a complex ratio (Bednarik 1984a). Radiocarbon dating of oxalate (Watchman 1990) or reprecipitated carbonate laminae (Bednarik 1985) may also become ineffective through the application of chalk, and it may even affect microerosion analysis (Bednarik 1992) of treated areas, due to the very high abrasion pH of chalk. Francis et al. (1993) have demonstrated that 13.5% of the 180 samples they collected at sites in Wyoming were heavily contaminated by calcium, especially at the two most frequently recorded sites, even though the chalk was no longer visible at the time of sampling.

Besides chalk, numerous other substances have been used for rock art enhancement. I have reported dye (in Siberia), lipstick (U.S.A.), pencil (central Europe), felt pen (Australia) and paint (Scandinavia), to name some examples. The use of pressure sensitive sheets not only discolours the rock, it also damages and contaminates surfaces. In some Scandinavian countries the use of paints to fill in entire petroglyph panels is not only widespread, it is still being defended by some of those charged with managing this priceless heritage. While in other parts of the world rock art conservators are willing to consider damaging methods to remove such paints (Bahn et al. 1995), in Scandinavia there are research programs dedicated to determining which types of paint to be used for this vandalism survive longest (Löfvendahl and Magnusson 2000).

The potential harm from recording techniques may not always be readily apparent to rock art recorders. While the mechanically damaging effect of petroglyph rubbings is obvious, it has been noted that rubbing of petroglyphs may change the chemistry in the rock surface or patina (Dorn 1990). Loendorf (1989) reports that radiocarbon dates can be affected by this method, after sampling before and after rubbing. Genge (1990) has observed that the transparent sheets used to trace rock art are often susceptible to electrostatic phenomena. If they are energised by the movement of felt pens, pencils or even just fingers, the film attracts poorly attached flakes of rock paint loosened by the action of the recording instrument. Finally, rock art recordings have often been obtained by casting, using a variety of materials (latex, plaster of Paris, *papier mâché*, thermoplastic resin etc.) that again either contaminate the substrate, or are applied without any attempt to understand their possible effects. Unless the petroglyphs subjected to such treatment are clearly to be destroyed in the short term, there is no justification for using such intrusive methods in this time and age, when it is possible to make entire facsimiles (see below) using non-contact methods based on digital technology (Bednarik 1990b). The only method of this type that can reasonably be tolerated in some cases is the use of aluminium foil tamped gently into petroglyphs, and backed by first more foil, then paper or cloth for stability (Clegg 1978). Other practices of mould making and rubbing of petroglyphs have now been widely eradicated, especially as a result of the conservation policies encouraged by IFRAO during the 1990s.

All these forms of interference either damage rock art, or they prejudice analytical methods of rock art studies that are in use now, or that may be developed in future centuries. One simple rule applies to all rock art recording work: if it prejudices any potential future method it would be irresponsible to use it. No-one can predict what kinds of analytical methods future generations of researchers may introduce, hence no contact with rock art is justifiable. The availability of a variety of non-contact recording methods (see below) renders the continued use of physical enhancement methods in the recording of rock art, or the deliberate compromising of its analytical potential, entirely unjustified. During the last decade IFRAO has conducted a systematic campaign to eradicate such practices which has been very successful worldwide, and it is now accepted universally that the use of any form of physical enhancement is inappropriate in rock art recording.

It is obvious from the above that, of the traditional methods employed in this, the use of transparent film is appropriate especially for petroglyphs on stable rock, as is the use of string grids or similar devices. Photographic recording involves no contact, and provided that it is done without physical enhancement of any kind it remains the favoured means in most circumstances. This becomes particularly obvious in the following chapters, when colour standardisation and manipulation are considered.

In considering traditional methods of recording rock art it is appropriate to make some comments about recording forms. It has long been a popular pastime of administrators in the cultural heritage management industry to design such forms for rock art sites, and over the decades I have had the opportunity of examining many dozens of them, from a great many countries. Practically all of them fail to fulfil the requirements of proper recording standards appropriate for rock art. Many are modelled on site cards for general archaeological sites and therefore of limited utility. They provide good administrative details (ownership status, location, access), reasonable archaeological details, and usually no details of the kind sought by the rock art scientist. The best to be found among them provide cursory information concerning rock and sediment type, predominant vegetation and type of nearest drinking water, and offer helpful details required by the rock art conservator. Standard recording forms specifically for rock art surveys are somewhat more useful, but usually suffer from focusing too much on the art and its morphology, or from soliciting misleading or subjective information (e.g. concerning 'style').

Rock art, however, is not a 'resource' particularly suited to adequate characterisation on a standard form. With the exception of fairly basic data, most of what rock art study is about is not suitable for a 'pigeonhole approach'. Each site has an infinite number of variables, whose combination is unique for each site. Some of these variables, like ambience, are impossible to quantify, and those that are of the greatest significance to the needs of rock art science almost invariably escape the attention of the site card approach. Hence while such systems are of some convenience, their potential in assisting the serious researcher is usually limited, and they are certainly not a reliable source for statistical data of any kind. This points to a principal problem with them, namely that they invite statistical misuse of selective, and always unreliable and profoundly incomplete, data.

Analytical and statistical recording work

Often the purpose of rock art recording is to prepare the data needed to describe a corpus quantitatively, and the end-product of this procedure is inevitably the use of the results in a variety of statistical analyses. Archaeologists, in particular, tend to favour this approach, reasoning that if a body of rock art at a locality is to be studied archaeologically, it must be treated like any other artefact form. In essence this means that each motif at the site must be assigned to a motif category, but objective motif categories are elusive. As in all of Pleistocene archaeology, which is entirely based on theoretical constructs of artefact types, this is not a testable, hence not a scientific, process.

While this limits the usefulness of the exercise and tends to generate irrelevant information and hypotheses, the more significant shortcoming of the idea that statistics are a way of introducing 'analytical' and empirical methods into rock art recording lies in its logic. The first part of the proposition it is based on is valid: an assemblage of rock art, such as that found at a specific site, can be described by stating, as it were, how many crosses and circles there are present in this corpus. The misconception occurs when we then take this finding and interpret it in archaeological terms. This involves several logical errors. First, with rock art it is always safe to assume that not all motifs have survived, or have survived in adequate variables to render their detection and identification possible. Therefore what we see on the rocks today is not representative of 'an art tradition', it is the product of very complex taphonomic processes as much as of cultural dynamics (Bednarik 1994a). Second, it is a fundamental error of logic, even in a purely archaeological sense, to accept a site corpus as representing *'a culture'*. There are hardly any rock art sites of any reasonable size that do not include in their inventory chronologically diverse components, hence the cumulative assemblage represents different times and cultures. It is the complete antithesis of everything archaeology stands for to combine the culturally diverse components of a site corpus, simply because it occurs at the one location, and treat it as defining one culture, one tradition. Yet this is precisely what the statistical inventory of an art site amounts to. Its logic is identical to that of excavating the Palaeolithic, Mesolithic and Neolithic layers of a site, and then combining all of the stone tools from all layers to 'analyse' them together, as the assemblage of a single culture. Until rock art scientists have separated the components of the corpus, archaeologists need to abstain from inventing mythologies about what the 'evidence' tells us, how one site connects with another, or contrasts, and what the art implies in terms of people movement, population densities and what not.

Next, we need to consider the definitions of *motif types*. Unfortunately most site corpora are not neatly dividable into crosses and circles. Demarcations between many motif types are arbitrary (see Ch. 8, 'Statistical interpretation'), and most certainly there is no reason to assume that the motif types invented by archaeologists would be shared by the producers of the rock art. Archaeologists are not able to separate the motifs at the site into chronological groups, let alone can they identify valid motif classes, in the way these would have been experienced by the makers of the art. The idea of the researchers that they can somehow put themselves into the place of the artist, see the art with his eyes, is undeniably a self-delusion (Mithen 1998: 181). And so is the belief that they can create an objective taxonomy, or that the taxonomy they do create has any practical meaning or significance — in the absence of any scientific information about the art.

To illustrate the point with an example, I select a motif type I call the CLM (convergent lines motif). It consists of a group of two to five lines, bunched together at one end. The most common form is made up of three lines, so that it resembles a bird track. It has been given many different names around the world (turkey track, emu track, vulva, arrow point, fish fin, nandu track, trident) — all based upon untestable propositions. But in 1993 I announced, as an experiment, that I had found numerous such trident glyphs in south-eastern Australia and that I knew their exact meaning. I offered a prize to any researcher who could tell me what the significance of the sets of CLMs was, illustrating two such sets. No rock art researcher in the world could guess the correct answer, therefore the 'identifications' of all self-appointed experts on this issue need to be rejected. (The glyphs I described were dendroglyphs, carved by the yellow-bellied glider, *Petaurus australis*, with its teeth; they were identical to motifs in nearby caves in every morphological respect; Bednarik 1993, 1994b.)

If we do not know what a motif class depicts, if we do not know the morphological parameters of a motif class, any taxonomy we devise is at best tentative, it has no objective or analytical function, it is merely a tool to describe subjectively (for more details, see Ch. 8). Any statistical treatment of such data will only reflect the subjectivity of the information it is necessarily based upon.

Finally, the perhaps least understood problem with quantified analyses of rock art is the role of *taphonomic logic* in processing the data so gained. Many of the variables of rock art (e.g. groove depth, patination, weathering, paint composition, pigment type, rock type, location, orientation, site morphology) are highly susceptible to taphonomic selection, therefore statistical data about rock art that have not been subjected to sophisticated treatment by taphonomic logic are almost always misleading. This is the most important of all objections to subjective taxonomies and recordings, and it is the least understood.

In summary, quantitative and statistical descriptions of rock art corpora are very useful in a limited way, but the tendency of using them as the basis of analyses that are thought to, somehow, mysteriously conjure up interpretations of many forms is to be rejected. Without having partitioned the corpus into chronological entities, without being able to define motif types reliably, and without being able to effectively account for taphonomy such interpretations will inevitably be worthless.

Recording standards

Giriraj Kumar, the dynamic founder of the Rock Art Society of India, has suggested the introduction in rock art recording of a system of standardised quality grading. This valuable suggestion certainly offers a great improvement, because until now the precision and reliability of a rock art recording was judged largely by subjective criteria. Yet it does make a considerable difference whether a recording has been made with painstaking care, or is merely a rough sketch of what a perhaps inexperienced observer thought was on the rock surface. Similar systems exist in other fields. For instance in speleocartography, the production of cave plans, standard grades are often applied to make it clear what precision one can expect of such details as direction, size and shape of cave passages. Without stating this on a cave map it would be difficult to know how reliable the document is.

Much the same applies to rock art recordings, yet interpreters of such records often base their hypotheses on the most minute details of what may well be a fairly imprecise likeness. Users of rock art recordings would stand to gain greatly from a reliable system of grading that tells them what level of precision they can expect from a recording. There has been no attempt to introduce such a standard system in rock art recording. It is recommended that the following system of grading be adopted and used for future recordings of rock art panels, beginning with the lowest grade of precision:

Grade 1: a freehand drawing of a panel, sufficient to indicate roughly what figures there are and how they are positioned on the surface. Dimensions, distances between motifs and appearance of motifs are unreliable.

Grade 2: a freehand drawing in which several dimensions were measured and transposed to scale. Reliable in terms of overall layout of the art, but not in respect of detail.

Grade 3: a scaled drawing in which use was made of a coarse recording grid that was laid out over the panel, with art details recorded to scale onto millimetre paper or similar aid; or a drawing made by projecting a slide onto paper and copying the design by hand.

Grade 4: a scaled drawing made with a fine grid (squares no greater than 5 × 5 cm), recording every detail of the art precisely in two-dimensional mode.

Grade 5: a precision recording made by a specialist on transparent sheets laid over the panel, including the colour shading of paintings or the finest details of engravings detectable by the unaided eye.

Grade 6: a three-dimensional topographic precision recording of petroglyphs, from which the shape of groove sections can be determined.

Grade 7: a micro-topographic or lasermicroscopic map of engravings, showing details well beyond the threshold of unaided vision. Similar to the work of F. d'Errico on portable material.

Grade 8: a recording similar to Grade 7, but of greater precision and entirely computer-generated and read. No such work has been undertaken as yet in rock art recording, but it would be achievable with current technology.

Grades 9 and 10 are reserved for greater, as yet unachievable precision that will no doubt become available in future centuries.

It is clear that most rock art recordings currently in use are of Grades 2 or 3, those of Grade 4 are much less common and mostly limited to the Upper Palaeolithic cave sites. Grade 5 might apply to some of the best work by Harald Pager, but has not been widely used, while Grades 6 and 7 have only been achieved in experimental work. This system can be supplemented by a number of additional techniques, such as photogrammetry or surface cartography, which would add detail other than that provided about the rock art motifs. Such information is of great value to the rock art scientist, but very limited use has been made of it so far.

GEOLOGY AND ROCK ART RECORDING

Geomorphic cartography

This recording method was introduced by François Soleilhavoup (1985) and although he has used it extensively, very few other rock art scientists have adopted it (Delluc et al. 1986; Soleilhavoup 1986, 1994). Independent of Soleilhavoup (Figure 26), and apparently without knowing about his system, Columbian rock art researchers led by Guillermo Muñoz have developed a similar cartographic system of recording rock art. The principal difference between the two is that the Columbian system (by GIPRI, the Grupo de Investigación de Arte Rupestre Indígena) includes the use of colour, which permits a much greater range of symbols than the monochrome French system. Some similarities in the results of these two independent initiatives seem to imply that the choices of symbols to be used for the various rock surface phenomena can be fairly self-evident. Nevertheless, the Columbian system is significantly more sophisticated, and capable of depicting such detail as differences in the lichen species or fungi present on a panel.

The principle of micro-geomorphic mapping of rock art panels is simple: whereas traditional recordings are almost universally limited to the perceived rock art motifs, Soleilhavoup and Muñoz include also information on other features of the rock panel, such as areas of exfoliation, lichen presence, taphonomic rock markings, patination, mineral accretions and salt efflorescence. The benefits of this cartography are not limited to those for the scientist, who is likely to refer to such micro-topographical information for a variety of analytical reasons; they are also of great significance to issues of rock art conservation. Indeed, in the latter area it seems self-evident that this form of recording is essential. The neglect hitherto of such an important tool of rock art research is symptomatic of a field dominated by nonscientific, humanistic preoccupations, such as what is depicted and why. It is part of the general pattern that has led to the shortage of empirical information about rock art, and the abundance of meaningless claims about meaning.

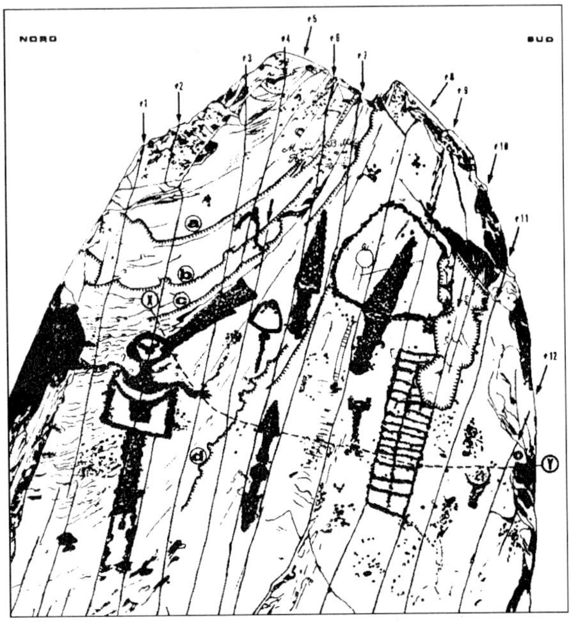

Figure 26. Example of geomorphic cartography by François Soleilhavoup.

It would be very useful to design a standardised and internationally accepted system of cartographic symbols for rock art recording. This would involve the use of marks and patterns denoting fissures, surface types (insolation spalling scar, exfoliated area, surface deposit or other feature covering an area), markings such as glacial striae, as well as the placement of the rock art relative to these features. Since so little of this type of work has so far been conducted it should be readily possible to introduce such a system without opposition, and IFRAO is best positioned to take the necessary initiatives of consultation, design and implementation.

Many of the world's rock art sites are in remote locations, and for the scientist the almost universal lack of surface cartographic information in recordings can be most frustrating: it can mean having to undertake a strenuous, long and costly expedition to a remote site simply to find out whether there are accretions or glacial striae present on a motif — information the previous recorders of the site could have easily provided and which, for all practical purposes, is much more useful than the kinds of information that *were* traditionally provided. It is obvious that the non-scientific preoccupations of rock art recorders often lead to wasteful duplication of logistical research efforts, because many rock art recorders are not equipped to appreciate what kinds of data are required. Perhaps one of the most important points to be made in this chapter about rock art recording is that a rudimentary understanding of micro-geomorphic phenomena commonly found with rock art is essential. It is certainly more important than an appreciation of the perceived archaeological context, which is often very tenuous or non-existent. While it is not a priority of this book to equip the rock art recorder with the relevant knowledge provided by the most important support disciplines, some basic information needs to be presented here. The very essence of proper rock art recording work is not just to record the details of the art faithfully, but also to define its chronological relationship to every discernible feature it is physically related to, be it directly or indirectly. This involves the sequencing of all phenomena near the art, especially spalling scars and their respective surface alterations. Therefore some introductory comments about such features are required here.

Rocks and their weathering

All types of rock are subject to weathering under natural conditions, but the rate at which it proceeds differs greatly among them, and is also determined by the weathering environment. The fundamental process of rock weathering is leaching by water, largely supplied by rain. The water found in rocks can be gravitational, capillary, hygroscopic or held in chemical combination. Apart from oxygen, the two most abundant chemical elements in the lithosphere are silicon and aluminium, and the most abundant minerals, with the exception of quartz, are aluminosilicates of various kinds. Therefore chemical weathering is principally concerned with aluminosilicate chemistry, and the principal products of rock weathering are the minerals that decay to clays. The processes involved in rock weathering are essentially solution, hydration, hydrolysis, ion exchange, chelation, oxidation and reduction. The morphological effects that are of significance to the rock art researcher are primarily surface retreat, saprolithisation (the initial decay phase of rock) and the development of weathering rinds.

Among common rock-forming minerals, susceptibility to weathering decreases roughly in the following order: calcite, dolomite, anorthite, olivine, augite, pyrite, magnetite, hornblende, biotite, ilmenite, albite, plagioclase, orthoclase, microcline, epidote, muscovite, quartz. Solution rates vary enormously under laboratory conditions, from 1 mm/31 days for calcite (Chou et al. 1989) to 1 mm/34 million years for crystalline quartz (Rimstidt and Barnes 1980).

In a more practical sense, the sequence is best expressed by the rate of surface retreat as determined from monumental masonry of known ages. Such retreat varies greatly according to local rock composition and climate, but the rock art student needs to be familiar with empirically determined ranges for common rock types, at least as a rough guide. These are, in millimetres per one thousand years, under 'central European climatic conditions':

Sandstone	5 – 50
Limestone	2 – 20
Schist	1 – 10
Marble	0.4 – 5
Dolomite	0.3 – 2.5
Serpentine	0.25 – 2.5
Diabase, porphyry	0.2 – 2
Gabbro	0.1 – 1.5
Diorite	0.1 – 1
Quartzite	0.1 – 0.5
Granite	0.05 – 0.2

Archaeological lack of such fundamental understanding of the interface between lithosphere and atmosphere has led to spectacular misconceptions. For instance it is unrealistic to expect to find

Pleistocene petroglyphs on a schist panel that was always fully exposed to precipitation, because at these rates of surface retreat (for schist 1–10 cm since the end of the Pleistocene) it is highly unlikely that any rock art could have survived under these conditions. Naturally preservation would be significantly better in an arid or Arctic climate, where the four last-listed rock types would show almost no surface deterioration over ten millennia. Indeed, petroglyphs on granite surfaces in northern Karelia are very well preserved after 4000 years, while historical, dated inscriptions on schist in the Côa valley of Portugal are barely decipherable after a few centuries (Bednarik 1995a). In the arid Pilbara of north-western Australia, petroglyphs have survived for many millennia on gabbro, and for several tens of thousands of years on granite (Bednarik 2002). These kinds of observations assist the rock art student greatly in gaining an initial understanding of the potential antiquity of petroglyphs. It is therefore absolutely essential that rock art recordings identify the rock type the art occurs on, and rock art researchers must possess some basic understanding of weathering rates of common minerals. This information is far more important than any perceived archaeological context in most instances.

The second type of weathering product, saprolite, is of less interest to rock art science. Decay of rock begins with the formation of a carious zone around individual grains where reaction with water occurs, and progressively leads to breakdown into detrital material. Feldspars generally change to mica or montmorillonite, then to kaolinite, and finally to gibbsite. Quartz, if present, remains largely unaltered, while in ferromagnesian minerals alteration starts by oxidation of Fe^{+2} to Fe^{+3}, followed by the removal of cations from pyroxene and amphibole. Muscovite micas adsorb hydrogen and other ions, reverting to illite-like minerals, and the less stable biotite micas tend to form chlorite-type minerals. Of particular interest is the saprolithisation of sandstone as the amorphous silica is leached out (it is about twenty times as soluble as quartz) and the detrital material disintegrates into quartz sand. This is important in appreciating the difficulties of applying thermoluminescence dating to the resulting sediments.

Of particular relevance to rock art science is the formation of weathering rinds, which on many rocks are quite pronounced zones of alteration whose thickness is clearly a function of exposure time. If the process could be calibrated it would be likely to yield rough estimates of geomorphic exposure ages. Černohouz and Solč (1966) attempted this with basalts, claiming to obtain reliability to within 10%–20%, but there has been no adequate attempt to pursue this possibility further (Colman and Pierce 1981). One of the principal difficulties is that the need for destructive sampling seems to exclude such methods from consideration in the case of rock art (but see Ch. 7, 'Patination and weathering'). This is a promising area for future research.

Another potential analytical method that needs to be appreciated by the rock art recorder concerns the spalling of boulders bearing rock art, be it by *Kernsprung*, insolation, kinetic impact, lightning strike or through brush or forest fires. Vast numbers of petroglyphs occur on boulders of various types of rock that are being subjected to gradual reduction by spalling. The various types of fracture can be recognised readily. Lightning generally strikes at the highest point of a target, and the impact area is often discoloured (e.g. greenish or bluish on iron-rich rocks, attributable to extreme temperatures; pers. comm. R. Connick 1988) or glazed where superficial vitrification occurred. Also, the fractures resemble impact fractures, often exhibiting a bulb of percussion or featuring radial stress lines. Spalling caused by brush fire is extremely common in some regions and results in thin flakes of up to 30 cm diameter, whose thickness reaches a couple of centimetres but always tapers off towards the sharp edges. Insolation and fire spalling essentially reduce a boulder of any shape to a sub-spherical form, so they gradually remove protruding aspects and acute edges, leaving behind always convex scars (Figure 27).

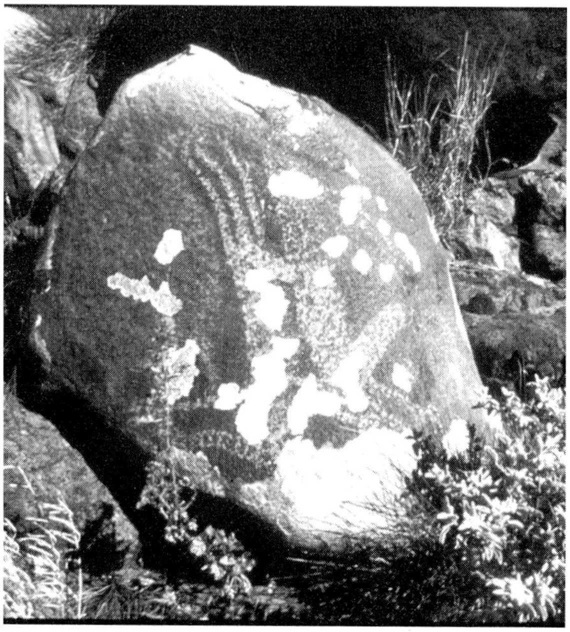

Figure 27. Fire spalling scars on a deeply patinated boulder with petroglyphs, Pilbara region, Australia.

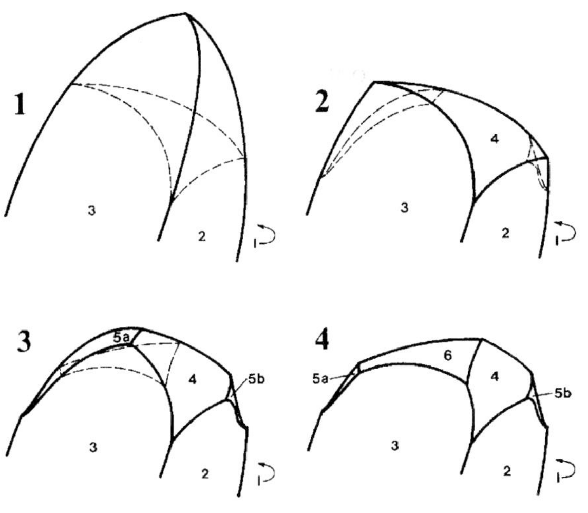

Figure 28. Schematic depiction of the chronological sequence of spalling events of a rock boulder.

The progressive reduction of a boulder through fracture, by whatever spalling process, results in many scars, often truncated by other scars. The chronological sequence of the spalling events can be reconstructed, as schematically depicted in Figure 28 (refer also Ch. 7). Since the analysis of the spalling sequence is within the means of a properly informed rock art recorder, it is reasonable to expect recordings of rock art on such boulders to include details of the analysis of such sequences. In other words, each relevant spalling scar needs to be identified and its chronological position relative to all other types of surface phenomena, including intentional anthropic marks (i.e. rock art), needs to be recorded. Direct dating of petroglyphs is best based on such sequencing of the traces of surface modifications, and on then locating the art within these sequences of events, the products of which can sometimes provide numerical age information directly relatable to the art.

Patination and petroglyphs

The word patina, in rock art science, defines a visually obvious surface feature that differs from the unaltered rock in colour or chemical composition. It is a collective, almost colloquial term for a great many phenomena, but all of them are acquired gradually over time. Hence they are an indication of antiquity, as researchers have appreciated for centuries. However, their use in age estimation has so far remained difficult and controversial, at least partly because of misunderstandings. For instance, there is a well-known polemic concerning the repatination of petroglyphs: if a groove has been cut into the weathering rind beneath a ferromanganous accretion, will its repatination occur at an accelerated rate relative to unaltered rock?

These archaeological conundrums indicate the need for some rudimentary understanding of the processes involved in patination. Unless the type of surface alteration is identified such controversies are futile: if the principal component of the patina were rock varnish, repatination would proceed independent of the substrate, but if the process relied largely on the oxidation of resident iron cations, then it would be affected by the state of the exposed substrate. To make this judgment it is essential to analyse the patination products responsible for the macroscopic appearance of the surface. This is certainly not beyond the means of the determined researcher, it involves the use of field microscopy (see Ch. 9) and some experience in the study of rock surface alteration phenomena.

Originally, the name *patina* referred to copper carbonate or copper sulphate, the corrosion skin that develops on copper and its alloys (*verdigris*) — although the term has earlier roots and derives from the Latin word for a 'shallow dish'. It was extended to the sheen or wear polish on antique surfaces, and to cutaneous alteration of rocks or stone tools that seemed to indicate great age. Such surface skins could be the result of bleaching or leaching (e.g. of sedimentary silicas; Bednarik 1980), limonite staining (Goodwin 1960), mineral accretion (e.g. by rock varnish; Engel and Sharp 1958), chemical alteration of substrate components (most rock weathering processes are candidates), and abrasion or polish (e.g. by sediment grains or biological agents). While this encompasses a great variety of causes, from the rubbing of animal bodies against a rock to the modification of optical properties through the etching of crystals, all of these processes are slow and gradual, resulting in cumulative products that represent lengthy time spans. Patinae have long been recognised as potential means of estimating the age of petroglyphs (for two centuries at least; see Ch. 7), but until recently the difficulties of quantifying and calibrating the processes involved have fostered the view that these are too intractable. Moreover, most rock surfaces experience more than one patination process, so what is simplistically called 'patination' is in fact the macroscopically visible outcome of several factors and their interplay. Their study involves intensive field microscopy.

Patinae can conveniently be divided into those involving the deposition of extraneous matter and endogenous alteration products (although some forms, such as the oxalate patina on marble statues, might be attributable to a combination of local and introduced substances; Del Monte and Sabbioni 1987; Lazzarini and Salvadori 1989). The form of patination most frequently encountered in the study of petroglyphs consists primarily of iron compounds, presenting themselves as the ubiquitous dark-brown coating of rock surfaces, particularly in arid and semi-arid regions. In all cases analysed this is not the product of just one process, and it frequently combines exogenous and endogenous components. Archaeologists frequently assume this to be either an oxidation product or a rock varnish. The latter term is often misused: it should be limited to a very thin (<0.5 mm), often shiny ferromanganous skin that covers even rocks entirely free of its contributing cations, and in whose laminar, stratified deposition micro-organisms are implicated (Scheffer et al. 1963). Other deposits of similar composition and appearance occur commonly and should be described as *dunkle Rinden* (Walther 1891).

To illuminate the issues concerning the relationships of weathering depths, petroglyph depths and repatination I designed a convention of graphically depicting them. Figure 29, first published in 1979, depicts these relationships for six core samples Crawford took from petroglyphs at Depuch Island, Western Australia (Trendall 1964). Two petroglyphs each had been classified as being of fresh, intermediate and deep patination. The mean weathering depth is compared with maximum and minimum weathering depth of each petroglyph, with the groove depth (*E*), the weathering zone thickness left beneath the petroglyph (*X*), and the position of the groove depth relative to weathering depth (*Y*).

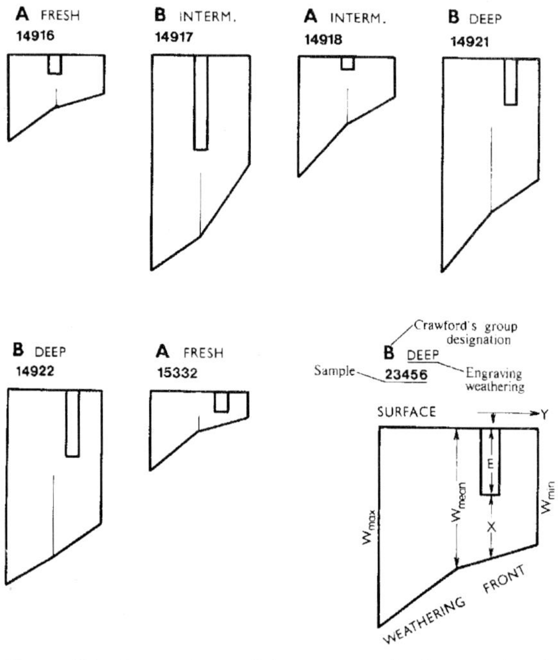

Figure 29. Comparison of six core samples from variously repatinated petroglyphs on Depuch Island, Western Australia, after data by Trendall (1964).

These diagrams illustrate other aspects of the relationships, e.g. the shape of the line representing the weathering front implies the relationship of median and mean weathering depth, and the diagrams demonstrate the lack of correlation between repatination intensity. I concluded:

> Whilst it is true that the three samples of heavy engraving patination coincide with those of deeply weathered rock they also correspond with the deeply engraved. Furthermore [the diagram] demonstrates the concurrence of the heavy engraving patination and greater distance between groove bottom and weathering front. The last-mentioned dimension steadily increases as a function of time, while it is probable that engraved groove depth decreases (although necessarily at a far slower rate), unless we postulate a complete absence of abrasive (aeolian) or other erosion. This argument introduces the possibility that of the oldest designs, only the deeply engraved remain discernible, while those of shallow depth have become unintelligible (Bednarik 1979: 22).

Microscopic examination of brown-patinated non-varnish surfaces usually presents evidence of a variety of processes. A surprisingly large component is clearly aeolian, especially on granites. Crusts of the *dunkle Rinden* type consist of several iron compounds that are subjected to progressive and continuous modification. For instance magnetite is metastable with respect to maghemite, which in turn ages to haematite, a process accelerated by solar radiation. Dehydration changes lepidocrocite to haematite, and heat can dehydrate even the much more stable goethite in the same direction, with attendant colour changes. Being the most stable form of Fe_2O_3, haematite tends to proportionally increase with time, even though it can be reduced to magnetite by high temperature. Its degree of agglomeration or particle size determines its colour — so larger the particles so redder the otherwise brown deposit — but saline solutions also influence the production of red haematite. While the colour is thus determined by the combination and state primarily of iron salts, especially through the taphonomy favouring haematite, other cations are also present, particularly manganese, and these crusts also comprise significant clays and aeolian detritus. I have observed quartz, tourmaline and other crystal grains, plant matter and even charcoal fragments in these accretions, caked together by iron compounds and amorphous silica. They are subjected to continuous modification by rainwater, which favours the formation of distinctively 'laced' or 'terraced' morphologies. However, such extraneous deposits are usually quite discontinuous, so that exposed surfaces can be found on all but the very oldest petroglyphs. Nevertheless, in the macroscopic sense these deposits form fairly consistently as a function of time. For instance in the Australian Pilbara, an incipient film becomes evident after a fresh surface has been exposed for 30–40 years, and after about 100 years, the deposit reaches a thickness locally of 30–50 mm, or 100–150 mm after 230 years (Bednarik 2002). Where a surface is not concealed by accretion, component minerals are subjected to conversion processes often similar to those affecting the accretions. They are here, however, much less effective as they are restricted to the weathering zone, particularly the immediate surface. The phenomenon we describe as 'patina' needs to be seen as usually comprising both types of products, extraneous and intrinsic, and their complex interplay and ongoing modification regime seem to imply that these phenomena are difficult to assess effectively.

Recent work, however, suggests that there may be a simple method to 'quantify' patination. The empirical observation that, in general, repatination does proceed fairly linearly overall may be well founded after all. The means suggested until recently of measuring the visual changes (e.g. by determination of reflectivity) are not expected to provide valid data, but the rapid development of computer programs to calibrate and quantify 'bulk colour' with incredible precision may render patination analysis viable. The results of recent work with colorimetry have been most encouraging (see Ch. 9). It remains necessary, therefore, that the rock art recorder has at least some rudimentary ability of describing the patination present on a petroglyph.

Accretionary mineral deposits

The same applies to more substantial deposits on rock surfaces, which are of importance for several reasons, and also need to be recorded to the extent of providing the specialist researcher with basic information about the type of deposit present, and its physical relationship with the rock art. There is no arbitrary division between the thin deposits termed 'patination', and the thicker layers to be discussed here. Thin ferromangenous patinae grade into thicker deposits of similar composition, but we also encounter various additional types of phenomena here. We are concerned with mineral skins and crusts consisting principally of silicas, oxalates and carbonates. Such mineral deposits are often layered, they can be datable or contain datable inclusions of a great variety, and most importantly, rock art may be sandwiched between two such layers. Both rock paintings and petroglyphs have been found between laminae of accretionary mineral deposits, or at least covered by them or executed on them. Where such clear physical relationships can be detected, they certainly need to be reported by the scholar recording the rock art.

Silica skins were formed through the precipitation of amorphous silica from aqueous solution of silicic acid ($Si[OH]_4$). They are rather thin (mostly <0.4 mm), of usually light colour or translucent, sometimes brown or grey, and they are of vermiform surface texture. They contain a great variety of inclusions, including bacteria, pollen, fungi and algae, which may yield AMS dates, and also numerous mineral substances such as clays and silts. In a classical stratigraphic study of siliceous accretions, Watchman (1996) documented the occurrence of two layers at Penascosa Panel 7 in the lower Côa valley of Portugal. The older is of whitish colour, the younger is of a silty brown appearance, consisting largely of weathered schist detritus and platy mica fragments. An animal figure abraded into Panel 7 cuts through the white layer, whereas the superimposed brown deposit also covers the engraved groove. Consequently the petroglyph postdates the older and predates the younger crust, and its age should lie between carbon dates Watchman derived from the two.

Oxalates are not only datable through the organic inclusions they may contain, but the oxalate itself is datable by virtue of being a salt of oxalic acid, a crystalline organic acid containing ultimately atmospheric carbon and therefore ^{14}C. While the origin of the oxalates Watchman (1990) has frequently identified in northern Australian sandstone shelters remains unresolved, their dating potential has already provided useful results (Watchman 1992, 2000). Oxalates occur as whewellite and weddellite and are generally darker than silica skins (dusty-brown to black) as well as thicker (>1 mm). They may occur in laminated deposits that include not only a variety of other minerals (e.g. gypsum) but also thin bands of pigment residues, such as ochres, which may have been applied as rock paintings. Quartz grains, clays, carbonates and charcoal have been observed in oxalate crusts at rock art sites, and their occasionally complex laminae have yielded entire sequences of painting episodes, separated by the deposition of layers of oxalates and other minerals. The most spectacular examples of such sequences, from Arnhem Land and north Queensland, include a recorded 2.11-mm-thick micro-section from Walkunder Arch Cave that yielded ten AMS carbon isotope determinations ranging from c. 29 700 to 3300 years ka BP (Campbell 2000; Watchman 2000). This illustrates the analytical value of such deposits and reinforces the need to mention their presence in rock art recordings.

The analytical principles Watchman applied in the Côa valley and elsewhere were much earlier employed to study carbonate accretions (Bednarik 1981, 1984a). Calcite, aragonite and dolomite are sedimentary rocks that are readily dissolved in an aqueous solution of carbon dioxide and then reprecipitated in a great variety of forms. Cutaneous travertine deposits occur frequently in limestone caves, covering considerable areas of ceilings and walls with a thickness that may reach some centimetres. Often these formations are faintly layered, and sometimes they contain petroglyphs (e.g. in several caves near Mt. Gamier, South Australia), the outlines of which remain visible on the surface. The rock art as such is sandwiched between two of the strata, having at some stage been engraved into the developing accretionary deposit. These carbonate speleothems are datable, with certain qualifications (Bednarik 1999), by several methods, especially carbon isotope and uranium series analysis (see Ch. 7).

Reprecipitated calcite crusts are not limited to caves, they occur commonly in semi-arid regions in the form of a light-coloured skin at the uppermost level of the sediment. Deposited over other weathering and patination phenomena, sometimes over petroglyphs (Bednarik 1987b) they might be datable. Their presence, like that of other mineral accretions (e.g. of gypsum or anhydrite), should be indicated on rock art recordings.

Other surface features

A scientific recording of rock art is very much about considering all of the many traces of processes that have had some form of impact on a rock panel. Among them is the rock art itself, which in a geomorphic sense is a form of 'biological weathering'. There may be other anthropic markings that are not rock art, markings made by animal species other than man, and even markings made by plants (see Ch. 3). Taphonomic markings are very commonly found on rock surfaces, and among them glacial striae are particularly ubiquitous. Found especially around the northern sector of the Northern Hemisphere, most surviving striae are from the late Pleistocene (earlier examples have survived very rarely), and indeed most are from the very end of the last glaciation. This is because the traces of earlier glacials have generally been obliterated by subsequent glacial erosion. In practical terms this means that, apart from areas where glaciers continued to be active, most surviving striae are between 9000 and 14 000 years old, depending on when the final Würm/ Weichsel/Wisconsin glaciers withdrew from a locality. Rock art, especially petroglyphs, is frequently found on rock panels scoured smooth by glacial debris, e.g. in the European Alps, Britain, Scandinavia, Russia, across parts of northern Asia and in northern North America. Such panels, if they are of a weathering-resistant rock, often still bear the subparallel striations caused by angular clasts dragged over them by the glacier, which can number in their millions per hectare of rock. Glacial striae have profitably been used in establishing calibration curves for microerosion analysis, because the age of the most recent ones can be estimated in areas where the recent glacial history has been studied (Bednarik 1992, 1997). For this and other potential work it is essential that the presence of any glacial striae be shown on rock art recordings, indicating their direction and weathering state.

Traces of damage by fire can often be observed at rock art sites. On very compact rock such as granite, such damage can be recognised by the exfoliation of characteristic spalls with very thin edges, and on rocks containing iron salts there is usually a reddening of the rock apparent. This is especially distinctive on sandstones, and is essentially a result of the dehydration of goethite to haematite, which occurs at about 130°C and can change the colour of a faintly yellow sandstone to a full red. Such discolourations are of relevance to the interpretation of a site, hence they too need to be reported by the rock art recorder.

COLOUR AND SIZE SCALE

Photographs, slides, film and video tape provide only subjective means (Bednarik and Seshadri 1995: 43–44) of rock art recording, their fidelity is limited by various inherent technical factors, and they are inevitably of limited life span. In particular, none of the dyes used in photography is fade-proof, and the collections of millions of colour slides and other records currently held in many institutes and private collections the world over are all doomed to eventual destruction. Rock art itself deteriorates world-wide, and despite our occasional efforts to delay the processes responsible, they cannot realistically be arrested. We are in urgent need of a system of recording rock art permanently and reliably, and photography as such is not the answer. It is therefore of greatest importance to the discipline to find a way of rendering photographic records permanent (Swartz 1991).

But the initial purpose of a standard scale is rather less ambitious. One of the most basic needs in photographic rock art recording is a precise indication of size, readily obtained by placing an object of known size into each picture taken. A scale also helps in focusing the camera because it provides straight edges of sharp contrast. Moreover, it serves to indicate how well a photograph was focused and processed. In the hope of creating a standard scale for rock art researchers, Taylor et al. (1979: 306) designed a simple black and white specimen, measuring 10 × 2 cm. It failed to be adopted and rock art recorders continued to use a wide assortment of designs and colours, not to mention matchboxes, sunglasses and lens-caps. The use of colour in whatever scale one used became increasingly important, to render photographs calibrated in both size and colour. The latter is particularly fundamental, because chroma, value and hue of the colour in all photographs, slides and films are distorted by such factors as lighting, dust, humidity, film type, optics, dyes used in photographic prints, even by the number of prints made since dyes were last replenished. To compensate for these many distortions, conscientious recorders used scientific or commercial standard colour charts, particularly the Munsell Chart, the Kodak Color Separation Guide and the Letraset Pantone colour chart.

Having long been concerned about the lack of size and colour calibration on most rock art photographs I realised that this was to some extent due to the lack of a suitable standard, a readily available scale designed specifically for use in rock art recording, and perhaps also due to an inadequate appreciation of the importance of this issue. After raising the matter on various occasions the need for an initiative became apparent to me, and in 1990, during field work in India, I decided to design, produce and distribute an appropriate colour scale (Bednarik 1991). Not only does the rock art recorder and photographer have to contend with the many technically unavoidable colour distortions, the inherent fading of all such records renders them ultimately worthless. Indeed, most rock art has a natural life expectancy dozens or hundreds of times greater than that of the records we can make of it, whatever traditional means we might use. What was needed was a means of cancelling out all the distortions as well as the inevitable fading resulting from the deterioration of the photographic dyes. Having further witnessed the phenomenal rise of desktop computers through the 1980s, and the incredible proliferation of software for colour manipulation, such as colour enhancement (Rip 1983, 1989), it became apparent to me that this technology offered a solution. If every rock art photograph bore a standard colour scale, it would be possible to recover from it the true colours of the rock art panel at the moment the picture was taken, irrespective of any photographic distortion or subsequent fading, by using the image of the colour scale as a *device profile*. Since the main colour chips on the scale are of precisely known colour values, an appropriately programmed computer would be able to compensate for all deviations in the image and reconstitute the true colours of the panel. In other words, the photograph itself is relegated to the role of intermediate field data device, and is no longer the ultimate recording medium.

I then presented a proposal for a standard scale combining colour and size scale and invited critical comments over a period of three years (Bednarik 1994c). After receiving suggestions and soliciting further advice I introduced the IFRAO Standard Scale in May 1994. Its final design met the need for simplicity, incorporating four colour chips that are well-spaced within the colour solid or the Cartesian colour cube, and four monochrome values (of reflection densities 0.0, 0.7, 1.6 and 2.0). There are two size scales, one for close-up photography, the other 10 cm long. To guard against fading of dyes the Scale also bears the printing date and will be replaced periodically. In the first decade since its introduction, over 50 000 specimens have been distributed worldwide, most of them free. The IFRAO Standard Scale is now not only the international colour calibration standard in rock art studies, it has also been adopted widely in numerous other disciplines, including archaeology, soil science,museology, palaeontology, forensic science and even medicine. In 1994 it became, as always intended, the device profile of the first system of digital colour reconstitution in scientific recording (Bednarik and Seshadri 1994). Since then its potential in research, documentation, conservation, condition monitoring of paint residues and patination has been widely realised, and it has also been the chosen standard in the development of new methods. For instance I have used the Scale to secure precise quantitative expressions of colour change due to repatination, in an effort to calibrate such changes against time, for the purpose of dating petroglyphs. Another recent application was its use by a British team to monitor changes in iron oxide pigment in a cave environment (Mirmehdi et al. n.d.).

COLOUR RE-CONSTITUTION

A collaborative project of the National Museum of Man in Bhopal, India, and the International

Federation of Rock Art Organisations (IFRAO) has led to the first attempt to reconstitute true colour from a rock art photograph (Bednarik and Seshadri 1995). This occurred on 8 December 1994 in Bhopal (Bednarik 1994d) and our immediate success prompted an intensive program of perfecting the procedures with the aim of producing comprehensive guidelines for rock art recorders. Essentially, this system works as follows. The photograph is first translated into digital information by one of the scanning processes available (Figure 30). The computer is then instructed to recall the true digital colour information contained in the reference device, and to compare it with that found in seven spot colour checks on the photograph's white, black, red, green, yellow and grey (two) colour chips. The software then compensates for all distortions in these primary colours, thus reconstituting them in the photographed colour calibration scale. To confirm the precision of the correction, it then checks that there is no distortion in the blue chip, which represents the least important colour in rock art photography. The entire image is then reconstituted on the basis of the known distortions in the primary colours, and this corrected image is output directly to the preferred format. This can include printer's four-colour separations, after the application of under-colour removal and grey-component replacement by proprietary software (Bednarik and Seshadri 1995).

When it involves a large number of images, the process of colour re-constitution as described is time consuming, cumbersome and repetitive. Since all of the world's rock art archives are expected to use this system eventually, millions of rock art images will be processed by it and stored digitally (or stored by some alternative, as yet unknown, future technology). Most of the operations involved in colour re-constitution can easily be accomplished by the computer, and indeed better than the human eye and judgment could expect to achieve. The computer manages colour information in a digital or mathematical format, i.e., entirely free of subjectivity. It was therefore obvious that colour re-constitution should be handled digitally, rather than manually as in the initial trials.

Software has been developed at the National Museum of Man of India which eliminates nearly all operator involvement. The computer scans the whole image, searching for angular shapes on it. Once it finds some of the colour chips on the photographed IFRAO Standard Scale, it determines the Scale's

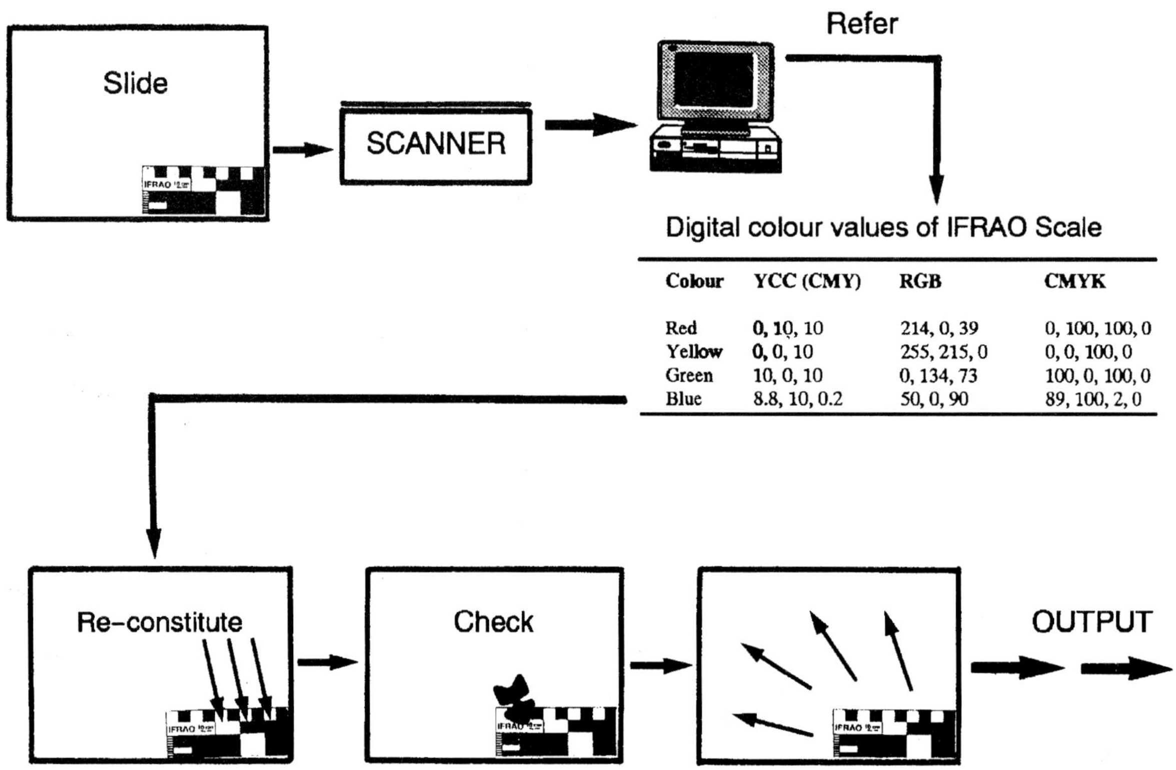

Colour	YCC (CMY)	RGB	CMYK
Red	0, 10, 10	214, 0, 39	0, 100, 100, 0
Yellow	0, 0, 10	255, 215, 0	0, 0, 100, 0
Green	10, 0, 10	0, 134, 73	100, 0, 100, 0
Blue	8.8, 10, 0.2	50, 0, 90	89, 100, 2, 0

Figure 30. Schematic depiction of the process of digitised colour re-constitution using the IFRAO Standard Scale.

relative size and orientation. In terms of software design this is the most difficult part of the operation. Having established these variables, the computer locates the various calibration sites on the Scale and determines a full set of digitised values from the mean values of a preset number of pixels from each of the various photographed colour chips. These are then digitally compared with the known values of the Scale, and the various distortions are determined almost instantly. From this information, the computer can readily calculate the correction required in each pixel of the image, using a commercially available colour management system. The image's true values are reconstituted, and all of this has been achieved without the operator having made any decision. Indeed, the operator's work is now limited to presenting the image for scanning, deciding the form of output, and adding archival identification data for retrieval. In the reconstituted image, the picture of the IFRAO Standard Scale has precisely the same colour as the actual Scale, and under reasonably favourable photographic conditions, the picture of the rock art matches precisely the colour information on the rock at the time it was photographed. All forms of distortion, irrespective of their causes, are compensated for (for further details, see Ch. 9)

COLOUR CALIBRATION

The main purpose of this project was not, however, simply to develop new technology, but to determine the optimal conditions for the use of the IFRAO Standard Scale, and to translate these into practical advice for rock art recorders. To be realistic it must be accepted that the common use of colour re-constitution, and the associated technology, are not likely to be universally available in the discipline for many years. Nor is this of immediate importance. Present digital storage means are not quite adequate, especially in terms of their durability. Computer technology is developing rapidly, so these considerations will be taken care of within a few decades. The most urgent requirement is merely the creation of the conditions for precise re-constitution. This means, very simply, that rock art photographs need to be colour calibrated, i.e. bear the image of the IFRAO Standard Scale. Naturally, they should be taken under conditions that are favourable for maximal precision in the colour re-constitution process.

The recommendations for optimum conditions (Bednarik and Seshadri 1995; Bednarik 1995b, 1995c) consist of several simple suggestions concerning medium, lighting, distance and positioning of the Scale. Slides and colour negatives are the preferred recording medium, unless video or digital photography is used. It is to be noted that colour veracity of different film makes can vary considerably, for instance Kodak Ektachrome Professional Plus enhances the primary colours, while Ektachrome 100 does not. Prints are not well suited, because their scanning is less accurate than that of the negatives. Natural lighting is preferred to artificial, and the Scale should be positioned near the margin where lighting is strongest. For full 100 per cent calibration and greatest colour precision through re-constitution, the Scale should occupy at least five per cent of the photograph's area. At distances ex ceeding 1.5 metres, two Scales should be included, one of them vertically on the upper left corner. With lenses of average focal lengths, no photographs should be taken at more than 4.5 metres distance. The Scale should be aligned parallel to the predominant plane of the rock art and at a similar distance from the camera lens (Figure 31). Finally, care must be taken to avoid direct reflection of the light from the Scale. Preferably the Scale should be perpendicular to the camera's focal axis if the light direction is from elsewhere, but not if the flash is mounted on the camera.

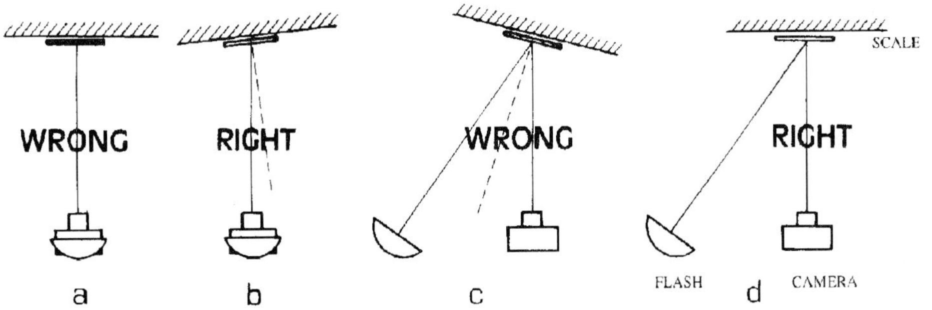

Figure 31. Recommended placement of camera, flash/strobe and scale relative to rock art panel: light and camera in the same position (a and b), and in two different positions (c and d).

An unexpected discovery during this work was that limited manual colour re-constitution of old photographs is even possible if they bear only a black and white scale. Under otherwise ideal conditions it may be possible to obtain as much as 70–80% colour correction. In some circumstances, even pictures without any scale lend themselves to limited correction, because they may include some colour features whose digital values can be determined. In particular, areas of full shadow may provide a reference for black, or Munsell field determinations of pigment or patina might provide fairly good reference points. White accretions, chalk marks, charcoal, freshly broken rock, or the hand of a person may all provide some limited means of calibration. Their use is laborious but it can provide a relative improvement in colour veracity in the absence of more precise means.

However, it will be self-evident that the use of a colour scale that has the backing of a digital colour re-constitution system is now essential. This measure renders rock art information recoverable in perpetuity. Most rock art of the world will not survive the third millennium, except in digital form, and to do so it must be colour calibrated. A further reason for the use of such a system is that it renders our records susceptible to electronic colour manipulation, including the important research tool of colour enhancement. Photographic records of rock art are relegated to the role of provisional, uncalibrated field data that are recorded only for temporary storage. Rock art recording of the future will be by several digital means, with re-constitution being done in the field as portable systems become available. As a first step we need to abandon our traditional reliance on photographs because of their obvious transience, and understand that they are simply a means of storing optical information temporarily, much of which is not even visible to the human eye. The computer can discriminate between colours with much greater precision then our visual system.

It will be obvious that the digitally stored imagery can then be interfaced with any number of computer applications, ranging from various scientific uses to publishing and so forth. For instance, from a customised library it will in the future be possible to engage search commands for specific pigment colours, motif types, even standardised stylistic characteristics. One will be able to monitor the fading or colour alteration of pigments with mathematical precision, and the same applies to deterioration of patinae. There are obvious applications in rock art conservation and site management, in comparison to which present monitoring means are quite primitive. The incorporation in archival systems, or in interactive systems intended for exhibition, provides numerous practical applications. It is obvious that colour veracity in printing and in producing exhibits will benefit enormously from this system, as anyone who has been involved in such projects will readily appreciate. Similarly, the system can be used for improving the procedures of creating rock art facsimiles. Here again, it is obvious that interfacing with other computer applications, such as three-dimensional modelling or CAD, is readily possible. There are various other possibilities, such as the incorporation of colour enhancement methods (Rip 1989) and other plug-ins (Mark and Newman 1995), but perhaps the most important application of this new technology will always be the ability to create permanently recoverable and accurate records of rock art.

DIGITAL IMAGE PROCESSING

The idea that digital processing of imagery offers a great many possibilities for the recording of rock art is not so new, but the technical means of doing this have only become widely available during the 1990s. When Rip (1983, 1989) pioneered the digital enhancement of rock art images he used the mainframe computer of the Hartebeeshoek Satellite Remote Sensing Centre in South Africa. When Dickman (1984) presented his vision of an image digitising and storage system for use in rock art research, it was greeted with scepticism: 'such a system will not (and does not seem intended to) replace more conventional means of motif illustration' (Rosenfeld 1984). Nothing could have been further from the truth: within ten years photographic means of illustrating rock art were relegated to the status of optical information *temporarily* storing visual and non-visual data for processing by more sophisticated media (Bednarik and Seshadri 1995). Sceptical commentators failed to appreciate two crucial points: that the photographic medium conveys more information, both quantitatively and qualitatively, than the human eye can process; and that Dickman's example was embryonic of a technological system that is amenable to almost limitless improvement. Human vision, entirely limited by the actinic effects on the retinal system, is in the short term immutable. Systems capable of discriminating additional information have incredible potential for development.

So far, only preliminary and isolated use has been made of such potential. Michael R. Rip succeeded in demonstrating the benefits of colour enhancement by digital image processing and intensity transformation (contrast enhancement) of a panel of South African paintings. He converted a colour slide image from analog to digital format through primary colour filters, transformed the Cartesian data to colour space, and then analysed and manipulated each of the three primary colour images according to brightness, hue and saturation. Enhancement was achieved by either stretching or compressing the top and/or bottom few per cent of the output images. After reconverting them to primary colours they were subjected to spatial filtering in order to enhance edges and boundaries (abrupt changes in brightness values). Finally the three RGB images were superimposed and a composite enhanced image reconstituted. Nowadays all of these steps can be achieved with proprietary software which, although still rather expensive, is now widely available (e.g. Clogg et al. 2000; McNiven et al. 2000; Mark and Billo 2002; Brady et al. 2004).

Jeffrey L. Dickman's work was carried out at about the same time, in 1982, when the technology he used had been available for about 15 years. He described simple enhancement functions of software already then commercially available, using a microcomputer with only 48K RAM, a 5¼ inch floppy drive and magnetic disks. He demonstrated not only the utility of such systems in modulating faded images or those difficult to recognise, he also considered the issue of storage of extensive digitised records — before the introduction of compact disks. His principal message, however, was that these kinds of media were evolving rapidly, and would be of particular importance in the future recording of rock art. Some readers naively assumed that the quality of output Dickman presented was indicative of what digitising was going to offer, when in fact he opened a window to incredible possibilities, some of which were realised in the subsequent 15 years. In a commentary on his paper, I predicted that the crucial question of perdurability of digital records would be resolved shortly, and that the archival and publishing potential of this evolving technology were enormous. I also proposed a system of recording very diffuse or weathered petroglyphs by eliminating the 'subjectivity' lighting imposes: taking a large number of exposed frames from a fixed position, each one differently lit, and having a computer program selecting those pixels that were exposed above a threshold level, chosen manually, that would most accurately record the image (Bednarik 1984b). This has never been tried.

Two British researchers, Phil Clogg and Margarita Díaz-Andreu, also recognised the difficulties of objectively recording rock art images under difficult conditions (e.g. the rock panel being a similar-colour, uneven granulate support surface). They have recently subjected a variously recorded bovid motif at Selva Pascuala site in Villar del Humo (Spain) to digital image processing. They noted that contrast and edge enhancement can facilitate the resolution of details and can also present the image in an unconventional manner, thus challenging our pre-conceived ideas of what we are seeing. They removed background interference, i.e. texture of the rock itself, and considered the very same procedure I had proposed, the processing of the image using multiple image operations. Using boundary-enhancing filters, they applied edge detection, and with a technique termed 'skeletonising' they reduced lines to a width of one pixel, thus providing a high level of detail. Problematic areas were further enhanced using the zoom function. This thresholding technique and edge detection sequence is a natural extension of the earlier pioneer studies.

With today's proprietary software programs of digital colour management, the old problem of separating paint residue from background to acquire a completely objective recording of a rock painting has become routine work achieved by a few automated commands. Few computer skills are required for this to be done effectively and within seconds. Not so many years ago this kind of work was painstaking and involved many days of work on a single motif. In appreciating this one cannot help but admire the work of those who persevered in the past, and appreciate how privileged we are, having today's immense possibilities of rock art recording at out disposal. Even in the early 1980s, Dickman still stored his work on optical disks, a medium now all but forgotten. They had the capacity to store 54 000 simple black and white images on each side. Storage is one of the most important aspects in the digital recording of rock art. The introduction of, first, the CD (compact disk) and then, in 1996, the DVD (digital video disk) has practically solved this issue. The CD stores about 700 MB of data, which corresponds to hundreds of good-resolution colour images, which is still dwarfed by the multi-gigabyte capacity of the DVD. In the years since Dickman's work the cost of the disks as well as of the equipment needed to record data on them permanently has plummeted due to mass production. Such equipment is now readily available even to most inadequately funded researchers, and in combination with other factors described in this chapter (particularly colour calibration and colour management) it offers the most efficient currently available system for the rock art recorder.

The primary concern with these media is the issue of their life expectancy. Subject to proper treatment in accordance with the manufacturers' recommendations, the longevity of CDs depends primarily on the dyes used on their recording surfaces. They are made from photosensitive organic compounds which are burned by the laser of the CD recorder, creating troughs or pits in the surface that can then be 'read' by another laser in a CD player. If this layer of dye deteriorates, the error rate in reading the CD increases and eventually becomes too great. The dye itself is of blue colour, but when a gold reflective backing is applied it appears green. With a backing of silver colour the blue colour is retained. The dye with the shortest life is cyanine, but well stored such a CD can still last for some decades. Its use is not recommended for archival rock art material. Phthalocyanine dye tends to be a lighter blue than cyanine, and phthalocyanine disks have a life expectancy of about 100 years. With a gold backing the phthalocyanine disks will have the longest life, well over a century. Another variable concerns the effectiveness of the laser diodes, which can vary over the life of a CD writer. This factor is probably responsible for reported variations in the quality of some colours between individual users of particular CD writers.

Combined with the facility of colour reconstitution as described above, CDs and DVDs provide a system of perpetual storage of rock art imagery. There should be no doubt that by, say, 2050 the means will be readily available to automatically check a CD recorded today for data deterioration and re-constitute its colour data if necessary, and to store it in some superior, then available, entirely permanent format. All that is really required at present is a colour-calibrated photographic record.

TOPOGRAPHY OF PETROGLYPHS

Topography refers to the detailed description and analysis of the geographical features of a comparatively small area. In the study of rock art, topography is of relevance at four distinctive dimensional levels: at the level of describing a site and its general setting, at the level of defining the morphology of an individual rock art panel, in recording and analysing such detail features as petroglyph grooves, and finally in the microscopic realm. While the technology used in each of these four cases may differ significantly, the theory as such is quite uniform, and the principles applicable to mapping the valley in which a site is located are no different from those of mapping an engraved groove only a millimetre wide. This point is well made with the use of multivariate characterisation of groove shape, which Urbani has used as profitably on a 57-m Venezuelan geoglyph as on small petroglyphs. In all cases topography provides solid empirical descriptive data.

Multivariate characterisation of groove shape

Urbani (1998) sought to find a way of objectively quantifying the shapes of petroglyph grooves. For his initial experiments he selected five metrical variables, chosen arbitrarily to roughly define a groove's cross-section. First he draws a line *C-D* from the deepest point of the groove perpendicular to a line *A-B* connecting its two rims (Figure 32). In the middle of the line dividing the groove into two parts, *C-D*, he draws a line *E-F* parallel to *A-B*. This enables the determination of five dimensions, *a* to *e*, in millimetres, to one decimal point. He then takes these measurements at numerous points along the grooves of a petroglyph and enters them into a matrix for digital processing in a spreadsheet format. This facilitates the calculation of average, minimum, maximum and standard deviation for each variable, or any ratio between them. With the averages of the five variables the mean shape of the petroglyph's groove cross-section is defined, which in turn facilitates univariate statistical comparisons between different motifs. Urbani also proposes the use of several indexes to characterise the shape of the groove: symmetry, sharpness, V-shape and flatness index.

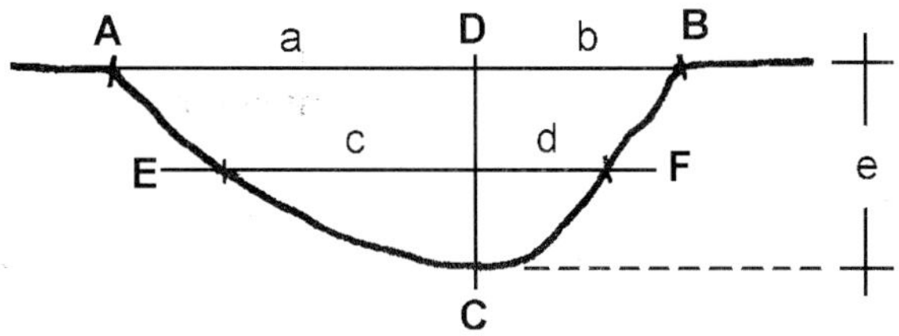

Figure 32. Diagram of a petroglyph groove section showing the variables in Urbani's method of multivariate characterisation of groove shape.

The multivariate statistical treatment of groove shape is performed on a micro-computer using proprietary software. It can include Q-mode cluster analysis, which presents the relationships of different samples in the form of a dendrogram. This can express, in an objective form, the similarity or difference of two petroglyphs on the basis of groove topography. Urbani has demonstrated the utility of this method by comparing two petroglyphs from Piedra del Indio, Venezuela.

Precisely the same principles were applied to a large geoglyph called La Rueda del Indio, located on a hillside near Chirgua, Carabobo state, Venezuela (Urbani and Urbani 2001). Because the grooves of the geoglyph are significantly larger, on average 36 cm deep, it was feasible to take measurements at depth intervals of 10 cm, so that in fact there were as many *E-F* lines as the depth of the groove permitted at this interval. A total of 42 sections were surveyed in this fashion, and the data were then also subjected to multivariate statistical treatment. In his work with the petroglyphs, Urbani (1998) acquired the data manually, using either a moulding clay that was pressed into the groove and then sectioned, or a comb-like tool used in metalworking, whose movable pins are adjusted to fit irregular shapes. It is obvious that this work could be rendered more accurate and comprehensive by using instead a digitised process employing a laser to take measurements at much smaller intervals (see below). This would also avoid the potential of damaging the petroglyph.

Laser scanner analysis of grooves

In her work on runic inscriptions in Scandinavia, Kitzler (2000) utilised a portable laser scanner probe controlled by a computer, which has a measuring accuracy of ± 2 microns. In the field, a movable arm could be used for vertical surfaces, but Kitzler chose instead to take casts with an elastic modelling clay. Her method is to measure depths at one millimetre intervals across a groove's width, and to then correct these for specific variables. First, the groove is 'straightened' by aligning the deepest points at each section measured and recording the seven depth values on each side of it, so that each set of dimensions spans a total of 14 mm. Next, the depth values are recalculated to refer to both adjacent rock surfaces rather than the plane on which the laser probe moves, and to which the primary data refer. This results in a matrix of variables that can be subjected to a variety of statistical analyses, just as that of Urbani's method.

The principal differences are that Kitzler uses only depth measurements and relies for a construction of profile on the regular distancing of values across a section. Urbani measures only one depth, to locate the deepest point, and then obtains the position of contour lines by measuring 'vertically' spaced widths. Both methods produce similar micro-topographical results, except that Kitzler's tends to be more precise, being significantly less laborious. Ease of application invites cross-sections to be taken at short regular intervals, rather than at a few random locations of a motif. Therefore the results of Kitzler's method are more likely to provide information about the 'flow' of engraved lines, or about characteristics of minor variations in the continuity of tool application. However, the equipment needed for this method is obviously sophisticated and not widely available.

Kitzler's express purpose is to distinguish between the handiwork of individual engravers, and while it remains to be established to what extent this can be done reliably, the quantitative methods she and Urbani have pioneered in describing grooves are certainly valid tools for a variety of research aims. They need to be developed further and they need to be applied to large samples. These techniques lead to another research topic of importance, the empirical differentiation between artificial grooves on surfaces, made intentionally by humans, and the often rather similar grooves made by a variety of natural agencies on several types of surfaces (Bednarik 1994e).

Lasermicroscopy

This was recently attempted in a study of the engraved bone objects from Bilzingsleben, Germany, which at an age of perhaps around 350000 years are the earliest currently known engravings on this material (Mania and Mania 1988). However, their status as intentional work has been challenged by various commentators, primarily those whose favoured models of human evolution were negated by the Bilzingsleben corpus. Here, the issue was not one of taphonomic (natural) versus anthropic markings, but whether the cut marks were incidental, ludic (playful) or intentional. For instance, it was suggested that the marks were the result of using the bones as cutting boards to cut strips of animal skin. That they had been made with stone tools was not disputed by anyone, and it was clear that many of them had been drawn with great care, being long and perfectly straight. Others had been made by repeated application of the same stone tool, so a good degree of purposefulness seemed apparent in many of the marks.

Steguweit (1999) applied lasermicroscopy to this problem, a method resembling the work of Urbani and Kitzler in that it quantifies a groove topographically. However, the precision of this equipment is considerably greater, and the ability to apply the method directly to the study surface rather than a replication cast eliminates the need to make contact with a perhaps fragile and valuable specimen. The method has been developed for metallurgical analysis, and it provides reference profiles at any intervals as well as three-dimensional modelling matrixes of individual sectors measuring 1.2 × 1.2 mm. The ability to detect topographic variations of a few microns renders this method suitable for grooves of under one millimetre width. Individual measurements, such as groove depth, are made to an accuracy of one tenth of a micron. The massive amount of data obtained is processed digitally.

In his Bilzingsleben analyses of four of the engraved objects, Steguweit demonstrated that the lines had been engraved with only light and very even pressure, and that each set of marks was made with just one tool point. More importantly, he showed that the complete absence of the irregularities in groove depth one finds in incidental marks resulting from use as a cutting base indicated that the cuts were not made through a skin or similar material: tool application was directly to the exposed bone surface. Moreover, in the case of two of the four objects the repeated application of the tool to individual marks excludes this possibility. This confirms the macroscopic observation that the Bilzingsleben marks were made purposefully and are non-utilitarian (Bednarik 1988).

While the relevance of the study of cut marks on bone may not readily be apparent to rock art research, potential applications of this technology are possible in rock art recording. In particular, some fine engravings on low metamorphism rocks ranging from mudstone to schist, especially slate and phyllite, could be subjected to similar analysis where they are not too much weathered. Similarly, the fine engravings often found on the limestone walls of deep caves are most certainly worthy of such attention, and would yield excellent micro-topographical modelling data of this type. Such information provides the opportunity of objective assessment of claims concerning the detailed morphology of engravings, it assists in 'internal analysis', and it can even help in arriving at deductive interpretations about intentionality. Moreover, it is also applicable to mobiliary art, especially plaques and slates (see Ch.10).

Digitised micro-topography

The rapid advances in digital technology have facilitated the development of another approach to topographical recording (Bertani et al. 1997). This optical technique involves the projection of 'structured light' in the form of a grid, and the recording of the effect produced by viewing the engraved panel from a position different to that of the light source. Using a high-resolution closed-circuit digital camera connected to a micro-computer, the algorithms derived from the digital interferometry create a three-dimensional image. The grid used by Bertani et al. is a pattern of black and white vertical stripes, and when it is projected onto an uneven surface the stripes will appear distorted if viewed from another perspective. This distortion will be a function of the angle between the focal axes of the light source and the camera. To avoid distortion of the perspective, the camera's axis is placed orthogonal to the surface being recorded and in its centre (Figure 33).

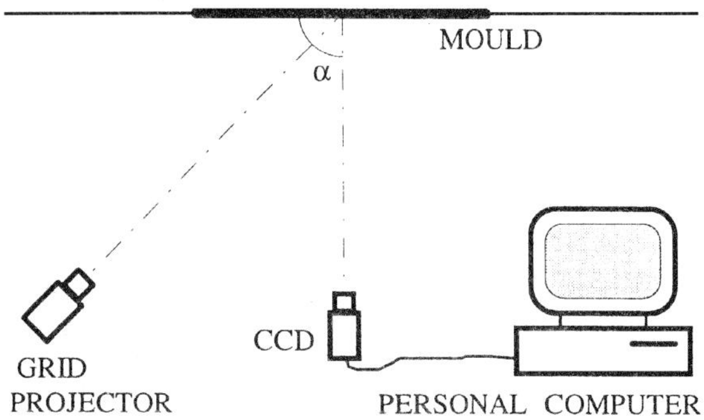

Figure 33. The components of the system of digitised micro-topography as applied by Bertani et al. (1997): a grid is projected onto the panel and recorded by a CCD camera.

Bertani et al. applied this recording method to a series of casts taken of the densely inscribed walls of an Italian site, Poesia Cave near Lecce. However, it can readily be applied to reasonably flat petroglyph panels, provided that there is adequate room in front of the panel (at least 2 m), and a portable power supply is available to operate the grated light source, CCD camera and computer. The camera Bertani et al. used had a 1300 × 1000 sensors focal plane array and was operated at a temperature of –35°C to minimise electronic noise. Camera and light projector were spaced at an angle of 11 degrees, and the grating consisted of 40 lines/mm. To minimise geometric distortion, high-quality 35 mm lenses were used on both the projector and the camera. The images acquired can be enhanced with high-pass digital filters, which 'flatten' the surface undulations of the rock panel by filtering out low spatial frequencies, while at the same time the high spatial frequencies of the petroglyph grooves can be enhanced. The filter changes the intensity of each pixel, taking into account local contrast, through the algorithm evaluation of adjacent pixels, comparing local averages. Thus the filter accentuates intensity changes mostly where contrast is poor. The resulting images are more legible than raking-light photographs in that they better reflect the appearance of the petroglyphs. However, if the contrast is increased too much, the spatial noise produced by fine irregularities in the limestone surface combines with instrumental noise and reduces legibility. The operator then has to choose a compromise between lack of resolution and excessive noise, which is easily done by adjusting the filter parameters.

A high-resolution digital surface map produced by this method facilitates a variety of manipulations of the primary data, each leading to a different visualisation of the data. The information content of such a numerical map is much greater than that of a photograph, and this recording method does not so much yield an end product, as a base line for a technology of handling micro-topographical information that has as yet to be explored.

OPTICAL AND ELECTRON MICROSCOPY

The two most important tools of the rock art scientist are the colour standard scale (see above) and the microscope. A science of rock art without microscopy is unthinkable, even though the microscope may not be thought of as a traditional tool in rock art recording. However, magnification is often required in the recording of both pictograms and petroglyphs, be it in petrography, the study of petroglyph-making stone tools, internal analysis or the identification of weathering and patination phenomena, to name just a few examples. It may be provided by magnifiers which range up to 20× magnification, and are found as large or small-diameter hand lenses or in the form of a pair of lenses mounted to a head frame strapped to the observer's head (magnification only 3× to 5×). The latter is essential in fieldwork involving the use of both hands, in which minimal magnification is adequate: initial survey of surface details, sample collection and coarse nano-stratigraphy. Hand-held monocular microscopes can be so small that they fit into a shirt pocket. Their research use is limited as their optical properties offer only a limited field of view, but their magnification is effective up to 50× or 60×, which is most adequate for many purposes required in recording work.

However, most specialised work in rock art research demands the field use of binocular microscopes, although there are some exceptions: the study of portable art objects, samples removed from sites, casts, exfoliated rock fragments and so forth. Unfortunately most binocular microscopes are not suitable for field microscopy. They are designed for laboratory use, or for placing small objects on their slide stage (for practical issues of field microscopy, see Ch. 9). Binocular microscopes perform well up to magnifications in the order of 160×, their upper limit is imposed by the wave length of natural light, which is about 0.2 micron. This translates into a maximum magnification of 200×. That range is entirely adequate for identifying patina types, weathering phenomena, nano-stratigraphic units, microerosion phenomena (and their quantification), petrographic studies and internal analysis of fine engravings, which in most cases exceeds the requirements for effective recording work.

Nevertheless, for a variety of specialised work, higher magnifications are required, which are provided by electron microscopes. Two types can be of use in rock art studies, the transmission electron microscope (TEM) and the scanning electron microscope (SEM). The TEM has a resolving power about ten times that of the SEM, or a thousand times better than that of an optical microscope. In a TEM, a fine electron beam emitted by a filament in the upper end of an evacuated column passes through the specimen, which therefore has to be extremely thin. The electrons are accelerated by a high voltage and form an image of the object on a fluorescent screen, which is recorded by a camera. Magnetic fields act as lenses focusing the electron beam and magnifying the image.

In palaeoart studies, however, samples are not often suitable for this technique, but the SEM has been found most useful (e.g. d'Errico 1988, 1989, 1991; Hyman et al. 1996; Mawk et al. 1996; Mawk and Rowe 1998; Watchman 1996; Watchman et al 1997). It produces three-dimensional images, magnified by up to 200 000×. Here, a fine beam of electrons is moved across the surface of the specimen, and electrons reflected from it are collected by a detector. The electrical signal they induce generates a point of brightness on a monitor, which scans rapidly over the screen, in phase with the scanning electron beam. An image of the specimen's surface emerges gradually. The resolution possible with this instrument depends on the size of the electron beam: the finer the beam, the higher the magnification obtained.

The use of SEM is entirely restricted to the laboratory, not only because the equipment is not portable, but because only small samples can be accommodated in it. Its use in palaeoart research is therefore limited to the study of material samples (paint residues, patinae) and minute casts (such as resin casts from rubber moulds) of fine engravings, be they replicative or archaeological. Nevertheless, surface profiling of such features has been shown to be of importance in conservation, in the detection of fakes, and in determining what caused morphological variations in marks carved on portable art objects (d'Errico 1996).

PHOTOGRAMMETRY AND CAD

Photogrammetry is defined as the science and technology of obtaining three-dimensional modelling information from physical objects by the use of multiple photographs, using cameras of precisely known lens and film geometry. By viewing a three-dimensional object from two horizontally displaced positions, it is possible to compute the distance to any point on the object by comparing the displacement of that point in its two images seen from the two positions. The standard procedure is to take pairs of photographs which, with a viewer, provide a likeness of an irregular surface, such as a rock panel, with depth of vision. Alternatively, the optical data so acquired can provide a contour map or comprehensive topographical description of the surface. Photogrammetry is certainly not a new method, it has been used in cartography for over a century, and in rock art recording for a few decades (Rivett 1977, 1978, 1983; Turpin 1979; Ogleby and Rivett 1985; Aujoulat 1987).

It is therefore evident that this method has applications in the recording of rock art, and that it would connect especially well with geomorphic cartography as introduced by Soleilhavoup (see above). Nevertheless, such work has not been attempted, and even straight photogrammetry has found only limited use in rock art recording. A number of limitations of the method have become apparent in rock art applications: the equipment is bulky and heavy, of limited focus range and film or plate choice, and the process of deriving drawings from photograph pairs presents obstacles (Ogleby 1995). It is probably best regarded as a method most suited for augmentation with others, particularly computer-assisted methods.

Kirsch and Kirsch (1996) have developed a variety of techniques of computer-processing photogrammetric images. To circumvent the difficulty of dealing with very uneven rock panels, they scan the two images and then correct them in the computer by using humanly recognisable fiducial points in the stereo pair (Brown 1992). They then distort the images to bring these points into correspondence. The corrected image pair should then approximate optimal conditions. From this Kirsch and Kirsch prepare a distance map, intended to record the depths of the petroglyph grooves and indentations relative to the 'flattened' rock panel. In doing so they can cancel distorting visual noise, such as chalk marks, because the image now ignores surface colour and records purely topography. Indeed, by rendering the panel plane black and the petroglyph white, with section profiles shown, they can produce what they call an 'artificially chalked' image of three-dimensional plasticity.

More recently an American resources consulting firm, C Dimensions, has also tried to combine traditional photogrammetry with new digital technologies. The process developed by Cooper (2000) involves gathering film stereo pairs in the field, followed by the scanning of the images and porting to a digital photogrammetric system for three-dimensional viewing, measuring and data extraction. The system allows one to zoom in on features for detailed data extraction, digitise and extract elements in three dimensions, produce very accurate elevation or contour models, and create sectionally rectified digital ortho-images (in which photographic distortion has been corrected).

Much the same has more recently been done by two other teams. Simpson et al. (2004) covered the rock area to be recorded with numerous self-adhesive dots as targets for a laser spotting device mounted in front of a digital camera. They produced a detailed three-dimensional rendition of the rock face they recorded, suitable for processing by a CAD program. The precision of the result depends on three factors: the density of targets across the rock surface, the quality of the lens and the resolution of the digital camera. Chandler et al. (2005) succeeded in eliminating the need to place targets with their entirely non-invasive method. They used two digital cameras to create pairs of photographs which, if calibrated, can produce accurate three-dimensional data of petroglyphs. To achieve this, fairly expensive photogrammetric software (such as Leica Photogrammetry System) is required to automatically acquire thousands of reference points on the rock surface. When combined with their ortho-photographs (produced digitally), these data can also be used to develop accurate Virtual Reality models. The fieldwork required for their system demands no experience with photogrammetry in most cases, and the field equipment is lightweight and cheap. Clearly, methodology is developing in this promising direction at present, and it is only to be hoped that the high cost of software can be reduced in the years to come.

In traditional photogrammetry the distance between the centre of the lens system and the film is invariant, i.e. the lens cannot be focused, but non-metric photogrammetry compensates for the distortions of the projection plane (the uneven rock panel) through calibration techniques (Ogleby 1995). Using the matrix of three-dimensional measurements obtained from computer-assisted photogrammetry, three-dimensional CAD files can then be created. The individual rock art motifs can be located on such digital surface models, but a difficulty in using *computer-aided design* programs is that they cannot deal with 'fuzzy' boundaries — as they are inevitably found on rock art motifs such as stencils and deteriorating paintings. However, with today's sophisticated proprietary software programs it is possible to treat images as texture maps, mapping them onto a CAD model of the site or rock panel. Images obtained with a video camera, a digital camera, or scanned from any other storage system can be digitised and subjected to image processing techniques (enhancement, colour calibration and others), and then transferred to the CAD workstation.

Ultimately the data so acquired can be used to create Virtual Reality models of rock art sites. Fundamental to such applications is the ability to view shapes, surfaces and textures from any perspective. Three-dimensional CAD programs now available commercially are capable of casting shadows, creating lighting directions and generating reflections, and of moving animated objects within their space. It is therefore now within the reach of the rock art recorder using this technology (which has been designed at great expense for other purposes, ranging from engineering applications to computer games) to produce Virtual Reality models that enable the viewer to 'walk through' a site. Once appropriately compressed, such data can be recorded effortlessly onto a CD with readily available technology.

Related to these methods is the use of global positioning systems (GPS) and geographical information systems (GIS). Depending on the precision of the equipment used, such instruments can be of help at various levels, ranging from locating a site geographically to precision geomatic applications (Mark and Billo 1999). With appropriate proprietary software and the use of electronic distance measuring devices, precision GPS offers the opportunity of simplifying site recording while at the same time increasing accuracy. This technology has so far not been widely applied in rock art recording, perhaps partly because the distance measuring devices available required the placing of physical targets for each measurement taken. But as target-less equipment becomes available, the opportunities of coupling these methods with CAD may render traditional photogrammetry obsolete in rock art recording work. Ultimately this will be decided by the way the technology is developed for other, commercially relevant applications.

PHOTOGRAPHY

The rendering of optical images on photosensitive surfaces, photography, is sometimes thought of as an objective means of depicting reality. This impression is perhaps attributable to the similarity of the photographic process with human vision itself: it duplicates to some extent what occurs in the eye. In both processes, selectively reflected light is collected by a focused lens and projected onto a surface of light-sensitive chemicals. Therefore photography results in a likeness of particular surface aspects resembling what human vision records of the same configuration of reflected light. The similarity between photographic image and visual perception is attributable to the similarity of two means of selectively processing information about surfaces in physical reality. Human neural reactions perceive visual information in this reality in a way similar to how the corresponding light patterns in the object world are recorded in a colour photograph. Nevertheless, photographs may still contain more information than can be detected by the human eye, as we have seen above. But being in tune with human vision does not mean that photography is objective.

This is not the place to offer basic information about how to photograph rock art, but there are some fundamental points that may profitably be made. Many rock art students have no access to most of the alternative recording methods listed in this chapter, and it needs to be emphasised that photography remains the most widely used and the most efficient method of rock art recording. Provided that it is colour calibrated it should retain this status for many years to come. A few basic observations need to be made here.

The quality of photographs depends significantly on lighting, of which three sources are generally used: solar radiation (direct or reflected), photographic flash or strobe, and movie lights. Irrespective of which of these provides the main source of lighting, its direction should generally not coincide with the focal axis of the camera, i.e. the light must come from a direction other than the camera position. Pictures taken with a camera-mounted flash inevitably lack depth. The use of portable reflectors is often an excellent means of illumination, but in the case of petroglyphs, particularly those of poor definition, photography by raking light remains the preferred choice. Except in caves and very dark rockshelters, the use of oblique artificial lighting demands night photography. A photographic flash can be operated either manually, or via a cable connected to the camera, or by a light sensor activated by another flash. Reflectors are generally used where the rock art is inadequately illuminated, but where direct sunlight is available nearby. Collapsible reflectors made of metallic fabric are ideal, and I have also used large mirrors with good results.

The most effective method of photographing rock art is with tungsten flood lights, because they can easily be moved until the best visual effect, the best balance between lit and unlit areas, is achieved. The procedure involves a team of two, one person monitoring the image at the camera and directing the other, who manoeuvres the light, varying distance, intensity, angle and direction as required. The high wattage of adequate lights renders a medium voltage power supply useful, but not necessary. I have since 1982 used a lead battery belt of the type TV reporters use, which facilitates photography (and filming) even in deep limestone caves and similarly inaccessible locations. Fully charged it powers a 250 Watt movie lamp for up to 15 to 20 minutes (depending on how much time the batteries are given to recover after each use). It is important to appreciate that these light sources generate considerable heat and must be kept an appropriate distance from the art surface.

Some recorders of rock art have experimented with a variety of special films and filters (e.g. narrow-band contrast filters), but recent technical developments seem to render some of this experimental work superseded. A new argument against the use of colour filters in rock art photography is that their products are less suitable for colour calibration treatment, and the novice would be well advised to aim for the best colour veracity possible, rather than experiment perhaps unnecessarily with filters. This does not extend, obviously, to filters used in monochrome photography, for instance the use of a blue filter to enhance orange-coloured paint residues, or red contrast filters to lighten red haematite pigment on a dark background. The use of infrared film needs to be mentioned, which Marshack (1975, 1986) and others have profitably turned to for enhancing near-invisible paint residues, or to distinguish between similarly coloured paints of different recipes. This can assist in separating superimposed paint applications, because infrared film treats red ochres as semi-transparent, detecting impurities rather than actual pigments. Because impurities are likely to differ among painting phases, the method often succeeds in separating motifs and in detecting the form of figures concealed by more recent paint application. Moreover, living organisms appear fluorescent when viewed under ultraviolet light, so where they are present in adequate concentrations they are rendered visible by the use of such light. This method has important applications in rock art conservation.

Of particular interest is a method described by Henderson (1995), who used polarised light to photograph rock art panels that are covered by silica skin, vandalised by surface scratching, or had simply faded. The objective is to separate surface reflectance (e.g. 'glare' from a silica skin or weathered paint residue) from internal backscattering so that the underlying diffuse reflections can be emphasised. The method has succeeded in improving the results of both colour and black-and-white photography. Electronic flashes as well as the camera itself are equipped with polarising filters which permit the passage of only those wavelengths of light that oscillate in a single plane. The primary surface reflection remains polarised in the same plane, and when it passes through a second filter (before entering the camera) that is rotated at 90°, the reflected light will be absorbed completely ('cross-polarised'). However, the diffused and backscattered component of the light, which reflects the partially masked pigment residues, becomes de-polarised and when it is reflected, part of it can pass through the second filter (Figure 34). Thus surface and interior reflections can be separated in this way. Even on well preserved paintings this method will improve visibility of the art by eliminating virtually all surface light reflection. Since it is not practical to attempt polarising sunlight, the method must use light sources whose radiation can be polarised, preferably two electronic strobes placed 30 to 40 degrees on either side of the camera position. The method results in considerably improved visibility of photographed pictograms, especially those covered by semitranslucent accretionary deposits.

In all of rock art photography, the overriding and most important rule is simply that no colour photograph, slide or film should be made without placing a calibrated standard scale into the frame. If it is considered to detract from the 'aesthetics' of the picture, it can be located at the very margin for later cropping. However, not including a colour standard is selfish and irresponsible. The preferred international size, colour and grey-scale standard is the IFRAO Standard Scale which is freely available to the world's rock art students.

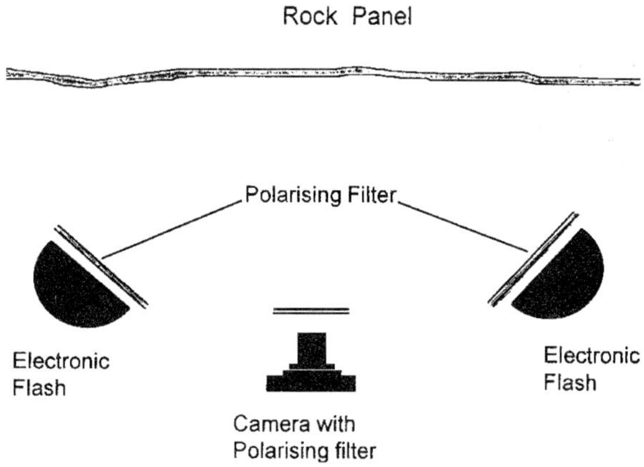

Figure 34. Positioning of equipment for cross-polarised photography. The polarising filters over each flash are rotated until their planes of polarisation are equal, and 90° opposite the axis of the filter on the camera (after J. W. Henderson).

FACSIMILES

The creation of physical rock art facsimiles could be regarded as the 'ultimate' method of recording rock art, and it is also the most time consuming. This is to be distinguished from taking casts or moulds from petroglyphs, such as plaster casts. Rock art facsimiles are nowadays made without any contact with the rock art, and their purpose is to produce a full-scale three-dimensional copy of the original rock panel, shelter or cave passage, in all details of shape, morphology, surface texture and colour. The quality of a rock art facsimile is measured by the closeness of its resemblance of the original. A facsimile may comprise just a small section of a panel, or it may involve a large part of a whole site.

The most celebrated rock art facsimile in the world is undoubtedly Lascaux 2, which is a partial copy of the famous cave of Lascaux in France. Created for the tourist industry when the significant deleterious effects of heavy human visitation on the limestone cave were recognised, it has been seen by millions of visitors, and its very significant original cost (several million dollars) was offset within a few years by the tourism trade it attracted. Lascaux 2 was constructed in a quarry near the site of the original cave (long closed to the public), and the standards set by this project remain the ideal. In this case there is no doubt that a replica has saved the original from slow destruction by algae, but there are other reasons for wanting to create rock art replicas. In particular, museums and exhibitions can in this way offer their visitors an experience that might otherwise involve travel to a very remote site, or that is not possible by other means because a site cannot be made available for public viewing. Numerous such situations exist but unfortunately the creation of good quality facsimiles of rock art is not only very expensive, it involves a great deal of expertise and the use of sophisticated equipment. Moreover, very few people worldwide possess the necessary experience and there is limited support for such work.

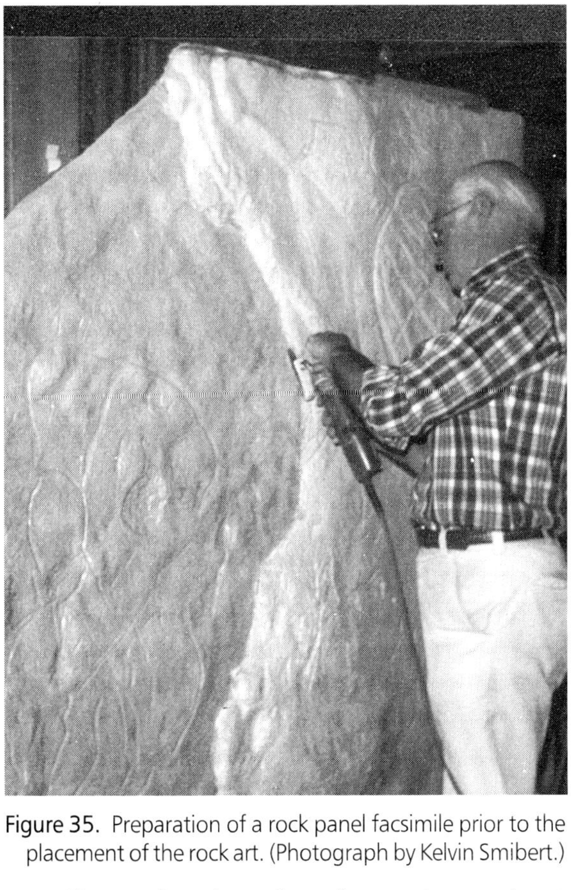

Figure 35. Preparation of a rock panel facsimile prior to the placement of the rock art. (Photograph by Kelvin Smibert.)

The preferred medium for modern rock art replicas is fibreglass, because of its excellent ratio of robustness versus lightness, its good workability, its resistance to various forms of deterioration, and the possibility of constructing panels in demountable sections. The work generally commences with a thorough photographic record of the panel to be replicated, and a three-dimensional survey of the support rock to establish its general shape. The latter is traditionally done either by photogrammetry or by using a precision theodolite, securing a vast number of dimensions, but obviously the same kinds of digitised systems described above can be used for acquiring these data more conveniently and perhaps more accurately. However, none of these methods lends itself to the cramped confines of some cave sites. In this environment Kelvin Smibert's method of scanning panels with a traversing laser system is much more accurate and the data obtained is directly and cheaply transferable to the construction phase. In the studio, construction begins with a frame on which these data are transformed into a likeness of the rock panel, first by creating the overall shape of the support, and then mapping on it the morphology, with all cracks, weathering features and so forth (Figure 35).

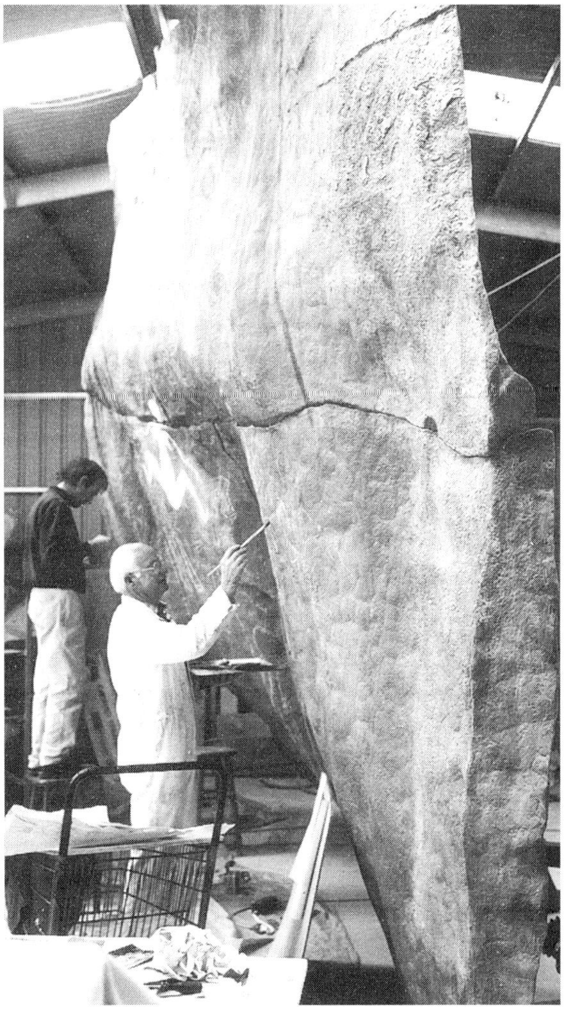

Figure 36. Re-creation of the rock art on a fibreglass facsimile of a rock art panel. (Photograph by Kelvin Smibert.)

This leads to replicating the finer details of surface textures, continually referring to the photographic record and re-visiting of the art site being copied for further checking of details. At this stage, experience becomes the crucial factor, because the re-creation of various types of rock surfaces involves considerable skill and artistic craft. For instance if the site being replicated is in a limestone cave, the panel is likely to show considerable variation in surface textures, attributable to various speleo-weathering patterns and to the great variability of travertine deposits, flowstone and stalagmitic formations. All of these many surface types can be replicated with great authenticity by a skilful craftsman, but only after years of training.

Finally the rock art is transferred from the record made of it, and again artistic competence is essential. There are various methods to do this effectively, for instance photographic images can be projected onto the panel to sketch in references, while the art work is carried out by methods rather similar to the way the original rock art was created (Figure 36). In the present context it is not relevant to examine the technical details of such work, which is clearly the preserve of specialists. Facsimiles are certainly a form of rock art record, but their making is not within the means of any but the most determined rock art recorders. There are simpler methods available to recreate less precise replicas, for instance a wall of my office bears a rendering of a petroglyph panel of two Thylacine images I discovered in the Australian Pilbara in 1968. It is made of cement render in the colour of the deeply patinated Pilbara rock, dark reddish-brown, so it does resemble texture and colour of the original rather well. I made this facsimile in 1972 by first placing a string grid over the wall, identical to the one I had used to record the figures, and then tracing the image as per my recording in the half-set coarse-grained cement render.

I emphasise that this is not a very precise facsimile. The best rock art facsimiles made in Australia are those of Kelvin Smibert of Mt Gambier, an artist who took an interest in the cave art I had discovered with my colleagues, Elfriede Bednarik and Geoffrey Aslin, in the general area around Mt Gambier (Bednarik 1990c). Smibert became interested in making facsimiles of cave petroglyph panels and I fostered his work with advice and encouragement for many years. He acquired a small factory to use as his studio, and after developing his skills he made and exhibited a good number of superb facsimiles of cave art as well as sandstone paintings. Among his painting replicas was one of the complete 25 square metres of the Anbangbang panel of Nourlangie Rock, Kakadu National Park, Australia. This commission is on permanent display at the Indira Gandhi National Centre for the Arts section for world rock art in New Delhi. Although he managed to secure some minor commissions since, his outstanding proficiency has not raised the interest it deserves.

CONCLUDING REMARKS

The records of rock art we produce collectively need to be stored in some form, and there have been a number of initiatives to house them. Naturally these records take many forms, ranging from CDs to serigraphs, from vast slide collections to kilometres of Mylar sheets or full facsimiles measuring many metres. They include relevant documentation and bibliographies, maps, films, videotapes, even audiotapes of interviews (for instance of traditional site custodians). Some of the world's rock art archives can be regarded as public collections, some are perhaps of a semi-public nature, while others are privately owned. Once in a while there is a call for a world archive of rock art in one continent or another, but the experiences with these initiatives are far from encouraging, nor is there any tangible evidence that such an institution would benefit the world discipline of rock art studies. It can easily be argued that a world centre would merely amass material, foster favouritism and create career opportunities. The initiatives in this respect we have seen so far have not succeeded in securing wide support, and the principal reason for this is that most students of rock art are individualistic, they tend to be sceptical of authority and power structures. Moreover, there is the important question of ownership of the rock art, even of copyright. In the case of Australia, all pre-Historic rock art was made by the Aboriginal people, whose descendants have inherited the cultural tradition in the full sense of the word, and who through their present-day custodians continue to hold 'copyright' in perpetuity. Also, we must not forget that a great deal of rock art is of a secret or sacred nature, and is not available for all to see. These kinds of limitations are not restricted to Australia, they exist in many other parts of the world, where they are being ignored to varying degrees. The conditions under which rock art is recorded thus differ from one world region to another, and a rock art archive in Capo di Ponte or at UCLA is not necessarily able to take all the relevant factors into account. It seems that non-centralised collections of rock art records are here to stay.

Nevertheless, it is also correct that in some respects, a degree of globalisation would be of benefit, although not at the level occasionally suggested in this context. The sort of preoccupations of many people calling for world rock art archives, such as comparing rock art motifs from Timbuktu with those from Newfoundland, is practically worthless and tends to lead to papers that are best left unpublished. International co-operation is important, specifically in conservation, site management, methodology and terminology. But experience so far suggests that these common goals are best served by an international structure that seeks no influence or control, but exists purely for altruistic purposes, such as IFRAO. Most importantly, IFRAO emphasises regionalisation in rock art research, and autonomy of its member organisations around the world. Thus the most promising way of creating an effective archival global network for rock art is through IFRAO: a non-formal affiliation of archival centres wherever they exist. Such a system will be criticised by those seeking a centralised system that can be taken over and controlled, but in this field it will, I believe, prevail. It is interesting to note that, in Australia, the largest archive of rock art is privately owned by one person (Takarakka Rock Art Centre, owned by Grahame Walsh), and the second-largest is the archive of a scholarly society, the Australian Rock Art Research Association. There are arguments both for and against such systems, but in the final analysis naturally evolving storage systems do work, enforced systems do not. People who favour centralised or at least state-owned archives need to be reminded that there is no tangible evidence that such agencies, where they exist, have resulted in better quality research. Rather they tend to stifle initiative and assist in the creation of academic technocracies.

This chapter should not be closed without some comment on the nexus between the recording of rock art and issues of conservation. Rock art exists today because it has managed to survive, and unless its preservation is threatened by new hazards it should in most cases survive the records we make of it. The greatest conservation threat to rock art comes from humans, and that certainly includes rock art students, especially through their misguided recording work. Often rock art has suffered degradation in the course of recording projects that were unnecessary duplications of previous work, or that yielded no useful records because they were inadequately conceived or executed, or records were never published or archived, and are thus of no use to the discipline. It should not need to be emphasised that the destruction of rock art and its fabric or research potential is never justified, but if it occurs in the course of ill-conceived and inconsequential activities then it is doubly regrettable.

There is one simple rule that governs all rock art recording work: the rock art records we produce are inadequate, provisional, deficient and mediocre. There are no exceptions. Whatever we do, however we acquire our records, we have no right to prejudice the work of generations of future researchers. We have a profound responsibility not to diminish the research potential of the rock art and its fabric, and unless we can predict what methods these future generations will bring to the task of conducting rock art science, we simply lack any justification for making contact with rock art in the course of our certainly primitive recording endeavours. I have no idea what methods rock art scientists of the 22nd or 23rd centuries will use. I venture to say that nobody else does either.

REFERENCES

AUJOULAT, N. 1987. *Le relevé des oeuvres parietales paléolithiques, enregistrement et traitement des donnes*. Documents d'Archelogie Française 9, Éditions de la Maison des Sciences de l'Homme, Paris.

BAHN, P. G., R. G. BEDNARIK and J. STEINBRING 1995. The Peterborough Petroglyph Site: reflections on massive intervention in rock art. *Rock Art Research* 12: 29–41.

BEDNARIK, R. G. 1979. The potential of rock patination analysis in Australian archaeology – part 1. *The Artefact* 4: 14–38

BEDNARIK, R. G. 1980. The potential of rock patination analysis in Australian archaeology – part 2. *The Artefact* 5: 47–77.

BEDNARIK, R. G. 1981. Finger lines, their medium, and their dating. Unpubl. MS, 34 pp., Archive of the Australian Rock Art Research Association, Melbourne.

BEDNARIK, R. G. 1984a. Die Bedeutung der paläolithischen Fingerlinientradition. *Anthropologie* 23: 73–79.

BEDNARIK, R. G. 1984b. Comment on L. L. Dickman, 'An image digitising and storage system for use in rock art research'. *Rock Art Research* 1: 33–34.

BEDNARIK, R. G. 1985. Parietal finger markings in Australia. *Bollettino del Centro Camuno di Studi Preistorici* 22: 83–88.

BEDNARIK, R. G. 1987a. The chalking of petroglyphs: a response. *La Pintura* 15(2+3): 12–13.

BEDNARIK, R. G. 1987b. No pictographs at end of Rochester Creek rainbow. *La Pintura* 15(2+3): 14–18.

BEDNARIK, R. G. 1988. Comment on D. Mania and U. Mania, 'Deliberate engravings on bone artefacts of *Homo erectus*'. *Rock Art Research* 5: 96–100.

BEDNARIK, R. G. 1990a. Sobre la practica de tizar los petroglifos. *SIARB Boletín* 4: 24–26.

BEDNARIK, R. G. 1990b. Petroglyph moulds and ethical standards. *Archaeology in New Zealand* 33: 209–13.

BEDNARIK, R. G. 1990c. The cave petroglyphs of Australia. *Australian Aboriginal Studies* 1990(2): 64–68.

BEDNARIK, R. G. 1991. The IFRAO Standard Scale. *Rock Art Research* 8: 78–80.

BEDNARIK, R. G. 1992. A new method to date petroglyphs. *Archaeometry* 34: 279–91.

BEDNARIK, R. G. 1993. Meaning of 'vulva' symbols established. *AURA Newsletter* 10(1): 4–5.

BEDNARIK, R. G. 1994a. A taphonomy of palaeoart. *Antiquity* 68: 68–74.

BEDNARIK, R. G. 1994b. No sex, please, we're gliders! *AURA Newsletter* 11(1): 1–2.

BEDNARIK, R. G. 1994c. Introducing the IFRAO Standard Scale. *Rock Art Research* 11: 74–5.

BEDNARIK, R. G. 1994d. Colour re-constitution achieved! Historical breakthrough in rock art research. *Rock Art Research* 11: 150.

BEDNARIK, R. G. 1994e. The discrimination of rock markings. *Rock Art Research* 11: 23–44.

BEDNARIK, R. G. 1995a. The age of the Côa valley petroglyphs in Portugal. *Rock Art Research* 12: 86–103.

BEDNARIK, R. G. 1995b. Computer colour re-constitution of rock art imagery. *Pictogram* 8(1): 24–28.

BEDNARIK, R. G. 1995c. Perpetual digital preservation of rock art imagery. *International Newsletter on Rock Art* 12: 25–27.

BEDNARIK, R. G. 1997. Microerosion analysis of petroglyphs in Valtellina, Italy. *Origini* 21: 7–22.

BEDNARIK, R. G. 1999. The speleothem medium of finger flutings and its isotopic geochemistry. *The Artefact* 22: 49–64.

BEDNARIK, R. G. 2002. About the age of Pilbara rock art. *Anthropos* 97(1): 201–15.

BEDNARIK, R. G. and K. SESHADRI 1995. Digital colour re-constitution in rock art photography. *Rock Art Research* 12: 42-51.

BERTANI, D., A. CAPANNI, M. CETICA, L. PEZZATI and C. PAGLIARI 1997. Digitised recording of petroglyphs in Poesia Cave, Italy. *Rock Art Research* 14: 137–42.

BOCK, A. J. 1981. To chalk ... or not to chalk ... response. *La Pintura* 7(4): 13–14, 17.

BRADY, L. M., B. DAVID, L. MANAS, THE MUALGAL CORPORATION and I. McNIVEN 2004. Rock paintings of Mua Island: initial results from western Torres Strait. *Rock Art Research* 21: 27–46.

BROWN, L. G. 1992. A survey of image registration techniques. *ACM Computing Surveys* 24: 4.

CAMPBELL, J. B. 2000. The Chillagoe and Laura laser-AMS dating project. In G. K. Ward and C. Tuniz (eds), *Advances in dating Australian rock-markings*, pp. 80–83. Occasional AURA Publication 10, Australian Rock Art Research Association, Melbourne.

ČERNOHOUZ, J. and I. SOLČ 1966. Use of sandstone wanes and weathered basaltic crust in absolute chronology. *Nature* 212: 806–7.

CHAFFEE, S. C., M. HYMAN and M. ROWE 1993. AMS ^{14}C dating of rock paintings. In J. Steinbring and A. Watchman (eds), *Time and space: dating and spatial considerations in rock art research*, pp. 67–73. Occasional AURA Publication 8, Australian Rock Art Research Association, Melbourne.

CHANDLER, J. H., J. G. FRYER and H. T. KNIEST 2005. Non-invasive recording of Aboriginal rock art using cost-effective digital photogrammetry. *Rock Art Research* 22.

CHOU, L., R. M. GARRELS and R. WOLLAST 1989. Comparative study of the kinetics and mechanisms of dissolution of carbonate minerals. *Chemistry and Geology* 78: 269–82.

CLEGG, J. 1978. Simple field techniques for recording engravings by casting and stereophotography. In C. Pearson (ed.), *Conservation of rock art*, pp. 22–26. Institute for the Conservation of Cultural Material, Sydney.

CLOGG, P., M. DIAZ-ANDREU and B. LARKMAN 2000. Digital image processing and the recording of rock art. *Journal of Archaeological Science* 27: 837–43.

COLMAN, S. M. and K. L. PIERCE 1981. *Weathering rinds on andesitic and basaltic stones as a Quaternary age indicator, western United States.* U.S. Geological Survey, Professional Paper 1210.

COOPER, E. S. 2000. Technological advances in rock art recording. *ESRARA Newsletter* 5(4): 15.

DELLUC, B., G. DELLUC, M. LEJEUNE and F. SOLEIL-HAVOUP 1986. Lecture analytique des supports rocheux et relevé synthétique. *L'Anthropologie* 90: 801–4.

DEL MONTE, M. and S. SABBIONI 1987. A study of the patina called 'scialbatura' on Imperial Roman marbles. *Studies in Conservation* 32: 114–21.

D'ERRICO, F. 1988. Lecture technologique de l'art mobilier grave nouvelles méthodes et premiers résultats sur les galets graves de Rochedane. *L'Anthropologie* 92: 101–22.

D'ERRICO, F. 1989. Palaeolithic lunar calendars: A case of wishful thinking? *Current Anthropology* 30: 117–18.

D'ERRICO, F. 1991. Microscopic and statistical criteria for the identification of prehistoric systems of notation. *Rock Art Research* 8: 83–93.

D'ERRICO, F. 1996. Image analysis and 3-D optical surface profiling of Upper Palaeolithic mobiliary art. *Microscopy and Analysis* 1996(1): 27–29.

DICKMAN, J. L. 1984. An image digitising and storage system for use in rock art research. *Rock Art Research* 1: 25–35.

DORN, R. I. 1990. Rock varnish dating of rock art: state of the art perspective. *La Pintura* 17(2): 1–2, 9–11.

ENGEL, C. E. and R. P. SHARP 1958. Chemical data on desert varnish. *Bulletin of the Geological Society of America* 69: 487–518.

FRANCIS, J., L. L. LOENDORF and R. I. DORN 1993. AMS radiocarbon and cation-ratio dating of rock art in the Bighorn Basin of Wyoming and Montana. *American Antiquity* 58: 711–37.

GENGE, P. 1990. Bravo Bednarik. *Pictogram* 3(2): 18.

GOODWIN, A. J. H. 1960. Chemical alteration (patination) of stone. In R. F. Heizer and S. F. Cook (eds), *The application of quantitative methods in archaeology*, pp. 300–312. Viking Fund Publications in Anthropology 28, New York.

HENDERSON, J. W. 1995. An improved procedure for the photographic enhancement of rock paintings. *Rock Art Research* 12: 75–85.

HYMAN, M., S. A. TURPIN and M. E. ZOLENSKY 1996. Pigment analyses from Panther Cave, Texas. *Rock Art Research* 13: 93–103.

KIRSCH, R. A. and J. L. KIRSCH 1996. New ways of viewing petroglyphs with computers. Paper presented at the SARARA Conference, Swakopmund, Namibia, August 1996.

KITZLER, L. 2000. Surface structure analysis of runic inscriptions on rock. A method for distinguishing between individual carvers. *Rock Art Research* 17: 85–98.

LAZZARINI, L. and O. SALVADORI 1989. A reassessment of the formation of the patina called *scialbatura*. *Studies in Conservation* 34: 20–26.

LEEN, D. 1981. To chalk or not to chalk. *La Pintura* 8 (3): 11.

LOENDORF, L. 1989. Nine rock art sites in the Piñon Canyon Maneuver Site, southeastern Colorado. Unpubl. report No. 248, to the National Parks Service, Rocky Mountain Regional Office, Denver, reference contract No. 110 1200-7-B061.

LOENDORF, L. 2001. Rock art recording. In D. S. Whitley (ed.), *Handbook of rock art research*, pp. 55–79. AltaMira Press, Walnut Creek, California.

LÖFVENDAHL, R. and J. MAGNUSSON 2000. Research and development — degradation and care. In K. Kallhovd and J. Magnusson (eds), *Rock carvings in the borderlands*, 47–72. INTERRED IIA Project, Bohuslän / Dalsland and Østfold.

McNIVEN, I. J., B. DAVID and L. BRADY 2002. Torres Strait rock art; and enhanced perspective. *Antiquity* 74: 759–60.

MANIA, D. and U. MANIA 1988. Deliberate engravings on bone artefacts of *Homo erectus*. *Rock Art Research* 5: 91–107.

MARK, R. and E. BILLO 1999. A stitch in time: digital panoramas and mosaics. *American Indian Rock Art* 25: 155–68.

MARK, R, and E. BILLO 2002. Application of digital image enhancement in rock art recording. American Indian Rock Art 28: 121–28.

MARK, R. and E. NEWMAN (BILLO) 1995. IFRAO calibration system as a plug-in. *Rock Art Research* 12: 129.

MARSHACK, A. 1975. Exploring the mind of Ice Age man. *National Geographic* January 1975: 65–89.

MARSHACK, A. 1986. Reply to Comments on A. Marshack, 'Theoretical concepts that lead to new analytic methods, modes of enquiry and classes of data'. *Rock Art Research* 3: 67–82.

MAWK, E. J., M. F. NOBBS and M. W. ROWE 1996. Analysis of white pigments from the Olary region, South Australia. *Rock Art Research* 13: 31–37.

MAWK, E. J. and M. W. ROWE 1998. Effect of water on Lower Pecos River rock paintings in Texas. *Rock Art Research* 15: 12–16.

MIRMEHDI, CHALMERS, BARHAM and GRIFFITH n.d. Automated analysis of environmental degradation of mineral pigments. MS in AURA Archive.

MITHEN, S. (ed.) 1998. *Creativity in human evolution and prehistory*. Routledge, New York.

OGLEBY, C. L. 1995. Digital technology in the documentation and management of rock art. In A. Thorn and J. Brunet (eds), *Preservation of rock art*, pp. 80-87. Occasional AURA Publication 9, Australian Rock Art Research Association, Melbourne.

OGLEBY, C. L. and L. J. RIVETT 1985. *Handbook of heritage photogrammetry*. Australian Government Publishing Service, Canberra.

RIMSTIDT, J. D. and H. L. BARNES 1980. The kinetics of silica-water reactions. *Geochimica et Cosmochimica Acta* 44: 1683–99.

RIP, M. R. 1983. Digital recording and image processing of rock art by computer. *South African Archaeological Bulletin* 38: 77–79.

RIP, M. R. 1989. Colour space transformations for the enhancement of rock art images by computer. *Rock Art Research* 6: 12–16.

RIVETT, L. 1977. *The application of photogrammetry to the recording of monuments and sites in Australia*. Bulletin No. 42, Department of Surveying, University of Melbourne.

RIVETT, L. 1978. Photogrammetry — its potential application to problems in Australian archaeology. In C. Pearson (ed.), *Conservation of rock art*, pp. 15–21. Institute for the Conservation of Cultural Material, Sydney.

RIVETT, L. 1983. The application of photogrammetry to the recording of rock art and archaeological sites in Kakadu National Park. In D. Gillespie (ed.), *Rock art sites of Kakadu National Park*, pp. 87–126. Australian National Parks and Wildlife Service, Canberra.

ROSENFELD, A. 1984. Review of *Rock Art Research*, Volume 1, Number 1. *Australian Archaeology* 19: 118–19.

SCHEFFER, F., B. MEYER and E. KALK 1963. Biologische Ursachen der Wüstenlackbildung. *Zeitschrift für Geomorphologie* 7: 112–19.

SIMPSON, A., P. CLOGG, M. DÍAZ-ANDREU and B. LARKMAN 2004. Towards three-dimensional non-invasive recording of incised rock art. *Antiquity* 78: 692–98.

SOLEILHAVOUP, F. 1985. Les paysages de l'art rupestre de plein air: vers une normalisation des méthodes d'étude et de conservation. *Rock Art Research* 2: 119–39.

SOLEILHAVOUP, F. 1986. Conventions de relevé analy-tique des surfaces rocheuses décorées par l'homme préhistorique. *Société Historique et Archéologique du Périgord* 113: 17–22.

SOLEILHAVOUP, F. 1994. Illusions et pertinences d'une approche sémiologique de l'art rupestre en plein air. *Musées / Homme* 4 (Jan.-March): 42–46.

STEGUWEIT, L. 1999. Intentionelle Schnittmarken auf Tierknochen von Bilzingsleben — Neue lasermikroskopische Untersuchungen. *Praehistoria Thuringica* 3: 64–79.

SWARTZ, B. K. 1991. Archival storage, digital enhancement and global transmission of rock art photographs: a practicable design from existing technology. In C. Pearson and B. K. Swartz (eds), *Rock art and posterity: conserving, managing and recording rock art*, pp. 119–120. Occasional AURA Publication 4, Australian Rock Art Research Association, Melbourne.

TAYLOR, J. M., W. BOKMAN and I. N. M. WAINWRIGHT 1979. Rock art conservation: some realities and practical considerations. In D. Lundy (ed.), *CRARA '77. Papers from the Fourth Biennial Conference of the Canadian Rock Art Research Associates*, pp. 293–323. Heritage Record 8, The British Columbia Provincial Museum, Victoria.

TRENDALL, A. F. 1964. Examination of rocks with Aboriginal engravings. In W. D. L. Ride and A. Neumann (eds), *Depuch Island*, pp. 83–88. Special Publication 2, Western Australian Museum, Perth.

TURPIN, S. A. 1979. Stereophotogrammetric documentation of exposed archaeological features. *Journal of Field Archaeology* 6: 329–37.

URBANI, F. 1998. A multivariate approach to characterise the groove shape of the linear parts of petroglyphs. *Rock Art Research* 15: 41–45.

URBANI, B. and F. URBANI 2001. The geoglyph of La Rueda del Indio, Chirgua, Venezuela. *Rock Art Research* 18: 33–39.

WALTHER, J. 1981. Die Denudation der Wüste. *Abhandlungen Mathematisch-Physikalischer Klasse der Königlichen Sächsischen Gesellschaft der Wissenschaften* 16: 112–42.

WATCHMAN, A. 1990. A summary of occurrences of oxalate-rich crusts in Australia. *Rock Art Research* 7: 44–50.

WATCHMAN, A. 1992. Composition, formation and age of some Australian silica skins. *Australian Aboriginal Studies* 1992(1): 61–66.

WATCHMAN, A. 1996. A review of the theory and assumptions in the AMS dating of the Foz Côa petroglyphs, Portugal. *Rock Art Research* 13: 21–30.

WATCHMAN, A. 2000. Micro-excavation and laser extraction methods for dating carbon in silica skins and oxalate crusts. In G. K. Ward and C. Tuniz (eds), *Advances in dating Australian rock-markings*, pp. 35–39. Occasional AURA Publication 10, Australian Rock Art Research Association, Melbourne.

WATCHMAN, A. L., G. L. WALSH, M. J. MORWOOD and C. TUNIZ 1997. AMS radiocarbon age estimates for early rock paintings in the Kimberley, N.W. Australia: preliminary results. *Rock Art Research* 14: 18–26.

6. The conservation of rock art

Introduction

Rock art is the principal research resource we have in palaeoart studies, the discipline whose ultimate scientific agenda it is to determine the origins of human constructs of reality. Consequently rock art is among the most important scientific evidence available to the species we call *Homo sapiens sapiens*: it would appear to be the major component of the corpus of evidence available to us to consider how that species constructed the conceptual artefact we consider to be the world we exist in. It is therefore reasonable to demand that the preservation and curation of this irreplaceable resource be afforded considerably more priority than has been given to it so far. Humanity lavishes billions of dollars annually on its art objects, its art repositories and its art industry. Yet from a scientific perspective the arts of historical periods are of almost trivial significance, at least in comparison to the arts externalising 'alternative' ontologies or metaphysical constructs.

Humanity's efforts in preventing the destruction of the immensely valuable and clearly irreplaceable resource of rock art remain minuscule (Swartz 1981). Loubser (2001: 82-3) points out that the very concern with preserving 'non-renewable cultural resources' is a relatively recent result of the expansionist milieu of the 20th century. In the case of rock art, this concern is largely a result of the formation of rock art organisations in most parts of the world over the last few decades. There is a distinct correlation between those parts of the world where such rock art organisations are most active and outspoken, and the geographical areas where government agencies and archaeologists have become most sensitive to concerns about rock art. In the not-so-distant past, government agencies in most parts of the world were quite aloof from these concerns. The present state is one of transition. While in some countries it has become standard procedure to, for instance, conceal rock art under protective covering while excavating sediments below it (Morwood 1994), in a few other countries archaeologists in charge of major rock art corpora continue to blatantly vandalise rock art. When challenged they defend their actions (Jaffe 1996; Swartz 1997a, 1997b), or they are themselves implicated in the destruction of rock art (Arcà et al. 2001). In such a transitional stage it may be useful to consider the currents that contribute to the changes, and to review the direction of the discipline from that perspective. This might give us an idea of the direction in which we are heading.

Sometimes visitors, or readers of books on rock art, are surprised to see how well preserved Australian rock art is, and they often assume this is because the traditions are recent. This is only partly true, more Australian than any other rock art is in fact of the Pleistocene. The reasons for its unusually good state of preservation are favourable environmental conditions (climatic, geological and morphological), a considerable geographical remoteness of much of the art, a lack of iconoclastic traditions, and a system of protection that is the envy of much of the world. The kinds of practices of some European connoisseurs of rock art, such as physical recording practices, would attract fines ranging from $5000 to $50 000 in Australia, depending on where the offence occurs and on other factors. The vandalistic practices of rock art recorders in some other regions — which include the application of various substances to petroglyphs, the wetting of paintings, and the production of rubbings and casts — have all been phased out in Australia for many years, if indeed they were ever introduced (Bednarik 1990a).

In the state of Western Australia it is even an offence to take a photograph of rock art for publication purposes without permission from the Traditional Custodians. It must be remembered that the rock art of Australia remains the cultural property of the Aboriginal people. Moreover, many rock art sites are sacred and may not be entered by uninitiated people, or by anyone other than initiated males or females, as the case may be. Consequently many of the most spectacular rock art sites or images of Australia have never been published — and will not be published. All information about them is of restricted access, and is not available at all outside of Australia.

In other cases, sites that are particularly sensitive to damage by human visitors (especially deep limestone caves with petroglyphs) are protected by a system of complete confidentiality about their locations (Bednarik 1990b). Indeed, the locations of some of the best cave art sites in the world are only known to two or three researchers, and their descriptions are published without providing any information about the site's location. After all, for a site to be scientifically useful, the exact location does not need to be available to other scholars. It is usually adequate to name the district or the general setting for such purposes. There is now a trend in rock art publishing not to reveal exact locations in print. Where well-known sites are involved, even their names are suppressed. There are several reasons for this emerging policy:

1. It keeps casual visitors and sightseers away, especially after reports have appeared in the printed or electronic mass media;
2. Scholarly publications are accessible to the public, and any determined person can search out the appropriate literature;
3. All rock art sites are regarded as the cultural property of the Aboriginal people, and researchers have no right to reveal the locations of these sites;
4. It is fundamentally wrong to assume that a site is 'safe' if it is accessible only to scholars. The most pernicious damage to rock art sites is often not that caused by tourists, site vandals, local villagers or children, as is so often claimed. It is by the researchers themselves (Bednarik 1990a, 1990c, 1990d, 1991a).

In general, it is agreed that conservation threats to rock art sites can be divided into two basic types: those that are attributable to human interference of some type, and those of natural deterioration. In practice, however, the two cannot always be separated effectively: a factor of natural deterioration may be indirectly attributable to human modification of the environment. Sometimes the connection may be very obscure, if indeed it can be determined. For instance, ecological imbalances introduced by humans are frequently responsible for new conservation threats. Experience shows that it is judicious to first look for a humanly introduced cause in most instances of rock art deterioration.

This should have been obvious from logic. Most rock art is of a considerable age, and to exist today it must have survived many threats. The older the art, the more potential threats it must have survived, and the higher the expectation that it will survive longer still (Bednarik 1990e). This is because the older art has attained a condition of near equilibrium with its natural environment, which can be threatened only by major environmental changes, or by human intervention. I have shown that therefore the oldest art is proportionally at a greater risk from human interference (Bednarik 1990e).

It follows from this that, as one evaluates the natural conservation threats to a site, one should pay special attention to any possible factors that may appear to be natural deterioration, but are in fact attributable to human agency, however indirectly. For instance, increasing acidity of rainwater (Laver and Wainwright 1995) is attributable to industrialisation. The lowering of ambient environmental pH leads to the erosion of rock varnish deposits formed over petroglyphs. The latter have so far often only survived under a protective varnish layer, and once this is lost the art cannot be expected to survive for much longer. The hydrology of a site may have been changed by human interference, now threatening an art that had managed to survive for a long time. Or morphological modifications of a site have affected its microclimatic regime, resulting in significantly differing environmental conditions which the art has not before experienced, and which pose a serious threat to it. An example is the deforestation that threatens many art sites in India. The removal of trees eliminates a protective shelter, exposes the site to rain, sun and aeolian erosion. At the same time it forces wild bees, which usually construct their hives in hollow trees, to occupy rockshelters instead, thereby damaging art (Tyagi 1991). In Australia it was found that damage by mud-daubing wasps subsided after the eradication of feral buffaloes. The disappearance of the buffalo wallows corrected an environmental imbalance and eliminated the supply of mud (Bednarik 1989). In short, there are many possible threats to rock art by what appear to be natural factors, but which are in reality humanly prompted changes. This is not to suggest that purely natural processes do not present conservation threats, only to say that the incidence of such threats is perhaps significantly smaller than sometimes intimated by commentators.

NATURAL DETERIORATION OF ROCK ART

The natural environment in which the art has managed to survive is essentially determined by climate, hydrology, geochemistry, geomorphology, and sometimes by geophysical and biospheric agents. In practice their effects cannot be readily separated; rather, issues of rock art conservation are governed by a delicate and complex interplay of many factors in practically every case. Nevertheless, to begin unravelling them and their effects it is essential to consider them separately.

Moisture

Arguably the most influential weathering factor is moisture, which occurs at rock art sites in various forms: as phreatic reservoirs (exposed aquifers, especially in limestone caves), as moving or stationery surface deposits (lakes, rivers, waterholes), as concealed aquifers, as surface run-off, as atmospheric precipitation, as gravitational water percolating through a rock mass, as capillary moisture rising in a porous rock mass, as condensation surface deposit, bound within the crystal structure of component minerals, as interstitial moisture in equilibrium with relative atmospheric humidity, and in the form of air humidity. The interdependence of many of these forms of moisture (e.g. capillary water requires a source such as an aquifer or episodic supply) is crucial in understanding the hydrological regime of a site, which in turn is essential in any remedial work.

There are several deleterious effects caused by most forms of water occurring at a site, while at the same time the presence of *some* moisture may be essential for preservation. Water travelling within the rock, be it gravitational or capillary, generally acquires solutes (numerous cations are candidates, but chlorides and carbonates are among the most readily soluble in most cases), especially because the pressure within a rock mass is significantly greater than atmospheric pressure (it can be hundreds of times greater). Pressure is one of the most important variables determining solubility, the others being temperature, kinetic turbulence, pH and presence of corrosive compounds. This means that when such vadose water re-emerges on a surface, where its pressure suddenly reverts to atmospheric conditions, most of its solute has to be precipitated. Stalactites, for instance, are formed by this process, as are numerous other forms of deposits found at rock art sites.

Weathering zones on rock are primarily the result of solution, hydration, hydrolysis, ion exchange, chelation, oxidation and reduction, leading to the selective removal of mineral mass. Moisture is thus heavily implicated in rock weathering, but as a cause of weathering zones it is usually most effective as direct precipitation. There are exceptions, however, particularly in the case of sandstones, where granular exfoliation of sheltered areas can greatly exceed the effects of weathering processes on surfaces fully exposed to precipitation. Only modest quantities of moisture are involved here, which are sufficient to gradually dissolve the carbonate or silica cement, and which are assisted by the formation of salts that wedge individual grains loose as they expand.

This leads to the next form of moisture-induced rock deterioration commonly seen at rock art sites, called *Salzsprengung* or salt-wedging. Typically, a zone of salt deposition (called 'subflorescence') develops some 5–15 mm beneath and parallel to the surface of a wall, corresponding to the frequent penetration zone of moisture or the extent of a surface zone that is accessible to periodic flushing or drying. The salt might be gypsum, anhydrite, a chloride, nitrate etc., and it has a tendency to increase its bulk, particularly with repeated wetting and drying cycles. This leads to the formation of a surface layer of rock that first becomes 'drummy', then lifts visibly and eventually exfoliates as spalls of a thickness corresponding to the alteration zone of the rock fabric. It is in fact this very process that is often the prime cause of the formation of the sandstone shelters of the former Gondwana facies, which I have studied in southern Africa, India, north eastern Brazil and northern Australia; in all these regions they are extremely rich in rock paintings. Because the results of laminar exfoliation of this type, rockshelters, are the most favoured site type for the production especially of pictograms, such exfoliation is one of the most destructive processes affecting rock art.

Another process causing shattering of rock is attributable to the formation of ice, or to *freeze-and-thaw cycles*. Liquid water is virtually incompressible, having its greatest density at +4°C; frozen, it expands by 1/11th of its volume. However, crystallisation of water as such does not cause fracturing of rocks, it can only exacerbate already existing cracking by penetrating fissures. In cracks that are less than a few tenth of a millimetre wide, even temperatures as low as -20°C will not induce water to relinquish its liquid state (Bednarik 1979: 16). On the other hand if openings exceed a few millimetres, congelifraction is not effective because the expansion of water through crystallisation will merely force water out. Rock fatigue due to freeze-and-thaw cycles is perhaps attributable to either the compression of air sealed off in voids by the developing ice (Tricart 1969) or to regelation (Schmid 1958). Be that as it may, the extremely high content of cryoclastics in stadial, entrance-near deposits in caves shows tellingly how effective congelifraction is on at least some rock types. Porous rocks (limestone and dolomite, for instance) are subjected to severe fracturing (Bednarik 1970), as are schists because of their laminate structure inviting penetration by gravitational water. I have suggested that the principal reason for the absence of Pleistocene cave art in central Europe is that the caves there, in contrast to south-western Europe with its more temperate climate, were subjected to extensive congelifraction during the final Würm stadial (Bednarik 1994a). Indeed, Palaeolithic rock art claimed to have been found in central Europe was reported from exfoliated clasts in German caves, having been destroyed by freezing and/or regelation (Hahn 1990; Conard and Uerpmann 2000). While this seemed to confirm my view, my subsequent investigation unfortunately resulted in the refutation of all claims made about German Pleistocene rock art (Bednarik 2002a).

Condensation water forms in caves and rockshelters when the relative air humidity is high and the ambient air temperature is greater than the rock face temperature. The dew point is the temperature at which air becomes saturated and dew is precipitated. Limestone caves frequently have a relative air humidity of 95% to 99%, yet condensation is not necessarily common in caves, particularly those where the speleoclimate is almost entirely independent of the atmospheric climate. Nor is the water, which condenses in distilled form, capable of dissolving the limestone in the absence of carbon dioxide. In a deep cave system, air temperature is buffered by rock temperature and therefore very stable. There is practically no convective temperature exchange in caves of a high air residence rate, and the temperature differences necessary to induce condensation do not exist. Condensation is more likely to appear near the entrance of a cave, or in rockshelters. It forms as water beads or as a film that can not only cause significant damage to paint residues (paints were often based on water as the solvent), it tends to attract cryptogamic growth within the reach of light (artificial or natural), and it can deposit a variety of dissolved salts. In the case of carbonate rock, such surface water deposits can even form carbonic acid in the presence of carbon dioxide, and convert the rock to water-soluble and mobile bicarbonate.

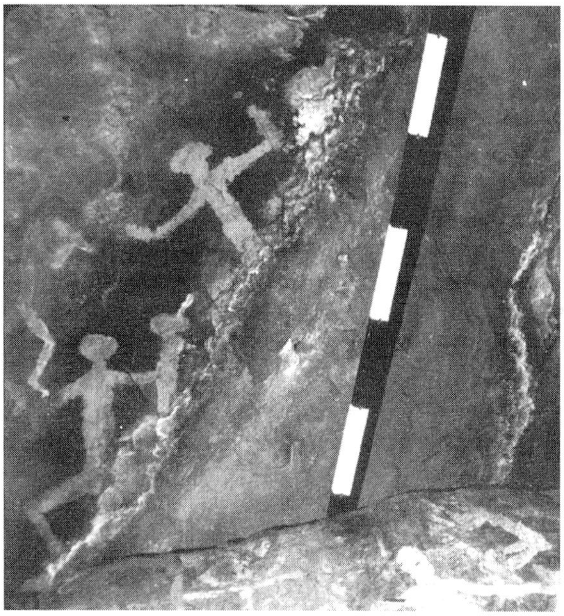

Figure 37. Destruction of pictograms by run-off water in sandstone shelter, Mt Grenfell, N.S.W., Australia.

Surface run-off is another factor frequently implicated in the destruction of rock art (Figure 37). On pictograms it can be highly effective, removing unconsolidated pigments rapidly. Where it occurs regularly, the establishment of mosses, fungi and lichens may be an unfavourable result. Mineral accretions, including ferromanganous crusts, may be deposited from solute-rich solutions. Rainwater is never pure water; it acquires numerous ions already before it reaches the ground, many of which assist it in converting or dissolving minerals. There is a distinct tendency for such inclusions, which are usually chlorides, sulphates, nitrates, phosphates and bicarbonates, to effect a lowering of the atmospheric water pH. It is well known that this has been exacerbated by the industrial development of recent centuries. However, organic acids are also present in rain-water. After noting the high contents of formate, acetate and proprionate in cloud and rainwater in tropical Australia (Noller et al. 1987), which is attributable to large-scale vegetation burning, Watchman (1990) suggested that these acids might cause the formation of oxalate crusts. Isoprene, found in many plants, is released into the atmosphere, converted by hydroxyl radicals to formaldehyde, which is then oxidised to formic acid. Similar photochemical reactions can convert other breakdown products of isoprene into oxalic acid, which can convert carbonates, including some rock art pigments, to oxalates.

Mass-exfoliation of discrete rock facies in stratified deposits can be caused by either gravitational or capillary moisture travelling within the rock. It is one of the more pernicious rock art conservation problems, because it not only destabilises otherwise perhaps quite well-preserved panels, but it is particularly difficult to address. Attempts to control capillary water, in particular, have a long history of failure. A comparatively stable rock art panel may be disintegrating because it depends on the structural support of another, less stable facies that is rapidly dissolving through moisture. Two different regimes are known, exemplified by two sites I have investigated. In the first case, at Shishkino in central Siberia, the rock art occurs on a vertical cliff, on a horizontal band of sound sandstone. Immediately below this stratum is a layer of argillaceous sandstone (almost mudstone), which decays rapidly from the action of internal water seepage. As it disintegrates, it leaves the stratum without support, which will eventually collapse from its own weight. In the second case, at Mootwingee in eastern Australia, a steep slope dipping at about 19° consists of relatively resistant siliceous sandstone. It bears the rock art, but is underlain by a layer cemented mainly by gypsum and hydrated aluminium silicates, both of which are removed readily. The upper layer develops fissures as a result, which in turn increases access by water and weathering of the lower stratum. Because of the slope's steepness individual blocks, which 'float' on this increasingly unstable support, then slide downwards. While this is seen as a form of physical weathering, the true source of the deterioration is primarily chemical action of moisture. Similar effects can work at a smaller scale, for instance Ollier's (1969) 'dirt cracking', which is essentially attributable to the swelling of clays deposited in fine rock fissures.

Physical weathering

While moisture does cause a variety of physical rock deterioration processes, such as flaking or exfoliation, other such processes involve no chemical changes wrought by moisture. They have been somewhat neglected in the rock art conservation literature, but they can have devastating effects on rock art and are often much easier to alleviate. While Rosenfeld (1985) lists here hydration, 'salt decay' and the removal of cementing medium, I limit the term physical rock weathering to purely physical processes.

Insolation or solar radiation is capable of breaking up some rock types through thermal expansion and contraction, particularly in arid or semi-arid regions experiencing significant diurnal temperature variations. Once controversial, the effectiveness of this process has been shown through the buckling of marble slabs. The ubiquitous sub-spherical boulders of some deserts are largely, though not entirely, the result of temperature stresses over great time spans. The rounding of boulders, most especially of granite, is the result of the geometry of temperature transference within the rock, which heats or cools protruding aspects or corners more readily. Over time the repetitiveness of the process along a stress zone leads to eventual material fatigue. Ideally the process would lead to a spherical shape (or more precisely, a body with the smallest possible surface area relative to mass), and the spalls are always of distinctly convex fracture surfaces. The process is assisted by fire damage, which has the same effect but yields quite different spalls. In my estimate, based on the repatination of successive fracture facets and limited dating information, a typical gabbro or dolerite boulder in an arid and hot region might experience one insolation spalling event every one to four millennia. A lesser rate applies to granite, even boulders engraved in the Pleistocene may not bear any subsequent facets. It is sometimes suggested that moisture within the rock increases susceptibility to insolation fracture. This is quite possible in some rock types, such as sandstones, but is probably less effective in granites, for instance. Thermal stress fatigue is believed to be responsible for a variety of fracturing patterns other than the described spherical reduction, which have also affected rock art sites, particularly in combination with other factors (Hall and Hall 1991; Meiklejohn 1995). The extensive exfoliation of the cupule-bearing walls of Daraki-Chattan Cave in India, one of the world's oldest known rock art sites, is conspicuously limited to the panels accessible to the sun, and is almost certainly attributable to insolation (Bednarik et al. 2005).

Lightning strikes result in often massive fracturing of boulders of any size, and their traces are easy to recognise (Figure 38). This is a major cause of rock reduction, especially in flat areas where rocky outcrops tend to be the only elevated features. Boulders near the peak or along upper ridges are favoured targets of lightning, which usually strikes the upper-most surface of boulders. A boulder may be broken in half, or a large chunk flaked off. At the point of impact the rock may be shattered, its surface is frequently glazed where surface minerals became fused and new ones formed instantaneously. If there are iron-rich rinds present, the minerals formed under very high temperatures of the electrical discharges tend to be of a light greenish to bluish colour. The fracture surfaces created by lightening resemble closely the fractures found on stone implements: point of percussion, positive and negative bulbs of percussion, and radial stress lines found on small stone flakes have their here much larger counterparts, on fractures sometimes measuring many square metres. Quite likely users of stone tools would have noticed such features in the landscape, and marvelled at the impact required to fracture such huge boulders.

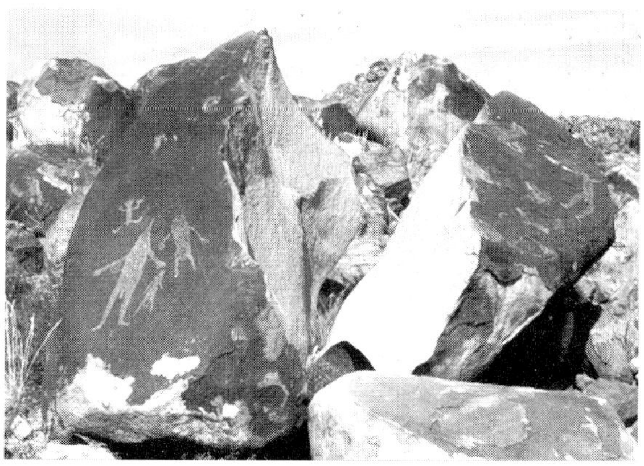

Figure 38. Recent lightning strike, petroglyph-covered granite boulder, Long Tin Creek site, Western Australia.

Brushfires are a highly active agent of physical weathering, especially on rock types that are less susceptible to other forms of weathering (Figure 39). The heat developed by the burning of often very resinous vegetation in arid regions can be quite intense (temperatures exceeding 800°C have been reported), resulting in rapid heating of a thin surface zone, and fatigue between this and the core mass of the boulder which is unaffected by this sudden temperature change. Due to the geometry of heat transference in a solid body, which obeys the same fundamental laws as wane formation (see microerosion analysis, Ch. 7), protruding aspects can heat up rapidly and the flakes detached are always convex on the inside. In general these flakes are under 20 mm maximum thickness, although thicker specimens have been observed.

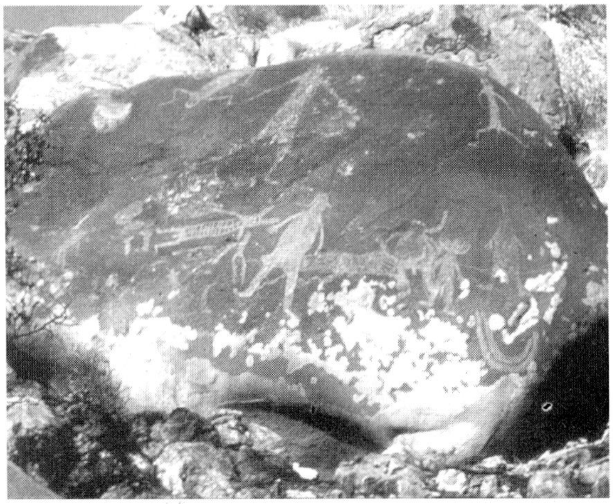

Figure 39. Typical damage by brushfire around the base of a granite boulder bearing petroglyphs, Spear Hill site 8, Western Australia.

On particularly compact, unweathered granite these heat spalls are as thin as one millimetre, and they tend to have sharp edges all around. Typically these spalls are of 15–30 cm diameter on weathered granite. A single fire can remove as much as a square metre of surface from a medium-sized boulder, and if there is any rock art present on this surface, the effect on it is devastating. Selkirk and Adamson (1981) report losses of 2–6 kg of rock per square metre of sandstone in a single intense forest fire. Another effect of fire is a reddening of many types of rock, where the reducing part of flames has converted any goethite present, be it in the rock fabric or on the surface, to haematite.

Kernsprung is a phenomenon of boulder fracture whose results resemble those of lightning strikes, but there is no impact apparent, nor any of the other features described above. The cause is not clearly established, but reports of extremely loud, explosion-like sounds in arid areas suggest that cumulative temperature-induced stresses could build up to the point of a spontaneous release, causing an apparently structurally sound boulder to split literally in half.

Tectonic changes in rock facies or rock structures can also affect rock art sites in a number of ways. These are structural responses, usually due to gravitational disequilibrium of some form. Not all such changes are attributable to natural causes, for instance subsidence due to underground extraction of coal is obviously an anthropic threat. Natural tectonic causes that have destroyed rock art are seismic activity, relocation of major sediment deposits which render rock structures unstable, and the effects of aquifer level fluctuations. The first two are fairly straightforward processes that destabilise rock masses bearing rock art. The third is less readily appreciated. Limestone cave systems often transect the upper limit of aquifers, and these water bodies can experience major oscillations. As the sea level has fluctuated by about 150 m during the Pleistocene, so did coastal aquifers. In the case of partially water-filled cave systems, this means that when the water table falls, rock masses that were tectonically stable under water become unstable once they emerge, because their gravity increases by one tonne per cubic metre. Gravitational equilibrium needs to be re-established, which means that formerly stable structures collapse, including false floors, load-bearing members and lintels, and sometimes cave roofs. Where cave art occurs its survival can be affected by such tectonic adjustments.

Petroglyphs often occur near rivers, even on boulders presently located in rivers (in the Amazon region, for instance), and other decorated boulders occur in shallow seawater (e.g. in the general region of Vancouver, Canada). Such boulders are exposed to yet another form of physical damage, due to the *kinetic energy* of water. They may be moved by the water, or sand moved by the water may act as an abrasive on them. The impact of such fluvial damage is illustrated with the example of the Siega Verde site in Spain, whose numerous petroglyphs archaeologists have assigned to the Upper Palaeolithic. All these petroglyphs occur on soft schist rock and boulders, all are submerged annually under high-energy flood waters. The sharp-edged coarse quartz sand then being rafted past gauges the schist so much that I have measured a retreat of up to 30 mm per century. Needless to say, in such an environment the petroglyphs will not survive more than a few centuries at most, and those of Siega Verde are certainly doomed to destruction. Sand-blasting is not, however, limited to water-propelled quartz sand, it also effects aeolian erosion. While this is barely effective on hard and structurally sound rock, *aeolian erosion* is highly effective on softer rock types, most especially on calcarenite, other soft sandstones, even limestone, especially in coastal and arid environments of high wind velocity. Sandblasting can destroy pictograms and even deep petroglyphs in a matter of a few decades. These weathering processes are often facilitated by weakening of the rock fabric through moisture or salt action.

Biological weathering factors

Non-human biological agents involved in the deterioration of rock art panels range from large mammals through to microfauna, from large plants through to cryptogamic growths, and include bacteria. All rock surfaces bear biotic substances, and all rock surfaces contain organic carbon (Bednarik 1979), which is the principal reason why carbon dating of rock surface features only yields questionable results in many circumstances (see Ch. 7). Rock surfaces are sometimes implicitly regarded as some-how 'sterile', when in fact bacteria occur even several kilometres deep in the lithosphere. Micro-organisms are also implicated in the formation and recycling of specific accretionary deposits as well as in the removal of various cations from numerous mineral components. Not only do such activities contribute to the weakening of rock fabric (Berthelin 1988), they are contingent upon the production of corrosive agents. Their metabolic products may also be corrosive (Eckhardt 1978). Broadly speaking, we are concerned with bacteria utilising atmospheric nitrogen (converting it to ammonia, or oxidising this to nitrous or nitric acid); those oxidising sulphur to sulphur dioxide and converting it to highly corrosive sulphuric acid or the weaker sulphurous acid; those oxidising iron and manganese from minerals, and those attacking silicates and phosphates with organic acids, in particular ketone-based compounds. However, two points need to be considered here: first, the quantities of such highly effective acids are extremely small; second, the processes they cause are not necessarily only corrosive. For instance *Ferrobacillus* sp. or *Thiobacillus* sp. do consume cations, but often from airborne material rather than the host rock, and they may accrete protective surface crusts that actually preserve petroglyphs. Similarly, the mobilisation of amorphous silica, for instance through 2-keto gluconic acid produced by bacteria, can lead to the deposition of silica skins, which have been observed to assist in consolidating both petroglyphs and pictograms. Therefore microbial action is not readily identifiable in most cases, nor are the processes readily definable. An exception is the effect of bacteria on some organic rock art paint residues, such as those reported by me from India (Bednarik 1992a: 148). At some sites in Madhya Pradesh, a white pigment is systematically transformed into black, generally from the margins of the coloured areas inwards. Similar bacterial action may occasionally account for other significant colour changes in paint residues (e.g. McNickle 1991).

The second group of Thallophyta, the fungi, also require no chlorophyll, they too can exist in complete darkness. Small airborne organic matter and moisture is all that is needed by many species. By producing oxalic or citric acid, some species can attack various minerals more aggressively than bacteria, except calcium-rich minerals which seem to be more susceptible to bacterial attack. The citric acid of fungi lead to hydrolysis of silicate minerals (Silverman and Munoz 1970; Winkler 1973). The only fungi (moulds) of interest to rock art science are saprotrophs, i.e. those feeding on dead organic matter, and they occur commonly in limestone caves and at other locations of high humidity. Fungi are further of interest as the symbiotic partners of algae in the formation of lichens, in which the latter provide atmospheric carbon and nitrogen through photosynthesis, while the fungi contribute water and minerals.

In contrast to fungi, algae require light for photosynthesis, although filtered and weak light suffices for some species. While algae range from single-celled forms to very complex multicellular seaweeds, two types are of particular interest to the rock art conservator. The blue-green algae (Cyanophyta), because of their involvement in the production of rock varnish (Scheffer et al. 1963), and the terrestrial green algae (Chlorophyta), which like the former class occur in lichen. Algae do not seem to attack rock surfaces directly, but they can have a damaging effect through their ability of moisture retention, and they depend on the presence of moisture. Especially on carbonates, this may effect minor solution in the presence of carbon dioxide. Algal growth can be unsightly when it occurs on or near rock art but is probably not a significant conservation threat.

Lichens, as already noted, result from a symbiosis between fungi, usually of the class Ascomycetes, and blue-green or green algae. They have been a favourite target in rock art conservation work, but there is very limited evidence of real damage lichens have caused to petroglyphs. Many reports appeal to issues of 'aesthetics', and most empirical claims appear to be anecdotic. Some authors even suggest that a lichen cover may reduce rock weathering rates (Wilson 1995), or while acknowledging deleterious effects have warned that removal of lichen may exacerbate substrate deterioration (Florian 1978). Jackson and Keller's (1970) study, while showing that the weathering zone under lichen cover is thicker than on nearby rock that is free of lichen, is inconclusive, because it cannot tell us whether this is because the lichen has prevented erosion, or because the weathering zone develops faster under the lichen (which I regard as unlikely). Cochrane and Berner (1992, 1993) report the preservation of a silica skin beneath colonising lichens, while other authors suggest that lichens could enhance rates of weathering (Fry 1924, 1927; Syers and Iskandar 1973). The significantly conflicting opinions of various investigators are perhaps easily explained: there are many lichen species to be considered, and it would be surprising if they all had similar effects on component minerals. By the same token each species certainly affects each rock type differently. So until we have acquired a great deal more knowledge about the effects of various lichens on various rock types we need to acknowledge that the jury is still out on lichens, and that it would be premature to favour large-scale lichen removal. On balance, the evidence currently available suggests that the principal problem with lichens is that they retain moisture, which may hasten weathering, but they may also stabilise surfaces on some types of rock, and their chemical weathering impact on most rock types is probably negligible.

Mosses have attracted considerably less ire from rock art site managers, although they are no doubt more effective in retaining moisture for extended periods of time and thus probably a greater conservation threat. Mosses are non-flowering plants that lack roots, but whose stems are equipped with rhizoids to anchor them. A rhizoid is a hairlike filament used to secure the plant to its substrate and it absorbs water and nutrients, operating like roots but of considerably simpler construction. Rhizoids are also found in fungi and lichens. Because of their often much greater bulk in comparison to lichens, mosses attract airborne debris and edaphic sediment to assist in colonising rock surfaces, which understandably conflicts with the survival of rock art.

Even larger plants, such as Gramineae, shrubs and trees can become major agents of rock weathering. In Chapter 3, two basic types of rock markings by plants were distinguished, 'kinetic' and 'chemical' marks. The first include those occasioned by large tufts of grass or plant branches rubbing against relatively soft rock surfaces over years; and marks made by tree roots hugging rocks for support, and moving slightly as the tree sways in the wind. The second type of marks, the 'chemical' marks, is particularly prominent on carbonate rocks, and is attributable to mycorrhizal action along the roots of plants, i.e. to respiratory carbon dioxide and possibly organic acids secreted by the mycelia of symbiotic fungi. While in some exceptional cases such rock markings resemble petroglyphs so closely that archaeologists have misidentified them as such, the influence of plants in the breakdown of rocks is much broader. It includes the widening of fractures with roots, the deposition of organic litter, the shade provided to encourage the colonisation of rocks by cryptogamic organisms, and the destruction or rock surfaces by brushfires.

There are well-known threats to rock art by several insect species, particularly mud-daubing wasps and termites. In Australia alone, four species of termites (Isoptera) have been reported to be causing damage to rock paintings through their construction of 'runways' over vertical walls (Watson and Flood 1987). These tunnel-shaped tracks connect the central nest with feeding areas, protecting the insects from predators and desiccation. Termites are an order of social insects that occur widely in tropical and subtropical regions and feed on complex carbohydrate cellulose. I have observed their runways, as they are preferably called, on rock art panels in numerous countries. These runways consist of an arched sheathing of soil, rock fragments and digested wood, and they are only built by a minority of the many termite species. Occasionally even the nest or mound structures are located at art sites, sometimes concealing part of a rock wall. The main damage, however, is through the runways radiating from the nest. In their construction, sand grains are removed from a supporting sandstone panel and placed on the surface of the runway sheath. In addition to this form of biological weathering, when the runways eventually exfoliate, any paint residues they cross are likely to flake off as well, leading to rapid destruction of the affected rock art.

Mud-daubing wasps (Hymenoptera) occur commonly in most if not all continents, and the nests of numerous species have been observed at rock art sites. A great variety of different structures (e.g. tubular, sub-hemispherical, polygonal) can even leave pigmented imprints on art panels after their exfoliation. Where bonding of the nest structure by salt precipitation has occurred, exfoliation is likely to remove some of the host rock's surface. The nests consist of locally derived fine sediment and organic ketones. There is no evidence that these insects erode the rock surface, therefore the damage they inflict on rock art is limited to the exfoliation phase of their nests, but as they tend to attract more nest-building activity the result can be unsightly colonies of such ultimately damaging structures (Naumann and Watson 1987). Bees can damage rock art in one of two ways. Many sites contain beehives made essentially of wax, but some species also burrow into soft rock types, such as calcarenite or weathered sandstone. Such nesting aggregations can include hundreds of closely adjacent entrances, each several millimetres in diameter.

The damage of mud nests to rock art is not restricted to those of insects. Swallows and martins often build their nests of mud pellets in rockshelters and limestone caves (Bednarik 1988a). Birds also damage rock art through the acidity of their droppings, which facilitates dissolving of rock varnish and other protective deposits (Bednarik 1979) and establishment of cryptogamic growths. In regions of deeply patinated rock outcrops, the highest points are inevitably free of patination, because they are the favourite perches of birds of prey. Therefore discolouration of such an aspect is not necessarily evidence of lightning strike.

Numerous larger animals visit rock art sites and damage the art in the process. In Australia, for instance, feral pigs, water buffaloes and domestic as well as feral cattle are among the main culprits. Hundreds of sites have been fenced in to keep these animals from rubbing their bodies against the walls of the rockshelters, and from raising dust which settles on the art. Perhaps the greatest problem with these animals is that many suffer from a variety of parasites that prompt them to rub parts of their bodies vigorously against the walls of rockshelters, whose relative coolness they are attracted to in a hot climate. This has devastating effects on any rock art present. Similar or other mammalian species affect rock art, especially pictograms, in most parts of the world, and while indigenous species do contribute to this damage, the impact of introduced species, both domesticated and feral varieties, is usually far greater. This is primarily because native megafauna has now been largely eliminated around the world, but on rock surfaces that have preserved earlier traces, particularly in deep caves, the picture is different. In the caves of Europe, the most prominent rock markings are not those of humans, but those of megafauna, particularly of Europe's cave bear. They consist not only of extensive scratch marks but also of the *Bärenschliffe*, polished walls where countless generations of bears polished cave walls with their bodies (see Ch. 3, 'Animal markings'). Animal markings occur in most caves and are a form of biological weathering, as are rock surface modifications by humans, such as bulldozer marks, mining quarries or rock art. Anthropic weathering, however, is so extensive that it warrants a separate section (see below).

Pictogram deterioration

Rosenfeld, in considering the weathering of rock paintings (1985: 49), states that minerals used in the paints are relatively stable 'under normal atmospheric conditions, the iron oxides in ochre pigments do not normally change colour'. This is incorrect. Not only can paint residues change their colour entirely (e.g. from white to black, as noted above, or from light-greenish to black), many of the pigments used are chemically mutable under natural conditions. The term ochre does not refer to a specific mineral, it describes a group of earthy mineral oxides and hydroxides of iron, all of which are metastable (Bednarik 1987a). This has been noted in Chapter 5 ('Patination and petroglyphs') and it also applies to pigments of iron compounds. Their red, yellow, brown and purple hues are attributable to reflective properties that are determined by the states of hydration, oxidation, reduction, hydrolysis, adsorption and grain size of the various components of such pigments. Therefore iron-rich pigments should be expected to age, striving for equilibrium conditions, which can also change with time. Even short-term changes in reflective characteristics, i.e. colour, occur in pictogram paints, and many rock art researchers have observed such changes according to relative air humidity. Such seasonal or even diurnal changes may not be substantial, but they are noticeable. For instance Australian observers have commented on the considerable differences in paint colour prompted by the very humid conditions of the annual wet season. Changes over long periods of time can be much more significant, and it is best not to assume that one can know in what precise colour a paint was originally applied.

These colour changes are not, however, random, there is a trend towards the more stable minerals. Under normal atmospheric conditions, haematite is the most stable of the iron compounds, therefore we need to expect the various components of an 'ochre' paint residue to age gradually towards the colour effect of haematite, which is dark red to 'mulberry'-coloured. It is hardly a coincidence that this is indeed the most common colour found in pictograms, most especially in the hot and dry environments of arid regions, which would particularly favour a trend towards the haematite phase.

With the recent advent of digitised colour management systems that are several times as accurate as human vision in detecting changes in colour it has at last become possible to monitor these effectively. This practically supersedes previous methods of colour monitoring, such as by the use of a chroma meter (Lambert 1995; but see Brammc

2004). However, to merely describe rock art paint residues or pigments as 'fading' is of little help in conservation, it needs to be established which specific process is responsible. Essentially three different effects may be involved: the conversion of the pigment involving a colour change, the gradual removal of pigment, or its masking by one or more of several potential agents. Simple unaided visual inspection may not suffice to establish which of these possibilities applies, but without such understanding it may well be futile, if not counterproductive, to design a preservation strategy. Pigment *conversion*, as noted above, can be by any number of processes that alter the chemical constitution of those components of paint residues that determine its colour. Pigment *removal*, on the other hand, involves a solvent, most likely water or an aqueous solution. Most rock art paints have presumably been applied with water, so unless the pigment component has been well bonded into the substrate's surface fabric by post-depositional processes, it can readily be remobilised with water. Alternatively a pigment might be quite stable, but its conversion renders it more fugitive, so there may be a combination of two processes at work. Finally, *masking* of a paint residue occurs generally through the accretion of a more or less translucent mineral precipitate, which perhaps most commonly is a silica skin. It may not affect the pigment directly, it merely conceals it gradually. So denser the cutaneous deposit, so more transparent it is, while a porous skin reflects more light and appears whitish. However, if it is sprayed with water to fill the interstitial spaces accessible to it, visibility of the concealed pigment layer tends to improve considerably.

One of the most feared forms of pictogram deterioration is the introduction of cryptogamic growths (see above) into deep limestone caves. This has occurred in European caves with Pleistocene rock paintings after they were exposed to large-scale public visitation over a number of years. Two factors are principally responsible, the introduction of organic matter on the clothing of visitors (pollen, spores etc.) which provided food for bacteria and fungi, and the installation of electric lighting which offered some algae the opportunity to colonise these subterranean environments. Ironically the lighting had been installed to eliminate the use of carbide lamps and torches, precisely to improve preservation conditions for the rock art.

The role of climate

A third factor in the deterioration of cave paintings that has attracted some attention is the role of the speleoclimate. The climatic regimes of deep caves operate largely independent of external conditions, particularly where the entrances are small and passages form air syphons. Air residency rates can be very high in caves with poor ventilation. In such conditions three factors are greatly affected by the frequent visits of large numbers of humans: air temperature, air humidity and level of respired carbon dioxide. The *temperature* in a small enclosed space rises markedly within minutes of the arrival of visitors, and interestingly it has been noted that juveniles give off relatively more heat than adults. The relative air *humidity* in a cave is so sensitive to humans that even the presence of a single person renders measurements unreliable and recording hygrometers need to be used. The effects of flooding caves with carbon dioxide can be a significant conservation threat because rocks tend to be moist and this renders the dilute carbonic acid the moisture forms with the CO_2 corrosive (Fernandez 1986). Many caves are close to the upper level of the aquifer, which retards drainage of the gas, which is heavier than air, and so prolongs exposure of the walls to it. In others, such as Chauvet Cave in France, high atmospheric concentration of CO_2 seems to be the result of high air residency attributable to well sealed convacuation spaces.

Closeness of the water table also prevents intake of warmer air, cool air is trapped, and buffered by both the water body and the rock mass, allowing its humidity to remain equally stable. When this equilibrium is threatened by convective heat in the entrance, the evaporation rate there increases, evaporation effects a lowering in temperature and thus protects the cool air below (Bednarik 1991b). In this system equilibrium is maintained, condensation does not occur, and rock paintings can survive for tens of thousands of years in almost original condition. This provides an illustration of the effectiveness of micro-climate in rock art preservation.

While it is not possible for a rockshelter to exercise the same influence on its local climate, it does nevertheless create its own climatic regime. This factor has been subjected to a good deal of research in several world regions, usually by the placement of recorders of ambient air temperature and relative air humidity. Much less attention has been given to other, similarly relevant factors, such as rock temperature, which in several of the European projects of monitoring deep cave climates has been taken care of. On the whole, these programs seem to have provided little tangible benefits in understanding the rather capricious micro-climates of rockshelters. However, it has been demonstrated that levels of relative air humidity and diurnal temperature oscillations in rockshelters are affected by tree cover.

ALLEVIATING NATURAL DETERIORATION

Moisture control

Of the various types of moisture affecting the survival of rock art, surface run-off is the easiest to address, and also the first to have been dealt with. The practice of diverting surface water away from decorated areas was known and applied by Australian Aborigines long before the arrival of Europeans (Mowaljarlai and Watchman 1989). In the wet season they placed spinifex, a grass-like plant (*Triodia* sp.), and flat rocks above rock paintings to prevent water from dribbling down the rock and washing the paint off. This was called *dundamarra*, which is the same word as for a windbreak. Aboriginal people also constructed artificial driplines made of beeswax below the lip of rockshelters to arrest surface water flow into the shelter and force the water to drip to the floor (Watchman 1990: 49). These two methods, the provision of guttering to divert water flow and the artificial dripline, remain the principal weapons in controlling destructive water flow at decorated rockshelters.

The modern artificial dripline is usually of a silicone sealing compound which is applied with a pressure gun. The silicone must have good bonding ability, but remain removable without damage to the rock, it must have a high thermal stability and resistance to moisture and ultra-violet radiation, and it should be of an unobtrusive colour (the clear version is favoured in Australia). At sites visited by the public it may be more advisable to use coloured silicone to match the colour of the rock, because it has been found that tourists tend to pull the silicone threads off the rock (Gillespie 1983). The nozzle of the pressure gun is adapted to specific applications. Rock surfaces need to be cleaned of organic deposits before the silicone is applied.

This method of water control is based on the fact that a thin laminar surface flow can be broken at or slightly below a natural dripline on the outer roof of a rockshelter, where much of the moisture follows gravity and drips to the floor. Part of the flow may continue, especially in conditions of heavy rain, and this can be encouraged to drip to the floor by a low (c. 5 mm) barrier whose inside is sloped upwards. The preferred position of the dripline is on the outer-most horizontal surface, just under the rim of the roof, where the water still has vertical flow velocity.

The extent of the use of this method in Australia is illustrated by the fact that, in one small region alone, the site managers have spent some $300 000 on such artificial driplines. The method has been introduced in other countries and will probably be adopted universally. However, it is most important to appreciate that many such driplines have been installed in unsuitable places (e.g. on vertical or inadequately sloped surfaces), and in such cases may in fact aggravate a conservation threat. It is therefore essential that the conservators using the method have been fully briefed concerning the placement of these barriers (Gillespie 1983). Other measures of diverting water flow include gutters (first used by M. Lorblanchet in Australia, in Glenisla Shelter, Grampians), small roofs and, in the case of caves with vertical entrances (sinkholes), surface channels or embankments (Bednarik 1988a).

Guttering has also been used in Australia to reduce excessive capillary action (e.g. at Mt Grenfell, NSW), in conjunction with modifications to vegetation to reduce retention of water (Walston and Dolanski 1976). Vegetation can also be introduced to soak up surface run-off above a site, especially a cave in a karst region (Bednarik 1991b). Deforestation can affect the hydrology of a site setting quite dramatically, for instance in Paroong Cave (South Australia) it resulted in occasional flash floods, one of which lowered the sediment deposit by some 80 cm. To arrest this trend I re-contoured the catchment area above the cave to reduce it by 98% and re-established the previous vegetation regime to 'soak up' the remaining precipitation (Bednarik 1988a). The area involved amounted to 18 150 m^2. Such indirect modification of site conditions can be very successful and it illustrates how important it is to consider the entire site environment rather than just the most immediately apparent conservation problem. It also shows that some hazards are best tackled at their source, well away from the actual rock art. This applies not just to surface run-off, but also to gravitational water (percolating through the rock fabric above the art). There are no practical means to control it at the rock art panel, the source must be determined. One example of this is the spectacular work of the Indian Archaeological Survey, Bhopal office, at Auditorium Rock, Bhimbetka. The 40-m-high quartzite tower was scaled to locate ingress openings of rainwater, which were grouted with waterproof cement. Similar work has been undertaken on a much smaller scale at various sites, such as Mt Grenfell, Australia.

While it is feasible, and often quite practicable, to control gravitational water, capillary moisture is virtually impossible to eradicate. Rising in porous rock, usually from an aquifer, it is probably the main factor in the formation of sandstone shelters at the base of cliffs (Lambert 1980). Moisture rises from the ground and the salt spalling it causes through wetting and drying cycles erodes the rock rapidly, but only above ground. The lack of exfoliation below ground, combined with the gradually rising sediment level leads to the formation of a sloping bedrock shelf and a receding inner wall, up to the height of the susceptible rock zone. The erosion process continues after rock art has been placed in the shelter, and short of preventing the aquifer from reaching the rock there is no realistic possibility of arresting the process. Attempts to control capillary moisture failed in an Australian project. However, if the moisture originates not from an aquifer, but from a moisture-buffered sediment, removal of such waterlogged material can be very effective in lowering moisture content in contiguous rock (Bednarik 1988a).

In theory, the deposition of condensation water is relatively easy to control, by modifying the climatic regime of the site. Since the dew point is determined by the difference between rock and air temperatures, the latter being higher, and very high air humidity, one can either raise rock temperature or lower air humidity. The practical application of such principles is not so simple, however. Schwartzbaum (1985) advocates the installation of electric heating coils, and while this would be effective in some instances, it is obviously not feasible in most affected rock art sites. In some caves containing rock art the ultimate technological solution has been to control the entire climate of the cave by air-conditioning equipment such as that installed at Lascaux and Font de Gaume in France (Brunet et al. 1995). This means that temperature and air humidity are set at appropriate levels thought best for the rock art. There are, however, much less intrusive methods of achieving a level of control over adverse microclimatic conditions in limestone caves. Since most condensation occurs near the cave entrance, well-designed alterations to nearby vegetation, to the configuration or size of the entrance or to sediment deposits in it can all affect the microclimate. To some extent this also applies to rockshelters, although when planting vegetation near rock art, the fire danger must always be taken into consideration.

Another form of water damage, through freeze-and-thaw cycles, can result in the gradual reduction of rock mass to cryoclastic detritus. Controlled experiments in Scandinavia have shown that this can be significantly alleviated by covering rock pavements (Bertilsson and Magnusson 2000). A variety of materials, ranging from sediment to synthetic sheets such as mineral wool ground insulation, can be used for this purpose. Vegetation has also been reported to have some effect by reducing exposure. A second option is to attempt control of the moisture source, but this is probably not readily possible in most cases. Finally, the ultimate solution at open sites is to enclose them, but if the structure has no walls the effect might not be great. A fully closed building might eliminate freezing but would introduce a completely new environment, whose effect on the rock art may well be more deleterious than that of ice (see 'Climate control', below).

Alleviating physical deterioration

A great deal of physical deterioration of rock art is attributable to the effects of moisture as discussed above: the deposition of various mineral skins (silica skins, rock varnish and similar ferromanganous laminae, oxalates, carbonates and others); the deposition of water-soluble salts (as surface efflorescence, interstitially or as subflorescence effecting surface spalling); the removal of soluble salts and subsequent granular or mass-exfoliation. Here, however, we are primarily concerned with temperature or insolation-induced stresses; hydration (for instance of a clay matrix) and subsequent mass-exfoliation; brush or forest fire spalling; the release of tectonic stresses; kinetic damage by fluvial transport; and damage by lightning strike. Several of the processes involved in these preservation hazards cannot realistically be arrested, but some palliative action may be possible.

Where physical processes are attributable to moisture, a site's hydrology can often be modified or managed indirectly as detailed above. Fracture by insolation or *Kernsprung* can only be averted by planting shade trees, but in the arid regions where this is most relevant such measures might not be feasible. Tectonic stresses in rock structures are unavoidable, unless geophysical damage is humanly caused (through mining or water extraction). Similarly it might be unrealistic in most cases to seek to arrest lightning damage at topographically prominent sites, although it is certainly possible to do so. Petroglyphs occurring in the seasonal flood zone of rivers are exposed to the abrasive action of sand and coarser material, which can be as effective in obliterating rock art as sand blasting. Again, there are no prospects of saving these petroglyphs in the long term, short of diverting the river. Where the petroglyphs occur on soft rock in high-velocity fluvial conditions, as at Siega Verde (Spain), it needs to be accepted that they will not survive the next few millennia.

However, damage from brush and grass fires is avoidable by keeping fuel away from the art panels. Back-burning is practised at some Australian sites, for instance in the Grampians. Fire is a particularly effective form of physical deterioration, because it focuses on the surface zone of rock, and depending on the availability of fuel, whole rock art panels can be stripped off in minutes. Therefore fuel control is one of the most important measures in the management of rock art sites.

The salt deposits caused mostly by capillary or gravitational water within the rock can occur either within the rock's fabric, or on the surface. In the latter case they are considered unsightly by site managers and visitors. Since these precipitates are readily water soluble, their removal is possible by compresses or poultices (Schwartzbaum 1985). Sheets of long-fibre, wet-strength tissue paper are applied with water and a flat bristle brush, from the bottom of the area to be treated to its top. The poultice is intended to soak up the dissolved salts. However, salts may retreat into the porous rock as well upon mobilisation, so the technique must be applied by experienced conservators. The same applies to the poultice treatment of pictogram panels in which specific solvents are introduced to target such unwanted substances as dust, soot or body grease.

At a number of sites, mass-exfoliation has led to programs of consolidating disintegrating panels by grouting and other physical means. The perhaps largest project of this type was at Mootwingee, New South Wales (Probert and Wallace 1970; Chestnut 1972), where in 1973 it was attempted to arrest the exfoliation of a massive layer of sandstone on a steep slope. Destabilised by the disintegration of the supporting substrate, large blocks of capstone were gradually sliding due to their weight, a condition aggravated by heavy visitor traffic. Large pins of stainless steel were installed in the gaps between blocks, with wooden and later plastic spacing blocks. This did not arrest deterioration, but introduced new factors leading to further remedial action in the form of grouting experiments. This interfered with the site's hydrology, and after catwalks were installed the site was eventually closed to tourism.

Small exfoliating rock fragments of the engraved pavement were occasionally fixed into position with epoxy resin at Mootwingee. The same method has been employed at another site in Australia, Trotman's Cave in the Great Sandy Desert. Here, J. Clarke reattached exfoliated fragments of a pictogram panel with epoxy resin, using only spots of this material to ensure that moisture could not be trapped in an impervious layer of resin. The same approach has been recommended to affix a thin exfoliating skin on sandstone at Shishkino, central Siberia (Bednarik 1992b). In Canada, polyester resin was used to arrest congelifraction of a metamorphosed limestone pavement near Peterborough. A large separated rock slab at Deer Corral, British Columbia, was reattached by grouting with a mixture of sand and acrylic resin (Kennedy 1979).

Exfoliating rock surfaces at rock art sites have been impregnated with various synthetic sealants, for instance in India and the United States, generally with negative results. Rather than alleviating the deterioration of porous rock, it is accelerated by the application of substances that produce an impervious skin, such as water repellents and resins. Interstitial moisture in rock must be free to move and evaporate. Therefore consolidants to be used must be pervious to moisture. Spry (1981) recommended the use of silicon esters (alkoxysilanes), silicones (polymerised alkoxysilanes) and acrylics or related polymers for building Masonry. However, the first do not bond well with rock and penetrate pores poorly, especially in hot surface conditions, while the silicones are adversely affected by ultraviolet radiation (Rosenfeld 1985: 61–63). Experiments conducted by Clarke (1978) suggest that the key to successful treatment is to get enough resin into the pigment layers to make them water repellent without rendering them impermeable. Such methods have been used only experimentally and no long-term results are available from them. It seems reasonable to conclude that there is no known 'safe' method of stabilising rock surfaces by concealing or impregnating them, be it with silicon esters, silicones or silanes.

The failure of such treatment has been reported from some regions, such as Siberia (Bednarik 1992b, 1995a; Bednarik and Devlet 1993). At the major sandstone site of Shishkino, exfoliation had been arrested with a preparation of eroded sand and tetraethoxysilane ($C_8H_{20}O_4Si$), which failed structurally within a year of application. Cracks developed between the repair grout and the rock — or to be more precise, within the weathering zone of the rock, 1 or 2 mm beneath the interface. So the net result was an acceleration of weathering. Similarly, the repair of rock varnish (Elvidge and Moore 1980) has been described as yielding unsatisfactory results (Bock and Bock 1990) and should thus be avoided.

After observing how rock paintings can survive very well under silica skins, Watchman has investigated the possibility of synthetically creating thin transparent epilithic silica deposits to protect paint residues. He attempted to use an artificial silica gel consolidant in the early 1990s (Watchman 1995).

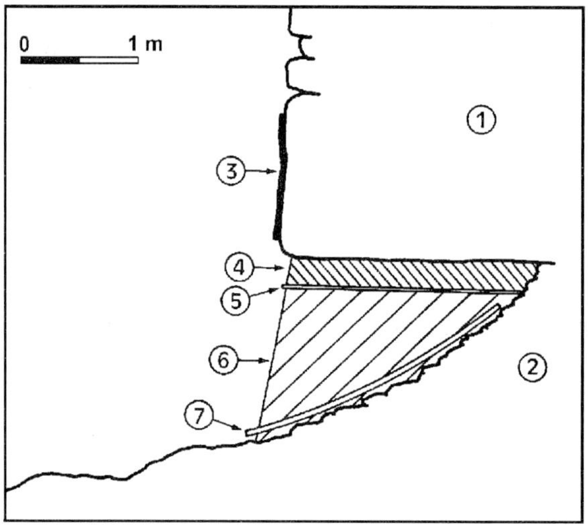

Figure 40. Schematic section of structural repair proposal, Shishkino, central Siberia: 1 - sound overlying rock, 2 - eroding facies, 3 - petroglyphs, 4 - dry-packed cement grout, 5 - elastomeric membrane, 6 - cast concrete, 7 - slotted drainage pipes in thin sand layer.

A viable form of structural repair of rock art sites concerns the rapid erosion and retreat of specific rock strata in vertical exposures bearing rock art. This can lead to the collapse of better-cemented rock above once it loses its support (Figure 40). The method of arresting such impending damage is to install a parcel of grout, together with an elastomeric membrane compensating for stresses and with provision of draining gravitational water from the rock's interior.

Most other tectonic adjustments in a rock mass, be they caused by seismic or other factors (e.g. oscillating aquifer level), are more difficult to deal with, and any action depends very much on the specific circumstances at a site. Nevertheless, remedial action of providing support structures for rock components of a site is certainly possible in many cases. It can take a number of different forms as required by site conditions and resources. Similarly, aeolian erosion in the form of sand blasting, which affects numerous sites, can be reduced considerably by artificial barriers, including vegetation. Some sites have been buried under sediment or other material, for this and other reasons (e.g. congelifraction). Examples are the fragile sandstone petroglyphs at Mt Cameron West, Tasmania (Blanks and Brown 1991) and the granite pavements at Tacompnum, Sweden (Bertilcompsson and Magnusson 2000: 100).

Biological deterioration

Bearing in mind that the most serious conservation threat to rock art is the one posed by humans, it is interesting that our most sustained conservation efforts seem to be directed at the eradication of lichens. The principal reason given is that they interfere with our aesthetic appreciation of rock art. It is also claimed frequently that they might affect the conservation of rock art, although the evidence presented for this seems to be largely anecdotal. The chemical effect of lichen on most rock substrates is probably negligible, and their principal contribution to the deterioration of rock is probably their longer retention of moisture relative to lichen-free rock. While the degradation lichens are claimed to cause remains largely unproven (Cochran and Berner 1993; Drever 1994), archaeologists and site managers around the world have waged chemical warfare on lichens, or scrubbed them away wherever they encountered them. Although their stated main motivation concerns 'aesthetics' (and one might reasonably argue that lichens also have aesthetic qualities), the subconscious reasons are perhaps more complex. In my view they are related to the perception of rock art as art, which must be kept free of 'blemishes', and to the phenomenon identified by Freeman (1994). Freeman found interesting connections between some aspects of rock art studies and religious practices concerning shrines and 'sanctuaries'. Psychologically, rock art sites need to be kept neat and free of the threatening anarchy of Nature, particularly in countries whose societies have been conditioned by religious values such as those of puritanism. However, lichens can assist in the scientific study of the rock art (see Ch. 7) and rock art researchers have begun to speak out against the vandalistic practices of lichen removal (Bahn et al. 1995; Tratebas and Chapman 1996; Walderhaug and Walderhaug 1998).

The methods used in the eradication of these 'pests' are particularly questionable. After all, the easiest and most obvious way of killing lichens is by depriving them of light. They can be covered by black plastic sheeting or, as has been done on Scandinavian pavements, by covering them with a thin layer of sand. Yet most publications on rock art conservation recommend instead a variety of highly toxic fungicides, requiring the wearing of protective clothing and masks (e.g. orthophenyl phenol in dehydrated ethanol), ammonium hydroxide (which destroys most forms of life), and fluorosilicates of zinc and magnesium. Some archaeologists have used bleach, compressed water jets and vigorous manual scrubbing 'with wooden tools' to remove even very light lichen growths on hundreds of quite fragile schist panels. Obviously this would have eliminated not only the lichens, but everything else on the rock surface, including paint traces, patination, mineral accretions, and even poorly anchored rock fragments. In addition, it compromised the research potential of the rock art so much that meaningful analytical work may no longer be possible at these sites.

Unless there is unambiguous evidence that the lichen concerned is threatening the survival of the rock art, specifically rock paintings, it is preferable to ignore lichens, or to remove only loose and exfoliating thalli and discourage growth indirectly. Dead lichens can be removed without vigorous mechanical action, and contamination with chemicals should always be avoided. Most importantly, all lichen thalli must be fully recorded before they are removed, and the species must be identified. Tratebas and Chapman (1996) have provided detailed guidelines for the correct procedure in lichen treatment. Mosses, however, are much more effective in retaining moisture than lichens, but they are also easier to remove without causing chemical or mechanical damage to the rock surface. At some sites in the Sydney sandstone region, organic material (presumably lichens, fungi and algae) has been mechanically removed from the grooves of petroglyphs to highlight them for the benefit of site visitors. This practice was, however, questioned and discontinued. Young and Wainwright (1995) have shown that algal growth can depend significantly on tree shade, and experimented with seven algicides on several species they identified on the marble pavement of the Peterborough site in Canada.

Plant roots can have corrosive effects on rock, especially through the organic carbon dioxide exhaled by the micro-organisms living on the root surfaces. In some cases tree roots have caused extensive damage to rock art panels, particularly in limestone caves. A panel of finger markings in Prungkart Cave, South Australia, was invaded by the root system of a pine tree (an introduced species in Australia), which followed the interface between the primary rock and a precipitated travertine layer bearing the rock art. This resulted in the exfoliation of much of the travertine lamina (Bednarik 1998). Other trees above the cave were then felled as a preventative measure. The activities of trees growing above limestone caves need to be monitored, even where the roof thickness is 20 or 30 m, and this applies particularly where a new species has been introduced in an area.

Similarly, all other conservation threats posed by plants are relatively easy to deal with. Plants whose parts rub against decorated rocks can be removed, and it is in any case preferable to remove most plant growth within a few metres of rock art. By far the greatest danger plants pose to rock art is through the fire threat they pose, particularly in regions where plant matter tends to be high in resins and oils.

There are two strategies to deal with termite infestation of rock art sites: to either destroy the central nest, which eliminates the integrative mechanisms on which the colony depends for its survival; or to place a chemical barrier at the base of the panel (a strip of soil is soaked with an insecticidal emulsion). The former method is clearly preferable, however. It is advisable to destroy all nests within 50 m of the art, and to return after a year to check whether any structures have been rebuilt (Watson and Flood 1987). The galleries traversing the art panel should not be removed. Nests of mud-daubing insects, however, should be removed (after first wetting them, or during the wet season in the tropics; but see below), because it has been found that existing nests attract new ones (Naumann and Watson 1987).

Some birds, too, construct mud nests at rock art sites in many parts of the world. Reports of damage to rock art are rare, however. In contrast, damage occasioned by large mammals is very common throughout the world. By far the most frequent culprits are domestic and feral grazing species. They favour rockshelters because of the shade and shelter they offer, they rub their bodies against the walls, depositing organic and sedimentary materials, they churn up archaeological deposits and walk on petroglyph pavements. In Australia, the significance of this threat is well appreciated and stock fences have been erected at numerous sites, particularly in the north of the continent. The most extensive fences for the protection of rock art, however, are probably those at Saudi Arabian sites — but they are primarily designed to keep out the most damaging animal of all.

ANTHROPIC DETERIORATION OF ROCK ART

Coming to terms with professional vandalism

The deterioration of rock art caused by one large mammal has to be considered in more detail than that by all other animals: the damage occasioned by just one single primate, man. It exceeds the damage of all other rock art deterioration factors combined, particularly when one includes indirect damage by human agency (e.g. through acid rain, domestic animals, aquifer changes). A disturbing aspect of anthropic damage of rock art is that the most severe threat to the research potential comes not from tourists, but from researchers themselves. This factor had not been examined in any detail until I began addressing it in a series of papers (Bednarik 1987b, 1990a, 1990c, 1990d, 1991a, 1992b). Whereas the tourist or casual visitor of a site may occasion rather obvious and usually localised damage, the damage caused by the scholar can be much more extensive, fundamental and systematic, compromising the site's research potential rather than its superficial appearance. Graffiti may deface a petroglyph, but covering it entirely with an organic substance or chalk for the sake of photography destroys its potential to be dated by many of the currently used methods of scientific 'dating'. Undated rock art, clearly, is of limited scientific significance, and non-datable rock art will always remain scientifically obscure. Recording work conducted by means that compromise the research potential of the art is therefore vandalistic.

Archaeologists have viewed rock art as an archaeological resource since the early 19th century, existing primarily to help them 'interpret the human past' (see Ch. 2). But there are several interest groups with claims relating to rock art, and some of them clearly have precedence (most especially indigenous people in those parts of the world where they own the art). Until it is properly dated, rock art is not even an archaeologically relevant resource. There exists no properly dated rock art in the world at the present time. Rock art scientists have provided age estimates or dating information of various levels of reliability and precision from a limited number of motifs located at sites in all continents (see Ch. 7). However, none of this dating evidence, however reliable some of it no doubt is, amounts to an actual 'dating' of the motif in question. Often one even reads the comment that a whole site has been 'dated'. The age of no whole pre-Historic rock art site assemblage has been even approximately determined, anywhere in the world. It is fair to say that dating information provided by rock art scientists has been systematically misinterpreted by archaeologists on most occasions when they commented on such data (Bednarik 1996; Watchman 1999).

One would hope that at least the recordings archaeologists have gathered by applying often inappropriate recording methods are useful. Unfortunately this is generally not the case, as explained in the previous Chapter. Many rock art recordings are subjective, the recorder superimposing his or her interpretation over what is actually on the rock surface. Many recorders seem preoccupied with idiosyncratic issues: to demonstrate the validity of their favourite interpretational hypothesis, to illustrate how ludicrous the ideas of their academic opponents are, to understand the meaning of the art, or to categorise the motifs in accordance with the arbitrarily imposed taxonomies of alien 'researchers'. The credibility of practically all statistical work on rock art can be questioned by simple taphonomic reasoning. Therefore the immense labour expended on such exercises was futile and the often elaborate interpretations of such records all lack credibility. Finally, photographic records obtained by physical enhancement generally lack colour coding by a device profile suitable for standardised electronic manipulation, so they are worthless in the long term. They are doomed to eventual loss (Bednarik 1994b), but they may have been acquired at a cost to the rock art.

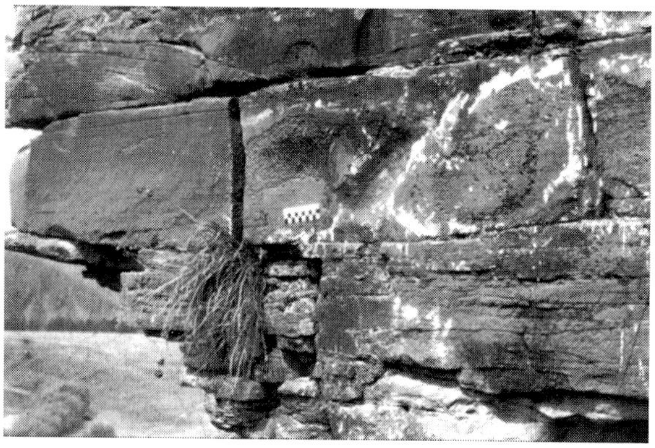

Figure 41. Residues of inexpertly applied latex casting at the remote Vorobiovo petroglyph site, Siberia.

Since the beginning of archaeology as a discipline, rock art vandalism has been widely practised by archaeologists, sometimes even in the most remote regions of the world (Bednarik and Devlet 1993). No distance was too great, no access too difficult, to apply latex, plaster of Paris, black films and a great variety of emphasising substances (Figure 41). In India and in the Sahara, the application of water to paintings was often standard archaeological procedure, while in Scandinavian countries, the practice of painting petroglyphs in gaudy colours continues to this day and is still being defended by some 'conservators'. Indeed, research is being conducted into the longevity of different paints for this very purpose (Löfvendahl and Magnusson 2000). In several other countries of Europe, thousands of petroglyph panels have been daubed by archaeologists with black and white organic paints for 'recording'. Whole rock art panels have been sawn off, at sites from Karelia (Peri Nos) to Australia (Panaramitee North), and transported to museums. Many archaeological excavations conducted at rock art sites have been sub-standard, for instance those in Lascaux (Bahn 1994) or the recent excavations in the Côa valley of

Portugal (Swartz 1997a). At most archaeological excavations of rock art sites no protection of the art panels was installed, of the type introduced by Morwood (1994). This has led to the deposition of dust on the rock art in the course of 'scientific' work. At some public sites in India, the site rangers had been instructed by archaeologists to daily sweep the dusty floor of the cave, resulting in extensive dust deposits on the cave walls. Another form of archaeological site vandalism is the excavation of sediments near petroglyph panels if the excavator lacks the knowledge support for identifying mur-e (petroglyph-making stone tools), leading to this key-evidence being discarded.

Since the early 1990s, a campaign has resulted in an extensive reassessment, and has largely eradicated a number of undesirable methodologies in many countries. However, there is still reluctance in some quarters to accept the validity of some of the points raised here. Nevertheless, rigorous self-criticism and criticism now form a cornerstone policy of the International Federation of Rock Art Organisations (IFRAO) and this is hoped to facilitate the establishment of a new awareness of human threats to rock art, including inadvertent threats by researchers.

Site tourism

Most human damage is not deliberate and can therefore be eradicated through well-directed education programs. In this sense the general public is more amenable to improvements than rock art students. In the area of rock art tourism such programs have been very successful in various continents.

The behaviour of rock art site visitors has been extensively studied in Australia, particularly through the work of Gale (1985). Children, organised tour groups and local visitors were identified as categories of high-risk visitors at publicly accessible sites, but it was also found that simple measures, such as signs, were most effective in modifying visitor behaviour, especially in the high-risk groups (Gale and Jacobs 1986, 1987). The results of Gale's studies have become the basis of Australia's national strategies of rock art site management, and have also been an influence in designing such policies elsewhere. Rock art sites have become prime destinations for 'cultural tourism' in many parts of the world. Sites or groups of sites attracting in excess of 100 000 annual visitors occur in France, Italy, India and Australia. It is therefore essential that sound management policies be designed and adhered to. The underlying philosophy is simple: all visitation contributes to the deterioration of a site, but the site manager is usually required to make some sites available for visitation. Many major rock art corpora are on public land, and if sites are not available for visitation, the public will seek alternative means of access. Since it is preferable that access be under controlled conditions, a few representative, easily accessible sites are ideally selected from a major art body, and 'sacrificed' to the public after they are carefully developed. A classical example is Kakadu National Park, where perhaps in the order of 5000 rock art sites exist. Of these, three sites were selected and developed with extensive walkways and interpretation signs. They are the only sites available for visitation in this National Park.

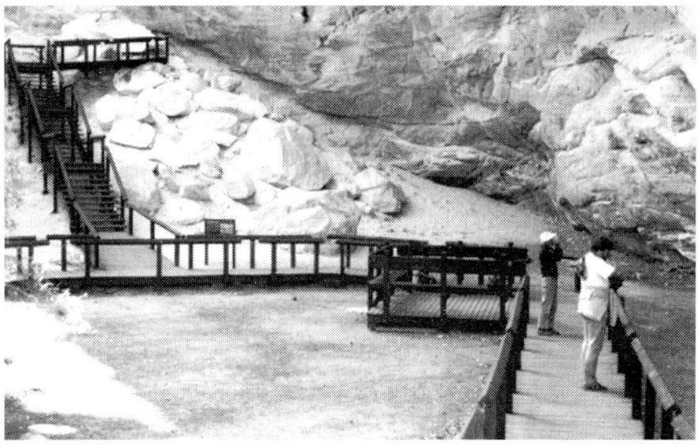

Figure 42. Wooden boardwalk system in Cathedral Cave stencil site, Carnarvon Gorge, Queensland, Australia.

It is appropriate to consider measures of visitor control by first describing Australian experiences, because the practices developed there are widely considered as exemplary and they are being adopted in other parts of the world, or adapted to the conditions there. Quite a number of such measures have been utilised at Australian rock art sites. The most frequent are boardwalks of steel or timber, often with elevated viewing platforms (Figure 42). They are designed to keep the visitors away from the art, while permitting a close-up view of it, and they prevent damage to the archaeological floor deposit. The erosion of floor sediments and the development of dust are often also controlled by floor covering in rockshelters, such as mats, gravel or wooden floorboards (Walsh 1991). Boardwalks need to be designed to blend with their particular setting, they need to meet several technical criteria (e.g. weight loadings) and they should permit a good flow of visitors, hence there should be no dead-ends in the layout. Of particular value are lectern-like signs, placed along the handrail facing the rock art panel and explaining aspects of the site. Visitor books have been found to be effective, and the Australian experience has shown that the visitor needs to be told what not to do, and is generally quite willing to comply with such directions. The fact that heavy fines apply in Australia to any form of interference with the rock art is without doubt a major deterrent, and it has also a second effect: it provides the visitor with a readily understood measure of significance. Nothing can ever be as effective in preventing damage to art from tourism than a simple sign stating that the prescribed penalty for touching the art is many thousands of dollars. However, signs also need to be positive in their messages, impressing on the visitors that the rock art is a major component of their cultural heritage. Importantly, they also need to inform visitors about the rock art. Signage at many Australian public sites is excellent and visitor orientated, offering adequate ethnographic, interpretational and environmental information.

This 'educational' approach is appropriate at very remote sites in the continent's north, which involve considerable effort on the part of the visitor just to reach them. It is less suitable at easily reached sites in the vicinity of major population centres. A large number of unsupervised sites in Australia, especially in the much more densely populated south east of the continent, have been fully enclosed in steel cages. While there is general agreement that these structures are highly obtrusive, it is equally true that they are most effective. There have been calls for their removal but they remain in use and have in some cases been replaced recently with better-constructed cages. In the case of the particularly vulnerable limestone cave sites, the preferred policy is to close the caves so that they can be visited only under supervision (Figure 43).

The perhaps best-protected rock art site in the world is Chauvet Cave, in the Ardèche of France. Vast resources have been lavished on this magnificent site since its discovery in late 1994. Access is through a strongroom door requiring dual handprint identification, constantly monitored via several CCTV cameras connected to a remote control room. Only members of the research team (presently seventy-four persons worldwide) are permitted to enter the site, and even their presence in the cave is subject to severe limitations of personnel number and duration of work sessions. All visitors must wear protective clothing and rubber booties that remain permanently at the site to eliminate the possibility of introducing organic contaminants. Photography is not permitted, except by instruction from management, and walking on the cave floors is strictly forbidden. Researchers, the only people entering the cave, move on walkways made of titanium alloy and stainless steel in the course of their work, and research is the only acceptable reason for entering the site. Hopefully, this jewel of Palaeolithic rock art is to enjoy this level of protection in perpetuity, and hopefully other countries will follow the French lead and strengthen their practices of site management.

In terms of protecting individual cave art sites, France is the undisputable world leader, having spent more money on protecting a single site than Australia has spent across the whole continent. In terms of efforts to control unauthorised access at open-air rock art sites, Saudi Arabia deserves special mention. The Deputy Ministry of Antiquities and Museums of the Kingdom has erected substantial fences at numerous remote desert sites, in some cases several kilometres long, at great expense (Bednarik and Khan 2002). Moreover, it is expected that there will be further enlightened initiatives concerning rock art visitation in Saudi Arabia in the near future.

A number of considerably less drastic and costly measures have been tested and in some cases employed in visitor control. These include the placing of 'psychological barriers', which may be low

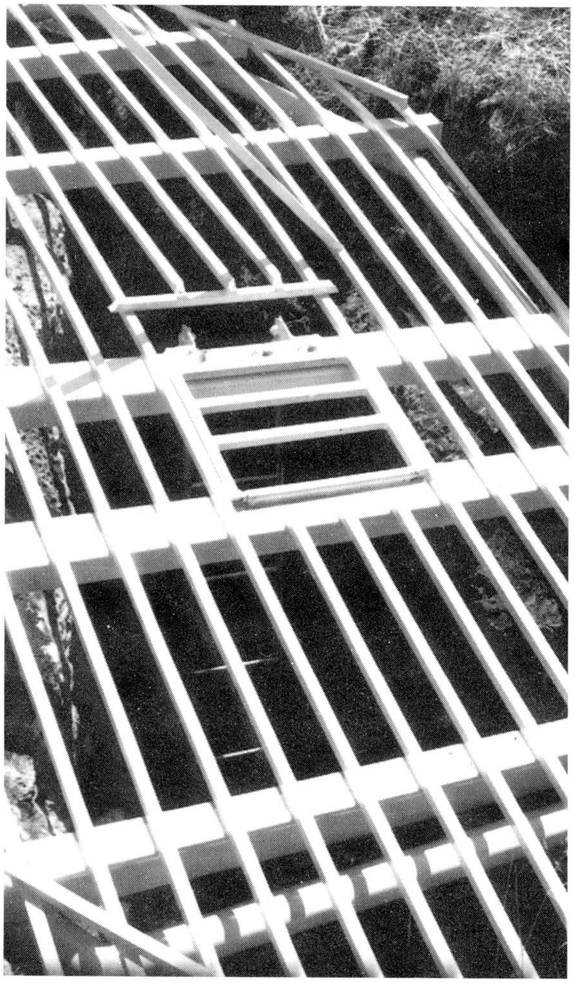

Figure 43. The vertical entrance of Paroong Cave, South Australia, closed by a steel frame to prevent accidents and to control access to the extensive cave petroglyphs.

fences, artificial rock ledges or some strategically placed prickly bushes. The effectiveness of such 'passive access-restricting measures' depends on local circumstances, particularly site topography and social context. Bearing in mind that it takes only one visitor with a can of spray paint to ruin a site, these measures cannot prevent blatant vandalism. They can be very effective, however, at some types of sites, as examples from Bolivia demonstrate. Omar Claure, Leo Ticlla and particularly Fernando Huaranca (1995) have developed access restriction to a fine art, by such measures as concealing or removing footholds on cliff sites and by strategically placed plants. These low-interference, costeffective, environmentally sound and innovative approaches to rock art conservation are also admirable applications of modern conservation philosophy.

Rock art graffiti

The visually most obvious threat from humans is the production of graffiti over rock art. In Australia, a combination of legislative protection prescribing heavy fines, and public education about the significance of the indigenous cultural heritage have widely eliminated the incidence of graffiti at rock art sites. Graffiti removal practices are vigorously pursued in some countries, such as the United States and Russia, but less enthusiastically in Australia — although excellent projects do provide some notable exceptions (e.g. Thorn 1991). The well-worn cliché that graffiti breed more graffiti may be true, but rock art also 'breeds' graffiti, and a great deal of what we describe as rock art began its existence as graffiti. Graffiti at rock art sites are a form of human response to rock art, and while clearly undesirable, the removal of existing graffiti may well do more damage to the scientific potential of the site than the graffiti being removed. While extant graffiti pose no major threat to the scientific potential of the rock art they disfigure, graffiti removal treatment does present such a threat, particularly where it involves the application of chemicals (Bednarik 1992c). Moreover, it has sometimes been observed that the laborious removal of huge graffiti prompted the almost immediate production of new ones in the area rendered 'vacant' (Bednarik 1992b). The laboriously 'reinstated' panel merely offered a fresh slate to graffiti artists.

It is also an important consideration that graffiti have been used most successfully in scientific work, for instance for the calibration of dating methods (Bednarik 1992d, 2001), to determine formation rates of carbonate speleothems, and in social studies of site visitors (Morwood and Kaiser-Glass 1991). Bearing in mind that rock art graffiti have been made for almost as long as rock art itself (since the Upper Palaeolithic; Clottes et al. 1992), they provide a record of human reactions to existing rock art whose study is just as important as that of the rock art they comment on. There are numerous graffiti from Pharaonic and Roman times. Other examples are the reactions of various religious movements to the rock art of the religions they sought to replace. They can be found, for instance, in much of the distribution area of Islam and in Spanish South America (Bednarik 1988b, 1992e). Few researchers would suggest that the religious Spanish graffiti at Andean sites ought to be removed, even though some were quite intentionally placed directly over earlier rock art motifs. Similarly, we have yet to hear American demands to remove the numerous graffiti at El Morro, New Mexico, where no less than 26 Spanish parties left their inscriptions between 1605 and 1774. There is no intention of removing the many historical graffiti in Rouffignac, France, dating from the early 19th century. In Australia, with its very short history, graffiti of that period are regarded as historical treasures, although many occur at rock art sites and were probably prompted by the presence of the earlier art (Gale and Jacobs 1987: Fig. 2). Even dated graffiti of the early 20th century are considered valuable historical documents, especially in the most recently colonised northern parts of the continent (Palmer 1991: 116). Thus the value of graffiti is derived from their age, certain social constructs and historical contingencies. It would seem that if the lewd inscription of today's graffiti artist should escape the attention of the graffiti remover long enough, it might in due course become a socio-political statement worthy of scholarly attention.

The definition of graffiti itself needs to be examined before we can attempt graffiti removal, otherwise we cannot know what is to be removed. One could argue that if the rock art was made by indigenes it is not graffiti. Is the recent Hopi inscription 'Tico and Liz' at Oraibi, Arizona (Ritter 1991: Fig. 3) to be removed? If it is to remain, how would a conservator decide which 'non-traditional' graffiti are by indigenes? Around the world there are traditional rock art sites where traditional societies continue painting today, but now paint slogans, motorcars, football teams or green frogs. The question of graffiti removal is not as clear-cut as if might appear to be. Rock art conservation is itself a sociopolitical phenomenon: the cultural remains of extinct or marginalised cultures are appropriated by the dominant culture in the name of preservation. Haskovec (1991) has warned against perceiving rock art conservation as self-evidently, intrinsically 'good', pointing out that it can also be a cultural ossification factor. Neither he nor I would ever advocate that graffiti practices be encouraged, but it is the role of the scientist to seek understanding, including of the dynamics of rock art conservation.

Moreover, the first condition of being able to prevent new graffiti is to understand the motivation of the graffiti artist, yet oddly enough the rock art conservation industry has not conducted sustained research into this issue, focusing on symptoms rather than the disease. Loubser (2001: 92) reports that in South Africa, pilgrims attending religious ceremonies in the wilderness write their names sometimes over rock art. He established that such names signify membership with credit unions and burial societies of the communities in question. Masao (1996) has reported similar observations in Tanzania. To illustrate the complexity of the issue, I cite an anecdote. When I observed the arrest of a graffiti artist at the Taj Mahal I requested to have him interviewed before police led him away. He had come from a village far away, at great expense, to declare his love for his sweetheart. The Taj is regarded as the ultimate monument to love and he was perfectly aware of the consequences of his action. Indeed, his apprehension and jailing was part of his declaration of commitment. Thus the fervour of the graffiti phobia also needs to be understood, its reminiscence of the puritan lichen-phobia mentioned above is obvious. Because such blind beliefs prevent rational analysis and understanding of phenomena they can themselves become obstacles to sound rock art preservation policy.

Nevertheless, in preparing rock art sites for public viewing it may be advisable to remove existing recent graffiti. As in rock art, additive (pigments) and reductive (carvings) versions occur, and need to be treated differently. In the first type, a great variety of graffiti materials have been observed, some of which can be readily identified; others require chemical or microscopic analysis. Wax crayon residues are fairly unstable when exposed to the sun and deteriorate, but if they need to be removed, poultices of cotton wool and sepiolite soaked in organic solvents are effective, as well as paint strippers (Rosenfeld 1985). Most paints can be removed with commercial paint strippers or mixtures of cellosolve acetate and acetone. A detailed description of paint removal at a granite site is provided by Thorn (1991), who used acetone poultices. If working close to rock art paint residues, care must be taken not to damage them. Well-bonded iron oxides and hydroxides are the most resistant, while white pigments are usually the most soluble. Graffiti of charcoal or lead pencil are also common, they are best removed by careful brushing with glass fibre brushes and swabbing with alcohol. However, graffiti can be stabilised by silica and other mineral deposits, which renders their removal much more difficult. It is also to be remembered that most chemicals used in graffiti removal will compromise the research potential of any rock art affected.

The removal of rust stains, which can be found at sites equipped with steel grids or cages, has been described in detail by Finn and Hall (1995). Many graffiti have been made by removal of rock mass, usually by means of steel tools or angular stones. The repair of such petroglyphs or lacunae with grouting materials has been attempted, but results have been unsatisfactory (Bednarik 1992b). Such materials have exfoliated within one or two years, for instance at Mootwingee, Australia. The alternative is to mask the effect of incised, carved or pounded areas, which can be done by one of several methods. Shallow scratchings can be camouflaged by brushing off crushed rock particles and establishing a 'patina' matching adjacent surfaces (e.g. simply by rubbing with soil). The graffiti can be removed entirely by abrasives, such as the use of a dry air abrasive unit. This consists of a supply of compressed air, hose and nozzle, and a means of introducing abrasive powder into the air stream (Ford 1995). The abrasive can be aluminium oxide powder (17–27 μm), glass beads (50 μm) or sodium bicarbonate (100 μm). This is particularly effective in masking engraved graffiti and has also been used on otherwise intractable painted graffiti, but its use must be restricted to the minimum as it also removes rock surface. On carbonate rock, hydrochloric acid has been used to mask engraved graffiti, followed by thorough cleaning of the chlorides formed.

Rock areas treated with graffiti removal techniques tend to be of 'fresh' appearance and need to be 'aged'. Where the adjacent surfaces are coated by rock varnish, the method developed by Elvidge and Moore (1980) can be considered. Initially applied at Newspaper Rock and Petrified Forest National Park, Arizona, it consists of the application of a preparation encouraging the precipitation of iron and manganese oxides. (It is rather similar to the chemicals probably used in preparing the Piltdown fakes in 1912.) The desired colour can be achieved by manipulation of concentrations, ratios and application (Elvidge 1979). However, Bock and Bock (1990) have reviewed this work a decade later, and report many problems. For instance the artificial coating has significantly darkened with time, which suggests that in such work natural colour should not be matched, but the repair work should initially be much lighter. Most certainly the method should only be used by experienced conservators, and only on small areas that are in need of repair.

Other anthropic threats

Geophysical damage of rock art sites can be occasioned by large-scale human modifications of the lithosphere. Examples are the extraction of minerals, such as coal, by the 'long-wall' mining method, or the extraction of oil, gas or aquifer water. These methods lead to subsidence of upper strata, and consequently affect features such as rockshelters in these surface facies. In Australia, such subsidence is attributable to underground coal mining in the Woronora Plateau where it has caused damage to shelters containing rock art (Sefton 1995). Monitoring provides the opportunity for appropriate conservation measures.

Dust can be a significant factor in the deterioration of sheltered rock art, particularly through trampling of the floor sediment and archaeological excavations (Morwood 1994). Moreover, Watchman (1998) has shown that dust raised from vehicular traffic on a nearby, unsealed road can be highly effective in establishing a dust cover over rock art. His painstaking work at Split Rock, north Queensland, has also shown that such dust particles can comprise carbon-rich compounds probably created in diesel exhausts, which become attached to the dust while still hot. Transported as aerosols in the wind, this material not only settles on rock art, it can significantly distort the carbon system of the surface deposit (the hydrocarbons are ^{14}C-free). Watchman rightly emphasises the importance of detailed observations of all aspects of a site before it is developed for tourism. Airborne dust occurs naturally, but many human activities exacerbate the problem significantly (construction, land degradation, deforestation etc.). While it is washed off by rain at open sites, it accumulates in sheltered locations and often becomes incorporated in surface mineral deposits.

Humanly caused phenomena impact in many other ways on rock art and its support. The perhaps most commonly cited is the anthropic acidification of rain, caused essentially by the industrialisation of recent centuries. (Actually, anthropic contamination of the atmosphere began long before the industrial revolution; for instance in response to the massive increase in inefficient silver smelting at Roman times, the lead content of aerosols rose rapidly.) A lowering of pH leads to the mobilisation especially of iron ions and thus the destruction of rock varnishes on which many petroglyphs depend for their survival. However, other cations are also affected, which leads to increased weathering rates. Substrates particularly affected are those of limestone, dolomite and carbonate-cemented sandstones.

Although the issue of atmospheric acidification is one of the most important in rock art conservation, almost no research has been conducted into its effects so far. The only long-term study of the effects of industrial emissions on rock art is that of the huge petroglyph complex of the Dampier Archipelago in Western Australia (Bednarik 2002b). Begun in 1968 and still continuing, it has shown a direct correlation between the onset of heavy acidic pollution in the mid-1980s and the bleaching of ferromanganous accretionary deposits into which the Dampier petroglyphs have been carved. Beginning with 2002, the Dampier rock art precinct became the site of history's most bitterly fought confrontation between rock art conservationists and a state (Bednarik 2003, 2004a, 2004b).

Rock art has also been destroyed by numerous development projects, including the construction of railways, roads, dwellings and particularly dams. In Portugal alone, hundreds of rock art sites have been inundated by hydroelectric schemes with the complicity of the state's archaeological protection authority (Arcà et al. 2001). Throughout the world, rock art has been shot at, painted over, hacked out and sawn off. Australia might pride itself in having an enlightened attitude — and some of the world's least damaged rock art. But great numbers of petroglyphs at Port Hedland and Dampier sites were needlessly sacrificed to 'economic progress', and no doubt elsewhere in the country too. Rock art has been dynamited in Rio Tinto Gorge, Western Australia, by a man who found Aboriginal art annoying. In other parts of the world the same kind of action has at least a 'rational' intent: for instance, in Bolivia (at Toro Muerto) and Macedonia, rock art is being destroyed in this way by treasure hunters who believe it indicates the presence of hidden riches. This depressing litany of humanly caused destruction to rock art could be continued ad infinitum. If there should be any doubt about what the principal threat to rock art is, it would be well to recall that some of the best-preserved rock art can be found within the exclusion zones of American radioactive waste dumps.

Changing policies

Because rock art conservation and site management is such a new and underdeveloped field, sound policies in this area are far from firmly established. There is a clear lack of basic research into almost any facet of this field and therefore underlying policies remain very much in flux. A few specific points are considered to illustrate this.

Termite tracks and the nests of a variety of mud-daubing wasps are such a common feature at tens of thousands of rock art sites the world over, that they have long attracted the ire of site managers in all continents except Europe. Some years ago we had clear expert recommendations by entomologists on how to deal with such 'infestations' (Watson and Flood 1987; Naumann and Watson 1987). For instance, the mud nests were to be removed because of aesthetic concerns and the damage they do to rock paintings, but also because the presence of wasp nests tends to attract the construction of more nests. Since the recent introduction of luminescence dating of quartz grains contained in these nests (Morwood et al. 1994; Roberts et al. 1997, 2000) it has become apparent that such research can only be conducted if these structures have remained intact. Much the same would apply to termite tracks. Moreover, at least in northern Australia it has been shown that rock paintings occur not only under wasp nests, but are often found painted over remains of such structures which may have survived for millennia. Naturally they may also contain organic matter, which can be dated. At some sites, notably in South America, the interstitial spaces in wasp nests have become mineralised, resulting in fossilised wasp nests that are as hard as limestone. One would certainly not recommend their removal, particularly as they are likely to yield considerable environmental information about the past if appropriately analysed, and are no doubt datable.

In the very short time of a decade, our attitude to insect structures at rock art sites has changed dramatically, from the fundamental doctrine of banishing from the vicinity of rock art everything that might possibly interfere with it, or with our 'aesthetic appreciation' of it, to the present, better informed attitude. This raises two relevant points: firstly, our knowledge of the extent of actual damage to rock art was based on conjecture, not on sound research in most cases. Secondly, the overriding consideration was the enjoyment of the human visitor: how easy the art is to see, how photogenic it is.

Precisely the same applies to the removal of lichen. As noted in Chapter 7, lichen can be useful in the dating of rock art, and in most circumstances there is no evidence that they contribute to deterioration of rock (Smith 1962; Walderhaug and Walderhaug 1998). Some lichenologists argue that lichen may reduce weathering rates, and there can be no doubt that they reduce anthropic damage where they conceal the petroglyphs successfully. Evidence concerning the effects of lichens seems limited to such chemically fragile rocks as limestone (Wainwright 1985) and shale (Fry 1924, 1927). Better metamorphosed facies, beginning with schists, are probably not much affected by lichens, especially where thalli are thin and patchy. Chemically resistant rock types apparently benefit from lichen cover in that it protects them. The occurrence of loose flakes beneath lichens is not evidence that it was caused by them, which is in fact unlikely; it is the lichen that has held such clasts in place. Most lichen species use the rock only for support, deriving their nutrients from airborne detritus. This is demonstrated by their ability to colonise inert surfaces such as pure quartz, aluminium, fibreglass and galvanised steel roofs. I have microscopically examined the surface of terracotta roof tiles that had been covered by lichens for about a century and have detected no corrosive traces that might be attributable to these plants.

Ten or twenty years ago, the construction of buildings to house rock art in situ was considered in quite a number of countries — and sometimes implemented without any comprehensive independent consultation. The placement of such buildings is one of the two basic forms of 'massive intervention', the other being the sawing off and removal of whole panels to transport them to a museum, which was last proposed in the Côa valley in Portugal, and defeated. The problems encountered in three such structures erected over petroglyph panels, in Canada, Russia and Sweden, have been critically reviewed (Bahn et al. 1995, 1996; Bahn and Hygen 1996). In all three cases the buildings are considered to be failures, primarily because massive intervention involves the creation of entirely different environmental conditions than those in which a rock art panel has managed to survive for centuries or millennia. While the rock art was certainly suffering some damage under conditions of natural weathering, the ameliorating effect of placing it inside a building may easily be negated by new threats due to new conditions which the rock had not previously experienced. Thus deterioration may well be accelerated by massive intervention. Again, a strategy of past years has become questionable after close scrutiny.

This applies also to the use of air abrasive equipment (Ford 1995) in emphasising patinated petroglyphs. Some years ago this method was applied to petroglyphs in the Sydney sandstone area of Australia, until members of the public objected and complained to an independent scholarly organisation, the Australian Rock Art Research Association. The practice was then discontinued, but the use of such equipment is still being advocated occasionally. There are legitimate applications for it, especially in the removal of modern graffiti — but once again we can see that the activities of rock art conservators need to be monitored by open peer review, and practitioners themselves need to be sensitive to such discussion. Another example is the widespread notion that graffiti beget more graffiti, hence to remove the existing graffiti may eliminate the motivation for the graffiti artist. This may well be true, but is at best a general rule of thumb. As detailed above, it has also been found that, when a small area in a graffiti-covered site was cleaned, within a year new graffiti appeared in the area left vacant by the graffiti removal (Bednarik 1992b).

An important recent development in rock art conservation work is the emerging emphasis on monitoring. In the past, resources were usually only made available for the duration of a particular project, and once this work was completed there were no funds and there was no further interest. Rock art preservation and site management measures need to be monitored over very long time spans. For the benefit of the global specialist community, both positive and negative effects must be determined and objectively reported. Without such measures, mistakes would be repeated over and over, thousands of times. Detailed follow-up technical reports are therefore required, and they need to be rendered accessible to the rock art conservators of the world. In view of the tendency of governments to re-organise their technocracies at rather regular intervals it is evident that no state agencies can be entrusted with such a long-term responsibility. Rather, universities and scholarly societies (specifically, the members of IFRAO) need to be entrusted with the necessary vigilance to ensure that such long-term monitoring is not neglected. Site monitoring is greatly facilitated by modern digitised equipment, which offers the benefit of facilitating types of research largely neglected until now: the measurement of surface retreat on fragile rock such as sandstones (see Ch. 7), the monitoring of weathering processes generally, of paint residue colours and of patination, among other variables.

A matter related to monitoring is the need to 'finger-print' interventions in rock art, in the way pioneered by Thorn (1993). Graphical documentation has long been considered appropriate, but Thorn introduced a new way of identifying interventions: by including in substances applied (such as paints or varnishes) materials the skilled researcher can readily identify as modern. For instance glass micro-spheres, ranging in size from 10–200 μm, are readily identifiable microscopically and by x-ray diffraction. They can be included in substances applied by the conservator, indicating that the intervention must postdate 1972 (when the glass spheres were first made). Similarly, certain colours used in toning incisions (e.g. synthetically manufactured ochres known as Mars colours, titanium white, manganese blue, platinum yellow) only became available at specific times in modern history, and they are readily identifiable microscopically. In contrast to the pigments used in pre-History, which contain many incidental inclusions, these synthetic substances are pure and of even particle size.

The introduction of peer review

The Côa example (Bednarik 1995b) and others recently published (Bednarik 2002b) have shown that the state authorities who have in the past conducted cultural heritage management (CRM) much as they saw fit are no longer immune to independent review. The establishment agencies supervising such matters, run by paid professionals with the 'independent' advice of paid consultants, are beginning to be subjected to genuinely independent peer review (Arcà et al. 2001).

While this is no doubt a healthy development, there has been opposition to it from some CRM quarters. It is relevant to cite from a pioneer of rock art conservation practices: 'I find that almost anywhere I go, when governments, corporations and even academic colleagues within the discipline [of archaeology] become involved with rock art conservation, the results are usually disastrous' (Swartz 1997a). This echoes the similar sentiments expressed by Bahn et al. (1996: 56–57) when they discuss the dynamics of CRM bureaucracy in general.

One of the responses to this new development has been the argument by CRM commentators that rock art conservators form a professional body that should not be criticised by outsiders, and that such criticisms are contrary to the interests of the discipline. There is perhaps some truth in this, even though the principle of developing a technocracy that is answerable only to its salaried practitioners needs to be rejected. It must be appreciated, however, that most rock art site management work in the world is not conducted by trained conservators, but by people with other and often almost unrelated training, especially by archaeologists. There is nothing in standard archaeological training that could possibly provide the necessary expertise to make executive decisions on sound conservation and management practices. Such practices must be based primarily on geochemical and geomorphological knowledge, and knowledge about the failures and successes of other such projects around the world. The CRM 'industry' has no policy of disseminating information about failures, and tends to react negatively when such experiences are made public (cf. Bahn et al. 1995 and subsequent comments). In the past the result has been that site management mistakes were repeated over and over elsewhere, because failures were not reported. It should be obvious that improvements are only possible by frank and open exchanges, and for this an open system of peer review is essential. Those who oppose this undermine the credibility of the industry more than those who criticise past practices.

Repainting of sites

In Australia, protective site works are more likely to be initiated by traditional Aboriginal owners or custodians than by archaeologists, and Aborigines are the principal stakeholders in any matter pertaining to Australian rock art (Ward and Sullivan 1989) or archaeology. They do not regard rock art as an archaeological resource, but as a very important physical manifestation of their tremendously rich spiritual culture. Cultural re-assertion expressed in the demand for control over cultural properties as experienced in Australia can reasonably be predicted to occur in due course in other parts of the world, such as the Americas, specific parts of Asia and perhaps southern Africa. Archaeologists there would be well advised not to repeat the mistake some of their Australian colleagues made, and oppose the curatorial aspirations of indigenous groups over indigenous cultural remains. In my own discussions with Aboriginal leaders they have themselves consistently expressed the desire for employing rock art conservators, and as they secure public funds for such projects it could well be that Aboriginal co-operatives and communities will become the major employer of rock art conservators.

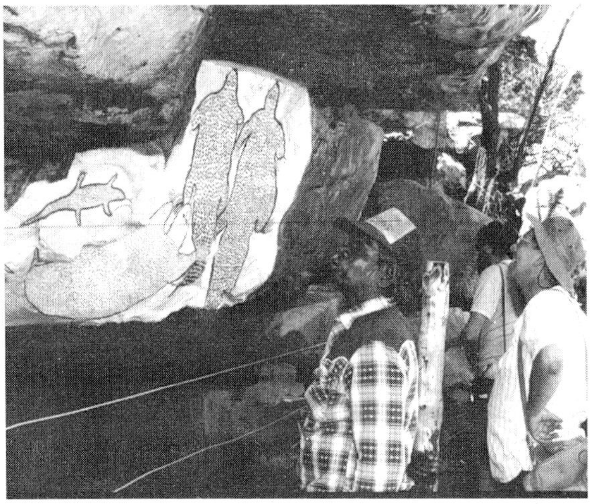

Figure 44. Wandjina site in the Kimberley, Australia, repainted in 1987, with traditional site custodian D. C., in 1988.

Australian archaeologists have been divided over how to respond to Aboriginal aspirations to regain control over their material cultural heritage. In the case of rock art sites, the traditional owners have had the support of the Australian Rock Art Research Association since its inception in 1983. A contentious key issue was whether present-day Aborigines should be permitted to continue the cyclical repainting of images (Chaloupka 1992), usually termed 'retouch'. Watchman (1992, 2000) has shown that this custom has existed for many millennia. It is a central tenet of Aboriginal beliefs that it is the sacred duty of the traditional custodians of a site to retouch or renew rock paintings when fading became evident. This responsibility has been handed down to them for countless generations, ever since the spirit beings that created much of the art had instructed the people to do so (Mowaljarlai 1992). Failure to comply with these instructions could result in malfunction of the natural order and punishment of the people concerned (Crawford 1968; Vinnicombe 1992). During European occupation of the continent, most surviving Aboriginal groups were removed from their traditional land, often forcibly, which led to the interruption of these traditional practices. In recent decades, however, there has been a trend to reinstate such practices to some degree, even in a revivalist sense (Morris and Hamm 1995). In the late 1980s this issue led to a confrontation between parties that either supported or opposed Aboriginal retouch of rock art sites, as a result of a specific project in the Kimberley region of north-western Australia (Ward 1992a; Clarke and Randolph 1992). The matter was extensively debated at the First AURA Congress, where a whole symposium was dedicated to it (Ward 1992b). While there is no clear-cut outcome evident, the extreme positions at either end of the spectrum appear no longer tenable, and Aboriginal communities have become increasingly empowered in their quest to regain their culture (Figure 44).

In Australia this has thus become a principal factor in rock art research as well as site management issues. Such matters are generally taking place in consultation with the relevant traditional custodians, and researchers working in Australia are now well aware that they do so under the authority of those who own indigenous Australian material culture. This new understanding of roles has been quite beneficial to European researchers, if only to remind them that their own metaphysical and academic reality is ethnocentric. Developments in the reassertion of ethnic identities in various parts of the world are likely to lead to similar endeavours there, once these societies appreciate that rock art corpora can become foci of cultural renewal. While repainting has so far been primarily an Australian feature, it is certainly not uniquely Australian. In North America, Spier (1930) reported the periodic repainting of rock art from the Columbia Plateau, and Loubser (2001) notes evidence of the practice in both southern Africa and Baja California.

Discussion

In rock art conservation the simplistic notion that 'the experts surely know best' is false. In precisely the same way as the methods and strategies of yesteryear's rock art conservator are superseded and outdated by contemporary thinking, our present priorities will be superseded in a very short time by ever more enlightened attitudes and practices. It is essential that this be fully understood by the rock art conservator, and that management decisions be based on reversibility of measures, and on the full appreciation of our severe limitations due to a chronic lack of relevant basic research. The overriding factor in all rock art management must be the understanding that we cannot afford to 'get it wrong': the resource is, after all, not renewable, and any alteration of the environment is likely to have unforeseeable effects as well as those one desires.

To appreciate these dynamics it is useful to consider certain parallels elsewhere. Recording methods that were accepted or at least tolerated just ten or twenty years ago are frowned upon today, or even thoroughly condemned in various cases. The reasons for these changes in attitude, be it in recording or in conservation, are largely attributable to the sudden rise of rock art science over the last decade or so, which introduced methods of analysing rock art and which promises to develop ever more sophisticated approaches. The general principle that has been espoused as a result over the past ten or fifteen years is that rock art recording work as well as any rock art conservation, preservation or site management work must be conducted in such a way as not to prejudice present and future scientific methods (Bednarik 1987b). Many people currently making decisions about rock art sites are not adequately familiar with present scientific research methods, and no-one, including rock art scientists themselves, can know the types of future methods. Hence the rule is very simply that direct interference with rock art is to be avoided in all except absolutely desperate cases.

In rock art conservation there are no standard diagnoses or treatments. Each site is different, and the management of each must be planned in a site-specific manner. One of the few truly universal rules that have emerged in recent decades refers to the concept of 'site fabric'. This is intended to mean all physical aspects of a rock art site, including accretionary deposits and lichens, the art itself, traces of later human responses, even of vandalism in cases, and also the general site setting, or what is described as its ambience. In modern rock art conservation, the integrity of the whole site is increasingly emphasised, as well as genuine consultation of those groups that are stakeholders in the rock art and the site. These ideals are central to the tenor of the IFRAO Code of Ethics (see Ch. 11).

Scientific information about rock art would be readily available, but it has attracted relatively little attention: how was the rock art created, when, and by whom? These questions are perfectly answerable through the use of refutable propositions, yet they have traditionally attracted little sustained research effort. For instance the amount of replicative research, so useful in the study of portable palaeoart, is diminutive in petroglyph studies. Studies of inclusions in rock art paints (brush fibres, airborne particles, extenders etc.) are in their infancy, as are studies of paint composition. Thus the speculations we have about 'meaning' and so forth lack any factual basis, they are simply the outcome of pure and often baseless conjecture. Management decisions have to be frequently based on the significance of rock art, and yet this significance is being decided on the basis of very questionable criteria.

Similarly, in the area of rock art conservation and site management, we have to contend with a widespread lack of appropriate basic research. This applies to the effects of lichen as much as to those of other biological factors, rainwater pH, insolation, wetting and drying as well as freezing and thawing cycles, not to mention those of humanly applied chemicals, or other human influence (Bednarik 1990e, 1991a). For instance, in South Africa, Meiklejohn's work (1995, 1997) has shown how little we really do know about fundamental issues that concern rock art management, and much the same has been found in other countries.

It seems that the best way to summarise present perceptions about rock art conservation and management is to say that this is not the domain of archaeologists, and that specialists with the appropriate knowledge need to appreciate the value of open peer review, and of frank dissemination of results from such projects. Rock art does not belong to the state, it was merely handed down to us by countless generations before us to pass on to countless generations after us. It is an immensely valuable scientific resource to some, a cherished cultural heritage to others. The generations that will follow us have the right to judge our performance in how we deal with the responsibility of managing this collective property of all of humanity's generations — past, present and future.

REFERENCES

ARCÀ, A., R. G. BEDNARIK, A. FOSSATI, L. JAFFE and M. SIMÕES DE ABREU 2001. Damned dams again: the plight of Portuguese rock art. *Rock Art Research* 18(1): i–iv.

BAHN 1994. Lascaux: composition or accumulation? *Zepyrvs* 47: 3–13.

BAHN, P. G., R. G. BEDNARIK and J. STEINBRING 1995. The Peterborough Petroglyph Site: reflections on massive intervention in rock art. *Rock Art Research* 12: 29–41.

BAHN, P. G., R. G. BEDNARIK and J. STEINBRING 1996. Peer review of massive intervention in rock art management practice. *Rock Art Research* 13: 54–60.

BAHN, P. G. and A.-S. HYGEN 1996. More on massive intervention: the Aspeberget structure. *Rock Art Research* 13: 137–38.

BEDNARIK, R. G. 1970. Die Grabungen in der Promenadensteighöhle (1961–1964). *Die Höhle* 21: 117–26.

BEDNARIK, R. G. 1979. The potential of rock patination analysis in Australian archaeology – part 1. *The Artefact* 4: 14–38.

BEDNARIK, R. G. 1987a. No pictographs at end of Rochester Creek rainbow. *La Pintura* 15(2+3): 14–18.

BEDNARIK, R. G. 1987b. The chalking of petroglyphs: a response. *La Pintura* 15(2+3): 12–13.

BEDNARIK, R. G. 1988a. *The Paroong Cave preservation project.* Occasional AURA Publication 1, Australian Rock Art Research Association, Melbourne.

BEDNARIK, R. G. 1988b. El arte rupestre Boliviano visto desde el exterior. *SIARB Boletín* 2: 22–28.

BEDNARIK, R. G. 1989. Priorities in rock art conservation. *Pictogram* 2(1): 5–6.

BEDNARIK, R. G. 1990a. About professional rock art vandals. *The Rock Art Quarterly* 1(1+2): 11–16.

BEDNARIK, R. G. 1990b. The cave petroglyphs of Australia. *Australian Aboriginal Studies* 1990/2: 64–68.

BEDNARIK, R. G. 1990c. Petroglyph moulds and ethical standards. *Archaeology in New Zealand* 33(4): 209–13.

BEDNARIK, R. G. 1990d. Sobre la practica de tizar los petroglifos. *SIARB Boletin* 4: 24–26.

BEDNARIK, R. G. 1990e. Priorità nella conservazione dell'arte rupestre. *Survey* 4: 13–19.

BEDNARIK, R. G. 1991a. Rock art researchers as rock art vandals. *Sahara* 4: 166–68.

BEDNARIK, R. G. 1991b. The Paroong Cave preservation project. In C. Pearson and B. K. Swartz (eds), *Rock art and posterity: conserving, managing and recording rock art*, pp. 66–70. Occasional AURA Publication 4, Australian Rock Art Research Association, Melbourne.

BEDNARIK, R. G. 1992a. Developments in rock art dating. *Acta Archaeologica* 63: 141–55.

BEDNARIK, R. G. 1992b. Prioritetnye napravleniya v rabotakh po konservatsii pamyatnikov naskal'nogo iskusstva. In *Naskal'nye risunki evrazil, Pervobytnoe iskusstvo*, pp. 8–13. Novosibirsk 'Nauka', Sibirskoe otdelenie, Novosibirsk.

BEDNARIK, R. G. 1992c. Permanence of art and transience of graffiti. *La Pintura* 19(2): 10–13.

BEDNARIK, R. G. 1992d. A new method to date petroglyphs. *Archaeometry* 34(2): 279–91.

BEDNARIK, R. G. 1992e. Acerca de la motivación del re-uso del arte rupestre: un ejemplo del Período Colonial de Bolivia. In R. Querejazu Lewis (ed.), *El arte rupestre colonial y republicano de Bolivia y paises vecinos*, pp. 28–35. Contribuciones al Estudio del Arte Rupestre Sudamericano 3. SIARB, La Paz.

BEDNARIK, R. G. 1994a. A taphonomy of palaeoart. *Antiquity* 68: 68–74.

BEDNARIK, R. G. 1994b. Introducing the IFRAO Standard Scale. *Pictogram* 7(1): 17–19.

BEDNARIK, R. G. 1995a. Rock art preservation in Siberia. In A. Thorn and J. Brunet (eds), *Preservation of rock art*, pp. 21–27. Occasional AURA Publication 9, Australian Rock Art Research Association Inc., Melbourne.

BEDNARIK, R. G. 1995b. The age of the Côa valley petroglyphs in Portugal. *Rock Art Research* 12: 86–103.

BEDNARIK, R. G. 1996. Only time will tell: a review of the methodology of direct rock art dating. *Archaeometry* 38: 1–13.

BEDNARIK, R. G. 1998. Direct dating results from Australian cave petroglyphs. *Geoarchaeology* 13(4): 411–18.

BEDNARIK, R. G. 2001. First dating of Pilbara petroglyphs. *Records of the Western Australian Museum* 20: 414–29.

BEDNARIK, R. G. 2002a. Paläolithische Felskunst in Deutschland? *Archäologische Informationen* 25(1-2): 107–17.

BEDNARIK, R. G. 2002b. The survival of the Murujuga (Burrup) petroglyphs. *Rock Art Research* 19: 29–40.

BEDNARIK, R. G. 2003. Dampier report April 2003. *AURA Newsletter* 20(1): 5–8.

BEDNARIK, R. G. 2004a. Dampier report May 2004. *AURA Newsletter* 21(1): 2–6.

BEDNARIK, R. G. 2004b. IFRAO's Dampier campaign. *Rock Art Research* 21: 207–10.

BEDNARIK, R. G. 2004c. Public archaeology and political dynamics in Portugal. *Public Archaeology* 3(3): 162–66.

BEDNARIK, R. G. and K. DEVLET 1993. Problemy konservatsiï pamyatnikov naskal'nogo iskusstva verkhneï Leny. *Sovremennye problemy isucheniya petroglifov*, pp. 37–48. Spornik Nauchnykh Trudov, Kemerovskiï Rocudarstvennyï Universitet, Kemerovo.

BEDNARIK, R. G. and M. KHAN 2002. The Saudi Arabian rock art mission of November 2001. *Atlal* 17: 75–99.

BEDNARIK, R. G., G. KUMAR, A. WATCHMAN and R. G. ROBERTS 2005. Preliminary results of the EIP Project: the status at the end of 2004. *Rock Art Research* 22.

BERNER, R. A. 1992. Weathering, plants, and the long-term carbon cycle. *Geochimica et Cosmochimica Acta* 56: 3225–31.

BERTHELIN, J. 1988. Microbial weathering processes in natural environments. In A. Lerman and M. Meybeck (eds), *Physical and chemical weathering in geochemical cycles*, pp. 33–59. Kluwer Academic Publishers, New York.

BERTILSSON, U. and J. MAGNUSSEN 2000. Documentation and care. In K. Kallhovd and J. Magnusson (eds), *Rock carvings in the borderlands*, pp. 73–106. Interreg IIA Project, Bohuslän/Dalsland and Østfold.

BLANKS, T. and S. BROWN 1991. Mt Cameron West rock art protection project: an assessment of the conservation program undertaken to June 1988. In C. Pearson and B. K. Swartz (eds), *Rock art and posterity: conserving, managing and recording rock art*, pp. 45–51. Occasional AURA Publication 4, Australian Rock Art Research Association, Melbourne.

BOCK, F. and A. J. BOCK 1990. A re-examination of an attempt to restore petroglyphs using artificial desert varnish at Petrified Forest. *Pictogram* 3(3): 5–11.

BRAMMC 2004. Summaries of proposed rock art monitoring studies, Burrup Rock Art Monitoring Management Committee. *AURA Newsletter* 21(1): 3–5.

BRUNET, J., J. VOUVÉ, P. VIDAL, P. MALAURENT and G. LACEZEDIEU 1995. Theories and practice of the conservation of our heritage of rock art: concrete examples of interventions in natural climatic environment. In A. Thorn and J. Brunet (eds), *Preservation of rock art*, pp. 1–12. Occasional AURA Publication 9, Australian Rock Art Research Association Inc., Melbourne.

CHALOUPKA, G. 1992. Retouch events. In G. K. Ward (ed.), *Retouch: maintenance and conservation of Aboriginal rock imagery*, pp. 12–16. Occasional AURA Publication 5, Australian Rock Art Research Association, Melbourne.

CHESTNUT, W. S. 1972. *Geological investigations of deterioration problems affecting Aboriginal art works at Mootwingee (Broken Hill) and Mount Grenfell (Cobar)*. Geological Survey of N.S.W., Department of Mines, Sydney.

CLARKE, J. 1978. Deterioration analysis of rock art sites. In C. Pearson (ed.), *Rock art conservation*, pp. 54–64. Institute for the Conservation of Cultural Material, Sydney.

CLARKE, J. and P. RANDOLPH 1992. Repainting of Kimberley Wandjina rock art sites. In G. K. Ward (ed.), *Retouch: maintenance and conservation of Aboriginal rock imagery*, pp. 17–22. Occasional AURA Publication 5, Australian Rock Art Research Association, Melbourne.

CLOTTES, J. J. COURTIN and H. VALLADAS 1992. A well-dated Palaeolithic cave: the Cosquer Cave at Marseille. *Rock Art Research* 9: 122–29.

COCHRAN, M. F. and R. A. BERNER 1992. The quantitative role of plants in weathering. In Y. K. Kharaka and A. S. Maest (eds), *Water-rock interaction*, pp. 473–76. Balkema, Rotterdam.

COCHRAN, M. F. and R. A. BERNER 1993. Reply to the comments on 'Weathering, plants, and the long-term carbon cycle'. *Geochimica et Cosmochimica Acta* 57: 2147–48.

CONARD, N. J and H.-P. UERPMANN 2000. New evidence for Paleolithic rock painting in central Europe. *Current Anthropology* 41: 853–56.

CRAWFORD, I. 1968. *The art of the Wandjina*. Oxford University Press, Melbourne.

DREVER, J. I. 1994. The effect of land plants on weathering rates of silicate minerals. *Geochimica et Cosmochimica Acta* 58: 2325–32.

ECKHARDT, F. E. W. 1978. Microorganisms and weathering of a sandstone monument. In W. E. K. Krumbein (ed.), *Environmental biochemistry and geomicrobiology*, pp. 675–686. Ann Arbor Science Publishers, Ann Arbor.

ELVIDGE, C. D. 1979. Experimental restoration to petroglyphs. MS at Western Archaeological Conservation Center, Tucson, Arizona.

ELVIDGE, C. D. and C. B. MOORE 1980. Restoration of petroglyphs with artificial desert varnish. *Studies in Conservation* 25: 108–17.

FERNANDEZ, P. L. 1986. Natural ventilation of the paintings room in the Altamira cave. *Nature* 321: 586–88.

FINN, P. and N. HALL 1995. Removal of iron fastenings and iron stains from sites in the Grampians (Gariwerd). In A. Thorn and J. Brunet (eds), *Preservation of rock art*, pp. 65–71. Occasional AURA Publication 9, Australian Rock Art Research Association, Melbourne.

FLORIAN, M. L. E. 1978. A review: the lichen role in rock art — dating, deterioration and control. In C. Pearson (ed.), *Conservation of rock art*, pp. 95–98. Institute for the Conservation of Cultural Material, Sydney.

FORD, B. 1995. Portable air abrasive unit for rock art graffiti removal. In A. Thorn and J. Brunet (eds), *Preservation of rock art*, pp. 72-76. Occasional AURA Publication 9, Australian Rock Art Research Association, Melbourne.

FREEMAN, L. G. 1994. The many faces of Altamira. *Complutum* 5: 331–42.

FRY, E. J. 1924. A suggested explanation of the mechanical action of lithophytic lichens on rocks (shale). *Annals of Botany* 38: 175–96.

FRY, E. J. 1927. The mechanical action of crustaceous lichens on substrata of shale, schist, gneiss, limestone, and obsidian. *Annals of Botany* 41: 437–60.

GALE, F. 1985. Monitoring visitor behaviour at rock art sites. *Rock Art Research* 2: 112–18.

GALE, F. and J. JACOBS 1986. Identifying high-risk visitors at Aboriginal art sites in Australia. *Rock Art Research* 3(1): 3–19.

GALE, F. and J. M. JACOBS 1987. *Tourists and the national estate. Procedures to protect Australia's heritage.* Special Australian Heritage Publication Series 6, Australian Government Publishing Service, Canberra.

GILLESPIE, D. A. 1983. The practice of rock art conservation and site management in Kakadu National Park. In D. A. Gillespie (ed.), *The rock art sites of Kakadu National Park.* Australian National Parks and Wildlife Service, Canberra.

HAHN, J. 1990. Höhlenkunst aus dem Hohlen Fels bei Schelklingen, Alb-Donau-Kreis. *Archäologische Ausgrabungen in Baden-Württemberg* 10: 19–22.

HALL, K. J. and A. HALL 1991. Thermal gradients and rock weathering at low temperatures: some simulation data. *Permafrost and Periglacial Processes* 2: 103–12.

HASKOVEC, I. P. 1991. On some non-technical issues of conservation. In C. Pearson and B. K. Swartz (eds), *Rock art and posterity: conserving, managing and recording rock art*, pp. 97–99. Occasional AURA Publication 4, Australian Rock Art Research Association, Melbourne.

HUARANCA, F. 1995. Protección de las pinturas rupestres del Parque Nacional de Torotoro, Dpto. de Potosí, Bolivia. In M. Strecker and F. Taboada Tellez (eds), *Administración y conservación de sitios de arte rupestre*, pp. 112–23. Sociedad de Investigación del Arte Rupestre de Bolivia, La Paz.

JACKSON, T. A. and W. D. KELLER 1970. A comparative study of the role of lichens and 'inorganic' processes in the chemical weathering of recent Hawaiian lava flows. *American Journal of Science* 269: 446–66.

JAFFE, L. 1996. Systematic vandalism and improper conduct in the Côa valley rock art area. *AURA Newsletter* 13(2): 12–13.

KENNEDY, B. 1979. Initial attempts at conservation work at rock art sites in British Columbia. *CRARA '77, Papers of the 4th biennial conference of the Canadian Rock Art Research Associates*, pp. 285–92.

LAMBERT, D. 1980. The influence of ground water salts in the formation of sandstone shelters near Gosford, NSW. *ICCM Bulletin* 6(3, 4): 29–34.

LAMBERT, D. 1995. Colour monitoring. In A. Thorn and J. Brunet (eds), *Preservation of rock art*, pp. 77–79. Occasional AURA Publication 9, Australian Rock Art Research Association, Melbourne.

LAVER, M. E. and I. N. M. WAINWRIGHT 1995. An investigation of the dissolution of a marble petroglyph site by acidic precipitation. *Studies in Conservation* 40: 265–73.

LÖFVENDAHL, R. and J. MAGNUSSON 2000. Research and development — degradation and care. In K. Kallhovd and J. Magnusson (eds), *Rock carvings in the borderlands*, pp. 47–72. Interreg IIA Project, Bohuslän /Dalsland and Østfold.

LOUBSER, J. 2001. Management planning for conservation. In D. S. Whitley (ed.), *Handbook of rock art research*, pp. 80–115. AltaMira Press, Walnut Creek, California.

McNICKLE, H. P. 1991. A survey of rock art in the Victoria River District, Northern Territory. *Rock Art Research* 8: 36–46.

MASAO, F. T. 1996. The rock art of Tanzania: status of conservation and research. *International Newsletter on Rock Art* 14: 26–8.

MEIKLEJOHN, K. I. 1995. The deterioration and preservation of rock art in the Kwazulu/Natal Clarens formation: a geomorphological perspective. *Pictogram* 8(1): 1–13.

MEIKLEJOHN, K. I. 1997. Rock art sites, deterioration, protection and utilisation. Paper presented to conference on 'Learning and teaching about rock art and the people who made it', African Window, Pretoria, 19 April 1997.

MORRIS, G. and G. HAMM 1995. Aboriginal use of traditional rock painting and engraving sites as a means of cultural revival. In G. K. Ward and L. A. Ward (eds), *Management of rock imagery*, pp. 63–70. Occasional AURA Publication 9, Australian Rock Art Research Association, Melbourne.

MORWOOD, M. J. 1994. Handy household hints for archaeological excavations at rock art sites. *Rock Art Research* 11: 10–12.

MORWOOD, M. J. and Y. KAISER-GLASS 1991. The use of graffiti in the monitoring of community attitudes towards Aboriginal rock art. *Rock Art Research* 8: 94–98.

MORWOOD, M. J., G. L. WALSH and A. WATCHMAN 1994. The dating potential of rock art in the Kimberley, N.W. Australia. *Rock Art Research* 11: 79–87.

MOWALJARLAI, D. 1992. A Ngarinyin perspective of repainting: Mowaljarlai's statement to the Symposium. In G. K. Ward (ed.), *Retouch: maintenance and conservation of Aboriginal rock imagery*, pp. 8–9. Occasional AURA Publication 5, Australian Rock Art Research Association, Melbourne.

MOWALJARLAI, D. and A. WATCHMAN 1989. An Aboriginal view of rock art management. *Rock Art Research* 6: 151–53.

NAUMANN, I. D. and J. A. L. WATSON 1987. Wasps and bees (Hymenoptera) on rock faces at Koolburra. *Rock Art Research* 4: 26–27.

NOLLER, B. N., N. CURREY, G. AYERS, R. GILLETT, A. HARRISON and R. A. RASMUSSEN 1987. Chemistry of rainwater acidity, nutrients and trace metals. In *Alligator Rivers Region Research Institute Annual Report Summary for 1985–86*, pp. 53–55. Australian Government Publishing Service, Canberra.

OLLIER, C. D. 1969 (revd. edn. 1975). *Weathering.* London.

PALMER, K. 1991. Indigenous art and the limits of social science. *Rock Art Research* 8: 113–18.

PROBERT, D. and I. WALLACE 1970. *Geological report on the preservation of a rock slope at Mootwingee Historic Site.* Geological Survey of N.S.W., Department of Mines, Sydney.

RITTER, E. W. 1991. Conservation and protection within the American Rock Art Research Association. In C.

Pearson and B. K. Swartz (eds), *Rock art and posterity: conserving, managing and recording rock art*, pp. 7–15. Occasional AURA Publication 4, Australian Rock Art Research Association, Melbourne.

ROBERTS, R., G. WALSH, A. MURRAY, J. OLLEY, R. JONES, M. MORWOOD, C. TUNIZ, E. LAWSON, M. MACPHAIL, D. BOWDERY and I. NAUMANN 1997. Luminescence dating of rock art and past environments using mud-wasp nests in northern Australia. *Nature* 387: 696–99.

ROBERTS, R. G., G. L. WALSH, J. M. OLLEY, A. S. MURRAY M. K. MACPHAIL, I. D. NAUMANN, R. JONES and M. J. MORWOOD 2000. Rock-picture chronologies and palaeoenvironmental records from fossil mud-wasp nests: preliminary investigations using optical dating. In G. K. Ward and C. Tuniz (eds), *Advances in dating Australian rock-markings*, pp. 40–44. Occasional AURA Publication 10, Australian Rock Art Research Association, Melbourne.

ROSENFELD, A. 1985. *Rock art conservation in Australia*. Special Australian Heritage Publication Series 6, Australian Government Publishing Service, Canberra.

SCHEFFER, F. B. MEYER and E. KALK 1963. Biologische Ursachen der Wüstenlackbildung. *Zeitschrift für Geomorphologie* 7: 112–19.

SCHMID, E. 1958. *Höhlenforschung und Sediment analyse*. Schriften des Institutes für Ur- und Frühgeschichte der Schweiz, Volume 13. Basle.

SCHWARTZBAUM, P. M. 1985. The role of conservation techniques in rock art conservation. *Rock Art Research* 2: 65–70.

SEFTON, C. 1995. Sandstone overhangs and subsidence: monitoring rock art for effects of mining activities. In A. Thorn and J. Brunet (eds), *Preservation of rock art*, pp. 55–59. Occasional AURA Publication 9, Australian Rock Art Research Association, Melbourne.

SELKIRK, P. M. and D. ADAMSON 1981. The effect of fire on Sydney sandstone. In P. Stanbury (ed.), *Bush fires: their effect on Australian life and landscapes*. Maclay Museum, Sydney University.

SILVERMAN, M. P. and E. F. MUNOZ 1970. Fungal attack on rock: solubilisation and altered infrared spectra. *Science* 169: 985–87.

SMITH, D. C. 1962. The biology of lichen thalli. *Biological Review* 37: 537–70.

SPIER, L. 1930. *Klamath ethnography*. University of California Publications in American Archaeology and Ethnology 30, Berkeley.

SPRY, A. H. 1981. *The conservation of Masonry materials in historic buildings*. Australian Mineral Development Laboratories, Department for the Environment of South Australia, Adelaide.

SWARTZ, B. K. 1981. Standards for the recording of petroglyphs and pictographs. *Current Anthropology* 22(1): 94–95.

SWARTZ, B. K. 1997a. An evaluation of rock art conservation practices at Foz Côa, northern Portugal. *Rock Art Research* 14: 73–75.

SWARTZ, B. K. 1997b. An investigation of the Portuguese government policies on the management of the Foz Côa sites. *Rock Art Research* 14: 75–76.

SYERS, J. K. and I. K. ISKANDAR 1973. Pedogenetic significance of lichens. In V. Ahmadjian and M. E. Hale (eds), *The lichens*, pp. 225–248. Academic Press, London.

THORN, A. 1991. The removal of recent overpaint from the image of Bunjil. In C. Pearson and B. K. Swartz (eds), *Rock art and posterity: conserving, managing and recording rock art*, pp. 71–79. Occasional AURA Publication 4, Australian Rock Art Research Association, Melbourne.

THORN, A. 1993. Dating intervention. *Rock Art Research* 10: 126–31.

TRATEBAS, A. M. and F. CHAPMAN 1996. Ethical and conservation issues in removing lichens from petroglyphs. *Rock Art Research* 13: 129–33.

TRICART, J. 1969. Étude expérimentale du problème de la gélivation. *Biuletyn Peryglacjanly* 2: 285–318.

TYAGI, G. S. 1991. Conservation of Indian rock art. In C. Pearson and B. K. Swartz (eds), *Rock art and posterity: conserving, managing and recording rock art*, pp. 28–29. Occasional AURA Publication 4, Australian Rock Art Research Association, Melbourne.

VINNICOMBE, P. 1992. Kimberley ideology and the maintenance of sites. In G. K. Ward (ed.), *Retouch: maintenance and conservation of Aboriginal rock imagery*, pp. 10–11. Occasional AURA Publication 5, Australian Rock Art Research Association, Melbourne.

WAINWRIGHT, I. N. M. 1985. Rock art conservation research in Canada. *Bollettino del Centro Camuno di Studi Preistorici* 22: 15–37.

WALDERHAUG, O. and E. M. WALDERHAUG 1998. Weathering of Norwegian rock art — a critical review. *Norwegian Archaeological Review* 31: 119–39.

WALSH, G. L. 1991. Flinders Group National Park site management: regional cultural resource evaluation, preservation and selective presentation in far north Queensland. In C. Pearson and B. K. Swartz (eds), *Rock art and posterity: conserving, managing and recording rock art*, pp. 34–44. Occasional AURA Publication 4, Australian Rock Art Research Association, Melbourne.

WALSTON, S. and J. DOLANSKI 1976. Two painted and engraved sandstone sites in Australia. *Studies in Conservation* 21: 1–17.

WARD, G. K. 1992a. Ochre and acrylic: conflicting ideologies and divergent discourses in the issue of re-painting of Aboriginal imagery. In G. K. Ward (ed.), *Retouch: maintenance and conservation of Aboriginal rock imagery*, pp. 31–38. Occasional AURA Publication 5, Australian Rock Art Research Association, Melbourne.

WARD, G. K. 1992b. The 'retouch' symposium of the First AURA Congress, Darwin: an introduction. In G. K. Ward (ed.), *Retouch: maintenance and conservation of Aboriginal rock imagery*, pp. 1–7. Occasional AURA Publication 5, Australian Rock Art Research Association, Melbourne.

WARD, G. K. and S. SULLIVAN 1989. The Australian Institute of Aboriginal Studies Rock Art Protection Program. *Rock Art Research* 6: 54–62.

WATCHMAN, A. 1990. A summary of occurrences of oxalate-rich crusts in Australia. *Rock Art Research* 7: 44–50.

WATCHMAN, A. 1992. Repainting or periodic-painting at Australian Aboriginal sites: evidence from rock surface crusts. In G. K. Ward (ed.), *Retouch: maintenance and conservation of Aboriginal rock imagery*, pp. 26–30. Occasional AURA Publication 5, Australian Rock Art Research Association, Melbourne.

WATCHMAN, A. 1995. Paint stabilisation by using an artificial silica gel consolidant. Unpubl. report to the Australian Institute of Aboriginal and Torres Strait Islander Studies, Canberra.

WATCHMAN, A. 1998. Composition and source of dust on Split Rock paintings, Australia. *Rock Art Research* 15: 36–40.

WATCHMAN, A. 1999. A universal standard for reporting the ages of petroglyphs and rock paintings. In M. Strecker and P. Bahn (eds), *Dating and the earliest known rock art*, pp. 1–3. Oxbow Books, Oxford.

WATCHMAN, A. 2000. Micro-excavation and laser extraction methods for dating carbon in silica skins and oxalate crusts. In G. K. Ward and C. Tuniz (eds), *Advances in dating Australian rock-markings*, pp. 35–39. Occasional AURA Publication 10, Australian Rock Art Research Association, Melbourne.

WATSON, J. A. L. and J. M. FLOOD 1987. Termite and wasp damage to Australian rock art. *Rock Art Research* 4: 17–26.

WILSON, M. J. 1995. Interactions between lichens and rocks; a review. *Cryptogamic Botany* 5: 299–305.

WINKLER, E. M. 1973. *Stone: properties, durability in man's environment.* Springer Verlag, New York.

YOUNG, G. S. and I. N. M. WAINWRIGHT 1995. The control of algal biodeterioration of a marble petroglyph site. *Studies in Conservation* 40: 82–92.

7. THE DATING OF ROCK ART

INTRODUCTION

It has long been apparent to philosophers of science that confusion concerning scientific matters is usually attributable to shortcomings of language. The term 'to date', for instance, has a variety of meanings, and confusion about the dating of rock art (or the dating of archaeological remains, for that matter) initially stems from this ambiguity. As a noun, 'date' may refer to the date shown on a coin, book or building, presumably representing the time of minting, printing or completion, i.e. an 'absolute date'. But it may alternatively refer to a time period of some considerable duration (e.g. hundreds of millennia) from which an archaeological, palaeontological or geological phenomenon supposedly 'dates'. The corruption imposed on the first meaning becomes apparent when the term is used in the second meaning but the precision implicit in the first meaning is often attributed to such usage.

Significant problems also arise when the scientific (i.e. refutable) dating information provided by archaeometrists is interpreted as if it referred to real ages. In nearly all cases, such data are subject to significant qualifications, which in archaeological use are not adequately taken into account. Even attempts to compensate for the routine misuses of dating results have been misguided. For instance, the introduction of once fashionable terms such as 'absolute dates' and 'relative dates', or the use of 'calibrated' radiocarbon dates have only provided cures worse than the disease; rather than correcting the problem they tried to conceal it. Apart from some rare exceptions, archaeometry does not provide results that could reasonably be defined as 'absolute dates', and radiocarbon assay results are no basis for calculating 'absolute calibrated dates'. Thus the practice of distinguishing between B.P. and b.p. carbon isotope 'dates' is misleading, in that it elicits a false sense of security in practitioners. Reference to a calibration curve proposed for bristlecone pine in some part of California does not compensate for the numerous inherent qualifications of radiocarbon results, it merely compounds interpretational confusion.

The difficulties of estimating the age of rock art are considerably greater than those of 'dating' archaeological finds in most cases, and the methodologies developed for these two entities differ considerably. Nevertheless, it is most instructive to consider the difficulties of archaeological dating before focusing on the dating of rock art.

Very few methods are known of absolute dating, such as dendrochronology (analysing the annual growth rings of sectioned tree trunks) and counting of annual ice layers (particularly in Greenland and Antarctica). Another possibility might be the annual luminescence banding in carbonate speleothems (Baker et al. 1993). All other methods used in dating yield results that cannot be expressed in calendar years, sidereal time or absolute historical time, irrespective of any 'calibration' used.

The radiometric method most used in estimating archaeological time is the analysis of carbon nuclides. Especially in the Anglo-American version of archaeological practice, this method now forms the chronological backbone of the discipline. All radiometric techniques (as well as some non-radiometric dating methods, such as fission-track analysis) provide sets of statistical information thought to relate to the age of samples; they do not yield sidereal or calendar ages. The probability statements they offer can be expressed at one, two or more standard deviations, which means that the true age of the sample would be within stated tolerance values if all secondary qualifications were ignored.

In the case of radiocarbon, the remnant content of an unstable and thus radioactive isotope of carbon is determined to estimate the time when its decay to nitrogen commenced. For this to be accurate it is necessary to know the initial concentration of carbon-12, 13 and 14; the decay rate; and that the process had not been influenced by other factors. There are problems with all these conditions:

1. The initial atmospheric concentrations of ^{14}C and $\delta^{13}C$ are not known to us. We can only make assumptions about past atmospheric carbon nuclide regimes, which introduces a significant unknown variable. Dendrochronology has documented major variations in past carbon regimes.
2. The decay rate is expressed in the half-life of radioactive substances. This is now thought to be about 5733 years for radiocarbon, but we continue to use Libby's original estimate of 5568 years, for consistency.
3. The assumption that the ratio of carbon isotopes in the carbon reservoir of the Earth are

the result of a complete and rapid equalisation is not necessarily valid.

4. The assumption that the ratios of carbon isotopes are only altered by radioactive decay is only approximately valid.
5. The levels of radiocarbon cannot be measured with real accuracy.

These issues are too complex to be examined in any detail here. They are well understood by radiocarbon scientists, but are not often reflected in the pronouncements of archaeologists about such results, as the excessive confidence in them indicates. Of greater concern still are the ways in which these results are then misused in the course of archaeological model building. For instance, it is commonly assumed that charcoal excavated in sediment strata provides secure dating for such deposits. All components of a geological sediment possess an 'age', most are significantly 'older' than the deposit and may have been redeposited many times by a variety of processes, while some are younger. Instead of referring to the 'age' of such a sediment or deposit it is more appropriate to refer to the time of its *most recent* deposition. Charcoal itself has no radiocarbon age, such an age denotes the time when the tree in question assimilated carbon dioxide from the atmosphere, not the time it stopped doing so, or the time the wood was incompletely burned (Schiffer 1986; Fetterman 1996). Moreover, due to its extremely low specific gravity relative to other sediment particles, charcoal tends to 'float' on top of a deposit through trampling or other disturbances, and it is easily transported by wind, water and biological agents (e.g. insects, burrowing animals). Its taphonomy ensures that few charcoal pieces are recovered from the locations of actual hearths, so there is no proof that they provide precise dates for the final deposition of the sediment they were recovered from (Bednarik 1989a). Even when the charcoal is extracted from a well-defined hearth, there is the possibility that charcoal or wood of various ages has been used. Moreover, the presence of charcoal in the vicinity of stone tools offers no proof that it is of anthropic origin, especially in a region that is prone to natural fires. These very brief comments should merely convey an inkling of the true complexity of dating issues, more details relating to carbon isotope analysis are given below.

TRADITIONAL METHODS OF ROCK ART DATING

Without at least some idea of the age of rock art, this class of evidence is of no help to the archaeologist, because except in rare cases, it can be linked to archaeological constructs only by one factor: its age. Therefore the question of antiquity has been foremost in the mind of researchers for as long as rock art has been studied. The methods that have been employed to this end until recent times can broadly be described as falling into the categories of iconographic determination, stylistic claims, presumed technique of execution, association with archaeological finds by excavation, 'dating' of final sealing off of cave or rockshelter; topographic proximity, weathering and patination study, superimposition of motifs, and a combination of two or more of these approaches.

Iconography

The theory of this very widespread approach consists of two parts. First, the observer attempts to determine the objects or activities depicted in the art in question, and then it is endeavoured to relate the content of this 'identified' iconography to supposedly dated archaeological or other time-related information. The most common applications of this method are the attempts to identify animal species, weapons or other objects supposedly depicted, or to identify ways of life observers believe they can discern in the art. Animal species may then be correlated with palaeozoological or ecological dating information, other objects (boats, ploughs, daggers, swords, halberds, rifles and so forth) with dated archaeological finds or historical documentation, supposed scenes of hunting with a hunting-foraging way of life, and supposed ceremonial depictions with archaeologically inferred practices.

This approach can produce useful supplementary information where the iconography in question is particularly detailed, but it has been widely over-used and misused. Most rock art of the world is not adequately detailed, and many interpreters of rock art seem to be unaware that there is no a priori reason to assume that the producers of the rock art shared the observer's cognitive strategies of locating iconicity in graphic production. On the contrary, we can safely assume that graphic conventions of the distant past differed more from those of modern Westerners than, say, the conventions of contemporary indigenous artists in many parts of the world. We know from the only blind test ever undertaken that a Western observer was entirely incapable of correctly identifying animal species in a non-Western rock art corpus. Macintosh (1977) demonstrated that he, a professional anatomist, misidentified 90% of the zoomorphs in Beswick Cave, a major rock painting gallery in northern Australia. This suggests that most identifications of animal species could be regarded doubtful.

To make matters worse for this approach, our knowledge of the past distribution and appearance of animal species is quite inadequate. Distribution patterns available to us, spatially and temporally, are not of animal species, but of the spatial and chronological distribution of the remains of these species. The past distribution pattern of a live species may differ very significantly from that of its palaeontological remains, as a result of taphonomic processes. To illustrate with an example: remains of Europe's cave bear have been found almost exclusively in limestone caves, which reflects neither endemism nor true geographical distribution, it is simply the result of a massive taphonomic bias (Bednarik 1994a).

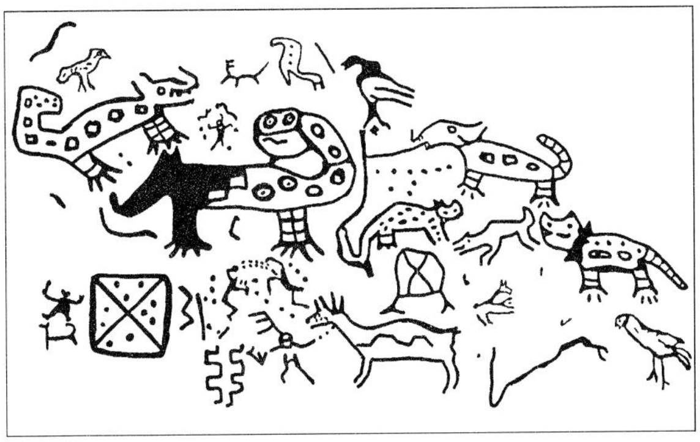

Figure 45. Peruvian petroglyphs depicting hallucinatory imagery.

But there are still other reasons why a zoomorphic iconography might prompt misleading deductions. For instance, the depiction of an extinct animal may have been prompted by its remains, such as a frozen carcass. Animal depictions may be based on iconic hallucinations (Figure 45), and it is perfectly possible to draw a picture of an animal not existing in one's physical world (narcotics such as harmaline and ibogane induce visions of large cats or snakes even in humans who have no concept of such real animals; Bednarik 1994b). It is perfectly possible that an animal was depicted that had never been seen by the members of a community, but by a traveller, or from descriptions. Even entirely fantastic animals may be, and commonly are, depicted in rock art, so it would be hasty to assume that all rock art imagery is necessarily a reliable reflection of the artist's actual rather than perceived physical environment. It would be just as logical to assume that unusual, exotic motifs are often depicted in art traditions, they are not necessarily faithful reflections of everyday domestic life. To appreciate the point one only needs to consider: does the religious art of any major faith typically depict domestic scenes? Most of it consists of unusual or mythological events or of allegoric iconographies far too complex to be understood by an alien. To assume that early cultures produced only simple depictive iconographies whose meaning is readily accessible to the uninitiated is not just akin to assuming that these were very simplistic societies, it contradicts what we know from ethnography (e.g. in Australia).

The literature on rock art is thickly littered with the pronouncements of scholars telling us which species are depicted in the alien iconography. They never mention what qualifies the inventers of these myths to make these pronouncements about an alien art whose age and cultural attribution remains elusive in most cases. The dating pronouncements they derive from their 'identifications' range from the plausible to the absurd. For instance, a Chinese scholar decided that some petroglyphs in the Helan Shan, Ningxia Hui, depict a group of giraffes, and since this is a Tertiary species in China he brazenly pronounced the rock art to date from the Tertiary. This may be an extreme example, but all similarly based dating claims are just as unsubstantiated, be they plausible or not. They have no scientific relevance, being based entirely on the visual perception of the observer, and his or her neural processing of phenomenal sensory input. In all humans this process is subjective — determined by the cultural, cognitive, religious, ontogenic and most particularly academic conditioning of the individual. They cannot therefore be tested by scientific means, as neither the interpreting subject nor the observer can analyse such claims in any meaningful way. If the subject believes that a marking on a rock depicts a human being with raised arms, he may impose his cultural conditioning over this perception and perceive an 'adorant'. Having been conditioned by observations of similar rigour that 'adorants' belong to Bronze Age traditions, he will assume to know the approximate age of this motif. Another observer, conditioned differently, may well perceive a line figure of an animal seen in plan view. Or perhaps he also perceives it as an adorant but places it in the Neolithic. All the time it remains a mystery why apparently human figures with apparently raised arms are defined as 'adorants' (worshippers, supplicants). After all, we have no idea in which posture the people of the Neolithic, Bronze Age etc. worshipped, if indeed they did so. Clearly, modern observers have imposed their own values and mores on the mute evidence. It may sound trite or overly economical, but it is quite correct to say that most interpretational and age claims about Eurasian rock art are of this calibre.

The subjectivity of human perception, particularly vision (see also Ch. 5, 'Photography'), excludes from scientific consideration judgments about what alien art motifs depict. This is not to say that such 'identifications' are necessarily false, it simply means that they are not refutable, as they refer entirely to what happens within the neural and cortical systems of subjective intelligent organisms.

Additional problems with the dating of palaeoarts via iconographic 'identifications' by 'experts' concern the interpretational claims based on them. For instance, if animals or hunting scenes are said to be depicted, it is claimed that the culture in question was one of hunters-foragers-fishers. This is based on the proposition that each culture paints and engraves motifs illustrating its daily life. This belief seems to indicate that its followers either think that the rock art consists of messages to them ("... and this, dear archaeologist, is how we lived"), or at least that the cultures in question took their domestic life very serious. Few if any historically understood art traditions focus on domestically representative iconographies, yet it is assumed that in pre-Historic times this applied inevitably. The absurdity of this belief is well demonstrated by the extensive and iconographically complex Gwion art traditions of the Kimberley, Australia (formerly known as Bradshaw traditions). There are no hunting depictions evident in it, almost no apparent animal figures, and there is not a single known female figure. Yet we have no evidence that these rich traditions relate to an agricultural people, or to a population that lacked females.

In various cases it has been proposed, based on perceived hunting arts, that these traditions must be pre-Neolithic, e.g. in the Spanish Levant, the Sahara and central India. These pronouncements are not accepted today (e.g. Beltrán 1982; Hernández Pérez et al. 1988; Muzzolini 1990), hence their basis was a false assumption about iconography in rock art. Similarly, rock art chronologies based on other iconographic 'identifications' are likely to be wrong. Some, no doubt, will be shown to have been right, but this kind of hit-and-miss approach, based essentially on the reputation of the proposer, is not a reliable method of dating rock art. It does not form a legitimate part of rock art science, except as subsidiary information. An exception may be the few known instances of relatively recent rock art comprising very distinctive motif types of known chronological ranges, such as images of Tsagiglalal (Keyser 1990) or possibly some of the examples Carlson (1990) offers. In particular, this applies to imagery of 'contact art', such as that dating from the time of European settlement. Numerous examples have been reported from Australia (e.g. McCarthy 1967; Edwards 1971; McNickle 1991; Chaloupka 1993; Chippindale and Taçon 1998), southern Africa (e.g. Thackeray 1983; Vinnicombe 1976) and North America (e.g. Grant 1967; Schaafsma 1980; Keyser 1979, 1987, 1992).

Style

This dating approach seems to be borrowed from art history, where historically documented art styles can assist in dating artworks. Nevertheless, the validity of extending this practice to traditions that are beyond ethnographic or historical access has not been demonstrated, nor can this procedure be said to be universally valid in art history itself. Stylistic conventions can be no more than social language forming a transmission system of differential messages (Ucko 1987). Individual artists may use different styles at different times (of their lives, or for different purposes; cf. Whitley 2001: 25), and reliable ethnographic work with contemporary producers of rock art provides no evidence that the artists of a specific group (clan, language group, even family) necessarily share a common distinctive style (see Mulvaney 1995; Novellino 1999, for pertinent ethnographic examples). Two closely related Aboriginal artists from the same family group and generation, living in the same locality, may depict the same object quite differently. Imagery relating to totemic ancestors, sorcery figures and secular meanings, produced by members of a common cultural tradition, can be distinguished by very different styles (Layton 2001: 315). While cultures do exhibit certain preferences in the genres of art they produce, there is nevertheless considerable scope for individual variation. Intra-cultural variability is almost never of a more narrow range than inter-cultural stylistic variability. Styles do exist, but to correctly identify them and their meaning and underlying rules, the 'visual grammar' needs to be known (Layton 1991). We have some understanding of this concerning Historic arts, but we lack it for pre-Historic art traditions.

The dependence of archaeological claims upon stylistic premises is by no means limited to palaeoart, it permeates every aspect of traditional archaeology. Practitioners construct the taxonomies of all forms of classes of material evidence on the basis of their own perceptions of reality (see Ch. 1). They invent categories of stone implements, spinning whorls, ceramic pots and whatever else they study, and then apply these pigeonholes (or 'egofacts', as they have been called; Consens 2000) to any further finds. Material that does not fit into the constructs so created is regarded as non-diagnostic or untypical, or is even viewed as irrelevant. The value of these tautological taxonomies needs to be questioned.

The classes of stone tools archaeologists are likely to invent and name do not coincide with those of the makers and users of such artefacts. The classifications of archaeologists are based on judgments about shape, form, working edge angle, ratios of dimensions and particularly on aspects of retouch. The experienced stone tool knapper tends to be sceptical of these well-honed academic definitions, and the same applies to the researcher who uses lithics in replication experiments. The original users of stone tools are much more concerned about aspects such as the technological properties of the lithic material, even its colour, and with the function of the tools, at least in known ethnographic contexts. It would be judicious to regard the taxonomies of archaeologists, be they of stone tools or any other categories they define, with some healthy scepticism. They are usually not refutable constructs. Microwear analysis is a scientific method in replication work, but when applied to archaeological specimens does not necessarily provide secure evidence. Observed similarity between wear traces is not conclusive proof, and the confidence expressed by some students of microwear is not warranted (Derndarski 1997).

The difficulties with stylistic taxonomic constructs of stone artefacts and other classes of material evidence apply also to rock art, where they are in fact amplified by the almost exclusively non-utilitarian nature of the medium. After all, lithics are at least partly utilitarian. That their classification is based especially on their perceived non-utilitarian variables (i.e. those of style) is of concern, and these are probably much less accessible to the alien researcher than their utilitarian aspects. In the case of petroglyphs and pictograms, claims to intuitively 'know' the stylistic conventions of the alien arts resemble the belief that one can 'communicate' with the societies in question, perhaps through some imagined human universals. It must not be over-looked that these claims refer to essentially undated motifs or whole art traditions. They seem to be based on the beliefs of their advocates to possess some special powers of detecting which variables shared by two or more pictures express ideological Gestalts that are specific and unique to a particular culture. Since such claims are made about artefacts whose age or attribution is otherwise unknown, they are inadequate proof of age and need to be substantially corroborated by more reliable evidence.

Another difficulty with the circular reasoning of 'stylistic dating' of rock art lies in the reluctance of its practitioners to present the basis of their pronouncements in a repeatable and testable format. Science has a clear preference for experiments that are repeatable, and processes of discrimination that are transparent. Attempts to render stylistic pronouncements transparent seem to founder on the intractable problem of translating subjective processes of perception into quantifiable, repeatable and thus testable entities.

Technique

Although numerous techniques have been used in producing rock art, most of them are repeated in various regions or periods. The possible techniques of making rock art, both as pictograms and petroglyphs, are necessarily limited — particularly those readily available to the peoples of early periods. The risks in using technique as a criterion of age or cultural provenience are therefore obvious. Nevertheless, such uses can be found in the literature.

There are two fundamental objections to this approach. First and foremost, there is the issue of recognising technique correctly. As discussed in Chapter 4, the technology of rock art has commonly been misjudged because of a combination of several circumstances: replicative experiments were rare and detailed scientific reports about them even more so; detailed studies of technology (especially by microscopy) were almost completely lacking; pronouncements about the technology of rock art were in nearly all cases made on the basis of subjective impression and superficial but uninformed examination; ethnographic evidence was in practically all such considerations ignored; and the few scientific comments made about the topic have been widely disregarded, even attacked. The judicious researcher will therefore disregard most published opinions about rock art technology.

Secondly, as already implied, identical treatment or technique guarantees no more cultural coherence than differences in technique guarantee the presence of culturally different traditions. The above observations about style apply even more to technique: individual artists may use different techniques at different times or for different purposes, while by the same token artists far removed spatially and chronologically may use an identical technique, because of the limited repertoire available to a hunter-forager. Simple logic offers a number of non-cultural explanations for continuity of technique. For instance, geological aspects of a region may be a major determinant of the kind of rock art found in it, and these are often strongly emphasised by taphonomic factors. The type of rock available for painting or engraving usually predetermines favoured techniques, much in the same way as the available lithic resources may determine stone tool types much more than cultural preferences do.

This is not to say that preferred or exclusive technique of rock art production may not be culturally determined. Certainly this may be the case, the problem is simply that the researcher must not base chronological claims on such an ambiguous variable. The use of these tenuous arguments is particularly misleading when they are offered together with one or more similarly weak hypotheses that are said to support the same finding. Confirmationist constructs drawing their support from two or more similarly slender arguments are particularly deceptive, in that they are designed to create confidence as if they were a substitute for solid or refutable evidence.

For instance no securely dated European Upper Palaeolithic petroglyphs have been made by impact, they are without exception engravings rather than percussion petroglyphs. This would seem to speak against the Iberian open-air petroglyphs on schist being of the Pleistocene, as many claim. But this argument, while probably quite correct, is still specious because we have no Palaeolithic cave art on schist, and the Palaeolithic artists could conceivably have used one method on one rock type, another elsewhere. Considerably more decisive evidence is needed in such reasoning.

Excavation

Where rock art has become covered by sediment, concealing strata may be considered as postdating the art. They may contain evidence that permits the estimation of the time of deposition, including artefacts presumed datable by their type, organic remains that contain residual radiocarbon, or mineral grains datable by such methods as TL or OSL analysis. While it is not acceptable to define the sediments themselves as being datable by such methods, under favourable conditions such dating information is likely to provide a fair idea of the time of their last deposition. Sediments used in this way must not have been disturbed subsequently, or be the result of deflation or colluvial processes. A recent example of a spectacularly false dating of excavated petroglyphs is provided by a vertical art panel at Fariseu in the Côa valley of Portugal, where it was claimed the petroglyphs must be in excess of 25 000 years old because the deposit contained purported Gravettian artefacts. The colluvium in question was in fact under 17 years old (Abreu and Bednarik 2000) and the assumed age of the perceived artefacts was entirely irrelevant to the age of the petroglyphs.

World-wide, the minimum dating of rock art by excavation has not been possible in more than a very few instances. Cases of pictograms that have been discovered under archaeological deposits are particularly rare, while the prospects are considerably better for petroglyphs. There have been attempts on most continents to relate pictograms to pigment traces found within a nearby sediment (Macintosh 1965; Wakankar 1983; Combier 1984; Linares 1988; Chippindale and Taçon 1998), but such a link has not been satisfactorily demonstrated in any one instance. A comment sometimes seen is that the ochreous pigment in the ground was found to be of the same hue as the paint on the wall. In reality, iron oxides and hydroxides are highly susceptible to chemical alterations that inevitably involve changes in reflective properties (colour), and it is naive even to assume that either the pigment on the wall or the pigment in the ground would retain the original colour. Both are likely to be modified differently, and will probably not match, bearing in mind the metastable character of all iron salts (which form the majority of pigments used in rock art).

Similarly, there are many claims in the archaeological literature that rock art dating has been achieved because the style or purported content of excavated and roughly dated portable art is identical or similar to that of otherwise undated rock art. None of these claims are listed or discussed here, because they have no scientific or falsifiable basis; they are anecdotal and refer to subjective perception. Besides, even if the presumed similarity were refutable, it would still be very possible that a rock art motif could be copied many millennia after its creation. Hence this kind of 'dating' is not evidence.

It must also be remembered that 'dating' via excavation is an indirect form of dating rock art, i.e. we have to accept inductive pronouncements on trust, such as the validity of the chronological association of charcoal and sediment, the claim that there was no recent contamination in the charcoal sample, and we must accept the archaeologist's pronouncements concerning sedimentological issues. Furthermore, dating of rock art by excavation provides never more than minimum ages, and it offers no evidence of how old the rock art was at the time it became concealed by the sediment. This unknown time span may be as long as a hundred millennia, or as short as a few hours.

Logically there are two different types of processes that may cover rock art by sediment strata. Rock art on either vertical or horizontal panels may be covered in situ, and such an occurrence was first roughly dated by Daleau (1896), at Pair-non-Pair, France, after fourteen years of investigation. Several subsequent minimum datings of petroglyphs by excavation have been reported (Lalanne and Breuil 1911; Lemozi 1920; David 1934; Passemard 1944; Ampoulange and Pintaud 1955; de Saint Mathurin 1975; Anati 1976: 34, 41; Rosenfeld et al. 1981;

Cannon and Ricks 1986; Steinbring et al. 1987; Crivelli et al. 1996). Pictograms are very rarely preserved below ground, but they were convincingly minimum-dated through a concealing sediment at Perna 1, Brazil (Bednarik 1989b; Pessis 1999).

Alternatively, a fragment of decorated rock may have exfoliated and fallen to the ground, where it eventually became covered by sediments. Several exfoliated petroglyph fragments have been minimum-dated in this fashion (Capitan et al. 1912; Hale and Tindale 1930; Mulvaney 1969: 176; Thackeray et al. 1981; Fullagar et al. 1996; Roberts et al. 1998; Bednarik et al. 2005), whereas similar claims for exfoliated fragments of pictograms have tended to be less persuasive (e.g. O'Connor 1995). Dating attempts of excavated petroglyph fragments may well provide a fairly precise timing for the event of exfoliation, which probably occurred very much later than the production of the rock art. Such information concerning the minimum age of the rock art offers the potential of using it in calibrating another time-dependent process that relates to the art. For instance, relative weathering or microerosion data from a panel may potentially provide relative age estimates of original petroglyph and exfoliation scar. If the time of exfoliation can be estimated, this may under favourable conditions lead to a fairly reliable age estimation for the rock art. For this or similar approaches to be successful, excavation needs to be combined with a direct dating method, and thus becomes supporting evidence. It is in this kind of framework that archaeological excavation can assist in securing convincing age estimates of rock art.

Proximity

It may seem self-evident that mere proximity of rock art to some datable evidence of occupation cannot be adequate proof of the rock art's age by any measure, and yet there are numerous instances on record, from many regions of the world, where archaeologists have deduced the age of rock art from evidence found merely nearby. Of course there may be cases where such precipitate claims were in fact correct, but this is hardly a justification for desperate proposals in the first place, and for presenting such mere guesses as admissible evidence without any corroborating support.

To appreciate the full shallowness of this strategy of dating rock art it is necessary to examine some points of logic. It is based loosely on the intuitive perception that different activity traces of the same period are more likely to occur together than at diverse locations. The concept of activity foci in an 'archaeological space' is thus ignored: the probability that two types of occupation traces found at one site are contemporaneous is millions of times greater at some randomly selected site in a featureless plain or desert, than it is at a site that was an occupation focus, such as a rockshelter, a cave, a spring or other favoured locality. In other words, if one discovered some petroglyphs together with stone artefacts at some seemingly 'random' locality on the Nullarbor Plain, the world's largest limestone karst, the chances that these two features dated from the same time would be very high indeed. If one discovered these petroglyphs and lithics in Koonalda Cave, a Nullarbor site of highly focused human activity over a long time period, the probability that they represented identical ages would be almost nil. In short, logic tells us that the lumping together of rock art and other evidence of human presence in places that were likely to be much frequented is a practice based on false premises.

A great deal of rock art in the world, possibly most rock art, occurs at localities that can be assumed to have been activity foci for as long as the region has seen human occupation. Rock art usually marks special places in the landscape, it is not distributed randomly in it, and ethnography has often shown why that is so. Similarly, occupation sites are not randomly distributed, their locations, too, are highly predictable. They often coincide with the types of localities favoured in rock art production. Therefore any attempt to extrapolate the dating of any such occupation evidence to the same site's rock art is unacceptable if it is not corroborated by alternative and credible methods.

The issue is best illustrated with an example. An extensive study of the rock art sites of the Koolburra Plateau in north Queensland (Flood 1987) has shown that 48% of these sites have no sediment deposits or traces of occupation, while another 16% have sediment cover over less than a quarter of their floor area. Stone tools were observed on the floor of only 4% of the sites. It follows that the majority of these sites offer no evidence of human presence other than the rock art. If we insisted that rock art must be accompanied by occupation evidence, it would logically follow that most Koolburra rock art should not even exist.

In many cultural contexts rock art production is segregated from domestic activities, and there are even societies who practise exclusion of some members from the cultural practices that result in some forms of rock art. Clearly in such cases it would need to be assumed that utilitarian occupation evidence found at a rock art site was likely to date from a time other than the time the art was made, because there would have been no domestic activity at the site when it served as a (perhaps sacred) ritual site.

A classical example of a claim to have dated rock art by proximity relates to the petroglyphs at Gum Tree Valley near Dampier, Australia. Lorblanhet (1992) secured a single radiocarbon 'date' of about 18 500 years from a large trumpet shell, a surface find from near the petroglyphs, which is over twice as old as all other dates from the site. On this basis alone he then confidently constructs an entire stylistic and formal chronology of the region's massive rock art assemblage spanning more than 18000 years (Lorblanchet 1992: Figs 20, 21), based on such feeble evidence as subjectively judged patination differences, spatial distribution and perceived subject matter. Although credible dating evidence is still lacking, the assemblage in question appears to be of the Holocene, and all other of Lorblanchet's dates are under 7000 radiocarbon-years. The archaeological occupation evidence consists of shell middens, which implies that the site became settled only when the present sea level was approached, i.e. during the early Holocene.

The practice of dating rock art through the proximity of supposedly datable occupation evidence may be valid occasionally, but on a logical basis it should be expected to provide false deductions much of the time. Statistically it may be as useful as reading tea leaves or animal entrails, which also results in occasionally valid predictions.

Patination and weathering

The study of rock surface alterations in the service of dating rock art was the forerunner of scientific methods to address this issue. It was through the analytical and microscopic study of time-related changes to rock surfaces that 'direct dating' was developed in the 1970s (Bednarik 1979). Such changes may be reductive (resulting in loss of mass, e.g. erosion), additive (resulting in addition of mass, e.g. accretion) or transformational (resulting in chemical or physical changes of the substrate). The aging process of rock surfaces has been considered relevant to estimating the ages of petroglyphs for at least 180 years: Belzoni (1820: 360-1) examined the numerous petroglyphs on Egyptian granite and noted the different stages of repatination, compared to the evenly dark-brown accretion on the unworked rock surface. The possibility of calculating the ages of the less patinated petroglyphs occurred to him:

> I beg my readers to pardon my thus speculating on a point which, in my humble capacity, can afford but little instruction; however, as the idea struck me, I lay it before the public.

The form of patination Belzoni considered was almost certainly desert varnish, a ferromanganous deposit that has been intensively studied by geomorphologists for over a century, but its use in speculating about rock art remained sporadic and plagued by confusion. Among the researchers using this approach were Basedow (1914), Rhotert (1938, 1952), Mori (1965), Goodwin (1960) and Anati (1960, 1961, 1963, 1968). But statements about patination colour were often imprecise and sometimes misunderstood. For instance, Anati's key observation was misrepresented by two Australian writers. Anati's careful formulation,

> [I]n this region we know of no engraved surface from [Iron Age to recent] with a patination identical to that of the original rock surface. This seems to mean that in this area it took a minimum of 2500 years to reach ... the natural colour of patina (Anati 1963: 189)

was rephrased thus:

> ... no engravings have re-weathered to match the natural dark rock surface. As some of them are associated with the Iron Age, Anati believes it takes a minimum of 2500 years for a thin, initial surface patination to form in that region (Edwards 1971: 361).

An almost identical error had earlier occurred in Mori (1965: 63), who corrected himself (Mori 1974: 89–90), substituting '*quasi scura quanto*' for '*tanto scura quanto*'.

There are other significant difficulties with using patination and weathering states in estimating ages of petroglyphs. To begin with, both weathering and patination processes are highly variable, depending on petrography, climate, topography, surface geometry, chemical environment and other factors. Secondly, there is no simplistic method of quantifying such changes, and attempts to do so (e.g. by measuring reflective properties of accretionary deposits such as rock varnish) have only resulted in unconvincing results. Moreover, the role of engraved groove depth remains poorly understood, as does the influence of cation-scavenging micro-organisms and other processes of re-cycling accretionary matter (see Ch. 5). For instance, one question that was raised in a debate concerning the use of patina colour in estimating petroglyph age is the issue, to what degree does groove depth affect repatination rates? Does a shallow groove repatinate faster than a deep groove? If the process is endogenous this would be likely, but not in exogenous patinae such as rock varnish. The use of such phenomena to estimate rock surface ages, including those within a petroglyph, requires an intimate understanding of the processes active in repatination, and most comments one finds in the existing rock art literature fail to provide any informed analytical data about the patinae. They elicit no confidence in the conclusions drawn from such observations. Indeed, there are numerous instances of quite evidently false or misleading statements about the nature and significance of such features in the literature, in which surface deposits are incorrectly described, or used as evidence to prop up grotesquely implausible chronological assertions. Repatination can be affected by numerous factors besides the underlying lithology, such as water presence, climate, epilithic organisms, coarseness of surface texture, and the proximity of cation sources, such as sediments or nearby accretions.

Weathering rinds are zones of oxidation, hydration or solution forming parallel to clast surfaces and their thickness is a function of time (Carroll 1974; Colman 1981; Colman and Pierce 1981; Crook 1986; Gellatly 1984). The growth rate of weathering rinds can be quantified for a given rock type under given climatic conditions if it can be calibrated by another dating method, but it only yields imprecise results. Černohouz and Solč (1966) developed a method for determining the ages of macro-wanes on sandstones, claiming an accuracy of ±10–20%. Although their hypothesis was subsequently refuted (Bednarik 1992), they correctly recognised that weathering rind thickness is a function of surface geometry, and that this aspect is the cause of wane formation (see below).

Surface rinds often suffer from mass loss due to abrasion, erosion, frost action, *Salzsprengung* or exfoliation, which introduces a major error source. It may be preferable to measure subsurface rinds on submerged rock, as Colman and Pierce (1981) did, examining a large sample of clasts from B-horizons of deposits. They proposed a logarithmic function in the form of

$$d = \log(a + bt) \qquad (1)$$

where a and b are constants, d is the rind thickness and time t can be determined. However, this is of limited use in estimating the age of petroglyphs. For instance, destructive sampling is usually out of the question, but in such cases one could consider the use of non-intrusive methods. In particular, the Schmidt hammer may be suitable for measuring degree of rock surface weathering (Birkeland et al. 1979; Burke and Birkeland 1979; McCarroll 1991). This instrument was originally designed to measure the surface hardness of concrete, but has been widely used on natural rock as well (Day and Goudie 1977).

The Schmidt hammer has almost never been used in rock art research (Campbell 1991; Sjöberg 1994; for a preliminary but unsubstantiated and inconclusive attempt, see Pope 2000), nor have there been any serious attempts so far to employ weathering rinds in estimating rock art ages in any more than the most cursory fashion. Clearly there is more research required in this area.

Superimposition

Similarly, there is considerable scope in the use of superimposition of motifs, which has hardly been explored so far. Some researchers have admitted that they find it difficult to decide which of two over lapping motifs precedes the other, especially for petroglyphs. This illustrates very well the inadequacies of rock art research as it has been widely practised. Microscopic study of superimpositions offers many means of distinguishing between peck marks of different ages, or between paint residues applied over or under others. Examination of the edges of areas of paint residue should certainly permit a clear definition of superimposition sequence. The only exceptions would be cases where significant mixing of paints has occurred, because the application of the superimposing paint layer has mobilised the earlier paint; or in cases of severe degradation of paintings or drawings. However, nano-stratigraphic studies of paint layers have been used very profitably in Australia, by A. Watchman, J. Clarke and others, and have shown well-defined stratigraphies of up to about forty-four layers of paint (Clarke 1976; cf. also Watchman 2000; Watchman and Campbell 1996).

Superimpositions of petroglyphs may seem more difficult to determine, especially if the time span between the two events is very short and differential weathering cannot be detected. However, even these cases yield their sequence if individual impact scars along the edge of the superimposition are examined under magnification. There are always diagnostic features, such as truncated scars. With abrasion petroglyphs, methods similar to those developed for portable art objects, called 'internal analysis' by Marshack (1972, 1975, 1985, 1989, 1992), are usually most helpful (see Ch. 8). They involve the examination of features such as crossing grooves under a binocular microscope, and they fail only in the case of heavily weathered engravings.

Superimposition as such provides of course only relative age information, as it does permit us to distinguish the older from the more recent motif. Naturally they may be separated by only a very brief time, even minutes, so traditional forms of studying superimpositions are of very limited use. However, if these studies were conducted in a more systematic and rigorous way, involving field microscopy, they are highly likely to yield considerably more reliable information. In particular, microscopic studies of this kind can include comparative studies of relative erosion (Bednarik 1995a). Indeed, when used together with methods of direct dating, the analysis of superimpositions can be a very potent tool of rock art science. While superimposition as such has been exploited by hundreds of researchers throughout the 20th century, more formal analysis has become available through the introduction of Harris matrices during the last decade (Chippindale and Taçon 1993; Loubser 1993, 1996; Magar and Davila 2004).

ESTIMATING THE AGE OF ROCK ART DIRECTLY

'Direct dating' of rock art is contingent upon two prerequisites: first, the physical relationship of the art and the dating criterion must be direct and indisputable; second, the propositions made concerning the chronological relationship of the rock art and the dating criterion should be scientifically testable (i.e. they should be refutable). The first requirement is met if the phenomenon being dated is directly relatable to the rock art: being either of the same age (e.g. a paint binder, or the fracture surfaces caused by the impact used to make a petroglyph), older than the art (e.g. its support surface, or a lichen thallus dissected by an engraved line), or younger than the art (e.g. a subsequent mineral deposit, or a fracture transecting the motif) (Bednarik 1981, 1996).

The second requirement of direct dating demands that the chronological data obtained for the dating criterion (e.g. the paint binder, the support surface, the mineral deposit) and its relationship with the actual age of the rock art must be testable by refutation. For instance, some archaeologists have included the subjects supposedly depicted in the art as a form of direct dating. This is unacceptable as direct dating, as explained above under 'Iconography', because the iconographic 'identifications' of archaeologists are not testable, they depend upon an untestable relationship between a form perceived by a subjective organism (the rock art 'interpreter') and the emic iconography of an alien culture. Archaeologists may well believe that they are able to identify depicted objects, and perhaps they are right occasionally, but science does not proceed by accepting such propositions as evidence — except when studying the perception of the scholar in question.

The criteria of direct rock art dating are clear, precise and rigorous. Direct dating does not produce actual ages of rock art, it generates testable propositions about the relevance of specific physical or chemical data to the true age of rock art. The interpretation of the relation demands a considerable understanding of the dating technique used; of the circumstances of sample collection, processing and distorting factors; and of the limitations and quite specific qualifications applying to the stated results. *None* of the methods used in direct dating of rock art produces results that can be conveyed by some simple numerical expression, which unfortunately is how they are often quoted in the archaeological literature. Therefore it is fair to say that archaeologically published results of direct dating are often presented in a misleading form. Such results should always be understood within the context they were acquired and within which the archaeometrists expect them to be seen (Bednarik 1996, 2000a; Watchman 1999).

Consider, for instance, the ubiquitous radiocarbon analysis results, and the way they are misused (see below, 'Pitfalls in rock art dating'). There are very few kinds of circumstances in which a carbon-14 result can directly be related to the age of rock art, and so far (in 2005) no rock art has been dated by radiocarbon. This is not what one would be led to believe if one sifted through recent archaeological commentaries.

Radiocarbon analysis of mineral accretions

The first technique to yield tangible direct dates for rock art was the determination of ^{14}C in a secondary calcite skin reprecipitated over petroglyphs in Malangine Cave, South Australia (Bednarik 1981, 1984). Radiocarbon occurs in such deposits because about one half of its carbon derives from atmospheric carbon dioxide:

$$x\mathrm{CaCO_3} + \mathrm{H_2O} + (x+y)\mathrm{CO_2} \rightleftharpoons x\mathrm{Ca(HCO_3)_2} + y\mathrm{CO_2}, \quad (2)$$

where x and y are the molecular concentrations of free and locked carbonic acid, and are subject to the correlation $y = \mathrm{K(T)}x^3$, K(T) being a temperature-related constant (Wendt et al. 1967). Actually, the relationship is significantly more complex than is suggested by this reaction, but it will suffice in the present context. The condition of electroneutrality pertaining to it can be summarised as:

$$C_{H^+} + 2C_{Ca^{2+}} - C_{OH^-} - C_{HCO_3^-} - 2C_{CO_3^{2-}} = 0, \quad (3)$$

where C_{H^+} is the concentration of hydrogen ions (moles/litre).

Limestone is dissolved by a combination of two processes which relate to the isotopic composition of the calcite precipitated in carbonate speleothems (Moore 1952): the open and the closed system. The carbon dioxide is usually derived from vegetation above the cave, which has either obtained it via photosynthesis and then released it after oxidation of dead plant matter, or has given rise to a community of mycorrhizal soil micro-organisms which then respire the gas.

The approximate age of reprecipitated calcite is therefore measurable by determination of its remnant content of radiocarbon, at least in theory. But there are, as with most dating methods, certain reservations. Carbonate speleothems may experience 'radiocarbon rejuvenation', for example where porosity is available for the deposition of younger carbonate, as well as through isotope exchange in the presence of moisture. An indication of the extent of such rejuvenation is given by the bulk carbon ratios from Malangine Cave, where an accretionary ceiling deposit over petroglyphs yielded 5550 ± 55 carbon years BP (Hv-10241), while an adjacent growth supplied a result of only 4425 ± 75 BP (Hv-10240) (Bednarik 1984). But a thorium-uranium analysis of the first deposit provided an age of 28 000 ± 2000 years BP (Bednarik 1997a), which gives an inkling of the massive distortion possible through the deposition of much younger solute in highly porous travertines.

Detailed research has shown that the most reliable dates of this type are from densely crystalline deposits, especially those of stalagmites (Bednarik 1981, 1998a), but we know of no instances in the world where stalagmites conceal rock art. Rock art occurs frequently on their surface, so they might provide a means of securing maximum ages for it. Stalactites sometimes do conceal rock art but their crystal structure is less dense, so they are less suitable. Recent research has also illustrated the great time span a travertine skin may take to form: the outer lamina of such a deposit in Prung-kart Cave, also in South Australia, has provided a result of 1150 ± 80 BP (ANU-6963B), while the inner (and older) part of the same thin cutaneous deposit yielded 2660 ± 70 BP (ANU-6963) (Bednarik 1998a). The complexities indicated are only some of those to be reckoned with, and they are also being illuminated by extraction and dating of organic matter from the laminae of complex sequences found in some cave sites (Figure 46).

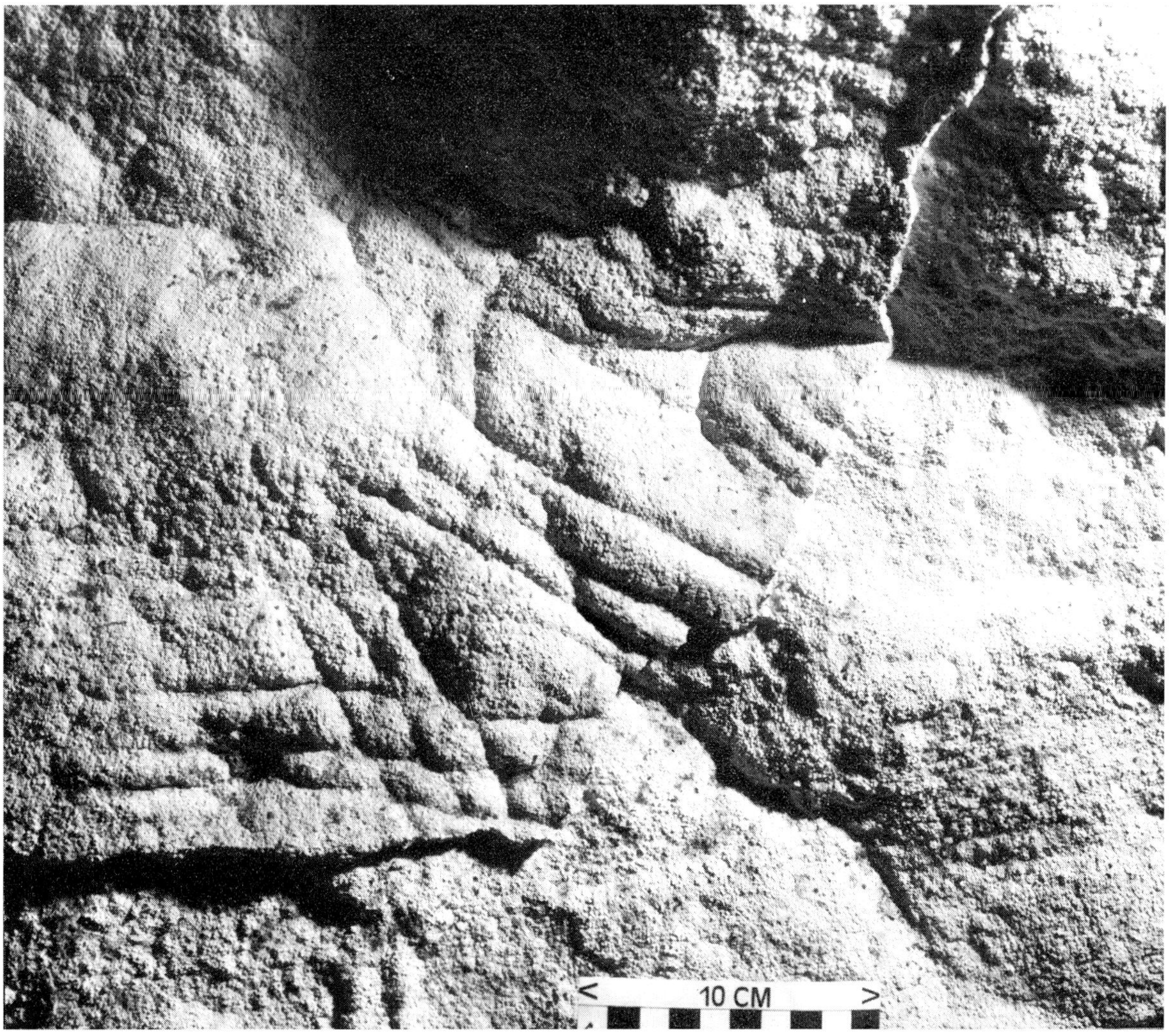

Figure 46. Exfoliating reprecipitated calcite skin containing within it sets of finger markings sandwiched between successive layers of formerly soft, but now hardened precipitate. The finger flutings can still be traced on the surface of the calcite skin, seen in situ on the left. Prung-kart Cave, South Australia.

Carbonates are not the only mineral accretions datable by radiocarbon. Oxalates, by virtue of being salts of oxalic acid derived from the atmosphere or organic sources, also contain ^{14}C. Their frequent occurrence at some rock art sites has prompted their use in estimating the ages of rock paintings (Watchman 1990, 1991, 2000; Watchman and Campbell 1996; Campbell 2000; cf. Muzzolini 1999a), but the problem of rejuvenation, which also applies to them, needs to be addressed. Ideally, the radiocarbon isotope concentrations in the accretionary strata sandwiching the rock art refer to the time the organisms in question absorbed or assimilated atmospheric carbon, but there is an obvious time lag between that event and the precipitation of an accretion. Once deposited, these mineral layers are not closed carbon systems, they remain in most cases open to several potential processes of distortion: rejuvenation through deposition of younger solute, deposition of organic matter of various sources, and isotopic exchange or fractionation. Alan Watchman (pers. comm. Sept. 1994) has observed interstices in crystallised whewellite, one of the oxalates, which permit the precipitation of younger minerals subsequent to the initial deposition of the accretion. However, this potential is probably lower for oxalates than for carbonates, which may be more porous. Most certainly the spectacular series of ten carbon isotope results from a very thin section (2.11 mm) of heavily laminated oxalate crust in Walkunder Arch Cave, Queensland, covering 26 000 radiocarbon years, were perfectly in sequence, and demonstrate the great potential of this medium.

In summary, direct dating of rock art by radiocarbon analysis of contiguous mineral accretions is possible in some circumstances, but the rigorous interpretation of such results is exceedingly difficult. At the present stage of our knowledge it cannot be expected to provide reasonably reliable results unless used in the context of independent data derived from alternative dating approaches.

Radiocarbon analysis of inclusions in accretions

Besides carbonates and oxalates there are many other forms of mineral accretionary deposits on rock surfaces that may conceal or underlie rock art, and while their essential components contain no radiocarbon, a variety of inclusions may be present in them. Among these residues are windborne particles, such as pollen and spores, micro-organisms and so forth. Others are derived from organisms occurring on the rock surface, such as algae or fungi. The most widely researched type of such mineral deposits are rock varnishes, dark-brown to almost black ferromanganous coatings found in many environments, but best preserved in arid regions due to their high-pH and low precipitation regimes.

Although exceedingly thin (mostly <2 to 500 microns), rock varnishes often comprise complex stratigraphies which contain small quantities of organic matter, derived either from aeolian deposition or from locally derived micro-organic remains, microbial metabolic products and plant-derived detritus. The involvement of micro-organisms in the formation of some forms of rock varnish was conclusively demonstrated by Scheffer et al. (1963), although earlier observations had pointed in that direction (e.g. Francis 1920). Analyses in the late 19th century and the first half of the 20th century had frequently implicated non-organic sources (e.g. Loew 1876; Merrill 1898; Walther 1924), while Blake (1905) recognised that the accretions must be at least partially of exogeneous origin. The comprehensive analytical work of Engel and Sharp (1958) ushered in modern studies of rock varnishes (Allen 1978; Krumbein 1969; Krumbein and Jens 1981; Perry and Adams 1978; Potter and Rossman 1977, 1979).

The cation re-cycling of such deposits by microbes accounts probably for at least some of the stratigraphical complexities of the varnishes, and it may also effect the incorporation of introduced matter, including carbonaceous matter. White (1924) suspected pollen to be a varnish-forming factor, mistakenly believing them to be rich in iron and manganese. They do, nevertheless, occur in rock varnish, as do other airborne particles. Its main components are essentially clay minerals, commonly accounting for two-thirds of the deposit's bulk. It needs to be emphasised that the terms rock varnish and desert varnish probably refer to the stable products of a number of quite heterogeneous processes and sources, which merely lead to similar end effects. The term has often been misused to describe a variety of *dunkle Rinden* and other accretionary deposits that do not resemble rock varnish. Even weathering rinds with some iron patination have been so misidentified at times (e.g. Pineda et al. 1988).

Since the early 1980s, Ronald Dorn sought to secure radiocarbon dates from supposedly organic substances extracted from rock varnishes, taking advantage of the AMS method which had been introduced in the 1970s. Initially he did not use it to date any rock art directly, but to obtain numerical-age controls at nearby calibration sites for his cation-ratio method (i.e. to calibrate CR ratios; see below). When the CR method (Dorn 1983, 1986, 1990, 1992; Dorn and Whitley 1984; Dorn et al. 1992; Nobbs and Dorn 1988) became widely rejected, with the advent of the 1990s, Dorn resorted to applying AMS analysis directly to samples taken from petroglyphs. By that time Watchman, who had played a pivotal role in refuting the CR method (Watchman 1992), was developing the FLECS method for the same purpose (Watchman 1993), and both researchers then sought to improve their respective approaches to the analysis of carbonaceous substances. Whereas Dorn continued to work almost exclusively with rock varnishes, Watchman diversified his technique and, having earlier experimented with oxalates, included analyses of other accretionary deposits, notably silica skins which he had previously worked with for conservation purposes.

Watchman's more rigorous approach is illustrated by a comparison of the two researchers' reports of their 1995 work at some of the Côa sites in Portugal, which they conducted under identical controlled conditions of a 'blind test' (Watchman 1995, 1996; Dorn 1997). Watchman sampled deposits postdating petroglyphs, but also collected two samples from older accretions that had been dissected by rock art. More importantly, he took control samples from a surface of known age, a railway cutting, thus realising that all the samples were contaminated. After locating the source of this distortion in graphite inclusions and correcting for it, he was able to provide minimum and maximum age estimates for a few petroglyphs. Dorn published his uncorrected results but at the same time rejected them, saying that he had lost confidence in the entire method of analysing carbonaceous inclusions in both varnishes and silica skins (Dorn 1996a, 1996b, 1997). In his 'change of perception' as he called it he admitted that he had noticed many 'anomalies' over the years, but this had apparently not prevented him from confidently publishing and defending his results. He admitted in 1996 that for over fifteen years he had made two critical mistakes which had 'blinded' him: he had falsely assumed homogeneity in his bulk samples even though it was clear that the organic matter was heterogeneous and of different ages; and he had assumed that the carbon was sealed into a closed system, until discovering that it was in fact an open system. 'To expect that no organic weathering occurred before a petroglyph panel was exposed by natural erosion was naive', he confessed (Dorn 1996a).

His mistakes were unnecessary, however, because in 1987 I had sent him my paper in which I had demonstrated that the carbon system of ferromanganous accretions is open, and that there are substantial differences in the composition, pH and organic matter concentrations within the nano-stratigraphy of such deposits. If he had studied my paper (Bednarik 1979) he would have realised his mistake almost a decade earlier, and he would have understood that his approach had always been futile — indeed, ironically, that I had solved the problems he was wrestling with before he even learnt of their existence. This episode illustrates the need to conduct a thorough survey of the relevant literature before embarking on any scientific work. Hundreds of archaeologists and geomorphologists have completely relied on Dorn's methods and results, which he has now recanted and disowned (for further problems with Dorn's work, see Dalton 1998; Dayton 1997; Beck et al. 1998; Malakoff 1998).

In contrast to the controversial status of the dating of rock varnish, the analysis of carbon-bearing substances found in silica crusts has yielded considerably more convincing results, primarily because the silica seems to provide a comparatively closed carbon system. In addition, silica skins do not suffer from recycling of cations by micro-organisms, as is assumed to be widely the case with rock varnish. Watchman (1996) has produced excellent results from layered silica skins, by separating a layer predating a petroglyph from a younger layer postdating the art, and securing organic carbon from both layers. Even though this procedure does not secure an actual dating for the rock art, it does provide tentative minimum and maximum ages for it.

Contrary to the tenor of Dorn's *mea culpa*, careful analysis of accretions remains a valid method of direct rock art dating (Watchman 2000; Campbell 2000). It does not provide numerical ages of rock art, but it does offer falsifiable data concerning the age of an entity that is physically related to the rock art in question. While there is a taphonomic problem in that the 'carbon age' of carbonaceous inclusions is probably not the same as the time of their deposition, the real qualifications that apply to such data are a great deal more complex than even Dorn has indicated lately. They are discussed below, under 'pitfalls'.

Lichenometry

The term lichenometry refers to a calibrated-age dating technique attempting to provide minimum dating of rock surfaces, using measurements of lichen thallus size or other indices of lichen growth. The use of lichens in the dating of archaeological remains was initially proposed by Renaud (1939) in Spain. Developed by Austrian Roland Beschel half a century ago, and first applied in the European Alps (Beschel 1950, 1957), this dating technique has been widely used in estimating the ages of recent geomorphic exposures, particularly glacial moraines (Worsley 1990). Apart from central Europe, its applications have been most common in Scandinavia, Iceland, New Zealand, the United States, Canada, Greenland and Antarctica, but there have also been applications in Kenya, Peru, Britain, Russia, China, central Asia and the Caucasus. Its use in archaeology has rarely been explored (Benedict 1975, 1985; Bettinger and Oglesby 1985; Broadbent 1987; Broadbent and Bergqvist 1986; Follmann 1961a, 1961b; Laundon 1980; Winchester 1988), and aside from myself, no rock art researcher has sought to apply lichenometry to rock art. I investigated its use in the age estimation of relatively recent Austrian Alpine petroglyphs in 1965, but later neglected to develop my experience further.

The extensive literature of geomorphic applications of the technique conveys the impression that the applicability of this method is limited to subpolar or alpine conditions, i.e. environments of limited rock art occurrence. This is not the case. The preferences of geomorphologists are attributable merely to the method's rather short effective time range: it can only be expected to provide valid data from the most recent millennia, and is particularly precise for ages in the order of up to some centuries. Although in favourable cases the method has been suggested to be effective to 9000 years BP and possibly even beyond (Miller and Andrews 1972), it is commonly only precise up to 500 or so years (Innes 1985). In geomorphological terms this makes it particularly useful for recent glacial deposits. However, most rock art of the world presumably falls within the effective range of the method, and some of it does occur together with lichen. Therefore the complete lack of interest rock art researchers have shown in lichenometry is astounding, bearing in mind its high reliability, robust simplicity and obvious economy, together with its non-intrusive nature.

This neglect is particularly frustrating when we consider the superb potential of lichenometry to be used in tandem with other dating methods, such as amino acid racemisation or radiocarbon analysis of thalli (Bednarik 1996) — another potential approach never used so far. The method involves no interference at all with the rock art itself, and if samples were taken of dead lichen matter their removal would not have any adverse effect, in contrast to sample removal for other dating methods. Clearly, for rock art of recent periods that can physically be related to lichen growths, lichenometry is one of the most desirable methods to use. Yet for decades archaeologists and others have been engaged in a relentless worldwide campaign to destroy lichen at petroglyph sites, claiming that they might affect the conservation of rock art (see Ch. 6). These misguided activities have resulted not only in the denuding of thousands of petroglyph sites, but also in the destruction or chemical contamination of accretionary deposits (Childers 1994), removal of mineral mass, and acceleration of deterioration while the claimed degradation by lichens remains unproven. Rock art scientists have begun to speak out against these vandalistic practices (Bahn et al. 1995; Tratebas and Chapman 1996; Walderhaug and Walderhaug 1998), but recent incidents in Portugal (Jaffe 1996) suggest that more drastic action may be required.

Two different approaches can be distinguished in lichenometry. In the direct approach, growth rates are determined by monitoring individual thalli over several years, typically of yellow-green specimens (subgenus *Rhizocarpon geographicum* agg.), which have provided the best results and are often abundant. The growth curves predict the thallus size through time. In the indirect approach, surfaces of known ages are used to calibrate growth rates empirically. Under ideal conditions, the lichenometric dating curves produced by both methods permit the age estimation of a thallus of unknown antiquity, but there are several qualifications. Ecesis (the establishment of a thallus) may not occur for a long time after the surface has become available, or it may occur almost immediately. This was countered by Beschel by focusing on the largest thalli present at a site. While the direct approach is more readily available, because it requires no chronological reference points in the construction of its curve, the indirect approach makes no assumption about ecesis lag and is less susceptible to environmentally determined growth fluctuations. Therefore the latter has been used in the majority of studies. It would also be the more relevant in future rock art dating.

Different metrical and statistical devices have been used to collect lichenometric data, including the determination of the longest axis present (Anderson and Sollid 1971; Bickerton and Matthews 1992; Bornfeldt and Österborg 1958), the mean of the longest and shortest axes (Erikstad and Sollid 1986; Hole and Sollid 1979), the shortest axis (Locke et al. 1979) and the largest thallus surface area. It has been found useful to measure the several largest thalli present, to avoid reliance on abnormally high values which may be attributable to contact growths or coalescence of multiple centre thalli. Optimal sampling area has been the subject of much research, bearing in mind that relative slope location does affect growth rates: values are 10–15 mm lower on moraine crests than near slope bases. In a full-scale analysis it is preferred to search at least ten sub-plots of no less than 400 m^2, measuring the ten largest thalli in each sub-plot.

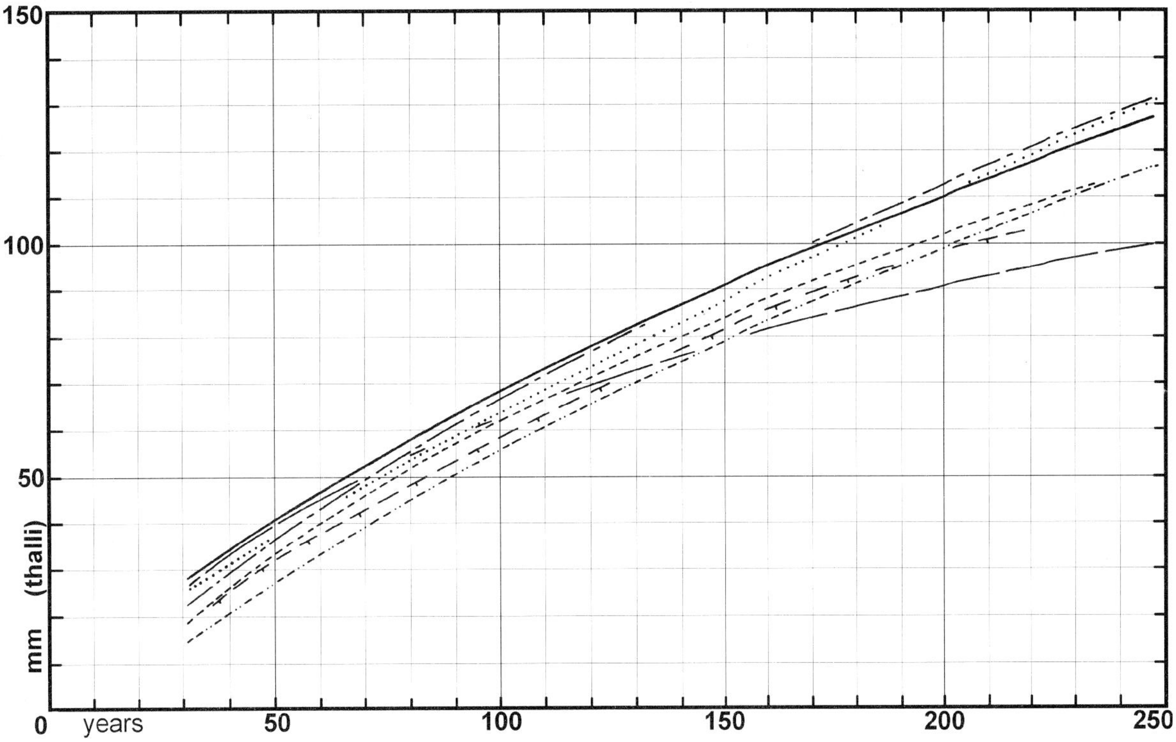

Figure 47. Comparison of seven lichenometric dating curves from southern Norway, suggesting a good overall correspondence in regression of thallus size (x) as function of moraine age (y) (adapted from Matthews 1994).

Lichenometric dating curves are slightly parabolic, with a decreasing growth rate as the thallus ages (Figure 47). They can be used two ways:

1. Where an engraved line has been made through an existing thallus, it must postdate it, and the lichen's growth will be impeded; the thallus provides a *terminus post quem* dating;
2. Where a thallus has formed over a petroglyph, or encroached on a petroglyph surface, it provides a *terminus ante quem* reference, although one involving certain qualifications (e.g. ecesis lag).

These kind of data can themselves lead to a fairly precise age estimate for a petroglyph, which could be cross-checked by removing dead plant matter from under the thallus, next to the engraved groove (maximum age) or from within the groove (minimum age). If such samples were collected from carefully chosen sites within the thallic topography they would be likely to provide dates very close to the age of the petroglyph. This would be an ideal combination of methods to determine such an age with great precision, particularly of comparatively recent rock art. Therefore the common destruction of lichen at petroglyph panels is most regrettable, and has done great damage to the scientific potential of rock art.

Microerosion analysis

The rationale of microerosion analysis is that, after a new rock surface has been created, by either natural or anthropic agents, it is subjected to chemical weathering processes. This applies especially in unsheltered locations, and it results in cumulative effects that are a function of time, among other factors. While this is a fairly self evident principle, the difficulty in using the results of such processes to estimate the age of a rock surface is that our understanding of them, of their effectiveness on different rock types, and of their susceptibility to environmental factors remain limited. We know that rock surfaces retreat with time, be it by solution (Acker and Bricker 1992; Busenberg and Clemency 1976; Lin and Clemency 1981; Oxburgh et al. 1994; Rimstidt and Barnes 1980; Williamson and Rimstidt 1994), physical wear, or a combination of the two. Empirical engineering data for natural building stone tells us that the amount of retreat differs greatly according to rock type (Schwegler 1995). Macroscopic rock erosion ranges up to fifty millimetres each one thousand years for poorly cemented sandstone, but can be as little as fifty microns on the non-quartz components of granite. This process of weathering is *surface retreat* (e.g. by granular exfoliation) and has sometimes been called 'micro erosion' (two words), although its products are certainly visible at the macroscopic level (Smith 1978) (see below under 'pitfalls').

The term '*microerosion*' (one word, unhyphenated) refers exclusively to solution processes whose effects can be seen only at the microscopic level. Hence, for the time-spans we are concerned with in dating petroglyphs, only comparatively erosion-resistant rock types are of interest. In most cases this excludes especially sedimentary rocks. It must also be emphasised that microerosion analysis is not one specific method, but a cluster of possible methods around a basic concept. Two have so far been applied practically: the measurement of micro-wanes on fractured crystals (Bednarik 1992, 1993), and the selective, often alveolar retreat in certain rock types of components that weather at vastly different rates (Bednarik 1995a). The effectiveness of the second approach has been confirmed by Pope (2000) when he tried to negate it. Pope effectively failed to appreciate the difference between these two approaches, perceiving microerosion analysis as a muddled combination of the two. There is no doubt that various alternative indices of microerosion may also prove to be useful, but, so far, their potential remains unexplored.

Macro-wanes on rock are the results of progressive rounding of freshly broken rock edges. Černohouz and Solč (1966) claimed to be able to estimate the ages of such wanes to within 10–20% accuracy on two rock types. After observing similar rounding at the microscopic scale, on individual mineral crystals that had been fractured, it occurred to me that these phenomena were likely to obey the same physical laws. I explained these fundamental laws geometrically and mathematically (Bednarik 1992, 1993), which made it possible to attempt dating by measuring wane sizes. These formulae explained how, under ideal conditions, wane development is related to time. (They explain also many other things in nature, for instance the geometry determining the course of temperature transfer within a solid object, the geometry explaining how a solid body melts, or how a liquid penetrates a porous body.)

The 'radius' of rock wanes (strictly speaking, wanes are not equicircular in section, but hyperbolic), at whatever magnitude of size, increases as a function of age. In wane formation (Figure 48), the ratio $h : r$ is constant for any angle α, irrespective of distance of retreat of the faces and the edge. Ratio $x : z$ is a function of α, and at $\alpha = 60°$, $x = 2z$. Dimension x can be expressed in algebraic fashion:

$$x = \sqrt{\left[\left(\frac{z}{tan\ 0.5\alpha}\right)^2 + z^2\right]} \qquad (4)$$

This leads to the prediction of β, the angle expressing the rate of wane development relative to surface retreat:

$$\beta = 2\ sin^{-1}\left(\frac{r}{x + h + r}\right) \qquad (5)$$

The relationship wane width A with age, irrespective of actual retreat, is ultimately determined by the ratio $\alpha : \beta$, which must be established empirically. It follows that the dimensions A, r, z, and angles α and β are all related geometrically and algebraically, and that the variables A, r, x, z and h are all proportionally equivalent, and increase linearly with age. Of these, A is most easily measured physically. It is therefore the variable used in micro-wane measurement. The analyst scans the rock surface microscopically to locate crystals that have been truncated (either fractured by impact or truncated by abrasion) by the event to be dated (e.g. the petroglyph production). A statistically significant sample of micro-wane widths along the edges of such truncation surfaces is recorded for a selected angle, and placed in a calibration curve. Age estimates are prefixed with a capital E, indicating that the result is erosion derived.

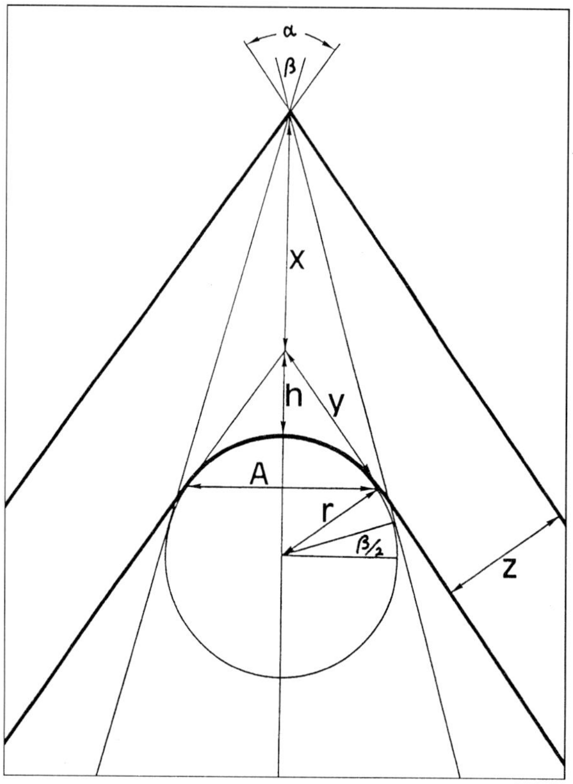

Figure 48. Diagram depicting the laws of wane formation in a simplified fashion.

Until we know much more about solution rates of common and suitable component minerals, we need to establish these rates regionally with calibration curves. In microerosion analysis, the use of two (or more) curves for two (or more) different component minerals is recommended. Since it is unlikely that different minerals would all react similarly to past environmental changes, one would expect to detect irregularities because the corresponding values of a sample would appear displaced in the calibration graph's ordinates. If solution of one component mineral had slowed or accelerated sufficiently to render the distortion detectable by such a comparatively coarse method, it would be reflected in the misalignment of the corresponding points on the curve. No other dating method currently used in archaeology offers such a self-checking mechanism.

The precision of the method is probably poor at this early stage, because it depends entirely on the number and precision of calibration points. The principal potential variables in microerosion are temperature, pH and moisture availability. The first two are regarded as unimportant: variations in mean temperatures were probably minor, even as far back as glacial peaks of the Pleistocene; they would not have affected solution rates appreciably. Variations in pH would certainly apply back through time, but in the case of both amorphous silica and quartz, there is almost no change in solubility below pH 9. For alumina it is negligible in the central region of the pH scale, which coincides with most natural conditions. Quartz, then, can serve as a control against which to check the effects of pH changes on other minerals (Rimstidt and Barnes 1980).

There is no doubt that precipitation would have varied at any site in the past, and it varies between different sites today. However, it is expected that significant changes in moisture availability would affect component minerals differently, and should thus be detectable by calibration. In this respect, the unknown sample — the surface to be dated — provides one of the points one can use to check reliability of the calibration curves, because its multi-mineral values, too, must lie on the same ordinate in the diagram.

The microerosion method by micro-wane measurement has been used on petroglyphs in six blind tests now, in Russia, Portugal, Italy and Bolivia (Bednarik 1992, 1993, 1995a, 1997b, 2000b, 2002). Archaeological expectations were matched in all cases except one, where, however, results matched those of other scientific analyses (Bednarik 1995b; Watchman 1995). Calibration curves are now available from Lake Onega (Russia), Vila Real (Portugal), Grosio (Italy), Jubbah and Najran (Saudi Arabia), Qinghai (China; Tang and Gao 2004) and the eastern Pilbara (Australia), and the technique has also been applied in India, Bolivia and South Africa. The method has a practical time range from the present to perhaps 50 000 years BP, which renders it particularly suitable for rock art. Results ranging from a few hundred years to thirty millennia have so far been obtained (Figure 49).

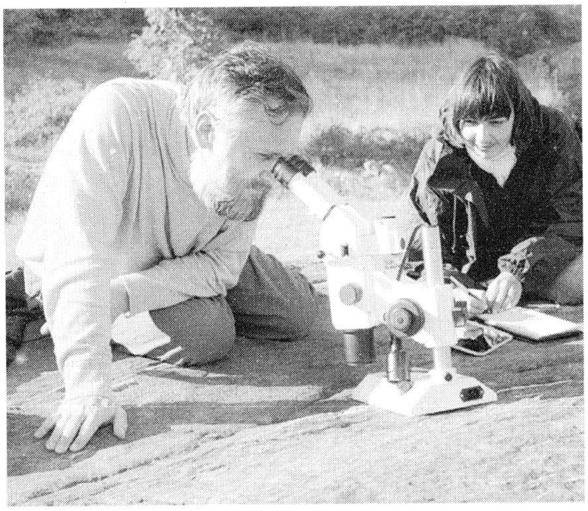

Figure 49. Microerosion analysis of petroglyphs on Rupe Magna, Valtellina, Italy.

While microerosion analysis is not thought to provide great accuracy, it is probably more reliable than most alternative methods of dating petroglyphs, and it is certainly cheaper and simpler than most. It requires no laboratory backing; the results can be determined in the field. It provides not a single result, but clusters of age-related values (the micro-wane widths) that can be converted into various statistical expressions — a luxury that nearly all other dating methods have to do without (OSL on individual mineral grains and multiple targeted applications of AMS ^{14}C to the same lamination might be broadly comparable). Importantly, it does not attempt to determine the age of some accretion or other feature somehow relatable to the rock art, it focuses on the age of the actual petroglyph, the 'target event' of Dunnell and Redhead (1988). No other method currently available does this. Microerosion analysis does satisfy the demand of Dunnell and Readhead for methods that are applicable directly to the feature about which chronological information is sought. Moreover, it is the only dating method that offers a means of internal checking, that is, of checking the validity of the result without recourse to another method (although again luminescence dating has a limited feature of this type, i.e. the possibility of checking whether the uranium and thorium decay chains are in equilibrium). Finally, microerosion analysis involves no removal of samples, or even contact with the rock art, being a purely optical, non-invasive method.

The valid arguments *against* microerosion analysis are that we have inadequate calibration curves for it, that its accuracy is inherently limited, that it can only be applied to certain rock types (principally those comprising crystalline quartz, until quartz-free rock types are calibrated), and that it is unsuitable where the rock surface may not have been continuously exposed to precipitation (i.e. where it may have been concealed in the past by sediment, mineral accretion etc.). An objection raised by (Dorn 2001: 171) is that there are different types of crystalline quartz, and only the weathering of alpha-quartz is well understood. However, until significant differences in solution rates are demonstrated, this should not detract from the method's utility in providing broad estimates of age. Dorn also fears that pre-existing weathering might be present in samples, which is a valid objection only where deep fractures truncated crystalline quartz veins and exposed them to water flow. I have described such an instance from one of the Penascosa panels in Portugal, which suggests that his fear is unfounded because such prior exposure is identifiable. Nevertheless, it is correct that there are significant inherent limitations in microerosion analysis, which have been emphasised in all publications about it, but these limitations are outweighed by the benefits of this method.

Perhaps the most telling example of its versatility is its recent use to date not petroglyphs, but the tools used in their production (see Ch. 4). This is an alternative application with indirect implications for rock art dating, but one of great promise. Quartz was frequently used as the material of petroglyph hammers, and in such cases where these tools remained on the surface, exposed to weathering, their fractured edges (or those on tiny spalls detached during their use) certainly lend themselves to microerosion analysis. This method has so far been used at only two sites, Kalatrancani 3 and Toro Muerto, both in central Bolivia (Bednarik 1998b: 32).

Luminescence dating

Although the use of thermoluminescence (TL) for archaeological purposes was first mentioned as early as 1953 (by F. Daniels; cf. Michels 1973: 189), the initial practical uses of TL were in the detection of nuclear and radiation hazards (Fleming 1979). The term TL refers to the release of energy by crystalline solids when heated or exposed to light. Ionising environmental alpha, beta and gamma radiation results in the release of electrons and other charge carriers ('holes') in these materials. Electrons become trapped in defects of their crystal lattice, such as impurities or chemical substitutions. These metastable charge carriers accumulate over time at a known and largely constant rate determined by the dose of the radiation. They can be ejected from their 'traps' by an input of additional energy, causing them to recombine, which releases their excess energy as light, measurable in photons. This energy (TL) is therefore, with some qualifications, a function of the time since the material was last heated (e.g. ceramics or heating stones) or exposed to light (e.g. crystalline mineral grains).

TL dating made its debut in archaeology primarily to help in estimating the ages of pottery remains (Aitken et al. 1968, 1971; Fagg and Fleming 1970; Fleming 1968, 1971, 1979; Kennedy and Knopf 1960; mejdahl 1969; Sampson et al. 1972; Zimmermann 1967, 1971). The use of its principles to determine when sand grains had last been exposed to sunlight is a more recent development (Aitken 1990; 1994; Huntley et al. 1985; Murray et al. 1997; Roberts and Jones 1994; Smith et al. 1990). It has been applied enthusiastically in Australia where archaeological dates exceeding 40 000 years were derived from two of the three luminescence methods now in use (Roberts and Jones 1994; Roberts et al. 1994, 1996). These are, besides standard TL analysis, optically stimulated luminescence (OSL) and infrared-stimulated luminescence (IRSL) analyses. The latter use either a green laser beam (OSL) or infrared light to free the trapped electrons.

Several technical difficulties apply to luminescence methods. An inherent problem concerns the annual environmental dose rate, which can be measured in the field or laboratory and which introduces the largest uncertainties into the method. For instance, substantial variability has been observed in K, Th and U, the principal sources of the environmental dose rate (Dunnell and Feathers 1994). Indeed, variations in sedimentary K may be directly related to former human occupation. For a field measurement the dosimeter would have to be placed virtually in the same location as the sample for a year, which is physically not feasible. Another difficulty concerns the moisture content, an important factor that cannot effectively be determined for the duration of the time in question.

Then there are specific problems relating to dating that relies on measurements taken from saprolithic or regolithic sediments, i.e. sediments that comprise grains from rock that decomposed in situ within the sediment. This is particularly crucial in sandstone shelters being formed by mass-exfoliation, one of the most common types of rock art sites. These shelters are usually not formed by fluvial, marine or tectonic action, but by the gradual exfoliation of degradation-susceptible sandstone facies. Rock fragments are prized from the walls and ceilings by *Salzsprengung* and other processes attributable to capillary moisture, they fall to the ground, become covered by sediment and then slowly decay due to ground moisture, becoming sand again. Only the surface grains of the rock fragments could have been exposed to daylight, while in the remainder of the material the 'TL-clock' has not been 'reset' (i.e. the traps have not been 'emptied' of electrons and holes). Therefore most of the sand formed by this process would show a TL age of millions of years, and any attempt to date such a sediment would combine essentially two groups of age readings. Significant errors through the misinterpretation attributable to this effect have already occurred in rock art dating, notably at the Australian site Jinmium. Here, archaeologists using TL analysis claimed an age of 58 000 to 75 000 years for petroglyphs that were clearly and obviously of the Holocene (Fullagar et al. 1996), and were subsequently shown to be so (Roberts et al. 1998). Such cases can readily be clarified by using OSL analysis instead, measuring each quartz grain separately and then discarding those results that are distinctly greater than the main cluster of data.

However, OSL dating, too, is not without significant qualifications. In TL dating it is traditionally customary to remove the outermost 2 mm of samples in the darkroom, to eliminate the need to account for dose rate alpha and beta radiation. This only penetrates to a depth in the order of microns, whereas gamma rays penetrate very much deeper. In the case of single-grain OSL analysis, this is obviously not possible, the grains are as a rule well under one millimetre in size. Their outermost rind may be removed by etching with hydrofluoric acid, but since the environmental radiation regime of the distant past cannot be known to us, absence of alpha-particle dose effects is not necessarily secured. Alpha and beta particles are far more ionising in their effects than gamma radiation. Consequently such results remain quite provisional, even in their order of magnitude, until they can be tested or the concerns can be dismissed. This applies especially to results secured from deposits on rock surfaces, such as mud-wasp nests. Disequilibrium in the uranium and thorium decay chains might occur more readily at such locations (Aitken 1985), and radon is very likely to be present in the sandstones concerned. These and other factors (changes in the hydrology due to past climatic changes) could have significant effects on past dose rates, which would yield correspondingly distorted age estimates. Examples of such experimental work are the OSL analyses recently conducted on quartz grains from mud-wasp nests in northern Australia, some of which are said to be physically related to rock paintings (Roberts et al. 1997, 2000). Their study involves the added difficulties of having to assume that the mud-nests were built in adequate daylight to bleach all grains, or that the inner parts of the droplets of mud transported by the wasps were always sufficiently exposed to the sun. The first set of results reported consists of fifteen OSL dates ranging up to 1800 years BP, plus three dates of about ten times that age. It is hard to believe that such fragile structures should survive for up to 24 000 years, particularly as the authors mention no evidence of mineralisation. I have observed fully mineralised mud-wasp nests at Toro Muerto, a rock art site in central Bolivia, which are only of the late Holocene. Moreover, the claim that one anthropomorphous painting at the site is more than 17 000 years old is difficult to reconcile with Watchman's radiocarbon dates of the late Holocene, for similar figures in the same region (Watchman et al. 1997). Finally, it is rendered less credible by the fact that nowhere else in the world is there a Pleistocene painting tradition that has survived in such large numbers of motifs outside of caves.

Of particular concern in OSL analysis is the issue of 'over-dispersion' of the OSL signal derived from many sediment samples. This issue is principally about distinguishing sediments containing multiple dose components (e.g. Bateman et al. 2003; Feathers 2003; Heimsath et al. 2002; Roberts et al. 1998, 1999; Spencer et al. 2003) from those comprising single dose components of broad dosage distributions (e.g. Holdaway et al. 2002). Unfortunately the causes of the spread in observed equivalent dose rates remains unexplained (Olley et al. 1999: 176; Jacobs et al. 2003a, 2003b); no compelling candidates have been identified (Galbraith et al. 2005: 304). Possible sources of 'overdispersion' showing this spread of OSL data include many candidates:

1. The possibility of a partial bleaching due to some coating having been present on the grains at the time in question.
2. A contribution to the OSL output from infrared radiation-sensitive mineral inclusions contained in the grains.
3. Uncertainty about the reproducibility with which the laser beam can be repositioned.

4. The possibility that grains contain radionuclide mineral inclusions that affect the OSL output.
5. Uncertainty about the maximal penetration depths of alpha and beta radiations.
6. Lower beta dose because of a grain's location in close proximity to a much larger, non-radioactive grain.
7. Higher beta dose rate because of a grain's proximity to a radioactive heavy mineral, such as zircon.
8. Unusual circumstances in the deposition of grains, preventing their full bleaching (especially transport at night).
9. Intrusion of grains from other sediment horizons.
10. The effects of moisture content.
11. Systematic uncertainty about the contribution of cosmic radiation to the dose rate.
12. The possibility that the sample includes grains that were significantly heated after their burial, e.g. by a campfire, and thus partially re-bleached.
13. Inherent sources of imprecision in the method, such as from the relative position of the stimulating light source.

It is to be hoped that the exciting claims from the Kimberley in Australia will withstand falsification attempts successfully, but for the time being the results will need to be considered carefully. They refer to the first attempt to introduce luminescence dating into rock art science and deserve every encouragement, but as with any pioneering endeavour of this type it is important that archaeologists exercise the requisite restraint in interpreting such preliminary and experimental results. Certainly this methodology is among the more promising in the age estimation of rock art. It applies not only to nests of mud-wasps, but also to similar structures by ants, termites and birds, all of which occur widely together with rock art.

A new development in rock art dating is the use of TL analysis to estimate the ages of calcite deposits in deep caves. Only two applications of this experimental method have so far been reported, one in Spain (Arias et al. 2000), the other in Piauí, Brazil. In the second case it was experimentally supplemented by electron spin resonance (ESR) dating, a method not so far used in rock art dating. If these approaches can be shown to provide accurate results it would be of considerable utility in determining the ages of cave art in both south-western Europe and Australia, where such art is most extensive and is frequently related physically to calcite speleothems.

Colorimetry of 'patinae'

Belzoni's (1820) idea of quantifying patination variations in petroglyphs has certainly been shared by many rock art researchers since, but none has made a controlled attempt to test it. The majority of descriptive or 'analytical' publications about petroglyphs contain comments on states of repatination and their relevance to antiquity, but hardly any of them even attempt to define the type of patination. The term 'patina' describes merely a visually obvious skin on rock surfaces that differs in colour or chemical composition from the unaltered rock and whose development is a function of time. It can be additive or accretionary, it can be reductive (result of solution), or it can have involved not a change in bulk, but one in the composition or surface characteristics of the substrate. In other words, stating that there is a change in colour with time without saying what caused it, or without quantifying that change and calibrating it with reference to time, is of little consequence to the matter at hand. Some 180 years after Belzoni presented his idea I attempted to address his question. Having discovered a series of dozens of dates hammered into a few granite boulders, which show distinctive scaling of colour relative to their ages, I conducted an analysis of them. Using the IFRAO Standard Scale and appropriate computer software to re-constitute true colours with very high precision, I plotted the measured colour changes against time, arriving at notably consistent results (Bednarik and Khan 2005). This experiment was conducted on rock almost identical to that referred to by Belzoni (coarse granite), in a region of very similar climate, the Australian Pilbara (very dry, sub-tropical), so it does provide a valid answer to him. It does not, however, provide the means for dating all re-patinated petroglyphs.

In this experimental study appropriate aliquot sizes, aliquot shapes and sample numbers had to be determined, and in the absence of dedicated software for processing sample matrices this had to be done manually. An unnecessarily large aliquot size would increase the amount of work exponentially, without a corresponding improvement in precision. Trials in 2002 suggested that thirty-six pixels was the smallest sample size offering reasonably representative data from the often quite variable repatination colours at the resolution range used (300–600 dpi), and for ease of handling a square sampling area was preferred over a circular one. Digital photographs were first colour corrected, using Adobe Photoshop software (Bednarik and Seshadri 1995). Visually obvious patches of dense precipitates, especially iron salts, were avoided in selecting suitable sampling sites, and for each sample multiple aliquots were selected and marked with surrounds of one pixel width. The RGB values of each pixel in each aliquot were then tabulated manually, and mean values determined from the resulting matrixes of thousands of readings, and plotted in logarithmic fashion, together with the RGB means. It became at once evident that the latter defined a distinctive, almost geometrically perfect trend. This convinced me that, against my own expectation, colorimetry of repatinated petroglyphs would be a useful analytical and quantifiable tool in rock art science.

Since then I have applied this new method at the extensive petroglyph complex north of Najran, at Jebel Qara in southern Saudi Arabia, partly in tandem with other dating methods such as microerosion and thorium-uranium analyses. The results of this pilot program are most encouraging, indicating the reliability of colorimetry in assessing the age of ferromanganous accretions on rock art and epigraphic features. As in all other rock art dating methods, there are significant qualification, in this case concerning applicability, calibration and appropriate interpretation. I have also used the same approach to assess sixteen red pictograms in Mladec Cave, Czech Republic, some of which had been mooted to date from the Pleistocene. Colorimetry and microscopy showed that these were almost certainly of the late 19th century.

Other possibilities

A group of radiometric or isotopic methods, *uranium-series dating*, is based on the decay series of the uranium isotopes to lead. Uranium-238 is by far the most abundant radioactive element in the Earth's crust, consequently its decay products are widely dispersed in the lithosphere. Precipitated in surface minerals it produces daughter isotopes, and where this process occurs in a closed system, it provides a good measure of the length of time since the formation of the mineral. Several specific decay processes have been used for dating, whose relevance and applicability depend upon their effective time range (determined by the half-life of the decaying isotope) and sample availability. In rock art dating we deal usually with Late Pleistocene and Holocene ages, and in this range only $^{230}Th/^{234}U$, $^{231}Pa/^{235}U$, ^{226}Ra, $^{231}Pa/^{230}Th$ and $^{230}Th/^{232}Th$ may be relevant. The preferred materials for analysis are carbonates (particularly reprecipitated carbonates, such as travertines, speleothems, corals and marl, also mollusc shells, bone and teeth) but other materials may be suitable. Only one of these methods has ever been applied to rock art, thorium-uranium dating. It was first used in 1982 to estimate the minimum ages of two petroglyph traditions in Malangine Cave, South Australia, which were both concealed by subsequent secondary calcite skins (speleothems). Among the results is one of the oldest credible rock art dates currently available, the conservative minimum age of 28 000 $\pm$ 2000 years BP for Karake type petroglyphs on the ceiling of the cave (Bednarik 1999).

The number of dating techniques that have potential applications in rock art dating but have apparently never been used is considerably greater than the number of those that have been applied. Even in the case of rock varnish, whose significance to direct rock art dating is beyond dispute, several dating methods appear to be more reliable than the much-used but now discredited CR technique. For instance, it is self-evident that this ferromanganous accretion would be well suited to palaeomagnetic dating, and yet none of the projects favouring CR dating has included a comparative study using this method (Clayton et al. 1990). Uranium was known to precipitate with the Mn-oxides of rock varnish even before the CR method was conceived (Knauss and Ku 1980) and uranium-series dating would provide more reliable information than the supposed leaching indices derived from the ratio of three cations. Rock varnishes contain clays that may be susceptible to potassium-argon dating where their ages are great enough, and if they conceal any quartz grains these may be datable by luminescence analysis. The latter would also offer far more reliable estimates of minimum age than the CR method is likely to provide, and yet again no comparative study has been attempted by the protagonists of CR dating.

The use of *potassium-argon analysis* may seem a desperate measure in this context, because it is widely seen as a method specifically for analysing lava flows of the middle time range (Miocene to Middle Pleistocene), but the method has been used even for Holocene materials (Evernden and Curtis 1965: 349; Miller 1970) and the half-life of ^{40}K (1.3 billion years) provides an effective range covering much of our planet's history. Also, the method can be applied to a wide variety of materials, including muscovite, biotite, orthoclase, microline, leucite, sanidine, obsidian, glauconite, illite, carnallite and others (Gentner and Lippolt 1970). Recent lava flows, tuffs and sedimentary rocks containing such minerals are often directly related to petroglyphs, and in such cases $^{40}Ar/^{40}K$ dating might be relevant. An alternative version of the method, intended to overcome the often non-homogenous distribution of the ^{40}K, is to irradiate the sample in a nuclear reactor to convert the ^{39}K into ^{39}Ar. The sample is then heated progressively to record the ratios of $^{39}Ar/^{40}Ar$ or $^{36}Ar/^{40}Ar$, and $^{39}Ar/^{36}Ar$. The slope of the curve of plotting the ratio $^{40}Ar/^{36}Ar$ against that of $^{39}Ar/^{36}Ar$ will be related to the age of the specimen (Miller 1970).

Besides these and other technologically complex potential methods for rock art age estimation, there are various readily available approaches that attract no interest. For instance, the formation of *macro-wanes* on rock is clearly time-related, and the processes involved seem reasonably straightforward. Just as the penetration rates of weathering processes are greatly influenced by surface contour (rocks weather faster on convex aspects), erosion affects protruding aspects more than flat surfaces. Černohouz and Solč (1996) have described a method for determining the ages of blunted edges on sandstone that uses two constants (*a* and *b*), the angle of the edge (φ) and the distance of retreat at the edge (*h*, in cm):

$$h = \frac{a\,t\,\sqrt{(2)}}{1 + b\,\sqrt{(t)}}\,cot\,\frac{\varphi}{2} \qquad (6)$$

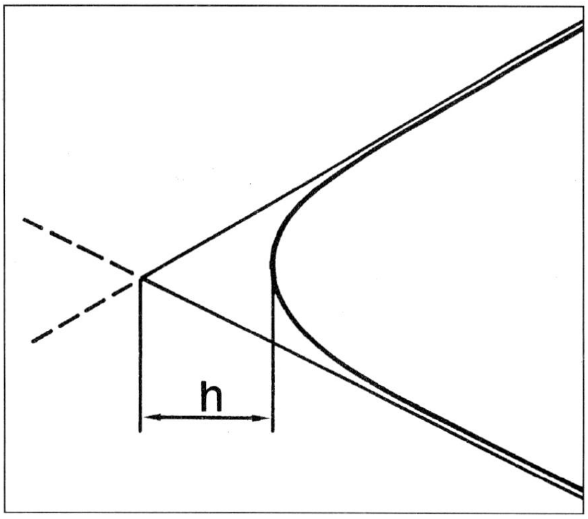

Figure 50. The development of sandstone wanes as assumed by Černohouz and Solč (1966).

Time *t* is thus obtained in millennia. While the intent of Černohouz and Solč is admirable, their theoretical model is false. Their dimension *h* is intended as a measure of retreat from the original sharp edge (Figure 50). However, the rock not only recedes at the edge, but also on the two surfaces forming the edge. The reason for the wane formation is precisely that the retreat proceeds markedly faster from the edge than from the flat surfaces. It should also be noted that the retreat of the edge does not occur as the circular curvature shown by Ollier (1969: Fig. 149), it consists of a hyperbola in section (Bednarik 1979: 28). Dimension *h* is therefore measured from the hypothetical section of two asymptotes, whose position cannot be determined numerically; therefore *h* cannot be measured. However, the underlying geometric principles of wane formation were subsequently explained (Bednarik 1992), and they apply to macro-wanes as much as to micro-wanes. No further research has been undertaken into using macro-wanes in geomorphic or rock art age estimation work.

Černohouz and Solč (1966) also examined weathering rinds of basalts, and such features have briefly been discussed above (see 'Patination and weathering'). They would be particularly useful in examining relative sequences of spalling facets such as those found on gabbro and granophyre boulders (Bednarik 1979: Fig. 1), which bear literally millions of petroglyphs worldwide. The progressive reduction of a boulder through fracture, by whatever spalling process, results in many scars, most of which are truncated by other scars. The chronological sequence of the spalling events can be reconstructed. If there are petroglyphs present on one or more of the facet surfaces, they are of necessity younger than the particular surface they are engraved on, but if they themselves have been truncated by a later spalling event, it must postdate them. This facilitates two potential analytical approaches. First, the various spalls, including any bearing truncated petroglyphs, may be found within datable sediment. Second, the chronological sequence of the spalling facets is reflected in patination of ages corresponding to each spalling event. Each and every fracture of a boulder results in two new surfaces and two new edges. Both the surfaces and edges may be datable entities, and it is clear that the rock art concerned occupies a discrete chronological position within this entire sequence of surfaces and edges. Its age relative to these surface features can be determined with complete confidence, and its radiometric age may be obtainable.

The idea of using patination and weathering in estimating the age of petroglyphs is, as noted, in the order of two centuries old, but so far very little tangible progress has been made in using such indices in geomorphic dating (for summary, see Knuepfer 1994), and practically none in rock art dating. *Weathering rinds* remain poorly understood and it would be premature to suggest that the many variables accounting for them can be quantified satisfactorily (cf. Bednarik 1979: Fig 2 for an attempt).

A very recent development in this area is the first attempt to estimate the age of rock art by *x-ray fluorescence spectrometry* (Lytle et al. 2004). In this method, the sample is bombarded with x-rays, and the wavelengths and quanta of the released energy, or fluorescent x-rays, are measured, thus determining the elemental composition of the sample's surface. The technique has long been used in archaeology, but portable XRF equipment has become available only recently. Lytle et al. determined the amounts of Mn and Fe in rock varnish deposits formed on petroglyphs at a site in Utah. Having established a calibration curve based on radiometric datings of geomorphic surfaces, they noted a consistent increase in the Mn+Fe concentration with increasing age. By projecting values taken from a series of petroglyphs into their calibration curve, they acquired age estimates for these ranging from about 500 to 4000 years BP.

This method offers several significant benefits. It involves no sample removal and, apart from contact, is non-invasive. It takes only about two minutes to take and record one measurement. Even if it were to be found ultimately that it does not provide viable estimates of petroglyph age, the use of portable XRF equipment is still an invaluable addition to the growing arsenal of the rock art scientist. At the very least is has obvious applications in analytical and sophisticated conservation work, providing most detailed compositional data of accretions and weathering phenomena. If it should also yield rough estimates of age (an accuracy of only about ±50% is being proposed), that would be a welcome bonus. The claims by Lytle et al. will need to be examined carefully, some aspects of their initial project are debatable. For instance, some of their calibration points were derived from questionable cosmogenic analyses and unreliable radiocarbon dates, and the diagenetic complexity of rock varnishes (in view of re-cycling of cations by microbes, and other causes of degradation) renders the idea of a linear enrichment implausible. Duplication of this work is therefore imperative.

To some degree the preceding comments reflect the state of the art of petroglyph dating: after neglect of this field of research it is at last being taken seriously since the 1980s. However, the science of rock art dating remains in its infancy, if not embryonic; catching up with the rest of science will require decades of effort.

Issues relating to the dating of pictograms

The state of our knowledge may seem somewhat better for pictograms than for petroglyphs, but impressions can be deceptive. The term pictogram is used here in accordance with the IFRAO Rock Art Glossary (Bednarik 2000c): a rock art motif that involved an additive process in its production, such as the application of paint, dry pigment or bees-wax; it includes essentially paintings, stencils, drawings and imprints. The basic division of rock art into petroglyphs and pictograms is useful not only in technological considerations, but analytical methods are also frequently related to it. Attempts to recover the mineral dust produced in petroglyph production have remained unsuccessful so far (despite attempts in Australia by George Susino), hence there is generally no substance available for dating, whereas such substances generally do exist in pictograms. Moreover, preservation and site management techniques may also differ between these two divisions.

While the availability of datable substances relating to the making of pictograms may foster an expectation that more reliable results can be secured from this form of rock art, this is not necessarily reflected in the results tendered so far. They range from very reliable to unconvincing and probably false claims, so it is important to consider each result on its own merits. This applies especially to startling or sensational claims, which differ significantly from expectations, as has been the case in several projects of recent years.

Beeswax figures are a local but widespread feature in northern Australian rock art, where they have been reported from western Arnhem Land (Brandl 1968; Chaloupka 1993), Kimberley (Welch 1995), Reynolds River, Keep River and Groote Eylandt. Of all the rock art types in the world, these figures are perhaps the most amenable for dating. Not only is there always adequate datable substance available, the physical properties of the beeswax render it unlikely that it would have been used in any but nearly fresh condition, so the time of the production of the wax, which approximates its radiocarbon age, is unlikely to differ significantly from the time the art was created. Numerous such dates have already been secured from beeswax figures (Nelson et al. 1995; Taçon and Garde 2000). Nelson (2000) reports radio-carbon age measurements from 137 figures at sixteen sites in the Northern Territory. They range from the present time to about 4000 BP, but the overwhelming majority of the ages falls within the last 500 years, and all except four are under 1500 years. The apparent rarity of the few significantly older samples as well as the dates' chronological distribution suggest that this is a result of taphonomic processes. The large number of available results renders it possible to detect a typical temporal distribution curve implying a taphonomic threshold (Bednarik 1994a) of about 800 years BP for beeswax figures (Bednarik 2001) (Figure 51).

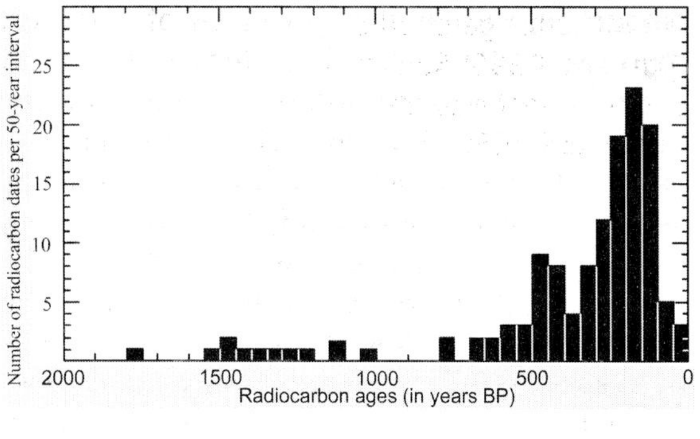

Figure 51. Radiocarbon ages for 135 of the 137 samples obtained from beeswax figures in northern Australia, after Nelson et al. (2000).

Residues of rock paintings, stencils or drawings have often been concealed by *accretionary deposits*, such as carbonate, silica and oxalate skins or crusts. These and the inclusions they frequently contain have been used to secure data intended to assist in estimating pictogram ages. In interpreting such data it is important to appreciate the many qualifications that apply to them (see also comments elsewhere in this chapter). The most spectacular results of such work are from Australia, where at several sites series of superimposed painting events, separated by deposition of accretions, have been analysed, and Watchman (2000) has even detected paint residues in substrates that lack any surface indication of the presence of rock art. At Walkunder Arch Cave, Queensland, a series of ten radiocarbon dates has been obtained from finely stratified accretions totalling only 2.11 mm thickness (Campbell 2000). These dates are in sequence and range from 29 700 to 3340 carbon-years, spanning a history of about 26 000 years. The sequence includes three painting events, at 28 100 ± 400, 16 100 ± 130 and 10 400 ± 90 carbon-years BP.

The extraordinary precision of these nano-stratigraphic techniques and the availability of sequences rather than individual 'dates' certainly enhances the credibility of such results, but they are still subject to a variety of qualifications. Most important of all, until radiocarbon sampling can be focused on specific compounds or substances, i.e. at the object or molecular level (Bednarik 1996), we cannot know what it is we are dating, and the ubiquitous presence of datable carbon in rock substrates, together with the openness of the carbon system, limits reliability of this approach.

The issue is well illustrated by another Australian project. Loy et al. (1990) claim to have identified blood residues at two Australian rock art sites. However, there are problems with this work at the site Laurie Creek (Northern Territory). Underlying sub-modern paintings, 'fragmentary panels of weathered dark red pigment' were reported from which Loy secured a proteinaceous substance he identified as human blood. An accelerator mass spectrometry radiocarbon date of 20 320 + 3100/ -2300 years BP was obtained from this substance. His co-author Erle Nelson, however, had 'second thoughts' about the results and returned to the site to re-sample the surface deposit (Nelson 1993). He found that the reported pigment layer was nothing more than naturally reprecipitated iron oxides of a type common on sandstone surfaces, and he detected organic matter at various surface locations that bore no paint. When he re-analysed the deposit from which the original data had been obtained, he found only very low concentrations of protein. He reports that 'the material dated was not proteinaceous, and therefore not a remnant of human blood. ... It is not a date with any archaeological meaning' (Nelson 1993: 894). Loy (1994) has responded to Nelson's correction, still maintaining that there was mammalian IgG present at the sampling site, and saying that Nelson's new data confirm the presence of organic carbon in the samples. Indeed they do, but the organic carbon is also present in the supposedly undecorated rock surface (cf. Bednarik 1979). However, Loy's views have been firmly refuted by Gillespie's (1997) subsequent research (cf. also Tuross and Barnes 1996).

Amino acid *racemisation* may have valid applications in rock art dating, despite the severe limitations imposed on this method by the extreme susceptibility of the reaction to temperature (Murray-Wallace 1993), and despite Denninger's (1971) refuted attempt to date South African rock paintings. Amino acid residues can certainly be preserved in rock paints (McCarthy et al. 1994).

Attempts to secure 'direct' *radiocarbon dates from paint residues* are based on the assumption that their organic content reflects binders or incidental vegetable inclusions that are of essentially the same age as the rock art. It was first introduced in South Africa (Van der Merwe et al. 1987; Hedges et al. 1987). Binders were frequently used in paint preparations, and presumed brush fibres and other material relating to paint preparation have been detected (Cole and Watchman 1992; Watchman and Cole 1993). However, unless the substances concerned are isolated and identified before processing for carbon analysis, there is no certainty that such radiocarbon dates refer to the age of the paintings concerned (Bednarik 1996). The most commonly used rock art pigments are ochres, i.e. oxides or hydroxides of iron, and Ridges et al. (2000) have shown that samples of such minerals from rock art regions comprise substantial amounts of organic matter, such as lichen and bacteria. Ridges et al. detected phototropic microbes, which could have radiocarbon ages that are unrelated to their actual antiquity, through recycling old organic carbon. Of particular concern should be their detection in one sample of approximately 5000-year-old unidentified organic matter. Had this sample been used in a rock painting, it would have provided a severely misleading carbon age. On the other hand, applied paints can be the target of bacteria and algal growths, as we know only too well from some decorated Palaeolithic caves in south-western Europe (but many other cases are known). Moreover, the ubiquitous presence of organic matter in probably most lithospheric substrates (Bednarik 1979; Nelson 1993) questions the reliability of such dates in any case. Whether the paint residues concerned are on the surface now or are sandwiched between layers of mineral accretion is in principle irrelevant. Even the availability of a sequence of dates is no guarantee, because if there were continuous contamination of a cumulative stratigraphic sequence the dates might well be in sequence, but they would still be invalid.

With carbon dates from paint residues dominated by *charcoal pigment*, these considerations are perhaps less paramount, though still applicable. Since such samples consist primarily of charcoal, the impact of distorting contaminations present would be somewhat lessened, but other reservations apply to such dates. The carbon isotope result of charcoal never refers to the event of rock painting, it can at best only indicate the time when the tree from whose wood the charcoal derives assimilated carbon dioxide from the atmosphere (Bednarik 1994c, 1996, 2000a). This is followed by the death of the tree or branch, its oxidation, and finally the selection of the resulting charcoal as pigment. This chain of events may occupy only decades or centuries, but it may equally well take tens of millennia. A documented example of this is provided by David et al. (1999): a dated charcoal inscription at a site in northern Queensland, Australia, apparently of 1894, yielded an age of over 1300 radiocarbon years. There is also the possibility, however remote, that fossil wood had been involved (Schiffer 1986; Fetterman 1996). Much more reliable is the method of analysing soot deposits on a cave ceiling, but this has so far been successful only at one site (Clottes et al. 1995).

Two specialised methods have been developed to process samples from pictograms for carbon nuclide analysis, and to guard against some possible contaminants. One uses low-temperature, low-pressure oxygen plasma to oxidise the organic matter (Armitage et al. 2000; Chaffee et al. 1993; Ilger et al. 1996; Russ et al. 1990). The second is 'focused laser extraction of carbon-bearing substances' (FLECS), followed by accelerator mass spectrometry (AMS) radiocarbon dating (Watchman 1993; Watchman and Lessard 1993). Here, a small sample of a rock art-related substance is combusted with the help of a laser, and the resulting carbon dioxide is then reduced to a graphite target for AMS dating. However, both methods cannot discriminate between different types of organic matter. They are certainly 'direct dating' methods in the sense of the term's definition, but their results are not readily relatable to the actual age of the art concerned. This is because they cannot be targeted on a particular substance, but may in fact provide composite results to which any organic matter present in the sample has contributed. This can include organic pigment or binder, microscopic biota, lipids, proteins, carbohydrates, vegetable remains such as brush fibres, airborne debris and so forth. It can also include natural graphite, whose presence at a rock art site Watchman (1995) has already demonstrated, and which has a significant 'ageing effect' on samples. It is therefore likely that two dating results from different locations on the same motif, using precisely the same technique, will provide different results, depending on the proportions of the contaminating components (see McDonald et al. 1990 for greatly incompatible results from charcoal of a single motif). This renders it even impossible to make precise allowance for the contaminants by determining them and their magnitudes chemically or microscopically from a control sample: their relative proportions may differ locally. Other concerns expressed about the uncritical acceptance by archaeologists of experimental data of this kind are that the petrology and morphology of the rock substrate may be inadequately accounted for; the presence of unknown contaminants; the neglect of ^{13}C measurements; effects of variations in techniques; and that indiscriminate sampling in the course of applications of this immature methodology may not be justified.

PITFALLS IN ROCK ART DATING

Radiocarbon analysis

This technique produces no calendar years or absolute dates, it yields radiocarbon years, which are expressed as sets of statistical probabilities. To treat them as actual ages or to 'calibrate' them as such is therefore unsatisfactory (Muzzolini 1999b). Usually results are expressed with tolerances stated at one standard deviation, which means that under ideal conditions (which do not exist), the true 'age' of the sample should lie between the tolerance values in 68.26% of cases. But in the first instance, there are many problems with this assumption, and in the second, even if they did not exist, such a result is not a 'date' that one can simply compare with some other data, such as another 'date' (Bednarik 1994c). In comparing two such results, the probability that the deductions we are likely to make from them are all true is only 46.59%, or 31.80% for three dates, and so on. If we compare statistical probabilities we must not treat them as finite facts or figures, and when we compare sets of probabilities derived from two different methods (e.g. ^{14}C and TL analyses) we are also bringing into correlation two sets of complex qualifications. We are truly comparing oranges and apples, and the logical underpinning becomes practically unmanageable.

But these simple qualifications refer to ideal conditions, which in any case do not exist in reality. We have already seen above that the technique relies on three false assumptions: that we know the atmospheric concentration of carbon isotopes in the distant past — we do not know it; that we know the isotope's true decay rate — we think we do but nevertheless use a wrong one; and that the decay process has not been influenced by factors other than the decay rate — we know this to be false. In considering just the first of these limiting factors in detail, we could examine just why the initial atmospheric concentrations of ^{14}C and $\delta^{13}C$ are not known. There is, for example, an intricate relationship between atmospheric $\delta^{13}C$, climate and vegetation: different plant communities facilitate specific carbon regimes. Shrub-dominated communities (C3 plants) provide values of between -12‰ and -10‰ $\delta^{13}C$ in respiratory CO_2, grasses (C4 plants) -3‰ to +1‰ (Cole and Monger 1994). C4 plants, so called because of the four-carbon acids in which carbon dioxide is initially captured in their outer mesophyll cells, have a physiological advantage over C3 plants in low atmospheric carbon dioxide concentrations (Robinson 1994). The latter are directly related to world climate and were significantly lower during the Pleistocene glacials. This introduces yet another variable, the effect of which is an unknown factor and questions the utility of all Pleistocene radiocarbon dates. Vulcanism would tilt the regime in favour of ^{12}C, rendering atmospheric carbon balance apparently 'older'. Further, the effects of cosmic rays cannot be known for past periods.

These systematic problems may sound disconcerting, but they are only the tip of an iceberg. They and other variables affecting the result (e.g. the de Vries effect, isotopic fractionation, differences in laboratory treatment, laboratory error) represent reasonable risks because they are to some extent expected. Contamination is always possible, before, during and after sample collection (e.g. oil film on supposedly sterile aluminium foil). Hedges et al. (1998) have found that the standard acid treatment (acid-base-acid washes) of radiocarbon samples does not necessarily remove oxalates. A similar observation was made by Armitage et al. (1999), who observed that four results from a sample of Mayan charcoal paint averaged about 1440 BP, using oxygen-plasma treatment, while the same sample yielded a date of about 11 770 BP, using standard pre-treatment. Bearing in mind that most of the rock paint samples so far analysed, particularly those from European caves, received this standard pre-treatment, it is obvious that such results need to be considered much more carefully than has been the case in the literature.

Just as serious is the plethora of general environmental variables that can significantly affect carbon isotopes. Among them is the hard water effect (the deposition of calcium and magnesium salts from aqueous solution in ground water), exchange with the atmosphere, humic acid, and especially the effect of the introduction of very old carbon from a variety of sources. Watchman (1998) has observed the occurrence of hydrocarbon aerosols derived from diesel exhausts, settling with airborne sand on a rock art site hundreds of metres from a road. Such deposits have the potential of significantly distorting the ratio of carbon isotopes in the surface deposit on an art panel. Just as a tree growing next to a busy motorway is likely to derive much of its carbon by assimilating exhaust fumes from vehicles burning ancient hydrocarbons, an animal or plant may contain high levels of carbon derived from a limestone environment. Thus the ^{14}C level in the ivory of an elephant, related to its food source, may differ according to the geology of the live animal's environment. The gaseous emissions of volcanic eruptions may age a sample, major forest or grass fires may make it appear younger, and past variations in cosmogenic radiation may have either effect.

Finally there is the whole class of problems relating to the fact that rock surface layers are usually open carbon systems, which can be quite significantly affected by a variety of processes (see section above on inclusions in accretions).

The greatest difficulty, however, is misinterpretation of results by archaeologists. A fragment of charcoal is *not* of the radiocarbon age derived from it (it is younger), and the soil from which it was excavated is *not* necessarily of the same age as the piece of charcoal (taphonomy sees to that). Archaeologists have introduced their inductive reasoning into rock art dating in several ways, especially through their favoured technique of carbon isotope analysis. Accordingly it has been assumed that charcoal pigment found in rock paintings must be of the same age as the picture. There is clearly no connection between the two, except that the picture should be more recent than the date secured from the charcoal, but the difference may be tens of millennia. When a motif yielded two different dates it was seen by various authors as proving that repainting had occurred, when in fact there are several alternatives possible:

a. The true age lies outside stated tolerances, of one or both samples;
b. Charcoal fragments of different ages were used at the same time;
c. The picture was retouched at a later time;
d. One or both samples are contaminated;
e. One or both samples provided erroneous results;
f. There were differences in laboratory procedures;
g. Or there could be any combination of some of the above factors.

Thus archaeological deductions drawn from charcoal paint dates may be essentially valid, or they may quite easily be false. Bearing in mind that as a rule these data were acquired by AMS analysis from exceedingly small samples, measuring only in the order of milligrams of carbon, the kinds of interpretations of these results we have already seen proliferate in the literature are certainly unwarranted.

Having said all this, it is timely to remember that, in the final analysis, radiocarbon dating remains one of the most reliable, most precise and most widely used techniques of estimating the age of rock art. This provides a fair measure of the very real complexity of dating issues, and of the qualifications concerning other, sometimes more experimental methods. Clearly this is a matter of judicious and careful assessment, without which rock art dating would soon be back in the wilderness from which it emerged only a few years ago. If this field of rock art science were to be judged on the basis of the distorted and uninformed interpretations some have made about it, direct dating would not be worthwhile. Fortunately the outlook is not that bleak, provided we can persuade archaeologists to take a greater interest in rock art science before they attempt interpreting such data.

Determination of cation leaching

This technique serves as a classical example of the pitfalls in rock art dating. Hailed as the miracle cure for rock art dating blues for about a decade, it has now been abandoned by all and sundry, particularly after its inventor and advocate effectively disowned it by rejecting his own method of calibration.

Cation-ratio dating (CR) provides results that must be expected to be highly variable depending on sampling site. This method seeks to calibrate the rate of leaching of the more soluble cations of rock varnish (potassium and calcium) relative to the supposedly more stable titanium content (Dorn 1983, 1986). After it was developed during the 1980s, its reliability and accuracy were seriously challenged (cf. Nobbs and Dorn 1988 and comments; see also Bednarik 1991; Bierman et al. 1991; Watchman 1992). Dorn has conceded that it is an inferior method (1990) and that it is susceptible to an excessively high number of variables (1994).

One of the numerous flaws of this technique is the great variability of the crucial indices, the cation ratios. For instance, sedimentary rocks have great variations in Ti on a millimetre scale, e.g. due to a single layer of heavy minerals, or spotting effects of low-grade metamorphism. Such differences of cation ratios in the host rock may be reflected in those of the varnish over the motif area. Anomalies can occur not only in Ti, but also in Ca and K. In addition, numerous other factors affect the CR of rock varnishes: the proximity of soil, oxalate, amorphous silica or organic matter; lichens, fungi, pH, water run-off; and of course relative exposure to leaching or weathering. Moreover, the ratio will differ laterally, depending on how the varnish spreads out from initial colonisation sites. Structurally, rock varnishes are as a rule highly variable, again on a millimetre scale, which is precisely why I abandoned the idea of using them for dating in the 1970s (Bednarik 1979). The extent of erosion episodes or of cation scavenging by micro-organisms, which certainly invalidate CR dates, is well demonstrated by SEM photographs of varnish stratigraphies. This applies also to episodes of microcolonial fungus attack or lichen activity. Even the fundamental proposition that cations are uniformly soluble is open to question. After all, they do not occur as pure elements and it would seem to be the solubility of the minerals they occur in that determines the relative leaching rates.

The solubility of diverse Ti-minerals relative to different Ca-minerals varies considerably. Some minerals, such as titanite, in fact contain both cations, which means that their removal will not affect the ratio at all. All of the factors determining the cation ratio of a weathered rock varnish are locally variable, besides distorting that ratio, and this probably explains the significantly discordant results of Watchman's (1992) re-sampling program.

CR analysis has not provided any accepted results, its methodology is fundamentally flawed and it does not offer a valid method of estimating the ages of rock art or geomorphic exposures. Following its demise, Dorn has focused on the possibility of using the nano-stratigraphy of rock varnish to estimate the ages of distinctive strata. These micro-laminations are viewed in ultra-thin sections (<5 microns), using a transmission light microscope (Liu and Dorn 1996; Dorn 2001). Dorn claims to recognise distinctive layers in samples from petroglyphs, layers he has observed and dated elsewhere. Sequences of such laminae have reportedly been dated by radiocarbon and uranium series analysis, spanning many tens of millennia. Dorn's own outspoken rejection of the carbon isotope analysis of accretionary deposits of this kind inspire no confidence in the precision he suggests for his results from such deposits. Moreover, rock varnish laminae are notoriously heterogeneous, because of their irregular deposition patterns, scavenging and recycling of cations by micro-organisms, and highly variable weathering patterns. Nevertheless, the possibility of nano-stratigraphic dating of varnish layers does need to be pursued, if only to test Dorn's claims.

Cosmogenic radiation nuclides

Another analytical method strongly supported by Dorn since at least 1990 is the determination of maximum rock exposure ages supposedly attainable from measuring the presence of cosmic ray-caused radiation products in rock. This can never provide actual age estimations of rock art, and even the claims that it can offer mere exposure ages need to be carefully qualified. The nuclides available for measurement by this method are ^{3}He, ^{10}Be, ^{14}C, ^{21}Ne, ^{26}Al, ^{36}Cl and ^{41}Ca, using accelerator mass spectrometry and noble gas mass spectrometry. Among the key qualifications are the need to be certain the sample comes from a closed system, and the production rates of the various nuclides need to be better calibrated than they are at present. There is a preference for using more than one radionuclide in tandem, and in particular the pair ^{10}Be and ^{26}Al is thought to give good results from quartz (Nishiizumi et al. 1989). Their half-lives are suitable for Quaternary deposits (1.5 Ma and 725 ka respectively), contamination can be dealt with effectively (Brown et al. 1991), and their production ratio of about six is not thought to be much affected by altitude and latitude. Another pair used is ^{3}He and ^{21}Ne, which is suitable for older surfaces, but helium data from radiocarbon-dated Hawaiian lava flows imply very coarse precision (Kurz et al. 1990; Rubin et al. 1987).

The production rates of the radionuclides in the substrate that result from cosmogenic radiation are variable according to topographic exposure, altitude, latitude, oscillations in radiation, overburden and time. Even past fluctuations in the earth's magnetic field may effect variations (Kurz et al. 1990). It is of concern that the method, which is almost as old as radiocarbon dating (Davis and Schaeffer 1955; Lal et al. 1958; Lal and Peters 1967), remains poorly calibrated. Its only two applications in archaeology, at Stonehenge (Williams-Thorpe et al. 1995) and Côa valley (Phillips et al. 1997) produced apparently false results (Bednarik 1998c). Estimates of production rates (Lal 1991; Yokoyama et al. 1977) remain severely hampered by the lack of appropriate reaction cross-sections for neutron-induced spallation. It has been difficult securing data from polished rock surfaces of known ages (Cerling 1990; Kurz et al. 1990; Nishiizumi et al. 1989; Phillips et al. 1986; Zreda et al. 1991). The well-established ages of lava flows are generally very young, usually of the Holocene (Poreda and Cerling 1992), which permits only the three nuclides with the shortest half-lives to be considered.

Cosmogenic radiation analysis has been applied at one rock art site, Penascosa in the Côa valley, northern Portugal (Phillips et al. 1997). Using the less attractive ^{36}Cl nuclide, geologically and historically unacceptable results were obtained, and the analysts made several crucial errors in their interpretation of their data. Most importantly, they ignored the high solubility and mobility of chlorides, and the susceptibility of subterranean strata to the nuclide conversion process, even though both factors were implied by their own data (Bednarik 1998c). Moreover, their method necessitates the assumption of a rate of erosion retreat (Phillips et al. 1990), while at the same time any surface retreat over tens of millennia would effectively exclude the survival of the petroglyphs they were trying to date. These several self-contradictions render the specific dating attempt of Phillips et al. (1997) refuted, but this does not imply that the method itself is discredited. Its use in estimating the age of geomorphic exposures is certainly valid, particularly in cases where exposure occurred on a massive scale, such as by meteor impact, major tectonic adjustment or quarrying operations. In such circumstances background radiation products would be either absent, or hopefully negligible. However, such conditions rarely apply in rock art dating, for which the determination of cosmogenic radiation nuclides therefore has little if any relevance.

Erosion retreat ('micro erosion') analysis

This method is of quite limited application in rock art analysis but it must be mentioned here because some archaeologists have confused it with microerosion dating (e.g. A. Rosenfeld, cited in Zilhão 1995). 'Micro erosion' is actually a misnomer, as it deals with processes that occur at the macroscopic rather than the microscopic level, and a more suitable name is *erosion retreat analysis*. It refers to the measurement of the retreat of rapidly eroding rock surfaces, especially those on sedimentary rocks (High and Hanna 1970; Atkinson and Smith 1976). Its primary use would be in rock art conservation research rather than dating applications (see Ch. 5, 'Rock and their weathering'). This retreat may be attributable to solution or granular exfoliation, and is often a combination of the two processes.

Essentially the method involves the use of an engineering precision dial gauge mounted on a frame supported by three legs, and the placement on the rock of a reference stud (Smith 1978). With this instrument, the gradual retreat of a rock surface can be monitored over a period of many years, and the data so gathered can provide good information concerning petroglyphs that have been subjected to similar surface retreat. Obviously this method would only be applicable to relatively recent rock art on such rocks as limestone and carbonate-cemented sandstone. However, it has not been used for estimating the age of any rock art so far and is likely to be of only limited applicability.

SUMMARY

Scientific dating of rock art has been conducted for about two decades, and has resulted in significant improvements in our understanding of rock art chronologies. It has also led to some spectacular changes in perception and fundamental misinterpretations of data.

Two types of radiocarbon results have been derived from mineral accretions over or under both paint residues and petroglyphs. In one type it has been attempted to estimate the time of the accretion's deposition from its principal component (carbonate or oxalate), while incidental inclusions were targeted in the second. Whereas the limitations of the first approach are appreciated (Bednarik 1998a, 1999), there is disagreement over the second. I had long been sceptical, at least in respect of specific types of deposits (particularly ferromanganous accretions), after establishing during the 1970s that their carbon isotope system was essentially open (Bednarik 1979), and that carbons occur widely in surfaces and substrates. Others, however, claimed for many years to obtain secure dates from such deposits. Dorn, in particular, argued strongly in support of radiocarbon analysis of rock varnishes, including its use in calibrating the cation-ratio method he developed (Dorn 1983). But in the mid-1990s he recanted his results, arguing against them and those of others using similar approaches. However, it might be premature to extrapolate concerns to all forms of accretion; the prospects of finding closed systems are better in silica skins and oxalates.

Carbon isotope analysis of inclusions in mineral accretions spatially related to rock art provides 'direct dating' evidence, but it does not date the rock art. To succeed in this, the analytical results should be determined either at the molecular level (i.e. be from a single identified compound) or specific object level (i.e. be from an identified organic object, such as a brush fibre). Bulk sampling by FLECS or oxygen plasma treatment permits no such discrimination and probably provides no reliable dating. Similarly, carbon dates from carbonates or oxalates are certainly 'direct', but presently available data do not permit us to test the true relationship between such results and the age of the rock art effectively. In all these cases results should be regarded as relevant 'preliminary dating information'.

Another crucial issue separates all dating approaches in rock art science into two groups: those expected to provide locally variable results, and those presumed to yield uniform results from any part of a specific rock art motif (Bednarik 1996). The first type fails to meet the demand of repeatability, which science favours philosophically, and includes techniques already considered to have failed (e.g. cation-ratio, cosmogenic radiation products). The second type includes particularly 'geochemical or geomorphological' approaches, using such phenomena as microerosion, weathering rinds, wanes, and possibly luminescence and others.

In relation to alternative methods, two factors stand out. First, only a minute portion of the possible options has been explored in detail, and there are numerous perfectly promising options that have not attracted any interest, have barely been attempted, or are used only rarely. Several of these alternative methods are evidently more robust and more reliable (particularly those focusing on geomorphic variables), which renders their neglect particularly perplexing. Second, most of the traditionally used, 'archaeological' methods of estimating rock art age are likely to lead to errors, and the use of proximity, iconography, style and technique in particular provides only supplementary or anecdotic data. Excavation and superimpositions can yield sound supporting evidence when used in combination with scientific data, and the physical and chemical analysis of patination and weathering phenomena has been utilised inadequately so far.

NOTE: A comprehensive list of direct dating results from rock art up to 1995 is given in Chapter 11.

REFERENCES

ABREU, M. S. DE and R. G. BEDNARIK 2000. Fariseu rock art not archaeologically dated. *Rock Art Research* 17: 65–68.

ACKER, J. G. and O. P. BRICKER 1992. The influence of pH on biotite dissolution and alteration kinetics at low temperature. *Geochimica et Cosmochimica Acta* 56: 3073–92.

AITKEN, M. J. 1985. *Thermoluminescence dating.* Academic Press, London.

AITKEN, M. J. 1990. *Science-based dating in archaeology.* Longman, London.

AITKEN, M. J. 1994. Optical dating: a non-specialist review. *Quaternary Science Reviews* 13: 503–8.

AITKEN, M. J., D. W. ZIMMERMANN and S. J. FLEMING 1968. Thermoluminescent dating of ancient pottery. *Nature* 219: 442–45.

AITKEN, M. J., P. R. S. MOOREY and P. J. UCKO 1971. The authenticity of vessels and figurines in the Hacilar style. *Archaeometry* 13: 89–142.

ALLEN, C. C. 1978. Desert varnish of the Sonoran Desert: optical and electron probe microanalysis. *Journal of Geology* 86: 743–52.

AMPOULANGE, U. and R. C. PINTAUD 1955. Une nouvelle gravure de la grotte de La Grèze (Dordogne). *Bulletin de la Société Préhistorique Française* 52: 249–51.

ANATI, E. 1960. *La civilisation du Val Camonica.* Mondes Anciens 4, Paris.

ANATI, E. 1961. La Grande Roche de Naquane. *Archives de l'Institut de Paléontologie Humaine* 31: 1–189.

ANATI, E. 1963. *Palestine before the Hebrews.* Alfred A. Knopf, New York.

ANATI, E. 1968. *Rock art in central Arabia* (2 volumes). Bibliothèque du Muséon 50, Institut Orientaliste Bibliothèque de l'Université Lovain.

ANATI, E. 1976. *Evolution and style in Camunian rock art.* Archivi 6, Capo di Ponte.

ANDERSON, J. L. and J. L. SOLLID 1971. Glacial chronology and glacial geomorphology in the marginal zones of the glaciers Midtdalsbreen and Nigardsbreen, south Norway. *Norsk Geografisk Tidsskrift* 25: 1–38.

ARIAS, P., T. CALDERÓN, C. GONZÁLEZ SAINZ, A. MILLÁN, A. MOURE ROMANILLO, R. ONTAÑON and R. RUIZ IDARRAGA 2000. Thermoluminescence dating of Palaeolithic rock engravings of Venta de la Perra (Carranza, Biscay, Spain). *International Newsletter on Rock Art* 26: 20–23.

ARMITAGE, R. A., J. E. BRADY, A. COBB, J. R. SOUTHON and M. W. ROWE 1999. Radiocarbon dates on charcoal pigments from three Mayan glyph texts in Naj Tunich Cave, Guatemala. Unpubl. MS.

ARMITAGE, R. A., M. HYMAN and M. W. ROWE 2000. Plasma-chemistry for dating pictographs by AMS. In G. K. Ward and C. Tuniz (eds), *Advances in dating Australian rock-markings*, pp. 31–34. Occasional AURA Publication 10, Australian Rock Art Research Association, Melbourne.

ATKINSON, T. C. and D. I. SMITH 1976. The erosion of limestones. In T. D. Ford and C. H. D. Cullingford (eds), *The science of speleology*, pp. 151–177. Academic Press, London.

BAHN, P. G., R. G. BEDNARIK and J. STENBRING 1995. The Peterborough petroglyph site: reflections on massive intervention in rock art. *Rock Art Research* 12: 29–41.

BAKER, A., P. L. SMART, R. LAWRENCE EDWARDS and D. A. RICHARDS 1993. Annual growth banding in a cave stalagmite. *Nature* 364: 518–20.

BASEDOW, H. 1914. Aboriginal rock carvings of great antiquity in South Australia. *Journal of the Royal Anthropological Institute* 44: 195–211.

BATEMAN, M. D., C. D. FREDERICK, M. K. JAISWAL and A. K. SINGHVI 2003. Investigations into the potential effects of pedoturbation on luminescence dating. *Quaternary Science Review* 22: 1169–76.

BECK, W., D. J. DONAHUE, A. J. T. JULL, G. BURR, W. S. BROECKER, G. BONANI, I. HAJDAS and E. MALOTKI 1998. Ambiguities in direct dating of rock surfaces using radiocarbon measurements; with response by R. I. DORN. *Science* 280: 2132–39.

BEDNARIK, R. G. 1979. The potential of rock patination analysis in Australian archaeology – part 1. *The Artefact* 4: 14–38.

BEDNARIK, R. G. 1981. Finger lines, their medium, and their dating. Unpubl. MS, 34 pp., Archive of the Australian Rock Art Research Association, Melbourne.

BEDNARIK, R. G. 1984. Die Bedeutung der paläolithischen Fingerlinientradition. *Anthropologie* 23: 73–79.

BEDNARIK, R. G. 1989a. Perspectives of Koongine Cave and scientistic archaeology. *Australian Archaeology* 29: 9–16.

BEDNARIK, R. G. 1989b. On the Pleistocene settlement of South America. *Antiquity* 63: 101–11.

BEDNARIK, R. G. 1991. Dating eons with cations. *La Pintura* 17(3): 8–9.

BEDNARIK, R. G. 1992. A new method to date petroglyphs. *Archaeometry* 34: 279–91.

BEDNARIK, R. G. 1993. Geoarchaeological dating of petroglyphs at Lake Onega, Russia. *Geoarchaeology* 8: 443–63.

BEDNARIK, R. G. 1994a. A taphonomy of palaeoart. *Antiquity* 68: 68–74.

BEDNARIK, R. G. 1994b. On the scientific study of palaeoart. *Semiotica* 100(2/4): 141–68.

BEDNARIK, R. G. 1994c. Conceptual pitfalls in dating of Palaeolithic rock art. *Préhistoire Anthropologie Méditerranéennes* 3: 95–102.

BEDNARIK, R. G. 1995a. The age of the Côa valley petroglyphs in Portugal. *Rock Art Research* 12: 86–103.

BEDNARIK, R. G. 1995b. The Côa petroglyphs: an obituary to the stylistic dating of Palaeolithic rock-art. *Antiquity* 69: 877–83.

BEDNARIK, R. G. 1996. Only time will tell: a review of the methodology of direct rock art dating. *Archaeometry* 38: 1–13.

BEDNARIK, R. G. 1997a. Direct dating results from rock art: a global review. *AURA Newsletter* 14(2): 9–12.

BEDNARIK, R. G. 1997b. Microerosion analysis of petroglyphs in Valtellina, Italy. *Origini* 21: 7–22.

BEDNARIK, R. G. 1998a. Direct dating results from Australian cave petroglyphs. *Geoarchaeology* 13: 411–18.

BEDNARIK, R. G. 1998b. The technology of petroglyphs. *Rock Art Research* 15: 23–35.

BEDNARIK, R. G. 1998c. Cosmogenic radiation nuclides in archaeology: a response to Phillips et al. *Antiquity* 72: 811–15.

BEDNARIK, R. G. 1999. The speleothem medium of finger flutings and its isotopic geochemistry. *The Artefact* 22: 49–64.

BEDNARIK, R. G. 2000a. Some problems with 'direct dating' of rock-pictures. In G. K. Ward and C. Tuniz (eds), *Advances in dating Australian rock-markings*, pp. 104–109. Occasional AURA Publication 10, Australian Rock Art Research Association, Melbourne.

BEDNARIK, R. G. 2000b. Age estimates for the petroglyph sequence of Inca Huasi, Mizque, Bolivia. *Andean Past* 6: 277–87.

BEDNARIK, R. G. 2000c. Rock art glossary. *Rock Art Research* 17: 147–55.

BEDNARIK, R. G. 2001. The taphonomy of beeswax figures. *Rock Art Research* 18: 91–95.

BEDNARIK, R. G. 2002. About the age of Pilbara rock art. *Anthropos* 97(1): 201–15.

BEDNARIK, R. G. and M. KHAN 2005. Scientific studies of Saudi Arabian rock art. *Rock Art Research* 22: 49–81

BEDNARIK, R. G., G. KUMAR, A. WATCHMAN and R. G. ROBERTS 2005. Preliminary results of the EIP Project: the status at the end of 2004. *Rock Art Research* 22.

BELTRÁN, A. 1992. Crisis in traditional ideas about European rock art: the question of diffusion and convergence. In M. Lorblanchet (ed.), *Rock art in the Old World*, pp. 401–413. IGNCA Rock Art Series 1, Indira Gandhi National Centre for the Arts, New Delhi.

BELZONI, G. 1820. *Narrative of the operations and recent discoveries within the pyramids, temples, tombs and excavations in Egypt and Nubia*, Vol. 1. London.

BENEDICT, J. B. 1975. The Murray Site: a Late Prehistoric game drive system in the Colorado Rocky Mountains. *Plains Anthropologist* 20: 169–74.

BENEDICT, J. B. 1985. Arapaho Pass: glacial geology and archaeology at the crest of the Colorado Front Range. *Center for Mountain Archaeology, Ward, Colorado, Research Reports* 3: 1–197.

BESCHEL, R. E. 1950. Flechten als Altersmaßstab rezenter Moränen. *Zeitschrift für Gletscherkunde und Glazialgeologie* 1: 152–61.

BESCHEL, R. E. 1957. Lichenometrie im Gletschervorfeld. *Jahrbuch des Vereins zum Schutze der Alpenpflanzen und -tiere* 22: 164–85.

BETTINGER, R. L. and R. OGLESBY 1985. Lichen dating of alpine villages in the White Mountains, California. *Journal of California and Great Basin Anthropology* 7: 202–24.

BICKERTON, R. W. and J. A. MATTHEWS 1992. On the accuracy of lichenometric dates: an assessment based on the 'Little Ice Age' moraine sequence at Nigardsbreen, southern Norway. *The Holocene* 2: 227–37.

BIERMAN, P. R., A. R. GILLESPIE and S. KUEHNER 1991. Precision of rock-varnish chemical analyses and cation-ratio ages. *Geology* 19: 135–38.

BIRKELAND, P. W., S. M. COLMAN, R. M. BURKE and T. C. MIERDING 1979. Nomenclature of alpine glacial deposits, or, what's in a name? *Geology* 7: 532–36.

BLAKE, W. P. 1905. Superficial blackening and discoloration of rocks especially in desert regions. *Transcripts of the American Institute of Mining Engineers* 35: 371–75.

BORNFELDT, F. and M. ÖSTERBORG 1958. Lavarter som hjälpmedel för datering av Ändmoräner vid Norska glaciärer. *Stockholms HögskolaGeografiska Proseminariet* 403: 1–37.

BRANDL, E. 1968. Aboriginal rock designs in beeswax and description of cave painting sites in western Arnhem Land. *Archaeology and Physical Anthropology in Oceania* 3: 19–29.

BROADBENT, N. D. 1987. Lichenometry and archaeology. Testing of lichen chronology on the Swedish north Bothnian coast. *Centre for Arctic Cultural Research, Umeå University, Research Reports* 2: 1–61.

BROADBENT, N. D. and K. I. BERGQVIST 1986. Lichenometric chronology and archaeological features on raised beaches: preliminary results from the Swedish north Bothnian coastal region. *Arctic and Alpine Research* 18: 297–306.

BROWN, E. T., J. M. EDMOND, G. M. RAISBECK, F. YIOU, M. D. KURZ and E. J. BROOK 1991. Examination of surface exposure ages of Antarctic moraines using *in situ* produced ^{10}Be and ^{26}Al. *Geochimica et Cosmochimica Acta* 55: 2269–83.

BURKE, R. M. and P. W. BIRKELAND 1979. Re-evaluation of multiparameter relative dating techniques and their application to the glacial sequence along the eastern escarpment of the Sierra Nevada, California. *Quaternary Research* 11: 21–51.

BUSENBERG, E. and C. V. CLEMENCY 1976. The dissolution kinetics of feldspars at 25°C and at 1 atm CO_2 partial pressure. *Geochimica et Cosmochimica Acta* 40: 41–50.

CAMPBELL, I. A. 1991. Classification of rock weathering at Writing-on-Stone Provincial Park, Alberta, Canada: a study in applied geomorphology. *Earth Surface Processes and Landforms* 16: 701–11.

CAMPBELL, J. B. 2000. The Chillagoe and Laura laser-AMS dating project. In G. K. Ward and C. Tuniz (eds), *Advances in dating Australian rock-markings*, pp. 80–83. Occasional AURA Publication 10, Australian Rock Art Research Association, Melbourne.

CANNON, W. J. and M. J. RICKS 1986. The Lake County, Oregon, rock art inventory: implications for prehistoric settlement and land use patterns. *Contributions to the Archaeology of Oregon* 3: 1–23.

CAPITAN, L., H. BREUIL and D. PEYRONY 1912. Les gravures sur cascade stalagmitique de la grotte de la Mairie à Teyat (Dordogne). *Congrès International d'Anthropologie et d'Archéologie Préhistorique, 16e session*, pp. 498–514. Geneva.

CARLSON, R. L. 1993. Content and chronology of Northwest Coast (North America) rock art. In J. Steinbring and A. Watchman (eds), *Time and space: dating considerations in rock art research*, pp. 7–12. Occasional AURA Publication 8. Australian Rock Art Research Association, Melbourne.

CARROLL, T. 1974. Relative age dating techniques and a Late Quaternary chronology, Arikaree Cirque, Colorado. *Geology* 2: 321–25.

CERLING, T. E. 1990. Dating geomorphologic surfaces using cosmogenic ^{3}He. *Quaternary Research* 33: 148–56.

ČERNOHOUZ, J. and I. SOLČ 1966. Use of sandstone wanes and weathered basaltic crust in absolute chronology. *Nature* 212: 806–7.

CHAFFEE, S. D., M. HYMAN and M. W. ROWE 1993. AMS ^{14}C dating of rock paintings. In J. Steinbring and A. Watchman (eds), *Time and space: dating considerations in rock art research*, pp. 67–73. Occasional AURA Publication 8. Australian Rock Art Research Association, Melbourne.

CHALOUPKA, G. 1993. *Journey in time*. Reed Books, Chatswood.

CHILDERS, B. C. 1994. Long-term lichen-removal experiments and petroglyph conservation: Fremont County, Wyoming, Ranch Petroglyph Site. *Rock Art Research* 11: 101–12.

CHIPPINDALE, C. and P. S. C. TAÇON 1993. Two old painted panels from Kakadu: variation and sequence in Arnhem Land rock art. In J. Steinbring and A. Watchman (eds), *Time and space: dating considerations in rock art research*, pp. 32–56. Occasional AURA Publication 8. Australian Rock Art Research Association, Melbourne.

CHIPPINDALE, C. and P. S. C. TAÇON 1998. The many ways of dating Arnhem Land rock art, north Australia. In C. Chippindale and P. S. C. Taçon (eds), *The archaeology of rock-art*, pp. 90–111. Cambridge University Press, Cambridge.

CLARKE, J. 1976. Two Aboriginal rock art pigments from Western Australia: their properties, use and durability. *Studies in Conservation* 21: 134–42.

CLAYTON, J. A., K. L. VEROSUB and C. D. HARRINGTON 1990. Magnetic techniques applied to the study of rock varnish. *Geophysical Research Letters* 17: 787–90.

CLOTTES, J., J.-M. CHAUVET, E. BRUNEL-DESCHAMPS, C. HILLAIRE, J.-P. DAUGAS, M. ARNOLD, H. CACHIER, J. EVIN, P. FORTIN, C. OBERLIN, N. TISNERAT and H. VALLADAS 1995. Les peintures paléolithiques de la Grotte Chauvet-Pont d'Arc, à Vallon-Pont-d'Arc (Ardèche, France): datations directes et indirectes par la méthode du radiocarbone. *Comptes Rendus de l'Académie des Sciences de Paris* 320: 1133–40.

COLE, D. R. and H. C. MONGER 1994. Influence of atmospheric CO_2 on the decline of C4 plants during the last deglaciation. *Nature* 368: 533–36.

COLE, N. and A. WATCHMAN 1992. Painting with plants: investigating fibres in Aboriginal rock paintings at Laura. North Queensland. *Rock Art Research* 9: 27–30.

COLMAN, S. M. 1981. Rock-weathering rates as functions of time. *Quaternary Research* 15: 250–64.

COLMAN, S. M. and K. L. PIERCE 1981. *Weathering rinds on andesitic and basaltic stones as a Quaternary age indicator, western United States*. U.S. Geological Survey, Professional Paper 1210.

COMBIER, J. 1984. Grotte de la Tête-du-Lion. In *L'Art des cavernes*, pp. 595–99. Ministère de la Culture, Paris.

CONSENS, M. 2000. Between artefacts and egofacts: the power of assigning names. Paper presented in Symposium C, 'Epistemology and rock art', Third AURA Congress, Alice Springs, 10 July 2000.

CRIVELLI MONTERO, E. A. and M. M. FERNÁNDEZ 1996. Palaeoindian bedrock petroglyphs at Epullán Grande Cave, northern Patagonia, Argentina. *Rock Art Research* 13: 112–17.

CROOK, R. 1986. Relative dating of Quaternary deposits based on P-wave velocities in weathered granitic clasts. *Quaternary Research* 25: 281–92.

DALEAU, F. 1896. Les gravures sur roche de la caverne de Pair-non-Pair. *Actes de la Société Archeologique de Bordeaux* 21: 235.

DALTON, R. 1998. Dating in doubt as researcher is probed. *Nature* 392: 218–19.

DAVID, B., R. A. ARMITAGE, M. HYMAN, M. W. ROWE and E. LAWSON 1999. How old is north Queensland rock art? A review of the evidence, with new AMS determinations. *Archaeology in Oceania* 34: 103–20.

DAVID, P. 1934. Abri de la Chaire à Calvin. *Congrès*

Préhistoire de France, 11e session, pp. 372–378. Périgueux.

DAVIS, R. and O. A. SCHAEFFER 1955. Chlorine-36 in nature. *Annals of the New York Academy of Sciences* 62: 107–21.

DAY, M. J. and A. S. GOUDIE 1977. Field assessment of rock hardness using the Schmidt hammer. *British Geomor-phological Research Group Technical Bulletin* 18:19–29.

DAYTON, L. 1997. Dating row divides rock art experts. *New Scientist* 153(2074): 10.

DENNINGER, E. 1971. The use of paper chromatography to determine the age of albuminous binders and its application to rock paintings. Rock paintings in southern Africa, supplement to the *South African Journal of Science*, Special Issue, 2: 80–84.

DERNDARSKI, M. 1997. Gebrauchsspurenanalyse nach Experimenten mit Geräten aus verschiedenen Gesteinsarten im Hinblick auf die jungpaläolithischen Steinartefakte aus Rosenburg am Kamp, Niederösterreich. *Archaeologia Austriaca* 81: 1–7.

DORN, R. I. 1983. Cation-ratio dating: a new rock varnish age-determination technique. *Quaternary Research* 20: 49–73.

DORN, R. I. 1986. Rock varnish as an indicator of aeolian environmental change. In W. G. Nickling (ed.), *Aeolian geomorphology*, pp. 291–307. Allen and Unwin, London.

DORN, R. I. 1990. Rock varnish dating of rock art: state of the art perspective. *La Pintura*, 17(2): 1–2, 9–11.

DORN, R. I. 1992. A review of rock varnish dating of rock engravings. *International Newsletter on Rock Art* 2: 10–14.

DORN, R. I. 1994. Dating petroglyphs with a three-tier rock varnish approach. In D. S. Whitley and L. L. Loendorf (eds), *New light on old art*, pp. 13–36. Monograph 36, Institute of Archaeology, University of California, Los Angeles.

DORN, R. I. 1996a. A change of perception. *La Pintura* 23(2): 10–11

DORN, R. I. 1996b. Uncertainties in ^{14}C ages for petroglyphs from the Olary province, South Australia. *Archaeology in Oceania* 31: 214–15.

DORN, R. I. 1997. Constraining the age of the Côa valley (Portugal) engravings with radiocarbon dating. *Antiquity* 71: 105–15.

DORN, R. I. 2001. Chronometric techniques: engravings. In D. S. Whitley (ed.), *Handbook of rock art research*, pp. 167–189. AltaMira Press, Walnut Creek, California.

DORN, R. I., P. B. CLARKSON, M. F. NOBBS, L. L. LOENDORF and D. S. WHITLEY 1992. New approach to the radio-carbon dating of rock varnish, with examples from drylands. *Annals of the Association of American Geographers* 82: 136–51.

DORN, R. I. AND D. S. WHITLEY 1984. Chronometric and relative age determination of petroglyphs in the western United States. *Annals of the Association of American Geographers* 42: 308–22.

DUNNELL, R. C. and J. K. FEATHERS 1994. Thermoluminescence dating of surficial archaeological material. In C. Beck (ed.), *Dating in exposed and surface contexts*, pp. 115–137. University of New Mexico Press, Albuquerque.

DUNNELL, R. C. and M. L. READHEAD 1988. The relation of dating and chronology: comments on Chatters and Hoover (1986) and Butler and Stein (1988). *Quaternary Research* 30: 232–33.

EDWARDS, R. 1971. Art and Aboriginal prehistory. In D. J. Mulvaney and J. Golson (eds), *Aboriginal man and environment in Australia*, pp. 356–367. Australian National University Press, Canberra.

ENGEL, C. E. and R. P. SHARP 1958. Chemical data on desert varnish. *Bulletin of the Geological Society of America* 69: 487–518.

ERIKSTAD, L. and J. L. SOLLID 1986. Neoglaciation in south Norway using lichenometric methods. *Norsk Geografisk Tidsskrift* 40: 85–105.

EVERNDEN, J. F. and G. H. CURTIS 1965. The potassium-argon dating of Late Cenozoic rocks in East Africa and Italy. *Current Anthropology* 6: 343–85.

FAGG, B. E. B. and S. J. FLEMING 1970. Thermoluminescent dating of a terra-cotta, of the Nok culture, Nigeria. *Archaeometry* 21: 53–55.

FEATHERS, J. K. 2003. Single-grain OSL dating of sediments from the Southern High Plains, USA. *Quaternary Science Review* 22: 1035–42.

FETTERMAN, J. 1996. Radiocarbon and tree-ring dating at early Navajo sites. In R. H. Towner (ed.), *The archaeology of Navajo origins*, pp. 71–82. University of Utah Press, Salt Lake City.

FLEMING, S. 1968. Thermoluminescent age studies on mineral inclusions separated from ancient pottery. In D. J. McDougall (ed.), *Thermoluminescence of geological materials*, pp. 431–440. Academic Press, New York.

FLEMING, S. 1971. Thermoluminescent authenticity testing of ancient ceramics: the effects of sampling by drilling. *Archaeometry* 13: 59–69.

FLEMING, S. 1979. *Thermoluminescence techniques in archaeology*. Clarendon Press, Oxford.

FLOOD, J. 1987. Rock art of the Koolburra Plateau, north Queensland. *Rock Art Research* 4: 91–126.

FOLLMANN, G. 1961a. Estudios liquenométricos en las monumentos prehistóricos de la Isla de Pacua. *Anales de la Academia Chilena de Ciencias Naturales* 24: 149–54.

FOLLMANN, G. 1961b. Lichenometrische Altersbestimmungen an vorchristlichen Steinsetzungen der polynesischen Osterinsel. *Naturwissenschaften* 48: 627–28.

FRANCIS, W. D. 1920. The origin of black coatings of iron and manganese oxides on rocks. *Proceedings of the Royal Society of Queensland* 32: 110–16.

FULLAGAR, R. L. K., D. M. PRICE and L. M. HEAD 1996. Early human occupation of northern Australia: archaeology and thermoluminescence dating of

Jinmium rock-shelter, Northern Territory. *Antiquity* 70: 751–73.

GAILBRAITH. R. F., R. G. ROBERTS and H. YOSHIDA 2005. Error variation in OSL palaeodose estimates from single aliquots of quartz: a factorial experiment. *Radiation Measurements* 39: 289–307.

GELLATLY, A. F. 1984. The use of rock weathering-rind thickness to redate moraines in Mount Cook National Park, New Zealand. *Arctic and Alpine Research* 16: 225–32.

GENTNER, W. and H. J. LIPPOLT 1970. The potassium-argon dating of Upper Tertiary and Pleistocene deposits. In D. Brothwell and E. Higgs (eds), *Science in archaeology*. Praeger, New York.

GILLESPIE, R. 1997. On human blood, rock art and calcium oxalate: further studies on organic carbon content and radiocarbon age of materials relating to Australian rock art. *Antiquity* 71: 430–7.

GOODWIN, A. J. H. 1960. Chemical alteration (patination) of stone. In R. F. Heizer and S. F. Cook (eds), *The application of quantitative methods in archaeology*, pp. 300–312. Viking Fund Publications in Anthropology 27, New York.

GRANT, C. 1967. *Rock art of the American Indian*. Thomas Y. Crowell Co., New York.

HALE, H. M. and N. B. TINDALE 1930. Notes on some human remains in the lower Murray valley, South Australia. *Records of the South Australian Museum* 4: 145–218.

HEDGES, R. E. M., R. A. HOUSLEY, I. A. LAW, C. PERRY and J. A. J. GOWLETT 1987. Radiocarbon dates from the Oxford AMS system: archaeometry datelist 6. *Archaeometry* 29: 289–306.

HEDGES, R. E. M., C. B. RAMSEY, G. J. VAN KLINKEN, P. B. PETTITT, C. NIELSEN-MARSH, A. ETCHEGOYEN, J. O. FERNANDEZ NIELLO, M. T. BOSCHIN and A. M. LLAMAZARES 1998. Methodological issues in the ^{14}C dating of rock paintings. *Radiocarbon* 40: 35–44.

HEIMSATH, A. M., J. CHAPPELL, N. A. SPOONER and D. G. QUESTIAUX 2002. Creeping soil. *Geology* 30: 111–14.

HERNÁNDEZ PÉREZ, M. S., P. FERRER I MARSET and E. CATALÁ FERRER 1988. *Arte rupestre en Alicante*. Fundación Banco de Alicante y Grupo Banco Exterior, Alicante.

HIGH, C. and F. K. HANNA 1970. A method for the direct measurement of erosion of rock surfaces. *British Geomorphological Research Corps, Technical Bulletin* 5: 24.

HOLDAWAY, R. N., R. G. ROBERTS, N. R. BEAVAN-ATHFIELD, J. M. OLLEY and T. H. WORTHY 2002. Optical dating of quartz sediments and accelerator mass spectrometry ^{14}C dating of bone gelatin and moa eggshell: a comparison of age estimates for non-archaeological deposits in New Zealand. *Journal of the Royal Society of New Zealand* 32: 463–505.

HOLE, N. and J. L. SOLLID 1979. Neoglaciation in western Norway — preliminary results. *Norsk Geografisk Tidsskrift* 33: 213–15.

HUNTLEY, D. J., D. I. GODFREY-SMITH and M. L. W. THEWALT 1985. Optical dating of sediments. *Nature* 313: 105–7.

ILGER, W. A., M. HYMAN, J. SOUTHON and M. W. ROWE 1996. Radiocarbon dating of ancient rock paintings. In M. V. Orna (ed.), *Archaeological chemistry: organic, inorganic, and biochemical analysis*, pp. 401–414. Advances in Chemistry Series. American Chemical Society, Washington, D.C.

INNES, J. L. 1985. Lichenometry. *Progress in Physical Geography* 9: 187–245.

JACOBS, Z., A. G. WINTLE and G. A. T. DULLER 2003a. Optical dating of dune sand from Blombos Cave, South Africa: I—multiple grain data. *Journal of Human Evolution* 44: 599–612.

JACOBS, Z., G. A. T. DULLER and A. G. WINTLE 2003b. Optical dating of dune sand from Blombos Cave, South Africa: II—single grain data. *Journal of Human Evolution* 44: 613–25.

JAFFE, L. 1996. Systematic vandalism and improper conduct in the Côa rock art area. *AURA Newsletter* 13(2): 12–13.

KENNEDY, G. and L. KNOPF 1960. Dating by thermoluminescence. *Archaeometry* 13: 137-48.

KEYSER, J. D. 1979. The Plains Indian war complex and the rock art of Writing-on-Stone, Alberta, Canada. *Journal of Field Archaeology* 6(1): 41–48.

KEYSER, J. D. 1987. Lexicon for Historic Plains Indian rock art: increasing interpretive potential. *Plains Anthropologist* 32: 42–71.

KEYSER, J. D. 1990. Tsagiglalal — She Who Watches: rock art as an interpretable phenomenon. *Journal of Interpretation* 14(2): S1–S4.

KEYSER, J. D. 1992. *Indian rock art of the Columbia Plateau*. University of Washington Press, Seattle.

KNAUSS, K. G. and T. L. KU 1980. Desert varnish: potential for age dating via uranium-series isotopes. *Journal of Geology* 88: 95–100.

KNUEPFER, P. L. K. 1994. Use of rock weathering rinds in dating geomorphic surfaces. In C. Beck (ed.), *Dating in exposed and surface contexts*, pp. 15–28. University of New Mexico Press, Albuquerque.

KRUMBEIN, W. E. 1969. Über den Einfluß der Mikroflora auf die exogene Dynamik (Verwitterung und Krustenbildung). *Geologische Rundschau* 58: 333–63.

KRUMBEIN, W. E. and K. JENS 1981. Biogenic rock varnishes of the Negev Desert (Israel): an ecological study of iron and manganese transformation by cyanobacteria and fungi. *Oecologia* 50: 25–38.

KURZ, M. D., D. COLODNER, T. W. TRULL, R. MOORE and K. O'BRIEN 1990. Cosmic ray exposure dating with *in-situ* produced cosmogenic ^{3}He: results from young Hawaiian lava flows. *Earth and Planetary Science Letters* 97: 177–89.

LAL, D. 1991. Cosmic ray labelling of erosion surfaces: *in situ* production rates and erosion models. *Earth and Planetary Science Letters* 104: 424–39.

LAL, D., P. K. MALHOTRA and B. PETERS 1958. On the production of radioisotopes in the atmosphere by cosmic radiation and their application to meteorology. *Journal of Atmospheric and Terrestrial Physics* 12: 306–28.

LAL, D. and B. PETERS 1967. Cosmic-ray produced radioactivity on the Earth. In S. Flugge (ed.), *Handbuch der Physik* 46/2, pp. 551–612. Springer Verlag, Berlin.

LALANNE, G. and H. BREUIL 1911. L'abri sculpté du Cap-Blanc à Laussel, Dordogne. *L'Anthropologie* 21: 385–402.

LAUNDON, J. R. 1980. The use of lichens for dating walls at Bradgate Park, Leicestershire. *Transactions of the Leicester Literary and Philosophical Society* 74: 11–30.

LAYTON, R. 1991. Figure, motif and symbol in the hunter-gatherer rock art of Europe and Australia. In P. Bahn and R. Rosenfeld (eds), *Rock art and prehistory*, pp. 23–38. Monograph 10, Oxbow Books, Oxford.

LAYTON, R. 2001. Ethnographic study and symbolic analysis. In D. S. Whitley (ed.), *Handbook of rock art research*, pp. 311–331. Altamira Press, Walnut Creek, California.

LEMOZI, A. 1920. Peintures et gravures paléolithiques découvertes dans les grottes des communes d'Espagnac, de Sainte-Eulalie et de Cabrerets. *Bulletin de la Société Préhistorique Française* 17: 256–63.

LIN, F. and C. V. CLEMENCY 1981. The kinetics of dissolution of muscovites at 25°C and 1 atm CO_2 partial pressure. *Geochimica et Cosmochimica Acta* 45: 571–76.

LINARES M., E. 1988. Arte mobiliar con tradición rupestre en el sur del Perú. *Rock Art Research* 5: 54–66.

LIU, T. and R. I. DORN 1996. Understanding spatial variability in environmental changes in drylands with rock varnish microlaminations. *Annals of the Association of American Geographers* 86: 187–212.

LOCKE, W. W., J. T. ANDREWS and P. J. WEBER 1979. A manual for lichenometry. *British Geomorphological Research Group, Technical Bulletin* 26: 1–47.

LOEW, O. 1876. *Annual report of the Geographical Survey west of the 100th Meridian*, p. 179.

LORBLANCHET, M. 1992. The rock engravings of Gum Tree Valley and Skew Valley. Dampier, Western Australia: chronology and functions of the sites. In J. McDonald and I. P. Haskovec (eds), *State of the art: regional rock art studies in Australia and Melanesia*, pp. 39–59. Occasional AURA Publication 6, Australian Rock Art Research Association, Melbourne.

LOUBSER, J. H. N. 1993. Guide to the rock paintings of Tandjesberg. *Navorsinge van die Nationale Museum* 9(11): 345–84.

LOUBSER, J. H. N. 1996. The use of Harris diagrams in recording, conserving, and interpreting rock paintings. *International Newsletter on Rock Art* 18: 14–21.

LOY, T. H. 1994. Direct dating of rock art at Laurie Creek (NT), Australia: a reply to Nelson. *Antiquity* 68: 147–48.

LOY, T. H., R. JONES, D. E. NELSON, B. MEEHAN, J. VOGEL, J. SOUTHON and R. COSGROVE 1990. Accelerator radiocarbon dating of human blood proteins in pigments from Late Pleistocene art sites in Australia. *Antiquity* 64: 110–16.

LYTLE, F., D. FERRIS-ROWLEY, P. ROWLEY, X. KRETSCHMER, M. DELGADO and N PINGITORE 2004. Determination of the age of petroglyphs at the Land Hill Site by x-ray fluorescence analysis. Paper presented at annual meeting of the Nevada Archaeological Association, Winnemucca, NV, 17 April 2004.

McCARROLL, D. 1991. The Schmidt Hammer, weathering and rock surface roughness. *Earth Surface Processes and Landforms* 16: 477–80.

McCARTHY, D. L. PAYEN and P. ENNIS 1994. Use of amino acid racemization methods on rock paintings at Motte Rimrock Reserve. *American Indian Rock Art* 13: 17–22.

McCARTHY, F. D. 1967. *Australian Aboriginal rock art* (3rd edn). Australian Museum, Sydney.

McDONALD, J., K. OFFICER, T. JULL, D. DONAHUE, J. HEAD and B. FORD 1990. Investigating ^{14}C AMS: dating prehistoric rock art in the Sydney Sandstone Basin, Australia. *Rock Art Research* 7: 83–92.

MACINTOSH, N. W. G. 1965. Dingo and horned anthropomorph in an Aboriginal rock shelter. *Oceania* 36: 85–101.

MACINTOSH, N. W. G. 1977. Beswick Creek cave two decades later: a reappraisal. In P. J. Ucko (ed.), *Form in indigenous art*, pp. 191–197. Australian Institute of Aboriginal Studies, Canberra.

McNICKLE, H. P. 1991. A survey of rock art in the Victoria River district, Northern Territory. *Rock Art Research* 8: 36–46.

MAGAR, V. and V. DAVILA 2004. Considerations on the dating of rock art from the Sierra de San Francisco, Baja California, Mexico. *Rock Art Research* 21: 129–36.

MALAKOFF, D. 1998. Rock dates thrown into doubt, researcher under fire. *Science* 280: 2041–42.

MARSHACK, A. 1972. *The roots of civilization*. McGraw-Hill, New York/Weidenfeld and Nicolson, London.

MARSHACK, A. 1975. Exploring the mind of Ice Age man. *National Geographic* 147: 62–89.

MARSHACK, A. 1985. Theoretical concepts that lead to new analytic methods, modes of enquiry and classes of data. *Rock Art Research* 2: 95–111.

MARSHACK, A. 1989. Methodology in the analysis and interpretation of Upper Palaeolithic image: theory versus contextual analysis. *Rock Art Research* 6: 17–38.

MARSHACK, A. 1992. An innovative analytical technology: discussion of its present and potential use. *Rock Art Research* 9: 37–64.

MATTHEWS, J. A. 1994. Lichenometric dating: a review with particular reference to 'Little Ice Age' moraines in southern Norway. In C. Beck (ed.), *Dating in exposed and surface contexts*, pp. 185–212. University of New Mexico Press, Albuquerque.

MEJDAHL, V. 1969. Thermoluminescence dating of

ancient Danish ceramics. *Archaeometry* 11: 99–104.

MERRILL. G. P. 1898. *U.S. Geological Survey Bulletin* No. 150: 389–91.

MICHELS, J. W. 1973. *Dating methods in archaeology.* Seminar Press, New York.

MILLER, G. H. and J. T. ANDREWS 1972. Quaternary history of northern Cumberland Peninsula, East Baffin Island, North West Territory, Canada. Part VI: Preliminary lichen growth curve. *Geological Society of America Bulletin* 83: 1133–38.

MILLER, J. A. 1970. Dating by the potassium-argon method — some advances in techniques. In D. Brothwell and E. Higgs (eds), *Science in archaeology.* Praeger, New York.

MOORE, G. W. 1952. Speleothem — a new cave term. *National Speleological Society News* 10: 2.

MORI, F. 1965. *Tadrart Acacus, arte rupestre e culture del Sahara preistorico.* Einaudi, Turin.

MORI, F. 1974. The earliest Saharan rock-engravings. *Antiquity* 48: 87–92.

MULVANEY, J. D. 1969. *The prehistory of Australia.* Thames and Hudson, London.

MULVANEY, K. 1995. What to do on a rainy day. Reminiscences of Mirriuwung and Gadjerong artists. *Rock Art Research* 13: 3–20.

MURRAY, A. S., R. G. ROBERTS and A. G. WINTLE 1997. Equivalent dose measurement using a single aliquot of quartz. *Radiation Measurements* 27: 171–84.

MURRAY-WALLACE, C. V. 1993. A review of the application of the amino acid racemisation reaction to archaeological dating. *The Artefact* 16: 19–26.

MUZZOLINI, A. 1990. The sheep in Saharan rock art. *Rock Art Research* 7: 93–109.

MUZZOLINI, A. 1999a. Sur la méthode de datation par les films de silice. *Cahiers de l'AARS* 5: 11.

MUZZOLINI, A. 1999b. La notation des dates au 14 C. *Cahiers de l'AARS* 16: 18–24.

NELSON, D. E. 1993. Second thoughts on a rock-art date. *Antiquity* 67: 893–95.

NELSON, D. E. (ed.) 2000. *The beeswax art of northern Australia.* Compact disk, Simon Fraser University, Burnaby, Canada.

NELSON, D. E., G. CHALOUPKA, C. CHIPPINDALE, M. S. ALDERSON and J. R. SOUTHON 1995. Radiocarbon dates for beeswax figures in the prehistoric rock art of northern Australia. *Archaeometry* 37: 151–56.

NISHIIZUMI, K., E. L. WINTERER, C. P. KOHL, J. KLEIN, R. MIDDLETON, D. LAL and J. R. ARNOLD 1989. Cosmic ray production rates of ^{10}Be and ^{26}Al in quartz from glacially polished rocks. *Journal of Geophysical Research* 94: 17 907–15.

NOBBS, M. F. and R. I. DORN 1988. Age determinations for rock varnish formation within petroglyphs: cation-ratio dating of 24 motifs from the Olary region, South Australia. *Rock Art Research* 5: 108–46.

NOVELLINO, D. 1999. Towards an understanding of Pälaqwan rock drawings: between visual and verbal expression. *Rock Art Research* 16: 3–24.

O'CONNOR, S. 1995. Carpenter's Gap Rockshelter 1: 40 000 years of Aboriginal occupation in the Napier Ranges, Kimberley, WA. *Australian Archaeology* 40: 58–59.

OLLEY, J. M., G. G. CAITCHEON and R. G. ROBERTS 1999. The origin of dose distributions in fluvial sediments, and the prospect of dating single grains of quartz from fluvial deposits using optically stimulated luminescence. *Radiation Measurements* 30: 207–17.

OLLIER, C. D. 1969 (revd. edn. 1975). *Weathering.* London.

OXBURGH, R., J. I. DREVER and Y.-T. SUN 1994. Mechanism of plagioclase dissolution in acid solution at 25°C. *Geochimica et Cosmochimica Acta* 58: 661–69.

PASSEMARD, E. 1944. La caverne d'Isturitz en pays basque. *Préhistoire* 13: 1–95.

PERRY, R. S. and J. B. ADAMS 1978. Desert varnish: evidence of cyclic deposition of manganese. *Nature* 276: 489–91.

PESSIS, A.-M. 1999. The chronology and evolution of the prehistoric rock paintings in the Serra da Capivara National Park, Piauí, Brazil. In M. Strecker and P. Bahn (eds), *Dating and the earliest known rock art*, pp. 41–47. Oxbow Books, Oxford.

PHILLIPS, F. M., B. D. LEAVY, N. D. JANNIK, D. ELMORE and P. W. KUBIK 1986. The accumulation of cosmogenic chlorine-36 in rocks: a method for surface exposure dating. *Science* 231: 41–43.

PHILLIPS, F. M., M. G. ZREDA, S. S. SMITH, D. ELMORE, P. W. KUBIK and P. SHARMA 1990. A cosmogenic chlorine-36 chronology for glacial deposits at Bloody Canyon, eastern Sierra Nevada, California. *Science* 248: 1529–32.

PHILLIPS, F. M., M. FLINSCH, D. ELMORE and P. SHARMA 1997. Maximum ages of the Côa valley (Portugal) engravings measured with chlorine-36. *Antiquity* 71: 100–4.

PINEDA, C. A., L. JACOBSON and M. PEISACH 1988. Ion beam analysis for the determination of cation-ratios as a means of dating southern African rock varnishes. *Nuclear Instruments and Methods in Physics Research* B35: 436–66.

POPE, G. A. 2000. Weathering of petroglyphs: direct assessment and implications for dating methods. *Antiquity* 74: 833–43.

POREDA, R. J. and T. E. CERLING 1992. Cosmogenic neon in recent lavas from the western United States. *Geophysical Research Letters* 19: 1863–66.

POTTER, R. M. and G. R. ROSSMAN 1977. Desert varnish: the importance of clay minerals. *Science* 196: 1446–48.

POTTER, R. M. and G. R. ROSSMAN 1979. Mineralogy of manganese dendrites and coatings. *American Mineralogist* 64: 1219–26.

RENAUD, E. B. 1939. Report on lichen of Spanish diggings. Quarterly report, *Works Projects Administration, Work Project* No. 885: 33.

RHOTERT, H. 1938. *Transjordanien. Vorgeschichtliche Forschungen*. Stuttgart.

RHOTERT, H. 1952. *Lybische Felsbilder*. Darmstadt.

RIDGES, M., I. DAVIDSON and D. TUCKER 2000. The organic environment of paintings on rock. In G. K. Ward and C. Tuniz (eds), *Advances in dating Australian rock-markings*, pp. 61–70. Occasional AURA Publication 10, Australian Rock Art Research Association, Melbourne.

RIMSTIDT, J. D. and H. L. BARNES 1980. The kinetics of silica-water reactions. *Geochimica et Cosmochimica Acta* 44: 1683–99.

ROBERTS, R. G. and R. M. JONES 1994. Luminescence dating of sediments: new light on the human colonisation of Australia. *Australian Aboriginal Studies* 1994/2: 2–17.

ROBERTS, R. G., R. M. JONES, N. A. SPOONER, M. J. HEAD, A. S. MURRAY and M. A. SMITH 1994. The human colonisation of Australia: optical dates of 53 000 and 60 000 years bracket human arrival at Deaf Adder Gorge, Northern Territory. *Quaternary Science Reviews* 13: 575–83.

ROBERTS, R. G., N. A. SPOONER, R. M. JONES, S. CANE, J. M. OLLEY, A. S. MURRAY and M. J. HEAD 1996. Preliminary luminescence dates for archaeological sediments on the Nullarbor Plain, South Australia. *Australian Archaeology* 42: 7–16.

ROBERTS, R., G. WALSH, A. MURRAY, J. OLLEY, R. JONES, M. MORWOOD, C. TUNIZ, E. LAWSON, M. MACPHAIL, D. BOWDERY and I. NAUMANN 1997. Luminescence dating of rock art and past environments using mud-wasp nests in northern Australia. *Nature* 387: 696–99.

ROBERTS, R. G., M. BIRD, J. OLLEY, R. GALBRAITH, E. LAWSON, G. LASLETT, H. YOSHIDA, R. JONES, R. FULLAGAR, G. JACOBSEN and Q. HUA 1998. Optical and radiocarbon dating at Jinmium rock shelter in northern Australia. *Nature* 393: 358–62.

ROBERTS, R. G., R. F. GALBRAITH, J. M. OLLEY, H. YOSHIDA and G. M. LASLETT 1999. Optical dating of single and multiple grains of quartz from Jinmium rock shelter, northern Australia: Part II, results and implications. *Archaeometry* 41: 365–95.

ROBERTS, R. G., G. L. WALSH, J. M. OLLEY, A. S. MURRAY M. K. MACPHAIL, I. D. NAUMANN, R. JONES and M. J. MORWOOD 2000. Rock-picture chronologies and palaeoenvironmental records from fossil mud-wasp nests: preliminary investigations using optical dating. In G. K. Ward and C. Tuniz (eds), *Advances in dating Australian rock-markings*, pp. 40–44. Occasional AURA Publication 10, Australian Rock Art Research Association, Melbourne.

ROBINSON, J. M. 1994. Atmospheric CO_2 and plants. *Nature* 368: 105–6.

ROSENFELD, A., D. HORTON and J. WINTER 1981. *Early Man in north Queensland*. Terra Australis No. 6, Australian National University, Canberra.

RUBIN, M., L. K. GARGULINSKI and J. P. McGEEHIN 1987. Hawaiian radiocarbon dates. *United States Geological Survey Professional Paper* 1350: 213–42.

RUSS, J., M. HYMAN, H. J. HAFER and M. W. ROWE 1990. Radiocarbon dating of prehistoric rock paintings by selective oxidation of organic carbon. *Nature* 348: 710–1.

SAINT MATHURIN, S. de 1975. Reliefs magdaléniens d'Angles-sur-l'Anglin (Vienne). *Antiquités Nationales* 7: 24–31.

SAMPSON, E. H., S. J. FLEMING and W. BRAY 1972. Thermoluminescent dating of Colombian pottery in the Yotoco style. *Archaeometry* 14: 119–26.

SCHAAFSMA, P. 1980. *Indian rock art of the Southwest*. University of New Mexico Press, Albuquerque.

SCHEFFER, F., B. MEYER and E. KALK 1963. Biologische Ursachen der Wüstenlackbildung. *Zeitschrift für Geomorphologie* 7: 112–19.

SCHIFFER, M. B. 1986. Radiocarbon dating and the 'old wood' problem: the case of the Hohokam chronology. *Journal of Archaeological Science* 13: 13–30.

SCHWEGLER, U. 1995. Datierung von Felszeichnungen und Schalensteinen. *Mitteilungen der Anisa* 16: 99–123.

SJÖBERG, R. 1994. Diagnosis of weathering on rock carving surfaces in northern Bohuslän, southwest Sweden. In D. A. Robinson and R. B. G. Williams (eds), *Rock weathering and landform evolution*, pp. 223–241. John Wiley & Sons, Chichester.

SMITH, B. W., E. J. RHODES, S. STOKES, N. A. SPOONER and M. J. AITKEN 1990. Optical dating of sediments: initial quartz results from Oxford. *Archaeometry* 32: 19–31.

SMITH, D. I. 1978. The micro erosion meter: its application to the weathering of rock surfaces. In C. Pearson (ed.), *Conservation of rock art*, pp. 44–53. Institute for the Conservation of Cultural Material, Sydney.

SPENCER, J. Q., D. C. W. SANDERSON, K. DECKERS and A. A. SOMMERVILLE 2003. Assessing mixed dose distributions in young sediments identified using small aliquots and a simple two-step SAR procedure: the F-statistic as a diagnostic tool. *Radiation Measurements* 37: 425–31.

STEINBRING, J., E. DANZIGER and R. CALLAGHAN 1987. Middle Archaic petroglyphs in northern North America. *Rock Art Research* 4: 3–16.

TANG HUISHENG and GAO ZHIWEI 2004. Dating analysis of rock art in the Qinghai-Tibetan Plateau. *Rock Art Research* 21: 161–72.

TAÇON, P. S. C. and M. GARDE 2000. Dating beeswax figures on rock art: the view from central Arnhem Land. In G. K. Ward and C. Tuniz (eds), *Advances in dating Australian rock-markings*, pp. 71–75. Occasional AURA Publication 10, Australian Rock Art Research Association, Inc., Melbourne.

THACKERAY, A. I. 1983. Dating the rock art of South Africa. In J. D. Lewis Williams (ed.), *New approaches to southern African rock art*, pp. 21–26. Goodwin Series 4, South African Archaeological Society, Johannesburg.

THACKERAY, A. I., J. F. THACKERAY, P. B. BEAUMONT and J. C. VOGEL 1981. Dated rock engravings from Wonderwork Cave, South Africa. *Science* 214: 64–67.

TRATEBAS, A. M. and F. CHAPMAN 1996. Ethical and conservation issues in removing lichens from petroglyphs. *Rock Art Research* 13: 129–33.

TUROSS, N. and I. BARNES 1996. Protein identification of blood residues on experimental stone tools. *Journal of Archaeological Science* 23: 289–96.

UCKO, P. I. 1987. Débuts illusoires dans la tradition artistique. *Préhistoire Ariégoise* 42: 15–81.

VAN DER MERWE, N. J., J. SEELY and R. YATES 1987. First accelerator carbon-14 date for pigment from a rock painting. *South African Journal of Science* 83: 56–57.

VINNICOMBE, P. 1976. *People of the eland: rock paintings of Drakensberg Bushmen as a reflection of their life and thought.* University of Natal Press, Pietermaritzburg.

WAKANKAR, V. S. 1983. The oldest works of art? *Science Today* 20: 43–48.

WALDERHAUG, O. and E. M. WALDERHAUG 1998. Weathering of Norwegian rock art — a critical review. *Norwegian Archaeological Review* 31: 119–39.

WALTHER, J. 1924. *Das Gesetz der Wüstenbildung*, 4th edn. Berlin.

WATCHMAN, A. 1990. A summary of occurrences of oxalate-rich crusts in Australia. *Rock Art Research* 7: 44–50.

WATCHMAN, A. 1991. Age and composition of oxalate-rich crusts in the Northern Territory, Australia. *Studies in Conservation* 36: 24–32.

WATCHMAN, A. 1992. Investigating the cation-ratio calibration curve: evidence from South Australia. *Rock Art Research* 9: 106–10.

WATCHMAN, A. 1993. The use of laser technology in rock art dating. *The Artefact* 16: 39–45.

WATCHMAN, A. 1995. Recent petroglyphs, Foz Côa, Portugal. *Rock Art Research* 12: 104–8.

WATCHMAN, A. 1996. A review of the theory and assumptions in the AMS dating of the Foz Côa petroglyphs, Portugal. *Rock Art Research* 13: 21–30.

WATCHMAN, A. 1998. Composition and source of dust on Split Rock paintings, Australia. *Rock Art Research* 15: 36–40.

WATCHMAN, A. 1999. A universal standard for reporting the ages of petroglyphs and rock paintings. In M. Strecker and P. Bahn (eds), *Dating and the earliest known rock art*, pp. 1–3. Oxbox Books, Oxford.

WATCHMAN, A. 2000. Micro-excavation and laser extraction methods for dating carbon in silica skins and oxalate crusts. In G. K. Ward and C. Tuniz (eds), *Advances in dating Australian rock-markings*, pp. 35–39. Occasional AURA Publication 10, Australian Rock Art Research Association, Melbourne.

WATCHMAN, A. and J. CAMPBELL 1996. Micro-stratigraphic analyses of laminated oxalate crusts in northern Australia. In M. Realini and L. Toniolo (eds), *The oxalate films in the conservation of works of art. Proceedings of the Second International Symposium, Milan, March 1996*, pp. 409–422. Centro CNR Gino Bozza, Bologna.

WATCHMAN, A. and N. COLE 1993. Accelerator radiocarbon dating of plant-fibre binders in rock paintings from northeastern Australia. *Antiquity* 67: 355–58.

WATCHMAN, A. and R. LESSARD 1993. Focused laser extraction of carbonaceous substances for AMS radiocarbon dating (FLECS-AMS). In J. Steinbring and A. Watchman (eds), *Time and space: dating considerations in rock art research*, pp. 74–77. Occasional AURA Publication 8. Australian Rock Art Research Association, Melbourne.

WATCHMAN, A. L., G. L. WALSH, M. J. MORWOOD and C. TUNIZ 1997. AMS radiocarbon age estimates for early rock paintings in the Kimberley, N.W. Australia: preliminary results. *Rock Art Research* 14: 18–26.

WELCH, D. 1995. Beeswax rock art in the Kimberley. *Rock Art Research* 12: 23–28.

WENDT, I., W. STAHL, M. A. GEYH and F. FAUTH 1967. Model experiments for ^{14}C-age determinations. In *Isotopes in hydrology*, p. 321. Proceedings of the IAEA, Vienna.

WHITE, C. H. 1924. Desert varnish. *American Journal of Science* 7(5th ser.): 413–20.

WHITLEY, D. S. 2001. Rock art and rock art research in a worldwide perspective: an introduction. In D. S. Whitley (ed.), *Handbook of rock art research*, pp. 7–51. AltaMira Press, Walnut Creek, California.

WILLIAMSON, M. A. and J. D. RIMSTIDT 1994. The kinetics and electrochemical rate-determining step of aqueous pyrite oxidation. *Geochimica et Cosmochimica Acta* 58: 5443–54.

WILLIAMS-THORPE, O., D. G. JENKINS, J. JENKINS and J. S. WATSON 1995. Chlorine-36 dating and the bluestones of Stonehenge. *Antiquity* 69: 1019–20.

WINCHESTER, V. 1988. An assessment of lichenometry as a method for dating recent stone movements in two stone circles in Cumbria and Oxfordshire. *Botanical Journal of the Linnean Society* 96: 57–68.

WORSLEY, P. 1990. Lichenometry. In A. Goudie (ed.), *Geomorphological techniques*, second edn. pp. 442–428. Unwin Hyman, London.

YOKOYAMA, Y., J.-L. REYSS and F. GUICHARD 1977. Production of radionuclides by cosmic rays at mountain altitudes. *Earth and Planetary Science Letters* 36: 44–50.

ZILHÃO, J. 1995. The age of the Côa valley (Portugal) rock-art: validation of archaeological dating to the Palaeolithic and refutation of 'scientific' dating to historic or proto-historic times. *Antiquity* 69: 883–901.

ZIMMERMANN, D. W. 1967. Thermoluminescence from fine grains from ancient pottery. *Archaeometry* 10: 26–28.

ZIMMERMANN, D. W. 1971. Uranium distributions in archaeologic ceramics: dating of radioactive inclusions. *Science* 174: 818–19.

ZREDA, M. G., F. M. PHILLIPS, D. ELMORE, P. W. KUBIK, P. SHARMA and R. I. DORN 1991. Cosmogenic ^{36}Cl production rates in terrestrial rocks. *Earth and Planetary Science Letters* 105: 94–109.

8. THE INTERPRETATION OF ROCK ART

TRADITIONAL APPROACHES OF INTERPRETATION

Traditional forms of interpreting rock art iconographies, which account for most published work in the field of 'rock art studies', are essentially autogenous formulations that were generated by auto-suggestion, the psychological process by which a person induces self-acceptance of an opinion or belief. With some rare exceptions there is nothing to tell us reliably what a rock art motif depicts or means, there is usually only autogenous suggestion based on the perception of one observer, or that of several observers, or of all observers. We need to remember that a consensus among even all contemporary observers is no substitute for testable (refutable) propositions about the meaning of rock art, which is not accessible by any of the means so far proposed in this field. It is essential to appreciate that the meaning of pre-Historic rock art is not a part of rock art science until ways are found to present propositions about it in a falsifiable format.

Globally, we have only a very limited range of interpretations by the artists themselves, or by their cultural peers, in the form of ethnographic interpretations (but see below). Our own perception does not define reality, and even less does it define the realities perceived by other cultures; it is heavily conditioned by culture ('culture' in the wider sense; scientifically, 'culture' is the result of non-genetic transfer of practice). This is a fundamental difficulty in rock art research, but there are several supplementary barriers preventing alien researchers from effective access to meaning.

One of the cardinal problems in the study of rock art is the traditional assumption that 'researchers' possess some special insight into the meaning of the iconography, somehow acquired through many years of 'observing' such art traditions. There is no rational explanation for the presumed acquisition of this ability, nor are there even published attempts to justify this form of self-delusion. I have long tried to discover the basis of this belief of some archaeologists that they 'communicate across vast time spans ... each time they ... visit a painted cave' (Mithen 1998: 181). I have not detected any significant difference between this belief system and the beliefs of other beholders of graphic productions that these arts communicate meanings to them. Children, for instance, are avid interpreters of rock art, and their interpretations, like those of any other intelligent organism not familiar with the graphic conventions of the artist's society, are excellent reflections of their own perception, cognition and visual skills. They are therefore instrumental in the study of the interpreting intellect and perception, but they are of no value in the scientific study of palaeoarts. The desire of intelligent organisms such as humans to detect meaning in anything from clouds to animal scratch marks or petroglyphs is most certainly of great interest in the study of, for instance, the origins of art-producing behaviour, but its results in the case of creative rock art interpreters are of no value to this discipline, be they the interpretations of juveniles, archaeologists or intergalactic visitors.

That is why, in rock art science, we place all motif designations or 'identifications' in quotation marks.

Iconographic identification

Maynard (1977: 399) is of the view that what she interprets as a motif of a man holding a boomerang is to be separated into two figures, 'because man and boomerang are separate motifs in their own right'. There are several reasons why this definition would be difficult to uphold. How many motifs would there be in a Saharan or Chinese rock art image of a 'horse-drawn chariot with a warrior'? Four horses, a chariot, a man, his shield, his lance, the reins ... . Would the wheels be separate motifs, and if not, why not? They may form part of the chariot, but they are detachable, whereas the man 'is not' a warrior without the lance and shield drawn. Or in the case of a Gwion anthropomorph from Kimberley, Australia (formerly called 'Bradshaw figure'): if the 'man' is one motif, and the various objects attached to his image are separate motifs, who decides what is and what is not 'detachable'? To determine this we would have to know what each aspect depicts (headdress or coiffure, *woomera* or Lightning Brothers' 'long thumb'?), which we certainly do not.

Therefore Maynard's definition of a motif is unworkable, and we need one that is practical and logically consistent. I favour the view that if the so-called boomerang is shown attached to the so-called hand, then it is part of the anthropomorphous motif. If it is separated from it than it represents a separate motif. While this may not necessarily reflect the intent of the artist, it is logically more consistent because we must not neglect to remember that Maynard's identifications as 'man' and 'boomerang' are themselves unsubstantiated assumptions, they are not real identifications in the sense that they are testable — even though they may well be valid. In other words, in a scientific perspective it must be unacceptable to employ subjective identifications of parts of motifs in deciding how many separate objects there are depicted in a composition. All we can say with some certainty is which parts of a composition are physically connected. Conversely, strong reasons would have to be offered to consider unconnected parts of a composition as forming parts of a single motif. Such reasons would include distinctive spatial relationship of elements, e.g. a centrally placed cross or cupule within a circle. In most cases I think a motif includes all parts that are shown together and are connected physically.

One of the most recent advocacies of the iconographic identification of rock art motifs is by Chippindale (2001), who (in the context of what purports to be a 'handbook' of rock art research) fails to cite a single justification for his own 'identifications'. He presents a number of rock art motifs and tells us what they depict, but he fails to inform us what qualifies him to make these pronouncements. Every one of his examples can readily be interpreted differently, and the interpretations of these same motifs by young children are more interesting, illuminating and relevant. To illustrate his academically vacuous approach, I cite his example of a tree-like petroglyph motif, which most juveniles seem to see as a fir or spruce tree, although to me it looks much more like an archaeologist's trowel. Chippindale claims it depicts a dagger, and because it resembles in his view Bronze Age daggers (which, actually, it does not, but this is an unimportant point) he goes on to assume that the petroglyphs are of such age. Presumably he would argue that the shape of the 'dagger' 'proves' it is of the Bronze Age, which confirms his dating claim. At no stage in his circular reasoning has Chippindale explained why his own iconographic perception should be relevant to the determination of subjects in an alien art, or how one is expected to test his tautological proposition without having full access to the neural processes of Chippindale's visual system. What he offers is reminiscent of Lewis-Williams' suggestion that one sees a circle as either an orange, a breast or a bomb, depending on one's preoccupations.

To illustrate the futility of iconographic identification in most rock art, many examples could be cited. I chose to select an example from Karelia, Russia: the 'identifications' of four specific motif types by eleven analysts are compared in Table 2, illustrating how pointless these preoccupations are. Much the same could be compiled from the existing literature about many rock art regions.

Researcher	Boat-like	Disc-like	Crescent-shaped	Spade-like
A. Bryusov	Boat	Trap	Trap	Trap
E. Ernits	Boat of nether world	Full moon	Half moon	Connected w. moon
C. Grewingk	Tally of killed game	Lake, clan sign	Crane, clan sign	-
K. Laushkin	Boat, sun boat	Lunar symbol	solar symbol	Staff, magic staff
A. Linewski	Boat	Trap	Trap	Projectile
F. Morozov	Sledge	Mirror	-	-
F. Ravdonikas	-	Lunar symbol	Lunar symbol	-
V. Ravdonikas	Boat, sun boat	Lunar symbol	Solar symbol	Staff for cosmic cult
Y. Savvateyev	Boat	Trap, lunar symbol	Trap, solar symbol	Projectile, staff
P. Schwedt	Saw	Dividers	Mirror	-
A. Stolyar	Boat of nether world	Lunar symbol	Solar symbol	Staff of nether world

Table 2. Interpretations of four Karelian petroglyph types by eleven scholars (adapted from Poikalainen and Ernits 1998).

ETHNOGRAPHIC INTERPRETATION

For ethnographic art, at least some levels of meaning remain accessible, and justify speculation about the function of such arts in the societies that produced them. In some rare cases one may be able to interview a producer or traditional consumer of the art, in others there are established cultural traditions maintaining a level of knowledge about the art that permits some access to its meaning.

However, the fallibility of ethnographic constructs, the problems of reconciling the indigenous and 'scientific' (alien) conceptualisations of meaning, and the significant question of whether ethnographic interpretations of meaning can be relevant in the 'text-free' record of the distant past all need to be considered. All humans, including ethnographers, lack the ability to think outside of their severely limited intellectual and cognitive universe. Huchet (1991, 1992) has examined numerous expressed or implied ethnographic analogies in archaeological specialist literature, and has found that there are hardly any instances of rigorous logic in the examples he considered. This, admittedly, refers to inadequate rigour, and does not negate the principle itself. However, at the more fundamental level, one can question the entire underlying logic. Relational analogy involves a demonstration of causal mechanisms or other factors in the similarities between source and subject that determine the presence and interrelationships of perceived properties (Wylie 1985). In practice, this is hardly possible, and analogic propositions must not be based on a simplistic acceptance of inferred properties in both the source and subject data. That record is itself never totally reliable, it has been filtered by a variety of cultural and cognitive biases.

Archaeologists have tried in a number of ways to deal with the problems of using ethnographic analogy, but there is no consensus of how it would be achieved scientifically. The leading protagonist of the so-called New Archaeology, Binford (1967), suggests that documented analogies should form a basis for postulates as to the relationship between 'archaeological forms' and their behavioural context in the past. Deductive hypotheses drawn from such postulates would then be used to test the postulates. But there are numerous pitfalls in this kind of procedure.

First, there is the nature of the archaeological raw data itself. When we consider the amount of reliable dating we have for rock art currently, it seems quite inappropriate to pretend that we can speak of specific rock art traditions and relate them to archaeological entities. Secure age estimates are unavailable for nearly all rock art of the world. Most age claims in the literature are merely statements about degree of consensus that a certain perceived stylistic latitude within an art corpus refers to a particular technological pigeonhole in archaeological time. This does not constitute evidence, it is opinion. Perceived styles are not real styles (Conkey and Hastorf 1991), they are only what untutored alien 'researchers' lump together for the sake of creating order in disorder, in accordance with their own conditioned ways of experiencing reality. The mere fact that they seem unable to agree among themselves as to how to define styles demonstrates that these are not intrinsic properties. Styles perceived by archaeologists, be they of rock paintings or stone artefacts or any other archaeologically perceived object classes, are never more than styles perceived by archaeologists; they are 'egofacts' (Consens 2000). Some may well be valid, that is perfectly possible, but to prove this in a scientific fashion would be extremely difficult and would require a great deal more work than is being invested. Studies must be conducted without assuming a validity that has not as yet been demonstrated with any semblance of scientific method (Bednarik 1991a).

There are greater problems still with archaeological information. Not having been qualified taphonomically, such data prompt greatly distorted perceived realities. While the archaeologist has always made some allowance for these distortions by simple common sense, without systematic correction one must expect that any interpretation of the record will be substantially distorted (Bednarik 1992a, 1993a, 1994a).

The ethnographic record: what is it?

Much of the ethnographic record has not been collected under ideal conditions, but, just for the sake of the argument, we shall assume that it was all secured under the best of conditions possible. So we assume that alien researchers, who interviewed indigenous people, recorded the information offered accurately. It would seem that this record, then, should be objective. But is it really?

The communication between informant and recorder is always by means of translation. Even where the interviewer speaks the language of the people being studied, he or she is usually not very proficient in their language. He certainly has little or no linguistic access to those aspects of the culture that are avoided, or indeed taboo. His interpretation of what he does have access to will be affected by inadequate understanding of these inherent limitations. In many cases he uses a third party, an interpreter, and what he obtains is quite literally a biased interpretation, and not a rigorous account. He then interprets this interpretation in a way that makes sense in his own linguistic and cognitive framework. Moreover, it is well known today that extant traditional cultures do not permit outsiders access to all aspects of their metaphysical world. For instance, students of the oldest surviving culture on earth, that of the Australian Aborigines, have found that the knowledge bestowed on them is intentionally limited in several directions. Not only is it incomplete in the sexual sense, because of the strict gender divisions in cultural knowledge (there are restrictions according to the gender of both informant and interviewer), but also there are explanations within explanations, in the fashion of Russian dolls: upon opening one, there is always another one inside it. Thus interviewers, including myself, have found that the same informant used a different, more elaborate explanation for a phenomenon many years after he had given a simpler one to the same interviewer ('But 25 years ago you didn't know much!'). Or, as a senior Aboriginal custodian once remarked: 'It took me 60 years to become an Aboriginal, so how could a young *balanda* (European) straight from university learn much in a matter of a few months or years!' (Figure 52).

Very simply, the explanations given to ethnographers are commensurate with a researcher's perceived competence and trustworthiness. This applies in any part of the world. For instance, a rock art motif may have many meanings, beginning from a very simple level. This is rather like an explanation a contemporary urban parent would give to a small child. Once it had become older, a more advanced explanation is considered appropriate, and so on. In indigenous or tribal societies, a great deal of knowledge is of restricted access. It may be of a secret or a sacred nature, and there may be levels of severity. In many such societies, serious breaches of sacred matters are traditionally punishable by death, and may be considered more serious crimes than murder, for instance. It is therefore inconceivable that information at the level of sacred knowledge would be passed on to uninitiated alien researchers, simply to satisfy their curiosity. Hence we can be certain that all the published ethnographic evidence of such metaphysical knowledge of tribal people is of the type given to people of inadequate understanding of the society in question. It should be obvious that this mechanism would have contributed to a simplification of ethnographic accounts: not only did the informants regularly observe the restrictions of tribal laws, they would have often felt obliged to simplify interpretations for untutored outsiders. At times they may have been forced to deceive their questioners in order to protect sacred knowledge. Ethnographers, often naively unaware of such factors as multiple meanings, may base their professional reputation and standing on their 'findings', and they may not be too willing to admit these severe limitations of their accounts. But that is understandable and we have to make allowances for such limitations.

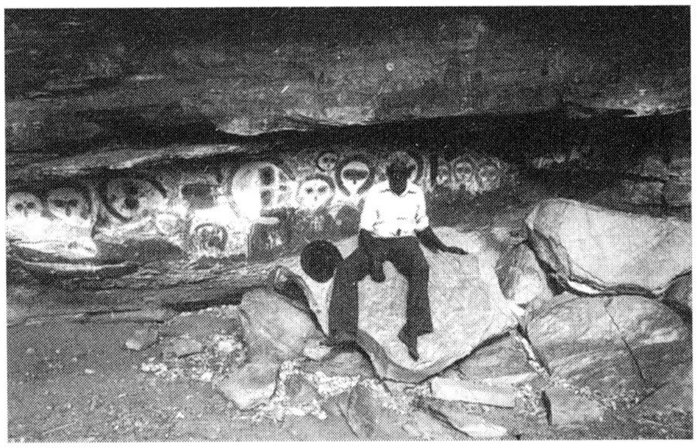

Figure 52. Senior traditional custodian of a Wandjina site in the Kimberley region of Western Australia.

The separation of religious and profane matters is not as clear in indigenous societies as it is in urban industrial societies. Since indigenous societies possess various levels of restrictions on metaphysical knowledge, these restrictions also affect the nature of the information that *can* be provided to uninitiated outsiders, such as researchers: one cannot explain to the interviewer every aspect of what appears to be, on the face of it, an economic and thus presumably profane aspect of the culture, because some of the meanings involved in a comprehensive explanation involve information of a secret nature. Hence even under the best possible conditions, the researcher will only obtain fragmentary, simplistic and even misleading explanations.

None of this is to negate that occasionally a non-indigenous researcher, through life-long endeavour, does reach a high level of understanding about the indigenous culture he partakes of. However, by the time he reaches such a state, he will have lost his desire to disseminate his knowledge 'academically', having learned that academic enquiry into sacred aspects of a society leads to its destruction — and having realised that he can celebrate his level of understanding without seeking the approval of his peers, through indiscriminate dissemination. Such a scholar, having risen above the need to prove himself to his peers, has no desire to inflict damage on the fabric of the culture of his teachers. Once again, knowledge 'of the highest degree', as it is regarded in Australia, will not become available for academic consumption.

Now we come to the main problem. In analogical interpretations of rock art we rely on two types of record: the source of the analogy (ethnographically 'determined' 'meanings', such as those just discussed) and the subject of the analogy (the empirical data acquired about a corpus of rock art). Archaeological data are severely distorted by many taphonomic processes and it is clear that the discipline has not as yet found systematic means of addressing this issue. A remedy is possible and some measures have been suggested (Bednarik 1994a), but this requires a sophisticated epistemology not realisable in the immediate future. The discipline is not capable of absorbing the required changes in a short time. We also know that most rock art is undated, or has only been attributed to some archaeological pigeonhole on the basis of inadequate assessment. Again, this is a shortcoming that can be addressed by improved research methodology and a great deal of hard work. Now we are trying to relate these biased and distorted archaeological data to the typically incomplete ethnographic interpretations that may be no more appropriate than children's stories. We would be naive to expect much of such a procedure, which cannot be proposed or supported by anyone who has seriously considered the issues. Yet this is precisely what 'archaeo-ethnographic interpretation' of rock art is.

Nevertheless, there are of course many instances where ethnographic information has been used profitably in rock art research. This is particularly the case when it demonstrates the futility of seeking to explain meanings in the complete absence of ethnography. A good example is the work of Michaelis (1981), who followed up Titiev's (1937) account of a journey of Pueblo Indians to collect salt. Titiev reports the practice of placing clan signs at the Willowsprings petroglyph site, and Michaelis found that nearly half of the known clan emblems of the Hopi occurred at that site. If the role of the petroglyphs had not been known ethnographically, researchers would have no means whatsoever of determining the meaning of the very diverse but also repetitive motifs. Similarly, if we were intergalactic visitors and found many rock art motifs with Christian crosses placed over them, we could not explain them. If we did discover the role of the cross, we would probably presume that it stands for death or resurrection. Its real role, iconoclasm, can only be known to us because we have some knowledge of the historical circumstances. It should be clear enough that for most rock art traditions, we certainly lack the necessary understanding of context, culture and ideology. In fact, most rock art cannot even be attributed to a specific cultural tradition at this stage.

THE FUTILITY OF CREATING ICONOGRAPHIC MEANINGS

By far the most common interpretation of meaning in rock art is the iconographic interpretation of motifs by the observer. We are told what the beholder of the art thinks it depicts. In many cases, the motif has such outstanding diagnostic features that these identifications do sound convincing, but in many other cases the picture is not at all clear-cut. Moreover, many researchers define various aspects of the motif in an entirely subjective fashion: they tell us that the subject is running, falling, swimming, pregnant, praying, dead or whatever else they happen to perceive in the art. Provided that all these interpretations are offered for the purpose of creating a folklore about the art, a new mythology, one could not possibly object to them. Indeed, such interpretations may even be useful to the scientist, because from them he can learn about the perception of the person interpreting the art. If the person speaks his language and is capable of analysing his own responses to the art (to tell, for instance, very precisely why he thinks an animal figure is of a dying individual), an analysable example of an ethnographic reaction to an alien art becomes available. The person whose perception is so analysed may be a 'tribal' person from Orissa or an ethnographer — the analysis of his perceptive processes is in both cases ethnographic work.

Many theories about rock art are based entirely on the identification of motifs in the art. These identifications are essentially subjective and they cannot be confirmed or refuted by any form of scientifically acceptable procedure (Bednarik 1991a, 1991b). Such identifications are non-refutable hypotheses based solely on the self-proclaimed abilities of 'interpreters'. In the only case the identifications of a researcher were checked against those of the artist himself, the 'scientific' interpreter of the art reported that he had failed abysmally (Macintosh 1977). The iconographic decisions of observers who have no access to the iconographic conventions of the pre-Historic culture in question, who are simply making up interpretations in the knowledge that they cannot be refuted, are not relevant to rock art science. Perhaps their conviction that their own cognitive processes of identifying and classifying iconicity are identical to those of the ancient artists is valid, but how would one demonstrate this?

Palaeoarts can be studied scientifically, but this is not served by striving to determine a quality that cannot be determined, such as meaning. We can either find out what else science can do, and can do properly — or we can abandon the rigour of science and take a shortcut to 'meaning', creating and projecting our own favoured interpretation of the art. It may involve shamans, metaphysics, arithmetic, lost tribes, trance visions, interstellar space travellers, blood-curdling rituals, virgins, head-hunting, aspects of religion, warfare, cannibalism, and a whole gamut of somewhat less entertaining interpretations. None of them can provide any insights about the rock art so interpreted, but they are always a revealing tool for exploring the psychology of the interpreter. Precisely the same applies to the iconographic interpretation of motifs: its only scientific function is to study the perception, cognition and cultural conditioning of the interpreter.

Provided we indulge in interpretation without physical interference with the art it is a perfectly harmless pastime, and there can be no objection to it. Rock art interpretation is highly stimulating, it enriches our experience and it can enrich our own art, culture and existence. It can help us create more myths about the past, we can invent our own favoured story of what happened in that past (in the fashion of Frankel's [1993] sculptor). Provided that in the process we do not belittle any other culture or inflict any damage on the rock art, there can be no objection to such quests — as long as we make no attempt of presenting them as science.

OBJECTIVE LINKS BETWEEN ART CORPORA

In the above critique of ethnographic constructs — the ideas ethnographers form about people and their social systems — the enormous differences we must expect to exist between the respective conceptualisations of meaning, reality and significance, of the informant and the interviewer were hardly even considered. The latter, with the rashness of Western science, assumes that his framework of reality, his metaphysical model of the world, is superior. Admittedly, in recent years it has become fashionable to treat alternative models of reality with less condescension than in the past, and this trend may even lead to a better quality in the information from such sources. There are three reasons for this recent trend: the gradual global improvement in the recognition of 'tribal' culture, the retreat of arrogant archaeology, and rapid developments in ethology. The latter have resulted in a general blurring of traditional humanistic divisions and in the challenge of the so-called social sciences by the biological sciences, such as ethology or neurophysiology (Plotkin 2002). The effect may be a better appreciation of the complexity of tribal cultures, but this does not help us in its actual understanding; it merely helps us to understand how difficult proper appreciation of such complexities might be. This is a step in the right direction, certainly, but still no help in interpreting palaeoarts. While ultimately all forms of art are in some way connected, it would serve no useful purpose to select two historically unrelated arts and to use one to interpret the other on the basis of one's own perceptions. If there is a sound historical connection possible, this is of course a different matter; there is no reason to assume that one form of art should not have affected another.

There is a second connection that may link the arts of a particular geographical region. Rock art has the unusual ability of surviving for a long time, and it occurs frequently in very prominent places within landscapes. Hence it is clear that rock arts of previous peoples were seen, interpreted and reacted to by later peoples occupying the same locality. Thus rock art has the outstanding ability of acting as a *cultural determinant* (Bednarik 1991/92). Indigenes in most parts of the world believe that the art of earlier traditions was not made by other humans, but was part of the original landscape (Flood 1995; Mowaljarlai and Vinnicombe 1995), having been placed by spirits, deities or creation heroes. Therefore rock art played a central role in the spiritual world of such tribes: it proved and confirmed, for all to see, the existence and power of the spiritual forces a group believed in — whatever those forces may have been. This validating role of rock art is fundamental to its significance to traditional societies. Naturally, such societies would adopt aspects of the earlier art's motif range into their own art, or they would adapt them to fit their own interpretations. In this way the older art served as a normative determinant of artistic expression, and there are rock art traditions that survived for tens of millennia without significant changes (Bednarik 1992b). This is not necessarily so because the region was occupied by just one definable ethnic group all this time, but because the successive occupiers or traditions adopted the earlier art into their cosmology, which led to an artistic conservatism of great durability. Other forms of art may have been developed alongside, but the most ancient form continued to exert its artistic influence through its relative permanence.

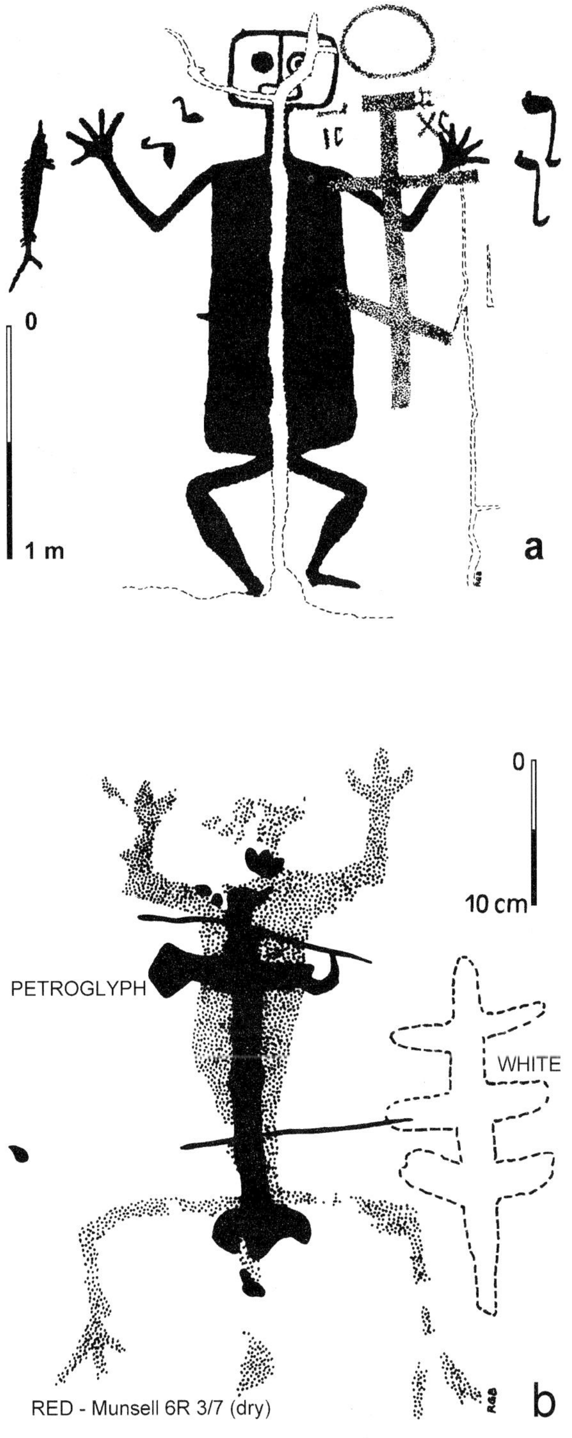

Figure 53. Two examples of religious iconoclasm of rock art motifs, (a) a petroglyph from Besov Nos, Karelia, and a pictogram from (b) Peña Escrita, central Bolivia, both with superimposed cross petroglyphs.

This, however, is not the only reaction documented in the evidence. One of several other forms of responses to rock art suggests vandalism, and rock art vandalism is almost as old as rock art itself. In Cosquer Cave, France, two phases of rock art are believed to be present: the first occupation may have been between 28 000 and 26 000 years BP, the second between 19 000 and 15 000 BP (Clottes et al. 1992). The more recent 'Solutrean' or 'Magdalenian people' destroyed or damaged much of the art of the earlier, 'Aurignacian' or 'Gravettian people'. Many of the hand stencils of the earlier occupiers were over-marked or tampered with, or the stalactites bearing them were smashed.

Graffiti or vandalism occur right through the periods of pre-History and History, and of particular interest are those of modern religions (Figure 53). For instance, Christian missionaries were notorious for over-marking or disfiguring early rock art (Bednarik 1991c), and the iconoclastic rock art vandalism of Moslems in western China and elsewhere was most extensive. In short, different peoples have responded to rock arts in different ways, which illustrates cultural dynamics. This type of information is much more reliable than vacuous speculations about the meaning of individual motifs, or about ethnocentrically perceived 'styles' — and it is much more useful. For instance, it may provide an opportunity for historical correlation, as in the case of documented Spanish policies in Andean regions in the 16th century, of 'exorcising' the spiritual dimensions from rock art sits (Querejazu-Lewis 1991/92).

UNIVERSALS IN ARTS

So far, two ways of studying relationships between different corpora of rock art have been defined. The first, development through cultural continuity, obviously requires such uninterruptedness, which is the factor providing the necessary link. In the second case, in which there are reactions to alien rock arts recorded (e.g. iconoclasm, commentary, correction, 'improvement', adoption), the link is not cultural, but spatial: it is provided simply by the location, through the relative permanence of the rock art at the site of its occurrence.

A third way of linking different bodies of rock art is neither cultural nor spatial. One can compare with it rock art corpora that occur in different continents, are from different periods and lack any cultural connection. This link is provided by the human brain and visual system, and the connection is made via universals in art. This approach is concerned with neural processes, motor actions and hominin endeavours of creating realities through art. Cognitive universals in art are a ferociously complex subject, and here is not the place to examine these complexities in any detail (cf. Bednarik 1990/91). This is not about simplistic applications of universals, as in the claims of shamanism, fertility imagery, hunting magic etc., but one can regard all forms of graphic art (rock art, portable two-dimensional art, tribal arts, body decoration, children's art, graffiti, subconscious doodling, fine arts etc.) as being tied together by certain forms of graphic universals. The perhaps most outstanding example are the phosphene motifs, derived from an autogeneous and involuntary phenomenon of the mammalian visual system. Their form constants cannot be influenced by cultural conditioning and seem to be ontogenically stable. Phosphene forms are any of the fifteen known standard form constants of phosphenes (Knoll and Kugler 1959; Kellogg et al. 1965; Eichmaier and Höfer 1974). They occur in many graphic art traditions, even to the complete exclusion of any other motif forms (Bednarik 1984, 1994b). For instance, all graphic art of infants prior to the acquisition of iconographic skills is thought to consist of phosphene forms, as apparently does all pre-iconic graphic palaeoart (i.e. prior to about 33 000 BP) (Figure 54). Since this proposition was first presented in 1984, it has never been falsified, but it has strongly been confirmed (Hodgson 2000).

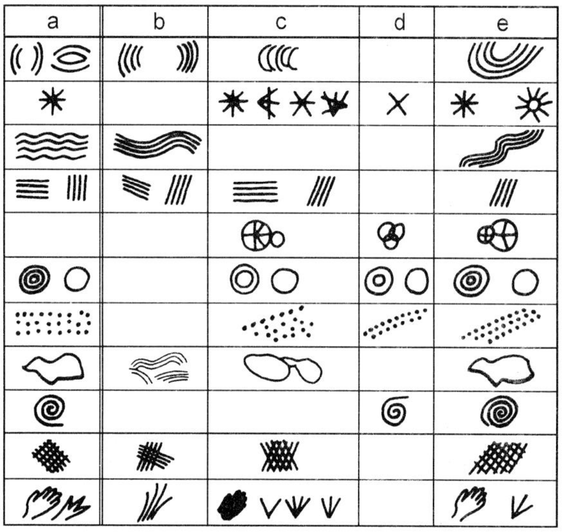

Figure 54. A comparison of (a) phosphene motifs with (b-e) the motif ranges of specific early graphic palaeoart traditions.

One more interpretational approach via universals is the semiotic study of rock art. Motifs can be regarded as signs or symbols, and their relationships with what they represent can be studied from the perspectives of semantics. However, to what extent such relationships, or the syntactic systems employed in rock art production, can be accessed without relying upon ethnography or archaeological constructs remains to be established. The several forays so far into the semiotic study of palaeoart systems, such as a special issue of the journal *Semiotica*, edited by Paul Bouissac in 1994, have not yielded sufficient substance to demonstrate a broad validity of this approach. Ultimately its future is likely to be decided by its ability to formulate its propositions in a refutable format.

SCIENTIFICALLY BASED INTERPRETATION

The obvious qualification of ethnographically and iconographically derived interpretations is, as mentioned above, that such mythologies must not be created in the name of science; it is not the business of science to create myths about the past (Bednarik 1992c). Science certainly does have a role to play in palaeoart studies, and although the application of scientific practice in rock art studies is a recent development, good progress has been made in recent years. Indeed, this discipline has progressed much more in the last fifteen years than in the previous two hundred years (see Ch. 2). An example is the recent proliferation in serious dating work. Among the specialised subjects being developed now are various technological studies and physico-chemical analyses; the identification of various types of residues (for instance, binders, proteins, lipids, extenders etc. in rock paints, or organic inclusions in mineral accretions over petroglyphs) (Clottes et al. 1990; Cole and Watchman 1992; Ridges et al. 2000); the use of computerised programs for image analysis, manipulation and colour standardisation (Rip 1989; Bednarik and Seshadri 1995); nano-stratigraphy of accretionary deposits and paint residues (Bednarik 1979; Watchman 1992); microscopic study and 'internal analysis' of tool marks in rock art and portable art (Marshack 1985); discrimination of anthropic and non-anthropic marks on rock and portable objects, and relevant ethology (Bednarik 1991d, 1993b); replication studies (d'Errico 1991; Bednarik 1997); erosion and microerosion studies (Bednarik 1992d); relationships between phylogenic and ontogenic development of logic and symbolism; the psychology of iconicity and its decipherment; concepts of type and typicalness in pre-Historic art, symbolism and psychology; distinction between mental and artistic representations; the application of taphonomic logic at both technical and epistemic levels (Bednarik 1994a); epistemology in the formulation of theories and in the interpretation of palaeoart; valid applications of statistics in the discipline; sound utilisation of universals in palaeoart studies (Bednarik 1990/91); and other experimental approaches. A few such approaches that can significantly assist interpretation are discussed below.

Internal analysis

This term was coined by Alexander Marshack to describe the microscopic study designed to determine various technological details of engravings, such as direction of tool application, handedness of operator and multiple tool application. Apart from one proviso concerning notational marks (see below), internal analysis has been very successfully used and tested by both d'Errico (1988, 1991, 1994) and myself (Bednarik 1984, 1988, 1992e), and more recently by others. Whereas Marshack and d'Errico applied this form of analysis only to portable objects, I extended it to rock art, especially engravings and finger flutings in limestone caves.

The principal difference between the work of Marshack and d'Errico is that the former researcher conducted little if any replicative work to underpin his theoretical constructs and pronouncements, relying essentially on visual judgment acquired from close familiarity with the materials. D'Errico has undertaken a great deal of experimental work in mark production and related fields. He also made extensive use of the scanning electron microscope, whereas Marshack and I only had access to optical microscopy. To examine striations and other details, d'Errico used not only the reflected-light microscope, he also created transparent cast replicas to study with a transmitted-light microscope, and resin casts to examine by scanning electron microscopy. He focused on incidental striae where tool aspects other than the point impacted upon a surface, and on changes in the pattern of contact, e.g. in response to variations in curvature of the engraved surface, or at points where the burin splintered.

D'Errico has shown through painstaking replicative studies that a good understanding of such minute tell-tale features in engraved lines, which can survive for many millennia on some surfaces, provides much reliable and testable information about the circumstances of mark production. The repeated application of the same tool point can be identified with great confidence, and it is often possible to determine the direction of tool application. Precedence in superimposition is another easily resolved issue, on sufficiently well preserved specimens.

It is often also possible to determine the type of material that was used in producing an engraved or incised (i.e. abraded) marking on rock, particularly on relatively soft rock (e.g. in a limestone cave, or on low metamorphism products such as slate, phyllite or schist). Applying blind tests I showed that an experienced observer can identify the experimental marks of metal points of utilitarian objects in nearly all cases, provided that the points had not been broken. The jagged ends of broken steel, for instance, yield marks resembling those of some stone points. Therefore it cannot be determined with confidence whether an engraved mark was made with a stone point, even if that does appear to be the case, whereas it is certainly possible to recognise the marks made by unbroken metal points with great confidence. Using this method I was able to establish that some of the supposedly Palaeolithic engravings in the Côa valley of northern Portugal had been made with steel points, and could therefore only be of final Holocene antiquity (Bednarik 1995a).

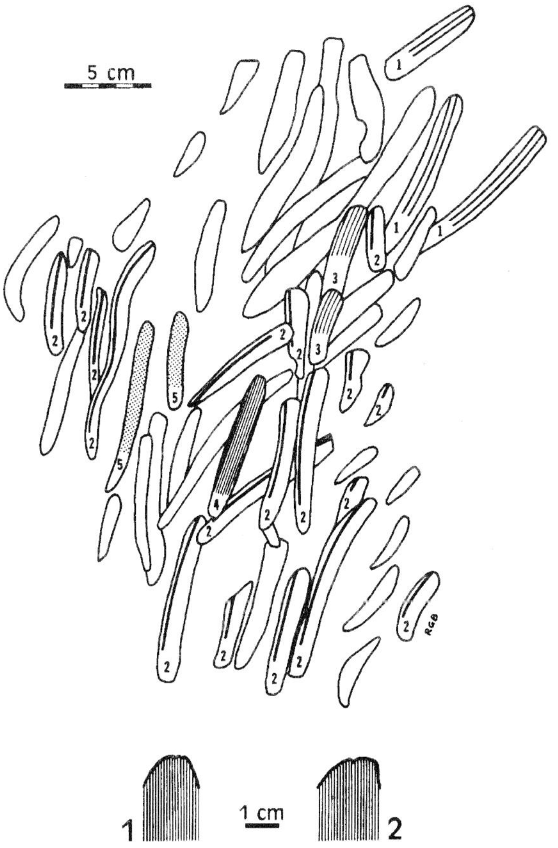

Figure 55. Internal analysis of tool markings on formerly soft wall deposit in Nung-kol Cave, South Australia. Where striation patterns are preserved, five apparently different tools have been identified, numbered 1-5. All marks were executed from top to bottom, with limestone clasts. The cross-sections of the tips (perpendicular to direction of movement) on two of the tools were determined, and are shown below (tool 1 and tool 2).

In some cases the method does not even involve a need for magnification (Figure 55). For instance, finger flutings in limestone caves are sometimes so well preserved that the direction of movement of the fingers is ascertainable from tiny tear-marks and other indicators (Bednarik 1986). Similarly, rock paintings would yield information about their execution by this approach, particularly where the paint was applied with fingers.

Marshack's internal analysis has become one of the most effective tools in the scientific interpretation of mark production processes. However, I contend that the primary purpose for which it was initially conceived, the recognition of notational markings (Marshack 1972, 1985, 1989), is not served by it. While the methods developed from Marshack's pioneering work have provided superb insights into questions of how engravings were made, they cannot furnish conclusive evidence for or against interpretation as notation (d'Errico 1989; Bednarik 1991e). Although it is certainly possible to determine that two or more marks were made by the same tool point, it is impossible to know if two different tools were used in any two different marks. This is because stone tool points are generally of non-symmetrical and irregular shape, so if the tool is put down briefly between applications, or if the grip or direction of application, even the angle of application, is changed between two marks, it may be impossible to recognise the repeated use of the same tool. Since a principal characteristic of notations is that a sequence of similar marks was made with interruptions, often using different tools, it follows that the issue cannot be resolved conclusively by this method. It cannot be demonstrated that two morphologically different markings could not have been made by the very same tool point.

Statistical interpretation

One of the most serious limitations of statistical analyses in rock art research is that posed by the inherent subjectivity of the primary data. Irrespective of the actual method used, statistics that address the content of rock arts always involve a taxonomy of motif elements, because the grouping of motifs perceived to be similar is a prerequisite for such treatment. Yet any such 'taxonomising' process is entirely based on the iconographic perceptions or graphic and depictive conventions defining the researcher's own system of reality. It does not reflect the artists' graphic cognition.

Empiricists seem to realise part of this problem, but their belief in their own objectivity still allows them to perceive meaningfulness in the arbitrary selection of criteria to create taxonomies. It would initially appear that nonfigurative art, consisting of 'geometric' arrangements, is more accessible to statistical analysis than figurative art. In fact the opposite is true, because while there might be some merit in assuming that the observer shares iconic perceptions of the artist, that cannot apply in noniconic art. No two rock art motifs are identical in every respect, yet in order to prepare a site's assemblage for statistical treatment, apparently similar motifs must be grouped and considered together. Without this process no statistical treatment of any corpus of rock art is possible. Each and every motif possesses thousands of variables, and the analyst must decide which ones are to be considered crucial in determining its taxon. Otherwise there will inevitably be as many motif types as there are motifs at any one site. Among the characteristics available for selection are metrical indices, qualitative or formal aspects, aspects of the motif's relationship to the site, to other motifs at the site, to the motifs at other sites, to the topography of the site, to petrological or past vegetational or hydrographic aspects of the site or of the surrounding landscape, spatial or syntactic context, the identity or status of the artist (is a circle engraved by a man the same motif type as one engraved by a woman?). Not only can single elements have wide ranges of 'meaning', definable only in terms of pre-Historic context (consider Munn 1973), the number of characteristics of each motif is practically unlimited. Many of those characteristics that defy archaeological definition may be crucial in identifying motif types (e.g. the sex of the artist). Thus the parameters the analyst chooses will inevitably reflect her/his personal, cultural, historical, ethnocentric and cognitive biases. Consequently the information so derived is useful only in studying the analyst's own culture and cognition, and in studying the way in which s/he applies these in examining the surviving graphic traces of cognitive systems to which s/he has no cognitive access. However, that information is not scientifically relevant to the study of the pre-Historic culture concerned, except for purely descriptive purposes. It cannot be expected to provide valid data for statistical analysis of the palaeoart.

This is one of the two fundamental objections to statistical interpretations of rock art, the second involves the application of taphonomic logic (see below). Both these concerns are fatal for the archaeological belief that rock art interpretation is possible through sophisticated statistical treatment. It needs to be emphasised that there certainly is a place for such treatment, namely in the empirical description of what there is on the rock surface today, and how a conditioned alien researcher perceives this legacy. For purely descriptive purposes such a site inventory is of limited usefulness (e.g. in conservation work), but it is not an adequate basis for further analysis. It must not be regarded as the raw data for any kind of 'scientific' treatment. For such purposes it is far too crude and inadequate. Any form of *analysis* of a corpus of rock art would have to be based on the *whole of the art* that was produced, and it would have to break down this whole into *temporal units*. If that is not done, or not possible, then statistical data about rock art are not scientific data.

Taphonomic interpretation

Metamorphology, the scientific version of archaeology, is a logic-based, refutable system of reviewing archaeological information to determine whether archaeological propositions could have scientific legitimacy. It is developed especially from taphonomic logic, which in turn hinges on the concept of cumulative data loss as a function of time (the principle is depicted graphically in Bednarik 1994: Fig. 2). It replaces uniformitarianism as a unified theory of archaeology (cf. Cameron 1993).

One of the greatest heuristic stumbling blocks of orthodox archaeology is that it tends to treat evidence — or what it calls the 'archaeological record', an essentially meaningless concept (Bednarik 1994c) — as a kind of random sample, as if it amounted to a *representative* selection of variables defining a particular culture. In the case of rock art, this is rendered particularly incongruous by two factors: that major rock art sites are usually cumulative records in mostly two-dimensional space (although there are exceptions, such as nano-stratigraphic sequences), and that the scientific dating of their chronological components continues to remain extremely difficult (Bednarik 1990-91). In other words, the rock art at such sites belongs to different periods, the artists of which contributed to the same corpus, perhaps reacting to pre-existing art at the site. Traditional archaeological approaches are practically pointless here, and the determination of what actually constitutes a valid sample is often extremely difficult, if indeed possible.

Expressed in epistemological language, there is a dependency relation called a supervenience: one set of properties, forming the historical event, is supervenient on a second, represented in the selected sample. There could not be a difference in the first without there being a difference in the second, though there could be a difference in the second with no difference in the first. Thus the relationship of the two sets of properties has to be explored by alternative means, not by direct deductive reasoning.

Metamorphology is the science of how forms of evidence change with time to become the forms as which they are perceived or understood by the individual archaeologist today (Bednarik 1995b). In accounting for the considerable gap that exists between the reality of what actually happened at some point of time in the distant past, and the abstraction of it as it is perceived by an archaeologist, metamorphology has to take into consideration such a myriad factors that it cannot be expected to provide precise interpretations. Like refutation in general, it instead provides us with models of what is unlikely to be valid, and so strengthens archaeology by weakening its dogmas. It also eschews the concepts of an 'archaeological record' and of a collective knowledge of the discipline.

The most obvious of these factors accounting for metamorphology, and thus for the gap between archaeologists' constructs and what really happened in the past, is taphonomy (Efremov 1940). Taphonomy deals with the logical underpinning of the idea that the quantified characteristics of a record of past events or systems are not an accurate reflection of what would have been a record of the live system or observed event. Taphonomy distorts archaeological evidence systematically, and it does so in forms that have often not been appreciated by archaeologists. Indeed, after the palaeontological concept of taphonomy was introduced into archaeology a couple of decades ago, it was soon misunderstood and effectively became a practice resembling actuopalaeontology — which ironically taphonomy was originally intended to replace (for an excellent discussion of this point, see Solomon 1990). Hence the potential of taphonomy in archaeology has remained significantly under-utilised.

In rock art science, *taphonomy* is the study of the processes affecting rock art after it has been executed, determining its present appearance and statistical properties. *Taphonomic logic* is a form of logic viewing rock art as the surviving remnant of a cumulative population that has been subjected to continuous degradation which selects in favour of specific properties facilitating longevity (Figure 56). It inevitably leads to the concept of the *taphonomic threshold*, which is the point in time at which instances of a specific class of material remains either begin to appear, or begin to appear in significant numbers. Before their respective taphonomic thresholds, all classes of material remains experienced a *taphonomic lag time*. This is the period during which the phenomena resulting in the material remains in question did exist, but from which we have found no such evidence — or so little that it is usually explained away as a 'running ahead of time' (Vishnyatsky 1994), or as incorrectly dated or identified. Until examined closely this may seem a minor issue, but for most classes of material remains, the taphonomic lag times are well in excess of 90% of the phenomenon's historical duration. Indeed, taphonomic lags in excess of 98% and 99% are quite common, they apply for instance to seafaring evidence (Bednarik 1999), and to most organic remains used as artefacts (e.g. hide, bark, wood, fibre, resin). Taphonomic logic is quantifiable, at least to the extent that it can be expressed as an integral function (Bednarik 1994a: 73).

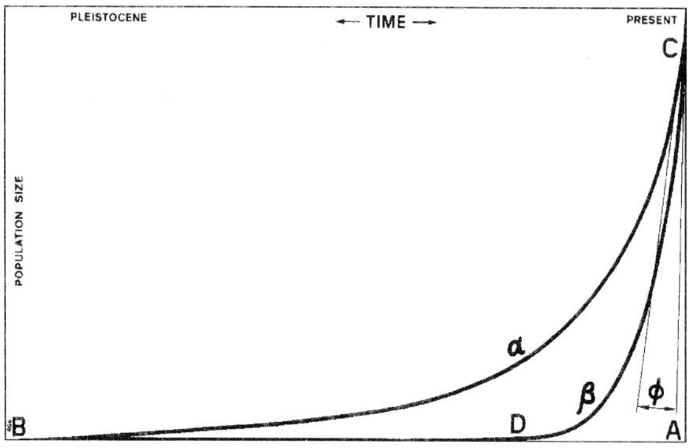

Figure 56. Principles of the relationship of total production of an archaeological phenomenon s_α to its surviving instances s_β as a function of angle φ. These principles are the basis of taphonomic logic.

In rock art, taphonomic lag times remain largely undetermined, but they would certainly differ greatly according to the climate, type of rock art and type of support rock. The taphonomic threshold of beeswax rock art in the Northern Territory of Australia (Nelson et al. 2000) has been estimated to be about 800 years BP (Bednarik 2001). One of the most common forms of surviving rock art consists of red paintings in sandstone shelters, and their threshold is believed to be in the order of 8000 years. For most other rock paintings the taphonomic threshold is lower. However, there are notable exceptions, especially art sites located in deep limestone caves offering extraordinary preservation conditions. In other words, the Palaeolithic 'cave art' traditions of Europe are known to us only because some of the art of the societies concerned was placed in 'fluke preservation conditions'. That evidence would probably not have survived elsewhere.

The ability of petroglyphs to survive in the open, i.e. exposed to precipitation, is governed largely by the rock they were made on. Those on limestone have a taphonomic threshold of well under 2000 years (Mandl 1996), while those on granite can easily survive from the Pleistocene, and recent dating evidence suggests that their threshold might be in the order of 30 000 or 50 000 years under some conditions (Bednarik 2002a). Other relevant variables are climate and geochemistry. Taphonomic logic demands that rock art of the various types was produced before all of these thresholds, but evidence of it should be either unavailable or extremely rare. Occurrence and distribution, as well as various characteristics of surviving rock art are all determined by taphonomic factors. Therefore it would be meaningless to state that a particular tradition produced only deep line petroglyphs, or painted only in caves, or left no open-air engravings. All characteristics of rock art that might contribute to their longevity (e.g. groove depth, location, type of rock support, morphology of site, composition of paint) are of no relevance to defining a tradition, because taphonomy selects in favour of them. For instance, the probably most common technological form of petroglyph is the sgraffito, made by the removal of a patina or weathering zone to reveal a differently coloured surface beneath. Sgraffiti tend to be obliterated by repatination processes within two or three millennia, therefore it is pointless to observe that the earliest petroglyphs of a region are consistently those that are deeply engraved. This observation, while valid, leads to misinterpretation of the sequence, unless moderated by taphonomic logic.

The mechanics of taphonomic logic are rather more complex than indicated in the present brief comments, but it must be emphasised that they are of crucial importance to the interpretation of primary data about rock art. This is the most important methodological tool so far developed in the interpretation of rock art data, and indeed, in archaeological interpretation of data and in hypothesis building. This form of logic is a recent introduction, it remains misunderstood by most archaeologists, yet it is crucial in transforming archaeology into a science. In rock art research, its introduction is probably easier, because the number of materials to be understood is quite limited, and also because the discipline is not as yet so much driven by, and committed to, dogma.

FADS AND BELIEFS

This raises a prominent aspect in the interpretation not only of rock art, but of general archaeology as well. The discipline is notoriously susceptible to faddish interpretations and in certain respects resembles a belief system (Freeman 1994). The structural causes of this tendency may appear complex, but the lack of falsifiability of purely archaeological propositions is no doubt a key factor. It permits the presentation of capricious hypotheses and encourages their energetic defence, relying on their lack of refutability. The history of archaeology can be seen as a succession of fads, which seem to arise when hypotheses, irrespective of their objective merits, happen to become popular. Kuckenburg (1997) has particularly well explained the historical dynamics that give rise to such favoured hypotheses. They inevitably reflect the social mood of the societies in which they arise, the political constellations and currents of the times, and similar essentially historical influences that reflect no systematic 'search for truth'. For instance, while it was fashionable to extol the virtues of competition and the survival of the fittest in the 'cynical' 1990s, the then popular tales of the genocide of the Neanderthals would not have gained any currency in the ideological climate of the 1960s. Throughout the period archaeology, a profoundly political discipline (Trigger 1989), exercised influence on social norms, through its 'explanations' of past societies. It operated in fact largely the reverse way: archaeological models and fads reflected the social currents of their times, rather than influencing public perceptions. Archaeologists subconsciously tailored their interpretations to suit the social mores of their societies, thus merely adding to historically contingent predispositions of their own social-cultural milieu. Political correctness is an integral factor in favoured models, which in turn feed the fantasies of both the public and the archaeologists.

While this already questions the ideological independence of the discipline, a second historical factor distorts archaeological preoccupations in a very different way. At any time in its history, the discipline's models depended on the information available to it, generally derived from finds made in an essentially random fashion. For instance, Palaeolithic tools were accepted historically before Palaeolithic art was reported, and for that reason the latter's authenticity was rejected: its sophistication was considered incompatible with the acknowledged tool technology of the period. Yet the sequence of discovery of all archaeological finds is without design, it is attributable largely to 'accidents of history'. Had Palaeolithic art been discovered before Palaeolithic implements, the latter would have no doubt been rejected because they would have been considered incompatible with the art. Hence in archaeology there is little system in the sequence of knowledge acquisition, which is often in contrast to the hard disciplines.

Since Boucher de Perthes had his 'worthless pebbles', the Acheulian tools, rejected for many years by establishment archaeologists, his experiences have been repeated over and over for almost two centuries, by dozens, even hundreds of scholars who challenged the discipline's beliefs (consider C. Fuhlrott, M. de Sautuola, E. Dubois, R. Dart, L. Leakey, A. Marshack). This pattern continues to the present day, and yet most of the major models Pleistocene archaeology offers today are either false or without adequate epistemological justification (Bednarik 2002b, 2003a). Scholars who present evidence or hypotheses contradicting its dogma are treated with contempt, and so archaeology remains the one discipline that manages to continue 'getting it wrong' more often than any other in all of scholarly endeavour (Bednarik 2003b).

Rock art research needs to appreciate these conditions — not just because archaeology often claims it as part of its discipline (the 'archaeological octopus' of Lorblanchet 1992: xxii) and imports its faulty epistemologies, but to avoid repeating the very same mistakes. Rock art study also is heavily influenced by fads, frequently derived from interpretations of its iconography. Their range includes *specific* beliefs, such as those that rock art is generally the work of shamans, and *general* beliefs in 'archaeolore', such as in the ability of experts to recognise Palaeolithicity in rock art. While it has been difficult in the past to test such beliefs, recent improvements in rock art science will render their falsification increasingly possible. Specific beliefs tend to be more short-lived, or they display alternating phases of growth and decline, oscillating in accord with societal preferences. For instance the shamanistic model has been advanced in several such cycles for at least a century, with minor modifications perhaps, but always without the presentation of testable hypotheses. General beliefs, on the other hand, can be long-lived and seemingly unassailable. For instance, the belief of all Palaeolithic art experts of Europe to possess the ability of determining the age of a rock art motif thought to be of the Upper Palaeolithic from its style alone was established early in the 20th century, and was not effectively challenged until refuted towards its end (Bednarik 1995c). This has not been conceded so far by most of the experts concerned, so their collective belief in their own capability, from which they derive their expert status within society, continues to be held and defended without rational justification.

The scientific issue here is how to test their belief, which would require that it be rendered quantifiable, repeatable and falsifiable. Style is not accessible to scientific definition, it is a subjective dimension that does not exist until it is perceived to exist. Since stylistic constructs in archaeology are autogenous formulations of self-appointed experts that have no independent existence outside of this belief system, it appears to be extremely difficult to analyse these self-proclaimed abilities. One possibility would be to devise blind tests, but efforts to conduct such work suggest that Palaeolithic art experts are reluctant to subject themselves to such tests. Indeed, it is said that 'blind tests are unethical' in archaeology, they are 'disrespectful' to colleagues (Zilhão 1995). Presumably this means that it is inconsiderate to practitioners to demonstrate that they are wrong. Freeman (1994) has examined the astonishing similarities between the procedures in validating religious shrines, especially in the Roman Catholic church, and validating the 'sanctuaries' in Palaeolithic art sites. He even observed similarities in the discovery myths disseminated for both types of sites, such as the involvement of 'innocents' (children, dogs, primitives; note the claimed involvement of dogs in finding both Altamira and Lascaux — no dog was involved in either case). Freeman concludes that 'these two manifestations of belief, reverence, and validation of experience have the same origin at a deeper structural level' (1994: 341). Again, the covert similarities with religion are evident, as they are also often in the terminology of those writing about Palaeolithic rock art. The term 'sanctuary', for instance, is widely used, yet there is no objective justification for its use.

The recent refutation of the belief of Palaeolithic art experts that they can determine the age of motifs from their style is based on the observation that all chronological stylistic constructs designed in the 20th century are negated by data presented in 1995. Some practitioners accept this to be the case, for instance Michel Lorblanchet admits that the discovery of Chauvet Cave in 1994 and the subsequent dating of paintings and soot traces was an 'earthquake' in pre-History. However, the majority of his colleagues have reacted in precisely the way one would expect the Catholic church to react to the claim that it has erred in validating religious shrines.

Not only has Chauvet Cave shown that a sound stylistic chronology of Palaeolithic rock art does not exist, the application of that chronology has also come to grief at other sites. Many Eurasian claims of Pleistocene age have been made for much younger rock art, especially on the Iberian peninsula, and they are all based entirely on the 'identification' of Palaeolithic style. The very same experts whose claims to be able to attribute rock art to specific Palaeolithic technological periods have been refuted are presenting the very same claims for a series of open-air petroglyph sites. A typical example would be the Spanish site Siega Verde, where numerous horse and bull pictures are claimed to be 15 000 or 17 000 years old. Yet the local villagers say that they were made by shepherds, and the first scientific examination showed that they could only be a few centuries old at most (Bednarik 2004). The nearby series of similar petroglyphs in the lower Côa valley occurs in identical geological and site-morphological conditions, most of it is also only in the order of centuries old, yet all Palaeolithic experts of Europe insist that it is of the Pleistocene. A major campaign to locate evidence for this claim (Aubry et al. 1998; Anonymous 2000) has become an acute embarrassment (Abreu and Bednarik 2000): no dating results were disclosed, sham claims were made, occupation layers with ceramic remains were pronounced Palaeolithic, and in one instance a colluvium was used to 'date' a rock art panel.

These examples show that the study of rock art should not be entrusted to a discipline that relies on autogeneous formulations about style in arriving at its chronological constructs, and then defends these in the fashion of a religion defending the foundations of its belief system. The dating and analysis of rock art needs to be conducted by rock art science. Fads, beliefs and controversies about rock art are no substitute for rigorous work.

REFERENCES

ABREU, M. S. DE and R. G. BEDNARIK 2000. Fariseu rock art not archaeologically dated. *Rock Art Research* 17: 65–68.

Anonymous 2000. 'Archaeologically dated Palaeolithic rock art' at Fariseu, Côa valley. *Rock Art Research* 17: 65.

AUBRY, T., A. F. CARVALHO, J. ZILHÃO 1997. Arqueologia: Salto do Boi – Cardina I. *Arte rupestre e pré-história do Vale do Côa (trabalhos de 1995–96)*, pp. 1–23. Relatório científico ao Governo da República Portuguesa, Lisbon.

BEDNARIK, R. G. 1979. The potential of rock patination analysis in Australian archaeology – part 1. *The Artefact* 4: 14–38.

BEDNARIK, R. G. 1984. Die Bedeutung der paläolithischen Fingerlinientradition. *Anthropologie* 23: 73–9.

BEDNARIK, R. G. 1986. Parietal finger markings in Europe and Australia. *Rock Art Research* 3: 30–61, 159–70.

BEDNARIK, R. G. 1988. Comment on D. Mania and U. Mania, 'Deliberate engravings on bone artefacts of *Homo erectus*'. *Rock Art Research* 5: 96–100.

BEDNARIK, R. G. 1990/91. Epistemology in palaeoart studies. *Origini* 15: 57–78.

BEDNARIK, R. G. 1991a. The emperor's clothes. *Purakala* 2(1): 18–21.

BEDNARIK, R. G. 1991b. Limits of knowledge. *Purakala* 2(1): 29–31.

BEDNARIK, R. G. 1991c. On the motivation of rock art reuse. *La Pintura* 18(2): 10–11, 13–14.

BEDNARIK, R. G. 1991d. On natural cave markings. *Helictite* 29(2): 27–41.

BEDNARIK, R.G., 1991e. Comment on F. d'Errico, 'Microscopic and statistical criteria for the identification of prehistoric systems of notation'. *Rock Art Research* 8: 89–91.

BEDNARIK, R. G. 1991/92. Rock art as a cultural determinant. *Survey* 5/6(7/8): 11–20.

BEDNARIK, R. G. 1992a. The stuff legends in archaeology are made of: a reply to critics. *Cambridge Archaeological Journal* 2: 262–65.

BEDNARIK, R. G. 1992b. Oldest dated rock art — a revision. *The Artefact* 15: 39.

BEDNARIK, R. G. 1992c. Palaeoart and archaeological myths. *Cambridge Archaeological Journal* 2: 27–43.

BEDNARIK, R. G. 1992d. A new method to date petroglyphs. *Archaeometry* 34: 279–91.

BEDNARIK, R. G. 1992e. Base pour des études de pointe des débuts de l'art. *L'Anthropologie* 96: 369–74.

BEDNARIK, R. G. 1993a. 1993. Who're we gonna call? The bias busters! In M. Lorblanchet and P. Bahn (eds), *Rock art studies: the post-stylistic era, or where do we go from here?*, pp. 207–211. Proceedings of Symposium A, Second AURA Congress. Oxbow Books, Oxford.

BEDNARIK, R. G. 1993b. Wall markings of the cave bear. *Studies in Speleology* 9: 51–70.

BEDNARIK, R. G. 1994a. A taphonomy of palaeoart. *Antiquity* 68: 68–74.

BEDNARIK, R. G. 1994b. On the scientific study of palaeoart. *Semiotica* 100(2/4): 141–68.

BEDNARIK, R. G. 1994c. Archaeology: empiricist determinism or cultural synthesis? *South African Archaeological Bulletin* 49: 96–99.

BEDNARIK, R. G. 1995a. The age of the Côa valley petroglyphs in Portugal. *Rock Art Research* 12: 86–103.

BEDNARIK, R. G. 1995b. Metamorphology: in lieu of uniformitarianism. *Oxford Journal of Archaeology* 14: 117–22.

BEDNARIK, R. G. 1995c. Refutation of stylistic constructs in Palaeolithic rock art. *Comptes Rendus de L'Académie de Sciences Paris* 321(série IIa, No. 9): 817–21.

BEDNARIK, R. G. 1997. The role of Pleistocene beads in documenting hominid cognition. *Rock Art Research* 14: 27–41.

BEDNARIK, R. G. 1999. Maritime navigation in the Lower and Middle Palaeolithic. *Comptes Rendus de l'Académie des Sciences Paris*, Earth and Planetary Sciences 328: 559–63.

BEDNARIK, R. G. 2001. The taphonomy of beeswax figures. *Rock Art Research* 18: 91–95.

BEDNARIK, R. G. 2002a. First dating of Pilbara petroglyphs. *Records of the Western Australian Museum* 20: 414–29.

BEDNARIK, R. G. 2002b. The human ascent: a critical review. *Anthropologie* 40(2): 101–5.

BEDNARIK, R. G. 2003a. A major change in archaeological paradigm. *Anthropos* 98: 511–20.

BEDNARIK, R. G. 2003b. Seafaring in the Pleistocene. *Cambridge Archaeological Journal* 13: 41–66.

BEDNARIK, R. G. 2004. New evidence from the Côa valley, Portugal. *Rock Art Research* 21: 137–44.

BEDNARIK, R. G. and K. SESHADRI 1995. Digital colour re-constitution in rock art photography. *Rock Art Research* 12: 42–51.

BINFORD, L. R. 1967. Smudge pits and hide smoking: the use of analogy in archaeological reasoning. *American Antiquity* 32: 1–12.

CAMERON, D. W. 1993. The archaeology of Upper Palaeolithic art: aspects of uniformitarianism. *Rock Art Research* 10: 3–17.

CHIPPINDALE, C. 2001. Studying ancient pictures as pictures. In D. S. Whitley (ed.), *Handbook of rock art research*, pp. 247–272. AltaMira, Walnut Creek, California.

CLOTTES, J., M. MENU and P. WALTER 1990. New light on the Niaux paintings. *Rock Art Research* 7: 21–26.

CLOTTES, J., J. COURTIN and H. VALLADAS 1992. A well-dated Palaeolithic cave: the Cosquer Cave at Marseille. *Rock Art Research* 9: 122–29.

COLE, N. and A. WATCHMAN 1992. Painting with plants: investigating fibres in Aboriginal rock paintings at Laura, north Queensland. *Rock Art Research* 9: 27–36.

CONSENS, M. 2000. Between artefacts and egofacts: the power of assigning names (abstract). In R. G. Bednarik (ed.), *Third AURA Congress, program and congress handbook*, p. 10. Occasional AURA Publication 11, Australian Rock Art Research Association, Melbourne.

CONKEY, M. W. and C. A. HASTORF (eds) 1991. *The uses of style in archaeology.* Cambridge University Press, Cambridge.

D'ERRICO, F. 1988. Lecture technologique de l'art mobilier grave nouvelles méthodes et premiers résultats sur les galets graves de Rochedane. *L'Anthropologie* (Paris) 92: 101–22.

D'ERRICO, F. 1989. Palaeolithic lunar calendars: A case of wishful thinking? *Current Anthropology* 30: 117–18.

D'ERRICO, F. 1991. Microscopic and statistical criteria for the identification of prehistoric systems of notation. *Rock Art Research* 8: 83–93.

D'ERRICO, F. 1994. *L'art gravé azilien.* 31e supplément, Gallia Préhistoire, CNRS Éditions, Paris.

EICHMAIER, J. and O. HÖFER (eds) 1974. *Endogene Bildmuster.* Urban and Schwarzenberg, Munich.

FLOOD, J. 1995. Copying the Dreamtime: anthropic marks

in early Aboriginal Australia. Paper presented to Symposium 1A of the International Rock Art Congress in Turin, September 1995.

FRANKEL, D. 1993. The excavator: creator or destroyer? *Antiquity* 67: 875–77.

FREEMAN, L. G. 1994. The many faces of Altamira. *Complutum* 5: 331–42.

HODGSON, D. 2000. Art, perception and information processing: an evolutionary perspective. *Rock Art Research* 17: 3–34.

HUCHET, B. M. J. 1991. The nature of analogies in Australian archaeology. *The Artefact* 14: 3–12.

HUCHET, B. M. J. 1992. Processual archaeology: discrepancies between norms and performances. *Norwegian Archaeological Review* 25: 111–19.

KELLOGG, R., M. KNOLL and J. KUGLER 1965. Form-similarity between phosphenes of adults and pre-school children's scribblings. *Nature* 208: 1129–30.

KNOLL, M. and J. KUGLER 1959. Subjective light pattern spectroscopy in the encephalographic frequency range. *Nature* 184: 1823–24.

KUCKENBURG, M. 1997. *Lag Eden im Neandertal? Auf der Suche nach dem frühen Menschen.* ECON Verlag, Düsseldorf and München.

LORBLANCHET, M. 1992. Introduction. In M. Lorblanchet (ed.), *Rock art in the Old World*, pp. xv–xxxii. IGNCA Rock Art Series 1, Indira Gandhi National Centre for the Arts, New Delhi.

MACINTOSH, N. W. G. 1977. Beswick Cave two decades later: a reappraisal. In P. J. Ucko (ed.), *Form in indigenous art*, pp. 191–197. Australian Institute of Aboriginal Studies, Canberra.

MANDL, F. 1996. Felsritzbilder auf dem Dachsteingebirge: Beiträge zur Datierung ostalpiner Felsritzbilder. *Mitteilungen der Anisa* 17(2/3): 136–56.

MARSHACK, A. 1972. *The roots of civilization.* McGraw-Hill, New York/Weidenfeld and Nicolson, London.

MARSHACK, A. 1985. Theoretical concepts that lead to new analytic methods, modes of enquiry and classes of data. *Rock Art Research* 2: 95–111.

MARSHACK, A. 1989. Methodology in the analysis and interpretation of Upper Palaeolithic image: theory versus contextual analysis. *Rock Art Research* 6: 17–38.

MAYNARD, L. 1977. Classification and terminology in Australian rock art. In P. J. Ucko (ed.), *Form in indigenous art*, pp. 387–402. Gerald Duckworth and Co. Ltd., London.

MICHAELIS, H. 1981. Willowsprings: a Hopi petroglyph site. *Journal of New World Archaeology* 4(2): 3–32.

MITHEN, S. (ed.) 1998. *Creativity in human evolution and prehistory.* Routledge, New York.

MOWALJARLAI, D. and P. VINNICOMBE 1995. Perspectives of the origin of rock images in the western Kimberley. In G. K. Ward and L. A. Ward (eds), *Management of rock imagery*, pp. 42–52. Occasional AURA Publication 9, Australian Rock Art Research Association, Melbourne.

MUNN, N. D. 1973. *Walbiri iconography.* Cornell University Press, Ithaca.

NELSON, D. E. (ed.) 2000. *The beeswax art of northern Australia.* Compact disk, Simon Fraser University, Burnaby, Canada.

PLOTKIN, H. 2002. *The imagined world made real: towards a natural science of culture.* Penguin Books, London.

POIKALAINEN, V. and E. ERNITS 1998. *Rock carvings of Lake Onega: the Vodla region.* Estonian Society of Prehistoric Rock Art, Tartu.

QUEREJAZU-LEWIS, R. 1991/92. Rock art as part of the popular Andean religiosity. *Survey* 5/6(7/8): 61–66.

RIDGES, M., I. DAVIDSON and D. TUCKER 2000. The organic environment of paintings on rock. In G. K. Ward and C. Tuniz (eds), *Advances in dating Australian rock-markings*, pp. 61–70. Occasional AURA Publication 10, Australian Rock Art Research Association, Melbourne.

RIP, M. R. 1989. Colour space transformations for the enhancement of rock art images by computer. *Rock Art Research* 6: 12–16.

SOLOMON, S. 1990. What is this thing taphonomy? In S. Solomon, I. Davidson and D. Watson (eds), *Problem solving in taphonomy: archaeological and palaeontological studies from Europe, Africa and Oceania*, pp. 25–33. Tempus 2, University of Queensland, St Lucia.

TITIEV, M. 1937. A Hopi salt expedition. *American Anthropologist* 39: 244–58.

TRIGGER, B. G. 1989. *A history of archaeological thought.* Cambridge University Press, Cambridge.

WATCHMAN, A. 1992. Repainting or periodic-painting at Australian Aboriginal sites: evidence from rock surface crusts. In G. K. Ward (ed.), *Retouch: maintenance and conservation of Aboriginal rock imagery*, pp. 26–30. Occasional AURA Publication 5, Australian Rock Art Research Association, Melbourne.

WYLIE, A. 1985. The reaction against analogy. In M. B. Schiffer (ed.), *Advances in archaeological method and theory*, Vol. 8, pp. 63–111. Academic Press, New York.

ZILHÃO, J. 1995. The age of the Côa valley (Portugal) rock-art: validation of archaeological dating to the Palaeolithic and refutation of 'scientific' dating to historic or proto-historic times. *Antiquity* 69: 883–901.

9. SOME METHODS OF ROCK ART SCIENCE

COLOUR CALIBRATION

In this chapter, some key methods of rock art science not considered in earlier chapters, or considered only inadequately, will be discussed. The principal method of recording rock art is colour photography, and the rock art archives and private collections of the world contain many millions of records in the form of slides, prints and films. The cost of having assembled this collective record, including travel and other related expenses, would have run into hundreds of millions of dollars. Yet all of this record is doomed to gradual deterioration and will eventually be lost, because photographic dyes are not permanent. In the majority of cases, the actual rock art will hopefully survive our photographic records of it. Nevertheless, even the rock art itself does deteriorate and will be lost eventually.

Digital preservation of rock art imagery, an alternative to preserving the actual rock art, has not been possible until very recently. Its development demands a significant review of our attitudes and priorities, in both rock art conservation and recording. The principle of digital preservation is that an image must be rendered susceptible to means of recovering its original visual properties inperpetuity. There were two impediments to digital preservation: standardised colour calibration (i.e. the use of a universal device profile) had not been introduced, and a method of re-constituting the colour and other reflective optical information of imagery was not available. The first step was therefore the introduction of a universal calibration standard, which was achieved with the production and world-wide distribution of the IFRAO Standard Scale in 1994/95 (Bednarik 1991, 1994). The Scale was not only distributed to all members of the then thirty-six IFRAO-affiliated organisations, and thus to most rock art specialists in the world, it has even been adopted by other disciplines since (Figure 57).

The second step has been achieved with the first colour re-constitution in collaboration between IFRAO and the National Museum of Man in India (Bednarik and Seshadri 1995). The technique can be applied routinely now, using commercially available software, but to simplify and completely standardise the method, customised software has been prepared. The digital colour re-constitution process is schematically depicted in Figure 30. Most of it can be handled by software, which limits manual input to decisions about calibration sampling sites (see Ch. 5).

Procedures of recording, conservation and study of rock art will be greatly influenced by this technology. Photographs are relegated to the role of an intermediate, provisional optical record of coded information that must be further processed to realise its full potential. They are no longer the central device of recording rock art, their place is taken by digital re-constitution coupled with digital colour management systems. This does not immediately affect rock art recording, except for one new requirement: all photographs, slides and films of rock art must now be colour-calibrated by a device profile that is backed by digital recovery software. The principal features of the system are that all rock art imagery recorded with the IFRAO Standard Scale will remain recoverable forever, irrespective of how faded a photograph is, how badly it has been scanned by a digital scanning device, or how distorted the photographic record itself is (e.g. through lighting). The re-constitution process cuts across all distortions by relying solely on the known (and digitally retrievable) characteristics of the standard device profile.

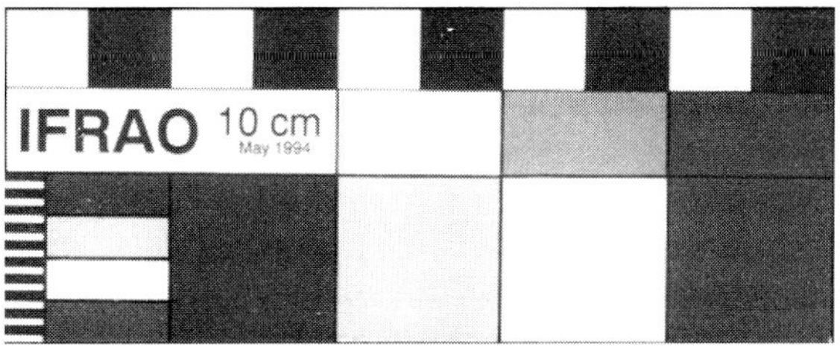

Figure 57. The IFRAO Standard Scale.

The long-term effects of this development will be very significant. To begin with, calibrated imagery can be rendered permanently true forever. We still lack proven perpetual (totally perdurable) digitised storage means, although compact discs are thought to preserve information for perhaps a century (Mark and Newman 1994). This is no longer an obstacle because we can now rejuvenate a calibrated image at any time. Therefore perpetual digital preservation of imagery (rock art or other) is available to us now. Truly permanent means of storage will become available in due course. High-fidelity records impact upon several aspects of conservation. Not only is physical preservation no longer our only alternative, the precision of this technology permits reliable monitoring of pigments and patinae for the first time (Mirmehdi et al. n.d.), replacing the awkward manual use of Munsell Charts with the mathematical precision of digital manipulation. Similarly, intra-site and inter-site cross-referencing, direct conversion to colour enhancement techniques (Rip 1989), certain dating and sourcing studies, and other possibilities have become readily available to us. There are further applications in conservation, for instance in lacunae repair or similar restoration work. But they are probably eclipsed by the changes and simplifications in colour printing. The days of painstaking checking of four-colour printing proofs are in the past. Colour re-constitution software can easily be coupled with under-colour removal and grey-component replacement techniques, superseding subjective processes and allowing perfect matching without the need of re-visiting sites. The entire process can be reduced to scanning or downloading a photographed image and outputting colour separations that will produce a true likeness of the rock art, rather than of the photograph.

While new recording technologies (e.g. digital cameras) are becoming widely available, traditional photography will remain in use for a long time yet. Facing the continual loss of rock art throughout the world, we have no choice but to make the best of the technology available to us. Whatever new technologies the future will deliver, it is certain that the only way of rendering rock art imagery fully recoverable forever is by colour-calibrating all rock art records. Not including the colour scale in our photographs is no longer an option. It would deprive the researchers of future generations of the possibility of using our photographs effectively. The photographs we take today may one day be the only records of a particular rock art. Even where this is not the case, they will always remain the only record of the rock art as it was at the time we photographed it, i.e. before it faded further. Just as we record site name and date with our photographs, we have to become accustomed to including on them the standard colour scale. If we feel that its presence detracts from the picture's perceived aesthetic quality, the scale can be placed on the edge of the negative and cropped from the print. The following guidelines have been established for the use of the IFRAO Standard Scale:

1. *Recording medium*: The colour calibration input should preferably be as slides (transparencies), colour negatives or digital images. This is because the scanning process presently required for paper prints is inferior to the digitisation directly from film, and colour transmission from photographs to CRT does not produce precise results.
2. *Lighting*: Natural lighting is superior to artificial light, which means that increased exposure times are preferable to the use of flash or other artificial lighting. Where necessary and possible, use a sunlight reflector. When using artificial lighting, use white light, not yellow halogen light.
3. *Direction*: Where artificial light is necessary, and especially for three-dimensional subjects (petroglyphs, cupules), the light source should preferably be from the upper left. The Scale should also be on the left upper corner of the frame.
4. *Area*: Full 100% calibration, which would result in a colour re-constitution adequate for rigorous technical and scientific purposes, requires that at least 5–10% of the photograph's area should be occupied by the Scale. With standard lenses this might correspond to a distance of about 0.5–0.8 m. There is a gradual but initially negligible loss in reliability as the image area occupied by the Scale decreases with distance.
5. *Distance*: One Scale suffices for distances of up to 1.5 m. If uneven lighting is unavoidable, place the Scale in the better lit section. For distances between 1.5 and 4.5 m, two scales must be used for optimal results: place one of them vertically and in the upper left corner of the frame. Beyond a distance of 4.5 m (i.e. using lenses of standard focal length), the Scale is too small to permit a calibration level approaching 100%, because at that distance the colour chips become too small to obtain precise digital readings from.
6. *Alignment*: Care must be taken to position the Scale so that it is parallel to the predominant plane of the rock art motif, and about the same distance from the camera lens. Misalignment will reduce the reliability of colour calibration.
7. *Reflection*: The Scale has been printed on matt stock, but this does not eliminate reflection entirely. If a camera-mounted flash is used, the scale must not be at right angle to the camera's focal axis, and if the subject is side-lit, the Scale should be perpendicular to the focal axis (Figure 31).

MICROSCOPY IN ROCK ART RESEARCH

There should be no doubt that this is one of the most important methods in rock art science. In a few respects it can take place in the laboratory, particularly in the analysis of mur-e (tools used in the making of petroglyphs), portable palaeoart objects, and in the study of samples taken from sites. However, the most useful and decisive microscopy work in this discipline takes place in the field, at sites of a great morphological variety.

Field microscopy differs significantly from

laboratory work, for several fairly obvious reasons. For one thing, there is rarely any ready power supply for lighting attachments at sites, and alternative light sources must be provided. Second, many rock art sites are geographically remote, and access is often very difficult and strenuous. Having hauled microscopes through equatorial jungles, over Arctic tundras and searing deserts, to high mountains and into deep caves, I assure the reader that a microscope chosen as a tool in rock art research needs to be carefully selected. Its choice is essentially a compromise between the lowest possible weight and the greatest possible robustness. The latter demands a sturdy construction, which adds to weight, but in choosing an instrument it is advisable to remember that ultimately one ends up carrying it for great distances. Then there is a very peculiar problem in working with rock art, the severe physical restrictions imposed: one must avoid making contact with the rock surface, and even stay clear of the rock surrounding the actual rock art motif. This may involve a variety of solutions that depend on circumstances, and some acrobatic skills could be an advantage at times.

Since the whole purpose of this work is to produce useful data, the design and technical properties of the equipment also need to be considered carefully. No commercially available optical microscope is designed for rock art study, in fact most models on the market are not intended for fieldwork at all. It is great to have a very expensive piece of equipment that requires two people just to carry it — when one has the help of a television crew, whose bus can be driven to within a few metres of the site. But I have found that such technological marvels are not even particularly suitable for our purposes, and besides, much of the time we may lack the luxury of help crews and may need to be as self-sufficient as possible.

Next is the problem that different applications may favour different equipment, particularly in terms of having adequate oculars and lenses. Here, optical versatility is obviously of great benefit, but the number of replacement lenses one carries needs to be strictly limited due to the extra weight. The following comments are guidelines in deciding what is most suitable for the work intended.

It is of benefit to consider initially what our technical field requirements are. Rock art sites vary greatly morphologically: horizontal pavements; more or less inclined panels, some with good standing room, others not; vertical surfaces, either in the open or in rockshelters or caves; and ceilings of enclosed spaces, under boulders, in caves or shelters. One circumstance that is in our favour here is that most rock art occurs in locations chosen for their convenience to humans: provided that there were no subsequent changes to the site's morphology, the art tends to be reasonably accessible to the human observer — though this is not always true by any means, as any rock art researcher will readily attest. Access can be severely affected by elevated floors resulting from sedimentation, by rock falls, tectonic changes and other factors. In general, however, rock art is often found in places offering some physical convenience to the human: at eye level perhaps, or where there was good room to apply blows with a hammer stone.

The first and most obvious requirement in optical field microscopy of rock art is that the equipment used must be suitable to place directly over the rock surface. Generally, binocular microscopes have a flat base and the specimen is placed above it, usually on a table. In some models there is a large opening through the base and the table can be removed, which would render them suitable for our type of work. Alternatively, the carriage can be rotated around the stand, thus avoiding the base. However, microscope bases tend to be very heavy, providing the instrument with stability, and they are a hindrance for our purposes. Moreover, at times we need to be able to focus the instrument onto vertical surfaces, even overhead surfaces, and a base would then be an impediment. In such applications it is necessary that the microscope be soundly attached to a supporting frame of some kind, and for this purpose it is most convenient that the carriage of the instrument is mounted on a rail of some type that can be attached to a robust support frame erected on site.

Here the researcher will benefit from some engineering experience, and from an ability to design and construct a stable support frame. The binocular microscope is mounted on this frame, which must facilitate the precision adjustment of focal distance to the surface to be examined. Needless to say, such a contraption must be sufficiently solid to allow lengthy work without vibration or accidental movement, and without the danger that the equipment could come into contact with the rock art (Figure 58). It must also be able to be transported to the site by means available to the researcher, it must be erected and dismantled, perhaps in a remote location. These are demanding specifications in a location with ready vehicular access, but in places of very difficult access (in caves, on mountains, or at sites involving hours of walking) they may create logistical nightmares. Nevertheless, I have for decades conducted such work, in all continents, often under difficult conditions and always without any public funding or support. This shows that with a little initiative and determination it is perfectly possible to conduct such work, even without a second person's help.

Optical requirements depend on the specific research task, which may be internal analysis, microerosion analysis, nano-stratigraphic study, sample removal, lichen identification, geomorphological examination, or one of a number of more specialised applications (e.g. study of micro-organic effects). Optical microscopes can range in magnification up to 200×, their resolution is limited by the wave length of natural light (about 0.2 micron). Instruments providing good resolution above 120× tend to be expensive, large and heavy, but fortunately most work with rock art is best conducted in the magnification range from 20× to 100×. For some purposes even magnifications of below 20× are perfectly adequate, if not preferable. In my experience, the principal range used in rock art work is from about 40× to 80×, and the use of higher magnification is usually quite pointless (I stress that there are some exceptions, such as young microerosion calibration points).

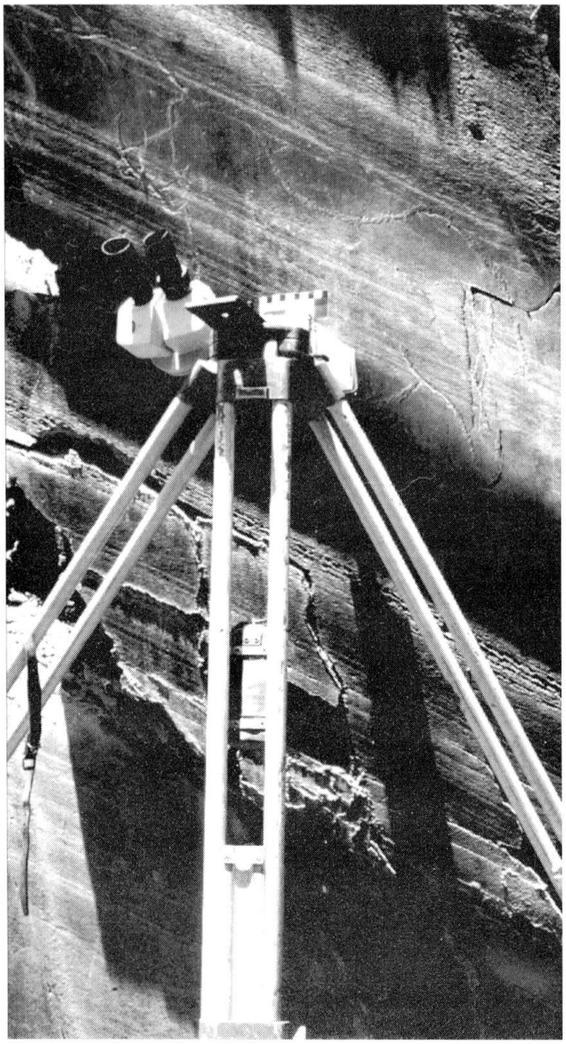

Figure 58. Rock art field microscopy. A binocular microscope has been mounted on a heavy tripod to examine the petroglyphs on a vertical rock face at Ribeira de Piscos, Côa valley, northern Portugal.

Nevertheless, it is useful in rugged working conditions to have a maximal number of lens combinations on the instrument rather than as loose replacements. It is ideal to have four or five primary magnifications, ranging from perhaps 5× to 40× or 50×, and a 1:2 cap lens. This provides the whole spectrum of magnifications usually required for work with rock art. A metric scale etched into one of the oculars, while not always essential, is an enormous practical help to have, especially for methods requiring the frequent determination of quantitative data. It is nearly indispensable for microerosion analysis, the alternative use of gauge wires being cumbersome and inaccurate. Its use is made easier by taking to the field a conversion table, because trying to calculate settings in the field can be an inconvenience and lead to errors. I tend to keep such a table attached to the base of the microscope.

After working at rock art sites for decades, using many models of Russian, German, Chinese and Japanese makers, a small but very robust binocular model constructed from parts of four different makers has become my favourite instrument. I equipped it with a simple lightweight aluminium base frame on three large rubber studs that has sufficient flexibility to permit focusing within a couple of dozen microns by gently pressing on the frame. This little trick has proved most useful because microscopic survey frequently concerns uneven (weathered or impact-damaged) rock surfaces where one has to constantly refocus within a narrow range to allow for the minor variation in objective lens distance.

The specific-purpose microscope I have designed for rock art work is easily dismantled and erected in seconds, and its components fit so snugly into a custom-made aluminium carry case that they cannot move during transport. The whole outfit including spare parts and case weighs only 8 kg (Figure 59). It may well be that over the period of more than 25 years that I have conducted field microscopy I have become too set in my ways, and another researcher might well find alternative equipment more suitable. Here I have merely tried to provide some guidelines for the inexperienced reader, even though they no doubt reflect personal preferences related to specific research priorities.

The importance of field microscopy in rock art science is so obvious that it requires no explanation. Many analytical projects depend on it entirely, such as microerosion analysis, internal analysis, identification of intervention markers (Thorn 1993), and analyses of patination products and nano-stratigraphy. Others, such as petrographic examination or the study of weathering phenomena, may be greatly facilitated by the field use of optical microscopes.

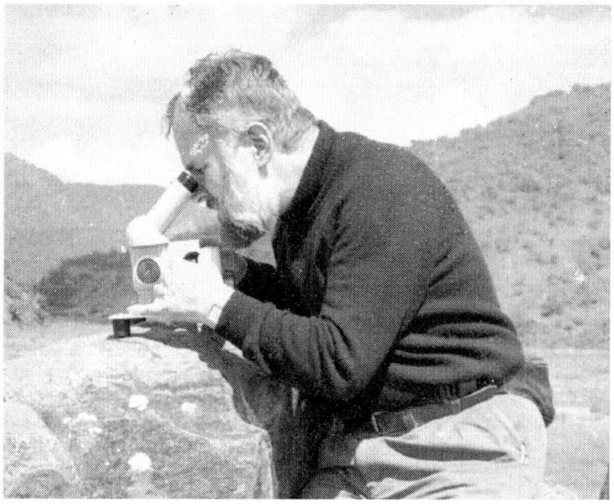

Figure 59. Custom-made binocular microscope used to examine cupules at Inca Huasi, Bolivia.

NANO-STRATIGRAPHIC EXCAVATION

I developed this method in 1977, specifically for analysing mechanically separated layers of ferromanganous mineral accretions. Essentially it involves exploration of microscopic strata of material physically related to rock art, through their controlled removal under a microscope. A number of research issues can be effectively tackled with this method, but broadly speaking it has been applied in two areas so far: in separating mineral accretionary strata to analyse them individually, and in exploring layers of paint residue. Both these applications are especially useful in dating studies, although certainly not limited to them.

The initial applications of nano-stratigraphic excavation (nano = relating to very small size, stratigraphy = the study of layered deposits whose strata provide a chronological sequence) were intended to provide an understanding of how iron- and manganese-rich accretions on rock are formed. Such crusts are usually under one millimetre thick, and I separated them into layers to analyse each one chemically, determining also their abrasion pH and studying their behaviour in aqueous exposure (Bednarik 1979). The results of this work contributed to a diagenetic understanding of the most common mineral accretions related to rock art (Figure 60), and they paved the way for the first attempts to estimate the ages of rock art by 'direct' means (see Ch. 7). Dorn has subsequently used a much coarser method to secure bulk samples of similar deposits (rock varnish), in his attempts to estimate their ages by determining the ratio of certain cations (Dorn 1983, 1994; Nobbs and Dorn 1988). His method (cation-ratio 'dating') assumes that such ratios reflect selective leaching of the more mobile cations, but now that the calibration method Dorn used has been discredited by himself the method has become redundant (see Ch. 7).

More recently, Watchman has made extensive use of nano-stratigraphic excavation for the removal of dating samples from petroglyphs, pictograms and adjacent rock surfaces. While continuing the use of mechanical excavation in his work (1995, 2000), Watchman has also pioneered an alternative approach, which is the use of a water-cooled krypton laser beam to combust selected laminae. The purpose of this method, called FLECS (focused laser extraction of carbon-bearing substances), is to extract carbon as CO_2 for carbon isotope analysis, usually for the age estimation of single layers within a sequence of accretionary deposits (Watchman 1993). Since the equipment is not portable, a sample has to be taken to the laboratory. A cross-section is cut through a sequence of deposits, from which specific nano-strata are then selected for ablation, based on analysis by polarised light microscopy, x-ray diffraction, Fourier transform infra-red spectroscopy and scanning electron microscopy/energy dispersive x-ray analysis. The carbon dioxide this procedure of highly focused combustion yields is then reduced to a graphite target for AMS radiocarbon dating.

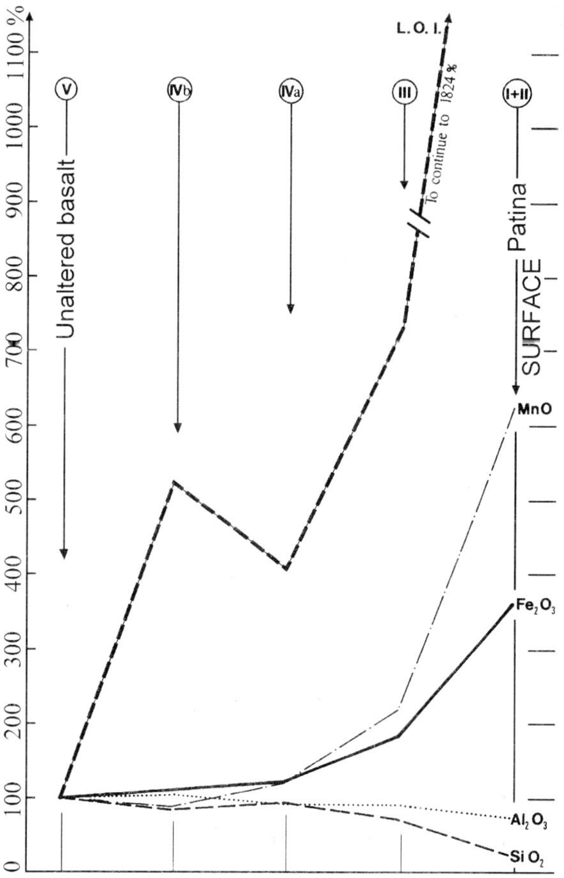

Figure 60. Some of the results of the first nano-stratigraphic analyses conducted in rock art science, in 1977. The graph depicts changes in chemical composition across a thin weathering skin of basalt, from the surface (on the right) to the unaltered rock (left). Of particular significance is the substantial increase of organic matter towards the surface.

For most purposes, however, nano-stratigraphic excavation remains a manual removal, layer by layer, under a microscope. Stainless steel dental tools are generally used, although they may be replaced by surgical blades in some cases, for instance, to remove identifiable organic objects, such as brush fibres or pollen. The low-power magnification required depends on the task at hand. Watchman uses 5× or even less, whilst my work is done at higher magnifications, at least 6.5× to 20×, sometimes greater. The process is essentially identical to archaeological excavation, with the surface-nearest stratum being the youngest, and strata truncated by a petroglyph being older than the figure in question. Needless to say, to excavate a deposit with a total depth of, say 700 microns manually and under field conditions is not a task for the novice, who will be expected to acquire considerable experience in this work before being ready to tackle deposits formed on rock art. Such work requires a thorough understanding of one's equipment and of geomorphic surfaces, not to mention a steady hand and considerable resourcefulness.

THE PHYSICAL SAMPLING OF ROCK ART

One of the technical questions I have been asked most frequently is how researchers should collect field samples for the 'direct dating' of rock art. Before considering this topic there are several important qualifications to be made.

First of all, in any dating of rock art, preference must always be given to non-destructive or 'non-invasive' analyses. A dating criterion may be a substance contained in the paint residue (e.g. a binder, brush fibre, pollen), it may be a mineral accretion that formed on top of the rock art (e.g. a silica skin, rock varnish, oxalate), a crack in the rock base transecting the motif and post-dating it, or a lichen thallus dissected by a petroglyph line — or any of many other things directly, physically and indisputably related to the rock art in question. The age of some of these features can be estimated by means involving no destructive sampling, or the sampling of material may be possible without damage to the art (e.g. mud-wasp nests or lichen covering it). Since physical sampling is generally a last-resort solution, all alternative possibilities must be explored before availing oneself of it.

Not even the leading practitioners of the various techniques can always successfully predict adequate or appropriate sampling requirements, and such an ability is well beyond the capacity of the general field archaeologist or other enthusiastic researcher. The available methods all remain experimental and the possible error factors applicable to their results are still to be established. It is clearly not possible at this stage to formulate standardised sampling requirements, or even to predict the favoured methodology of years to come. The sampling requirements most appropriate for specific methods under specific site conditions should be determined only by experienced specialists, and in full collaboration with the intended analytical laboratory. Physical sampling of rock art and related features should be undertaken only within the context of an integrated research design and not simply in response to a desire to 'know the age of the art'.

The true age of rock art cannot be determined with present technology; all that can and should be provided is falsifiable information relating to the age of the art. The precise interpretation of such information, too, remains the preserve of the specialist at this stage. Valid justification in terms of 'necessity' of destructive research is always required, as well as a valid research design. This means, among other things, that alternative approaches to a research problem have been considered. In selecting a research strategy it is essential that priority be given to methods on the following basis, in descending order of priority:

1. Methods that involve no physical contact with the rock art. The classical example is microerosion analysis, which is by microscopy, and which is also the most reliable of all rock art dating methods, though one of the less accurate. Only data samples are taken, not samples of physical substances.
2. Methods involving physical contact, e.g. to take measurements, but without the removal of physical samples. There is no damage of the rock art involved, and only very minor potential for contamination. Examples would be traditional lichenometry and XRF analysis.
3. Methods involving the removal of physical samples of a substance directly related to the rock art, but not forming any part of the actual rock art. Typical examples would be the removal of mineral accretions over or adjacent to the rock art. With appropriate care, damage to the rock art should be either avoidable or minimal.
4. Methods involving the removal of material forming part of the rock art, e.g. the surface fabric of a petroglyph or the paint residue of a pictogram. A typical example is the removal of paint residues for radiocarbon analysis.

In addition, there are several further considerations in ranking dating methods, such as the preference of methods providing 'locally uniform indices' over those yielding 'locally variable indices' (Bednarik 1996); considerations of precision and reliability, of cost, and of compatibility with previous research.

There is one exception to the harsh opposition to destructive sampling. Many sites experience exfoliation of paint residues or mineral accretion laminae from walls and ceilings. Clearly there is no objection to the collection of exfoliated fragments from the floors of shelters or caves, and to their destructive analysis. Such exfoliated fragments need to be collected without coming into contact with organic substances. The use of sterile surgical gloves is recommended, or the use of sterile metal pincers. If aluminium foil is used to collect the flakes in, care must be taken that it is not coated with oil (as domestic aluminium foil is), which is a hydrocarbon derivative and thus a significant source of contamination. The preferred collecting vessel is a sealable glass phial that has been thoroughly sterilised before use. There are various dental and optical tools used in the collection of in-situ samples, but this is not relevant here because the removal of in-situ samples by inexperienced personnel is not appropriate.

Obviously every effort must be made to determine which painting the sample has exfoliated from, and this may involve detailed field microscopy. The collecting phial must be reliably identified (site, motif, date of collection, condition of the floor it was in contact with, contact details of the collecting researcher) and related to a photographic record of the motif and the collecting site. Once in the laboratory, the sample's carbon content should be established to ensure that a radiocarbon determination is warranted. A microscopic study may be appropriate to determine whether any organic objects can be detected, such as brush fibres, charcoal grains, airborne plant material or incidental inclusions in a paint residue. Processing involves pre-treatment to remove a number of contaminants, such as humic acid, oxalates and carbonates (by washing in acids and bases), and finally the production of a carbon dioxide or graphite target for counting in the accelerator.

Samples for processing by luminescence analysis need to be collected by a specialist, not only to avoid contamination, but especially because the collecting site's background radiation needs to be measured. This is done with a gamma spectrometer and a caesium probe. The radiation derived from K, Th and U are measured, and other information required includes the morphology of the sampling site, its rock cover, elevation and precise longitude and latitide.

Concerning the possible sampling of pristine or in-situ paint residues, the conditions prescribed in the IFRAO Code of Ethics are as follows:

(a) The sample removal is to form part of a larger and specific research design that has peer approval;
(b) The sample removal has been approved in writing by two peer researchers (i.e. scientists specialising in the analytical study of rock art);
(c) The funds necessary for the best possible analytical laboratory support have been secured;
(d) The analyst has extensive first-hand experience in sampling geomorphic surfaces;
(e) Traditional indigenous custodians, where they have jurisdiction, have approved the sample removal;
(f) The relevant local or national authorities have approved the sample removal.

Accordingly, a researcher who has acquired the requisite expertise in rock art dating would, in justifying the collection of paint samples, begin with the design of a research project: why is it necessary, have all alternatives been considered exhaustively, what are the research issues and questions demanding the sampling? The project proposal then has to be peer reviewed, independent of any issues of funding. Once approved by the researcher's peers, the support of an appropriate analytical laboratory (and relevant funding) is to be secured, in addition to that of the AMS facility (or other final processor of the samples). Only after all of these steps have been satisfied is the proposal ready for consideration by the appropriate authorities. This lengthy process will not only ensure that the proposal is well-designed and likely to succeed, it will also eliminate any trivial or poorly conceived projects. It is in the interest of all concerned — including rock art owners, rock art researchers, conservators, funding agencies and laboratories — to prevent inadequately planned projects from securing support.

REFERENCES

BEDNARIK, R. G. 1979. The potential of rock patination analysis in Australian archaeology — part 1. *The Artefact* 4: 14–38

BEDNARIK, R. G. 1991. The IFRAO Standard Scale. *Rock Art Research* 8: 78–79.

BEDNARIK, R. G. 1994. Introducing the IFRAO Standard Scale. *Rock Art Research* 11: 74–75.

BEDNARIK, R. G. 1996. Only time will tell: a review of the methodology of direct rock art dating. *Archaeometry* 38: 1–13.

BEDNARIK, R. G. and K. SESHADRI 1995. Digital colour re-constitution in rock art photography. *Rock Art Research* 12: 42–51.

DORN, R. I. 1983. Cation-ratio dating: a new rock varnish age-determination technique. *Quaternary Research* 20: 49–73.

DORN, R. I. 1994. Dating petroglyphs with a three-tier rock varnish approach. In D. S. Whitley and L. L. Loendorf (eds), *New light on old art*, pp. 13–36. Monograph 36, Institute of Archaeology, University of California, Los Angeles.

MARK, R. K. and E. B. NEWMAN 1994. Applications of Photo CD and image processing technology. Paper presented to the International Rock Art Congress, Flagstaff, Arizona.

MIRMEHDI, CHALMERS, BARHAM and GRIFFITH n.d. Automated analysis of environmental degradation of mineral pigments. MS in AURA Archive.

NOBBS, M. F. and R. I. DORN 1988. Age determinations for rock varnish formation within petroglyphs: cation-ratio dating of 24 motifs from the Olary region, South Australia. *Rock Art Research* 5: 108–46.

RIP, M. R. 1989. Colour space transformations for the enhancement of rock art images by computer. *Rock Art Research* 6: 12–16.

THORN, A. 1993. Dating intervention. *Rock Art Research* 10: 126–31.

WATCHMAN, A. 1993. The use of laser technology in rock art dating. *The Artefact* 16: 39–45.

WATCHMAN, A. 1995. Recent petroglyphs, Foz Côa, Portugal. *Rock Art Research* 12: 104–8.

WATCHMAN, A. 2000. Micro-excavation and laser extraction methods for dating carbon in silica skins and oxalate crusts. In G. K. Ward and C. Tuniz (eds), *Advances in dating Australian rock-markings*, pp. 35–39. Occasional AURA Publication 10, Australian Rock Art Research Association, Inc., Melbourne.

10. PORTABLE PALAEOART

INTRODUCTION

Portable palaeoart, obviously, is not rock art, and it could well be argued that it should not be included for consideration in this book. However, most academic practitioners will agree that the separation of the two forms of evidence is arbitrary, counterproductive, not in keeping with indigenous views, and likely to impede the flow of information. While it is true that a number of technological and methodological issues are not shared by rock art and other palaeoart, on the balance of all relevant considerations it is certainly appropriate that portable material be discussed here, however briefly.

Essentially, 'palaeoart' is the collective term describing all art-like manifestations of the distant past. This definition does not stipulate what time periods should be included (e.g. it does not resort to the inappropriate term 'prehistoric'), nor is it concerned with the irrelevant but often heard question, 'is it art?' Unless the questioner offers a scientific (i.e. testable and refutable) definition of 'art' that question is superfluous. Palaeoart is what it is: all physical evidence considered to refer to non-utilitarian practices of humans in the distant past. Perhaps a more precise definition of palaeoart is that it consists of materials whose non-utilitarian aspects are thought to significantly exceed the utilitarian ones. After all, most artefacts thought of as utilitarian (knives, arrow shafts, laurel leaf points ...) in fact also convey a great deal of non-utilitarian information, related for instance to design, fashion, group affiliation or status. So there is no hard and fast separation of utilitarian and non-utilitarian objects, nor do either of them necessarily have to be artefacts. Portable palaeoart certainly includes manuports (e.g. naturally perforated objects worn as beads, quartz crystals used by a sorcerer), which may bear no traces of human modification, but may have had a symbolic, communicative or emblemic function, for instance. Finally, use is always inferred in such ancient remains, never demonstrated.

It is estimated that most surviving palaeoart, certainly over 90% of it, consists of rock art. The much smaller component, portable palaeoart, is made up of a diversity of materials, whose key determining feature it is that they are small enough to be carried around easily by humans, and which in many cases can be worn on the human body in some fashion. Included in this are beads and pendants, as well as other 'decorative' objects; mnemonic devices (such as 'message sticks'), portable engravings and figurines, plaques, objects bearing series of notches or lines, and ceremonial objects (e.g. in Australia *tjuringas* and cylcons); and manuports such as crystal prisms, fossil casts, unusually coloured or shaped stones and used mineral pigment pieces.

One aspect many of these classes of objects share with rock art is their susceptibility to misidentification by archaeologists. In the majority of such published cases, natural objects bearing no evidence of anthropic modification or use have been pronounced to be art objects, but there are also many cases on record of authentic palaeoart objects that were claimed to be natural phenomena. A study of the reasons for such misidentifications reveals significant differences between these two basic types. While the former, the pronouncement of natural markings or objects as artificial, is most common in non-Western countries, the latter, typical in some Western countries, often seems inspired by the perceived need to explain away evidence that seems to contradict faddish interpretations in archaeology. Some examples are cited below. In an analytical sense it is important to note the considerable similarities between these epistemological issues and those in misidentification of rock art. Indeed, in some cases the problems involved are identical — for instance when animal scratches on a cave wall have exfoliated in small pieces and their markings are claimed to be human handiwork (Bednarik 1998a).

MANUPORTS AND VERY EARLY PALAEOART

Manuports are unmodified objects transported and deposited by hominins, and they are distinguished by being of a usually striking material clearly foreign to the sediment containing the occupation deposit they occur in. Indeed, there is one singular instance of a manuport suggested to have been deposited by a pre-human, the Makapansgat cobble (Bednarik 1998b). Although the involvement of an australopithecine has been favoured in the past, that of a very early and as yet unknown hominin cannot be excluded. The age of its sediment, the level 3 pink stony bone breccia (Partridge's Member 4; cf. Oakley 1981: 205), is between two and three million years, and closer to the higher figure (McFadden et al. 1979). While this is beyond the widely accepted chronological range of Homo, the discovery of *Kenyanthropus platyops* offers an alternative attribution of the cobble. The former dolerite cave of Makapansgat, South Africa, contained substantial deposits of australopithecine-bearing breccia, and it was among these remains that a jasperite cobble was excavated in 1925, which had been carried to the site over a distance of at least several kilometres. The red-coloured cobble bears such striking markings that archaeologists have suggested they might have been made, or at least emphasised, artificially (Figure 61). Yet for 72 years it was never subjected to analysis, until detailed microscopic analysis established that its various markings are all entirely natural (Bednarik 1998b, 1999a). Nevertheless, it was carried into the cave either by *Australopithecus africanus*, or by an as yet unknown hominin. Almost certainly this was because of its conspicuous colour, shape and markings — most especially the 'staring eyes motif' formed by two equal-sized, symmetrically located depressions iconographically related to a mouth-like marking.

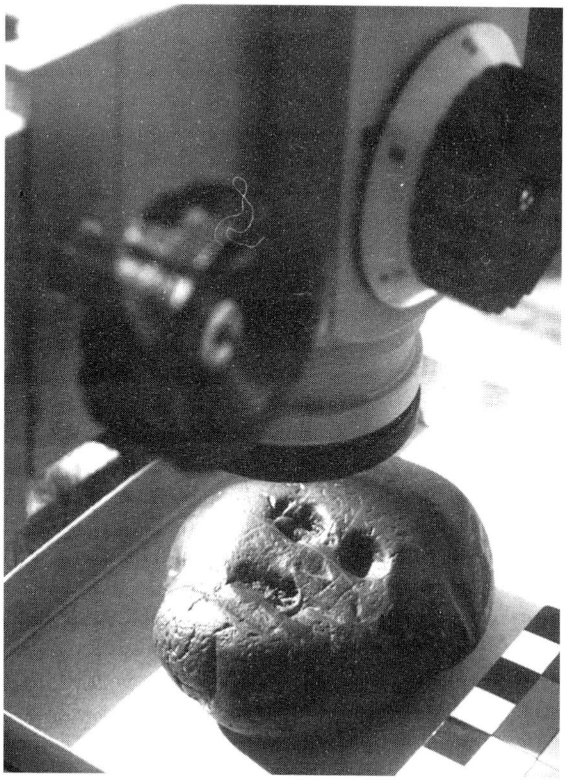

Figure 61. The Makapansgat jasperite manuport, South Africa. Although not a hominin product, it can be regarded as the oldest known palaeoart object.

While this find does not necessarily imply iconographic comprehension (the 'staring eyes' motif can be detected even by birds and insects) it does demonstrate that such an object has attracted sufficient curiosity to have been carried around for some time. This manuport qualifies as palaeoart in the sense that it conveyed non-inherent properties to its collectors that were imposed by neural processes and involved an incipient form of consciousness.

The Makapansgat cobble is the oldest known object of this kind in the world, and for more than one half of the duration of human history it remains alone on our extremely fragmentary archaeological record. Perhaps a million years BP *Homo erectus* took to the sea, no doubt progressively venturing out further and further, until by about 850 ka ago he managed to cross several stretches of sea to colonise first the Indonesian island of Flores, and subsequently Timor (Bednarik 1999b; Bednarik and Kuckenburg 1999). This point in time seems significant, because it is also between 800 and 900 ka ago that the first use of pigment becomes detectable (in South Africa and perhaps India), and around the same time the practice of collecting crystal prisms seems to begin (Bednarik 1994a).

These two activities are of great significance. Pigment is of little practical use other than for colouring (be it rock surfaces, artefacts or human skin), and it is therefore used for largely non-utilitarian and cultural purposes. The oldest apparent evidence we have of rock art does not, in fact, consist of rock art, but of a haematite crayon excavated at the Lower Acheulian occupation site of Hunsgi, India (Bednarik 1990a). At one end the pebble bears a facet made when it was repeatedly rubbed hard against a coarse granular rock surface. We cannot possibly know what kind of marking was produced; perhaps it was no more complex than the doodles chimpanzees create when encouraged by primatologists. But we do know from this indirect evidence that coloured rock markings were produced at the time. More recently, in the Upper Acheulian and through the Middle Palaeolithic, ochre or haematite use becomes more evident (Bednarik 1992a) and there are numerous finds of such materials from occupation sites in Africa, Europe, Asia and, finally, Australia. Obviously this kind of evidence is of great relevance to the rock art scientist, even if it does not consist of rock art, and although the actual use of the pigment can in most cases not be established.

Crystals and other 'unusual' natural objects are of interest because they indicate that the hominins collecting and 'curating' them had acquired the faculty of distinguishing between 'ordinary' objects and 'exotic' objects. They had begun to 'consciously' create taxonomies, using a dualist or binary system to do so initially. The neural structures supporting such concept-building made their imposition on an 'orderless' reality possible, creating 'consciousness' (Bednarik 1990b). They led to humanly perceptible externalisations of such mental formulations and their imposition on physical reality. This, in a nutshell, is how what we might call 'art' began. The earliest such perceptible externalisations we have found so far are the engravings from the Lower Palaeolithic period (Bednarik 2003a).

PORTABLE ENGRAVINGS

The earliest known engravings on portable objects of bone, ivory and stone occur in the Lower Palaeolithic, but just as rock art of this period, they are rare finds. They include five engraved bone fragments (Figure 62) from the Holstein interglacial, >250 000 BP, at Bilzingsleben, Germany (Mania and Mania 1988), as well as a quartzite slab with arcuate engraving from the same site (Bednarik 1995a); a scoria pebble with several deep, apparently anthropic grooves that underline the object's shape of a female figure, Acheulian, >230 000 years, Berekhat Ram, Israel (Goren-Inbar 1986; Goren-Inbar and Peltz 1995; d'Errico and Nowell 2000); a human figurine of quartzitic sandstone, also of the Acheulian, 300 000 to 500 000 years old, Tan Tan, Morocco (Bednarik 2003b); the grid pattern engraved on a Fauresmith grindstone Laidler (1933) found at the Blind River mouth in South Africa; two banded ironstone slabs bearing engraved sub-parallel lines of the Middle Pleistocene from Wonderwork Cave, also in South Africa (Imbrie et al. 1984); and a fragment of bone, probably of a horse, bearing ten cuts along its edge, from the Upper Acheulian of Sainte Anne I, at Polignac, Haute-Loire, France (Raynal and Séguy 1986; cf. Crémades 1996.).

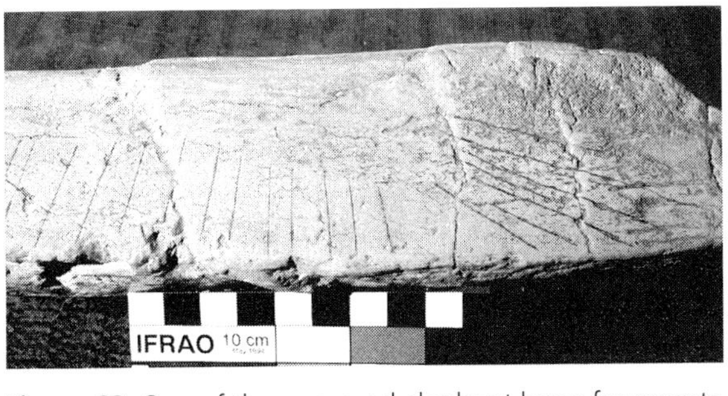

Figure 62. One of the engraved elephant bone fragments from Bilzingsleben, Germany, >250 000 years old.

The subsequent Middle Palaeolithic period (Middle Stone Age in sub-Saharan Africa) has yielded a considerably greater number of such finds. Bone fragments bearing engravings or serrations cut by stone tools are common, such as those from Schulen, Belgium (Huyge 1990); Bacho Kiro, Bulgaria (Marshack 1976); La Quina, France (Martin 1907-10; Marshack 1991); La Ferrassie, France (Capitan and Peyrony 1921; Marshack 1976); Tagliente shelter, Italy (Leonardi 1988); Cueva Morín, Spain (Freeman and Gonzalez Echegaray 1983); Taubach near Weimar, Germany (Kuckenburg 1997); Wyhlen near Lörrach, Germany (Kuckenburg 1996: 141, 1997); three engraved bone fragments from Oldisleben, also Germany (Bednarik 2003a); Abri Suard, Le Chaise-de-Vouthon, Charente, France (Duport 1960; Debénath and Duport 1971; Crémades 1996); Petit Puymoyen and Montgaudier (Débenath and Duport 1971; Crémades 1996); Peyrere 1 Cave, also called Noisetier Cave, near Arreau, Aure valley, France (d'Errico and Allard 1997); Prolom 2, Crimean Peninsula (Stepanchuk 1993); Kebara Cave, Israel (Davis 1974); Klasies River Mouth, South Africa (Singer and Wymer 1982); Border Cave, Swaziland (Beaumont et al. 1978); and Apollo 11 Cave, Namibia (Wendt 1974). Similar engravings of the Middle Stone Age are known from three ostrich eggshell fragments in Dieplkloof Cave, South Africa. A notched fragment of antler comes from Grotte Vaufrey, France (Vincent 1988), and the Micoquian of Prolom 2 in Ukraine yielded an engraved horse canine (Stepanchuk 1993) (Figure 63).

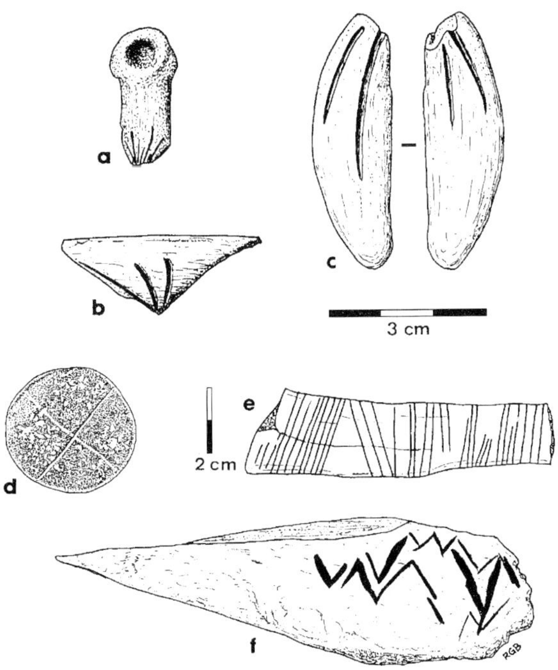

Figure 63. Some Middle Palaeolithic engravings from Europe: (a, b) engraved bones from Prolom 2, Ukraine; (c) engraved horse tooth, also Prolom 2; (d) engraved fossil nummulite from Tata, Hungary; (e) engraved bone, La Ferrassie, France; (f) engraved bone fragment from Bacho Kiro, Bulgaria.

Middle Palaeolithic engravings are also known from several stone objects, including stone tools: from Temnata Cave near Karlukovo, Bulgaria (Crémades et al. 1995); Grotta dell'Alto, Italy (Leonardi 1988); Tagliente and Solinas shelters (Leonardi 1988); Tata, Hungary (Bednarik 1995a); Quneitra, Israel (Goren-Inbar 1990; Marshack 1996); Qafzeh Cave, Israel (Hovers et al. 1997); and two haematite pieces from the MSA of Blombos Cave, South Africa, bearing geometric engravings (Henshilwood et al. 2002). With so many pre-Upper Palaeolithic engravings now known, it is possible to formulate the first generalising propositions about early art systems (Bednarik 1984, 1990c; Hodgson 2000), and it is salient that these differ most significantly from the dominant models traditional archaeology has produced over the past century or more. Combined with the careful application of taphonomic logic (see Ch. 8), these revisionary theories promise to review the history of human cognitive evolution. It is important to appreciate that, in addressing entrenched misconceptions about the human past — which certainly exist widely in orthodox archaeology — palaeoart science needs to be radical and persistent (Bednarik 1999c). The evidence provided by palaeoart clearly refutes the most widely held views about art origins, and this needs to be pursued effectively.

ABOUT BEADS AND PENDANTS

Nowhere is this more transparent than with Pleistocene beads and pendants, which can tell us a great deal about both the technology and the culture of their makers and users. Technologically they illustrate not only the ability to drill through brittle or very hard materials, but also they imply the use of cordage. The very essence of a bead or pendant is to be threaded onto a string, in antiquity it would simply have been pointless to perforate a small object for a purpose other than to pass a string though it. However, the use of cordage also suggests the use of knots, because a string needs to be closed to form a loop to be effective. Although the ends of a string may be joined by means other than a knot, e.g. by the use of adhesive or by plaiting, these alternative means are either impracticable or they are technologically even more complex than the use of knotting (Warner and Bednarik 1996). The diachronic availability of Pleistocene remains of cordage (Leroi-Gourhan 1982; Nadel et al. 1994; Pringle 1997) is of no relevance to the issue, because that class of material evidence obviously possesses an exceptionally high taphonomic lag time (Bednarik 1994b). Therefore, what beads tell us about the technology of the people who used them is well in excess of deductions concerning their manufacture.

Of more importance are the cultural and cognitive deductions beads make possible. They can be used in a number of ways or for several purposes; they provide various forms of information about the wearer and his or her status in society. Availability for marriage, political status, state of mourning might be such possible symbolic meanings. To explain beads simply as body adornment is almost certainly an over-simplification. Even if vanity were the motivation for wearing such items, stating this explains not why they are perceived as 'decorative'. The concept itself is anthropocentric, we do not assume that other animals perceive the information imparted by the beads as meaningful. In human culture, however, various forms or levels of meaning may be encoded in such objects, as well as in other kinds of body adornment (tattoos, body painting, cicatrices, infibulations, anklets, armbands etc.). In ethnography, beads sewn onto apparel or worn on necklaces may signify complex social, economic, ethnic, ideological, religious or emblemic meanings, all of which are only accessible to a participant of the culture in question. To name just one example: beads or pendants may function as charms, they may be a means of protection against evil spells or spirits.

While none of this information is archaeologically recoverable, all of it refers to a level of cultural sophistication most archaeologists would not currently be prepared to concede to humans prior to about 35 000 years ago. And yet, hundreds of such Lower and Middle Palaeolithic objects are reported in the literature, although there is often no reliable evidence that the perforation is anthropic. Some materials can be perforated by natural processes. For instance, bones can be chewed through by animal canines or partially digested by stomach acids, while mollusc shells are commonly perforated by parasitic organisms. But while it is preferable to rely only on specimens bearing clear evidence of human work or use when dealing with a period from which bead use has not as yet been conclusively demonstrated, it is to be emphasised that the perforation of a bead or pendant certainly does not need to be man-made, as d'Errico and Villa (1997) erroneously assume. Naturally perforated objects are commonly used in ethnographic specimens (as are perishable materials) and it seems likely that such natural beads were also used in the past. Indeed, the earliest beads ever used quite possibly had natural perforations.

Small perforated objects of the Pleistocene may have been beads or pendants, or they could have been quanging tools, pulling handles or buckles as reported ethnographically (Boas 1888: Figs 15, 17, 121d; Kroeber 1900: Fig. 8; Nelson 1899: Pl. 17). However, most of the utilitarian objects of this type are not only of a quite typical shape or design, they exhibit specific wear traces and material properties. Small circular objects with central perforation are considered to be beads, especially when they occur repeatedly. Similarly, objects such as animal teeth, perforated near one end (near the root), are not thought to be pulling handles, nor are objects that are too fragile to function as such utilitarian equipment (e.g. ostrich eggshell beads). Evidence that a bead was drilled with a stone tool includes a distinctive bi-conical and 'machined' section and sometimes rotation striae. The wear of pendants can often be observed on archaeological specimens, including those made of stone (Bednarik 1997b), and is also quite typical.

The earliest mention of possible beads of the Lower Palaeolithic relates to the first Palaeolithic tools ever reported, from the very type site of the Acheulian. In the famous paper by Prestwich (1859), in which he recognised the authenticity of the St. Acheul stone tools Jacques Boucher de Perthes had been collecting for many years, the occurrence of possible beads of a fossilised sponge (*Coscinopora globularis*) is noted. In some of them the hole seems 'to have been enlarged and completed' (Prestwich 1859: 52). Smith (1894: 272–76) has reported about 200 specimens of the very same species from another Acheulian site, Bedford in England. Keeley (1980: 164), with his splendid experience in the microscopic examination of very early material, thinks that 'there is no doubt that some of these fossils show artificial enlargement of their natural orifices'. When I examined several hundred of these objects, from both French and English sites, I found that they were actually of a different species than previously claimed, *Porosphaera globularis* Phillips 1829. But I also found that many of them had not only been modified, many also featured extensive wear that showed conclusively that they had been threaded onto strings and worn for considerable periods of time. Some bore deep conical wear rims around their openings, and there can be no doubt that they were used as beads (Figure 64).

Circular, discoid fossil casts have been found at another Acheulian site, Gesher Benot Ya'aqov, Israel. They are crinoid columnar segments of *Millericrinus* sp. but there is no evidence of modification or use (Goren-Inbar et al. 1991). Finally, a series of disc beads laboriously made from ostrich eggshell has been excavated and dated to about 200 000 years BP at yet another Acheulian site, El Greifa E near Ubari, Libya (Bednarik 1997a).

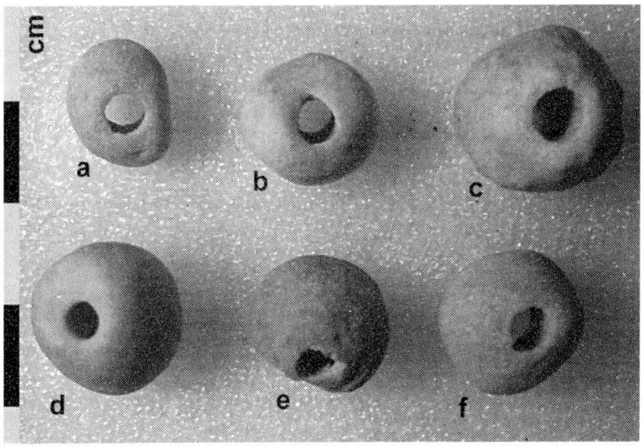

Figure 64. Six of the Acheulian beads made from *Porosphaera globularis* fossils found at Bedford, England.

Initially only three specimens were recovered, but more have been found since. Some of the earliest objects with indisputably human-made perforations we know of are the two perforated pendants from the Repolust Cave in Styria, Austria. One is a wolf incisor, very expertly drilled near its root (Figure 65), the second is a flaked bone point, roughly triangular and perforated near one corner (Mottl 1951; Bednarik 1997a, 2001a). They were excavated with undated Lower Palaeolithic remains thought to be around 300 000 years old.

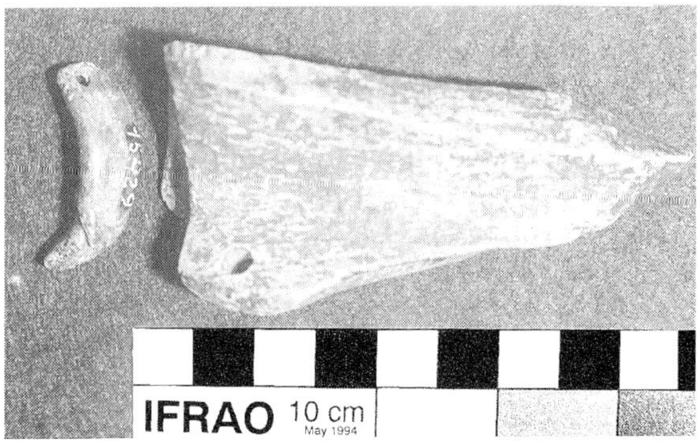

Figure 65. Perforated wolf's canine and bone fragment, Repolust Cave, Austria.

In replicating the three Acheulian beads initially excavated in Libya it was found that their consistency in size and the near-perfect rounding of all preserved edges, internal and external, suggests the use of a standardised manufacturing process (Bednarik 1997a). Their roundness can be obtained only by constant checking of the shape during the final abrading process, using not just a developed sense of symmetry, but possessing a clear concept of a geometric form. It is the outcome of a distinctive abstract construct of form — a concept-mediated, geometrically perfect product (Figure 66).

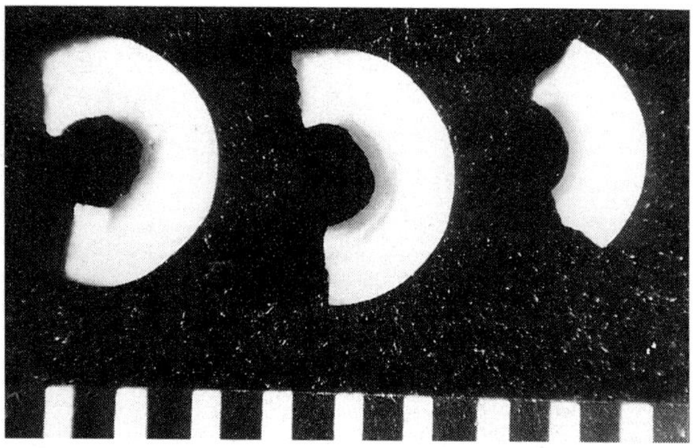

Figure 66. Three replicative fragments of ostrich eggshell beads, Acheulian, showing the perfection of these artefacts.

Moreover, it is the result of a determined effort to produce best-quality work, and to make the beads as small as practicable. The most parsimonious explanation for both the size and the form of these objects is that these characteristics reflect a developed abstract value system and a *concept of perfection*, and thus a considerable social complexity in the society that made and used these objects. It seems impossible to account for the empirical characteristics of the evidence without assuming a cultural impetus placing value and meaning on such perfect forms, and on an utmost standard of craftsmanship. In this way we can extract much information from some types of palaeoart finds, leading to the formulation of reasonable propositions about the cognitive, cultural and social capabilities of the hominins concerned. This information has a direct bearing on what we can deduce from the earliest forms of rock art we have managed to recover, from two Indian sites (Bednarik 2001b, 2003a).

FIGURINES AND PLAQUES

While palaeoart of the Lower and Middle Palaeolithic is limited to beads, pendants, pigment, certain types of manuports and a number of relatively simple engraved marks on various types of materials, fully made figurines and more complex marked plaques only appear about 35 000 to 30 000 years ago. The above finds from Makapansgat and Berekhat Ram are not sculptures, even though in both cases some appreciation of iconic features may reasonably be inferred. In the case of the Tan Tan figurine, however, the term proto-sculpture seems justified, even though its maker still began with a natural form. From time to time it is proposed that a series of modified stone objects from western Europe, usually of flint, exhibits iconic features, but these interpretations have not been accepted by archaeology. If iconic sculptures were made prior to the Upper Palaeolithic, no persuasive examples of them have been presented so far.

The possibly earliest known fully sculpted iconic figurine may be the presumed bear head from Tolbaga, Siberia, if the proposed dating of about 34 800 BP were correct (Bednarik 1994a). The most notable series of early sculptures comes from a number of very early Upper Palaeolithic sites in central Europe. They are the Galgenberg female figurine of serpentine, from Austria (Bednarik 1989) (Figure 67), and finds from three German sites: the ivory therianthrope from the Stadel at Hohler Stein (Schmid 1989), a small anthropomorphous relief carving from Geißenklösterle, and several animal figurines from Vogelherd (Riek 1934, 1960). These early sculptures are iconographically sophisticated and full of expression, implying a preceding tradition of which we lack any such finds (Marshack 1985). They are followed by various Upper Palaeolithic traditions of producing anthropomorphous and zoomorphic figurines of stone, burnt clay, ivory and bone — materials capable of surviving in adequate numbers to render the tradition archaeologically visible. The geographical distribution of these materials encompasses especially south-western, central and eastern Europe, central Siberia and the Levant.

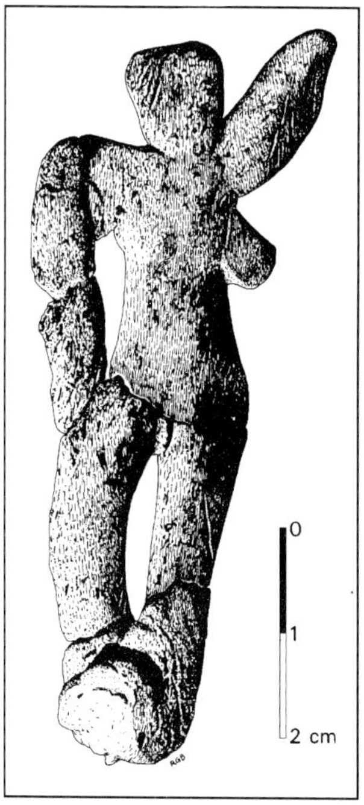

Figure 67. Serpentine figurine of the early Aurignacian, c. 31 790 BP, Galgenberg, Austria.

The most frequently discussed figurines of pre-History are the so-called 'Venus' figurines of the

Eurasian Upper Palaeolithic. They have been subjected to an unparalleled attention of interpretational fervour, characterised by several common features: the interpretations are often ideologically motivated, they are taphonomically naive, they are presented by inadequately informed commentators who often had not studied any of the evidence or sites first hand, and their epistemology is often inadequate. The underlying idea of all of these hypotheses is that there is a corpus of some 100 to 140 female figurines, whose distribution from the Pyrenees to Lake Baikal indicates a Gravettian tradition concerned with fertility, or with a mother goddess cult, with Palaeolithic pornography or whatever other imagined cultural activity. None of these studies attempts to define the sample spatially or temporally, by stating a rationale for including or excluding specimens. All omit numerous known examples that would fall well within the stated or implied parameters of such studies. Most of the figurines in question exhibit no clear evidence of female attributes, they are not corpulent or large-breasted as frequently claimed (most have no breasts, and one male figurine also has small breasts), some appear to be fully clothed, very few might be pregnant, and fewer still could reasonably be classified as steatopygous. Most of these specimens are either undated, or they are not from a Gravettian context. Indeed, these anthropomorphous figurines originate from all periods of the Upper Palaeolithic, and some of them may be as yet undetected fakes (e.g. from Brassempouy; Bahn 1993).

To analyse an arbitrarily selected, chronologically and formally undefined, incomplete sample such as this collection is not a scientifically promising procedure. Apart from usually a priori assumptions about meaning, it is not even clear what the sample is intended to be representative of (Bednarik 1996). The sample has been defined largely on the basis of ideological, cultural and academic conditioning of how to detect the visual clues of an alien culture, and by arbitrary (and invalid) variables of spatial and chronological distribution. Consequently the sample will include specimens that are 20 000 years and 6000 km apart, but it will exclude those from the very same site and only a few millennia younger (of the Holocene). It will exclude other forms of female depiction of the same period, and it will perceive differences in iconography as culturally conditioned, when in fact they are more likely the outcome of technological factors (Bednarik 1990d).

The analysis of a sample should not be accepted if the sample was defined by excluding those specimens that would contradict a desired finding. Hence we need to start by defining a sample without anticipating what we are going to find. Since such a definition of sample cannot be free of theory, we would do well to abandon all ideological baggage. This has not been done in the study of the figurines colloquially known as 'Venuses'. Consequently the extensive interpretive literature on the supposedly female figurines of the Eurasian Upper Palaeolithic, with its references to fecundity and so forth, consists largely of androcentric, gynocentric, heterocentric, feminist-inspired and Eurocentric polemic. This deservedly harsh judgment does not extend to purely descriptive and ideology-free works on this material, which are rare and receive much less attention (e.g. Rosenfeld 1977; Russell 2006; Gvozdover 1997). The figurines in question are of greatly differing formal attributes, antiquities, cultural affiliations, geographic provenience and materials. Almost certainly they do not represent a homogeneous tradition, but have been lumped together by scholars seeking confirmation of preconceived explanations (Figure 68).

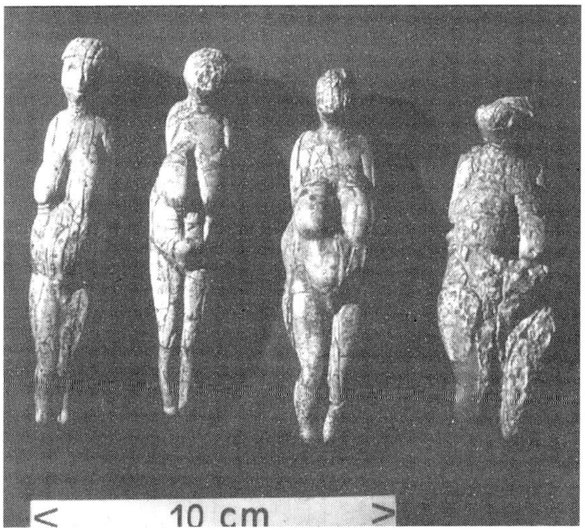

Figure 68. Some of the many Russian female figurines of the Upper Palaeolithic. These specimens are, from left, Avdeevo Nos 7, 8, 6, 9.

While three-dimensional iconographic art of the Upper Palaeolithic is widely found in Eurasia, the distribution of two-dimensional iconic palaeoart differs significantly. East of Germany and Italy, across all of Eurasia, Pleistocene graphic art is almost exclusively noniconic, be it portable or on rock. There are only a few exceptions (Bednarik 1995b). No explanation is available for this glaring distributional discrepancy, nor has it even attracted interest. The graphic Pleistocene art of most of Eurasia consists of 'geometric' designs that are often of great complexity, especially at Russian sites. Most of this palaeoart is found on plaques of stone, bone and ivory. The thousands of engraved Upper Palaeolithic plaques of western Europe, by contrast, feature a rich array of iconic markings, at such sites as Rochedane, Mas d'Azil, La Marche, Gönnersdorf and Parpalló.

Engraved plaques and similar portable objects of the Pleistocene are not, however, restricted to Eurasia. While their number elsewhere is considerably smaller (Bednarik 1994a), this is at least to some degree a predictable outcome of uneven research efforts and of research biases. The point is illustrated by the remarkable concentrations of Palaeolithic palaeoart objects in the two regions that have experienced the most sustained research efforts in all of Asia, the area around Irkutsk and the Levant. Elsewhere on this huge continent, such early art objects are exceedingly rare (Bednarik 1994a). Art traditions no doubt existed, but almost none of the surviving evidence has so far been located (consider China, where only one engraved Palaeolithic object has been found; Bednarik 1992b).

Australia, with its particularly rich heritage of Pleistocene rock art, has a notable absence of portable art objects of that period. The few published exceptions of early stone plaques, from Devil's Lair and Koonalda Cave, have been rejected after specialist analysis (see below). The mysterious 'cylcons', cylindrical-conical stone objects from eastern inland Australia, often bear engravings, and they may well be of the Pleistocene. However, no attention has been given to that issue so far.

FAKES AND MISIDENTIFICATIONS

A problem with the corpus of 'Pleistocene art', especially portable objects, is the existence of fakes. They occur also in rock art, but in mobiliary art they seem to be more common and harder to detect. Generally, fakes in archaeology can be divided into two basic types. The first are those made for economic gain. They are purported to be from many different periods and cultures, but rarely from the Pleistocene. In some parts of the world, these commercial fakes support whole local industries. Interestingly, in certain other regions no archaeological fakes at all seem to exist (e.g. in Australia).

The second type of fake is much more likely to be of purported Pleistocene antiquity. It is often not made for material gain, but merely to deceive. The motivation may be complex, and it appears relevant that such fakes seem to be limited entirely to Europe and North America. The majority of them concern portable art objects. It would be fascinating to explore the reasons why people in these two regions have such a penchant for providing false evidence from this particular period, an issue I have already tried to address analytically. It seems to be linked to factors such as archaeological value judgments and the mechanisms of authenticating religious shrines (Bednarik 1999c). One might argue that such cases are common in south-western Europe because the palaeoart is also common there, but this is easily falsified. Pleistocene portable palaeoart is just as prominent in Russia and Siberia, yet not a single fake has ever been reported from that art region. On the other hand, Pleistocene art is almost entirely lacking in North America, yet a number of fakes or suspected fakes are known there. Hence there is no reason to assume that there is an inherent geographical correlation between fakes and find regions. The existence of fake Palaeolithic art is best explained in cultural and social terms. It seems to be related to the academic predisposition, in the same regions, of attributing Pleistocene antiquity to recent art corpora.

Many fakes have been recognised over the years in palaeoart, ranging from hundreds of Azilian painted cobbles to engraved plaques and to figurines carved from genuine mammoth ivory (for some examples see Bahn 1984, 1990, 1993; Bednarik 1998a). The probable existence of further fakes in Palaeolithic art continues to be a significant problem, because still undetected fakes would presumably be central in the perceived stylistic spectrum of this art. For a fake to be successful, the perpetrator must share with the authenticator certain perceptions of what constitutes the essence of Palaeolithic art. This means, in practical terms, that if there are still fakes among Palaeolithic art, they are likely to distort perceptions of what constitutes Palaeolithic style in favour of already shared biases, and so are likely to amplify these. This illustrates how precarious an understanding of 'Palaeolithicity' as a stylistic property really is.

While fake palaeoart objects are a phenomenon specifically of a few world regions, misidentifications of mobiliary art have been much more widespread. In Asia, for example, fakes are virtually unknown, but there are hundreds of known erroneous claims in that continent alone. For instance, in China I have had to reject every one of the c. 600 'engraved' bone fragments from the wenhua Shiyu site, after a microscopic examination revealed that all these objects bore surface markings derived from four different natural causes (see below). Detailed iconographic interpretations of some of the markings had been published, such as the markings on a horse humerus fragment supposedly showing two separate hunting scenes (You 1984). In India I travelled widely to see all forty-six known 'engraved' ostrich eggshell fragments of the Palaeolithic, only to find that forty-five of them bear natural markings, while only one was actually engraved by human hand. My study of sometimes heavily marked ivory objects from Siberia produced similar results, and eventually led to understanding the natural process that produced the mysterious markings Marshack had first described from ancient bone surfaces in Spain. When he examined some of the claimed Mousterian engravings of Cueva Morín microscopically, Marshack (1991: 54) was 'astonished' to find that narrow grooves 'dipped below the surface of the bone and then reappeared on the surface some millimetres ahead'. Similar markings are quite common on materials consisting primarily of calcium carbonate and calcium phosphate, such as ivory, bone, antler, ostrich eggshell, and even on marl or limestone. After becoming aware of this, I focused on Bronze Age mammoth ivory objects from Irkutsk and observed that their heavy marking was the result of mycorrhizal action (Bednarik 1992c). Numerous plant species have symbiotic associations of the mycelium of a fungus with their roots, which often extend to bacteria in the root systems of plants. The respiratory carbon dioxide of these micro-organisms reacts with moisture and dissolves carbonate locally (ivory is a dense form of dentine, which consists largely of $CaCO_3$). Thus these grooves effectively trace the course of former tiny plant rootlets of specific species that are particularly effective in forming them. This is readily observable on the large ivory objects I examined, whereas the many objects that had been misidentified by archaeologists were usually tiny fragments on which the markings are perhaps more difficult to explain. However, a careful microscopic study can always clarify the status of such markings.

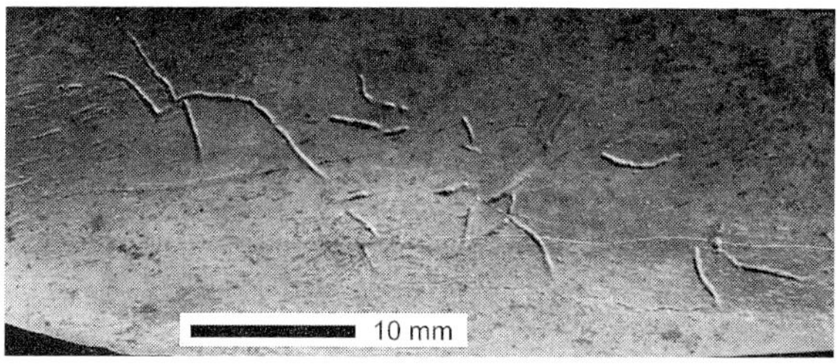

Figure 69. Natural markings on a horse humerus fragment that have been interpreted as depicting two hunting scenes; Shiyu, China, c. 28 135 BP.

Fossil, collagen-free bone consists largely of calcium phosphate and calcium carbonate, and it is therefore susceptible to the process just described. The previously mentioned numerous 'engraved' bone objects from the Shiyu site bear a rich body of surface markings (Figure 69). They are from the transition of Middle to Upper Palaeolithic industries and roughly 30 000 years old (Bednarik and You 1991). In this large collection of marked bone fragments mycorrhyzal marks represent only a small proportion of the repertoire. Nearly all specimens bear abrasion marks, which are typically short and broad, consisting of numerous parallel striae, and are most numerous on prominent surface aspects. Occasionally there are gouge marks indicating taphonomic damage by stone points pressed against the bone surfaces. Finally, there are linear incision marks, randomly orientated, sometimes with a hooked end or *stries parasites* present near one of the ends. No instances were observed of intentionally engraved lines, on the hundreds of specimens. Since the site's sediment is rich in stone implements, many of the incisions were quite probably caused taphonomically by the points of chert flakes.

In Australia, the six 'engraved plaques' from Devil's Lair provide an example of yet another form of archaeological misidentification. Excavated in the mid-1970s, this series of marked pieces of soft aeolian limestone or marl has since been described numerous times as bearing noniconic Pleistocene engravings, together with a perforated object described as a stone pendant (Dortch 1976, 1984). However, doubts were expressed and to resolve the controversy the Museum of Western Australia asked me in 1997 to conduct a detailed study of the objects (Bednarik 1998a). I noted that the perforation in the pendant was fully natural, contrary to what archaeologists had reported. Despite this setback I was able to demonstrate that the object had indeed been used as a pendant. In examining such pieces for use or wear traces one focuses on the inside of their perforation, on the surface opposite the object's centre of gravity. In precisely that location I detected four distinctive grooves that indicated that the pendant had been supported and worn on a string, and I was even able to estimate the approximate diameter of that string (Bednarik 1997b).

However, none of the six marked limestone pieces, two of which had been published as engraved plaques, were found to bear any intentional anthropic marks. The limestone fragments from Devil's Lair exhibit a variety of taphonomic markings which present an initially confusing picture to the observer, but which can be untangled and analysed through detailed observation in combination with various replication experiments. Not a single marking on these objects can be attributed to a stone tool, and there is a complete lack of diagnostic characteristics of stone tool incisions, including longitudinal striations, *stries parasites*, *sillons rectilignes* and others (see e.g. d'Errico 1994; Bednarik 1992d, 1994c, 1995c, 1997c). Among the many hundreds of macroscopic and microscopic markings on the Devil's Lair objects are kinetic markings caused by quartz sand grains or projections from other stones, minute solution pits and animal scratches of various species. Numerically they are dominated by the traces of various types of modern damage. This includes innumerable faint lines caused when the objects were cleaned with nylon toothbrushes. Many microscopic bristle fragments and shavings were found still attached to the surface. Visually the animal claw marks dominate, and those of two species of very different body sizes occur. One is about the size of a Tasmanian devil, the other about the size of a small mouse (Bednarik 1998a).

TECHNOLOGICAL ANALYSES

The above consideration of the frequency of misidentifications is perhaps one of the principal concerns in analytical work on portable palaeoart, although certainly not the only impetus for such studies. The authentication of portable objects or the markings they bear is a specialist task, much in the same way as this applies to the discrimination of doubtful rock markings (see Ch. 3). Nevertheless, it will be useful to illustrate some basic principles here. To continue with the last example, the various types of markings found on six limestone pieces from an Australian Late Pleistocene deposit: how can the analyst determine that an incised line was not made with a chert point, but with an animal claw? How does one discriminate between different types of linear markings on soft rock?

Animal claw marks are among the most common rock markings in the world, being about as common as glacial striae. To recognise individual animal marks requires considerable experience, because their morphologies differ greatly according to the species' climbing ability and method, 'speleo-behaviour', mobility, relative length of extremities, shape of claws or talons and their mechanics of application, and according to the shape of the claw points. The latter, for instance, can vary according to local conditions, the specimen's age, and so forth. Moreover, great variations can be caused by the lithology or state of the support rock (by relative hardness, moisture content, relative air humidity etc.), and most particularly by modification processes (weathering, including speleo-weathering, the deposition of speleothems, and the deforming action of some precipitates, notably certain types of carbonate deposits). It is therefore necessary to appreciate that there are no simple, ready-made rules for discriminating between animal scratch marks and other, similar rock marks. Rather, this is a process of elimination in which many factors need to be taken into account, and in which alternatives have to be discounted systematically.

The empirical basis of this discrimination process consists of two bodies of evidence: the study of markings that can securely be attributed to particular animal species (Bednarik 1993a), and the study of 'experimental' animal markings. The latter have involved a number of species, and in Australia especially possums (*Trichosurus vulpecula*). In that continent, four broad categories of animal scratch marks on rock surfaces have been distinguished (Bednarik 1991). Large accumulations of claw marks are usually much easier to identify than isolated or single marks. One of the distinguishing characteristics refers to the relative positions of multiple marks constituting a 'set', and the relative course of individual grooves of a multi-pronged instrument such as an animal paw. Small rock fragments may only bear one or two grooves of a set (having either exfoliated from a wall, or been marked within the sediment), which renders discrimination more difficult than on a cave wall. Other variables to be consulted include longitudinal striations frequently present in lines engraved with stone tools (animal scratches typically bear no striations); claw points are always rounded and comparatively symmetrical, stone points are rarely so; in cross-section, a claw-caused groove is rather U-shaped, with the side walls steep, and *stries parasites* are never present; and morphologically, claw marks are frequently of 'cuneiform' appearance, i.e. with one end deeper and abrupt, and the other shallow and 'fading'. This applies especially to short marks, and where such a mark is well preserved, the deeper and wider end can provide a fairly good impression of the shape of the claw point. An important source of relevant information is replicative experimentation with a number of potential materials (Bednarik 1987). Stone tool marks have been identified on the walls of about a dozen Australian limestone caves and they have been subjected to detailed 'internal analysis' (see Ch. 8).

Another already mentioned discrimination of natural and artificial markings on portable specimens is that of grooves found on ostrich eggshell fragments. This is a material widely used in decorated form, in many regions of Africa and Asia, and in all periods beginning with the Palaeolithic (Bednarik 1993b). Again, the binocular microscope is indispensable in the analytical work. Ostrich eggshell consists of three layers, the outermost of which is less than 0.1 mm thick (Sahni et al. 1990). When the shell is engraved with a stone tool, the resulting groove is cut to well below this thin veneer, but along the edges of the groove pressure scars form a jagged, angular fringe. This is where the outermost layer of the shell splintered, and sometimes it is even possible to detect the direction of tool application from the orientation of these scars. The grooves of root marks, by contrast, are distinctly rounded in section, and clearly attributable to a solution process rather than mechanical force (Figure 70). There are other features to differentiate between the two types of marking, but the described characteristics are adequate for secure discrimination if the markings have not been subjected to subsequent corrosion that obliterated such telltale features.

Clastic movement marks occur frequently on portable objects, including mobiliary art items. They are also among the most common rock marks in the world (see Ch. 3), and they are attributable mainly to glacial action, fluviatile sedimentary movement, animal borrowing, gravity and tectonic movement (e.g. through adjustment in cave systems with a sub-floor phreatic reservoir). They grade into 'general taphonomic marks', which include those caused by cryoturbation, solifluction and trampling. There are numerous examples on record, in most continents, of archaeologists describing taphonomic and clastic markings as anthropic engravings (e.g. Bednarik 1994d).

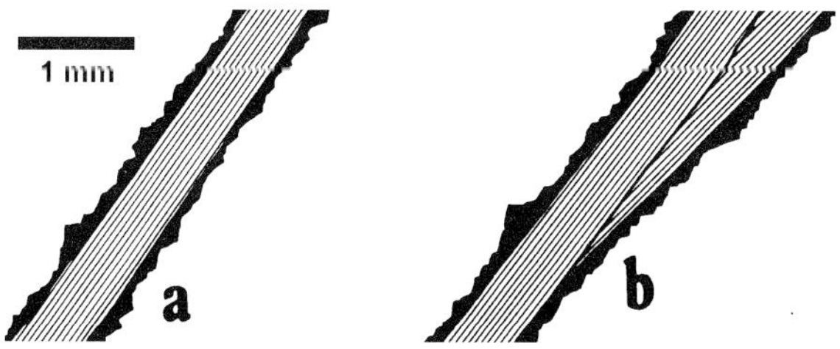

Figure 70A. Engraved grooves on ostrich eggshell in plan view: (a) a single line; (b) a second line engraved over a previous mark. The jagged margins are caused by the splintering of the outermost layer of the shell.

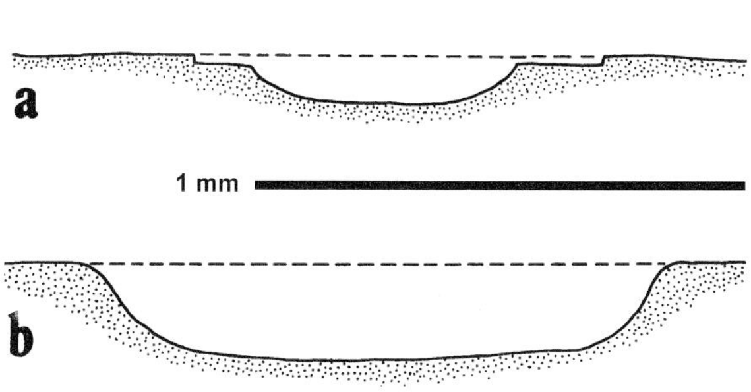

Figure 70B. Schematic sections of (a) an engraved groove on ostrich eggshell and (b) a natural solution groove on the same material; note the splintered margins in (a).

Technological analysis of portable palaeoart objects is, however, not limited to the question of discriminating between natural and anthropic markings. It covers a range of subjects and techniques that cannot be covered adequately in this short chapter. Much research has been lavished on the 'internal analysis' of engravings on portable specimens of stone, ivory, antler, bone and amber, particularly of the European Upper Palaeolithic and Mesolithic periods (Ch. 9). Less popular, but just as important, is the determination of the materials used in the production of markings on portable objects, especially engraved grooves. In particular, the discrimination of metal and stone points used in engraving can be crucial, because metal points were entirely unavailable prior to the Bronze Age. In forms suitable for such purposes they became widely available only between 2000 and 3000 years ago in Eurasia, and later still in other parts of the world. In Australia, for instance, metal tools cannot predate the arrival of Macassans and Europeans. In the coastal zone they became widely available only about 200 years ago, and inland later still. Hence the identification of metal tool marks in Australian portable engravings (Bednarik 1997c) or rock art (Bednarik 2000) delimits their possible antiquity quite significantly.

Of particular importance is the analysis of presumed Pleistocene engraved marks on bone. Not only is this one of the most common portable palaeoart finds of this period, the identification and interpretation of groove markings on bone and other materials of the Lower and Middle Palaeolithic has been the subject of much polemical discussion, because of greatly varying standards of documentation and proof. This has significantly retarded discussion and research of cognitive aspects of human evolution, and has led to polarisation among scholars considering related subjects. It is therefore essential that uniform standards for recognising very early intentional engravings, especially those on bone, be applied. Having examined thousands of purported Pleistocene engravings on bone, dozens on ostrich eggshell fragments, and many more on ivory and stone, I developed the following procedure.

The first task must be to determine whether there are among these usually linear grooves markings that were made with either the point or the cutting edge of a stone tool. If there are no anthropic marks present, no further analytical effort is needed, unless one has resolved to also study natural markings. If there are, it needs to be established whether these stone tool markings are intentional or are the unintended by-product of a utilitarian process — which is often rather more difficult. The markings a stone tool creates on fresh ('green' or 'greasy') bone are quite different from those made on a dry and brittle bone surface. The former have a better rounded cross-section and are of smoother appearance, whereas in the latter case, the greater brittleness of the bone is reflected in jagged edges and coarser groove floors. The issue of intentionality can be illuminated by 'internal analysis' (see Ch. 8) and detailed examination of the organisation of individual marks in relation to each other as well as to spatial features of the object surface.

Steps one and two have thus established whether the marks we examine were made with stone tools, and precisely *how* they were made. We have thus gained a great deal of insight into the physics and history of their production, but we may not yet be in a position of determining whether they were made deliberately, or are simply incidental, like the grooves on a kitchen cutting board. If the arrangement is undeniably iconographic and the object is not a fake or a recent intrusion into an older deposit, no further examination may be warranted. But so far we have only one possibly iconographic engraved motif from the older Palaeolithic periods, one of the three Oldisleben specimens (Bednarik 2006). All other materials of this kind reported to date are merely arrangements or quasi-geometric compositions of linear grooves. It is therefore necessary to establish acceptable guidelines for recognising 'intentionality' — itself a slippery concept in any scientific context — in a set of engraved grooves.

The fact that we have already established, as far as this is possible, in what direction the lines were made and possibly even in what sequence now becomes most helpful. I divide the aspects that favour their interpretation as intentional engravings into the following groups: (A) those that suggest intentionality but do not demand it, because incidental utilitarian markings could conceivably be found with similar properties, however remote that may seem; (B) those that demonstrate intentionality because they cannot reasonably be expected to occur in utilitarian stone tool marks; and (C) those that are not intrinsic to the possibility of the markings being utilitarian. Importantly, the first two groups are of attributes whose strength is enhanced if it can be demonstrated that all or many of the individual marks of an arrangement have been made by the same stone tool:

- A1. Fairly equal spacings between sub-parallel grooves;
- A2. Individual marks of a set, such as sub-parallel grooves, were made in a spatial sequence (e.g. from left to right, suggesting right-handedness);
- A3. Repeated shape or angling of the elements of a set of markings;
- A4. Arrangement or orientation of the elements of a set of marks appears to reflect spatial attributes of the given surface geometry;
- A5. A set of elements, such as straight grooves, is orientated so that its components point to or emphasise a common focus.
- A6. Individual grooves exhibit consistent profile depth and margins over their full length, which reduces the probability that the tool cut through a secondary material, such as hide (Steguweit 1999).

- B1. Individual elements of a set of marks are so arranged that their ends meet or 'connect';
- B2. Some elements of a set or group of marks have been made by the repeated application of a tool, either deepening a groove or duplicating or extending it;
- B3. The arrangement of the elements of a set of marks appears to have been marked out before execution, as if to secure equal spacing of a given number of marks;
- B4. The arrangement of marks is accompanied by subsidiary markings suggesting that, before the principal grooves were produced, the maker hesitated or deliberated the placement of each groove.

- C1. The graphic pattern evident in the arrangement has been previously recognised in another ancient find;
- C2. The repeated use of the same stone tool point or edge is evident among the elements of a set of marks.

My factors B3 and B4 may in practice be hard to separate, and C1 would be expected to apply only in exceptional cases that would be of special interest to further research. Once any of the above factors have been detected, the arrangement of engraved marks becomes a candidate for deliberate execution. In a strictly scientific sense this cannot, however, be proved, rather it needs to be refuted that it is a non-intentional, fortuitous or utilitarian set of marks made with stone tools. As is usual in science, this can never be demonstrated in a finite sense; it can only be expressed in a formulation of relative plausibility. This is achieved in the following manner.

Factors of the first group (A) are weaker evidence than those in the two other groups, because each attribute of the latter does, by itself, almost exclude the possibility that we are dealing with a fortuitous product. In my work, if one of the B or C factors occurs in combination with at least two other factors, I am satisfied that intentionality has been demonstrated. If only one of the A factors is present, but no other supporting evidence, I would consider the marking to be a candidate but one whose status as deliberate engraving should not be accepted. Any ranking intermediate between these two would indicate a commensurate strength of the evidence. For instance if any group B variable co-occurs with just one group A factor, the acceptance of intentionality would be justified, though not as decisively as if two group B factors were present in an arrangement. This is a rigorous and repeatable way of judging the evidence, and it is also a sensible procedure: 'intentionality' (whatever this may mean in this context, or any other) in mark production must inevitably 'fade out' as we proceed back in time in human evolution, to a point where it had not yet been 'introduced'.

Another form of technological analysis is almost entirely restricted to the study of small portable palaeoart objects, namely the microscopic study of perforations. Most accepted beads and pendants bear artificial drill holes, and since in pre-History they have been made almost exclusively with stone points it follows that, on authentic specimens, the perforations should show distinctive diagnostic features. Indeed, these holes are generally conical or bi-conical until Neolithic times, when bow drills were introduced. If the surfaces are not too corroded, rotational striations may be visible even to the unaided eye. The tools used in this work were reamers rather than drills, and as Semenov (1964: 78) observed, these holes are often not circular. The rotating movement of the hand holding the reamer describes no full circle. The point of the reamer does not maintain its axial position, it deviates from it to follow the shape of the hole. The result is a vaguely conical but more or less distorted hole, although Palaeolithic perforations of excellent circularity are also known. True cylindrical boring or drilling only appears with the advent of the bow drill.

The bi-conical opening often observed in beads and pendants is attributable to the application of tapered stone points from both surfaces, but in many if not most cases the initial opening was achieved working only from one side. Extensive replicative work of producing disc beads identical to Pleistocene specimens, using Palaeolithic stone tool replicas, has shown that it is quite impracticable to alternatively work from both surfaces. It is difficult to meet up with the centre of the first indentation, and it is easier to ream out the new opening after the boring tool has broken through from only one side (Bednarik 1997a).

This highlights again the importance of replicative experimentation, which is an integral component of any technological analysis of portable palaeoart — irrespective of whether it is concerned with engravings, figurines or pendants. Micro-wear analysis as used in archaeology to gain insights into technological processes is closely related to much of this work. However, on the whole the potential of such analytical studies of mobiliary art remains inadequately explored, and is the preserve of very few researchers worldwide. Clearly, as in most other specialised areas of palaeoart science, we have seen little more than isolated pioneering efforts, and yet without more comprehensive research programs we will largely remain at the mercy of untestable and idiosyncratic archaeological interpretations. Analytical and replicative work of the type indicated here is absolutely crucial in enlarging our still tiny knowledge base, and in widening the horizons of palaeoart science.

REFERENCES

BAHN, P. G. 1984. How to spot a fake Azilian pebble. *Nature* 308: 229.

BAHN, P. G. 1990. Familiar fakes and unfamiliar faces. *European Cultural Heritage Newsletter on Research* 4(1): 51–53.

BAHN, P. G. 1993. The 'dead wood stage' of prehistoric art studies: style is not enough. In: M. Lorblanchet and P. G. Bahn (eds), *Rock art studies: the post-stylistic era, or, where do we go from here?*, pp. 51–59. Oxbow Monograph 35, Oxbow Books, Oxford.

BEAUMONT, P., H. DE VILLIERS and J. VOGEL 1978. Modern man in sub-Saharan Africa prior to 49 000 B.P.: a review and evaluation with particular reference to Border Cave. *South African Journal of Science* 74: 409–19.

BEDNARIK, R. G. 1984. On the nature of psychograms. *The Artefact* 8: 27–33.

BEDNARIK, R. G. 1987. The cave art of Western Australia. *The Artefact* 12: 1–16.

BEDNARIK, R. G. 1989. The Galgenberg figurine from Krems, Austria. *Rock Art Research* 6: 118–25.

BEDNARIK, R. G. 1990a. An Acheulian haematite pebble with striations. *Rock Art Research* 7: 75.

BEDNARIK, R. G. 1990b. On the cognitive development of hominids. *Man and Environment* 15(2): 1–7.

BEDNARIK, R. G. 1990c. On neuropsychology and shamanism in rock art. *Current Anthropology* 31: 77–80.

BEDNARIK, R. G. 1990d. More to Palaeolithic females than meets the eye. *Rock Art Research* 7: 133–37.

BEDNARIK, R. G. 1991. On natural cave markings. *Helictite* 29(2): 27–41.

BEDNARIK, R. G. 1992a. Palaeoart and archaeological myths. *Cambridge Archaeological Journal* 2(1): 27–43.

BEDNARIK, R. G. 1992b. Palaeolithic art found in China. *Nature* 356: 116.

BEDNARIK, R. G. 1992c. Natural line markings on Palaeolithic objects. *Anthropologie* 29: 233–40.

BEDNARIK, R. G. 1992d. Base pour des études de pointe des débuts de l'art. *L'Anthropologie* 96: 369–74.

BEDNARIK, R. G. 1993a. Wall markings of the cave bear. *Studies in Speleology* 9: 51–70.

BEDNARIK, R. G. 1993b. About Palaeolithic ostrich eggshell in India. *Indo-Pacific Prehistory Association Bulletin* 13: 34–43.

BEDNARIK, R. G. 1994a. The Pleistocene art of Asia. *Journal of World Prehistory* 8: 351–75.

BEDNARIK, R. G. 1994b. A taphonomy of palaeoart. *Antiquity* 68: 68–74.

BEDNARIK, R. G. 1994c. On the scientific study of palaeoart. *Semiotica* 100: 141–68.

BEDNARIK, R. G. 1994d. The discrimination of rock markings. *Rock Art Research* 11: 23–44.

BEDNARIK, R. G. 1995a. Concept-mediated marking in the Lower Palaeolithic. *Current Anthropology* 36: 605–34.

BEDNARIK, R. G. 1995b. Contexte eurasien de l'art paléolithique chinois. *L'Anthropologie* 99: 459–66.

BEDNARIK, R. G. 1995c. The age of the Côa valley petroglyphs in Portugal. *Rock Art Research* 12: 86–103.

BEDNARIK, R. G. 1996. Palaeolithic love goddesses of feminism. *Anthropos* 91: 183–90.

BEDNARIK, R. G. 1997a. The role of Pleistocene beads in documenting hominid cognition. *Rock Art Research* 14: 27–41.

BEDNARIK, R. G. 1997b. Pleistocene stone pendant from Western Australia. *Australian Archaeology* 45: 32–34.

BEDNARIK, R. G. 1997c. An engraved slate fragment from Walyunga, Western Australia. *Records of the Western Australian Museum* 18: 317–21.

BEDNARIK, R. G. 1998a. Microscopic analysis of 'engraved plaques' and other objects from Devil's Lair. *Journal of the Royal Society of Western Australia* 81: 23–33.

BEDNARIK, R. G. 1998b. The 'australopithecine' cobble from Makapansgat, South Africa. *South African Archaeological Bulletin* 53: 4–8.

BEDNARIK, R. G. 1999a. Der Kiesel von Makapansgat. Früheste Urkunst der Welt? *Anthropos* 94: 199–204.

BEDNARIK, R. G. 1999b. Maritime navigation in the Lower and Middle Palaeolithic. *Comptes Rendus de l'Académie des Sciences Paris*, Earth and Planetary Sciences 328: 559–63.

BEDNARIK, R. G. 1999c. Nicht-paläolithische "paläolithische" Felskunst. *Mitteilungen der Anisa* 19(1-2): 7–16.

BEDNARIK, R. G. 2000. Earliest known Historical rock art in Australia. *Rock Art Research* 17: 131–33.

BEDNARIK, R. G. 2001a. Beads and pendants of the Pleistocene. *Anthropos* 96: 1–12.

BEDNARIK, R. G. 2001b. The oldest known rock art in the world. *Anthropologie* 39: 81–89.

BEDNARIK, R. G. 2003a. The earliest evidence of palaeoart. *Rock Art Research* 20: 89–135.

BEDNARIK, R. G. 2003b. A figurine from the African Acheulian. *Current Anthropology* 44(3): 405–13.

BEDNARIK, R. G. 2006. The Middle Palaeolithic engravings from Oldisleben, Germany. *Anthropologie.*

BEDNARIK, R. G. and M. KUCKENBURG 1999. *Nale Tasih: Eine Floßfahrt in die Steinzeit.* Thorbecke, Stuttgart.

BEDNARIK R. G. and YOU YUZHU 1991. Palaeolithic art from China. *Rock Art Research* 8: 119–23.

BOAS, F. 1888. *The Central Eskimo*, reprinted 1964. University of Nebraska Press, Lincoln.

CAPITAN, L. and D. PEYRONY 1921. Les origines de l'art à l'Aurignacien moyen: La Ferrassie. *Revue Archéologique* 31: 92–112.

CRÉMADES, M. 1996. L'expression graphique au paléolithique inférieur et moyen: l'exemple de l'Abri Suard (La Chaise-de-Vouthon, Charente. *Bulletin de la Société Préhistorique Française* 93: 494–501.

CRÉMADES, M., H. LAVILLE, N. SIRAKOV and J. K. KOZLOWSKI 1995. Une pierre gravée de 50 000 ans B.P. dans les Balkans. *Palaeo* 7(Dec.): 201–9.

DAVIS, S. 1974. Incised bones from the Mousterian of Kebara Cave (Mount Carmel) and the Aurignacian of Ha-Yonim Cave (Western Galilee), Israel. *Paléorient* 2: 181–82.

DÉBENATH, A. and L. DUPORT 1971. *Os travaillés et os utilisés de quelques gisements préhistoriques charentais.* Mémoires, Société Archéologique et Historique de la Charente, pp. 189–202.

D'ERRICO, F. 1994. *L'art gravé azilien.* 31e supplément, Gallia Préhistoire, CNRS Éditions, Paris.

D'ERRICO, F. and M. ALLARD 1997. The Mousterian engraved bone of the Grotte de Peyrere 1 (Hautes-Pyrenées, France. Abstract in M. Strecker (ed.), *Congreso Internacional de Arte Rupestre, Cochabamba, Bolivia, 1-6 de Abril de 1997*, p. 41. SIARB, La Paz.

D'ERRICO, F. and A. NOWELL 2000. A new look at the Berekhat Ram figurine: implications for the origins of symbolism. *Cambridge Archaeological Journal* 10: 123–67.

D'ERRICO, F. and P. VILLA 1997. Holes and grooves: the contribution of microscopy and taphonomy to the problem of art origins. *Journal of Human Evolution* 33: 1–31.

DORTCH, C. E. 1976. Two engraved stone plaques of late Pleistocene age from Devil's Lair, Western Australia.

Archaeology and Physical Anthropology in Oceania 11: 32–44.

DORTCH, C. E. 1984. *Devil's Lair, a study in prehistory.* Western Australian Museum, Perth.

DUPORT, L. 1960. Les gisements préhistoriques de la vallée des Eaux-Claires III. Os moustérien peut-être gravé. *Bulletin de la Société Archéologique et Historique de la Charente* 1960: 55–59.

FREEMAN, L. G. and J. GONZÁLEZ ECHEGARAY 1983. Tally-marked bone from Mousterian levels at Cueva Morín (Santander, Spain). In *Homenaje al Prof. M. Almagro Basch*, Vol. I, pp. 143–147. Ministerio de Cultura, Madrid.

GOREN-INBAR, N. 1986. A figurine from the Acheulian site of Berekhat Ram. *Mi'Tekufat Ha'Even* 19: 7–12.

GOREN-INBAR, N. 1990. *Quneitra — a Mousterian site on the Golan Heights.* Quedem 31. Institute of Archaeology, Jerusalem.

GOREN-INBAR, N., Z. LEWY and M. E. KISLEV 1991. The taphonomy of a bead-like fossil from the Acheulian of Gesher Benot Ya'aqov, Israel. *Rock Art Research* 8: 83–87.

GOREN-INBAR, N. and S. PELTZ 1995. Additional remarks on the Berekhat Ram figurine. *Rock Art Research* 12: 153–54.

GVOZDOVER, M. 1995. *Art of the mammoth hunters: the finds from Avdeevo.* Oxbow Monograph 49, Oxbow Books, Oxford.

HENSHILWOOD, C., F. D'ERRICO, R. YATES, Z. JACOBS, C. TRIBOLO, G. A. T. DULLER, N. MERCIER, J. C. SEALY, H. VALLADAS, I. WATTS and A. G. WINTLE 2002. Emergence of modern human behavior: Middle Stone age engravings from South Africa. *Science* 295: 1278-80.

HODGSON, D. 2000. Art, perception and information processing: an evolutionary perspective. *Rock Art Research* 17: 3–34.

HOVERS, E., B. VANDERMEERSCH and O. BAR-YOSEF 1997. A Middle Palaeolithic engraved artefact from Qafzeh Cave, Israel. *Rock Art Research* 14: 79–87.

HUYGE, D. 1990. Mousterian skiffle? Note on a Middle Palaeolithic engraved bone from Schulen, Belgium. *Rock Art Research* 7: 125–32.

IMBRIE, J., J. D. HAYS, D. G. MARTINSON, A. MCINTYRE, A. C. MIX, J. J. MARLEY, N. G. PISIAS, W. L. PRELL and N. J. SHACKLETON 1984. The orbital theory of Pleistocene climate: support from a revised chronology of the marine ä^{18}0 record. In A. L. Berger, J. Imbrie, J. Hays, G. Kukla and B. Saltzman (eds), *Milankovitch and climate, Part 1*, pp. 269–305. Reidel, Dordrecht.

KEELEY, L. H. 1980. *Experimental determination of stone tool uses.* Chicago.

KROEBER, A. L. 1900. The Eskimo of Smith Sound. *Bulletin of the American Museum of Natural History* 12: 265–327.

KUCKENBURG, M. 1996. *... und sprachen das erste Wort. Die Entstehung von Sprache und Schrift.* Econ Verlag, Düsseldorf.

KUCKENBURG, M. 1997. *Lag Eden im Neandertal? Auf der Suche nach dem frühen Menschen.* Econ Verlag, Düsseldorf and München.

LAIDLER, P. W. 1933. Dating evidence concerning the Middle Stone Ages and a Capsio-Wilton culture, in the South-East Cape. *South African Journal of Science* 30: 530–42.

LEONARDI, P. 1988. Art Paléolithique mobilier et pariétal en Italie. *L'Anthropologie* 92: 139–202.

LEROI-GOURHAN, A. 1982. The archaeology of Lascaux Cave. *Scientific American* 246(6): 80–8.

McFADDEN, P. L., A. BROCK and T. C. PARTRIDGE 1979. Palaeomagnetism and the age of the Makapansgat hominid site. *Earth Planetary Science Letters* 44: 373–82.

MANIA, D. and MANIA, U. 1988. Deliberate engravings on bone artefacts of *Homo erectus. Rock Art Research* 5: 91–107.

MARSHACK, A. 1976. Some implications of the Paleolithic symbolic evidence for the origin of language. *Current Anthropology* 17: 274–82.

MARSHACK, A. 1985. Theoretical concepts that lead to new analytic methods, modes of enquiry and classes of data. *Rock Art Research* 2: 95–111.

MARSHACK, A. 1991: A reply to Davidson on Mania and Mania. *Rock Art Research* 8: 47–58.

MARSHACK, A. 1996. A Middle Palaeolithic symbolic composition from the Golan Heights: the earliest known depictive image. *Current Anthropology* 37: 357–65.

MARTIN, H. 1907–10. *Récherches sur l'évolution du Moustérien dans le gisement de la Quina (Charente). Industrie osseuse*, Vol. 1. Schleicher Frères, Paris.

MOTTL, M. 1951. Die Repolust-Höhle bei Peggau (Steiermark) und ihre eiszeitlichen Bewohner. *Archaeologica Austriaca* 8: 1–78.

NADEL, D., A. DANIN, E. WERKER, T. SCHICK, M. E. KISLEV and K. STEWART 1994. 19 000-year-old twisted fibers from Ohalo II. *Current Anthropology* 35: 451–57.

NELSON, E. W. 1899. The Eskimo about Bering Strait. In *Eighteenth Annual Report of the Bureau of American Ethnology to the Secretary of the Smithsonian Institution, 1896–97,* Part I, pp. 19–526.

OAKLEY, K. P. 1981. Emergence of higher thought, 3.0–0.2 Ma B.P. *Philosophical Transactions of the Royal Society of London* B292: 205–11.

PRESTWICH, J. 1859. On the occurrence of flint-implements, associated with the remains of extinct mammalia, in undisturbed beds of a late geological period. *Proceedings of the Royal Society of London* 10: 50–59.

PRINGLE, H. 1997. Ice Age communities may be earliest known net hunters. *Science* 277: 1203–4.

RAYNAL, J.-P. and R. SÉGUY 1986. Os incisé acheuléen de Sainte-Anne 1 (Polignac, Haute-Loire). *RACF* 25: 79–80.

RIEK, G. 1934. *Die Eiszeitjägerstation am Vogelherd im Lonetal*, Vol. 1, Die Kulturen. Tübingen.

RIEK, G. 1960. Das Paläolithikum der Höhlen des Lone- und des Brenztales. *Jahreshefte für Karst- und Höhlenkunde* 1: 57–104.

ROSENFELD, A. 1977. Profile figures: schematisation of the human figure in the Magdalenian culture of Europe. In P. J. Ucko (ed.), *Form in indigenous art*, pp. 90–109. Australian Institute of Aboriginal Studies, Canberra.

RUSSELL, P. 2006. Learning from curves: the female figure in Palaeolithic Europe. *Rock Art Research* 23: 41-49.

SAHNI, A., G. KUMAR, S. BAJPAI and S. SRINIVASAN 1990. A review of Late Pleistocene ostriches (*Struthio* sp.) in India. *Man and Environment* 15(1): 41–47.

SCHMID, E. 1989. Die altsteinzeitliche Elfenbeinstatuette aus der Höhle Stadel im Hohlenstein bei Asselfingen, Alb-Donau-Kreis. *Fundberichte aus Baden-Württemberg* 14: 33–96.

SINGER, R. and J. WYMER 1982. *The Middle Stone Age at Klasies River Mouth in South Africa.* University of Chicago Press, Chicago.

SEMENOV, S. A. 1964. *Prehistoric technology* (transl. by M. W. Thompson). Cory, Adams and Mackay, London.

SMITH, W. G. 1894. *Man the primeval savage.* Edward Stanford, London.

STEGUWEIT, L. 1999. Intentionelle Schnittmarken auf Tierknochen von Bilzingsleben — Neue lasermikroskopische Untersuchungen. *Praehistoria Thuringica* 3: 64–79.

STEPANCHUK, V. N. 1993. Prolom II, a Middle Palaeolithic cave site in the eastern Crimea with non-utilitarian bone artefacts. *Proceedings of the Prehistoric Society* 59: 17–37.

VINCENT, A. 1988. L'os comme artefact au Paléolithique moyen: principes d'étude et premiers résultats. In *L'Homme de Néandertal, Vol. 4: La technique*, pp. 185–196. Études et Recherches Archéologiques de l'Université de Liège 31, Liège.

WARNER, C. and R. G. BEDNARIK 1996. Pleistocene knotting. In J. C. Turner and P. van de Griend (eds), *History and science of knots*, pp. 3–18. World Scientific, Singapore.

WENDT, W. E. 1974. Art mobilier aus der Apollo 11 Grotte in Südwest-Afrika. *Acta Praehistorica et Archaeologica* 5: 1–42.

YOU YOUZHU 1984. Preliminary study of a Palaeolithic bone engraving. *Kexue Tongbao* 29(1): 80–82.

11. Resources in rock art research

Rock art research organisations of the world

Office of the Convener of IFRAO:
Robert G. Bednarik
International Federation of Rock Art Organisations
P.O. Box 216
CAULFIELD SOUTH, Vic. 3162
Australia
E-mail: auraweb@hotmail.com

Office of the IFRAO-UNESCO Liaison Officer:
Professor Dario Seglie
Viale Giolitti, 1
10064 PINEROLO (TO)
Italy
E-mail: CeSMAP@cesmap.it

Offices of the IFRAO Representatives
Professor B. K. Swartz, Jr
American Committee to Advance the Study of Petroglyphs and Pictographs (ACASPP)
Dept of Anthropology
Ball State University
MUNCIE, IN 47306
U.S.A.
E-mail: 01bkswartz@bsuvc.bsu.edu

Leigh Marymor
c/o American Rock Art Research Association (ARARA)
Box 210026
Tucson, AZ 85721-0026
U.S.A.
E-mail: MLeighM@aol.com

Professor Ara Demirkhanian
Armenian Centre of Prehistoric Art Study
National Academy of Sciences of Armenia
Institute of Arts
Marshal Bagramian Prosp. 24 G
YEREVAN-19
375019 Armenia

Fernando Javier Costas Goberna
Asociación Arqueológica Viguesa (AAV)
Museo Municipal
Parque de Castrelos c/n
36213 VIGO
Spain

D. Hipólito Collado Giraldo
Asociación Cultural 'Colectivo Barbaón' (ACCB)
Míralrío, we 13, 3e E
10002 Cáceres
Spain
E-mail: hipolitocollado@ozu.es

Professor Roy Querejazu Lewis
Asociación de Estudios del Arte Rupestre de Cochabamba (AEARC)
Casilla 4243
Cochabamba,
Bolivia
E-mail: aearc@hotmail.com

Professor Edithe da Silva Pereira
Associaçao Brasileira de Arte Rupestre (ABAR)
Museu Paraense Emílio Goeldi
Av. Magalhòes Barata, 376
CEP: 66040 - Belém
Brazil
E-mail: edithe@museu-goeldi.br

Professor Mila Simões de Abreu
Associaçao Portuguesa de Arte e Arqueologia Rupestre (APAAR)
c/o Departamento de Geologia, Unidade de Arqueologia
Universidade de Trás-os-Montes e Alto Douro
Apartado 1013
5000-911 VILA REAL
Portugal
E-mail: msabreu@utad.pt

Dr Joerg W. Hansen
Association des Amis de L'Art Rupestre Saharien (AARS)
5, rue des Nobles
F - 09190 SAINT LIZIER
France
E-mail: hansenj@dial.oleane.com

Dr Abdelkhalek Lemjidi
Association Marocaine d'Art Rupestre (AMAR)
Massira III, C
Tarablous residence, IMM.685, N°26
46001-Marrakech
Morocco
E-mail: idijmel@yahoo.fr

Dr Jean Clottes
Association pour le Rayonnement de L'Art Pariétal Européen (ARAPE)
11, rue du Fourcat
09000 FOIX
France
E-mail: j.clottes@wanadoo.fr

Robert G. Bednarik
Australian Rock Art Research Association (AURA)
P.O. Box 216
CAULFIELD SOUTH, Vic. 3162
Australia
E-mail: auraweb@hotmail.com

Robert G. Bednarik
Cave Art Research Association (CARA)
P.O. Box 216
CAULFIELD SOUTH, Vic. 3162
Australia
E-mail: ca1ra1@hotmail.com

Professor Mario Consens
Centro de Investigación de Arte Rupestre del Uruguay (CIARU)
C.C. 18.007
MONTEVIDEO
Uruguay
E-mail: consens@adinet.com.uy

Professor Dario Seglie
Centro Studi e Museo d'Arte Preistorica (CeSMAP)
Viale Giolitti, 1
10064 PINEROLO (TO)
Italy
E-mail: CeSMAP@cesmap.it

Lic. María Mercedes Podestá
Comite de Investigación del Arte Rupestre de la Sociedad Argentina de Antropología
Av. Santa Fe 983, 4 piso A
1059 BUENOS AIRES
Argentina
E-mail: mercedespodesta@yahoo.com

Dr Thomas W. Wyrwoll
Deutsche Gesellschaft für Petroikonologie e.V. (DGP)
Albert-Schweitzer-Straße 52
D060437 FRANKFURT AM MAIN
Germany
E-Mail: Thomas.Wyrwoll@gmx.de

Dr Fidelis T. Masao
East African Rock Art Research Association (EARARA)
Biocultural Research
P.O. Box 70566
DAR ES SALAM
Tanzania
E-mail: fitman60@hotmail.com

Dr Carol Diaz-Granados
Eastern States Rock Art Research Association (ESRARA)
Department of Anthropology
Campus Box 1114
Washington University
1 Brookings Drive
Saint Louis, Missouri 63130-4899
E-mail: cdiazgra@artsci.wustl.edu

Dr Lothar Wanke
Gesellschaft für Vergleichende Felsbildforschung (GE.FE.BI.)
Geidorfgürtel 40
A-8010 GRAZ
Austria

Professor Guillermo Muñoz C.
Grupo de Investigación de Arte Rupestre Indigena (GIPRI)
Carrera 54A 174-12
SANTAFÉ DE BOGOTÁ, D.C.
Colombia
E-mail: gipri@col1.telecom.com.co

Dr George Dimitriadis
Hellenic Rock Art Centre (HERAC)
Philippi
GR 640 03 Krinides
Greece
E-mail: webmaster@herac.4t.com

Professor Werner Pichler
Institutum Canarium (IC)
Wagrainerstraße 9
A-4840 VÖCKLABRUCK
Austria
E-mail: we.pichler@asn-linz.ac.at

Professor Nobuhiro Yoshida
Japan Petrograph Society (JPS)
P.O. Box 11
Kokuranishi Post Office
KITAKYUSYU-CITY, 803
Japan
E-mail: jps@qd5.so-net.ne.jp

Professor Jack Steinbring
Mid-America Geographic Foundation, Inc. (MAGF)
Department of Anthropology
Ripon College
P.O. Box 248
RIPON, Wisconsin 54971
U.S.A.
E-mail: SteinbringJ@Mail.Ripon.EDU

Dr Arsen Faradjev
Moscow Centre of Rock Art and Bioindication Research
Ramenki, 11/1, 33
MOSCOW 117607
Russia
E-mail: farajev@hotmail.com

Dr Alanah Woody
Nevada Rock Art Foundation (NRAF)
305 South Arlington Street
Reno, Nevada 89501
U.S.A.
E-mail: info@nevadarockart.org

David Morris
Northern Cape Rock Art Trust
Archaeology Department
McGregor Museum
P.O. Box 316
Kimberley 8300
South Africa
E-mail: dmorris@museumsnc.co.za

Eileen C. Brownlie
Pictish Arts Society (PAS)
12 Dean Park Mews
EDINBURGH, EH4 1ED
United Kingdom
E-mail: info@pictarts.demon.co.uk

Rob Burrett
Prehistory Society of Zimbabwe (PSZ)
P. O. Box 876
HARARE
Zimbabwe
E-mail: Burrett@zol.co.zw

Professor Jack Steinbring
Rock Art Association of Manitoba (RAAM)
Dept of Anthropology
Ripon College
P.O. Box 248
RIPON, Wisc. 54971-0248
U.S.A.
E-mail: SteinbringJ@Mail.Ripon.EDU

Professor Chen Zhao Fu
Rock Art Research Association of China (RARAC)
Central Institute for Nationalities
100081 BEIJING
P. R. China
E-mail: chen525@vip.sohu.net

Dr Giriraj Kumar
Rock Art Society of India (RASI)
Faculty of Arts
Dayalbagh Educational Institute
DAYALBAGH, Agra 282 005
India
E-mail: girirajrasi@yahoo.com

Professor Yakov A. Sher
Siberian Association of Prehistoric Art Researches (SAPAR)
State University of Kemerovo
Krasnaya Street 6
KEMEROVO 650043
Russia
E-mail: sher@kemsu.ru

Lic. Freddy Taboada
Sociedad de Investigación del Arte Rupestre de Bolivia (SIARB)
c/o Matthias Strecker
Casilla 3091
LA PAZ
Bolivia
E-mail: siarb@acelerate.com

Dr Angelo Fossati
Società Cooperativa Archeologica Le Orme dell'Uomo
Piazzale Donatori di Sangue, 1
25040 CERVENO (Brescia)
Italy
E-mail: aarca@inrete.it

Dr Jean Clottes
Société Préhistorique Ariège-Pyrénées
11, rue du Fourcat
09000 FOIX
France
E-mail: j.clottes@wanadoo.fr

Dr Anne Solomon
Southern African Rock Art Research Association (SARARA)
Natal Museum
Private Bag 9070
PIETERMARITZBURG 3200
South Africa

Professor Vadim A. Ranov
Tadjik Centre for the Study of Petroglyphs (TCSP)
Institute of History, Archaeology and Ethnography
Tadjik Academy of Sciences
Dushanbe
Tadjikistan
E-mail: ranov@ac.tajik.net

David Coulson
The Trust for African Rock Art (TARA)
P.O. Box 24122
00502, Nairobi
Kenya
E-mail: tara@swiftkenya.com

Charles Robert Bailey
Upper Midwest Rock Art Research Association (UMRARA)
1513 72nd Avenue North
BROOKLYN CENTER, Minnesota 55430
U.S.A.
E-mail: cbailey@tcinternet.net

Prof. Dr Herta Mandl-Neumann
Verein Anisa
A-8967 HAUS i. E.
Austria
E-mail: anisa@aon.at

ROCK ART LIBRARIES AND ARCHIVES

The AURA Archive
P.O. Box 216
CAULFIELD SOUTH, Vic. 3162
Australia
E-mail: auraweb@hotmail.com

This collection includes substantial holdings of prints, transparencies, books, journals and reprints, as well as serigraphs, facsimiles, films, compact discs and audio tapes, all relating to rock art and its study. The AURA Archive distributes the IFRAO Standard Scale worldwide.

The Library
Centro Camuno di Studi Preistorici
25044 CAPO DI PONTE (Bs)
Italy
E-mail: ccspreist@tin.it

The CCSP holds substantial printed records as well as other material relevant to rock art. Its world rock art archive comprises one of the world's largest collections of photographic material.

Rock Art Research Unit
Archaeology Department
University of the Witwatersrand
Private Bag 3, WITS 2050
South Africa

This dedicated section of a university department specialises in the teaching of rock art studies, and holds a major literature and transparencies collection. It comprises also a research laboratory.

The Library
Indira Gandhi National Centre for the Arts
Janpath, NEW DELHI 110 001
India

The IGNCA library and archive has major holdings of a wide range of literature, a substantial collection of photographic material, and one of the world's best collections of rock art facsimiles.

Rock Art Archive
Ball State University
Department of Anthropology
MUNCIE, IN 47306
U.S.A.

This electronic repository of rock art material is maintained by Philip Shaffer, Ball State Computer Services. The site collects images of all pre-Historic rock art worldwide by anyone who wishes to submit. The URL is:
http://web.bsu.edu/rockart/
Administrator: Professor B. K. Swartz, Jr.
E-mail: 01bkswartz@bsuvc.bsu.edu

UCLA Rock Art Archive
Department of Archaeology
University of California, Los Angeles
U.S.A.

Takarakka Rock Art Research Centre
36 Bonros Place
THE GAP, Qld 4061
Australia
E-mail: gwalsh@uq.net.au

This privately owned archive includes one of the world's largest collections of photographic rock art material.

IFRAO Code of Ethics

The following Code of Ethics was ratified by the full IFRAO meeting on 14 July 2000 in Alice Springs, Australia. It represents the recommended minimum ethical standards for conducting rock art research anywhere.

1. Preamble

1(1). This Code of Ethics describes general guidelines which IFRAO recommends to its members.

1(2). Rock art provides a window to our collective past, helps us make sense of the present and contributes to our future. Some of it has been handed down to us by many generations preceding us, to safeguard it for many generations to follow us. Unless we can trace our lineage directly to those who created the rock art and have retained aspects of its original cultural context, it does not belong to us in any way.

1(3). The cultural significance of a rock art site is embodied in the entire fabric of the site, in addition to the actual art present; in the traditional use of the place and the activities that occurred there; and in the meanings and intangible qualities of the place.

1(4). Understanding the cultural significance of a place is fundamental to its care, and where such understanding is inadequate, any interference may be regarded as inappropriate.

1(5). The 'patina of history' apparent in the fabric of a rock art site is important evidence and forms an integral part of that fabric. It includes natural or artificial changes or traces.

2. Definitions

Fabric: all physical aspects of a rock art site, including accretionary deposits, the art itself, traces of later human responses, modifications, even traces of vandalism in cases, lichen, and so forth.

Geomorphic exposure: any rock surface.

Graffiti: collective term describing recent anthropic graphic markings or inscriptions that are incompatible with the known or presumed uses of the rock art on the same panels.

IFRAO: the International Federation of Rock Art Organisations.

Indigenous cultural custodians: descendants of people who created rock art, who are obligated by their cultural traditions or beliefs to act as the custodians or curators of rock art.

Management: administrative control over the management of rock art sites, including preservation, access control, public presentation.

Massive intervention: significant changes to the environmental conditions under which the rock art survives. This includes housing in a building, or removal of the supporting bedrock to another location.

Members: the members of IFRAO.

Peer approval: the approval of an action or proposed action by relevant specialists who have no pecuniary involvement in the project in question.

Rock art: the surviving graphic markings of cultural activities found on rock surfaces.

Triumvirate of IFRAO: the ruling council of IFRAO, consisting of the immediate past president, president and incoming president.

Traditional owners: see Indigenous cultural custodians.

3. Issues of ownership

3(1). *Traditional owners and indigenous cultural custodians*: In areas where indigenous peoples live whose lifestyles and beliefs continue traditions associated with rock art, members recognise their ownership of the sites, and all research, conservation or management of such sites are subject to the full approval of the traditional owners. In areas where such indigenous peoples and traditions are no longer present, members shall endeavour to understand and promote management practices consistent with such beliefs in so far as they are known from ethnographic or archaeological evidence. In the absence of such evidence to the contrary, provisional concepts of such beliefs (e.g. non-human sources of authority, nature of the sacred, non-linear time/space) should be projected from similar societies and traditions elsewhere.

3(2). *Local antiquities and cultural heritage laws*: Members shall abide by all local, state or national laws protecting archaeological sites and monuments, and comply with heritage protection laws generally.

3(3). *Non-traditional ownership of sites*: Members shall respect the rules, laws or requests of any individuals or organisations possessing legal ownership of the land rock art sites are located on, or the land that must be traversed in order to reach the sites.

3(4). *Copyright and ownership of records*: In regions where traditional indigenous owners exist, they possess copyright of the rock art designs. Members wishing to reproduce such designs shall make appropriate applications. Records made of rock art remain the cultural property of the rock artists, or collectively of the societies these lived amongst.

4. Recording of rock art

4(1). *Methods of recording*: Members shall not physically interfere with rock art except as provided in Clauses 5(2) and 6. No substances shall be applied to rock art for recording purposes, except substances that are regularly applied to individual panels by natural processes (e.g. water at open air sites).

4(2). *Coverage of recording*: All recordings of rock art are incomplete. Therefore rock art recordings need to be as comprehensive as possible, and by multi-disciplinary means.

4(3). *Conduct at sites*: New uses of sites, including for purposes of research, shall not change the fabric of a site, and shall respect associations and meanings of the site and its contents.

4(4). *Conduct in foreign countries*: In addition to other requirements listed herein, researchers working in foreign countries shall do so in consultation with the region's rock art organisation, and shall provide copies of reports and publications to that organisation.

5. Removal of samples

5(1). *Archaeological research*: No excavation shall be undertaken at a rock art site unless it forms part of an appropriately authorised archaeological research project. This includes the removal of any sediment to uncover rock art images. Similarly, no archaeological surface remains shall be removed or relocated.

5(2). *Sampling of rock art and adjacent geomorphic exposures*: No samples shall be removed of paint residue, accretionary deposits of any kind, or of the support rock, except after the following requirements have been satisfied:

(a) The sample removal is to form part of a larger and specific research design that has peer approval;

(b) The sample removal has been approved in writing by two peer researchers (i.e. scientists specialising in the analytical study of rock art);

(c) The funds necessary for the best possible analytical laboratory support have been secured;

(d) The analyst has extensive first-hand experience in sampling geomorphic surfaces;

(e) Traditional indigenous custodians, where they have jurisdiction, have approved the sample removal;

(f) The relevant local or national authorities have approved the sample removal;

5(3). *Excavation*: No excavations shall be undertaken at a rock art site unless the expertise of identifying rock art-making tools is available to the researchers proposing such excavation.

6. Conservation

6(1). *Setting*: The area around a rock art site, its setting, may contain features associated with the rock art and other evidence of its history. The visual, historical and other relationships between a site and its setting which contribute to its significance shall be retained in all conservation or preservation work.

6(2). *Site fabric*: In all conservation, preservation or management work at and near rock art sites, the visual, historical and scientific significance of the site fabric shall be retained. The removal or palliation of 'graffiti' shall be undertaken only after approval of the relevant authorities, and be effected only under the guidance of qualified rock art conservators. Massive intervention is to be reserved for situations of extreme threats to rock art, and shall be undertaken only after extensive peer review and approval.

6(3). *Protection*: Members will not disclose the locations of non-public and unprotected rock art sites to the general public. Ultimately, the best protection will depend on the awareness of the general public of the value of rock art. Part of any conservation effort should include the education of the public towards respect for rock art wherever it occurs.

7. Disputes

7(1). *Conduct*: Members shall endeavour to treat other members in a courteous manner. In regions where traditional indigenous owners exist, members shall ensure that they are kept informed about all aspects of research work, and that copies of completed reports are made available to them. Where such reports appear in technical jargon, ordinary-language versions are to be made available.

7(2). *Plagiarism*: Members shall acknowledge the use of other researcher's recordings, published comments and ideas.

7(3). *Dispute settlement*: Members shall make every endeavour to settle disputes among themselves, as IFRAO is reluctant to settle disputes among its members. Where a dispute cannot be settled and threatens the integrity of IFRAO, application for arbitration shall be made to the President of IFRAO, providing the relevant documentation. The dispute will then be arbitrated by a Triumvirate of IFRAO if its resolution is urgent, but preferably at the subsequent General Meeting of IFRAO.

EARLY DATING RESULTS

List of the projects of 'direct dating' of rock art up to 1995, and the results obtained by them

1980 - Malangine Cave, South Australia - Radiocarbon dating of reprecipitated carbonate over and under petroglyphs - Two - Minimum age of c. 5550 BP for some petroglyphs - R. G. Bednarik, Australia.

1982 - Malangine Cave, South Australia - Uranium / thorium dating of reprecipitated carbonate over and under petroglyphs - Two - Minimum age of c. 28 000 BP for some petroglyphs - R. G. Bednarik, H. H. Veeh, Australia.

1987 - Boontjieskloof, South Africa - AMS radiocarbon dating of charcoal pigment - One - 500 BP - N. J. van der Merwe, J. Sealy, R. Yates, South Africa.

1987 - Huashan, China - Radiocarbon dating of reprecipitated carbonate over and under painting - Two for one motif - 2370 BP max. and 2115 BP min. - Qin Shengmin, China.

1990 - Kakadu National Park, Australia - Radiocarbon dating of oxalate associated with paintings - Two - Up to c. 8880 BP - A. Watchman, Australia.

1990 - Lake Onega, Russia - Microerosion dating of petroglyph - One - E4000 BP - R. G. Bednarik, Australia.

1990 - Cougnac Cave, France - AMS dating of charcoal pigment - One - 14 300 BP - M. Lorblanchet, France.

1990 - Gnatalia Creek, Australia - AMS dating of charcoal pigment - Two - 6000 BP and 29 800 BP from one motif - J. McDonald, K. Officer, T. Jull, D. Donahue, H. Head, B. Ford, Australia.

1990 - Waterfall Cave, Australia - AMS dating of charcoal pigment - One - 600 BP - J. McDonald, K. Officer, T. Jull, D. Donahue, H. Head, B. Ford, Australia.

1990 - Judds Cavern, Tasmania - AMS dating of blood residue in pigment - Two - 10 000 BP - T. H. Loy, R. Jones, D. E. Nelson, B. Meehan, J. Vogel, J. Southon, R. Cosgrove, Australia-Canada.

1990 - Laurie Creek, Australia - AMS dating of blood residue in pigment - One - C. 20 000 BP - T. H. Loy, R. Jones, D. E. Nelson, B. Meehan, J. Vogel, J. Southon, R. Cosgrove, Australia-Canada. (This result is now doubtful.)

1990 - Seminole Canyon, Texas - AMS dating of organic carbon in pigment - One - 3900 BP - J. Russ, M. Hyman, H. J. hafer, M. W. Rowe, USA.

1990 - Cangyuan, China - Radiocarbon dating of reprecipitated carbonate under and over painting - Several for one motif - 3100 BP max. and 2960 BP min. - Woo Sheh Ming, China.

1992 - Cosquer Cave, France - AMS dating of charcoal pigment - Seven - Ranging from c. 18 000 BP to 27 900 BP - J. Clottes, J. Courtin, H. Valladas, France.

1992 - Niaux, France - AMS dating of charcoal pigment - Three - Ranging from c. 12 900 BP to 13 850 BP - H. Valladas, H. Cachier, M. Arnold, F. Bernaldo de Quiros, J. Clottes, P. Uzquiano, France-Spain.

1992 - Altamira, Spain - AMS dating of charcoal pigment - Three - Ranging from 13 600 BP to 14 300 BP - H. Valladas, H. Cachier, M. Arnold, F. Bernaldo de Quiros, J. Clottes, P. Uzquiano, France-Spain.

1992 - Castillo, Spain - AMS dating of charcoal pigment - Two - C. 13 000 BP - H. Valladas, H. Cachier, M. Arnold, F. Bernaldo de Quiros, J. Clottes, P. Uzquiano, France-Spain.

1992 - Laura South, Australia - AMS dating of oxalate containing paint residue - One - 24 600 BP - A. Watchman, Australia.

1992 - Lower Pecos River region, Texas - AMS dating of organic carbon in pigment - Two - Both c. 3000 BP - J. Russ, M. Hyman, M. W. Rowe, USA.

1993 - Olary Province, Australia - AMS dating from organics on petroglyphs - Nineteen - Ranging from c. 1500 BP to 43 140 BP - M. Nobbs, R. Dorn, Australia-USA.

1993 - Cougnac, France - AMS dating of charcoal pigment - Five - Ranging from c. 13 800 BP to 25 100 BP - M. Lorblanchet, France.

1993 - Yam Camp, Laura, Australia - AMS dating of plant-fibre binders in rock paintings - Two - Both c. 700 BP - A. Watchman, N. Cole, Australia.

1993 - Lower Pecos River region, Texas - AMS dating of organic carbon in pigment - Two - 3000 and 4200 BP - S. D. Chaffee, M. Hyman, M. W. Rowe, USA.

1993 - Arnhem Land, Australia - AMS dating of beeswax figures - Several - Up to 4000 BP - D. E. Nelson, C. Chippindale, G. Chaloupka, P. Taçon, J. Southon, Canada-Australia-U.K.-USA.

1994 - Pryor Mountains, Montana - AMS dating of organic carbon in pigment - One - 840 BP - S. D. Chaffee, L. L. Loendorf, M. Hyman, M. W. Rowe, USA.

1994 - Canyonlands National Park, Utah - AMS dating of charcoal pigment and organic carbon in pigment - Two - 600 and 750 BP - S. D. Chaffee, M. Hyman, M. W. Rowe, N. J. Coulam, A. Schroedl, K. Hogue, USA.

1994 - All American Man painting, Utah, U.S.A. - AMS dating of paint residue - Two - 575 BP and 753 BP - S. D. Chaffee, M. Hyman, M. W. Rowe, N. J. Coulam, A. Schroedl, K. Hogue, U.S.A.

1994 - El Raton, Baja California Sur, Mexico - AMS dating of paints - Four - 300 BP to 5000 BP (probably contaminated) - J. M. Fullola, V. del Castillo, M. A. Petit, A. Rubio, E. Sarrià, R. Viñas, Spain.

1994 - Auditorium Cave, India - Microerosion dating of petroglyphs - One - Beyond range of method - R. G. Bednarik, Australia.

1995 - Le portel, France - AMS dating of charcoal pigment - Two - 11 600 and 12 200 BP - W. A. Ilger, M. Dauvois, M. Hyman, M. Menu, M. W. Rowe, J. Vezian, P. Walter, USA-France.

1995 - Grotte Chauvet, France - AMS dating of charcoal pigment and torch soot - Nine - Ranging from c. 26 100 to 32 400 BP - J. Clottes, J.-M. Chauvet, E. Brunel-Deschamps, C. Hillaire, J.-P. Daugas, M. Arnold, H. Cachier, J. Evin, P. Fortin, C. Oberlin, N. Tisnerat, H. Valladas, France.

1995 - Pech Merle, France - AMS dating of charcoal pigment - One - C. 24 600 BP - M. Lorblanchet, H. Cachier, H. Valla-das, France.

1995 - Drakensburg, Natal, South Africa - AMS dating from plant fibre binders - Two - Of c. 300 and 400 BP - A. Mazel, A. Watchman, South Africa-Canada.

1995 - Walkunder Arch, Chillagoe, Australia - AMS dating of oxalates associated with paintings - Four - from c. 6800 - 28 100 BP - A. Watchman, J. Campbell, C. Tuniz, Canada-Australia.

1995 - Côa site complex, Portugal - AMS dating from organics on petroglyphs and adjacent surfaces - Eight - Primary dates ranging from c. 2000 to 7000 BP, corrected to 100 BP to 1700 BP - A. Watchman, Canada.

1995 - Côa site complex, Portugal - AMS dating from organics on petroglyphs - Ten - Primary dates from c. 2000 to 5100 BP - R. Dorn, USA.

1995 - Côa site complex, Portugal - Microerosion analyses of petroglyphs - Numerous - Oldest figure c. E6500 BP, youngest a few centuries - R. G. Bednarik, Australia.

1995 - Grosio, Italy - Microerosion dating of petroglyph - One - E4900 BP - R. G. Bednarik, Australia.

1995 - Lewis Canyon, Texas - AMS dating of organic carbon in pigment - One - 1100 BP - W. A. Ilger, M. Hyman, J. Southon, M. W. Rowe, USA.

1995 - Opeleva Cave, Angola - AMS dating of organic charcoal in pigment - Two - Both c. 1900 BP - W. A. Ilger, M. Hyman, J. Southon, M. W. Rowe, USA.

1995 - Seminole Canyon, Texas - AMS dating of organic carbon in pigment - Four replicates - From 2950 to 3600 BP - W. A. Ilger, M. Hyman, J. Southon, M. W. Rowe, USA.

IFRAO STANDARD SCALE

The IFRAO Standard Scale is distributed worldwide by AURA, P.O. Box 216, Caulfield South, Vic. 3162, Australia; auraweb@hotmail.com

The Scale is provided free to individual members of IFRAO-affiliated organisations (listed above) and to researchers in developing countries. The cost for others depends on the number ordered, and is in the order of $0.50-2.00 per specimen.

ROCK ART PERIODICALS

Journals

Rock Art Research is the refereed premier academic journal of the discipline, appearing biannually since 1984. It comprises major articles and brief papers on any aspect of rock art science, covering all regions. Most papers are in English. *RAR* is the official organ of the International Federation of Rock Art Organisations (IFRAO), the Australian Rock Art Research Association (AURA) and the Cave Art Research Association (CARA). The editorial address is:
Robert G. Bednarik
P.O. Box 216
CAULFIELD SOUTH, Vic. 3162
Australia
E-mail: auraweb@hotmail.com

The *Bollettino del Centro Camuno di Studi Preistorici* is the oldest of the major rock art journals in the world. It has featured world rock art articles as well as general and Italian archaeology for well over thirty years. Articles published in this serial are in English, French and Italian. Its editorial address is:
Professor Emmanuel Anati
General Editor, BCSP
Centro Camuno di Studi Preistorici
25044 CAPO DI PONTE (Bs.)
Italy
E-mail: ccspreist@tin.it

An important Spanish language rock art journal is *SIARB Boletín*, produced annually by the Sociedad de Investigación del Arte Rupestre de Bolivia (SIARB). To contact the editor, write to:
Matthias Strecker
Editor, SIARB Boletín
Casilla 3091, LA PAZ
Bolivia
E-mail: siarb@latinwide.com

Another Spanish language journal is the recent newcomer, *Rupestre - Arte Rupestre en Colombia*. It is very well produced by the Grupo de Investigación de Arte Rupestre Indigena (GIPRI), with Volume 3 having appeared in 2000. The editorial address is:
Guillermo Muñoz C.
Grupo de Investigación de Arte Rupestre Indigena (GIPRI)
Carrera 54A # 174-12
SANTAFÉ DE BOGOTÁ, D.C.
Colombia
E-mail: gipri@col1.telecom.com.co

Purakala is a refereed, English-language rock art journal of substance issued by the Rock Art Society of India. It focuses on Indian issues and discoveries, but features also international contributions. The editor is:
Dr Giriraj Kumar
c/o Department of Indian Culture
Faculty of Arts
Dayalbagh Educational Institute
DAYALBAGH, AGRA 282 005
India
E-mail: girirajrasi@yahoo.com

The *Mitteilungen der ANISA* is a major journal of Alpine rock art and early montane settlement studies, produced by the Verein Anisa. It is very well produced, contributions are usually in German. Volume 21 appeared in 2000. The editorial address is:
Franz Mandl
Verein Anisa
A-8967 HAUS i. E.
Austria
E-mail: anisa@aon.at

Almogaren is a well-established refereed German-language journal focusing on the Canary Islands and related topics, with a strong emphasis on rock art. Volume 31 appeared in 2000. It is produced by the Institutum Canarium, manuscripts to be sent to:
Hans-Joachim Ulbrich
Grabenstraße 30/1
D-71404 KORB
Germany

Newsletters

A particularly valuable source is the fully bilingual *International Newsletter on Rock Art* of the Association pour le Rayonnement de l'Art Pariétal Européen (ARAPE), appearing three times per year in French and English. Contact:
Dr Jean Clottes
11, rue du Fourcat
9000 FOIX
France
E-mail: j.clottes@wanadoo.fr

SAPAR Bulletin is fully bi-lingual, in Russian and English. Produced by the Siberian Association of Prehistoric Art Researches (SAPAR), it features short articles primarily on Siberian issues. The editor is:
Professor Yakov A. Sher
State University of Kemerovo
Krasnaya Street 6
KEMEROVO 650043
Russia
E-mail: sher@kemsu.ru

La Pintura is the newsletter of the American Rock Art Research Association (ARARA) and appears four times a year. Contact:
Ken Hedges
8153 Cinderella Pl.
LEMON GROVE, CA 91945-3000
U.S.A.

Bay Area Rock Art News focuses on rock art in the San Francisco area of the U.S.A. Contact:
Dr Paul Freeman
1959 Webster Street
SAN FRANCISCO, CA 94115
U.S.A.

The *E.S.R.A.R.A. Newsletter* is a quarterly produced by the Eastern States Rock Art Research Association in the U.S.A. Contact:
Kevin L. Callahan
1102 26th Avenue S.E.
MINNEAPOLIS, Minnesota 55414
U.S.A.

A newsletter dealing with Saharan rock art, *Cahiers de l'AARS,* is produced in French by the Associaçao Portuguesa de Arte e Arqueologia Rupestre (AARS). Write to:
Dr Joerg W. Hansen
5, rue des Nobles
F - 09190 SAINT LIZIER
France
E-mail: hansenj@dial.oleane.com

Internet sites

Home-pages of some of the IFRAO member organisations:

Rock Art Society of China: http://chenzhaofu.nease.net

American Rock Art Research Association: http://www.arara.org/

Association des Amis de l'Art Rupestre Saharien: http://aars.site.voila.fr/

Australian Rock Art Research Association: http://mc2.vicnet.net.au/home/aura/web/index.html

Centro de Investigación de Arte Rupestre del Uruguay: http://www.geocities.com/Athens/ Parthenon/6994/indexi.htm

Centro Studi e Museo d'Arte Preistorica: http://www.cesmap.it/

Eastern States Rock Art Research Association: http://www.public.asu.edu/~rexweeks/Eastern_States_Rock_Art_Re.htm

Cave Art Research Association: http://mc2.vicnet.net.au/home/cara13/web/index.html

Institutum Canarium: http://www.Institutum-canarium.org/start_e.html

Nevada Rock Art Foundation: http://nevadarockart.org/

Northern Cape Rock Art Trust: http://www.museumsnc.co.za/McGregor/ departments Archaeology/rockarttrust.htm

Siberian Association of Prehistoric Art Researches: http://www.kemsu.ru/org/sapar/engl/mainengl.html

Società Cooperativa Archeologica Le Orme: dell'Uomo: http://rupestre.net/orme/

Upper Midwest Rock Art Research Association: http://www.tcinternet.net/users/cbailey/

Verein Anisa: http://members.aon.at/anisa/index-2.htm

Bolivian Rock Art Research Society: http://www.siarb-bolivia.org

Grupo de Investigacion de Arte Rupestre (Columbia): http://mc2.vicnet.net.au/home/gipri/web/index.html

12. ROCK ART GLOSSARY

A

abrade - to wear or scrape away through repeated abrasive movement of a tool.

abrasion petroglyph - a technological class of rock marking, produced by a process of abrasion removing rock mass.

abri - a concavity in a rock wall, formed by one or more natural processes, most commonly of erosion. French equivalent of 'rockshelter'.

absolute age - a numerical age in calendar years, rarely able to be determined in rock art research or archaeology.

abstract motif - a rock art motif that, to most Western observers, offers no iconic information elements.

accelerator mass spectrometry - a technique of determining the quantities of specific isotopes or nuclides in a sample, by separating them in a mass spectrometer and counting their individual atoms. In rock art science, cosmogenic nuclides may be determined in this way, including carbon-14.

accretion - an externally added, naturally deposited material on a rock surface, usually consisting of chiefly mineral matter.

Acheulian - a lithic tradition of the Lower Palaeolithic, characterised especially by 'handaxes', and found widely in the Old World, from southern Africa to India; named after the site of Saint-Acheul, Somme valley, France.

adze - a small stone tool, usually made from a flake, steeply retouched, mounted on a handle and used in wood working.

aeolian - pertaining to, caused by, or carried by the wind; aeolian erosion can affect rock surfaces.

ahu - a rectangular ceremonial platform on Easter Island/Rapa Nui, where it sometimes supports large anthropomorphous stone statues, and on the Society Islands.

ales (pl. alites) - a therianthrope with wings or arms in wing-like posture, found among southern African pictograms.

alignment - an anthropic arrangement of boulders or cobbles in relation to each other.

alluvial - of, pertaining to, or composed of sediment deposited by flowing water.

amino acid racemisation - a dating technique utilising the time-dependent conversion process (called racemisation) of L-isomers, the amino acids in living matter, to D-isomers.

amorphous - without definite shape or form, or lacking crystalline structure.

AMS - see accelerator mass spectrometry.

analogy - a form of logical inference based on the assumption that if two things are known to be alike in some respects, then they must be alike in other respects.

anamorphosis - an image distorted so that it can be viewed without distortion only from a particular perspective.

Ancestral Heroes - in various traditional ontologies, the beings who created the landscape and the living things in it.

animal scratch marks - rock markings made with the claws of a great variety of animal species, found commonly in limestone caves.

anthropic - pertaining to or made by human beings.

anthropomorph - an object or picture providing adequate visual information to most contemporary humans as resembling human form.

anthropomorphic - a deity's resemblance of human form; human motivation, characteristics or motivation attributed to animals, inanimate objects or natural phenomena.

anthropomorphous - providing visual information recognised by most contemporary humans as resembling human form.

archaeology - the study of the human past through the recovery of taphonomically distorted material evidence thought to relate to human cultural information; cf. culture.

archaeomagnetic dating - see palaeomagnetism.

archaeometry - the use of techniques of the sciences in interpreting material remains recovered by archaeology.

archaeozoology - palaeontological work in the context of archaeological parameters, which includes also the subjective identification of rock art motifs thought to depict animals.

art - the medium conveying awareness of a perceived reality to the sensory perception of other humans, i.e. the basis of denoting anthropocentric reality. More generally, the production or arrangement of sensory information (sounds, colours, forms, movements) for human use and consumption.

artefact - an object that has been modified, manufactured or even just used by a human or hominoid, usually but not necessarily portable.

ASL system - the sediment classification system of the Archaeological Soil Lab, Australia.

assemblage - a group of artefacts archaeologists consider as a single analytical unit.

astromorph - an object or picture providing adequate visual information to contemporary humans as resembling astral or lunar form.

attribute - a specific variable of rock art, such as size, inclination, colour, groove depth.

Aurignacian - an early Upper Palaeolithic tradition of southern Europe and the Near East, roughly 40-28 ka; named after the Aurignac rockshelter in the Pyrenees, France.

axe-grinding groove - elongate, concave shape abraded into near-horizontal rock, a result of reducing ground axe heads to the desired finish.

Azilian - a final Palaeolithic to early Mesolithic tradition of south-western Europe, roughly 11-10 ka; noted for its schist cobbles bearing red paint markings.

B

back lighting - in photography, the technique of lighting an object from behind, or from an angle between 135 and 225 degrees from focal axis.

bark painting - an Australian painting, traditionally of mineral or vegetal colours, executed on flattened and cured tree bark.

barred lines - a rock art motif consisting of a series of parallel or sub-parallel, usually vertical lines of similar lengths.

bas-relief - a sculpture of low relief, or a carving on a flat surface, in which figures are raised only slightly from background.

bead - a small circular or spherical object, with central perforation or otherwise attachable to string.

bedrock - the solid rock that underlies all sediments or detrital deposits, or lies exposed as the ground surface.

beeswax figure - a rock art motif made by applying shaped beeswax to rock surfaces, found in northern Australia.

bichrome - a pictogram executed in two different colours.

binder - a component of rock art paint, assisting uniform consistency, solidification or adhesion.

biomorph - an object or picture providing adequate visual information to contemporary humans as resembling a biological form.

boulder - a granulometric division, designating the largest fraction of gravel, according to the ASL system larger than 250 mm in diameter.

BP, bp - before present, meaning before A.D. 1950; used for dates in radiocarbon years. These are not calendar years but statistical expressions of radiocarbon ratios.

Bradshaw figure - superseded term, see *gwion.*

breccia - a rock composed of angular rock fragments larger than the sand fraction, cemented in a fine-grained matrix.

bridging argument - an argument linking the material remains studied in archaeology with their interpretations as components of living cultural systems.

bruise - to pound a rock surface lightly, but sufficient to remove some of its weathering zone.

bruising - a rock marking produced by light direct percussion, through removal of weathered material; see also sgraffito.

burin - a stone tool with a short transverse working-edge formed by the removal of a narrow spall, used in engraving.

C

cairn - an anthropic mound of stones.

calcification - an impregnation with calcium salts, especially calcium carbonate, with consequent hardening or fossilisation.

calcrete - a sandstone formed with calcium carbonate as the cement.

calibrated age - an age estimate derived from a method determining individual rates of particular processes that must be calibrated by independent chronological control.

calibration - a systematic standardisation of a quantitative expression by means of a reference factor.

carving - a design cut into a surface with a sharp instrument, such as a knife or carving chisel.

cast - a negative impression formed by a mould or matrix, such as a petroglyph cast formed by plaster of Paris.

cation-ratio dating - a technique once thought to date geomorphic and petroglyph surfaces, based on the premise of a time-related decrease of the ratio of calcium and potassium to titanium, now refuted; developed by R. I. Dorn.

cave - a hollow space in bedrock, which may or may not be accessible from the surface, and may contain a variety of solid and liquid bodies, including sediments, speleothems and phreatic systems; cf. rockshelter.

cave art - a rock art tradition found in caves, but not necessarily endemic to them; occurs in all continents except Antarctica.

cenote - a karst phenomenon, caused by the collapse of a cave roof into a phreatic reservoir, resulting in a water-filled sinkhole.

Chalcolithic - a technological period marked by the introduction of copper use, applied especially in India and Near East, elsewhere often termed Copper Age or Eneolithic.

chert - a collective term for sedimentary microcrystalline silica rock formed by selective replacement of limestone; in some regions occurring as flint.

chevron - a pattern of repeated V-shapes.

chronology - the arrangement of past events or manifestations according to their temporal sequence, and the science of providing dates for them.

chronometric dating - the dating methods that report results as numerical age estimations, in most cases qualified by expressions of uncertainty and other factors; cf. relative dating.

churinga - see tjuringa.

cicatrice - a form of body decoration, a deliberately made body scar, usually cut with a stone knife.

clast - a fragment of rock of any size, but used especially to denote cobble-sized angular breakdown debris.; synonymous to detritus.

claviform - being club shaped.

clay - the smallest of the granulometric fractions, according to the ASL system grains of under 2 microns diameter; also a textural class designation relative to sand and silt; and a descriptive term of sediment dominated by clay-size particles.

CLM - see convergent lines motif.

cluster - a configuration of elements gathered or occurring closely together.

cobble - a granulometric division, according to the ASL system designating clasts between 60 and 250 mm in diameter.

cognitive archaeology - the branch of archaeology that investigates the development of human cognition.

colluvium - a loose deposit of rock debris formed at the base of a cliff or slope, such as a talus scree.

colour - the wavelength of light emitted or reflected by an object, perceived as the sum of the constituent values of hue, saturation (chroma) and lightness (tone).

colour reconstitution - the method of recovering original colour information at time of photographic recording, compensating for the photographic process and other distortions through digitised re-calibration against a known standard; cf. IFRAO Standard Scale.

complex, site complex - a group of rock art sites or galleries in close geographical proximity, arranged over an area of up to some square kilometres.

composition - the arrangement of parts of a rock art motif so as to form a meaningfully juxtaposed whole; cf. scene.

concentric circles - an arrangement of two or more circles, each nested centrally within the next larger.

concretion - a coalesced deposit of mineral matter formed through the deposition of a cementing mineral precipitate, such as carbonate, silica or iron salts.

conservation - the practice of preserving from natural or anthropic deterioration by means of specific measures.

contact art - a form of rock art pertaining to the period of initial contact with European colonisers or other aliens, characterised by the occurrence of depictions of imported objects or ideas.

contamination - a chemical or physical component that distorts the result of an analytical process.

context - the circumstances in which a particular event occurred, which may be crucial in an archaeological interpretation of it.

convergent lines motif - a common rock art motif, consisting of two or more lines converging at one end, but not necessarily connecting. When it consists of three connecting digits it is often defined as a bird track, vulva, arrow etc.; see trident.

core - an intact cylindrical sample taken of a solid substance (rock, sediment, bone, ice etc.) by means of a core drill. The term is also used to define the nucleus that remains after stone flakes are knapped.

core tool - a stone tool made from a nucleus, not from a flake of blade, bearing retouch or use wear.

correlated age - an age estimate produced through correlation (association) with independently dated events.

correlation - a causal, complementary, parallel or reciprocal relationship, especially a structural, functional or qualitative correspondence between comparable entities.

cortex - a surface zone on rock which may be the result of weathering, but more often refers to the porous but hard zone of incomplete silicification found on chert nodules.

cosmogenic radiation dating - a technique of estimating geomorphic exposure ages, based on the production of nuclides by cosmic ray bombardment and using noble gas mass spectrometry and accelerator mass spectrometry.

cosmography - description of a perceived world or universe; the way in which a cosmology has been recorded.

cosmology - a belief system or world-view of a society, creating an ordered universe.

CRM - the abbreviation of cultural resource management, which refers to the protection of sites by the state.

cross-dating - the attempt to date an artefact on the basis that what is perceived to be a similar artefact has been dated by a scientific method elsewhere.

cross-hatching - two or more sets of parallel or sub-parallel fine lines in contrary directions, used to fill in some engraved outline motifs.

cruciform - having the shape of a cross.

culture - the transference of practice by non-genetic means, and the behaviour based on such transference.

cuneiform - being wedge shaped.

cup-and-ring mark - a common petroglyph motif in some regions, consisting of a central cupule and one or several concentric circles surrounding it.

cup mark - see cupule.

cupule - a hemispherical percussion petroglyph, which may occur on a horizontal or vertical surface.

curation - the practice of keeping artefacts or manuports in custody for a period of time, of looking after them, and sometimes of reworking them.
curvilinear - consisting of curved lines.
custodian - an indigenous or autochthon person with traditional curatorial rights for a rock art site, often determined by a metaphysical belief system.
cylcon - a cylindrical-conical stone object of unknown purpose with a tapered end, found especially in western New South Wales, Australia, which may or may not be incised with engravings.

D

dating - a method of estimating the age of a deposit or artefact.
dendrochronology - a dating technique based on the sequences of annual tree-rings found in the trunks of trees, and in timbers used in anthropic structures. This is the principal method of absolute dating.
dendroglyph - a motif cut or painted into or onto the bark or wood of a living tree trunk.
dent - a small hollow made on a rock surface when struck with a hammerstone by direct percussion; cf. nick.
desert varnish - see rock varnish.
diachronic - pertaining to development through time.
diffusion - a transference of material culture or ideas from one society to another.
digital fluting - see finger fluting.
diluent - a liquid used in the preparation of rock art paint, which may be water, blood, urine or other.
direct dating - the dating of rock art by direct physical relationship of art and dating criterion, and falsifiable propositions concerning this relationship; introduced by R. G. Bednarik.
direct percussion - a method of producing petroglyphs with the impact of one hand-held tool.
drawing - a technological class of pictogram, consisting of dry applied pigment.
Dreaming - a parallel time frame that in Australia overlaps with the present through ceremony and ritual.
dripline - the outline of the furthest projection of the roof of a rockshelter or cave entrance.
dripline, artificial - a barrier erected on the underside of a rockshelter roof to prevent rain water from spilling onto the ceiling area, usually made of silicone applied with a pressure gun.
dry application - an application of pigment to a rock surface without the use of a diluent, usually by crayons of charcoal or iron compounds; cf. drawing.
dynamic figures - a corpus of rock art consisting of anthropomorphs or zoomorphs shown in apparent poses of movement.

E

Early Pleistocene - the earliest geological period of the Quaternary, from about 1.8 million years ago to 780 000 years ago.
electron probe microanalysis - a form of non-destructive chemical analysis, in which a sample bombarded by electrons emits recordable x-rays which reveal the presence and concentrations of chemical elements.
electron spin resonance dating - a radiogenic dating technique detecting electrons trapped in charge-deficit sites which result from natural irradiation.
emblemic - pertaining to a distinctive sign of the state, status or class of a person, recognisable by participants in the culture concerned.
Eneolithic - see Chalcolithic.
engraving - a rock marking produced by a process of abrasion with a pointed graver or burin.
enhancement - a process of increasing specific values or contrasts of a photographic or digitised image, commonly by electronic manipulation.
entoptic phenomenon - an image created by the visual neural system without retinal input, as in dreams and through phosphenes or hallucinations.
epistemology - the science of the origins, nature, methods and limits of human constructs of knowledge, evaluating the veracity of human knowledge.
erosion - a natural process by which mineral or earth matter is removed, including dissolution, weathering, abrasion, corrosion or transportation.
ESR - see electron spin resonance dating.
exfoliation - a form of geological weathering, involving the progressive detachment of cutaneous flakes or scales from a rock surface.
extender - a substance added to rock art paint to dilute it or to give it additional body.

F

facies - a stratigraphic body distinguished from others by appearance or composition, representing a specific period of time.
faded - having lost original brightness, brilliance or colour contrast.
figurative - providing visual information recognised by contemporary humans as resembling the form of an object.
figure - a design or pattern painted, drawn, pressed or engraved on a rock surface; a rock art motif.
figurine - a sculptural representation providing visual information recognised by contemporary humans as resembling human or animal form.
finger fluting - a form of rock art resulting from dragging human fingers over a soft surface in a limestone cave, usually of *Mondmilch*, and consisting of sub-parallel grooves (*sillons digitaux paralleles*).
finger marking - a form of rock art made with human fingers, which may consist of finger-applied paint or of finger flutings.
FLECS - the technique of using combustion by a

laser beam to oxidise organic matter contained in mineral accretions under or over rock art for AMS radiocarbon analysis, called Focused Laser Extraction of Carbon-bearing Substances; developed by A. Watchman.

frieze - a continuous panel of rock art located along a vertical wall, usually of considerable horizontal extent.

G

gallery - a large concentration of rock art, not necessarily continuous, consisting of a number of panels.

genre - a category of rock art perceived by contemporary humans as forming a distinctive entity; cf. style.

geofact - a naturally formed stone object that resembles a stone tool closely enough to be mistaken for one.

geoglyph - a large motif (usually >4 m) or design produced on the ground, either by arranging clasts (positive geoglyph, stone arrangement/alignment, petroform, earth mound) or by removing patinated clasts to expose unpatinated ground (negative geoglyph).

geometric motif - a rock art motif of simple geometrical form or design, such as circle, line, cupule, CLM, barred lines.

gestalt - a unified symbolic configuration having properties that cannot be derived from its parts.

Global positioning system - a satellite-based navigation system, a network of satellites in several orbits, which enables precise geographical location to be determined with a receiver that calculates the differences in time between receiving the signals from four satellites.

glyph - a petroglyph motif; in archaeology, a symbol in a writing system.

gouge - a scooped out or deeply carved indentation in soft rock, made with a gouging tool.

GPS - see Global positioning system.

graffito (pl. graffiti) - a drawing or inscription superimposed over or in proximity of rock art and distinctively more recent, often judged crude or unwelcome.

gravel - see pebble.

Gravettian - an Upper Palaeolithic tradition of south-western, central and eastern Europe, about 28 000 to 20 000 years old; named after La Gravette in the Dordogne, France.

grid motif - see lattice motif.

grinding groove - a groove on a rock pavement, the incidental result of making or sharpening a ground stone tool such as an axe or hatchet; also grinding hollow.

groove - an elongate indentation abraded or hammered (or both) into a rock surface.

ground art - a petroglyph produced by abrasive action, especially referring to the infilled area of an intaglio.

gwion - a small, often animate or dynamic anthropomorphous red painting in the Kimberley region, Western Australia, preceding the region's Wandjina art phase; this authentic name supersedes the former term 'Bradshaw figure'.

H

hammerstone - a pebble or cobble used in the production of percussion petroglyphs.

hand print - a positive pigmented imprint of a human hand, made by pressing a paint-covered hand against the rock surface.

hand sign language - a form of non-verbal human communication consisting of hand signs, which has been suggested to be depicted in some rock art traditions.

hand stencil - a negative pigmented imprint of a human hand, made by spraying paint over the hand's outline while it is pressed against the rock surface.

hard water effect - the distorting effect aqueous salts of calcium and magnesium can have on radiocarbon analysis results.

hatching - the parallel or sub-parallel fine lines used to fill in some engraved outline motifs.

history - the generic term of past events.

History - the specific time period beginning with the introduction of writing by some members of a human species.

Holocene - the geological present, the final period of the Quaternary, from 10 500 years ago to the present time.

hypothetico-deductive reasoning - a form of reasoning in which predictions deduced from a hypothesis are tested by empirical data.

I

iconic, iconographic - providing visual information recognised by most contemporary humans as resembling the form of an object.

IFRAO Standard Scale - a calibrated colour and size standard used in rock art photography for precise colour manipulation with digital technology, introduced in 1994.

igneous - a rock formed by solidification from a molten or partially molten state.

incision - a shallow rock marking produced with a single application of a pointed tool, consisting of a narrow smooth groove.

increase site - a location where supplication rituals are or were performed that encouraged the propagation of a specific species associated with the site's Ancestral Hero.

indirect percussion - a method of producing petroglyphs with the impact of a chisel or punch held in one hand, struck by a hammer in the other hand; identifiable by bipolar flaking of mur-e.

indirect superimposition - a superimposition involving three or more motifs, the first and last of which are not physically related.

industry - a group of stone tools archaeologists consider representative of a specific culture; sometimes used as synonym for assemblage.

infill - the treatment of the surface area enclosed by the outline of a rock art motif, which may be additive or reductive.

in situ - being in its original place, usually referring to the location or position of an object's last use or its burial.

intaglio - a petroglyph motif whose internal surface area is ground or pounded, either to remove a dark varnish (sgraffito) or to create an area of relief; also called an infilled figure.

internal analysis - the microscopic study of engravings to determine various technological details, such as tool type, direction of application, handedness, multiple tool application; introduced by A. Marshack.

intrusion - an intrusive rock mass or facies forced into an existing formation.

isotopic replacement - a chemical process that affects some dating methods, in which an isotope or nuclide used in the dating analysis has been partially replaced by another isotope of the same element.

K

ka - the abbreviation indicating 'thousand years'.

karst - a region of carbonate rock (limestone or dolomite) characterised by underground drainage and various karst phenomena, such as caves, sinkholes, cenotes, dolines, karren and kamenitsa.

keystone - the wedge-shaped piece at the top of a stone arch, regarded as holding the structure in place.

L

lacunae - a gap in a pictogram caused by exfoliation or vandalism.

laser oxidation - a controlled burning of carbonaceous matter in a substance related to rock art, such as a mineral accretion or a paint residue.

Late Pleistocene - the geological period from 127 000 to 10 500 years ago.

lattice motif - a rock art motif consisting of a repeated pattern, particularly of sets of parallel lines crossing each other.

Levantine art - the rockshelter art of Mediterranean eastern Spain, thought to be of the mid to late Holocene.

lichenometry - the technique of estimating the age of lichen thalli from their relative sizes, calibrated against another standard; developed by R. E. Beschel.

linear - of or relating to a straight line, or composed of straight lines.

lithic - having been made from stone; in archaeology referring to stone tools.

lithophone - a rock, stalactite or stalagmite that has been used to produce sound.

Lower Palaeolithic - the oldest chronological division of the Older Stone Age of the Old World, roughly 2.5 Ma to 180 ka.

M

Ma - the abbreviation indicating 'million years'.

macaroni art - a form of randomly meandering finger flutings.

Magdalenian - a late Upper Palaeolithic tradition of western and central Europe, roughly 16-10 ka; named after La Madeleine abri, Dordogne, France.

manuport - an unmodified object transported and deposited by humans or hominoids.

mark, marking - a visible trace or impression on a surface, here particularly a rock surface. It may be a xenolith, a glacial striae, an animal scratch, or a petroglyph.

material culture - the physical remains of human activities recovered by archaeology.

maze motif - a rock art motif of an intricate network of lines offering no obvious iconographic interpretation.

meander - a rock art motif of circulinear arrangements offering no obvious iconographic interpretation.

medium - the materials used in producing art, particularly the solvent of paint, and by extension the type of artistic technique.

megafauna - the large-bodied animal species which in various parts of the world suffered extinction during the final Pleistocene and the Holocene.

megalithic art - the Neolithic petroglyphs found on arranged stones such as stelae and tombs.

Mesolithic - the Middle Stone Age of Eurasia, commencing at the end of the Pleistocene 10 500 years ago and ending with the advent of the Neolithic, which differs in various regions.

metamorphism - the alteration in composition, texture or structure of rock masses, caused by heat and pressure within the Earth's crust.

metamorphology - the science of how forms of archaeological evidence change with time and how they are perceived or understood by the individual archaeologist today.

methodology - the system of assumptions, principles, theories and practices applied in rock art research.

microerosion analysis - the methods of direct petroglyph dating using microscopic erosion criteria, such as the micro-wanes forming on fracture edges of mineral crystals; developed by R. G. Bednarik.

microlith - a small stone tool of under 5 cm length, made from bladelets or blade fragments, set in hafts and typical of the final Upper Palaeolithic, the Mesolithic and the Neolithic periods of Eurasia.

micro-wane - the result of non-kinetic progressive rounding processes on crystal edges, at the microscopic level.

Middle Palaeolithic - the middle chronological division of the Older Stone Age of Eurasia and northern Africa, roughly 180 to 30 ka; in sub-Saharan Africa called the Middle Stone Age and ending later.

Middle Pleistocene - the geological period from 780 000 to 127 000 years ago.

middle-range theory - a set of hypotheses that lead to archaeological propositions about past human behaviour.

mineral precipitate dating - the methods of direct-dating rock art by analysing contiguous mineral accretions, such as reprecipitated calcite (via radiocarbon or uranium series dating) or oxalate (via radiocarbon analysis) layers.

mobiliary art - a form of palaeoart consisting of or made on objects small enough to be easily carried by humans.

Mondmilch, *Montmilch*, **moonmilk** - a white speleothem of calcium carbonate, resembling snow or consisting of a dough-like mass, forming the medium of finger fluting.

monochrome - concerning a pictogram executed in one single colour.

motif - an anthropic mark or connected arrangement of marks on rock, perceived by contemporary humans as forming a single design.

mould - a negative cast of a petroglyph, made from an initially fluid or plastic substance which hardens subsequent to application.

Mousterian - a Middle Palaeolithic tradition of Europe, western Asia and northern Africa, roughly 180 to 30 ka old; named after the lower abri of Le Moustier, Dordogne, France.

Munsell Soil Color Charts - a standardised colour identification system used in rock art research to describe paint residues and rock patinae, produced by the Kollmorgen Corporation in Baltimore, U.S.A.

mur-e - a tool used in the production of a petroglyph.

mutilated hand stencil - a hand negative made by spraying paint over a hand, in which one or more fingers are shortened, probably because they were intentionally bent rather than mutilated.

N

nano-stratigraphy - the stratigraphy of pictogram paint residues, or mineral accretions formed over and under rock art, studied by microscopic excavation; introduced by R. G. Bednarik.

naturalistic - providing visual information recognised by contemporary humans, particularly Westerners, as resembling an object.

naturefact - a portable object which resembles an artefact, but has not been modified or demonstrably used or handled by humans; cf. geofact.

negative - see stencil.

Neolithic - a vague technological division of the Stone Age, referring to traditions of cultivation and domestication which still lack the use of metals for tools; the advent of ceramics and ground stone tools is often falsely attributed to the Neolithic.

niche - a concavity found especially in sedimentary rocks, formed by exfoliation and measuring no more than a few metres.

nick - a small hollow made on a rock surface when struck with a chisel in indirect percussion; cf. dent.

non-figurative - providing no visual information recognised by contemporary humans as resembling the form of an object.

non-iconic - see non-figurative.

non-utilitarian - possessing characteristics that seem to exclude interpretation as utilitarian, suggestive of possessing artistic or ritual significance.

normative - relating to a deterministic view of culture, in which each society produces a uniform patterning of archaeologically visible material remains through standardised practices.

notational - possessing attributes that may represent numbers, quantities or other facts or values.

numerical age - an age estimate derived from a method yielding results on a ratio (or absolute) scale, that may have uncertainties attached.

O

object imprint - a form of pictogram made by pressing or throwing paint-covered objects against a rock surface.

object stencil - a form of pictogram made by holding an object against a rock surface and spraying paint around all or part of its edge.

ochre - an earthy mineral oxide or hydroxide of iron of red, brown or yellow colour; the most common surviving pigment of pictograms.

open site - a place of occupation, artefact manufacture, mineral extraction or rock art production which is fully exposed to weathering processes.

optically stimulated luminescence dating (OSL) - a radiogenic technique in which the luminescence emitted by individual mineral grains when exposed to visible light is measured to determine when it was last exposed to sunlight.

orientation - the positioning of a rock art motif or panel relative to specified referents.

oxalate - a salt or ester of oxalic acid, often occurring as a mineral accretion with rock art.

oxygen isotope dating - a technique of determining the ratio of $^{18}O/^{16}O$ of materials, such as calcium carbonate and ice, to determine temperature fluctuation of the past.

oxygen plasma dating method - the technique of extracting organic carbon from rock art paint residues by coupling high vacuum with a low-temperature oxygen plasma, before dating it by AMS; introduced by M. Rowe.

P

paint - a liquid mixture consisting of at least a pigment and a solvent, which may also contain a binder, extender, and a great variety of incidental inclusions, such as airborne matter or brush fibres.

painted petroglyph - a petroglyph bearing traces of paint which are thought to have been applied to colour the figure.

painting - see rock painting.

palaeoart - the collective term describing all art-like manifestations of the distant past.

palaeoclimate - the climatic regimes of the distant past.

Palaeoindian - the earliest archaeological period in North America, ending c. 7000 BP.

Palaeolithic - the first 99.6% of human history in the Old World, ending 10 500 years ago.

Palaeolithic art - the surviving palaeoart of the Pleistocene, from the Lower Palaeolithic to the end of the Upper Palaeolithic.

palaeomagnetism - the polarisation of magnetic particles in rocks and sediments of previous geological periods, which indicates that the Earth's magnetic field has been repeatedly reversed, which is used for approximate dating of these substances.

palynology - the scientific determination of fossil and extant pollen and spores, e.g. those found in paint residues or mineral accretions, which can assist in relative dating and environmental studies.

panel - a group of rock art motifs occurring in very close proximity, on a rock surface of reasonably uniform orientation.

parietal art - rock art located on the walls or ceilings of a cavity, usually a limestone cave.

patina - a visually obvious skin on rock surfaces which differs in colour or chemical composition from the unaltered rock and whose development is a function of time.

pavement - a predominantly horizontal expanse of exposed bedrock.

patterned hand print - a hand print in which a pattern has been painted on the hand prior to printing.

pebble - a granulometric division, according to the ASL system designating clasts between 2 and 60 mm in diameter.

pecked petroglyph, pecking - a rock marking produced by a process of indirect percussion, involving the use of a hammer in one hand and a chisel, gad or bit in the other.

pendant - an object suspended on a string, often but not necessarily perforated near one end.

percussion petroglyph - an anthropic rock marking produced by the removal of rock mass through impact.

petroform - a geoglyph consisting of clasts placed on the ground to form a motif.

petroglyph - a rock art motif that involved a reductive process in its production, such as percussion or abrasion.

petroglyph-producing implement - see mur-e.

petrological microscopy - a technique of examining thin sections of rock samples under a microscope to determine its components from the diagnostic way they refract polarised light.

phosphene - an autogeneous and involuntary phenomenon of the mammalian visual system whose form constants cannot be influenced by cultural conditioning and which seem to be ontogenically stable.

phosphene form - one of the fifteen known standard form constants of phosphenes, most of which are common in very early rock art traditions.

photogrammetry - a technique of extracting three-dimensional modelling information from photographs using a camera of known lens and film geometry taking multiple photographs of a subject.

photomicrograph - a photograph of an object taken by a camera mounted on and focused through a microscope.

phreatic - pertaining to the water of an aquifer or ground water.

pictogram - a rock art motif that involved an additive process in its production, such as the application of paint, dry pigment, beeswax.

pictograph - a writing character of figurative appearance, representing a word or a syllable; a hieroglyph.

pigment - a colouring substance used to produce pictograms, such as rock paintings, stencils and drawings.

pipeclay - a very fine-grained white clay, principally of kaolinite, widely used as white pigment in rock art production.

pisciform - having the form of a fish.

pit, pitting, pit mark - see cupule.

pit and groove petroglyph - an early petroglyph tradition of the Americas, consisting of cupules and abraded grooves.

plaque, plaquette - a flat plate bearing engraved or painted markings, consisting of stone, bone, ivory or other materials.

Pleistocene - the geological period also known as the Ice Age, from c. 1.8 million to 10 500 years ago.

podomorphic - having the form of a foot.
polychrome - concerning a pictogram executed in three or more colours.
portable art - see mobiliary art.
post-processual archaeology - a school of archaeological theory that perceives culture as a system of context-specific symbols and meanings, rejecting its deterministic interpretations.
post-stylistic - referring to the phase of rock art research that eschews reliance on stylistic predictions of alien researchers about rock art ages and cultural attributions.
potassium-argon dating - a radiometric technique of dating volcanic deposits that utilises the decay of ^{40}K to ^{40}Ar to estimate the time when these deposit were formed by eruptions.
pounded petroglyph, pounding - a rock marking produced by a process of direct percussion with a hammerstone.
prehistory - with lower case h: a colloquial and illogical term, as there can be no period before the past; cf. history.
pre-History - the period before the beginning of History, ending with the introduction of writing by some members of a human species; cf. History.
print - a rock marking made by pressing a paint-covered object against the rock surface.
processual archaeology - a school of archaeological theory that emphasises the need to explicitly state assumptions and use specific scientific procedures; also called New Archaeology.

Q

Quaternary - the most recent of the major geological divisions of time, comprising the Pleistocene and the Holocene.
quartzite - a metamorphosed siliceous sandstone, the result of recrystallisation under great heat and pressure.

R

radiocarbon dating - a radiometric dating technique of late Quaternary carbon-bearing materials that utilises the decay of ^{14}C to nitrogen to estimate when they absorbed carbon from the atmosphere.
radiometric dating - a method of estimating age based on the decay of radioactive isotopes contained in a sample.
Rainbow Serpent - the most powerful Australian Dreamtime being, responsible for creating features of the landscape.
referent - the object or idea which a rock art motif depicts, not necessarily by iconographic resemblance; also signified.
referrer - the rock art motif depicting an object or idea, not necessarily by iconographic resemblance; also signifier.
reification - the treatment of an abstraction or idea as if it had concrete or material existence.
relative dating - a method of estimating age relative to other features, providing no numerical results; cf. chronometric dating.
repainting - the cultural practice of placing a rock painting over an existing motif, closely following the form, colour and style of the previous design.
replication - the method of studying past technologies by reproducing their products as precisely as possible, and under similar conditions.
representational - see figurative.
residue analysis - the study of remaining material traces that have been subjected to reductive physical or chemical processes.
resin - any of a class of semisolid organic substances obtained from plant exudates, and used archaeologically for a variety of purposes, including as paint binder.
retouch - the modification or renewal of a rock art motif, particularly where required by cultural practice.
re-use - the modification of an earlier produced rock art motif, to alter it, to comment upon it, or to renew it.
Rillenkarren - a karst phenomenon, consisting of subparallel solution grooves of regular spacing on a sloping rock surface exposed to atmospheric weathering.
rock art - non-utilitarian anthropic markings on rock surfaces, made either by an additive process (pictogram) or by a reductive process (petroglyph).
rock art science - the systematic study of rock art by means of falsifiable propositions about observations.
rock bruising - a technological class of petroglyph, made by the removal or partial removal of a patina or weathering zone through percussion; cf. sgraffito.
rock-hole - an unmodified depression in bedrock where rainwater collects; cf. waterhole.
rock marking - any arrangement of surface properties on rock discernible by the human visual system; it may be a natural marking, a utilitarian anthropic marking or a non-utilitarian anthropic marking (rock art).
rock painting - a technological class of pictogram, consisting of paint which was applied wet with fingers or a brush-like tool.
rockshelter - a concavity in a rock wall, formed by one or more natural processes, most commonly of erosion; it is wider than deep; cf. niche, scallop.
rock varnish - a ferromanganeous surface accretion on rocks, particularly common in arid regions, of dark-brown to near-black colour; formerly called desert varnish.
rock-well - a rock-hole modified through enlargement, covering etc.; cf. waterhole.
rubbed petroglyph - a technological class of petroglyph, made by the removal or partial

removal of a patina or weathering zone through abrasion; cf. sgraffito.

S

sacred site - a locality of particular religious or spiritual significance, a place infused with the creative force of the ancestral being who created that element in the landscape.

sand - a granulometric division, according to the ASL system designating grains between 0.06 and 2 mm in diameter.

scalariform - having the form of a ladder, having rungs.

scallop - a shallow concavity resembling a niche, but where the erosion process is impeded by formations of previously consolidated sub-surface.

scanning electron microscope - an instrument producing three-dimensional images magnified 10-200 000 times, by scanning a surface with a fine beam of electrons, focused by electromagnets.

scene - a presumed depiction of a real or imagined episode involving more than one rock art motif.

schematic - relating to or of the nature of a plan, diagram or scheme.

scratched petroglyph - a technological class of petroglyph, made by shallow linear incision of a rock surface.

secret-sacred - referring to religious information which is of restricted access.

sediment - an aggregate of grains deposited by water, wind, ice or biological agents, primarily of mineral matter but including organic debris.

seismic - relating to, like, or caused by an earthquake or earth vibration.

SEM - see scanning electron microscope.

semantic - pertaining to signs or meaning.

semiotics - the science dealing with signs and sign language.

sequence - a chronological succession of rock art motifs, genres or traditions.

seriation - a technique of relative dating in which perceived motif classes are temporally organised according to their relative popularity.

serpentiform - having the form of a serpent or snake.

sgraffito (pl. sgraffiti) - a technological class of petroglyph, made by the removal of a patina or weathering zone to reveal a differently coloured surface beneath; cf. graffito.

shamanism - the religious practices of certain Asian and North American populations whose professional priests are capable of summoning or consulting the spirits.

sign - an entity that stands for another, a referrer; in the Palaeolithic rock art of south-western Europe, an apparently non-figurative conventionalised motif.

silica skin - a cutaneous accretionary deposit of amorphous silica.

sillons rectilignes - parallel striations observed microscopically in an engraved line which indicate where the engraving function is taken over by alternative projections of a multiple-pointed stone tool.

silt - a granulometric division, according to the ASL system designating grains between 2 and 60 microns in diameter.

sinkhole - a karst phenomenon caused by the collapse of a cave roof, a vertical opening in the ground with vertical or overhanging walls.

site - any place where evidence for past human behaviour has been found, or which is of significance to contemporary indigenes.

slope wash - the sediment recently washed down a slope that truncates other strata in section.

soak - an unmodified depression in sand or soil where rainwater collects; cf. waterhole.

soil - an aggregate of grains of mineral or organic materials occurring at or near the land surface.

solute - a substance dissolved in another, usually the component of a solution.

Solutrean - an Upper Palaeolithic tradition of south-western Europe, roughly 19-16 ka; named after the open-air site Solutré, France.

solvent - the component of a solution that is present in excess or that is intended to evaporate subsequent to application.

sorcery art - a rock art motif produced as malignant sympathetic art, as part of a ritual supplicating spirit beings to perform harmful actions.

spall - a small, thin and elongated chip of stone flaked from a stone tool, such as a burin.

spatial - pertaining to or having the nature of space.

spearthrower - a device for increasing propulsion force of a spear or dart, consisting of an elongate form with a small hook at the rear; also atlatl, woomera.

speleothem - a secondary mineral deposit, most often a carbonate, precipitated in air-filled caves from vadose aqueous solution enriched with mineral solute.

spring - a location where an aquifer periodically or permanently discharges; cf. waterhole.

stele (pl. stelae) - an upright stone slab erected in its position by humans, which may bear an inscription or graphic element.

stencil - a technological class of pictogram, made with paint sprayed over an object, usually from the mouth, resulting in a silhouette image; also called a negative.

stick figure - an anthropomorphous or zoomorphic rock art motif in which all body parts are depicted as single lines.

stochastic - denoting or characterised by conjecture, referring to random process.

stone arrangement - see geoglyph.

stratigraphy - the study of the formation, composition, sequence and correlation of layered sedimentary or accretionary deposits, providing a relative reference frame for chronology.

striae - striations made by a clast transported by a glacier over the surface marked by it.

striation - a groove cut into a rock surface, especially one of a group of such parallel marks produced in a single abrasive event; the term applies to microscopic as well as macroscopic forms.

stries parasites - subsidiary parallel striations observed microscopically, found especially on convex aspects of the medium.

structural archaeology - a school of archaeological theory studying past cultures as sets of symbols and codes that determine how individuals acted in society; cf. post-processual archaeology.

stupa - a monument of stone, usually erected by Buddhists.

style - a combination of distinctive features of artistic expression or execution peculiar to a particular person, people, school or era; cf. genre.

superimposition - an instance of one rock art motif having been placed over another, earlier motif; cf. indirect superimposition.

support - the rock surface upon which a motif has been executed, be it a petroglyph or a pictogram.

symbol - an entity representing another by resemblance, association or culturally determined convention.

sympathetic magic - a rock art motif produced as part of a ritual supplicating spirit beings to achieve desired outcomes, such as success in hunt or the death of a person.

synchronic - pertaining to contemporaneity.

T

tally marks - a set of sub-parallel vertical marks of similar length and spacing, often suggested to be of notational significance; better referred to as bar set.

talus - loose accumulation of pebble and cobble-size clasts at the foot of a cliff or slope.

taphonomy - the study of the processes affecting rock art after it has been executed, determining its present appearance and statistical properties.

taphonomic logic - a form of logic viewing rock art as the surviving remnant of a cumulative population that has been subjected to continuous degradation which selects in favour of specific properties facilitating longevity.

technique - the method of execution, such as painting, incision, direct percussion.

tectiform - being roof-shaped or dwelling-like.

tectonic - pertaining to structure, which may be that of a building, a cave, the crust of the Earth or a work of art.

terminus ante quem - the reference time before which something occurred.

terminus post quem - the reference time after which something occurred.

therianthrope - a biomorph possessing both human and animal features.

theriomorph - see zoomorph.

thermoluminescence dating - a radiogenic method in which the luminescence emitted by a number of mineral grains when exposed to visible light is measured to determine when they were last exposed to sunlight.

tjuringa - an Australian ceremonial board of stone or wood, often decorated with sacred designs, whose access is restricted to fully initiated men; also churinga, *atywerrenge*, *tywerrenge*.

tool marks - a form of anthropic rock marking on soft cave deposits that has been made with tools rather than fingers, and appears to be non-utilitarian.

tracing - a recording of rock art made by placing a flexible transparent sheet over the motif and tracing the image upon it, which may damage rock art.

tradition - the elements of a culture passed down from generation to generation; in rock art, the forms of expression collectively regarded as belonging to a specific ethnic entity.

travertine - a deposit of reprecipitated calcite at springs and in caves, formed by the precipitation of calcium bicarbonate from a solution.

trident - a CLM with three connecting digits, often called a bird track, vulva, arrow etc., frequently without proof.

twisted perspective - a form of depiction found in many rock art traditions, in which different elements of an apparently depicted object, usually a biomorph, are shown from different perspectives; also called bi-angular perspective.

typology - the classification of a series of motifs that are thought to belong to a single tradition, on the basis of subjectively chosen attributes such as perceived morphology.

U

Upper Palaeolithic - the final chronological division of the Older Stone Age of Eurasia and northern Africa, roughly 40 to 10 ka; in sub-Saharan Africa called the Late Stone Age and commencing later.

uranium series dating - a group of radiometric dating techniques based on the decay series of the uranium isotopes deposited through precipitation in travertine, marl, coral, mollusc shells, bone, teeth and other materials.

use-wear - the microscopic edge and surface modifications of an artefact that have resulted from its use.

utilitarian - being intended, made or used for practical as opposed to ritual purposes.

V

vadose - pertaining to ground water that re-emerges at the atmosphere, e.g. in a cave or at the foot of a cliff, often supersaturated with mineral solute.

vandalism - the defacing or destruction of rock art, or impairing of its scientific potential.

vesicle - a small bubble-like gas pocket formed in volcanic rock during solidification.

W

wane - a rounded edge on a clast, particularly a boulder, resulting from non-kinetic progressive wear processes such as insolation, exfoliation or solution.

waterhole - a natural depression in which rain water collects, or a location where an aquifer is periodically or permanently exposed; cf. soak, well, spring, rock-hole, rock-well.

weathering - the chemical and physical processes by which rocks exposed to the atmosphere decay to soil.

weathering zone - a cutaneous layer of chemically or physically altered rock whose thickness approximates exposure age.

well - a soak modified through enlargement, covering etc.; cf. waterhole.

X

xenolith - foreign inclusion in igneous rock which may effect a surface marking resembling a petroglyph.

x-ray art - a form of rock art in which internal properties of an object are depicted as if they were normally visible, occasionally found in many parts of the world, but strongly developed in Arnhem Land, Australia.

x-ray diffraction analysis - a technique of studying the atomic and molecular structure of crystalline substances by using the diffraction of x-rays to determine the shape and size of atoms.

Z

zoomorph - an object or picture providing adequate visual information to contemporary humans as resembling animal form.

zoomorphic - pertaining to a zoomorph.

*

Acknowledgments: Bahn (1992) and Flood (1995, 1997) have been profitably consulted in formulating some of the definitions. Of particular value have been the contributions of Jane Kolber, R. G. Kimber, H. C. Woodhouse and particularly Dr Charles Warner, who have suggested hundreds of possible inclusions. Constructive comments on the first published draft (Bednarik 1999) were gratefully received from Dr Friedrich Berger, Mario Consens, Dr Fred E. Coy, Christian Eckart-Ublagger, R. G. Gunn, Jr, Dr Dirk Huyge, Prof. Dr Herta Mandl-Neumann, Dr Alfred Muzzolini and Professor Yakov A. Sher. However, I alone bear the responsibility for the shortcomings of this glossary.
R. G. Bednarik

REFERENCES

BAHN, P. (ed.) 1992. *Collins dictionary of archaeology*. Harper Collins, Glasgow.

BEDNARIK, R. G. 1999. Proposed glossary of rock art research. *AURA Newsletter* 16(1): 3-10.

FLOOD, J. 1995. *Archaeology of the Dreamtime* (revd. edn). Angus & Robertson, Sydney.

FLOOD, J. 1997. *Rock art of the Dreamtime*. Angus & Robertson, Sydney.

Index

X

Y

Z